MAKING DYSTOPIA

Professor James Stevens Curl has established an international reputation as one of the few architectural historians who manages to absorb prodigious research which he imparts seemingly effortlessly in sustained and lively narrative. He was twice Visiting Fellow at Peterhouse, University of Cambridge, and is a Member of the Royal Irish Academy, a Fellow of the Society of Antiquaries of London, and a Fellow of the Royal Incorporation of Architects in Scotland. In 2014, De Montfort University awarded him an Honorary Doctorate of Arts in recognition of his 'distinctive contribution . . . to the intellectual and cultural life of the nation and region'. His many publications include studies of Classical, Georgian, and Victorian architecture, and the most recent edition of his acclaimed *Oxford Dictionary of Architecture* (with contributions on landscape from Susan Wilson) was published by Oxford University Press in 2015. In 2017 he was presented with the President's Medal of the British Academy for 'outstanding service to the cause of the humanities' in his 'wider study of the History of Architecture in Britain and Ireland', and was later honoured with a 2019 Arthur Ross Award for Excellence in the Classical Tradition for History & Writing by the Institute of Classical Architecture & Art (ICAA), USA.

BY THE SAME AUTHOR

The Victorian Celebration of Death (Harlech: Heritage Ebooks 2015)

The Oxford Dictionary of Architecture (with Susan Wilson) (Oxford: Oxford University Press 2015, 2016)

Funerary Monuments & Memorials in the Church of Ireland (Anglican) Cathedral of St Patrick, Armagh (Whitstable: Historical Publications Ltd. 2013)

Georgian Architecture in the British Isles 1714–1830 (Swindon: English Heritage 2011)

Freemasonry & the Enlightenment: Architecture, Symbols, & Influences (London: Historical Publications Ltd. 2011)

Spas, Wells, & Pleasure-Gardens of London (London: Historical Publications Ltd. 2010)

Victorian Architecture: Diversity & Invention (Reading: Spire Books Ltd. 2007)

The Egyptian Revival: Ancient Egypt as the Inspiration for Design Motifs in the West (London & New York: Taylor & Francis Group 2005)

Classical Architecture: An Introduction to its Vocabulary and Essentials, with a Select Glossary of Terms (London & New York: W.W. Norton 2003)

Piety Proclaimed: An Introduction to Places of Worship in Victorian England (London: Historical Publications Ltd. 2002)

Kensal Green Cemetery: The Origins & Development of the General Cemetery of All Souls, Kensal Green, London, 1824–2001 (edited, with various contributions from other scholars) (Chichester: Phillimore & Co. Ltd. 2001)

The Honourable The Irish Society 1608–2000 and the Plantation of Ulster. The City of London and the Colonisation of County Londonderry in the Province of Ulster in Ireland. A History & Critique (Chichester: Phillimore & Co. Ltd. 2000)

Encyclopaedia of Architectural Terms (London: Donhead Publishing 1992)

The Londonderry Plantation 1609–1914: The History, Architecture, and Planning of the Estates of the City of London and its Livery Companies in Ulster (Chichester: Phillimore & Co. Ltd. 1986)

The Life and Work of Henry Roberts (1803–76), Architect: The Evangelical Conscience and the Campaign for Model Housing and Healthy Nations (Chichester: Phillimore & Co. Ltd. 1983)

A Celebration of Death. An Introduction to some of the buildings, monuments, and settings of funerary architecture in the Western European tradition (London: Constable & Co. Ltd. 1980)

The Erosion of Oxford (Oxford: Oxford Illustrated Press Ltd. 1977)

City of London Pubs: A Practical and Historical Guide (with Timothy M. Richards) (Newton Abbot: David & Charles [Holdings] Ltd. 1973)

Praise for *Making Dystopia*

'This brilliant text is a timely marvel...*Making Dystopia* is unquestionably a major contribution...and quite possibly the most important publication in Stevens Curl's enormously prodigious *oeuvre*...[He] has penned a magisterial *tour de force* that exposes the conceits and folly of architectural Modernism. It exhibits the work of a scholar at the height of his perceptive powers and provides a penetrating and judicious interrogation into one of the greatest shams in the history of architecture.'

Frank Albo, Adjunct Professor of History,
University of Winnipeg

'a spirited, scholarly assault on the tin gods of Modernism..., this book's scholarship is precise. Prepare to be shocked...'

Clive Aslet, *Country Life*

'An important and necessary book...Professor Curl has dug behind and chiselled away at the details of a history veneered over by decades of received modernist mythmaking.'

Graham Cunningham, *The New Criterion*

'Written with passion and eloquence,...a work of rare intellectual magnitude, to be recognized as an important, imperative contribution to the culture of our times. It promises to become essential reading...'

Giovanna L Costantini, *Leonardo Reviews Archive*

'Stevens Curl gets his teeth into "the disaster that has been post-1945 British architecture and town planning", tackling the thorny subject with verve, wit and tremendous erudition...This great book, in showing categorically, and cogently, what went wrong, makes an unarguable case...'

Patricia Craig, *The Times Literary Supplement*

'In this scholarly,...enjoyably polemical book, Professor Curl recounts...the devastating effects of architectural modernism...[It is] an essential, uncompromising, learned...critique of one of the worst and most significant legacies of the 20th century...[for never]...in world history had such technical incompetence been so powerfully allied with...total aesthetic insensitivity...His book...is a loud and salutary clarion call to resist further architectural fascism.'

Theodore Dalrymple, *New English Review*

'A storm is brewing in the world of architecture thanks to James Stevens Curl's lightning bolt of a book...although Curl's polemic is fierce, and well-written to boot, it is far from a blinkered rant'.

Jonathan Glancey, *The Daily Telegraph*

'This is a book to be read, discussed and debated by anyone with an interest in our built environment ... This is a full-blooded, no-holds-barred, scholarly treatise stemming from a lifetime of study and experience and an unwillingness to bow down to popular but often unsubstantiated opinion. [It] ramps up the debate with a passionate argument meticulously backed up by detailed notes and a vast range of source material much of which is new ... This scholarly and challenging book deserves to be widely read.'

Karen Latimer, *Journal of the Royal Society of Ulster Architects*

'Curl, a veteran architectural historian with a string of big books to his name, certainly tells us what he thinks ... This massive *cri-de-coeur*, ... argued with a pathological attention to detail, ... is ... a blistering broadside ...'

Richard Morrison, *The Times*

'This ... erudite polemic [has] a scholarly solidity ... and a relentlessness to the argument that means ... you won't so easily throw off the memory of its message. It sticks in the mind ...'

Newsletter of The Ancient Monuments Society

'*Making Dystopia* is meticulously researched and convincingly argued: it ... empties out the contents of modernism for all to see and holds them up to the light for judgement ... Here, finally, is an authoritative critique of the ... nature of modernism ... a contentious, highly thought-provoking study, ... it is also in places very funny.'

Patrick O'Keeffe, *Architecture Today*

' ... encyclopaedic in its range ... it is a powerful and passionate indictment. The dogs of anger are always straining at the leash.'

Bernard Richards, *Oxford Magazine*

'Curl ... is not wrong ... *Making Dystopia* [is] ... an impassioned bomb-throwing jeremiad ... [containing] underlying truths ... The ultimate failure of modern architecture ... is that while [it] suppressed an architectural language that had taken hundreds of years to evolve, it proved incapable of developing a successful substitute.'

Witold Rybczynski, *Journal of the American Institute of Architects*

'A coruscating, driven, and passionately committed book which should be read by anyone who believes that a house is more than a machine for living.'

Katharine Wilson, author of *Fictions of Authorship*
in Late Elizabethan Narratives: Euphues in Arcadia

'Modernist principles ... often led to atrocious results. Le Corbusier's "vertical gardens" became vertical slums, and there is only a sliver of difference between Walter Gropius's lofty Bauhaus ideals and a crap council estate.'

Stephen Bayley, *The Spectator*

MAKING
DYSTOPIA

THE STRANGE RISE
AND SURVIVAL OF
ARCHITECTURAL BARBARISM

JAMES STEVENS CURL

with a

Prolegomenon

by

Timothy Brittain-Catlin

OXFORD
UNIVERSITY PRESS

OXFORD
UNIVERSITY PRESS

Great Clarendon Street, Oxford, OX2 6DP,
United Kingdom

Oxford University Press is a department of the University of Oxford.
It furthers the University's objective of excellence in research, scholarship,
and education by publishing worldwide. Oxford is a registered trade mark of
Oxford University Press in the UK and in certain other countries

© James Stevens Curl 2018

The moral rights of the author have been asserted

First published 2018
First published in paperback 2019

Published in the United States of America by Oxford University Press
198 Madison Avenue, New York, NY 10016, United States of America

British Library Cataloguing in Publication Data
Data available

Library of Congress Cataloging in Publication Data
Data available

ISBN 978–0–19–875369–8 (Hbk.)
ISBN 978–0–19–882086–4 (Pbk.)

Printed and bound by
CPI Group (UK) Ltd, Croydon, CR0 4YY

AdfG

Gratia, Musa, tibi: Nam tu solacia praebes
Tu curae requies, tu medicina venis…
PUBLIUS OVIDIUS NASO (43 BC–c.AD 17): *Tristia* **iv** x 117–18

Frontispiece *They are Weighed in the Balance and Found Wanting: with respectful apologies to A.W.N. Pugin.* An assortment of structures, including an International-Style tower resembling a pile of sandwiches, a tortured piece of Deconstructivism, some Blobism, *pilotis*, a sub-Corbusian block, and other familiar Modernist elements, is weighed against a selection of Classical works of architecture by John Nash, Robert Smirke, and others, and found unworthy

Contents

Prolegomenon

It is a foolish thing to make a long prologue,
and to be short in the story itself.

APOCRYPHA (Before AD 70): II Maccabees II 32

This revealing and well-argued book is about a cultural and environmental Catastrophe, a process by which the accumulated knowledge of expertise in construction and ornament that architects used to pass on from one generation to the next in the West over many centuries was abandoned after the First World War. There had been previous periods of rise and fall in construction standards—many of the decorative applied arts in building had been forgotten in Britain before A.W.N. Pugin and the Puginites revived them in the 1840s—but this Catastrophe was something new: it was the result of a divisive and active campaign to destroy knowledge and a practice-base, perpetrated mainly by people who were not only members of peculiar cults and held extreme (and wildly swinging) political convictions, but who had, for the most part, limited design skills. Walter Gropius, it emerges from the author's researches, is unlikely to have designed singlehandedly any of the works conventionally attributed to him, and Le Corbusier appears to have been associated with Fascist sympathies, but found the collaborationist Vichy *régime* in France uncongenially liberal for his tastes.

However, it cannot be doubted, as the author acknowledges, that experimental architecture after 1918 varied tremendously in quality and content. Some of the best-known Western buildings of that period, such as the *Bauhaus* complex at Dessau (completed 1926) and the *Villa Savoie* at Poissy (1928–31), inspired many as forms of inhabited sculpture (so long as they were well maintained and the weather was good). Furthermore, there were buildings by Miës van der Rohe, as he was known in the 1920s and 1930s, that brought aesthetic gratification to some, whilst at the same time, according to Detlef Mertins's recent study,[1] were intended to represent the ideas of the philosopher of religion, Romano Guardini, by imposing an external visual 'order' onto the various demands of what were then modern building programmes. However weird and unpleasant Le Corbusier was as a person—and he was evidently both of these—his wildly original sculptural buildings such as the pilgrimage chapel of *Notre-Dame-du-Haut*, on its isolated site at Ronchamp, near Besançon, on the edge of the Jura mountains in France (1950–5), are known to have had, and continue to have, strong effects on people, perhaps in part because of their disruptive effect on their immediate surroundings. Many who grew up in dismal architectural environments felt elevated by their first encounters with Modernist pavilions in gardens, festivals, or on the beach, which instilled a lifelong love of bright, cheery spaces.

But the Catastrophe is not that experimental architecture existed at all: it is that eventually any kind of architecture that deviated from the style of one or other of its most famous and warring protagonists was gradually dismissed by critics and by fashionable people. The results of this were extreme, and absurd, and the examples many. The 'architecture' section of the *Thirties* exhibition at the Hayward Gallery in London (1979) consisted only of a handful of freak Modernist buildings;[2] architectural historians would not be taken seriously if they deviated from a dogmatic Modernist line; young architects were for a period no longer taught the primacy of construction method and the basic organization of form; historical references in buildings were abandoned entirely, for irrelevant reasons; pseudo-scientific processes were introduced all over the place, no more useful than phrenology in its day; a kind of crude simplistic aesthetics was applied to the detailing and shape of huge buildings that demanded much more to make their bulk acceptable; ornament was jettisoned almost completely, apart from an unrelated high-art panel or a sculpture arbitrarily added here and there; and the language used to describe new buildings became declamatory, abusive, moralistic, and above all, unconnected with the experiences of most people who had to use them.

Architects are not good at describing what they are doing; they tend to cling on to what they hear, especially from their potential clients. All creative artists therefore need critics if they want to make a public case for their work, but the puritanical streak in Anglo-Saxon culture is perpetuated by the fact that, generally speaking, the eloquence of cheap literary style is taken more seriously than costly aesthetics. Thus loquacious critics from John Ruskin to Reyner Banham exerted short-term influence apparently greater than that of the designers they championed. There was a debate some years ago about whether the then Lord Chancellor should have decorated his rooms in the Palace of Westminster with revived Pugin wallpaper at public expense: we all heard from prim commentators about the supposed disgrace of 'wasting public money', but that Pugin was one of the most creative designers Britain has ever seen, which in turn led to a flowering of design and, not least, the employment of many talented craftsmen, was something ignored. The argument often resurfaces when critics who see themselves as 'progressive' or 'left-wing' discuss the future of abandoned country houses; the impression is that they would rather see such buildings burn down than be restored or recreated for other uses, no matter how rich their history, or the fact that they often stand as the only records of the hard-worked people who invested their life-skills in designing, constructing, and decorating them. And this burning down of the house is what the Catastrophe brought about.

The Catastrophe has had a major and long-lasting impact on the way in which architecture is taught: one can still witness its terrible effects at first hand. One phenomenon that never ceases to astonish is when students, not even twenty years old, justify their design for a white-rendered block of a building with long horizontal windows as 'modern' or even 'contemporary' when in fact it would have been familiar or even old-fashioned to their great- or even great-great-grandparents. Far worse is the habit of using affected, poisonous, bullying language at public critiques of student work, which seems to have emerged from banter between tutors at the Architectural Association and, earlier, at Harvard (Marcel Breuer finally walked out on his mentor Walter Gropius after one of these).[3] There may have been occasional humour in some of these early performances, but, as the method filtered down to reach every critique in every architectural school across the Western world, their entertainment value somewhat palled. Thus it came about that, for at least a couple of decades towards the end of the twentieth century, discussion at critiques of students' work focused more on whether the young designer had fallen in line with the mesmeric appeal of their tutors' current fashionable preoccupations—political, social, or whatever they were—than on the construction, or tradition, or even simply the visual appeal of the project in hand.

It was and it remains a mystery to me how this approach—the direct, unadulterated progeny of the Catastrophe, completely unrelated to design, to material, to spirit, to anything positive at all—has a useful rôle to play in architectural education. The world has changed a lot since then, but this particular mine of bombastic aggression has probably not yet been exhausted. A short film posted to *YouTube* in August 2008 shows one of the world's most celebrated architects humiliatingly laying into a student's work in a way that viewers have described as rude, self-righteous, and narcissistic.[4] Where did this nonsense come from?

This book offers a scholarly and passionate analysis of the whole unfortunate and destructive process, written by a distinguished architectural historian, one of the very few whose authority, accuracy, and incisiveness are beyond question in every subject he addresses.

Timothy Brittain-Catlin
Broadstairs
Kent
Summer 2017

List of Plates

List of Figures

Preface & Acknowledgements

Essence of the Argument; Afterword & Acknowledgements

> The preface is the most important part of the book...
> Even reviewers read a preface.
>
> <div align="right">PHILIP GUEDALLA (1889–1944): 'Conversation with a Caller'
in <i>The Missing Muse: and Other Essays</i>
(London: Hodder & Stoughton 1929) VIII</div>

> Should you, my LORD,[5] a wretched Picture view;
> Which some unskilful Copying-*Painter* drew,
> Without Design, Intolerably bad,
> Would you not smile, and think the Man was mad?
> Just so a tasteless Structure; where each Part
> Is void of *Order, Symmetry*, or *Art*:
> Alike offends, when we the Mimick Place;
> Compare with *Beauty, Harmony*, or *Grace*.[6]
>
> <div align="right">ROBERT MORRIS (1703–54): <i>The Art of Architecture, a Poem.</i>
In Imitation of <i>HORACE's Art of Poetry</i> (London: R. Dodsley 1742)[7]</div>

Essence of the Argument

This is not a history of Modernism[8] in architectural or urban design. The term presents difficulties of definition, and it is probably easier to think of it as opposed to academicism, historicism, and tradition, embracing that which is self-consciously new or fashionable, with pronounced tendencies towards abstraction. The word was used from the 1920s to suggest the new architecture from which all ornament, historical allusions, and traditional forms had been expunged: promoted by architects such as Miës van der Rohe, Le Corbusier, and Walter Gropius, it had 'flat'[9] roofs, plain, smooth, white rendered walls, long horizontal strips of window, some sort of frame construction so that external and internal walls were non-structural, and often depended on factory-made components (*see* **Figures 4.2, 4.4, 4.5, 5.1, 5.2**).

Indeed there would be a 'general consensus' regarding what can be 'readily identified' as Modernist buildings that began to appear shortly after the end of the 1914–18 war,[10] and that, despite denials they were in any 'style', their progeny continued to proliferate well into the 1970s. Stylistically recognizable, often with 'curtain-walled' façades (*see* **Figure 6.4**), such buildings were representative of what became known as the 'Modern Movement' in architecture, more specifically of what was termed 'The International Style',[11] so called because its protagonists insisted it must be applied globally, no matter what were local conditions of climate, skills, industrialization, traditions, culture, or much else, for that matter.

Nor is this study an attack on that Modern Movement in architecture as such. There were certain aspects of Modernism, such as the liberation of rooms from being boxes and experiments in the flowing of one internal space into another (made easier by structural innovations), that were positive, but there was a coercive, dogmatic side to it (especially in the pronouncements of Le Corbusier and his followers) that was unattractive, and that has led to a great deal of bad architecture and disruptive interference with old-established urban fabric. It questions some of the means by which the Modern Movement in architecture and town planning became not only accepted, but virtually compulsory, the only 'appropriate' way of designing buildings and urban structures, according to its devotees, after 1945.[12] It assumes in the reader a smattering of knowledge concerning the subject, otherwise the volume would have to be very much larger than it actually is.

The aims of this book are to attempt to explain, expose, and outline the complex factors[13] that have managed to create so many Dystopias in which, arguably, an 'architecture' devoid of any coherent language or meaning has been foisted on the world by cliques convinced they knew or know all the answers, yet demonstrated or demonstrate an incompetence with buildings that fail as architecture at almost every level and by almost every criterion. It became clear many years ago that all was not well, and that enormous damage had been done to cities, towns, and the countryside, and was continuing, backed by spurious arguments and questionable posturings, including the central tenet of Modernism that tradition was dead (it was Modernism which did its best to kill it, and put enormous numbers of craftsmen out of a job).

Osbert Lancaster's *Pillar to Post: English Architecture without Tears*[14] first appeared in 1938, followed in 1939 by *Homes Sweet Homes*:[15] consisting of cleverly economical drawings, each opposite a page of pithy text. These volumes describe styles with clarity and wit. Together, they comprise what is

probably the best and most succinct textbook on architecture ever published, even though the author, in the Foreword to *Pillar and Post*, entitled
'Order to View', opens with a disclaimer: the 'book is not a text-book'[16] at
all. A great satirist, Lancaster knew exactly when something was both true
and untrue. He used irony (something clearly beyond the comprehension
of Le Corbusier and other Modernists) with devastating effect, at the same
time pointing out that everything built is architecture (in contrast to the
questionable and dogmatic positions adopted by Sigfried Giedion, Nikolaus
Pevsner, John Ruskin, and others). Moreover, Lancaster demystified architecture, and, by so doing, enabled everybody uncowed by the pretensions of
aggressive architectural critics to have opinions of their own about the subject. He deplored the establishment of critical 'compounds'[17] and obfuscatory 'specialist' language that excluded normal people from all debate about
their surroundings in daily life. He even had the temerity, having worked for
a time (from 1934) as an assistant editor at *The Architectural Review*, to refer
to the outpourings of certain enthusiasts of the Modern Movement as 'that
Bauhaus balls'.[18]

In 1949, Lancaster brought out *Drayneflete Revealed*,[19] in which he showed
that of all ideologies which threatened British urban and rural landscapes,
the most destructive was that of Corbusianity (ubiquitous worship of the
Swiss-French architect, C.-É. Jeanneret-Gris, who from *c.* 1920 pretentiously
called himself 'Le Corbusier'), as the hearts were torn out of countless towns
and cities in the dubious name of 'progress'. People were condemned to an
unpleasant existence in badly designed and built high-rise blocks of flats and
to rat-runs of dark, smelly, threatening underpasses, leaving what was left of
the earth's ruined surface to motor traffic. *Drayneflete* chronicled the historical
evolution and final wrecking of an English town from prehistoric times
to its terrible demise ('The Drayneflete of Tomorrow')[20] as a Modernist
Dystopia dominated by roads and tower blocks on *pilotis*, with only four old
buildings ludicrously 'preserved' as 'Cultural Monuments' (one marooned
on a traffic roundabout) (**Figure P.1**). The Corbusian device of *piloti* (one
of several piers supporting a building above the ground), which elevated
the lowest floor to first-floor level, leaving an open area below, was widely
adopted, and resulted in countless unpleasant spaces.[21] Drayneflete's remaining fabric was completely obliterated to create an inhumane environment
of empty, stupefying, memoryless banality, devoid of beauty or anything uplifting to the spirit: its succinctly observed fate, as recorded by Lancaster in his
wonderful book, sums up what happened up to 1949 and was to happen in

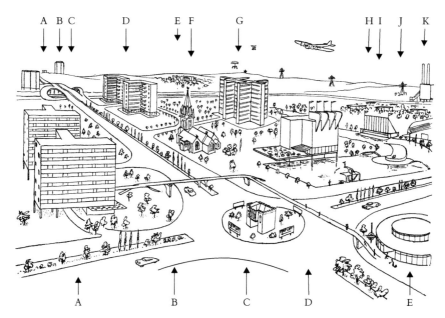

Figure Preface P.1. 'The Drayneflete of Tomorrow'. Osbert Lancaster's vision of an English Town with virtually everything of its old fabric obliterated, apart from: 'Poet's Corner'; the former stately home of the Littlehamptons, now serving as a Lunatic Asylum, set in its Park; the parish church with all traces of its burial-ground obliterated; and the gateway to the former Augustinian Priory marooned on a traffic-island. Nothing resembling a traditional street remains: Le Corbusier had decreed streets should be abolished

Key to Illustration

Top:

A: Cultural Monument scheduled under National Trust ('Poet's Corner')
B: Gasometer
C: Clover-leaf Crossing and Bridge
D: Communal Housing-Block on *pilotis*
E: Lunatic Asylum and Littlehampton Memorial Park
F: Cultural Monument scheduled under National Trust
G: Municipal Offices including Community Centre, Psychiatric Clinic, Crèche, and Helicopter Landing-Strip on the Roof
H: Housing-Estate for Higher-Income Brackets
I: Communal Sports-Centre, Yacht-Club, and Football-Ground
J: Floating Concert-Hall for Audience of 2,500 and full Symphony Orchestra
K: Power-Station

Bottom:

A: Communal Housing-Blocks on *pilotis*
B: High-Level Pedestrian Road Bridge
C: Cultural Monument scheduled under National Trust
D: People's Restaurant, Swimming-Club, Bathing-Pool, Cinema, and Amenities Centre
E: Underground Station

the next three decades, as Modernists enforced 'a monopoly of uglifiers',[22] as Sir Roger Scruton has aptly put it.

As each year passes, so-called 'iconic'[23] erections become more and more bizarre, unsettling, outrageous, incredibly expensive, and wasteful, ignoring established contexts, destroying townscapes, and cutting across old-established geometries and urban grain. If these represent a 'new paradigm', as some have claimed,[24] then an unpleasant future for a Dystopian universe is assured. This is especially true as something resembling gross irresponsibility was manifest in London,[25] where the property bubble was being inflated to obscene dimensions at the expense of social cohesion at the time this study was being written. When cities become dominated by enormously wasteful 'icons' and affordable housing lies beyond the reach of most people, the development of shanty-towns around them is more than likely.

Such models exist elsewhere in the world where Modernists were given free rein. Brasília, Federal Capital of Brasil, designed (1956–7) by the 'left-wing' Modernists Oscar Niemeyer and Lúcio Costa,[26] encapsulated many principles laid down by the *Congrès Internationaux d'Architecture Moderne* (CIAM) in Le Corbusier's Athens Charter:[27] these included demands for 'autonomous sectors' for four major 'functions' of cities, and thus enshrined the notion of rigid zoning in urban planning widely adopted for urban reconstruction after the 1939–45 war with disastrous results. The plans for Brasília were praised to the skies in Modernist architectural circles when they were first revealed, but the place has not worn well.[28] It is completely lacking in human scale. Dominated by the motor-car,[29] it has dated painfully, with a handful of large official 'iconic' buildings as its centre, but around it satellite- and shanty-towns in the outskirts have proliferated. Exacerbation of this trend on a global scale can only lead eventually to social disintegration and ungovernable violence.

The world has already experienced several manifestations of extreme anger against aspects of Western life not unconnected with architecture. The prognosis is not encouraging, as, almost daily, Modernist architects inflict damage on the already weakened fabric of cities that have been subjected to nearly a century of ideological tinkering, and even export their outlandish computer-generated Parametricist[30] fancies to places where their incongruities insult and contribute to the wrecking of what survives of indigenous cultures. Parametricism owes its origins to digital animation techniques. It implies that all elements and aspects of an architectural composition are parametrically malleable, and makes unprecedented use of computational design tools and methods of fabrication. It has been claimed[31] as the great new 'style' (succeeding Modernism, Post-Modernism, Deconstructivism, and Minimalism). It is supposed to have superior capacities to articulate programmatic complexity, enabling architecture to translate convoluted contemporary life processes in the global Post-Fordist (meaning mass-production, presumably) network society. It is said to offer functional and formal heuristics based on a set of general abstract rules distilled from a very complex ecosystem of sustained *avant-garde* design research.[32]

In the face of such 'clarity' of expression, it is little wonder ordinary human beings hesitate to question the pretensions of the incomprehensible. Obfuscatory language is an effective camouflage for a massive programme to impose a new architectural style on a global scale. Parametricist architects and their disciples seem to be oblivious as to the impact of what they are doing or have done as they bask in the adulation of a handful of critics adept in the fancy jargon of what has become a cult.[33] The assumption by so-called 'star' architects and their acolytes that only they have the right to insist on the excellence of Modernist 'icons' must be challenged: they are wrong. Only those persons who have to live in, use, or endure the sight of what those 'stars' impose on the rest of us have the *exclusive* right to criticize, to weigh in the balance, and decide. Architecture is ubiquitous. It is not a mystery to be guarded and protected by the high-priests of obscure cults: it is everywhere, and the public should be its judges, not a small coterie promoting its own agenda.[34]

A lifetime studying architecture and looking at hundreds of villages, towns, and cities has provided the essence for what lies within this volume. The book attempts to explain how an extraordinary state of affairs occurred to channel the noble art of architecture into stony paths beset with problems over the last century or so. Much of this work, therefore, is based on personal observations made during travels looking (and drawing, because that is the most effective way of *really looking*) at buildings in their contexts in Europe and America; on careful perusals of original texts (as opposed to what commentators have written about those texts); on painfully acquired knowledge of historic fabric (and the terminology associated with it,[35] something that is clearly lacking in contemporary 'education'); and on quiet contemplation (often leading to great regret and sadness).

Several influential *dramatis personae* will appear: many of these took stances that were inconsistent, demonstrably illogical, and frequently just plain wrong. It is not just the theorists and practitioners who created difficulties for the historian. Apologists for certain almost deified Modernists constructed mythologies and made connections with earlier architects and architecture that are simply untenable once subjected to careful analysis. They fabricated narratives that were swallowed whole by the gullible. I shall attempt, therefore, to point out some of the more glaring errors in widely accepted texts, theories, and dogmas, though space precludes an analysis of every one of them, as the 'literature' is so vast.

Reactions to certain writers, including Jane Jacobs's critique of the damage being done to American cities by Modernism,[36] were examples of the vindictiveness of believers in the cult. A title given to a review by Lewis Mumford,[37] of all people, was unquestionably sexist in tone ('Mother Jacobs' Home Remedies'[38]): this was all the more unpleasant because Mumford had once written perceptively on Utopias,[39] on the need for an indigenous American architecture as an antidote to the puritanical, fanatical, and political extremists of European Modernism,[40] and (despite helping to organize the exhibition *International Style* at the Museum of Modern Art [MoMA], New York [1932]) on the dangers of that style, particularly the dogmatic theories of 'Le Corbusier'.

In the same year, however (1962), Mumford was to write an article entitled 'The Case Against Modern Architecture'[41] in which he questioned much, not least a blind belief in mechanical progress as an end in itself. Nevertheless, there was a cacophonous chorus of damnation of someone (especially a mere woman, it would seem) with the temerity to question the professionals, their entrenched beliefs, and (especially) the unholy mess they had managed to make of countless places. Oddly, Mumford's 'Case Against Modern Architecture' came out in April 1962, and his unpleasant attack on Jane Jacobs was published in December of that year: it is difficult to understand what prompted such a thoroughgoing change of mind, and even more difficult to avoid the suspicion that he may have been leant on. There were many other predictable denunciations of Jacobs by Modernists[42] who believed but could not see: enthusiasts may pursue these dreary effusions if so inclined, but an assurance that they were published will have to suffice here.

Another weapon, of course, is to damn by ignoring any criticism, which was almost the fate of David Watkin's *Morality and Architecture*,[43] published by Oxford University Press, until Denys Sutton printed an approving review in *Apollo* (which he edited 1962–86), noting the 'trouncing' meted out to the 'collectivists' who had 'had their way far too long in intellectual circles' thanks to a general and cowardly 'appeasement of the Left'.[44] Thereafter came a flood of hostile reviews, including a specimen in the *Times Literary Supplement*[45] by one always on the lookout for a fashionable attitude, Reyner Banham, 'willing as usual to go too far'[46] with his unpleasant jibes (including one about the 'kind of vindictiveness of which only Christians seem capable',[47] which was particularly significant given the anti-historical, anti-cultural, and anti-religious nature of much in Modernism). Stephen Bayley drew on an arsenal of barbs, describing the book as an 'addled, sly, knowing, superior, rancorous, smarmy, sneering stinker':[48] and *Building Design* called it 'waspish', 'spiteful', and obsessed with 'reds under the beds'.[49] Question the priests of the cult at your peril, it would seem, but there are times in one's life when one has to put one's head above the protective screen of the crenellations.

Now one of the many reasons for such attacks were Watkin's criticisms of Nikolaus Pevsner who, by that time, had almost been beatified, if not canonized, by received opinion: Pevsner's utterances, having acquired an 'almost Mosaic authority', were eagerly embraced, became ideology, and were repeated, as his biographer, Susie Harries, observed, without any qualification the man himself might have applied to them.[50] Some commentators even referred to Pevsner's 'sacred cow-dom' that had ensured his 'highly debatable views' became 'all too acceptable to influential people'.[51] Pevsner's achievements were immense, not least as the originator of the marvellous *Buildings of England* series and their progeny, the *Buildings of Scotland*, *Wales*, and *Ireland*. He was extremely generous with information to young scholars, including myself at the start of my career, but that does not mean scholars have no right to suggest that some of his work, especially his considerable part in constructing the very questionable 'Grand Narratives' of the Modern Movement, might have been based on error. When some of those Pevsner described as 'pioneers' (of something they themselves detested) denied that they were anything of the sort, he and his followers continued to insist on the opposite view. So it might be sensible to suggest that Pevsner's categorizations were perhaps odd or even flew in the face of facts: his construct should be recognized as part of a deliberately fabricated propaganda exercise.

Arthur Korn (who had worked with Erich Mendelsohn and was a member of Berlin's *avant-garde*, including *Der Ring*) supervised one of my early research projects: a delightful and generous man, a real friend, he, like Pevsner, tended to construct a seamless history linking Modernism with millennia of historical developments, when in fact what had happened was a complete and absolute rupture. So this book will cast doubt on Korn's views too. This does not constitute an attack, personally, on either Pevsner or Korn at all: what it does mean is that, despite holding both men in high esteem, and being grateful to both of them for many reasons, it is neither dishonourable nor 'spiteful' to suggest that they might, in some respects, have been severely and seriously mistaken, even to the extent of contributing to a great deal of damage.

When marvellous publications[52] of the past demonstrate what beautifully designed, sensitive, and carefully detailed works of real architectural quality were being created in the United Kingdom alone in the years before 1914, a sense of great loss is inevitable, and comparisons with much-lauded productions by today's architects might suggest that something like a massive cultural disruption has occurred. This ought to be cause for concern, yet seems to be merely accepted as part of a general, inevitable, resigned attitude to the incomprehensible and to current fashion. Thus this book is inevitably filled with regret, but it also contains critical examinations of what seem to be absurdities that have been supinely adopted as bases for what is happening in the world of architecture. What is needed now, perhaps more than ever before, is a surgical, thorough, methodical *exposé* of the ideologies of those responsible for an environmental and cultural disaster on a massive scale, and no punches should be pulled when compiling it.

There appears to be a yawning chasm between architectural criticism and the facts of architectural history: in a lifetime reading about architecture and looking at it, I have been amazed, time and time again, to perceive how many authors have proved they are incapable of seeing that which is in front of them, or that they wilfully distort what is visible in that about which they write.[53] Whole generations have been informed that works by distinguished Arts-and-Crafts architects were 'pioneering' designs of the Modern Movement,[54] which is simply untrue, as anyone who really looks clear-sightedly at buildings by C.R. Mackintosh, C.F.A. Voysey, and others would immediately be able to understand. It is a curious problem, but it suggests that those who uncritically accepted such assertions are unable to use their eyes, and can only believe what they are told: indeed, they are not looking at all, but are superimposing the opinions of others, overlayering what they could see with what others wish them to see. In other words, they look with their ears.

I recall reading essays by students, all of which claimed that the Glasgow School of Art contained nothing derived from period styles, something I knew was untrue. When I questioned the students it was clear they had all lifted this uncritically from Pevsner's *Pioneers*,[55] so I asked them each in turn if they had ever seen the building, or bothered to study pictures of it. One had 'seen' the building, and a few admitted to having glanced at the photograph in Pevsner's book, but none had actually studied it and tested the evidence of what could be viewed in the image against what Pevsner had claimed for the architecture. When I showed them good, comprehensive, clear photographs of the building, picking out details, comparing them with images of *Art-Nouveau* details and canted bay-windows from English vernacular buildings, and then displayed a photograph of Lutyens's house known as *Le Bois des Moutiers*, they were profoundly shaken, but it taught them a salutary lesson: to check statements made against what could actually be seen, and not to take printed opinions by polemicists as truths without testing them. Many thanked me later for what to them at the time was a shocking revelation.

Is this the result of having a word-based culture rather than a visual one; or is it intellectual idleness or mere cowardice in being unable to see facts for what they are? Or is it, perhaps, the result of brainwashing and indoctrination? Architects, curiously more than most, seem to be afflicted with a chronic inability to see and think with clarity: even in the early nineteenth century, certain architects claimed their designs for crenellated houses had been derived from ecclesiastical architecture, yet it is obvious that was not so.[56]

The strange thing about the almost universal embrace of architectural Modernism and Corbusier-inspired town planning is that it occurred at all. This cannot be explained only in terms of a few proselytisers, pedagogues, practitioners, loaded 'histories' that were essentially polemics, well-publicized exemplars, or claims for their 'rationalism' or 'functionalism' (both of which soon turned out to be neither, but were just concerned with appearance, packaging, and the creation of images that *suggested* these). Something more was required to propel the Modern Movement into global acceptance. First of all, in the 1930s it captivated wealthy, fashionable society in the USA through the taste-formers associated with the Museum of Modern Art in New York;[57] secondly, its possibilities were quickly grasped in America by large commercial/financial concerns, such as General Motors, which lobbied both public opinion and politicians to back it;[58] thirdly, it was seen after the 1939–45 war as the antithesis of the sort of grandiose stripped Classicism that had been favoured for public, official architecture by German National Socialism and during the Cold War by the Stalinist Soviet Union, so was promoted by groups working against the Soviet Union;[59] fourthly, its association with *émigrés* from Germany (some of whom had attempted to work for the National-Socialist *régime*, but that inconvenient fact was suppressed) gave it a kind of kudos, a tenuous connection with a righteousness that was founded on fantasy; fifthly, its dogmatic assertions, 'energised by a heady mix of economic power and quixotic idealism',[60] were not countered intellectually by the traditional architectural profession, which was increasingly sidelined as irrelevant, with '*bourgeois*' 'reactionary' values, and browbeaten into silence; and sixthly, the combination of product-marketing, the manufacture of industrialized building components and systems, and designers who abandoned everything in order to serve the machine-minimalism claimed as 'objective', 'functional', 'rational', and so on, produced environments that enriched those involved in their creation but impoverished those who had to live and work in them.

Architecture itself, once a respected art, was tragically corrupted by the industrialization of the human habitat, serving not society and the betterment of the human condition but the interests of enormous conglomerates and financial/commercial corporations only concerned with ever-greater profits and ever-increasing production. Many key figures of the Modern Movement and their successors today embraced a 'vehement ideological rigidity'[61] and a 'cognitive bias' similar to that occurring in other forms of fundamentalism.[62] A by-product of this is the curious blindness of architects to the many negative and unpleasant effects of their own work: such 'architectural myopia'[63] rejects the views of ordinary people, the public, who wonder why architects, and architectural students, want to create strange, unpleasant, expensive, crude structures, ill-mannered interlopers that damage the environment today. In other words, there is, and has been for some time, a 'remarkable divergence between the way architects see their work and the way non-architects do'.[64]

Some of these matters will be described below, and this book will make a plea for clear-sightedness, for a more humane and pleasant environment, and for a stop to outlandish fashions that only serve advertisers, corporate greed, and 'celebrity culture' (which has nothing in common with real culture of any value).[65] It will also regret the widespread infantilism that seems to be endemic: infantilism was already a tendency present in John Ruskin's writings in the nineteenth century, but is now so widespread it threatens everything that is actually important. When attention-spans become ever-shorter, reading a whole book is too much to expect of many undergraduates, and whole groups feel 'challenged' or 'threatened' by anything they cannot be bothered to study, it becomes clear that the infantilization of society proceeds.[66]

This is a gloomy, even frightening, prospect for the future, but there are some glimmerings of hope that real architecture might once more be revived. Apart from the School of Architecture at the University of Notre Dame, South Bend, Indiana, USA,[67] there are several organizations devoted to the study and practice of the art and craft of architecture, including the Traditional Architecture Group (TAG) and the International Network for Traditional Building, Architecture, & Urbanism (INTBAU), both of which were founded by the English architect, Robert Adam.[68] INTBAU runs a Summer School in Sweden in which Adam and other members of ADAM Architecture (the practice established in Winchester, Hampshire, and London) participate. Adam, too, has been involved with the Council for European Urbanism, with the British Academy of Urbanism, and with the Prince of Wales's Foundation for Building Community. The MArch design-studio, Kingston University, Surrey, teaches the *application* of the Classical language of architecture to contemporary design, making explicit issues of scale, proportion, order, and relief, all neglected in much modern education. The environment and climate-change have not been ignored either.

In the USA, too, many architects have turned away from the aridities of Modernism, yet have seen their work as a branch of Modernism, freed from its stultifying stylistic shackles. R.A.M. Stern, for example, has spoken of architecture having a 'public responsibility': its future, as well as the fabric of Western civilization as a whole, depends on society's ability and willingness to seek precedents in the massive riches of its inheritance rather than ditching that great legacy. He has expressed his belief that the past can 'release us from the tyranny of the present' as well as help to create a future in which scientific and technological innovation will support the enhancement of daily life.[69] To him, architecture is a 'meditation of the present on the past' as well as a 'speculation of the present on the future': 'Modern architecture' in the 1960s was defined as 'buildings your mother and practically everyone else hated', and he had no doubt where the blame for that lay. European Modernists (and their American supporters) had 'combined to rob American architects of the courage to continue their dialogue with the past',[70] yet architecture is 'not a private meditation': it is 'a public art'.[71]

Several students, too, are beginning to show an interest in historical architecture and what it can offer for inspiration and even emulation: those brave enough are finding meaning, metaphor, and much else in works by great architects of the past, although they may have to do so in a clandestine manner, concealing the fact from their 'Modernist' tutors for whom they have to conform to something in which they do not believe. Some of my own students, realizing the implication of those Modernists who took over the Royal Institute of British Architects (RIBA) from the 1950s onwards in corrupting what architecture should be all about, refused to join that institution after they qualified as architects: some joined the Art Workers' Guild instead, a body that still values aspects of creative activity long ditched by the *apparatchiks* of the Modern Movement.

In January 2017 I met a young man who had spent five years studying architecture in a state of some bewilderment, not finding much intellectual stimulation in the sort of stuff to which he had been subjected by his tutors. Then, through a new tutor who knew something of architectural history and its wider culture, he discovered Hawksmoor, one of the greatest architects England had ever produced after the Middle Ages: this was a revelation, and the student began to devour every book he could find which featured the work of Hawksmoor, discovering the tensions and possibilities of the juxtaposition of masses of masonry, the drama and power of modelling, light, and dark in vigorous design, and design-triggers from Antiquity, the Renaissance, and the mediaeval period that informed an architecture of immense emotional resonance wholly absent in the flabbiness, shallowness, and superfluities of so much 'modern' architecture. The student told me that in two weeks not only had he learned more than in the previous five years when he felt architecture had no real meaning, but now he was galvanized, enthused, and belatedly discovered a whole world of amazing richness, beauty, and possibility.

In Petrarch's celebration of Scipio Africanus,[72] there is a passage relevant to this topic:

> Poterunt discussis forte tenebris
> Ad purum priscumque iubar remeare nepotes[73]
> (Then perhaps, with the darkness dispelled,
> Our descendants will be able to return to the pure radiance of the past).

Regrettably, that 'pure radiance' was noticeably absent from the Modern Movement in architecture and urban planning: Dystopias it created were not celebrated for illumination other than garish advertisements for trivialities that are not needed, and no references to the past were permitted in their urban deserts. An historical vacuum was the result of the widespread adoption of the Modern Movement. That cannot be filled with what Robert Adam has aptly described as 'glib eclecticism':[74] it requires nothing less than a rebuilding of education with a respect for the past, an immersion in history and culture, including a religious dimension, and an end to the inglorious separation of 'academic' education from technical and craft teaching (and, indeed, the deplorable compartmentalization of the 'Humanities' and the 'Sciences'). Architecture is far too important to be entrusted to the products of talking-shops: as a public art, it matters hugely, and it cannot succeed unless it connects with the public in a positive way, conveys meanings, arouses resonances, reaches back to the past and forward to the future, and has the appearance of stability. All great architecture turns gravitational thrust to aesthetic advantage, expressed historically in the Orders and in Gothic construction, for example. Architecture only succeeds as architecture as an expression of gravitational control and stability:[75] if it fails in these respects, it induces anxiety. Coventry Patmore understood the importance of this, and had no truck with contemporary critics such as Ruskin and their shallow, fallacious arguments about ornament, morality, and an impoverished, restrictive palette of supposedly 'acceptable' styles.[76]

Deconstructivism and Parametricism, by rejecting all that went before and failing to provide clear values as replacements, can be seen as intentional aggression on human senses, abusing perceptive mechanisms in order to generate unease, dislocation, and discomfort. But that attack, that aggression, began a century ago, gaining impetus after 1945 (backed largely by American money and political clout, and catalysed by 'Grand Narrative' polemics masquerading as history):[77] it managed almost complete victory some thirty years later, yet its protagonists were blind to the ravages of what they had done.[78] Subsequent branches of Modernism have made a Dystopia even more alien and unhumane: it is time for a complete rethink.

Afterword & Acknowledgements

Any author owes much to earlier writers: the sources to which this study is indebted are many, but only those which have been major influences are given within. All my life I have read voraciously, and days without books and journals (more and more usual for most people these days) would be unbearable to me. Matter, absorbed over a lifetime from books, journals, and conversations, has imperceptibly become unconsciously part of my own intellectual make-up, and its origins have simply been forgotten with the passing of time, so publications cited represent only a fraction of what has prompted the contents of this volume. Obligations to acknowledge such long-assimilated knowledge or opinions are the hardest to make, for that reason, because when one has come to believe they are one's own, the memories of original sources have entirely faded. The many authors of works read by me over the last seventy years or so are therefore thanked for enriching, disturbing, or irritating: whatever my reactions, they all stimulated thought, and that is what counts. The notes and bibliography acknowledge material by others used in this study, and also include works that have some indirect bearing on the subjects discussed: they could have been much more extensive, and no doubt will be criticized for not incorporating this or that volume or paper favoured by pundits. Nevertheless, in my judgement, everything included is there for a reason, not a mere whim.

Dates of individuals will not appear in the texts. A decision was made with the publishers not to include them there, because the flow can be interrupted if a page is littered with dates, so the years of birth and death (if known) are given in the *index only*: the information is there if required by the reader.

Many years of travel, study, and looking with unclouded eyes rather than ears have contributed to the making of this book. Thanks are recorded to the British Council, which arranged for two major study visits (1986–7) to the former *Deutsche Demokratische Republik* (DDR), the Ministry of Culture of which facilitated delvings in numerous places, especially Weimar, Dessau, Berlin, and Dresden, thus providing a fairly comprehensive understanding of the convoluted history of Modernism, not least that connected with the *Bauhaus* and the shifting sands of politics: in my DDR journeyings, benefit was derived from the assistance of Eva Eissmann in cutting through tedious bureaucratic obstructions. Later, in a reunited Germany, Andreas Förderer arranged a memorable visit with Jan Snoek to the *Mathildenhöhe*, Darmstadt,[79] a real eye-opener; Georg Friedrich Kempter kindly discussed the Column in its various manifestations, meanings, and uses;[80] and David Lehrman generously provided information on Poznań.

Gratitude is due to several persons who helped to make this book possible: first of all, my father, the late George Stevens Curl, who refused facile arguments, insisted on testing attitudes, and had a fine eye (and well-tuned ear); secondly, the late A.H. Buck, who insisted on clarity of expression and avoidance of obfuscation; thirdly, Judith Wilson and Matthew Cotton of Oxford University Press, who saw the point, and without whose backing nothing would have been written at all. Unfortunately, Matthew Cotton fell seriously ill when the book was being written, so his duties were assumed by Luciana O'Flaherty, assisted by Martha Cunneen: from the summer of 2017 Matthew Cotton, Martha Cunneen, Hannah Newport-Watson, and

Gemma Wilkins (later Alec Swann) took over, and Paul Dines dealt with the onerous task of copy-editing, so their efforts helped to steer the work through the choppy processes leading to publication. Kim Behrens and Kate Shepherd efficiently managed publicity, Dorothy McCarthy read the proofs with me, and Auriol Griffith-Jones prepared the splendid Index with her customary expertise. Finally, my wife, Dorota Iwaniec, with rare grace and patience, put up with the inconveniences, tedium, and distractions inevitable during the book's gestation, construction, and completion: she helped in a great many ways (not least tracking down useful material) to ease it to the finish, for which she has my humble thanks.

Among many others who helped in different ways were Frank Albo, whose infectious enthusiasm and encouragement spurred me to proceed with what turned out to be a huge task; Maureen Alden, who, with great generosity of spirit, made helpful suggestions for improvements to the text, and heroically corrected several clangers; the late Stephen Dykes Bower, who provided insights into the repugnant tactics of Modernist bullies; Timothy Brittain-Catlin, who courageously allowed quotations from his publications, shared some thoughts with me, and very kindly wrote the *Prolegomenon*; Madeleine Compagnon of the Monacelli Press, who organized permission to quote from the work of R.A.M. Stern; Carol Conlin, Gregory Dunstan, and their colleagues in Armagh Public Library for their unfailing kindness and courtesy; Inge Drew, who corrected my clumsy translations from her native language; Lucas Elkin, formerly of the University of Cambridge Library, who managed to dig out some obscure stuff with great speed, humour, and efficiency; Susan Halpert, Reference Librarian, Houghton Library, Harvard University, for invaluable help with some unpleasant correspondence connected with Mendelsohn and Gropius; Clare Hastings, for permission to use an illustration by Osbert Lancaster; Simon Jenkins, who permitted the use of material from his perceptive writings; Ian Johnson, whose friendship and backing always raised morale; the late Arthur Korn, whose support greatly helped a young man, and with whom lively arguments sparked the heretical thought that Korn's 'leftist-Modernist' orthodoxy might be mistaken; the late Arthur Ling, whose trenchant views expressed in kindly and timely terms stimulated early musings on matters mentioned in this book; Nicholas Llewellyn, with help regarding reproduction of a drawing by Osbert Lancaster; Lutz Luithlen, who made useful comments; Scott McMaster, who came to the rescue when IT mysteries or infections had to be unravelled or cured; Malcolm Millais, who supplied some interesting technical material based on his original studies of the *Unité d'Habitation* at Marseilles; Ulrike Möhlenbeck, *Leiterin des Historischen Archivs*, *Akademie der Künste*, Berlin, who helped with material relating to what was the Prussian Academy of Arts; Tanya O'Sullivan, who assisted with biblio-graphical matters and illustrations; the writings of the late Coventry Patmore,[81] which revealed many basic architectural truths that have been forgotten, especially in the Deconstructivist and Parametricist miasmas; the late Nikolaus Pevsner, who generously provided leads concerning several Victorian archi-tects, especially Henry Roberts; the late Georges-Henri Pingusson, who shared insights concerning the 1930s and after; Tanja Poppelreuter, who kindly sent the author her perceptive paper on Miës van der Rohe's concept of the 'dweller', 1926–30; the staff of the Linen Hall Library, Belfast, who managed to get material through inter-library loans with amazing speed and absence of tedious bureaucracy; Nikos Salingaros, who sent some very useful material and was kindness itself in his copious generosity with criticisms, ideas, references, and suggestions; Nina Schönig and Erika Babatz of the *Bauhaus-Archiv/Museum für Gestaltung*, Berlin; Megan Schwenke, Senior Archivist/Records Manager, Harvard Art Museums, for help with docu-ments; the late Albert Speer, who suggested looking at the works of certain architects active in the 1930s; the late Gavin Stamp, for liberally sharing infor-mation and warm friendship over many years, and who provided encourage-ment for the project; Anthony Symondson, SJ, for discussing the works of Comper and Dykes Bower with me over a long and agreeable luncheon at his Club; Peter Walker, for exploring with me useful ideas concerning the way forward for architectural education; the late David Watkin, for invaluable support; Nigel Wilkins, Archive Services Officers, Historic England, for help with illustrations; and Nicola Willmot-Noller for her insights, taste, expertise, and speed in assisting with the design of the wrapper. I am also extremely grateful to Geoff Brandwood, Lawrence Matheson, the late Gavin Stamp, and Mark Watson for their great kindness in supplying images (some taken especially for this book, at extremely short notice) to replace those of Historic England's photographs which had become financially out of reach; Jason Canham, Simon Edwards, Tricia Lawton, Richard Reed, and Cathy Wilson of the RIBA Library and Information Centre, London, for assistance in check-ing journal references (and their patience in so doing); Gill and the late Hal Wilson, who enthusiastically endorsed the project, read the first drafts, offered constructive criticism, and encouraged me to get on with the work, despite exhaustion and self-doubt; Katharine Wilson, for allotting a considerable amount of time to propose perspicacious and extremely helpful tweaks of the text; Vicky Wilson, Assistant Curator, RIBA Drawings & Archives Collection,

Victoria & Albert Museum, London; and, last, but not least, Susan Wilson, who loyally, in friendship, in 2013 argued (mindful of the problems inherent in what is a convoluted subject) that I should propose the topic to Oxford University Press (with which publisher we had worked for several years to produce our *Oxford Dictionary of Architecture* [2015 & 2016]), as she recognized I had long been deeply concerned about the future of architecture and urban design, and needed to get many of my thoughts and views on the matter coherently down on paper and out of my system, especially in relation to reversing the general attitude in architectural circles that was anti-history. Learning from historical precedents has always been the means to successful development across the arts until that was not only discouraged but actively forbidden by doctrinaire Modernist theorists and teachers.

After the appearance of the UK hardback edition, published in August 2018, I was greatly encouraged by many colleagues, critics, and friends in these islands and on the European Continent, including George Bain, David Black, Tim Brittain-Catlin, Robert Cooper, Patricia Craig, Graham Cunningham, Anthony Daniels, Audun Engh, Brian Hamilton, Michael Harris, Hugh Kavanagh, Robert Lane, Karen Latimer, David Lee, Colum Mulhern, Patrick O'Keeffe, Caro Skyrme, John Smylie, Anthony Sully, Marjo Uotila, and Susan Wilson, as well as generously supported by gallant allies 'across The Pond' following the issue of the book in the USA, including Frank Albo, Steve Bass, David Brussat, Nir Buras, Giovanna Costantini, Christine Franck, Joscelyn Godwin, Mark Alan Hewitt, Kendra Mallock, Michael Mehaffy, Nikos Salingaros, and Brian G. Scott. Their assistance, unstintingly given, is herewith recorded with my warmest appreciation and gratitude: no author could have received more or better from anybody, and their generosity and wisdom have been amazing, heart-warming, and hugely morale-boosting. Kizzy Taylor-Richelieu of Oxford University Press oversaw the preparation of the paperback, and has my thanks for her meticulous work, as has Matthew Cotton for his unwavering support and faith in the book.

James Stevens Curl

Berlin, Broadfans, Cambridge,
Chicago, Darmstadt, Dublin,
Glasgow, Holywood, London,
New York, Oxford, Paris, Rutland,
Weimar, Winchester, and Wrocław

1970–2019

I

Origins of a Catastrophe

Introduction: A Few Definitions; The Modern Movement; A Strange Aberration; Pugin, the Ruskin Problem, Perils of Uncritical Acceptance, & Some Perceptive Critics; Hermann Muthesius; Harry Kessler, van de Velde, & Weimar; The Deutscher Werkbund; The Werkbund Exhibition, Cologne, 1914; Epilogue

> *An der heutigen, mit verkrüppeltem Kunstorgan behafteten Gesellschaft ist vielleicht nichts bezeichnender, als die vollkommene Unfähigkeit, irgend ein Verhältnis zur Architektur zu gewinnen. Malerei und Bildhauerei interessieren ja wenigstens durch die Anekdote, die Architektur bleibt aber ganz unverständlich* (Nothing is more characteristic of modern society's atrophied appreciation of the arts than its complete inability to form any kind of relationship with architecture. Painting and sculpture may appeal through their anecdotal content, but architecture remains completely unintelligible).
>
> HERMANN MUTHESIUS (1861–1927): *Das Englische Haus: Entwicklung,*
> *Bedingungen Anlage, Aufbau, Einrichtung und Innenraum* i
> (Berlin: Ernst Wasmuth 1908–11) 7

> *Modernismus* is an hysterical state, the climax of a succession of false starts. It began on the Continent before the War.[1] In France and Germany, the break-up of tradition and the loss of all standards in the Arts went very much further and at the same time there was a rapid advance in applied science resulting in a tendency to mechanize everything. Modernists translated the Arts into terms of mechanical science yet they should have concentrated on finding the right balance between the two. However, with the 'recklessness of ignorance' they threw everything overboard...
>
> SIR REGINALD THEODORE BLOMFIELD (1856–1942): *Modernismus*
> (London: Macmillan & Co. Ltd 1934) 171

Introduction: A Few Definitions

It is best, at the beginning, to clarify a few terms used in this book. A place, state, or condition, ideally perfect in respect of politics, laws, customs, and conditions has been described as *Utopia* (from the Greek οὐ [= not] + τόπος

[= a place]), once imagined by Thomas More as an island that enjoyed a perfect social, legal, and political system,[2] though some have interpreted his work as a satire on Tudor government. More, or his friend, Peter (Pieter) Giles (Gilles *or* Gillis), of Antwerp, printer, Humanist, and city official, used the word *Eutopia* (from the Greek εὖ [= good or well] and τόπος [= a place]) to signify a region of ideal happiness or good order: in other words, a positive Utopia.

Of course there were earlier versions of ideal societies, including *The Republic* of Plato. The concept of a city suggests a reality which is both ideal and empirical. Throughout history the city has been the centre of civilization, set apart from the barbarous, hostile countryside, and the Ideal City may be viewed in terms of *Revelation*[3] as the City of God, a regular, symmetrical creation that may have its roots in the human sub-conscious. The symbolic aspects of designs for ideal cities cannot be over-stressed, and emphasize the desire for wholeness, completeness, and unity expressed in the shapes and plans. Such plans have affinities with the designs for labyrinths, such as that in the centre of Chartres Cathedral, France, representing a journey, a ritual pilgrimage, an allegory of life's journey, with its trials, tribulations, and false turnings, yet a goal at the very centre (**Figures 1.1a & b**).[4]

The notion of the Ideal City influenced many designs for geometrical symmetrical plans for settlements during the Renaissance period: all of these

Figure 1.1a. Labyrinth of inlays of blue and white stones in the centre of the nave of Chartres cathedral, measuring some 13 metres (43 feet) in diameter. The way to the central point (called the *Paradise* or *Jerusalem*) was 230 metres (775 feet) long, representing a journey, a ritual pilgrimage, progress through life itself, with all its false turnings

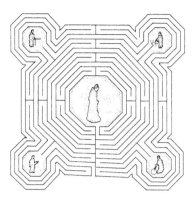

Figure 1.1*b*. Labyrinth formerly in Rheims cathedral, from a sixteenth-century representation (it was destroyed in the eighteenth century). Four master-masons were shown with compasses, square, etc., and the archbishop was depicted in the centre

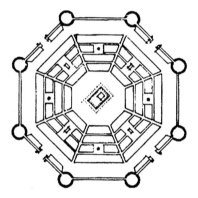

Figure 1.2. Ideal-City plan created during the Renaissance based on ideas in Vitruvius

were variants on patterns established during the reign of the Roman Emperor Augustus by Vitruvius (Marcus Vitruvius Pollio) (**Figure 1.2**), who, in turn, may have derived his typology from more ancient sources, now lost. Renaissance architects of the *città ideale* froze elements into formal patterns on which Man imposed his ideals and heroic dimensions (**Figure 1.3**),[5] often with a central structure (e.g. a fortified building or a church) as an expression of the social order. Such perfect geometrical plans also symbolized the yearning for Utopia, the perfect State, and even the City of God, the *New Jerusalem*, and include works by Antonio di Pietro Averlino (known as *Il Filarete* [from the Greek φιλάρετος = lover of excellence]) (**Figure 1.4***a*),

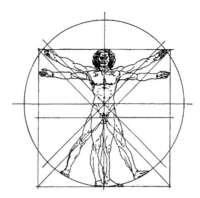

Figure 1.3. Vitruvian Man imposing his own dimensions upon the elemental forms (the square and the circle) of the Ideal City

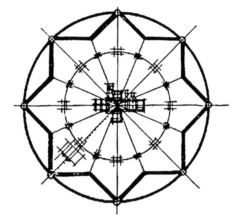

Figure 1.4*a*. Sforzinda, by Filarete (*c.*1457–64)

Pietro Cataneo, Albrecht Dürer, Bonaiuto Lorini, Francesco (Maurizio) di Giorgio Martini, Jacques Perret, Giulio Savorgnano, Vincenzo Scamozzi, Heinrich Schickhardt, and others (**Figures 1.4*b*–*c*).**[6]

Figure 1.4*b* (*facing page*). Renaissance Ideal-City plans with massive fortifications: (*top*) proposal by Bonaiuto Lorini (*c.*1590s) showing a central octagonal space with radiating streets and six squares in the centres of densely packed urban fabric; (*centre*) design by Pietro Cataneo (published 1554) for a heptagonal arrangement of fortifications within which is a grid pattern of streets and blocks, a large central square, and other squares disposed within the grid; and (*bottom*) Vincenzo Scamozzi's version (published 1615) of a grid with one central rectangular space, four squares, and a grid pattern set within a dodecagon held within a geometrically arranged set of bastions

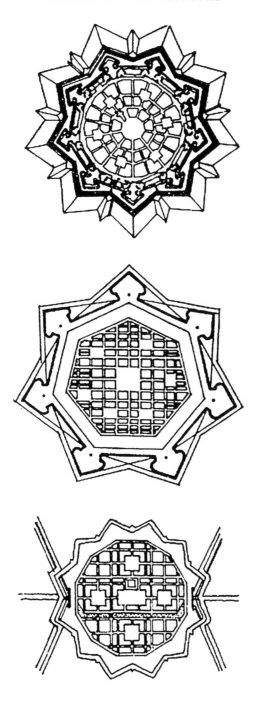

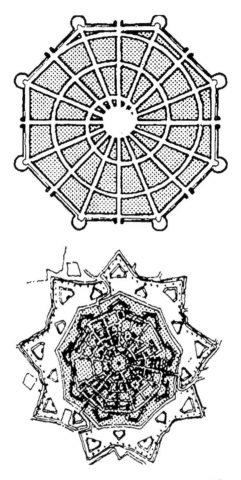

Figure 1.4c. (*top*) Ideal-City plan by Giorgio Martini with spiral street-pattern leading to central circular open space; (*bottom*) plan of the unfinished town of Palmanova, the fortress-town of Venice (1593–8), designed by Giulio Savorgnano, Lorini, and Scamozzi

It follows that *Dystopia* (the opposite of *Utopia*) is a place or condition in which everything is as bad as possible. Aldous Huxley's *Brave New World*[7] and George Orwell's *Nineteen Eighty-Four*[8] are about *Dystopias*. 'They describe not a world we should like to live in, but one we must be sure to avoid':[9] however, as the quality of the environment, notably in terms of architecture, infrastructure, and urban devastation, deteriorates, to a very great extent because of matters discussed in this book, 'our real future is more likely to be dystopian',[10] a grim prospect indeed.[11]

And what do we mean by 'Modern Architecture', 'Modernism', 'Modernist', the 'Modern Movement'? 'Modern' has meant whatever one might want it to mean.[12] If we look at such sumptuous volumes as the Dutch *Moderne Architectuur* (1927)[13] most of the exemplars therein would hardly be described as 'modern' today. Otto Wagner's *Moderne Architektur*[14] is *fin-de-siècle* Austro-Hungary steeped in Baroque, Neo-Classicism, *Jugendstil*, and it contains nothing of what might be perceived as 'modern' now (even though Wagner [who conveniently died in 1918, a few months before the collapse of the Empire he had served so well] was reinvented by the compilers of the hitherto widely accepted Modernist cult-narrative as a proto-Modernist). Werner Hegemann's *Façades of Buildings* (1929) illustrates over 500 buildings, only a fraction of which could be regarded as 'modern', and demonstrates a refreshingly undogmatic stylistic approach to early twentieth-century architecture.[15] In 1922, Hegemann had collaborated with Elbert Peets on *The American Vitruvius*, one of the finest twentieth-century publications dealing with urban design and architecture, and although skyscrapers and a good medley of modern buildings are included, their selection is eclectic, giving a full flavour of the vast range of stylistic choice available in the 1920s before the authoritarian zealots of International Modernism dictated their architectural agenda.[16]

Confusingly, the word *Moderne* refers also to the Art-Deco style. *Modernismo* is Spanish *Art Nouveau*, also called *Estilo Modernista*, and mostly associated with Catalonia, where it was called *Modernisme*, connected with an assertion of regional (even nationalistic) identity: yet its architectural expression lay in the incorporation of eclectic elements derived from historic styles (notably Moorish and Gothic), in the exploitation of materials (especially brick and tile) to express structure as well as to embellish every visible part of the fabric, and exuberant use of enrichment, applied or integral to the structure. Its most celebrated protagonists were Domènech i Montaner, Gaudí i Cornet, and Puig i Cadafalch, none of whom, by any torturing of facts, could ever be regarded as a Modernist, 'pioneer' or otherwise.[17] The '*Modern Style*' was a term also applied to *Art Nouveau*, called *Nieuwe Kunst* in The Netherlands, *Jugendstil* (Youth Style) in German-speaking countries (though in parts of German-speaking Europe, notably Austria-Hungary, it was identified as *Sezessionstil* because it was associated with those artists who seceded from traditional, conservative academies to show their works), and *Stile Liberty* or *Stile Floreale* in Italy.

The style conveniently labelled *Art Nouveau* was abhorred by converts to the Modern Movement, who clung to deliberately unnatural abstractions.

It had its roots in the late Gothic Revival: the flowing forms that were such a feature of the style were also found in sixteenth-, seventeenth-, and eighteenth-century Auricular and Rococo ornament.[18] Viollet-le-Duc's *Entretiens* (1858–72) disseminated images of free-flowing curved forms throughout Europe and America, and there are many instances in the Gothic Revival where *Art-Nouveau* motifs[19] occur much earlier than suggested by many commentators. The Gothic Revival, however, was the main source for *Art Nouveau*, albeit with much attenuated emphasis.

None of this could ever be regarded as having any connection with the so-called 'Modern Movement', nor did those who promoted that 'Modern Movement' approve of *Art Nouveau*. Even Hermann Muthesius, in *Das englische Haus*, made overt his antipathy to what some have described as a '*movement, not a style*',[20] despite the fact that there was a time when '*Modern Style*' referred specifically to *Art Nouveau*.

The Modern Movement

A short explanation of the essence of Modernism in architecture was included in the Preface. The term 'Modern Architecture' may refer to all buildings of the modern period, but more often it signals a narrow stylistic/ideological approach, usually associated with International Modernism and with a handful of architects and their disciples approved of by its theorists, apologists, and protagonists.[21]

'Modernist' can also suggest an architectural style (1920s/30s) incorporating decorative devices that owed not a little to Art-Deco, Aztec, and Ancient-Egyptian styles, prompted by the discovery (1922) of the tomb of King Tutankhamun and by the Paris *Exposition Internationale des Arts-Décoratifs et Industriels Modernes* (1924–5). Among commoner motifs were chevrons, canted and corbelled pseudo-arches, medallions, wave-scrolls, flutings, mouldings stepped over surfaces, and strong geometrical patterns. Colours were vivid, influenced by Ancient-Egyptian artefacts such as those associated with Tutankhamun, so blacks, vermilions, greens, yellows, blues, and lots of gilt and chrome were *de rigueur*, often in enamels and even glazed openings.[22] 'Modernistic' buildings (as they are often called) also incorporated streamlining and curved walls: a good example of Modernistic architecture (**Plate 1.1**) is the former Hoover Building, Western Avenue, London (1931–8), by Wallis, Gilbert, & Partners (Nikolaus Pevsner hated it, primly

Plate 1.1. Egyptianizing, Art-Deco, Modernistic former Hoover factory, Western Avenue, London (1931–8), by Wallis, Gilbert, & Partners: the long front, with battered sides, is a version of an Egyptian temple-front, whilst *loculi*-like openings are recalled in the windows of the towers (which also sport tall windows with heads composed of the chamfered or canted pseudo-arch)

dubbing it 'offensive' and a 'modernistic atrocity' because it did not fit neatly into his *Bauhaus*-slanted, Gropius-worshipping narrative).[23] 'Modernist' also can mean a person subscribing to the doctrines and principles of the 'Modern Movement'.[24]

The term 'Modern Movement' is used to encompass disparate twentieth-century architectural tendencies (also called 'Modernism')[25] that sought to sunder all stylistic/historic links with the past, despising context, and demanding replacement of existing buildings so that there could be no comparisons between the new and the old. There was much debate in the nineteenth century about how a *style* suitable for the times could be found. Attempts to achieve this involved eclecticism and mingling to produce so-called 'free' or 'mixed' styles, the optimistic idea being that something fresh might emerge from the well-spiced *mélange*: others claimed that 'function', 'honest' expression of structure and materials, and a 'rational' approach to design problems based on first principles freed from constraints of style were sufficient to point the way forward to a 'New Architecture'.[26]

Early twentieth-century movements associated with totalitarianism (such as Futurism and Constructivism) sought answers in machinery, technology, and the expression of industrialized power, while the search for a 'machine aesthetic' became at times an end in itself.[27] To some (notably Le Corbusier), grain-silos, ocean-going liners of the *Titanic* vintage, motor-cars, and aeroplanes were paradigms of a desirable new aesthetic (*see* **Figures 5.3, 6.1–2**),[28] but others held that all art, all aesthetics, and all refinement were *bourgeois* affectations and therefore should be avoided. Aims of Modernism were radical, concerned with the suppression of all ornament and historical allusions, counterbalanced by the search for so-called *Sachlichkeit* (variously translated as functionalism, impartiality, objectivity, pertinence, practicality, realism, reality, relevance) and the wholesale adoption of industrialized methods of construction.

Some Modernist groups (e.g., those associated with the Dutch *De Stijl*) advocated abstractions and purity of expression, and there were various different emphases within what was never a unified movement; but virtually all were agreed on the need for 'rational' responses to contemporary requirements using modern materials, mass-produced building components, and experimental, industrial methods of building (which brought in their wake many problems, including spectacular *functional* failures). While idealistic iconoclasm, allied with 'leftist' political attitudes, was endemic, the more extreme protagonists advocated violence: slogan-making and rabid polemics all too often suppressed all pretensions to 'rational' argument. 'Functionalism'[29] was supposed to be common ground, but even that term was subjected to objections in the search for an architecture freed from tiresome constraints, not only from the past and aesthetics, but from use as well. Some advocated that the purest architecture was that which remained on paper, or, even better, in the mind, uncorrupted by any processes involving getting it down in drawn form or being built, let alone used by imperfect, untidy human beings.

The so-called 'pioneer'[30] phase of the Modern Movement has been deliberately (but arguably erroneously [see Chapter II, *passim*]) identified with the British Arts-and-Crafts Movement, with *Art Nouveau*, and with other themes, personalities (notably C.F.A. Voysey and C.R. Mackintosh, neither of whom, despite the efforts of various writers, can be regarded by the clear-sighted as 'pioneer' Modernists), and supposed precedents. The Movement itself seems to have originated around the time of the 1914–18 war, and especially in the aftermath of that catastrophe. Its protagonists shared a concern of many nineteenth-century architects in that they sought an 'appropriate' contemporary mode of design. But what made it different from earlier stylistic movements was its absolutist nature not unconnected with 'left-wing' political stances. There had been tyrannical attitudes to Taste in English Palladianism, and the dogmatic 'moral' imperatives in the writings of A.W.N. Pugin and John Ruskin associated with religion certainly had unpleasant undercurrents. But the violently expressed coercion, aggression, and intolerance that permeated Modernist sloganizing were more than sinister, and were something new.

Secondly, Modernism's apologists created a 'Grand Narrative' which attempted to connect the extraordinarily fecund artistic movements and creative personalities (dubbed 'pioneers' by those apologists) of c.1880–1914 with what happened after 1918, but close and clear-sighted examination of that narrative exposes its obvious weaknesses. Through exhibitions, manifestos, publications, and exemplars, Modernist proselytizing succeeded in establishing Modern Movement roots in most Western countries, with the major aim, assumed to be a political necessity, of destroying the boundaries between aesthetics, technologies, and society. Architecture became a means by which, allegedly, social aims (or engineering) could be achieved.[31] Supposedly influenced by the writings of Friedrich Engels, Karl Marx, William Morris, and John Ruskin, among others, many accepted that the proletariat had been brutalized by mechanization and division of labour, leading to psychological impoverishment: so the alienated masses were seen as the victims of capitalism, and, ultimately, as machine-gun and high-explosives fodder for the slaughterhouse of 1914–18. Theorists noted further that since design was an essential element in the production of commodities, and therefore with wealth-creation, it was capable of changing the conditions of the proletariat, and so, the argument went, alienation could be reversed.[32]

Malign seeds of 'moral' confusion in architecture may be detected in Pugin's urgings[33] about architectural design. Ruskin, too, followed with dogmatic assertions regarding acceptable styles and 'morality', and these curious arguments formed the kernel of beliefs among Modern-Movement architects, although in that kernel there were no longer any religious or historical connotations. Faith in the possibilities of modes of building, freed from human imperfections, that grew logically as a result of some irrefutable, inevitable process, evolved into a quasi-religious belief in 'functionalism' and 'truth' in respect of materials. Yet what resulted was all about appearance and image and nothing about 'truth' at all. 'Truth', a *moral* value, became a supposed *aesthetic* value, not least to protagonists of the Modern Movement. The search for 'truth' went even further, rejecting decoration: and that meant discarding mouldings as well, even though those could help a building to weather naturally and with grace by throwing water off plain vertical walls below.

But we must now return to the origins of all this in the years before the 1914–18 war.

A Strange Aberration

If one looks at old photographs of streets in the British Isles taken just before the catastrophe of 1914, it is apparent that the architecture of the buildings lining those streets consists of series of predominantly *vertical* elements (**Plate 1.2a**). Pictures of the same streets (if those streets have survived) taken from the 1950s onwards show alien intruders with aggressive *horizontal* bands of windows, ground-floor insertions utterly unrelated in any way to what happens above, failure to respond to roof-pitches, and a lamentable demonstration of what can be described as not only architectural

Plate 1.2a. High Street, Belfast, *c.*1910 (the tramways were electrified in 1905), looking towards the Clock-Tower (1865–9) commemorating Albert, Prince Consort, designed by W.J. Barre. The third building from the left topped by urns (1888–9) is No. 16, called Washington House, probably designed by W.J. Gilliland. Each element in the street is characterized by a series of vertical elements

bad manners, but as an assault on the essence of architectural aesthetics (**Plate 1.2*b***). The deliberate disruption of established geometries was a direct result of the Modern Movement, and especially derives from designs by Maria Ludwig Michael Miës van der Rohe, Erich Mendelsohn, Charles-Édouard Jeanneret-Gris (*known as* 'Le Corbusier' from the early 1920s), and their legions of imitators. Yet this is not a contrast of aesthetics, but a fundamental clash with physiology: human beings evolved to accommodate forms responding to gravity, not to predominantly horizontal ones.[34] Gravitation and its counteraction[35] once informed all legitimate structural design to create an imagery of perceptible stability, 'the secret of beauty in architecture',[36] and Coventry Patmore, drawing on Kugler,[37] grasped both the essence of the *aesthetic development* of the principles of trabeation

Plate 1.2*b*. High Street, Belfast, 2016. Washington House is on the left, minus its urns and with its ground floor wrecked. Beyond it is a work of 1957–9 in the Festival-of-Britain manner, by Young & Mackenzie, then an uninspired block in the Neo-Georgian style (1955) by the same architects; but the aggressive *horizontals* of River House (Nos. 48–60) demonstrate the damage the Modern Movement could do to grain and character, typical of the way in which established geometries were destroyed by Modernist interventions that paid no heed whatsoever to context. In 2017–18 River House was re-clad, eliminating the horizontals, but nothing could be done about its bulk

(essentially, beams supported on columns or piers) in ancient Greek architecture and that of what the Germans call *emporstreben* (rise *or* tower *or* soar up) in Gothic architecture, with the 'transcendent symbolic potential' of the pointed arch.[38] Patmore also pointed out that architectural ornament, as in Gothic, was not *decorative*, but *expressive of structure*, a response to the laws of gravity, and therefore of physics, a view contrary to that of Ruskin, and completely incomprehensible to devotees of the Modern Movement.

It seems that, despite expensive so-called 'architectural education'[39] spanning several years of 'study', many, perhaps most, architects no longer understand the street (because they were told to ignore it in the writings of 'Le Corbusier', and obediently did so).[40] It would appear that conventionally trained Modernist architects are no longer capable of designing an aesthetically agreeable street, let alone intervene without making matters worse. The pleasures of walking down an old-established street are becoming rare, as Alain de Botton has noted: it is impossible to create pleasant, ordinary, humane streets or places when every architect is straining to be 'original', which really means cribbing exemplars of the latest fad, be it Deconstructivism, Parametricism, or whatever, an activity that can hardly be described as 'original'.[41] There was another factor that put paid to the street: in the 1930s a campaign in the USA to promote motor-cars as essential accessories proposed driving highways into towns and cities, destroying traditional streets, discouraging pedestrians, and making cars penetrate every part of the urban fabric.[42]

Throughout the ages, humankind has embellished its creations with ornament. If one considers exemplars of the architecture of ancient Mesopotamia, of ancient Egypt, of China, of Japan, of India, of Hellenic and Hellenistic culture, of the Roman Empire, of Islam, of Carolingian and Romanesque Europe, of the Middle Ages, of the Renaissance, Baroque, and Neo-Classical periods, of nineteenth-century Historicism, of the Arts-and-Crafts Movement, and indeed of any period in human history, ornament has played no small part in them all.

The exception has been the 'International Style'[43] that emerged from the 1920s, lauded as 'patently in accordance with the new social and industrial situation of architecture'.[44] With 'its refusal to accept craftsmanship and whims of design'[45] it was 'eminently suitable for a large anonymous clientele'.[46] Its 'sheer surfaces and minimum of mouldings for the industrial production of parts'[47] received the *imprimatur* of Nikolaus Pevsner and others.

The problems with the 'refusal to accept craftsmanship' and 'sheer surfaces and minimum of mouldings' were that buildings did not age gracefully, and indeed failed spectacularly, but succeeded as uncouth interlopers in established streets, towns, and cities. As Osbert Lancaster put it, the

> voice of the new Puritans, nourished in the doctrines of Gropius, Le Corbusier, and Mumford, first attained an authoritative ring in the late 'twenties, but even in the succeeding ten years, while it was listened to with ever-increasing respect, the number of persons who felt compelled to act upon such advice as it so generously gave remained disappointingly small.[48]

That voice, however, was hearkened to among 'progressive' persons, with startling results, but the chief catalysts were those intimately connected with commerce, finance, and politics.

It became apparent that something very strange had occurred: an aberration, something alien to the history of humanity, something destructive aesthetically and spiritually, something ugly and unpleasant, something that was inhumane and abnormal, yet something that was almost universally accepted in architectural circles, like some fundamentalist quasi-religious cult that demanded total allegiance, obedience, and subservience. What is more, the Modern Movement claimed to abolish 'style' by preventing any choice in the matter through the imposition of one single style (which it was at pains to claim was not a 'style' at all: one of the apostles of Modernism, Walter Gropius, for example, insisted, not entirely ingenuously, that the object of his creation, the *Bauhaus*, 'was not to propagate any "style", system, or dogma, but simply to exert a revitalising influence on design').[49]

Yet if disciples of the apostles and evangelists of Modernism had acquainted themselves with the huge stylistic choices available to architects of the latter part of the eighteenth and beginning of the nineteenth centuries, when the Picturesque was the subject of much consideration,[50] they might have understood that eclecticism represents freedom of thought and is a hallmark of sophisticated societies antipathetic to slavish adherence to imposed dogma. Regrettably, however, blinded by myopia, deafened by slogans shouted at *fortissimo* volume (notably by Le Corbusier), and cowed into submission for fear of being cast into critical outer darkness, they obeyed the *Diktat*, hearkened to the herd instinct, and adopted stylistic conformity.[51] Modernists did not actually want choice at all: their agenda were to *impose* that stylistic dictatorship by any means possible.

Clément Vautel denounced[52] such tendencies as *snobisme* based on the anxiety of the dim not to be left behind or out of the gloomy procession of obedience:[53] the Modernist asserts 'all authority and precedent should be abandoned'.[54] As Sir Reginald Blomfield observed, 'the "New Architecture" was a conscious and deliberate change in the whole orientation of architecture... dashing off to an extreme of crude and unabashed brutality, and total disregard of the amenities of town and country'.[55] The most curious aspect of all this is that the ideologies of European Modernism of the 1920s (with all the *lacunae* in their claims) were so widely accepted, apparently uncritically too (apart from a few brave souls who spoke out against them, to their own detriment): their ferocity, their evangelical sloganizing, and their intolerance seem to have provided illusions of probity[56] attractive to confused minds and puritanical dispositions. 'Traditionalists', Blomfield firmly declared, should 'refuse to be bullied by clamour and violent assertion',[57] but such aggressively declaimed posturings were universally accepted after 1945 for a strange *mélange* of reasons that coalesced in the aftermath of war.

Human beings are affected by their everyday surroundings: ugly, threatening, cacophonous, visually chaotic environments do not soothe the battered spirit. The harmonious, the unassuming, the ordinary, can contribute to an environment in which it is possible to live without anxiety, stress, or affronts to the sensibilities. *Deutsche Kunst und Dekoration*,[58] edited by Alexander Koch, was an important monthly publication that promoted modern design, and therefore the artists who created it: as an influence on design, and especially on architecture, it was highly significant in Germanophone countries from 1897 until the end of the Weimar Republic in 1933. Adolf Loos, hailed by commentators as a 'pioneer' of Modernism, stated that the

> best form is always readily at hand and nobody should be afraid to use it, even though it may come almost entirely from someone else. Enough of 'geniuses' and their originality! Let us repeat ourselves again and again! Let one building be similar to another! For doing that we will not be published in *Deutsche Kunst und Dekoration*, and we will not be appointed professors of applied Art, but we will have served our times, ourselves, our nation, and humanity to the best of our ability.[59]

Genius, indeed, 'is as rare among architects as among the rest of us'.[60] This was also realized during the Georgian period (1714–1830), so pattern-books were made available, enabling those without genius to design and erect buildings which did not offend or jar, fitted into contexts, and were at ease with themselves and with humanity.[61]

Pugin, the Ruskin Problem, Perils of Uncritical Acceptance, & Some Perceptive Critics

Long before Loos expressed those views, A. W. N. Pugin wrote of the 'Babel of confusion' where private judgement ran 'riot' and every architect had 'a theory of his own, a beau ideal' he had 'himself created; a disguise with which to invest the building' he erected...'Styles' were '*adopted* instead of *generated*, and ornament and design *adapted to*, instead of *originated by*, the edifices themselves', all of which could only lead to a veritable '*carnival* of architecture'.[62]

Pugin, a recent convert to Roman Catholicism, used the 'moral' argument to promote his vision of Gothic, and fourteenth-century Gothic at that, as well as his concept of the 'True Picturesque' by which three-dimensional forms grew naturally and unforced from plans.[63] Pugin's claims for what was 'true' or 'false', morally depraved or uplifting, and 'honest' or 'dishonest' included statements that 'there should be no features about a building which are not necessary for convenience, construction, or propriety';[64] that 'all ornament should consist of enrichment of the essential construction of the building';[65] that 'the smallest detail should have a meaning or serve a purpose';[66] that 'the construction itself should vary with the material employed';[67] that designs 'should be adapted to the material in which they are executed';[68] and that it was in 'pointed architecture [i.e. Gothic] alone that these great principles' could be demonstrated. Pugin's 'convenience', 'construction', and 'propriety' obviously owe debts to the paraphrases 'commodity', 'firmness', and 'delight' of Sir Henry Wotton,[69] 'durability [soundness or strength], convenience [utility], and beauty [attractiveness]'[70] (*firmitas, utilitas, venustas*) of Vitruvius,[71] and 'beauty', 'firmness', and 'convenience' of Sir Christopher Wren.[72]

It is significant that Pugin replaced 'delight' and 'beauty' with 'propriety', thus moving from a world of Picturesque sensation to a new (and dangerous) realm of moral judgement whereby the 'propriety' of the architecture depends upon whether or not it is 'proper' or appropriate for the use to which a building is put. Pugin's message was loud and clear: Classical architecture was no better than primitive Stonehenge in its columnar-and-trabeated structure, and was 'Pagan'[73] anyway, whereas 'pointed' architecture was not a style, but a principle, a moral crusade, and the only mode of building for a 'Christian' (by which he meant Roman Catholic) nation (which is what he earnestly hoped England would become).[74]

Interestingly, he did not think much of Greek temples, because when the Greeks started building with stone, 'the properties of this material did not suggest to them some different and improved mode of construction': they set up stone columns as they

> had set up trunks of wood; they laid stone lintels as they had laid wood ones, *flat across*; they even made the construction appear still more similar to wood, by carving triglyphs, which are merely a representation of the beam ends. The finest temple of the Greeks is constructed on the *same principle* as a large wooden cabin…but as for [it] being held up as the standard of architectural excellence,…it is a monstrous absurdity.[75]

All of which is somewhat different from the inaccuracies[76] later spouted by Le Corbusier (e.g. on the *guttae* below the frieze of the Athenian Parthenon: 'this plastic machinery is realized in marble with the rigour that we have learned to apply in the machine. The impression is of naked polished steel',[77] which, to anyone who has studied the Greek Doric entablature,[78] is a strangely perverse interpretation).

There can be no doubting the enormous influence Pugin had, for better or for worse, but one of the downsides was that he suggested to later generations that there might be a possibility of building something that was not marked by human imperfections, and which represented some sort of 'inescapable reality'.[79] Pugin stated that 'the severity of Christian architecture is opposed to all deception. We should never make a building erected to God appear better than it really is by artificial means',[80] but what he failed to note is that *all* buildings, without exception, *are* artificial. *The Architectural Review*, taking its cue from Pevsner and others, promoted Pugin as a founding-father of the Modern Movement; but Pugin, the Romantic, the champion of craftsmanship, the Gothic revivalist, the deeply religious Roman Catholic, the hardworking, scholarly designer steeped in history, and the enemy of falsehoods, simply cannot have been a founder or 'pioneer' of twentieth-century materialistic Modernism, with its insistence on the *tabula rasa*, its contempt for the *genius loci*, and its indifference to religion.

When one considers what Pugin actually wrote,[81] it is wholly impossible to see him as a prophet of 'High-Tech', Modernism, or Functionalism. With only slight modifications, his words could easily be applied to the situation today: 'The moderns…are constantly producing the greatest anomalies; and we are called upon to admire their thrice-cooked hashes…as fine national monuments of the present age.'[82] And he went on about the 'junta' who had 'disfigured the face of the country' (he was referring to those architects who had dominated the profession in the last two decades of the eighteenth and the first three of the nineteenth century):[83]

> Their works will hardly be endured for the time they have to run, and the remembrance of them will be the laughing-stock of posterity; and when the ancient glories of our native land are restored, and this generation of pretenders have passed away, men will be amazed that a period could have existed when they were permitted to disfigure and destroy, unchecked and unreproved.[84]

Pugin's prophecy led to a lack of appreciation of the works of numerous architects of whom he disapproved, and who worked with the Classical style, but were not averse to other styles as well: Nash's legacy, especially, suffered greatly, but the eclectic works of the 'junta' were later seen in more favourable lights. However, in the early decades of the twenty-first century, an obsession with expensive 'iconic' structures, conceived as though there were no context into which they were set, was very much apparent, so the second Puginian quotation could equally well apply to the contemporary situation. The desire to be 'original' has destroyed uniformity, yet uniformity is what makes many historical streets and towns agreeable.[85] The Georgian pattern-book had its uses, because it provided the alphabets, grammar, and vocabulary which enabled harmonious architecture to be created, even by modest talents.[86]

Variety, on the other hand, became *de rigueur*, with individuality, the fantastical, and even the whimsical jockeying for positions in what had been serenely understated street-frontages: and very often the people or groups who paid for the buildings went further, demanding vulgarity, individuality, and 'originality'. The assumption persists that a new architecture had to be invented from scratch every time a new school or other building-type was required. It is not possible to create decent, civilized environments when every Tom, Dick, or Harry of an architect is trying to be 'original' and create an 'icon'. Ordinary places are important, but courteous ordinariness is not what most modern architects seek to achieve in their works.

Pugin was not responsible for this state of affairs, though his name has been recruited to the cause of Modernism, notably in schools of architecture, where he might be mentioned to justify every kind of horror. Yet in the experience of the present writer, few students will turn out to have read him, but only to have heard what others have written or said about him, especially in relation to 'morality', 'honesty', and designing from the inside out. It is a sad state of affairs, but it is certainly arguable that Pugin's fanaticism and the power of his rhetoric in relation to architectural concerns have sometimes had less than beneficial effects.[87]

John Ruskin, too, observed that a 'day never passes without our hearing our English architects called upon to be original, and to invent a new style … We want no new style of architecture … But we want *some* style'.[88] However, when the stylistic exemplars he arbitrarily judged worthy of emulation were Pisan Romanesque, early Gothic of Western Italy, Venetian Gothic, and English Second Pointed (*aka* Decorated) of the fourteenth century, his readers might be permitted a twitch of the eyebrow. Ruskin found certain styles (e.g. Baroque) unacceptable, not only because of their associations with Roman Catholicism, but because they exploited illusion, and therefore could not be considered 'truthful'. The interchangeability of truth and beauty[89] seems to have originated with Keats, but Ruskin, though he went on at length about such matters 'in a score of thick volumes',[90] failed to give precise reasons or provide reasoned arguments as to why any one style of building should be more 'true' than any other. Indeed his texts remain, as Osbert Lancaster observed, with truth, 'impenetrably obscure'.[91]

This moral disapprobation to justify an aesthetic stance has been a dangerous weapon in the hands of International Modernists: the claim of Walter Gropius, for example, to have been influenced by Ruskin's writings,[92] would have surprised, even shocked, the Englishman himself. One might be excused for questioning Gropius's supposed admiration for someone who pulled four mediaeval styles out of his critical hat as models to be followed in the middle of the nineteenth century, for Gropius's works show no traces of any of them.

It is highly doubtful, however, if the 'style' that was universally adopted in the twentieth century would have met with Ruskin's approval anyway, and it certainly would have horrified Pugin. Yet Pugin, by linking beauty,[93] function, morality, propriety, and utility, and claiming that any *building that is treated naturally, without disguise or concealment, cannot fail to look well,*[94] sowed pernicious seeds, not least by substituting ethical/religious/moral notions for the earlier visual and associationist values by which a building was perceived as pleasant because it looked stable and suitable for what it was supposed to do.[95]

Sir Reginald Blomfield set out the problem with clarity. He pointed out that 'literature and the written word established a disastrous domination in arts not their own, and all sorts of strange ideals were introduced and pursued with an enthusiasm which constantly missed the mark, because most of its aims were irrelevant to the art of architecture'. He referred particularly to 'Ruskin and Morris,...men of...uneven judgment, who constantly translated architecture into terms of socialism and craftsmanship'.[96] Yet those two men were revered as gurus, and their names constantly recur in the writings of apologists for the Modern Movement.[97]

Blomfield went on to write that it

> was peculiarly unfortunate that there should have appeared in England in the middle of the last century a writer...of ample private means, of unbalanced temperament, and of a wholly uncritical enthusiasm, who should have devoted his...eloquence to the study of...architecture. For some fifty years Ruskin riveted his misconception of architecture on the educated English public, and so made confusion worse confounded, and paved the way not only for the revolt of Modernism, but also for the dominance of architecture and the arts not by artists, but by writers who regard the arts only as excellent copy.[98]

Osbert Lancaster observed that architecture was a topic about which the average man cares little and knows less: such views as he may have are founded 'on a variety of misconceptions'.[99] In earlier times 'every well-educated' person could express an opinion 'about the moulding of a cornice or the disposition of a pilaster', and was 'possessed of sufficient knowledge to lend it weight', but in the nineteenth century architecture 'was removed from the sphere of everyday life and placed under the jealous guardianship of experts and aesthetes. Faith became a substitute for knowledge', and very soon the 'ordinary person came to consider architecture...as something which he could never hope properly to understand', and 'possessed of a scale of values that he must take on trust. With the advent of Mr Ruskin, whose distinction it was to express in prose of incomparable grandeur' thought of 'unparalleled confusion, this divorce from reality became complete, and in less than no time the whole theory of architecture had become hopelessly confounded' with morals, religion, and a 'great many other things with which it had not the least connection'. Worse, the actual practice of architecture 'went rapidly to pot'.[100]

It is a strange business, inexplicable unless one accepts the predominance of the written word and its authority over mere visual matters. Perception of the city as a malign growth was widespread during the nineteenth century, and doubtless encouraged by the writings of Ruskin: his intemperate pronouncements and violently anti-urban language captured the attention of many, especially in public life and *Academe*. A curious fact is that the Victorians, who made possible the first modern predominantly urban society, were, to a very great extent, antipathetic to their own creation: therein lay a huge problem, a failure to appreciate and value real achievements.[101] For this state of affairs many were to blame, but there can be no doubt that their high-priest was Ruskin. Nevertheless, some perceptive commentators saw through Ruskin. Robert Kerr opposed him and all he stood for, and 'Greek' Thomson, arguably one of the greatest architects of the nineteenth century anywhere, did not think much of him either, considering that nobody had done more 'to mislead the public mind in matters of Art than he', for his books were 'hailed as . . . a way of escape from the tiresome necessity of learning, . . . a complete immunity from the duty of thinking'.[102] That difficulty has not gone away or become less significant with the passing of the years, for there has been a problem with much 'architectural' writing, uncritically accepted without demur. Gropius's claims to have been influenced by Ruskin and Morris, for example, have been widely accepted, without serious analysis: I believe them to be mere statements, lip-service to a supposed moral position, wholly without foundation in fact.

Thomson held that fashion is a hindrance to progress, for its demands are imperative and unassailable by reason: he perceived the contradictory, inconsistent, illogical ramblings of Ruskin with devastating accuracy, and made his views on those very clear.[103] For example, Ruskin found triglyphs in the Doric Order 'ugly' because they were not based on any 'organic' form, and denounced geometrical fret ornament because the type was only found in crystals of bismuth.[104] He then declared of Venetian billet-mouldings that nothing could ever be invented fitter for its purpose;[105] but to detect natural forms in billet-mouldings and unnatural ones in geometrical fret seems perverse, to be mild about it.

Architectural theories, however, are not reckoned by their context: they are judged by their influence. For instance, Ruskin's advocacy of north-Italian Gothic missed the point, and created 'just another system of secular decoration'.[106] Coventry Patmore deplored the fact that in Italian Gothic the shafts and mouldings were 'maimed in their upward flight by horizontal bands of colour':[107] Ruskin completely failed to understand about architecture responding to the realities of gravity, not only in terms of structure and form, but in embellishment as well, decoration that was expressive of that response.

Ruskin's prolixity and shifting positions have always been problematic. His influence on architecture would probably have ceased to matter by around 1875, had interest in him not been reawakened by his attitudes to work, to the problems in society, and to the lot of the craftsman. In other words, Ruskin continued to be significant because of the Romantic Socialism of the New Jerusalemers that began to evolve. Some influential writers, however, were unrelenting in their criticisms: H.H. Statham said of him that 'his only principle was that of saying the most effective and picturesque thing that had occurred to him at the moment',[108] and viewed *The Stones of Venice* as 'an immense rhetorical rhapsody of exaggerated and unwieldly dimensions…lacking any sort of logic or sequence'.[109] Blomfield felt that Ruskin's architectural theories were 'preposterous clap-trap', based on fallacious and infantile-Romantic analogies between architecture and Nature, whereas Nature has nothing whatsoever to do with architecture (although architecture should respect Nature, not abuse it). Moreover, Ruskin knew nothing of planning or structure, and Blomfield hoped the public were 'beginning to find him out', adding that he had had enough of Ruskin's 'twaddle'.[110]

Blomfield observed that Ruskin 'attracted amateurs and sentimentalists… by treating art and morals as interchangeable' and expressed amazement at the pernicious influence of 'fifty years[111] of unchallenged dogmatism.'[112] He also pinpointed three major problems with Ruskin: first, his claim that there was a distinction between building and architecture. If such a distinction were to exist, he got it hopelessly wrong (as did Pevsner, who wrote 'a bicycle shed is a building; Lincoln Cathedral is a piece of architecture');[113] second, he could not see the wood for the trees, ignoring plans and sections (in other words he was incapable of thinking in terms of architecture); and, third, he did not know that aesthetic appreciation was autonomous, and should not be mixed up with pseudo-morality, undisciplined writings about ornament, and inappropriate sentimentality.[114] He castigated Ruskin's childish 'outcries'[115] and vaporous notions,[116] expressed in mellifluous babblings. Blomfield was not alone when he detected infantilism, a phenomenon that is the result of sentimentality, lack of rigour, and widespread acceptance of falsehoods through received opinion or intellectual idleness.

Such damage has been long-lasting: it seems that all critical faculties have been suspended, and that absurdities are accepted wholesale as easy substitutes for thought. One might be forgiven for suspecting that this was because, faced with the need to survive, the deities themselves had had to adapt, and, having adapted beyond recognition, ceased to matter, so that their very symbols, too, were simply forgotten. Architecture, like much else of worth, began to lie well off the beaten track, beyond the reach of contemporary experience, and finally became incomprehensible to ordinary mortals. Perhaps this was because of the cacophonous Babel of corrupted architectural languages, but more likely it was a loss of meaning itself, accelerated by a softening of manners leading to arrested development in critical matters associated with visual things. In recent times, weak-mindedness has become endemic, and serious debate hardly exists.

Most commentators on Ruskin seem to have been over-awed by his Victorian reputation, and appear to excuse or gloss over his grotesque contradictions and messianic wrong-headedness. (Was that very messianic tendency the reason why he was revered at a time when the interminable rantings of evangelical preachers were inexplicably valued?) Mention of his frequent use of infantile language is usually avoided, and his bouts of mental incapacity are treated more like attacks of influenza than as symptoms of a more serious malady. A careful reading of Ruskin's works arouses serious misgivings, suggesting that he was unbalanced for most of his life.[117] His influence is difficult to explain: part of the problem is probably fright, part is lack of rigour in dissecting his prose, part may lie in snobbery, and part seems to be a sentimentalized tendency to wishful thinking about Nature, the supposed 'nobility' of work, and what things were 'morally' acceptable and what were not. Much about the second half of the nineteenth century in Britain and elsewhere suggests a massive distortion of ancient artistic and social standards and relationships.[118] The distortion was exacerbated thereafter until it caused fractures and collapse.

That people like Gropius claimed Ruskin as a major influence perhaps goes some way in explaining what went wrong with twentieth-century architecture: supposedly 'scientific' and so-called 'objective' pretensions were unlikely to emanate from any utterance of Ruskin, and Gropius's suggestion deserves to be treated with scepticism. However, even during his lifetime, there were some who objected to Ruskin's view. Matthew Digby Wyatt, for example, regretted that Ruskin could not recognize inevitable tendencies of his own age and consider how those tendencies might be improved: he

> puts up his back against their further development, or would attempt to bring back the world of art to what its course of action was four centuries ago.[119] Our course in this nineteenth century may be hateful, if you please; denounce it, but as it *is* our course, wise men should recognise the fact.[120]

The same criticism, of course, could apply to Morris.

Ruskin's influence on those advocates of a 'New Jerusalem' who were to promote such wholesale destruction of the Victorian and earlier fabric of

Britain after 1945, and who were to foist a ruinously expensive Dystopia on a financially strapped nation, cannot be denied.[121] If Pugin and Ruskin could be disingenuous or worse, other, later writers were also guilty of gross misrepresentation; yet their works, also, have been accepted almost without a murmur, among them Pevsner's *An Outline of European Architecture*,[122] which first appeared in 1943, and attempted (successfully, to judge from its critical acclaim and sales) to link the richly varied architecture of two millennia in Europe to a highly selective sample of Modernist buildings approved of by the author, omitting everything that did not fit a preconceived programme. Pevsner's *Pioneers of the Modern Movement from William Morris to Walter Gropius* (1936),[123] which will be discussed later, was also highly selective to the point of distortion, and included individuals who themselves objected to being seen as 'pioneers' of a movement they regarded as an abomination.

Pevsner, to his credit, seems to have been exasperated by Ruskin on many fronts,[124] not least because the latter did not acknowledge Pugin's influence on his own position (something Pevsner ascribed to Ruskin's 'questionable personal character', for which we should read 'bigotry', as Ruskin's detestation of Roman Catholicism coloured his views of the great Goth).[125] Perhaps more tellingly, he was unable to recruit him as a 'pioneer' of modern design, recognizing, perhaps, the hopelessness of that connection, despite claims by Gropius *et al.* that they had been influenced by Ruskin's works. More than many of his contemporaries, Ruskin could see how things might develop in the twentieth century, and truly hated what he saw (and for that he too deserves credit).

Hermann Muthesius

In 1896, the architect Hermann Muthesius was appointed technical *attaché*[126] to the Imperial German embassy in London, a post he held until 1903. His brief included the preparation of reports on railways, industrial concerns, and other matters, but he also began, from 1897, to collect material on English domestic architecture, for he held that no nation was more committed to the development of the private house, and that England had produced unique and outstanding exemplars worthy of the closest study. From that time he had in mind a thorough investigation and exposition of the English house, a project heartily supported by the artistic Grand Duke Karl

Alexander of Saxe-Weimar-Eisenach,[127] who, in 1860, had founded the *Großherzoglich-Sächsische Kunstschule Weimar*,[128] later (1910) the *Großherzoglich-Sächsische Hochschule für bildende Kunst*.[129] The Grand Duke opined that such a comprehensive publication would be of great value in Germany, where notions of 'home comforts' were less developed than they were in England. During his time in England Muthesius got to know several architects and artists, including Walter Crane, Francis Henry Newbery (who headed the progressive Glasgow School of Art from 1885 until 1917), Newbery's wife (Jessie Wylie Rowat [one of the 'Glasgow Girls' (active 1880–1920)]), Charles Rennie Mackintosh and his wife (Margaret Macdonald), James Henry McNair and his wife (Frances Macdonald), and many others.

Interest in contemporary English domestic architecture had already been stimulated in Germany by the publication of *Das englische Haus* by Robert Dohme,[130] to whose work Muthesius paid due tribute. The perceptive Muthesius chose the same title for his monumental study, subtitled *Historical Development, Conditions, Layout, Construction, Furnishing and Appliances, and Interior Space*, splendidly published in three volumes by Wasmuth in Berlin, 1904–5. In the preface to that first edition, he noted the indebtedness of the modern English house to *historical traditions*, without knowledge of which it would be unintelligible. Only in history, he wrote, 'can we trace the steps by which the domestic culture that is so highly evolved today has developed'[131] (an opinion that was anathema to Modernists, who therefore ignored it). He noted the unostentatious taste, breathing simplicity, that had produced the English house, sometimes verging on the vernacular, free of 'sham modernity' and 'whimsical artificiality', but in its unaffected design, firmly rooted in well-observed tradition, far more truly modern than all the 'fantastic excesses' of a 'so-called modern style.'[132] Tellingly, he observed there were no 'disconcerting exhibition-pieces',[133] and, 'thanks be to God, no trace of Art Nouveau'.[134]

The success of the first edition led to a second, also published by Wasmuth, in 1908–11,[135] with a revised and updated text, but the essence of the book remained the same. Here were distinguished works Muthesius admired, by architects including William Arthur Smith Benson, William Henry Bidlake, Cecil Claude Brewer, Walter Frederick Cave, Thomas Edward Collcutt, John Douglas, Ernest George, Ralph Heaton, Gerald Callcott Horsley, William Richard Lethaby, Robert Stodart Lorimer, Edwin Landseer Lutyens, Charles Rennie Mackintosh, Arthur George Sydney Mitchell, James Archibald Morris, William Eden Nesfield, Ernest Newton, Harold Ainsworth Peto, Mackay

Hugh Baillie Scott, John Dando Sedding, Richard Norman Shaw, Leonard Aloysius Scott Stokes, Charles Francis Annesley Voysey, George Walton, Philip Speakman Webb, Henry Wilson, and Edgar Wood.

Many of these were associated with the Art Workers' Guild (founded 1884) and with the Arts-and-Crafts Movement.[136] Muthesius stressed the debts they owed to history, and indeed he singled out Norman Shaw and his pupils for 'not wishing to develop new forms', restricting themselves to 'native' themes and local traditions. Moreover, the importance of craftsmanship was stressed, when the best English architects of the time began to follow the traditions of the old master-masons, building simply and rationally, using materials with sensitivity and understanding, and studying surviving examples of vernacular architecture (some of which were illustrated in *Das englische Haus*) that had hitherto been overlooked and undervalued.[137] Indeed, Muthesius praised Norman Shaw for retaining motifs of the old, indigenous domestic architecture for the small and medium-sized houses he built. Other talented architects succeeded in creating pleasing designs through 'painstaking and assiduous study'[138] of old buildings and details, thus recovering 'accumulated traditions',[139] activities of which the *Bauhäusler* and their apologists (notably Pevsner) would definitely not approve. Interestingly, Ernest Newton's Red Court, Scotland Lane, Haslemere, Surrey (1894–5), was hailed by Muthesius as illustrating his 'plain, broad, austere manner', an 'ideal example' of a 'good house'. This opinion contrasts with that of Nikolaus Pevsner, who described Red Court as an 'ominous house with some sterile Neo-Georgianism just around the corner', having 'segmental windows combined with gables in an acid way', and displaying a 'fundamental and fatal pettiness of scale and detail'.[140]

In discussing Voysey's work, Muthesius perceptively noted the simplicity of 'his means of expression', and that there was always an 'air of primitivism' about his houses: this lent them 'their charm, for deliberate originality in architecture can lead those who are less than brilliant into absurdities'.[141] Voysey's use of 'rough plaster on his walls', 'broad, tapering buttresses', roofs covered with English slates projecting 'a long way beyond the walls' (the overhangs supported by 'slender wrought-iron brackets'), tapering chimney stacks, and 'strips of small, narrow windows, the frames of which' were painted green, hardly sounds at all like anything one could associate with Modernism, 'pioneering' or otherwise,[142] and a glance at Voysey's drawings for numerous houses will be sufficient to confirm there is no connection whatsoever with the Modern Movement, no matter what Pevsner and others later claimed.[143]

Muthesius himself designed numerous *Landhäuser* (villas, country-houses, or weekend retreats) in which certain influences from English exemplars, not least the planning, may be detected: the Freudenberg house, *Rehwiese*, *Nikolaßee*, Berlin (1905–7), for example, owed not a little to the English X- or 'Butterfly' planning of houses such as The Barn, Exmouth, Devon (1895–7), by Edward Schroeder Prior,[144] another architect Muthesius greatly admired.

The German-born critic, Julius Posener, who had grown up in a house[145] in the '*englischen Landhaus-stil*' designed by Fritz Crzellitzer for his father, the painter Moritz Moses Posener, at 79 *Baselerstraße* in the *Villenkolonie* of Lichterfelde-West, Berlin, in 1909, wrote perceptively on Muthesius's work in his preface to the 1979 single-volume English translation of *Das englische Haus*, reissued in paperback in 1987.[146] At that time he observed that the English house (*c.*1860–1900) had received 'scant attention' until, as Lethaby noted, Muthesius

> was to become the historian—in the German language—of English free architecture. All architects, who about this time [1900] [had] built anything were studied, classified, registered, and…understood. Then, just as our English building became real, or at least very, very nearly real, a pusillanimous reaction set in…[147]

Posener's remark is itself of interest, for Lethaby referred to 'building' more often than 'architecture' because English (and Scots) 'free architecture' owed more to simple unpretentious historical buildings, often impossible to categorize stylistically, although they could be dated. And that 'free architecture', in the hands of the masters listed by Muthesius, began to be dismissed by English critics, who increasingly ignored it, just as the intelligent German extolled it: it was finally buried by Geoffrey Scott in his *The Architecture of Humanism* (1914), in which he defended Renaissance architecture as a standard, and attacked the multiplicity of styles that had informed the work of Norman Shaw, Philip Webb, Richard Lethaby, and others whose works grace *Das englische Haus*.

The odd thing is that English writers and architects of the time, influenced by the writings of Pugin and those who held similar views, put internal planning, shapes of rooms, circulation, aspect, and the relationships with outdoor areas before elevations: with the result that external appearances were actually very freely composed, asymmetrical, and employed various themes and devices in what sometimes appeared to be a disparate collection of elements drawn from numerous precedents. They never attempted clear analyses of this new type of domestic architecture, nor did they trace its origins back to mediaeval and vernacular exemplars, yet Muthesius did just that: the first part of his great work included a useful, concise account of the development of the English house from pre-Conquest times, through the Middle Ages into the Elizabethan and Jacobean periods, then Palladianism, and the Georgian, Regency, and early-Victorian eras up to 1860.[148]

Muthesius 'discovered the English house. For him, and for Germany at that moment, the discovery was of vital importance'.[149] He also understood the significance of history in determining the 'free architecture' he so admired, something Modernists were to ignore and suppress.

Harry Kessler, van de Velde, & Weimar

Muthesius's Weimar connections were significant for what was to follow. The Belgian architect, artist, and designer, Henry van de Velde, was also inspired by the British Arts-and-Crafts Movement, and he was instrumental in introducing ideas drawn from it into his native country. In 1895 he was invited by the art dealer Siegfried (Pevsner called him 'Samuel')[150] Bing to design three rooms for the latter's new gallery in Paris, which Bing called *L'Art Nouveau*, and when these were exhibited (1897) in Dresden, van de Velde's name became intimately associated with *Jugendstil* (the German version of *Art Nouveau*): many German commissions followed, not least through the influence of that remarkable aesthete, the Anglo-Irish-German Count Harry Kessler, who had seen van de Velde's work in Bing's gallery in 1895. Kessler commissioned van de Velde to design the furnishings and interiors of his new Berlin apartment, and it was through him that van de Velde was introduced to Elisabeth Förster-Nietzsche, the notoriously anti-Semitic sister of Friedrich Nietzsche (whose ideas concerning humankind freed from the restricting tenets [as he saw them] of Christianity had caused more than a ripple throughout the German-speaking world). Frau Förster-Nietzsche established the Nietzsche archive in Weimar, aided by a generous donation from Kessler, who was able to visit the philosopher, then laid low in his final illness. Van de Velde was commissioned to design a luxurious edition of Nietzsche's *Also sprach Zarathustra*, and the Belgian's association with Weimar took a further turn on the death of the reigning Grand Duke Karl Alexander, who was succeeded by his grandson, Wilhelm Ernst, in 1901.

The possibilities of a new golden age of culture in Weimar gained ground
from this time, Förster-Nietzsche and Kessler being two of the catalysts. But
there was a rival near Darmstadt, where, on the *Mathildenhöhe*, from 1899,
the young Ernst Ludwig, Grand Duke of Hesse, had invited various German
and Austrian designers, including Peter Behrens, Rudolf Bosselt, Paul Burck,
Hans Christiansen, Ludwig Habich, Patriz Huber, Albin Müller, and Joseph
M. Olbrich, to form a permanent community of artists, with buildings
designed by Behrens and Olbrich. Previously, the Grand Duke, a grandson of
Queen Victoria, who was familiar with the British Arts-and-Crafts Movement,
had commissioned Baillie Scott to design furnishings for his own residence
in Darmstadt, so the Grand Duchy had become a magnet for those interested in the 'New Art'. Despite damage in the 1939–45 war, the *Mathildenhöhe*
complex remains an extraordinary creation where the inventiveness of
Jugendstil is displayed.[151]

Kessler and van de Velde visited the *Mathildenhöhe*, but their opinions
were less than enthusiastic: it consisted of 'architecture for a bordello, and
what's more, a bad bordello',[152] as van de Velde described it. Kessler was
equally scathing.[153] It occurred to him that there was a golden opportunity
to get van de Velde appointed to an official post in Weimar where he could
bring the entire craft industry of the little State under his influence: Kessler
emphasized that van de Velde did not wish to break with tradition, but
would give the Thuringian craftsmen the knowledge to continue their own
traditions, reinvigorated with new ideas (something the *Bauhaus* was later to
completely reverse and destroy). With Förster-Nietzsche's backing, van de
Velde was duly appointed head of the new Grand-Ducal school of arts and
crafts in Weimar in 1901, and Kessler himself took over the Directorship of
the Grand-Ducal museum for arts and crafts in 1902: the stage was set for
the building of the 'new Weimar'.[154]

Artefacts designed by van de Velde were soon being manufactured: furniture, jewellery, bookbindings, tea-services, vases were found in all the major
cities of the German Empire, and a new building, also the work of van de Velde,
was erected (1904–11) to house the school. Van de Velde's Berlin interiors,
notably the Havana Company cigar-shop (1899–1900)[155] and Haby's barber-
shop (1900–1), were firmly *Art-Nouveau* in style: at the new Weimar school,
however, ornament was eschewed, mouldings were kept to a minimum, and
large, factory-type studio windows with exposed steel lintels dominated the
main elevation (an even more severe treatment than Mackintosh had given
to the first phase of his Glasgow school of art [1897–9]).[156] Van de Velde also

designed a Nietzsche memorial (which was not realized): but this long-drawn-out saga exasperated Kessler, who complained that the Belgian could not 'free himself from designing from the inside out',[157] whereas he should have tried to express an idea encompassing feelings, heroism, joy, and the essence of Nietzsche's Dionysian writings. Kessler compared van de Velde's proposals unfavourably with those of Wilhelm Kreis for the Bismarck memorials,[158] because Kreis managed to express Bismarck's personality, whereas van de Velde's initial attempts failed to rise to the occasion. Kessler demanded a 'grand architectural formula inspired by Nietzsche's personality alone'. In other words, Kessler wanted an *expressive* rather than a *constructive* architecture.[159]

By 1911, what emerged was a design for a huge stadium based on the dimensions of the antique Athenian exemplar, and a temple based on a square plan that was to celebrate Nietzsche's ideas and would contain works by several of the foremost modern artists. In this scheme can be detected Expressionist themes: stirrings of a movement that, like some early warning before a violent storm, influenced German architecture in the period c.1910–23. It owed much to literary origins in the works of Nietzsche, who had reappraised Greek art and culture, questioning the sun-drenched Apollonian interpretation of Ancient Greece promoted by Goethe and Winckelmann, among others, and substituting the idea of the irrational, the tragic, the wild, excessive, joyous realms of Dionysus. Nietzsche envisioned the freeing of humankind from received ideas, life-denying religion (but not spirituality), and suffocating 'tradition', in order to embrace nature and the acceptance of life, unfettered by the dead hand of respectability and custom. By creating works of art in the white heat of ecstasy, life itself is enhanced, and both spiritual and creative forces unite.

However, the anti-Christian undercurrents in Nietzsche's work had repercussions: he deplored a religion of anti-rationalism, anti-science, vengefulness, judgement, and negation, and was especially critical of Christianity's philology in its treatment of the Old Testament, which he regarded as profoundly dishonest, making false connections that simply were far-fetched. He further denounced the self-deception in a religion he perceived as born of weakness, failure, and resentment, the enemy of reason, of the body (sex especially), and of joy, freedom, and the realities of the earth. In particular, he regarded 'morality' as designating a social code that equates being 'moral' with conformity to a cult or something worse.

Regrettably, many commentators deliberately and irresponsibly perverted Nietzsche's work, emphasizing what he called the 'will-to-power' to justify brutality, cruelty, and trampling the helpless underfoot. Like Baudelaire, he regarded 'progress' as a modern idea, and a damaging, dangerous, false one. He was immersed in European culture, and when he called himself an 'immoralist' he obviously did not mean he favoured a lack of self-discipline. Instead, he argued that without long, hard discipline, humankind could not achieve the means by which life on earth is worthwhile in virtue, music, art, reason, and spirituality, and so his 'immoralism' was a passionate, civilized, learned nonconformity founded in open-mindedness and refusal to be confined within the straitjacket of a cult. That Nietzsche was profoundly religious, and recognized the necessity of a spiritual aspect to culture and life, is clear. What he might have made of the Modern Movement in architecture (from which the erotic was entirely absent) is intriguing to contemplate.

Assisting with the Nietzsche archive in Weimar was Rudolf Steiner,[160] who saw Nietzsche as the complement of Goethe, and who founded the Anthroposophical Society, which seems to have aimed to embrace both Goethean and Nietzschean ideas, and was one of many pseudo-religious sects that evolved in Germany during the early years of the twentieth century. He designed the *Goetheanum*, Dornach, near Basel, Switzerland (1913–20), in which Expressionist, *Jugendstil*, and Symbolist themes coalesced. This building burned down, and was replaced by *Goetheanum II* (1924, completed 1962): both owed something to the notion of *Einfühlung* (empathy), by which feelings could be expressed in the forms of the architecture, and different, seemingly unrelated parts would merge in a harmonious whole. A building, according to Steiner, should be a living organism.[161]

So what are we to make of Weimar in the early years of the twentieth century?[162] The French artist, Maurice Denis, described the paganism, the obsessions with 'sickly art', the arrogant Classicism, the rejection of Western values, the cosmopolitanism, the boredom, the permanent seeking for new sensations, the ever-present shadows of Goethe and Nietzsche, the Hellenism. To him, these all seemed rather unhealthy and slightly alarming, especially within Weimar's small-town setting.[163] Karl Scheffler, who edited the influential *Kunst und Künstler* (Art and Artist—1903–33), published by Bruno Cassirer, decided that living in rooms within the *Hohenhof*, Hagen, Nordrhein-Westfalen (designed 1907–8 by van de Velde for Karl Ernst Osthaus, the Maecenas of Hagen) induced a peculiar strain, because the mood in them was sombre, and not at all ingenuous: an atmosphere was created that compelled earnest diligence, a 'spiritual' attitude, and this was extremely oppressive.

Kessler found the melancholy, tubercular atmosphere of Osthaus's *Hohenhof* impossible,[164] despite having been van de Velde's patron and supporter. Helene von Nostitz-Wallwitz described Kessler's own rooms as a 'temple of art', filled with a feeling of energy and movement, in which heat and coolness, distance and intimacy, purity and multi-coloured splendour, renunciation and envelopment, and all things contradictory, were contained. A chill serenity pervaded everything.[165] There was something of the rarefied hothouse about pre-1914 Weimar,[166] as there certainly was about the *Mathildenhöhe* at Darmstadt and the *Sezessionstil* in Austria-Hungary (especially in Vienna).

What is absolutely clear from numerous accounts of Weimar, the attitudes of the protagonists of the *Werkbund*, and the utterances of the leaders of the various artistic movements which might be described as *avant-garde* in the Second Reich, is that there were many programmes to provide models for *Lebensführung* (style of living, or conduct of life) that were preceptive, most definitely *élitist*, culturally ambitious, and widespread throughout the various Modernist movements in Germany. The 'Circle' around Stefan George, for instance, partly centred on Heidelberg, was an interesting example: anti-democratic, opposed to '*bourgeois*' values, hostile to Enlightenment notions of rationality, equality, and personal freedom, it promulgated a hierarchically ordered society ruled by a supreme, omnipotent *Führer* (Leader, Guide, or Chief—a title George and his disciples did much to promote) to whom everyone should submit. A prime exemplar to be emulated was Friedrich II Hohenstaufen, Holy Roman Emperor and King of Sicily and Jerusalem, known as *Stupor Mundi*, the mightiest ruler of the Middle Ages, whose biography, by Ernst Kantorowicz,[167] an intimate of George, was an immediate success.[168]

There was a 'we know best' coercive attitude present in a great many groups and 'circles' which flourished in Germany before and after the 1914–18 war. It is worth noting that Claus, Graf von Stauffenberg, among others influenced by George, was implicated in the July 1944 plot to kill Hitler, having come to the rather late conclusion that the *Führer* was leading Germany into the Abyss, and paid for his failure with his life. However, there was much in National-Socialist ideology that appealed to many Germans in the 1920s and '30s, including men like Stauffenberg: only after the war started to go wrong for Germany did they belatedly see flaws in the *Führerprinzip* (authoritarian principle). But in Germany that authoritarianism was by no means unusual or strange: it was pervasive, and in the short-lived

Weimar Republic (which did not command universal support by any means)
there were numerous societies, associations, parties, 'circles', and the like
which were *élitist*, hierarchical, authoritarian, all certain they were right, and
knew what should be done, so were prepared to force others to conform.
Such attitudes were certainly carried on well into the 1970s by those who
had embraced the Modern Movement, and they were by then the majority
in architectural and town-planning circles.

The seeds, however, were planted in Germany early in the twentieth
century, the young plants were nurtured in Weimar and elsewhere both before
and after the 1914–18 war, and in turn their progeny became established
globally. It was an astonishing turn of events.

The *Deutscher Werkbund*

Muthesius, as noted above, designed several fine houses after he returned to
Germany, but he also turned his attention to the very real problem of how
to maintain high standards of design and craftsmanship in an industrial age.
Unlike Morris and Ruskin, he did not reject the machine, which would
have been difficult anyway, as Germany had eagerly and efficiently embraced
mechanized production, and had made hugely impressive advances in that
respect: so Muthesius anticipated the concept of industrial design, arguing
for an amalgamation of sound design principles and manufacture using
machines. Early on, he was critical of *Art Nouveau* and its German equivalent of *Jugendstil*,[169] correctly seeing (unlike Pevsner *et al.*) that these were
not 'new', but rather derived from earlier styles; but, more importantly,
he was inimical to the dogmatic embrace of any 'style'. That is why he
wrote perceptively about the British Arts-and-Crafts Movement, for what
mattered there was good building and fine craftsmanship, and 'design' drew
on a vast cornucopia of motifs, themes, and elements derived from many
historical exemplars and sources, often of differing styles, mixed with
imagination and skill, with eclectic results, often brilliantly assembled to
form a coherent whole.

Good architecture, Muthesius felt, could transcend illogical insistence on
using one style only,[170] as was clear from his own work as an architect. Style,
after all, should not be objected to on principle, for it can neither 'mar nor
make the beauty of what it conveys',[171] though devotees of the International
Modern Movement insisted that 'flat' roofs, absence of any mouldings, and

long strips of glass were 'functional' and nothing to do with 'style'.[172] Fashions may pass, but style remains, yet most architects associated with Modernism in its various guises denied there was any validity in the concept of style: despite Barr, Hitchcock, and Johnson having given a label to the 'International Style' (this will be elaborated upon in Chapters IV and V);[173] despite Le Corbusier's bow ties and large circular spectacle frames; despite Frank Lloyd Wright's pork-pie hats and capes; and despite the gloomy, pseudo-clerical, sartorial affectations of Deconstructivists and Parametricists.[174]

Muthesius obviously believed that the British Arts-and-Crafts Movement provided the soundest exemplars for future developments in architecture elsewhere,[175] unlike the tortured, rather unwholesome excesses of *Art Nouveau*,[176] the various Secession styles, or those persons Pevsner called the 'Anti-Rationalists'.[177] With his many friends and colleagues, and drawing on his experiences in Britain, Muthesius sought to establish what might be described as cultural enlightenment throughout Germany, using the information he had gathered for his monumental *Das englische Haus* to promote improvements, and as an official of the Prussian Ministry of Trade, to advocate a revolution in the German craft industries by massive advances in rational design and manufacture. In the Spring of 1907 (the year in which his edited volume entitled *Landhaus und Garten* was published),[178] Muthesius gave a lecture in Berlin in which he argued for simplicity and other virtues in design, attributes which had begun to emerge in the third German Arts-and-Crafts exhibition held in Dresden in 1906, but which upset many of the established makers of domestic furnishings and decorations.

Acrimonious debates led to the establishment of the *Deutscher Werkbund*, a group of professionals united in their views, with the aims of ennobling commerce by the collaboration of art, industry, and craftsmanship through education, publications, lectures, and other means.[179] Founding members included Muthesius, Peter Behrens,[180] Theodor Fischer,[181] Fritz Schumacher,[182] and Heinrich Tessenow.[183] The three first secretaries were Wolf Dohrn, Alfons Paquet, and Ernst Jäckh, all of whom were influenced by the political theorist, Friedrich Naumann. This ensured that the *Werkbund*, from its beginnings, was strongly nationalist (Naumann wrote that the *Werkbund* should aim to extend Germany's economic power): indeed, the emphasis on a coming together of the best artistic and commercial/industrial minds was perceived as elevating German culture to a superior plane.[184] Proceedings of annual conferences were published, and included essays by Muthesius on German skills to arrive at universally valid design solutions,[185] Gropius (ominously) on American grain-silos and other structures that were to be admired by Modernists in the 1920s,[186] and Behrens on modern form, space, and time.[187]

The *Werkbund* embraced a disparate range of artistic aims as well as many large industrial and commercial interests. Behrens was appointed (1907) artistic adviser to the electrical giant, *Allgemeine Elektrizitäts-Gesellschaft* (AEG— General Electricity Company), for which he designed the huge high-voltage factory, Wedding (1909–10—with stripped rudimentary nods to Classicism), and the *Turbinenfabrik*, Moabit (1909—a steel-framed hall with battered, rounded, non-structural corners made of reinforced-concrete elements separated by steel bands, suggesting a massive rusticated effect at the gable end), both in Berlin. However, Behrens also designed many artefacts, fixtures, and fittings for AEG: his work created suitable images for marketing purposes, including logos, stationery, and advertisements, all carefully considered from both commercial and aesthetic standpoints. Indeed, he can be considered one of the first architects to exploit the possibilities of what became known as 'corporate branding', so was of immense significance as a true pioneer of a new age of standardization and mass-production.[188]

A corollary of this was that if architects were to abandon designing buildings that used local materials, craft methods, and respected context, using instead factory-made standardized components and a very limited architectural vocabulary stripped of all 'unessential' elements (such as ornament), how were they to begin to produce aesthetically distinctive works? Behrens showed the way by introducing what became known as 'theming', a kind of 'house-style', capable of being produced by industry, so architects, designing with self-imposed limitations demanded by the new 'Modern' aesthetic minimalism, could join with client companies to suggest visions of bright, clean, ordered, technologically advanced futures, the realities, moreover, which would quickly date and become tarnished, so this deliberately planned obsolescence could soon create a demand for new, 'improved' products in their place.

In these apparently innocuous beginnings lay the poisonous seeds of an architectural and environmental calamity, but that would only become all too obvious half a century later. They go a long way to explain the short life much Modern-Movement architecture actually had: the possibilities of industrialized architecture were not lost on young men who worked for a time in Behrens's office in Berlin, especially Walter Gropius, C.-É. Jeanneret-Gris (later 'Le Corbusier'), and Ludwig Mies (later Miës van der Rohe), three architects who ruthlessly promoted 'total' architecture, industrialized building, and a minimalist aesthetic which became so minimalized that Henry-Russell Hitchcock was to observe of the Seagram building in New York (1954–8—by Mies van der Rohe [as he had become by then] with Philip Johnson and others) that he had 'never seen more of less',[189] a clever inversion of Mies' much-trumpeted claim that 'less is more'.

Much of Behrens's architectural work was influenced by that of the great Prussian architect Karl Friedrich Schinkel, especially his clear, rational planning and his severe interpretations of Classicism: both aspects informed the Imperial German embassy, at the corner of *Isaakiyevskaya Ploshchad* and *Bolshaya Morskaya Ulitsa*, St Petersburg, Russia (1911–12—a building later admired by Adolf Hitler and Albert Speer). Built of red-grey Finnish granite, it is essentially a town palace (**Plate 1.3**), owing much to Behrens's earlier AEG *Kleinmotorenfabrik, Voltastraße*, Berlin (1909–13), as well as to Roman *palazzi*, but there are echoes of Schinkel's designs for *Schloß Orianda in der Krim*, the same architect's *Altes Museum,* Schlüter's great *Schloß*, and even Langhans' *Brandenburger Tor*, all three in Berlin. This important exemplar of what became known as *stripped Classicism* had a profound influence on the official architecture of the Third Reich, and also that of the USSR under Stalin, but it also affected architectural design elsewhere, notably in Sweden. On the plinth in the centre of the long colonnaded façade above the main cornice were monumental statues of the Διόσκουροι [*Dioscuri*][190] and their

Plate 1.3. Former Imperial German embassy, corner of *Isaakiyevskaya Ploshchad* and *Bolshaya Morskaya Ulitsa*, St Petersburg, Russia, by Peter Behrens (1911–13), a town palace in the stripped-Classical style. The plinth above the centre of the colonnaded façade once supported statues by Eberhard Encke of the *Dioscuri* with their horses

two horses designed and made by Eberhard Encke as the crowning central feature of the embassy building: they stood, stiff and almost crude, anticipating, perhaps, the architectural sculpture of the Third Reich. Indeed it was Neo-Classicism, more than anything, that permeated Behrens's architecture in the period 1907–14, even to the extent of using severe unfluted Greek Doric in the Wiegand house, Berlin-Dahlem (1911–12). The pedimented entrance of Behrens's *Festhalle* for the *Werkbund* exhibition in Cologne (1914) suggested a paraphrase of a Roman triumphal-arch further transformed at the façade of Sant'Andrea, Mantua (commenced 1470), designed by Leon Battista Alberti. The stripped Neo-Classical flavour was emphasized by a cast of Encke's *Dioscuri* for the St Petersburg embassy.

In 1906–7 the Eduard Müller crematorium at Delstern-bei-Hagen (**Figure 1.5**) had been erected to Behrens's designs: in essence its plan was reminiscent of an Early-Christian basilica, and the external marble cladding suggested that the building owed something to the church of San Miniato al Monte (eleventh to twelfth centuries), high above Florence, intermingled with quotations from the façade of the Pazzi chapel (built

Figure 1.5. Crematorium (1906–7) at Delstern-bei-Hagen, North-Rhine-Westphalia, Germany, by Peter Behrens. The long colonnade of the columbarium to the right was never realized: it was based on that of the mortuary temple of Queen Hatshepsut at Deïr-el-Bahari, Egypt (*c.*1479–58 BC)

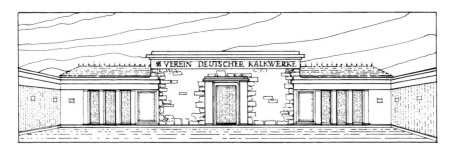

Figure 1.6. *Hof des Vereins Deutscher Kalk-Werke* for the *Ton- Zement-, und Kalkindustrieauβtellung*, Berlin-Treptow, 1910, by Behrens, owing debts to both the Queen Hatshepsut temple at Deïr-el-Bahari and the temple at Medinet Habu (*c.*1479–36 BC)

1472) at Santa Croce, also in Florence, supposedly designed (*c.*1423–4) by Brunelleschi (*see* **Plate 7.7**). A further Italian allusion was to the *campanile*-like element attached to the main building, which, instead of emitting joyful peals of bells, belched smoke. The long, low columbarium behind the crematorium was never realized, although it was to have long ranges of square columns reminiscent of those at the mortuary temple of Queen Hatshepsut at Deïr-el-Bahari, Egypt, designed by Senmut;[191] and there were other works by Behrens in which the Ancient-Egyptian influence was clear, for example the *Hof des Vereins Deutscher Kalk-Werke* (court of the association of German lime-works) (**Figure 1.6**) for the *Ton-, Zement-, und Kalkindustrieauβtellung* (clay-, cement-, and lime-industry exhibition), Berlin-Treptow, 1910.[192]

The *Werkbund* Exhibition, Cologne, 1914

It was at the Cologne exhibition of 1914 that the disparate approaches to design and aims came to a head. Muthesius gave a somewhat confused paper (his literary style was not among the most felicitous)[193] in which, although he accepted that certain archetypes had evolved over a long period, he thought standardization of types would be more appropriate for industrialized production. A re-reading of what he advocated gives a clue as to why delegates including van de Velde, August Endell, Hermann Obrist, Walter Gropius, and Bruno Taut took issue with him, seeing his paper as an attack on artistic freedom; but the main problem was that its message was unclear. Behrens, too, was unsure of what Muthesius was driving at. There was certainly a feeling that the elevated, perhaps Nietzsche-inspired, position of creative artists was beginning to be threatened by the interests of industrialists and the commercial world.

Van de Velde had designed the theatre for the Cologne exhibition, a slightly sinister building, the front of which resembled a crouching crab. The plan was symmetrical and Classically inspired, contrasting with the moulded forms of the exterior. Some commentators have observed that with this building van de Velde 'disassociated himself completely'[194] from *Jugendstil*, and leant towards Expressionism, but the *Werkbund-Theater* seems to me to display more than a few hints of that rejected style. Bruno Taut's crystalline, circular, Glass Pavilion (financed by the German glass industries to promote the use of glass in building) featured an internal waterfall, glass-block walls, and glass mosaics. Set around the base of the faceted cupola were aphorisms by Paul Scheerbart making startling claims (symptomatic, perhaps, of the many curious notions current in the Second Reich) that coloured glass destroys hatred, that glass brings a new era, that without a glass palace life becomes a burden, and that building with brick does humans harm.[195] Taut saw his building as a paradigm of all religious building ('the Gothic Cathedral is the Prelude to a Glass Architecture', he claimed), which, together with the beliefs it would inspire, would become an essential element in the restructuring of society. However, the fact that industrial concerns paid for the Pavilion belies the Utopian claims: the building was really about selling glass through architecture, so was less to do with spiritual uplift and more linked to commerce.[196]

Later, the architect Adolf Behne would claim that glass architecture would bring about a new culture, wrenching *bourgeois* humankind out of its alleged smugness. The quasi-evangelical sloganizing makes uncomfortable reading (as was intended), but there is no mistaking the messianic tone, the suggestion of compulsion, and the questionable beliefs underlying the declaimed certainties. Such tendencies were to become more aggressive, and the language of the cult (already painfully obvious in the Germany of the Second Reich)[197] ever more strident, notably in what was to become the *Bauhaus*.

Gropius and Adolf Meyer designed the Fagus shoe-last factory, Alfeld-an-der Leine (1910–11): the treatment of its curtain-walling was to have an enormous influence on the International Style between the wars. They were also responsible for the model factory at the Cologne exhibition. Its administration block had a symmetrical façade with glazed elements at each end that may have been suggested by Mackintosh's Scotland-Street school of 1904–6 in Glasgow, with its partially glazed staircase-towers. The rest of the front owed something to the work of Frank Lloyd Wright (whose architectural designs had been lavishly published [1911] by Wasmuth) (**Plate 1.4**). But one aspect of the design has been missed by most commentators, *videlicet* the relationship of the plan to that of the Ptolemaïc temple of Horus at Edfu (80–51 BC) (**Figure 1.7**), a reconstruction of which had been shown at the *Große Berliner Gewerbe-Außtellung* (Great Berlin Industrial Exposition), 1896.[198] Gropius had worked in Behrens's office from 1907 to 1910, just at the time Behrens was quoting from Ancient-Egyptian buildings.[199]

However, the arguments which set artistic freedom against standardization were overtaken by the outbreak of war in 1914. Van de Velde, as a Belgian, lost his position as head of the Grand-Ducal Saxon School of Arts and Crafts at Weimar, and proposed Endell, Gropius, or Obrist as his successor: in the event Gropius was appointed, but was unable to take up the position immediately, as he was serving in the German army. Van de Velde's later career was marked by his claims to have been an early protagonist of the Modern Movement, and his attitude towards the retrospective *Art-Nouveau* exhibition in Zürich (1952) was equivocal, if not hostile: it seems he feared it would draw attention to his skills in a style he had repudiated, even though it is apparent that his best work was carried out before 1915.[200]

Plate 1.4. View of the model factory designed by Walter Gropius and Adolf Meyer for the *Werkbund* exhibition, Cologne (1914). The pylon-like towers and strongly axial composition suggest an Egyptian influence

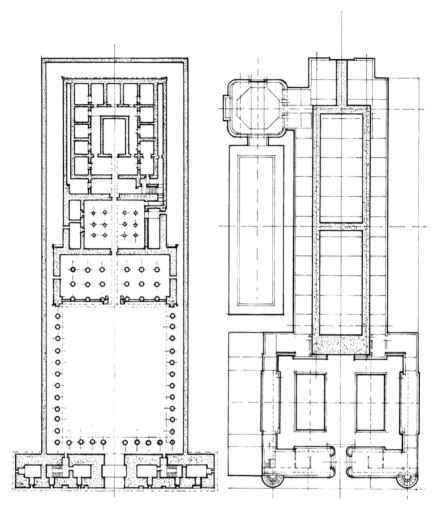

Figure 1.7. (*left*) Plan of the Ptolemaïc temple of Horus at Edfu (80–51 BC) compared with (*right*) plan of the model factory designed by Gropius and Meyer for the *Werkbund* exhibition, Cologne (1914). The plans are not drawn to the same scale, and are shown only for comparison purposes

Epilogue

The *Werkbund*'s ethos changed with the outbreak of hostilities in 1914; in 1915 its yearbook was concerned with 'German Form in the War Year', and in 1916/17 with war-graves and war-cemeteries, although at the annual conference of 1916 in Bamberg, the arguments about standardization and machinery were again rehearsed. Exhibitions such as those held in Basel, Bern, Copenhagen, and Winterthur had flavours of propaganda, laced with a fading nationalist fervour; and there was a competition (1917) for a German House of Friendship for Constantinople, intended to cement ties between the Ottoman and German Empires, then allies in the war. Hans Poelzig's entry showed a huge terraced building, with hanging gardens, and the architecture, with its long ranges of arches, was an attempt to free the design from European precedents.[201]

Poelzig had been appointed, through Muthesius's influence, to head the Academy of Arts and Crafts at Breslau (now Wrocław, Poland), where he also had his own architectural practice. While there he designed the Expressionist water-tower and exhibition-hall, Posen (1910–11—now Poznań, Poland), and other buildings included an office-block (1911–13) at what used to be *Junkernstraße* (now 38/40 *Ofiar Oświęcimskich*) in central Breslau, with horizontal strip-windows (anticipating International Modernism of the following decades) (**Plate 1.5**), a chemical factory and workers' housing at Luban (now Lubań, Poland) (1911–12), and the Four Domes Pavilion and other elements (1910–13) for the Centennial Exhibition (*Jahrhundertfeier*) in the outskirts of Breslau to mark the centenary of Napoléon's defeat at Leipzig (1813) (**Plate 1.6**). For this, and the landscaping of the Exhibition (opened in a great ceremony by Crown Prince Wilhelm of Germany), Poelzig collaborated with Max Berg, whose massive reinforced-concrete *Jahrhunderthalle* (1910–13) still dominates the southern part of Szczytnicki Park, Wrocław (**Plate 1.7**). The Pavilion employed a simplified Greek Doric Order, all in reinforced concrete, which Poelzig thought was expressive of the early nineteenth-century period celebrated by the Exhibition, and Berg's great Hall itself was not without its stripped-Classical allusions. What was the German city of Breslau saw several fine exemplars of pioneering reinforced-concrete architecture all of which was steeped in historical precedent: an early masterpiece was the Market Hall (1906–8) by Richard Plüddemann. In 1916 Poelzig moved to Dresden, and in 1920 returned to Berlin.[202]

Germany's defeat in 1918, the complete disintegration of the monarchies, national bankruptcy, the huge reduction of the former industrial base, the denting of nationalist fervour, and the collapse of the mighty export-driven economy were all realities when the *Werkbund* held its first major post-war conference in 1919 in Stuttgart. Despite the obvious change of Germany's fortunes, the *Werkbund*'s President Peter Bruckmann seemed not to have noticed, and spoke about the importance of the organization for nationalist

Plate 1.5. Office-block, 38/40 *Ofiar Oświęcimskich* (formerly *Junkernstraße*) where that street joins *ulica Łaciarska* (formerly *Altbüsserstraße*), Wrocław (formerly Breslau), by Poelzig (1911–13), a very early type of the office-block that was to become common in later years

Kulturpolitik, as though nothing had changed. The resulting uproar made it clear that there were many members who were anti-industrialist and anti-capitalist, supporting hand-craftsmanship and denouncing industrialized prefabrication. There were armed uprisings in Germany, and attempts by Communists to seize power, resulting in near anarchy in some areas: so it was a very unsettled time, with numerous groups jockeying for position in the vacuum left by the discredited *Kaiserreich*, now replaced by the Weimar Republic, which had to call on elements from the military to restore order in certain cities. Bruckmann was replaced by Poelzig, representing the Expressionists and supported by Gropius, César Klein (a founder

Plate 1.6. Four Domes Pavilion, Szczytnicki Park, Wrocław (formerly Breslau), by Poelzig (1910–13), employing a simplified Greek Doric Order all in concrete

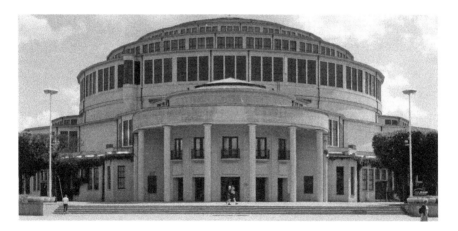

Plate 1.7. *Jahrhunderthalle*, Szczytnicki Park, Wrocław (formerly Breslau), by Max Berg (1910–13)

of the *Novembergruppe*), Osthaus, Bernhard Pankok (who was to design, among much else, the passenger compartments of four *Zeppelin* airships), and Bruno Taut.

Some of Poelzig's utterances in his famous speech to the *Werkbund* (1919) should be recalled: 'architecture is the product of a national state of mind',[203] only achievable 'where the conviction has been established that we have to create for eternity'; this recalls Sir Christopher Wren's 'Architecture aims at Eternity', though Wren went on to say 'and therefore is the only Thing uncapable of Modes and Fashions in its Principals, the *Orders*',[204] something no Modernist would ever accept. It also suggests Ruskin's 'when we build, let us think that we build for ever'.[205] His address to the *Werkbund* reflected the difficult times in which it was given. He stressed that the *Werkbund* originated from a spiritual, not an economic, position, but that its ethos had faded under the pressures of political and industrial/commercial interests, so it was high time its essence should be restored. The Arts and Crafts were the two foundations on which the *Werkbund* was based: they were meant to be one and the same, interjoined. Poelzig drove home his belief that the handicrafts were purely spiritual, and not merely centred on mechanical skills. Forms should be created with great thought and love, and during that process no attention should be given to considerations of how the results should be economically exploited.

Industry, on the other hand, is concerned with technical matters, guided by economic principles. Arts and handicrafts involve the creation of things that have eternal value: the artist or artisan who does not wish to make things of eternal value does not deserve to be called either an artist or an artisan, Poelzig claimed. If the *Werkbund* did not want to be merely something like a mediator or a promoter of industrial art, which is subject to fashion and change, it should turn to first principles of 'true art and true handicraft'. He noted that young artists who sought 'cheap fame' came to harm, and questioned the growing obsessions among architects with the design of motor-cars, aeroplanes, and all sorts of machines (pointedly, he said that most of the water-towers, grain-silos, and so on that attracted some Modernists could not be compared with the splendid aqueducts, fortifications, and great barns of the past). All buildings which were likely to stand for at least half a century or so should have forms originating from the 'architectonic urge' to create something that yet strictly observed the technical principles of sound construction. Dwellings could not be created from technical-hygienic principles alone, or from mere theorizing or supposedly 'scientific' considerations: observance of senses of values beyond mere construction, no matter how practicable, should be paramount.[206]

Given that Germany was entering a period of impoverishment, the opportunity had arisen to divest architecture of that which was superfluous. Cheap fancy should be avoided, and adherence to strict forms and discipline was essential. Poelzig went on to state that deplorable architecture is the result of psychic corruption, of the desire to seek only material gain, and of a mentality which had lost the psychic connection with Nature, with the nation's 'native soil'. The *Werkbund*'s aim should be to reconnect that which had been fractured, and a change of attitude was necessary to achieve such reconnection. It would be necessary to resuscitate satisfaction in work, something both Morris and Ruskin, among others, had advocated for many years. Art must be inspiring, and must be closely interwoven with the collective soul of a people: its creators should be indifferent to the commercial value imposed on works of art. Fundamental improvements would only be possible after architects received an education in how to build, to create works of art, with the understanding of how materials behave, and to respect the architectonic-musical character of creative processes.[207]

Despite Poelzig's rather typical Germanic contortions of expression, none of that speech to the *Werkbund* sounds like a harbinger of the sort of Modernism that became *de rigueur*, especially after Hitchcock and Johnson gave it their *imprimatur*, and the limited vocabulary of the International Style became the only possible one to be employed. Music, understanding of materials and how they are put together, and the handicrafts were far from the agenda established in the 1920s. They are even further away now with Parametricism's impact, the dependence on electronic machines to design buildings, and the sorry state of the Arts and Crafts.

Given what was to happen later, it is odd that Gropius supported Poelzig, although it would not be unreasonable to suggest that his stance may have been more political, a jockeying for position, and a seeking for as wide a sphere of influence as possible. That Gropius was more a politician than a good architect can hardly be doubted,[208] especially since the *Werkbund* was lobbying for a *Reichskunstwart* (state art advisor), and succeeded when Edwin Redslob, the *Werkbund*'s representative in Thuringia, was appointed to that position in 1919. In that year, however, Poelzig was associated with *Formenrausch*, a Nietzschean term, which might be translated as the 'ecstasy of creating designs/forms', and it is to that short-lived phase that we will shortly turn.

II

Makers of Mythologies & False Analogies

Introduction; Voysey as a Pevsnerian 'Pioneer'; Further Objections to the Pevsnerian Position; Baillie Scott; The Religious Factor; Unfortunate Treatment of Berlage, Comper, & Dykes Bower

> The young modernist, heedless that 'modernity' is not quality, is inclined to throw over the good as well as what there may be of bad in his heritage, and goes to excess, like all revolutionaries, in his desire at all costs to express himself.
>
> Sir Herbert Baker (1862–1946): *Architecture & Personalities*
> (London: Country Life Ltd 1944) 182

> Herbert Read stated[1] that Modern Art was not so much a revolution, but rather a break-up. Its character is catastrophic.
>
> Sir Reginald Theodore Blomfield (1856–1942): *Modernismus*
> (London: Macmillan & Co. Ltd 1934) 62

> There is ... an easy belief proclaimed that Mackintosh ... and the others of the Glasgow group were disregarded clairvoyants; that during a long period of neglect over here their visionary germs were cultured abroad in a gelatinous 'ismus,' that the European war stirred the minds of our architects to discontent with their former productions; until a new courage, a new originality, and a new truth, popped conveniently out of the laboratory bottles.
>
> Harry Stuart Goodhart-Rendel (1887–1959): *English Architecture since the Regency* (London: Constable & Co. Ltd 1953) 224

Introduction

Hermann Muthesius 'had discovered for his countrymen the great domestic architecture England produced before 1900'.[2] The foreword by Dennis Sharp to the superlative[3] three-volume English version of *Das englische*

Haus states that Muthesius 'transmitted an informed view of the English domestic architectural tradition of his times, emphasising the influence of the English Arts and Crafts to his German compatriots'.[4] Muthesius shared the belief of William Morris that the Middle Ages provided exemplars for the way forward, not in terms of slavishly copying elements, but in the organization of craft-guilds (Gropius claimed he believed in something similar, though what actually resulted from his works was, to understate it, rather different), the understanding of materials, fine workmanship, and the huge amount of domestic architecture from that period that survived and provided so many models for the protagonists of the 'free architecture' celebrated in his magnificent book.[5] The importance Muthesius gave to the works of Ernest George, Edwin Lutyens, Norman Shaw, and C.F.A. Voysey can be judged from the amount of space devoted to them in *Das englische Haus*.

It should be pointed out, however, that 'English' is misleading, because there were distinguished designs by Scots architects in Muthesius's work. Shaw was born in Scotland of a Scots mother and an Irish father; Mervyn Edmund Macartney was London-born of a County Armagh, Ireland, family; R.S. Lorimer was a Scot, as was William Flockhart; and of course C.R. Mackintosh was a Scot too. Given Muthesius's antipathy towards *Art Nouveau*, it is curious he was so enthusiastic about Mackintosh and Macdonald, for their work was often more than influenced by *Art Nouveau*: he stated that the Mackintoshes, the McNairs, and their circle 'all spoke the same artistic language with great conviction'.[6] But Mackintosh, like so many of his contemporaries, went rapidly out of fashion at a time when not only was *Art Nouveau* regarded as decadent and *passé*, but 'free architecture' was being rejected in favour of a *Beaux-Arts* Classicism embraced by numerous practitioners, including Norman Shaw himself (e.g. Alliance Assurance office, St James's [1901–5], and the huge Piccadilly hotel [early 1900s], both in London) and especially the Glasgow-born John James Burnet, whose Edward VII galleries, the extension to the British Museum (1904–14), made his reputation.

The catastrophic fire-damage sustained (2014) by Mackintosh's Glasgow School of Art (1896–1909) has led to an outpouring of claims for funds to restore this mis-called 'pioneering work of the Modern Movement'.[7] However, any observant critic will perceive the building as a brilliant *eclectic* design, drawing on *Art-Nouveau* themes: the motif above the main entrance is a typical example of that style, as are the wrought-iron brackets attached to the huge studio-windows and the clusters of iron buds on the railings.

English vernacular architecture is recalled in the canted bay-window to the left of the main entrance, suggesting an element from cottages in Broadway, Worcestershire, sketched by Mackintosh in 1894 (**Plate 2.1**). The west façade, with its tall oriel windows, seems to owe more to Lutyens's *Le Bois-des-Moutiers*, a house at Varengeville-sur-Mer, Seine-Maritime, Haute-Normandie, France (1897–8),[8] than to 'national tradition' exemplified in the 'Scottish baronial past'.[9] No one accustomed to studying real Scottish historic buildings[10] would see references to them in the Glasgow School of Art.

So what are the origins of these notions that eclectic architects, steeped in the language of *Art Nouveau*, southern-English vernacular details, and traditional methods of building, were 'pioneers' of 'Modern design'? They certainly did not emerge with Muthesius's book. Critics such as Philip Morton Shand saw clearly that Mackintosh was 'far less of a constructor

Plate 2.1. Detail of the entrance to the School of Art, Glasgow, showing the *Art-Nouveau* motif over the door and the canted bay-window derived from English vernacular exemplars sketched by Mackintosh

than a decorator', whose status as a 'functionalist pioneer' was itself a construction that did not stand up.[11] H.S. Goodhart-Rendel's views on the matter were unequivocal.

The culprit is easily traced: he was Pevsner, whose incredibly influential *Pioneers of the Modern Movement from William Morris to Walter Gropius* (1936), later revised as *Pioneers of Modern Design*, claimed that in the first part of the Glasgow School of Art to be completed (1899), not 'a single feature' was 'derived from period styles'.[12] This is patently untrue: he went on to mention 'playful Art Nouveau ornaments' and the 'intertwined tentacles of iron' on the brackets attached to the studio windows, the source of which was 'clearly the Celtic and Viking art of Britain'.[13] He also spotted *Art-Nouveau* tendencies in the library balustrades running from the parapets of the gallery to the 'pillars' (to describe the vertical timber posts as 'pillars'[14] is unfortunate). So Pevsner identified *Art-Nouveau* elements, Celtic and Viking sources, and missed the Lutyens connection entirely, yet 'not a single feature' had been 'derived from period styles'. He then hailed Mackintosh as one of the few 'true forerunners of that most ingenious juggler of space: Le Corbusier'.[15]

Such contradictions and serious misjudgements explain why 'few now accept the view of Nikolaus Pevsner, put forward in his influential *Pioneers of the Modern Movement* (1936), of Arts and Crafts as an antecedent of modernism, to which it had contributed a functionalist and stripped-down aesthetic'.[16]

Pevsner's agenda are clear from the subtitle of his simplistic and distorted text: *from William Morris to Walter Gropius.*[17] His highly selective polemic was part of a campaign by convinced Modernists against what they regarded as 'reactionary' architecture. Numerous hagiographies of the so-called 'pioneers' Pevsner canonized have been published, but until comparatively recently, masters he either ignored or scorned (like Ernest Newton) have been neglected, and his approved architects, such as Baillie Scott and C.F.A. Voysey, were largely observed 'through Pevsner-approved Bauhaus-tinted spectacles', as the late Roderick Gradidge sagely observed.[18]

The choice of Gropius's name in the subtitle is also revealing. Pevsner seems to have been mesmerized by Gropius's personality and physical presence: he had never before met anyone in whom discipline and integrity were united so powerfully in one man;[19] he regarded Gropius as a 'moral force';[20] he felt extraordinary emotions resembling 'the excitement of someone in love' when he anticipated dining with him; and his biographer wrote that 'Pevsner's admiration amounted almost to infatuation'.[21] There were some who felt that Pevsner's idolization was excessive. Philip Johnson believed Gropius (who could not draw) had never designed anything, whether it appeared over his name or not. As it happens, Gropius did design some individual buildings, but his solo efforts were unimpressive.[22] What is more, Johnson detested Gropius (who 'never learned'),[23] and he was by no means alone in this opinion. Johnson felt that *From William Morris to Walter Gropius* was 'too much of a compliment to our estimable and excellent pedagogue, Walter Gropius'.[24]

Even the *Bauhaus* at Dessau was originally credited to Gropius *and* Meyer[25] (though Meyer's involvement has been expunged in most accounts), but in fact much of the design work was carried out, not by Gropius at all, but by Carl Fieger (who also came from the Behrens stable) and Ernst Neufert.[26] Fieger had worked on the design of the interiors of the German embassy in St Petersburg (*see* **Plate 1.3**) before he joined Gropius in practice in 1912: indeed he continued to work for Gropius on and off until 1934, and after that practised anonymously.[27] His work on his own account was in a quite distinguished International-Modern style (**Figure 2.1**), and after the 1939–45 war he returned to Dessau to help with the reconstruction after widespread war-damage. Under the aegis of Richard Paulick he was appointed (1952) to the German Building Academy.[28]

Neufert became an expert on prefabrication and standardization, and wrote his influential *Bauentwurfslehre* (later published in English as *Architects' data*),[29] which went into a great many subsequent editions: some of Neufert's illustrations seem to have been adapted by Le Corbusier a decade later for

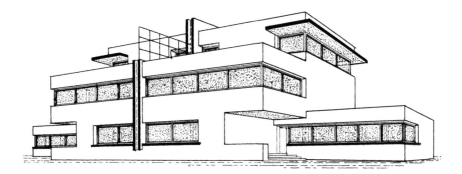

Figure 2.1. Design for a 'double dwelling-house' (i.e. semi-detached pair) by Karl Fieger, *c.*1926

his *Modulor* system.[30] The success of *Bauentwurfslehre* dissuaded Neufert from emigrating to the USA, and in 1939 Albert Speer appointed him to work on the standardization of German industrial architecture. This appointment is yet another instance of a former *Bauhaus* student (hereafter termed *Bauhäusler*) rising to a position of some eminence under National Socialism. Gropius was dismissive of Neufert's achievements, not least because of his work on standardization and industrialized components for Nazi Germany (and his involvement in the design of the Dessau *Bauhaus*).[31] There are disturbing elements in this, though: Neufert's seemingly unassuming technical approach to standardization is uncomfortably related to the notion of reducing human beings to systems of measurement. *Existenzminimum* can overlap from a disinterested scientific study of how to apply minimum standards to how many can be crammed into a dormitory, or, perhaps, even into a cattle-truck. There was undoubtedly a very dark side to the amoral, dehumanized, supposedly 'scientific' application of measurable data to the built environment, and that crepuscular obscurity contributed to a failure to see where Modernism might lead, and indeed it led to catastrophe.

In the 1930s some protagonists of Modern architecture felt they had to connect it with some carefully selected buildings of the past (in attempts to give it a spurious historical pedigree in order to disguise its disruptive character and pretend it derived from respectable antecedents), while simultaneously denying what Pevsner called 'Historicism'[32] and *demanding* the *tabula rasa*: contradictory positions indeed. The building up of certain individuals as Modernist heroes (what Banham called a 'Stephen Dedalus thirst for respectable father figures')[33] was rightly considered by some to produce, in John Summerson's words, 'sentimental psycho-biographies'.[34] Pevsner used the 'father-figures' more as links in an imaginary chain supporting his argument, but his selectivity and *Bauhaus*-tinted views warped the structure, even the essence, of *Pioneers*. One wonders, reading it today, how it could have been so successful as a key element in what might be termed the 'Grand Narrative' of the Modern Movement which Pevsner undoubtedly tried to legitimize by giving it a fabricated historical pedigree. His book was also propaganda to establish the agenda of the Modern Movement in England: hence his build-up of Gropius.[35] Even Alfred Kurlbaum, Pevsner's father-in-law, made clear that he felt Gropius had been given far too much space and attention in *Pioneers*, and that Gropius was not really interested in 'art for all': he compared his attitudes in that respect unfavourably with National-Socialist policies concerning design and the arts.[36]

Pevsner insisted that the Modern Movement began with Morris, that it formed an historical unity in its development to the time of Gropius, and that with Gropius its character was ultimately determined. 'It is the creative energy of this world in which we live and work and which we want to master, a world of science and technique, of speed and danger, of hard struggles and no personal security, that is glorified in Gropius's architecture',[37] wrote Pevsner. He also considered, in regard to the German's work at the *Werkbund* exhibition, Cologne, 1914, and the Fagus shoe-last factory, Alfeld-an-der-Leine, 1911 (with both of which Adolf Meyer was more involved than has been generally credited), that never 'since the Sainte Chapelle and the choir of Beauvais had the human art of building been so triumphant over matter';[38] a piece of hyperbole that seems to have been accepted, unquestioningly and inexplicably, as serious, considered comment. Furthermore, there is a phrase in the first edition of *Pioneers* concerning 'this new style [the Modern Movement] of the twentieth century': 'because it is a genuine style as opposed to a passing fashion, [it is] totalitarian'.[39] This revealing admission was subsequently changed: in the 2005 edition, 'totalitarian' became 'universal'.[40]

It is difficult, when considering the rather embarrassing adulation Pevsner heaped on Gropius, not to conclude that he may have felt a multitude of conflicting emotions, not unconnected with his Russian-Jewish origins, his upbringing in the Saxon city of Leipzig, and his perception of the older Gropius as somehow a superior being (with a Prussian background, service with an *élite* cavalry regiment in the 1914–18 war, connections with a family long associated with the profession of architecture in Berlin, and an elevated position within the social *milieu* of pre-war Vienna, including marriage to the anti-Semitic and formidable widow of the distinguished composer, Gustav Mahler).[41]

In short, Pevsner, for all his intellectual equipment and considerable culture, may have felt some sort of social inferiority to his hero, yet could hardly have been unaware of the many unpleasant sides of Gropius.

P. Morton Shand commented in a letter (17 February 1934—written in German from London) to Gropius on the possible involvement of the German-Jewish architect, Erich Mendelsohn, in an exhibition to be mounted at the Royal Institute of British Architects (RIBA) that year. Soon Gropius would, like Mendelsohn, be living as an *émigré* in England, but Mendelsohn found more and more that he was being treated as an outsider, and that other European Modernists increasingly had the ear of architectural sympathizers resident in England. Mendelsohn had been one of the most successful founders of architectural Modernism during the Weimar Republic, but Pevsner did not include him in the first edition of *Pioneers* at all. Mendelsohn had not been involved in the *Congrès Internationaux d'Architecture Moderne* (CIAM hereafter), and as a result was refused membership of the Modern Architecture Research Group (MARS hereafter, effectively the London branch of CIAM, but from *c.*1937 a major influence *on* CIAM).[42] His exclusion was snidely justified by Wells Coates on the grounds that if this 'ex-German' were admitted, it would 'not be helpful' to the interests of the Group.[43] Shand, who is described as 'casually anti-Semitic'[44] (which, to judge from the evidence, seems to be an understatement), held that the RIBA and Maxwell Fry deemed it essential (*wichtig*) that the exhibition (*Außtellung*) should display (*zeigt*) the work of a 'pure' (*rein*) German architect, which was not to be confused (*verwechseln*) with creations of the 'unpatriotic' (*vaterlandslosen*) Mendelsohn. He went on to reveal himself as 'no special friend of the Jew' (*ich selbst kein sonderlicher Freund der Juden bin*), and that only 'significant work' (*bedeutende Werk*) of a 'full and entirely German citizen' (*eines ganz und gar deutschen Staatsbürgers* [i.e. Gropius]) should be shown.[45]

This may have been something to do with Mendelsohn's Zionist sympathies, and the fact that he had worked almost exclusively for German-Jewish clients like the Schockens, but Shand's views (clearly known to his English associates, such as Fry) seem distasteful, at the very least. When we consider that Gropius never overtly objected to the Hitler *régime*, indeed made many attempts to come to terms with it, at the very least an anti-Semitic 'tendency' (borne out by disagreeable remarks that have been quoted elsewhere)[46] can be attributed to him, so Pevsner's attitude towards Gropius raises all sorts of issues and questions. Indeed, not only Gropius but other *Bauhäusler* displayed odious anti-Semitic attitudes.[47] The fact remains that Mendelsohn's work was no less central than that of Gropius and others to modern architecture in Germany between the wars.[48]

Although Pevsner converted to Lutheranism in 1921, partly in order to become a 'normal German'[49] and partly to open doors that would usually be closed to a Jew, like many such converts he found it cut no ice with either the Nazis or with many non-Jewish Germans. A sensitive man like Pevsner would have been all too aware of how he was perceived by certain of his compatriots who, despite his Lutheranism and his embrace of all things German, would still have regarded him as not quite German enough.[50]

Voysey as a Pevsnerian 'Pioneer'

Among the architects to whom Muthesius devoted several pages in *Das englische Haus* were Baillie Scott and Voysey, although the latter's designs for metalwork, fireplaces, and various features were often suffused with *Art-Nouveau* elements which Muthesius found unpalatable elsewhere. One of Voysey's houses singled out in *Das englische Haus*[51] was Broadleys, Bowness-on-Windermere, Westmorland (1898–9), which has three bows on the elevation facing the lake (**Plate 2.2**). These bows, constructed of stone, with plain, unmoulded mullions and transoms, have leaded lights, and two of the bows are partially rendered:[52] Pevsner hailed them as coming 'amazingly close to the twentieth-century concrete and glass grid'.[53] In *An Outline of European Architecture*, first published (1943) in Pelican Books, he claimed Voysey's use of 'bare walls and long horizontal bands of windows' (as in the house called 'Grey Friars', Puttenham, Surrey [1896–7]) 'came nearest to the idiom of the Modern Movement';[54] and then, in the next paragraph, announced that for the 'next forty years...no English name need here be mentioned'.[55] These Pevsnerian utterances deserve consideration, not least because they have been influential, although based on what might charitably be regarded as misjudgements.

In *Elseviers Geïllustreed Maandschrift*,[56] Pevsner wrote that Voysey's 'roughcast walls, decorative buttresses with pronounced batter, a big reassuring roof and horizontal mullioned windows' were based on the 'English yeoman's house of the seventeenth century... *there can be no doubt about that*'.[57] Well, quite so: if one looks at buildings such as West End Farm, West Street, Pembridge, Herefordshire (*c.*1425); seventeenth-century merchants' houses at Sandhill, Newcastle upon Tyne (where the horizontal bands of windows are spectacular); the former White Hart Inn at the south-east corner of the Market Place, Newark, Nottinghamshire, with its much-restored late-fifteenth-century façade featuring rows of Gothic canopies over tiny figures set beneath rows of windows separated by mullions, a feature slightly reminiscent of the Prior's House at Much Wenlock Priory, Shropshire (**Plate 2.3**); the long range of mullioned-and-transomed windows illuminating the long gallery at Little Moreton Hall, Cheshire (late-sixteenth century, but curiously linked by F. R. S. Yorke to fenestration by Le Corbusier)[58] (**Plate 2.4**); and numerous examples of the timber-framed buildings with which England was once so blessed, it is not difficult to

Plate 2.2. Bow-windows with plain stone mullions and transoms at Broadleys, Bowness-on-Windermere, Westmorland (1898–9), by C. F. A. Voysey. Pevsner fancifully perceived them through *Bauhaus*-tinted spectacles as coming 'amazingly close to the twentieth-century concrete and glass grid' (Pevsner [1968a] ii 148)

Plate 2.3. Restored Market-Place frontage of the fifteenth-century former White Hart Inn, Newark, Nottinghamshire, showing the ranges of windows separated by timber mullions

Plate 2.4. The late-sixteenth-century timber-framed Little Moreton Hall, Cheshire, showing the long ranges of windows with timber mullions

imagine how unmoulded timber mullions and transoms could be models for petrified versions. But to hail such exemplars as harbingers of Modernism is questionable, at the very least, and stretching facts to breaking-point.

Fine timber-framed buildings, such as those of Lancashire and Suffolk, provide good exemplars for long bands of fenestration subdivided by unmoulded uprights, patterns which could easily trigger interpretations of similar features in stone. Long ranks of windows with plain mullions occur at Townsford Mill, Halstead, Essex (late eighteenth century, converted for silk-throwing and weaving purposes by Samuel Courtauld in 1825); another range of horizontal windows with plain mullions survives at Abbey Mill, Little Coggeshall, Essex (mid-eighteenth century, converted as a silk-throwing mill, c. 1820); and various other eighteenth- and nineteenth-century industrial buildings. Weavers' houses in Charles Lane, Milnrow, Lancashire (mid-nineteenth century) (**Plate 2.5**), and the Hazelhurst engineering-works, Ramsbottom, Lancashire (c. 1840), are but two examples. But none of these has any resemblance to the long strip-windows of International Modernism, with no mullions subdividing the aggressive horizontals of glass, and very different structural systems supporting the floors.

C.F.A. Voysey had been a pupil (1874–9) of John Pollard Seddon before briefly joining (1879) the office of Henry Saxon Snell. Then he worked as

Plate 2.5. Weavers' houses, 25–9 Charles Lane, Milnrow, Lancashire (mid-nineteenth century), showing the grids of simple squared stone mullions, heads, and cills, set flush with the walls, allowing the windows to be opened or blocked up as required

an 'improver' in George Devey's office (1880–1) before setting up his own practice. Devey, incidentally, was a member of the Theistic Church founded by Voysey's father, the Revd Charles Voysey, who had been expelled from the Anglican Church in 1871 for his 'heretical doctrines'.[59] Voysey gained invaluable experience with Seddon (no mean architect himself), Snell (who specialized in hospital-design and was meticulous in his attention to detail), and Devey. The last carried out numerous extensions to old houses, and was a *true pioneer* in the revived interest in English vernacular buildings. His very sensitive domestic architecture at Penshurst, Kent (1849–50—greatly admired and drawn by, among others, W.E. Nesfield and Norman Shaw), undoubtedly influenced the evolution of the 'Old English' style of the Domestic Revival, and had a huge impact on the architecture of the English house as diligently recorded by Muthesius.

That Voysey was influenced by his time with Devey cannot be doubted, and some of the features he employed in his own work have echoes of the older architect's designs, notably at Penshurst. Devey's substantial interventions (1874–84) at Smithills Hall, Bolton, Lancashire (fourteenth to sixteenth

Plate 2.6. Twin early-seventeenth-century bay-windows with stone mullions and transoms at Kirby Hall, Northamptonshire

centuries with later additions and alterations), coincided with the time Voysey was with him: 'Devey's influence on Voysey as a designer quite out-weighed what he had learned with Seddon',[60] observed Devey's biographer, and that is undoubtedly true. So Devey's work informed Voysey, who was erroneously supposed to be a 'pioneer' of Modernism,[61] yet Modernists' 'histories' have tended not to claim Devey as one of their so-called 'pioneers'.

As for the bays of Broadleys, various precedents, such as the south-eastern tower of the town walls, Blackfriars Road, Great Yarmouth, Norfolk (early fourteenth century), suggest themselves. There were certainly mullioned-and-transomed windows of stone on earlier plans that were segments of a circle or almost half-circles: they include the remarkable example, cinque-foil on plan, in the south range of Thornbury Castle, Gloucestershire (c. 1510–14); the immense twin bays at Kirby Hall, Northamptonshire (early seventeenth century) (**Plate 2.6**); the bay-window at Fountains Hall, Yorkshire (c. 1611); and the central bay of the oak-framed façade of the house in Bishopsgate, London (known as that of Sir Paul Pindar), now preserved in the Victoria & Albert Museum (**Plate 2.7**). Voysey used three projecting bays on semicircular plans with unmoulded stone mullions at 14/16 Hans Road, Knightsbridge, London (1892).

Plate 2.7. The timber-framed (oak) front of the Sir Paul Pindar Tavern (formerly the dwelling of Sir Paul Pindar), Bishopsgate, London, demolished 1890, showing the bay-windows. The façade is now in the Victoria & Albert Museum

The writings of A.W.N. Pugin influenced the work of mid-nineteeth-century architects long before the advent of what we call the Arts-and-Crafts Movement. Two architects in particular, William Butterfield and George Edmund Street, both Gothic Revivalists, designed houses which responded to Pugin's demands that the three-dimensional form of a building should grow, unforced and naturally, out of the plan (something he called the 'True Picturesque'); that locally available materials should be used honestly; and that structure should be expressed and not hidden. Butterfield's parsonage at Coalpit Heath, Gloucestershire (1844–5), was an important precedent for the free domestic compositions of architects such as Nesfield, Shaw, and Webb, because fenestration was placed where needed to illuminate the volumes inside, and all traces of the straitjacket of Classical symmetry were expunged (**Plate 2.8**).[62] Street's essay (1853) in *The Ecclesiologist* on the revival of the 'Ancient Style of Domestic Architecture' was a milestone in the upsurge of interest in vernacular buildings, and had a considerable

Plate 2.8. The former St Saviour's Vicarage, Coalpit Heath, Westerleigh, Gloucestershire (1845), by Butterfield, designed on Puginian principles that elevations should develop logically from the ground plan

impact on the Domestic Revival of the Arts-and-Crafts Movement.[63] Among the most important catalysts for that Domestic Revival was *Some Account of Domestic Architecture in England*, commenced by Thomas Hudson Turner, completed by John Henry Parker, and profusely and beautifully illustrated.[64]

By the 1850s, two further themes joined Pugin's 'principles', namely that local building traditions deserved study and should be triggers for design, and that a wider aesthetic freedom should be available for any architect. Devey's work of the 1850s at Penshurst was remarkably prescient, for his new work there harmonized with existing fabric, and he used tile-hanging, external rendering, half-timbering, tall chimneys, jetties, fretted barge-boards, brick, and rubble with freedom, firmly establishing a fluency in the vernacular language of building as an important ingredient in English domestic design.[65] One can see in his architectural treatments various pre-cedents that obviously informed developments in Voysey's design language. At Penshurst, too, Devey employed simple windows of five lights subdivided by plain timber mullions, but two lights were at right angles to three, so the five lights actually turn a corner, an unusual feature, and one that was a very free interpretation of traditional domestic architecture (**Plate 2.9**). Voysey used variants of this in his designs for a studio house, St Dunstan's Road,

Plate 2.9. Work of the 1850s by Devey at Penshurst, Kent, showing (*on the right*) windows turning a corner, a device later used by Voysey and others

Hammersmith, London (c.1897),[66] The Homestead, Frinton-on-Sea, Essex (1905–6), and at Holly Mount, near Beaconsfield, Buckinghamshire (1905),[67] but at Broadleys he wrapped a continuous window around three sides of the first floor to illuminate the staircase: here the lights were divided by timber mullions, and turn two corners.[68]

Pevsner did admit (1940) that Devey was 'a domestic architect of far greater interest and importance than is realised',[69] but he did not analyse the elements in Voysey's work that may have been derived (however indirectly) from Devey's designs.[70] His insistence on Voysey as a 'pioneer' of the Modern Movement is founded on highly dubious premises, and it has had a long life, but the odd thing is that Pevsner was not the first to categorize Voysey thus. John Betjeman, when an assistant editor of *The Architectural Review* (from 1930, even before Pevsner's utterances on the man), adopted Voysey as one of three 'true pioneers' (the other two being Ruskin and Le Corbusier),[71] but he retreated from this position as he began to realize what was being done (and was likely to be done) to towns and cities by Modernists: some early doubts and concerns started to appear in his *Ghastly Good Taste*, subtitled *A Depressing Story of the Rise and Fall of English Architecture*.[72] By that time the damage was done.

Even earlier, an anonymous series of articles on Voysey, the man and his work, was published (1927) in *The Architect & Building News* which presented him as a rock-like super-hero of artistic integrity, a kind of John the Baptist, the harbinger of the Modern Movement.[73] The late John Brandon-Jones, who was to publish a more balanced memoir of Voysey in 1957,[74] suggested[75] that the author of the 1927 articles might have been H.B. Creswell, who, under the initials H.B.C., wrote a piece about Voysey in the *RIBA Journal* in the same year.[76] Although there are stylistic hints that Creswell was indeed responsible, his authorship has not been proven beyond doubt.

Voysey himself deplored being categorized at all. J.M. Richards[77] had joined the office of Charles Cowles Voysey (C.F.A. Voysey's son),[78] before becoming (1933) assistant editor of the *Architects' Journal*. Later (1937) he took over the editorship of *The Architectural Review*, in which capacity, with Pevsner and others, he zealously promoted the Modern Movement. When he approached Voysey to discuss his inclusion as a 'pioneer' in Richards's own book on modern architecture, the old man objected to being included 'among the originators of an architecture he heartily disliked'.[79] Despite Voysey's indignation, Richards named him.[80]

When we consider that Voysey indeed stated in no uncertain terms that the architecture of the Modern Movement

> was pitifully full of such faults as proportions that were vulgarly agressive [*sic*], mountebank eccentricities in detail, and windows built lying down on their sides. Like rude children we had broken away and turned our backs on tradition. This was false originality, the true originality having been for all time the spiritual something given to the development of traditional forms by the individual artist.[81]

Obviously he did not see any connection between his long ranges of mullioned windows (which derived from English historical architecture) and the 'windows lying on their sides' so favoured by those (like Le Corbusier) who lifted images from ocean-going liners (now almost a century old, or even more) as their sources (*see* **Figure 5.3**).

Several commentators saw Voysey as the natural successor of William Morris, but he himself objected to that spurious relationship for reasons given below. Pevsner perceived Arthur Heygate Mackmurdo as a major influence on the young Voysey (though they later quarrelled), and as a 'pioneer' of *Art Nouveau* (e.g. Mackmurdo's 'proto-Art Nouveau…title-page to his book on *Wren's City Churches*' [1883][82] and his chair-back of the same year).[83] Yet *Art Nouveau* really grew out of the Gothic Revival,[84] as can be seen in the capitals of the clustered piers that carried the lines of the former London, Chatham, & Dover Railway over the Thames at Blackfriars, London: they were designed, it would appear, by Joseph Cubitt, Henry Carr, Frederick Thomas Turner, and John Taylor Jr, and date from 1862–4, long before Mackmurdo's forays into 'proto-Art Nouveau' (**Plate 2.10a**).

William Haywood's Holborn Viaduct, London (1863–4), where it crosses Farringdon Street on a cast-iron bridge (made by John Cochrane) carried on hexagonal granite piers, has delicate metalwork capitals fixed to the granite that also herald *Art-Nouveau* forms (**Plate 2.10b**). The bronze statues on the bridge were by Farmer & Brindley and H. Burshill. Thomas Blashill assisted Haywood with the architectural detail, so it was presumably Blashill who designed or supervised the making of these remarkable and very beautiful capitals. The essence of *Art-Nouveau* themes was therefore certainly in place in England in the early 1860s, for John Francis Bentley designed the exquisite high-altar and reredos for the church of St Francis of Assisi, Pottery Lane, Northern Kensington, with pronounced *Art-Nouveau* inlays of black foliate patterns in its first super-altar (1863). These *true heralds* of *Art Nouveau* were in place, designed, and manufactured,

Plate 2.10a. Clustered piers that carried the lines of the former London, Chatham, & Dover Railway over the Thames at Blackfriars, London (1862–4), showing the proto-*Art-Nouveau* capitals

twenty years before Mackmurdo's works were realized, later claimed as 'pioneering' by Pevsner.[85]

Although there were many artefacts designed by the fastidious Voysey that obviously drew on *Art-Nouveau* themes,[86] he found aspects of the 'New Art' 'distinctly unhealthy and revolting',[87] and heartily disliked the work of Mackintosh, even though the latter's enthusiasts (including Betjeman and Newbery) claimed the Scotsman was inspired by Voysey's *oeuvre*,[88] something that did not please the Englishman at all.[89] English rejection of *Art Nouveau* was not unconnected with the disgrace of Oscar Wilde (1895) and associations, therefore, with *The Yellow Book* and other publications, notably those with illustrations by Aubrey Beardsley.[90] This animosity towards *Art Nouveau* was also apparent in the writings of Muthesius[91] (even though the covers of the three-volume set of *Das englische Haus* published by Wasmuth featured an embossed-gilt floral design that was very much in that style, and two interiors by Mackintosh where *Art-Nouveau* influences were obvious

Plate 2.10*b*. Granite pier with capital embellished with gilded metal at Holborn Viaduct, Farringdon Street, London (1863–9)

featured in volume one):[92] the rejection of *Art Nouveau* was part of the wholesale rejection of what Pevsner called 'Historicism' by those German Modernists who rose to pre-eminence after 1918, notably the *Bauhäusler*.

In Britain, however, the Wilde story tended to become submerged under blankets of national prudishness until the 1960s, when that writer was rediscovered, and something like an *Art-Nouveau* revival and rehabilitation began. Wilde, like other aesthetes, considered morality and art to be mutually exclusive, the antithesis of the position adopted by Ruskin and his circle,[93] but Modernists, fixed in their dogmas, continued to reject and ignore *Art Nouveau*, even though, or perhaps because, it became popular once again. Pevsner himself had the grace to admit in print that Voysey was 'cross' with him for 'having discussed his work as pioneer work of the twentieth century style' (*sic*) which he 'disliked'. Voysey told Pevsner that 'the new architecture cannot last. The architects have no religion. They have nothing exalted which they could try to approach; they are like designers who draw flowers and trees without remembering and honouring Him who created them.'[94]

Pevsner and others like him, however, knew better, and overrode such scruples. Selectivity and exaggerated claims were essential elements of the 'Grand Narrative' of Modernism, and Pevsner was not the only one to employ them, although he was among the most influential. *Space, Time and Architecture*, subtitled *The Growth of a New Tradition*,[95] by Sigfried Giedion, the Swiss *apparatchik* of that powerful *Politburo* of Modernism, CIAM, was also selective, linking an account of historical architecture and town planning with an aberration that, by no stretch of any uncorrupted imagination, could be in any way connected with the long history of European civilization.

Arthur Korn, in his *History Builds the Town* (1953),[96] attempted the pretence that Ancient-Egyptian, Babylonian, Assyrian, Persian, Greek, Roman, mediaeval-European, Renaissance, Baroque, Rococo, Georgian, and Neo-Classical town plans led inevitably to Le Corbusier's conceptions; the appallingly destructive, but fortunately unrealized MARS proposals for London;[97] the County of London Plan (1943—by Patrick Abercrombie and J.H. Forshaw);[98] the British New Towns post-1945; the designs for towns (e.g. Tirgan) by Ernst May and (e.g. Magnitogorsk) by N.A. Milyutin in the Soviet Union;[99] and the entire evolution of Soviet Planning after 1945, notably in Poland.[100] He concluded his book with the statement that our

> capitalist society of poverty and wealth experiences growing difficulties in the field of reconstruction. The developments in the U.S.S.R. and Eastern Europe, on the other hand, have made essential contributions to the realisation of co-ordinated planning. Between 1925 and 1930 a strong mutual influence could be recognised: the East trying to catch up with modern Western technique, calling in teams of western planners for reconstruction of new towns; the West being impressed by the possibility of controlled planning on a national scale.[101]

What is more, he considered the May towns, and many Modernist schemes that have not mellowed well, as 'works of art': some might disagree. There are many more exemplars of unsustainable attempts to link the past with later Dystopian presents, and some of that twisted thinking must stem from people like Ruskin.

Nevertheless, the blurb on the back of Pevsner's *Pioneers* (1975 paperback edition)[102] states that 'Voysey and Mackintosh in Britain were among the early masters of the Modern Movement. Louis Sullivan and Frank Lloyd Wright in America,[103] the Sezession School, Adolf Loos and Otto Wagner in Vienna[104] and, finally, Gropius and his Bauhaus colleagues perfected the style.' The 2005 edition of *Pioneers* stated that Pevsner 'saw Modernism as a synthesis of three main sources: William Morris and his followers, the work of nineteenth-century engineers, and Art Nouveau'. He considered 'the role of these sources in the work of early Modernists and looks at such masters of the movement as C.F.A. Voysey and Charles Rennie Mackintosh in Britain, Louis Sullivan and Frank Lloyd Wright in America, and Adolf Loos and Otto Wagner in Vienna'.[105] *The Art and Architecture of C.F.A. Voysey: English Pioneer Modernist Architect*[106] was published in 2015, so Pevsner's label still sticks, regardless of facts and the hot denials of men like Voysey himself.

Further Objections to the Pevsnerian Position

The revised and expanded edition of *Pioneers*[107] seemed to accept uncritically much of Pevsner's extraordinarily influential text, but Alan Crawford raised some real objections, finding the original book 'scrappy': he was appalled by its 'looseness and...lack of detail'.[108] He pointed out that as Pevsner was driving 'towards his Modernist goal, picking out this individual here and that feature there, leaving the rest by the wayside, he did not bother to give weight or substance to his story'.[109] He began to think that the Arts-and-Crafts Movement might be the *opposite* of what Pevsner *claimed* it was. Crawford noted that Pevsner had used Ashbee's statement that 'Modern Civilisation rests on Machinery, and no system for the endowment, or encouragement, or the teaching of art can be sound that does not recognise this'[110] to insist that Ashbee had 'abandoned the doctrine of the Arts and Crafts and adopted one of the basic premises of the Modern Movement'.[111] Crawford held that Pevsner's 'version of Ashbee was inaccurate, unbalanced and unsympathetic':[112] he went on to describe Ashbee's 'little band of medievalizing craftsmen' retreating 'to the country'; his antipathy towards 'the culture, individualism and economic life of the bourgeoisie'; and his joining of 'hands with Bohemia and the workmen of Mile End'. Crawford's Ashbee was 'a full-blown, drastic, Romantic anti-Modernist, shaking his cultured fist at the birth of the modern world'.[113] Crawford wrote that he 'never normally' took issue 'with other writers', but made 'an exception in this case...because Pevsner's influence was so great'.[114]

Crawford then proceeded to call the 'ghost' of William Morris as a witness. The Arts-and-Crafts Movement made more sense in terms of how it had evolved rather than where it was supposedly leading. Pevsner claimed that the establishment of Morris's firm in 1861 marked 'the beginning of a new era in Western art':[115] thus he gave the impression of 'starting with a clean slate, as if nothing had gone before', yet the truth was that the whole Arts-and-Crafts Movement grew from the Gothic Revival.[116] Crawford's second 'ghost witness' was Edward Johnston, the Arts-and-Crafts calligrapher and typographer, who, from 1910 to 1930, had designed type for Graf Harry Kessler's *Cranach Presse*, Weimar, and from 1916 to 1929 was responsible for the alphabet of block letters for London Transport designs and posters, initially commissioned (1913) by Frank Pick.[117]

Johnston, in turn, had been strongly influenced by the works of W.H. Cowlishaw, Walter Crane, Selwyn Image, W.R. Lethaby, Morris, Edward F. Strange, Voysey, and other figures of the Arts-and-Crafts Movement. Johnston gave important lectures in Dresden (1912) and Leipzig (1914), and his considerable influence on German typographical design certainly informed aspects of typography produced later by the *Bauhäusler*. Johnston was a leading member of the Guild of St Joseph and St Dominic; was president of the Arts and Crafts Society (1933–6); and he taught many well-known artists, including Eric Gill and Irene Wellington,[118] through whom his (and therefore the Arts-and-Crafts) influence continued some half a century beyond the time Pevsner claimed that Movement had run out of steam. Indeed, through people like Wellington, aspects of Arts and Crafts continued well into the 1950s.

The fact that the Arts-and-Crafts Movement was based on the ideal of making things in small workshops did not fit conveniently with Pevsner's Grand and Neat (too neat) Narrative of the inevitable onward march of styles and movements. Pevsner's articles on Frank Pick,[119] Gordon Russell,[120] and the Design and Industries Association (DIA)[121] contributed to a history of English Modernism between the wars. In the words of Crawford, Russell was 'drenched in'[122] Arts-and-Crafts values, and Johnston was too, so arguably both men kept the flame alight long after Pevsner said it had gone out. The DIA rejected those values to a certain extent, but it also encouraged continuation of aspects of the Movement, despite the prominence given to figures such as Maxwell Fry. Crawford's 'ghostly witness' for the workshops was Ashbee, who spoke of the 'ordinary people, too small for the sweep of'[123] Pevsner's art history.

Then Crawford conjured up Ernest Gimson,[124] who had laid the foundations for his own creative work by measuring and drawing old buildings and artefacts, once the way in which budding designers got to know how things were put together using real materials. Pevsner recognized that Gimson 'was more responsive to English tradition, and did not despise the forms invented in the past':[125] thus he was labelled an 'unrevolutionary spirit'.[126] Where Pevsner used the term 'Historicism', Arts-and-Crafts protagonists referred affectionately to 'Old Work', which they often perceived as a catalyst or inspiration for design, yet the Modernist in Pevsner, seeking what he mistakenly thought was 'originality', refused to see it that way.

Crawford ended his essay by stating something that is undoubtedly true: the 'spirit of the Arts and Crafts was very different from the spirit of the Modern Movement'.[127] It is known that Morris had a mercurial temperament, and was given to outbursts of rage (aspects that repelled the fastidious Voysey): Crawford called Morris again, as his last ghostly witness, to say that if he had lived to read *Pioneers* he 'should have had a fit to end all fits', and that he might have killed himself, seeing that Pevsner's 'words destroyed much of what made life worth living..., the beauty of the earth, the inspiration of past times, the sense that a man can stand up and create for himself, and so go on from day to day with dignity'.[128] The wraith of Morris ended by ruefully remarking that if it is true, as Pevsner insisted, that a path leads from Morris to Gropius, 'something precious has got lost along the way.'[129] This reaction is similar to that of Berlage (1928), who accused doctrinaire Modernists of demolishing everything he had tried to achieve.[130]

In short, the connections and links constructed by Pevsner were, quite simply, based on wishful thinking; no more than political agenda, they had hardly a tenuous relationship to facts, reality, or truth. They were called up as propaganda, to serve a cause. That is not history.

Baillie Scott

Blackwell, Bowness-on-Windermere, Westmorland (1898–1900—by Baillie Scott), was featured prominently in *Das englische Haus*:[131] it is an asymmetrical composition, stylistically based on the vernacular architecture of the English Lake District, yet with some curiously unsettling Tudoresque details and Voyseyesque fireplaces. Pevsner saw Baillie Scott as 'maybe...more revolutionary than Voysey', and mentions him in relation to the designs he prepared for Ernst Ludwig, Grand Duke of Hesse, at Darmstadt,[132] in his *Sources of Modern Architecture and Design*.[133] Baillie Scott's three-dimensional treatment of interior volumes is perhaps the most interesting feature of Blackwell. Even so, commentators like James David Kornwolf claimed (in his *Baillie*

Scott and the Arts and Crafts Movement, subtitled [presumably with a nod to Pevsnerian orthodoxy] *Pioneers of Modern Design*)[134] that the gallery room breaking into the 'mono-spatial'[135] two-storey hall at Blackwell (**Plate 2.11**) 'found further expression...later in'[136] the *Atelier* (1923–4) for Amédée Ozenfant in Paris,[137] designed by Le Corbusier and A.-A.-P. Jeanneret.[138] The hall at Blackwell is not outstandingly original anyway,[139] because clearly it was influenced by the great Ernest George[140] and Norman Shaw.[141] However, the suggestion that factory-windows and a glazed ceiling (**Figure 2.2**) above which were saw-toothed industrial skylights[142] had any resemblances whatsoever to Baillie Scott's complex spaces and uses of finely crafted traditional materials at Blackwell is twisting truth, and creating a connection where in fact there is none. Gradidge understandably dismissed Kornwolf's notion with a contemptuous 'save the mark'.[143]

Although Pevsner considered that Baillie Scott's work was 'maybe...more revolutionary' than Voysey's, the man himself rejected such stuff. Scott and his co-author, Arthur Edgar Beresford, with whom he was in partnership from 1905, wrote that it

Plate 2.11. The hall at Blackwell, Bowness-on-Windermere, by Baillie Scott (1898–1900), a design firmly embedded in the Arts-and-Crafts Movement, also drawing on English timber-framing details, which some wished Scott had had the courage to abandon so that the interior could be said to lead to the Corbusier-Jeanneret *Atelier* depicted in **Figure 2.2**

Figure 2.2. Interior of *Atelier* (1923–4) for Amédée Ozenfant in Paris by Le Corbusier and A.-A.-P. Jeanneret, absurdly claimed by some to have a 'substantial affinity' to Baillie Scott's hall at Blackwell because of the way in which the tiny study (*top left*) projects into the room (*see* **Plate 2.11**)

is fashionable nowadays to disparage the value of tradition in building design. Why, we are asked, should we not strike out in an entirely new direction; break new ground, develop a really modern style? When, on rare occasions, the daily Press ventures to publish anything about house-building (a subject, incidentally, of far greater importance to its readers than many which are commented upon every day) the note is invariably one of criticism of the stupidity of architects and builders who continue to use the old methods and obsolete styles; whilst the only commendation is reserved for the novel and iconoclastic efforts of certain Continental modernists and their imitators.[144]

They warned that 'a mere breaking-up of old laws, unless we have better ones to take their place, means not progress, but disorder and futility...no new style in building has ever been able to disregard its precedents'.[145]

Unfortunately, that is exactly what has occurred, thanks to Modernist insistence: Scott and Beresford noted that 'whenever the modernist in architecture appears to stumble across an old principle, in horror he at once proceeds to demolish it'.[146] Instead of starting 'with a clean slate', they felt, it would have been 'wiser...to leave on it for our guidance those old sums which have worked out all right'.[147] They emphasized the value of

precedent, deploring the 'harsh and inflexible utilitarianism' of the Modern
Movement, and the transformation of the home into a 'workshop, an effi-
cient, scientifically equipped laboratory, a dustproof, up-to-date machine'.[148]

Scott and Beresford, drawing partly on the opinions of St John Greer
Ervine, perceived the conceit and folly of imagining that only those things
which have occurred in our own time are of interest or value. Those who
claim that the work of humankind throughout the ages is of no importance
to us today are guilty of fatuous vanity. Few of us, they wrote,

> have souls so dead that we shall not ask for something beyond mere utility
> in our houses. In the old days the hopes of humanity were centred on some
> ultimate home for the human soul, and old houses and cottages in rural
> England seem to represent an attempt to realise the earthly equivalent of that
> ultimate ideal. Compared with these dwellings, so friendly and inviting, so
> absolutely in harmony with trees and fields and flowers, the mechanical pro-
> ductions of the modernist designer, with their repellent and startling incon-
> gruities, are not only practically absurd but destructive of all that natural
> beauty of the world... which the old builders knew so well how to emphasise
> and adorn: that beauty which so many modern building developments dese-
> crate and destroy. We cannot but deplore the spirit of base materialism which
> is content to accept the theory that the modern house should be merely a
> 'machine to live in'. It should rather be considered as a temple of the house-
> hold gods—a place which ministers not merely to our physical comfort but
> also satisfies our hearts' desire, not by mere superficial aestheticism but in the
> very essence of its being.[149]

Their reference to the 'household gods' is revealing, as is the concept of a
dwelling as a 'temple': this sort of religious reference is completely absent in
the standard texts of the Modern Movement. They denounced the 'mechanical conjunction of glass, steel and concrete':[150] instead of that 'uninspiring
and rather tiresome slogan, "Fitness for Purpose" which any pigsty can fulfil',
and instead of 'turning his back on the splendid work of his fathers', the
modern architect should 'find his inspiration in the buildings which have
given us the precious heritage of rural England', rather than 'go to Sweden'.[151]
So Scott and Beresford were specifically criticizing 'Le Corbusier' and his
facile sloganeering, as well as those who sought salvation in contemporary
foreign architectural exemplars.

They also managed a dig or two at 'critics... who write with such authority
about building... and are... but blind leaders of the blind'.[152] 'The greater
number of modernist designers seem to be concerned merely with material
ends and do not consider the claims of beauty at all'.[153] In the 1970s, the

scholar-architect Stephen Ernest Dykes Bower, who believed passionately in the continuity of historical memory, in using natural materials, in encouraging fine craftsmanship, and who was in the front rank of ecclesiastical architect/decorators, lamented the fact that the word 'beauty' had been abolished by Modernists, who had also succeeded in eliminating all traces of anything beautiful in their inhumane and doctrinaire productions.[154] Scott and Beresford warned that so much Modernist work, instead of improving with age, would merely become dingy and dilapidated, out-of-date and discredited, and give way to later fashions.[155]

In 1954 Reyner Banham proclaimed that 'façade treatments do not form part of the common theory of the Modern Movement...the problem of the façade does not exist; form follows function, and when the problems of the interior have been correctly resolved, the exterior form will be found to have crystallized into an unarguable solution'.[156] Summerson declared that the chief contribution of Modern architecture was 'social', and that the source of its unified approach lay in the architect's 'programme', which he defined as the 'description of spatial dimensions, spatial relationships and other physical conditions required for the convenient performance of specific functions...and the resultant unity...is the unity of a process'.[157] Any possibility that a work of architecture might have any emotional or aesthetic impact was ignored: the Movement insisted all that was required was 'designing' a building from the inside out. These factors go a long way to explaining why the Modern Movement failed to present anything like an agreeable face to the world, let alone to the street.[158]

Historically, architecture involved choice, a certain freedom of action, conscious attempts to establish hierarchies of values, and design concerned with metaphors through which those sets of values were made overt and expressed. It was not 'all about structure', as doctrinaire Modernists would hold, and it was not about the sort of minimal effort that produced far too many badly functioning, seedy, leaking, industrialized, ugly buildings in response to loudly trumpeted manifestos and slogans. The Modern Movement's pseudo-moralizing fixations on supposed 'function', industrialized methods of construction, rejection of everything in favour of the 'clean slate', and scary proclamations concerning 'total architecture'[159] have produced painfully obvious failures in the context of the urban environment.[160]

Le Corbusier wrote of a time when the cathedrals were 'white': that, too, was incorrect. They never were white, and indeed were often coloured, even garishly so. Lubetkin noted that for too long modern architectural solutions were regarded in terms of abstract principles with formal expression left to itself as a functional resultant. The principles of composition, the emotional impact of the visual, were brushed aside as irrelevant. Yet this is the very material with which the architect operates; it is in this sphere that he is sole master, by virtue of his training and tradition... Turning utility, practicality, and functional economy of resources into the sole criterion of quality is the best way to divest architecture of that living richness and complexity that have throughout history given it significance and purpose.[161]

However, Lubetkin's incorporation of *caryatides* at Highpoint II success-fully enraged the stupid,[162] made him suspect as a Modernist and, worse, a 'formalist', a favourite term of abuse used under the Soviet system to denounce anyone who strayed from the approved Party Line (**Plate 2.12**). Lubetkin was found guilty of 'divergence' from and 'betrayal' of 'the cause', and, horror of horrors, of using 'ideas as a motive force in design'.[163] Anthony Cox, the critic of Highpoint II, later stated the position of English Modernists who were not interested in architecture as 'a cultural object for the indi-vidual, nor as a status symbol for the official or commercial organization. The notion of the monument' in architecture 'was anathema', and so was the so-called 'prima donna' architect.[164] It should be remembered, however, that one of the main driving forces of the Modern Movement in architecture

Plate 2.12. Highpoint II, Highgate North, London (1938), by Lubetkin and Tecton, showing (*left*) the *caryatides* supporting the porch roof, an example of Surrealism in which the familiar is made unusual in the surprise setting, and the figures are shorn of their original meaning. Their incorporation in the design was denounced by doc-trinaire Modernists. On the right is part of Highpoint I (1933–5), by the same archi-tects, fancifully likened by Le Corbusier to a 'vertical garden city'. Note the *pilotis*

and planning was a huge commercial corporation called General Motors, and that Movement would never have succeeded globally without the financial backing of American industries[165] and other organizations.[166] H.S. Goodhart-Rendel deplored International Modernism's insistence on spurious 'moral' values, its rejection of aesthetic value-systems, its puritanical, prim-lipped, negative attitudes, and its claims to use architecture as an instrument of moral good. He saw these claims as futile and ridiculous. To Goodhart-Rendel, Le Corbusier had been born old-fashioned, and held the 'worst Victorian ethical view' of architecture.[167]

Houses and Gardens contains ample evidence that Scott and Beresford detested the kind of thing Pevsner *et al.* claimed to admire and worked unceasingly to promote. They wrote that 'there is no reasonable excuse for continuous' horizontal ribbons of fenestration 'which destroy the apparent stability of a building', and asked 'to be spared those windows which are vertically linked together', ignoring the expression of the floor lines. Pevsner, however, saw nothing amiss with either motif, and stated that the Modern Movement was a style 'of the twentieth century completely independent of the past', which 'originated during the last years of Queen Victoria's reign, mainly in Britain',[168] harking back to his attempt to link the achievements of British architects such as Voysey *et al.* to the International Modern Movement. Yet Pevsner traced the origins of fenestration in vertical strips where 'no horizontal appears'[169] to Alfred Messel's Wertheim Department Store, *Leipziger Straße/Platz*, Berlin (1897–1904) (*see* **Plate 4.7**). Scott and Beresford, however, had no truck with that: to them, the Modern Movement was a 'ruthless perversion',[170] which, perhaps, is not far off the mark.[171]

The sumptuous 1933 version of *Houses and Gardens* differs enormously from the 1906 edition,[172] and the tone of the text is almost bitter in its refutations of the tenets and affectations of Modernism which Scott and Beresford perceived as an aberration, a fracturing, a total break with millennia of evolution, with no discernible ancestry, despite the efforts by Pevsner *et al.* to give it a respectable pedigree. The book absolutely denies legitimacy to the Modernism Pevsner and others were strenuously promoting, so any claims that Baillie Scott was a 'revolutionary'[173] are refuted by what Scott himself wrote, and by examination of his designs. Scott was a gifted architect, unlike Pevsner, who, like Ruskin, did not think architecturally.

Baillie Scott's texts extol nature and the necessity of not only respecting it but letting buildings respond to, rather than damage it. Nature, to him, was a 'creation essentially divine, a world decorated with miracles of design in trees and flowers'.[174] Scott and Beresford stated firmly that the 'modern architect...[should]...add his contribution to this natural beauty of the world with buildings which are in harmony with it',[175] yet 'in whatever direction one looks, modern building, almost without exception, is destructive of the natural beauty of the world'.[176] Those responsible for development have succeeded in the destruction of local character, and it does not seem to have occurred to their apologists that by allowing, permitting, acquiescing in, and carrying out such enormities 'they are accessories in a crime which has deliberately destroyed the beauty of that bit of England which is their heritage'.[177]

It should be stated very firmly that the opinions quoted above, and those set out in Baillie Scott's 1906 volume,[178] are most definitely not those of a 'pioneer' of the Modern Movement: there can be no doubt whatsoever that Baillie Scott detested the Modern Movement and everything it stood for. He saw it as a massive error, as an agent of destruction and ugliness, and as a phenomenon based on falsehoods and folly. Scott and Beresford mentioned the work of Voysey as 'remarkable for its ascetic restraint and its essentially practical qualities of fitness and simplicity', and its 'expression of human "thought and feeling"...beyond utilitarian values,...[an]...expression of emotion or sentiment, some soul in the composition which cannot be assessed' in monetary terms 'or in definitely practical values'.[179]

Voysey has been named over and over again as a 'pioneer' which he himself indignantly refuted, and claims that he was do not survive close examination. Evidence that others were supposed 'pioneers' does not stand up either: careful sifting through it is enough to convince that those *dramatis personae* were nothing of the sort, and indeed those who were still alive objected strongly when they were thus labelled. Those who had died could not defend themselves, but it can be argued that they suffered posthumously from a grave injustice.

The Religious Factor

Now there is something in Scott's, Beresford's, and Voysey's writings and views that is completely absent from the works of those who promoted, created, and finally *imposed* the Modern Movement on us all: it is a reference to the 'soul' and to the Deity. Indeed, Scott and Beresford quoted[180] from *My New-cut Ashlar* by Rudyard Kipling:

> Who, lest all thought of Eden fade,
> Bring'st Eden to the craftsman's brain,
> Godlike to muse o'er his own Trade
> And Manlike stand with God again.[181]

They wrote that nothing filled them 'with a greater despair than the cold and calculating intellectualism of much architectural criticism of to-day: the art of building, if it is to be revived, needs warm-hearted human enthusiasm far more than…detached and inhuman methods…'[182]

Voysey, too, condemned materialism, and his insistence on the importance of 'ideas in things' and of 'thought and feeling' as fundamentals in all forms of creative activity was repeated constantly: he held that works of art were to be valued according to their 'spiritual qualities',[183] that nature was an expression of God's work, and that 'through thought and feeling man was in direct communication with God'.[184] In fact, Voysey's religious faith was 'fundamental to his life and work',[185] and he firmly believed in a 'beneficent and omnipotent controlling power'.[186] Voysey objected to William Morris's scepticism in matters of religious belief, was repelled by his ebullient, larger-than-life, over-emphatic personality, and shrank from his enthusiastic advocacy of 'reconstructive' Socialism. Morris, of course, was another figure Pevsner[187] claimed as a proto-Modernist, but he was, in fact, despite the lip-service paid to him by Gropius and countless others, a conservative designer steeped in the crafts and architecture of the Middle Ages, who had a profound influence on the Arts-and-Crafts Movement, and was anything but a 'pioneer' of mechanized Modernism:[188] indeed, he abhorred everything the Modern Movement was to admire and promote.

Morris's hatred of large windows that let far too much light into a room,[189] his loathing of machinery, industrial processes, and the covering over of England with 'hideous hovels'[190] suggest he would not have found greatly to his taste the environment created in the twentieth and twenty-first centuries by disciples of the apostles of the Modern Movement. Morris's first principle of design was that there was only one style on which it was possible to found a true living art, and that was Gothic architecture,[191] which is definitely not a position any devotee of the Modern Movement would dream of taking. What seems clear about Morris is that he perceived Gothic as providing the foundations for design: he wrote that he saw 'nothing for it but that the form, as well as the spirit, must be Gothic',[192] and that the principles of Gothic 'belonged to the aesthetics of all art in all countries'.[193]

Those remarks could not possibly be made by any proto-Modernist, and commentators who have tied themselves in knots to claim Morris was a 'pioneer' of Modernity have simply twisted the facts to fit their fanciful and destructive propaganda. Voysey's connections with Gothic, however, were virtually non-existent, although he was obviously influenced by certain aspects of mediaeval and vernacular domestic architecture.[194]

Osbert Lancaster, keenly observant as ever, wryly noted that 'if...left-wing housing experts' had their way, the dwelling of the agricultural labourer would have wide expanses of glazing 'admitting buckets of light and air', even though the inhabitant, who usually 'had his fill of both commodities during his day's work, might perhaps prefer the shuttered gloom which he is still in a few cases allowed to inhabit'. Permitted sparse decorations would include a 'clever little camera study' of Magnitogorsk (much lauded by left-ist writers, especially Korn)[195] and 'bracing slogans' such as 'religion is the opium of the people' in a 'functional type, for ideological reasons devoid of capitals'.[196]

The French Benedictine monk/architect Dom Paul Bellot also believed that the modern architect should emulate (not imitate) the lessons of the Middle Ages, and like Pugin,[197] held that religious belief was of fundamental importance to successful architectural design. Bellot roundly denounced Le Corbusier as an *'architecte bolchéviste militant'*,[198] even though the evidence points to the Franco-Swiss architect as having more pronounced sympathies for groups associated with Fascism, vicious anti-Semitism, and, of course, totalitarianism.[199] Bellot's target was, naturally, an atheist.

In view of the perhaps unpalatable fact that religion, in an extreme form, has not gone away, but has become a menacing and destructive force, it is odd that the worries of men like Bellot, Baillie Scott, and Voysey concerning lack of belief and its effects on architecture have been glossed over. Bellot's masterpiece, Quarr Abbey, Isle of Wight (1907–14), astonished even Pevsner (who declared Bellot 'one of the pioneers of C20 Expressionism'). However, Pevsner saw in Bellot's work aspects that were 'curiously reminiscent'[200] of the creations of Antoni Gaudí i Cornet, a deeply religious Catalan architect and candidate for beatification, whose *Santa Colonna de Cervelló*, near Barcelona (from 1898), Pevsner described as 'horrible', and whose stylistic inventions the same Pevsner proscribed, revealingly, as 'intransigent'.[201] Besides, anyone who did not conform to the rigidities of International Modernism was dismissed as an 'anti-Rationalist'.[202]

Unfortunate Treatment of Berlage, Comper, & Dykes Bower

One of the many British architects ignored or damned by Pevsner was John Ninian Comper, a great designer who, like Dykes Bower, was not afraid of the word 'beauty'.[203] In the quest for it he acquired an unrivalled knowledge of ecclesiastical art and architecture as he searched for spiritual values for his own time. His deep understanding of the Christian tradition was accretive: he favoured 'unity by inclusion' and drew on many precedents to create a vital English style.[204] The finest exemplar of his work is St Mary's Church, Wellingborough, Northamptonshire (1904–31). Betjeman considered that Comper did for ecclesiastical design what Baillie Scott and Voysey had done for domestic architecture. Like those two great architects, Comper loathed Modernism and all its pretensions, and said of St Mary's that 'only to its contemporaries does it owe nothing'.[205]

Comper's stance (and perhaps his devoutness?) attracted Pevsner's hostility:

> Comper's principal antagonist in the second half of the twentieth century was Sir Nikolaus Pevsner who rarely missed an opportunity to dismiss or overlook his work in *The Buildings of England*.[206] It was Pevsner's moralistic condemnation of historicism, of modern architecture conceived in the Classical and Gothic language of architecture, that won the day in his relentless campaign to establish the ideology of the International Modern Style, with its machine and functionalist aesthetic, as the architectural style of all time. He desired a clean break with the past. To do otherwise resulted in architecture that was not only bad, he believed, but also immoral in that it attempted to resist social progress. He achieved lasting damage to Comper's reputation by persuading his readers that his work was artistically and architecturally valueless. The only building that made him melt was St Mary's, Wellingborough... When asked why, he replied: because the dates are right.[207]

The whole question of critical Modernist hostility to those Christian religious beliefs needs forensic examination. It does seem peculiar (or perhaps it explains much), that totalitarian anti-Semites with Fascist and National-Socialist sympathies should be lauded in Modernist writings, while scholars and gifted designers who were also Christians should be dismissed, ignored, or falsely categorized as 'pioneers' of the Modern Movement.

Pevsner's 'pioneers' were not confined to Britain, of course. He named the Dutchman, Hendrik Petrus Berlage, citing his *Koopmansbeurs* in Amsterdam (1897–1903) as 'parallel to the moderate and judicious contemporary innovations of a man like Voysey in domestic architecture'.[208] He suggested Berlage's work was a 'source'[209] for Dutch Modernism. But Berlage, like his British contemporaries, was no revolutionary, no slogan-shouting advocate of the destruction of all extant architectural fabric: he drew on the native Netherlandish traditions of finely-crafted brickwork, and on much else besides. A close study of Berlage's Merchants' or Commodities' Exchange demonstrates that the building is firmly grounded in a sophisticated under- standing of arcuated brick-and-masonry load-bearing construction in which stone abutments, caps, corbels, and quoins are employed in logical, traditional ways. As with numerous nineteenth-century buildings, the metal roof- structure over the central space is beautifully related to the load-bearing walls from which the trusses spring. Berlage, in short, was a genuinely creative designer who did not discard the past, but drew inspiration from fine exemplars of architecture in his innovative designs. The *Koopmansbeurs* is a carefully crafted late-nineteenth-century building with echoes of several historical styles, though freed from self-conscious allusions to Gothic, Romanesque, or anything other than sound, traditional construction. And it is clear that Berlage obtained certain ideas from the prolix but obfuscatory writings of Gottfried Semper, from which, on occasion, he liberally quoted.[210]

An obvious influence on Berlage was the *Entretiens* (Discourses) of Eugène-Emmanuel Viollet-le-Duc.[211] The Dutchman also believed that cultural improvements could only be achieved through the production of well-designed, finely-made objects, including buildings: in this he shared the views of Muthesius. It should also be emphasized that Berlage believed in the *cultural* importance of the city, and deplored the *suburbanizing* tenden- cies of English enthusiasts for Garden Suburbs and Garden Cities,[212] perhaps one of the more unfortunate by-products of the Domestic Revival and the Arts-and-Crafts Movement.

Berlage was also profoundly aware of the decline of spiritual and com- munal interests as personal greed and materialism gained ever more ground at their expense. Like others of his time, he looked back to the mediaeval European city as an ideal, and frequently quoted Brugge (Bruges) as its epitome. He deplored the lack of respect for beautiful buildings of the past, and towards the end of his life he was truly horrified by the iconoclastic tone of *avant-garde* Modernists of the 1920s who 'demanded' a 'specifically new understanding of the building task', and refused 'to adopt for their works the design principles of earlier epochs'.[213] At the end of the first meeting (1928) of the malign CIAM (*see* Select Glossary), which was to do so much damage to countless towns and cities in the course of the twentieth century, Berlage made his revulsion and opposition clear.

The meeting, called at the request of a rich patron, Madame Hélène de Mandrot, was organized by Sigfried Giedion (Secretary-General of CIAM until 1956. His pernicious writings[214] were major contributions to the 'Grand Narrative' of Modernism). It took place, incongruously, in the mediaeval castle owned by Madame de Mandrot at La Sarraz, Canton Vaud, situated halfway between Morges on Lac Léman (*or* Lac de Genève) and Yverdon on Lac de Neuchâtel in La Suisse Romande. The meeting established the Modern Movement as an organized body, and dictated its trajectory for many years thereafter. It drew up a draconian manifesto and statutes, and set up an executive organ called *Comité International pour la Résolution des Problèmes de l'Architecture Contemporaine* (CIRPAC), charged with organizing congresses and exhibitions, publicizing the programme, proselytizing, and recruiting new members. The list of signatories to CIAM's aims included Le Corbusier, A.É.L. Lurçat, Hannes Meyer, and G.T. Rietveld.

Although Berlage's name appears on the list, he disapproved of the flavour of the congress, did not take part in events, sat outside, and spent his time drawing the *château*. When asked to join the party for a group-photograph at the end of the conference, he refused, and told Rietveld that he and the other zealots and *apparatchiks* were destroying everything he had tried to create.[215] CIAM was to insist on frame-construction, multi-level high-rise cities, propaganda to popularize the 'already established style of the Modern Movement', 'dialectical manipulation' of categories, replacement of existing buildings and cities with new 'categorically formulated elements', and the production of agreed prototypical buildings and master-plans for 'urban programmes' that would be universally imposed, irrespective of location. What was proposed was nothing less than architectural and town-planning dictatorship. It is little wonder a great architect of Berlage's stature would dissent from such a simplistic, destructive series of objectives.

Voysey obviously felt similar disappointment and disgust at being claimed as a 'pioneer' of something he loathed,[216] and architects, like Comper and Dykes Bower, who were steeped in Western civilization and revered beauty, had to repudiate International Modernism because its ideology was based on a complete break with the past. It was also governed by the supposed social and 'scientific' principles embedded in a collectivist view of society from which religion was to be eliminated, and so was closely associated with atheistic principles.

In the world valued by Comper, Dykes Bower,[217] and the few who had the courage to resist the Modern Movement, language, dignity, mystery, the 'historically sanctified symbols of a transcendent reality',[218] and the striving after the *primacy of beauty* were principles which governed their creative lives. But beauty has largely been repudiated in following the mantra of 'building for our own time', which, like *aggiornamento* (bringing in up-to-date religious liturgies), actually meant the expulsion of all concepts of beauty. In churches, enormous damage took place under the banner of supposed 'reform' following the Second Vatican Council (1962–5): this was likened, with staggering inappropriateness, to 'slum-clearance' by Cardinal (from 1965) J.C. Heenan, Archbishop of Westminster from 1963, in a Pastoral Letter of 1965,[219] with ecclesiastical results as devastating as the widespread destruction at secular levels.

Dykes Bower suffered at the hands of critics such as Pevsner: his church of the Good Shepherd, Mansel Road, Arbury, Cambridge, was unpleasantly and unjustifiably denounced as 'reactionary to a degree almost unbelievable in 1957–8'[220] and as an 'embarrassment':[221] in fact it is a beautifully crafted building of banded brick, and has worn very well compared with many of the buildings Pevsner praised, numerous examples of which have had to be demolished. Dykes Bower (who was very musical, and indeed could perform competently on the keyboard) always insisted on the *imperative* of beauty, as well as the value of continuity, craftsmanship, respect for materials, and style instead of the frantic search for originality and narcissistic self-expression. For him, like Comper and others, architecture ought to speak of eternity, not of the present which so quickly becomes the past. Viciously attacked in his lifetime, and badly hurt by such ungracious treatment,[222] he nevertheless achieved much that was fine and wonderful, believing not only in beauty, but in the necessity of keeping alive the language, syntax, and grammar of a real and enduring architecture.[223]

III

Modernism in Germany in the Aftermath of the 1914–18 War

Introduction: Expressionist Interlude; The Bauhaus *at Weimar; The* Bauhaus *at Dessau;*
A Department of Architecture at Dessau; Epilogue

> *Heute lebt der Künstler in einer dogmalosen Zeit der Auflösung. Er steht geistig*
> *allein da. Die alten Formen sind zerbrochen, die erstarrte Welt ist aufgelockert, der*
> *alte Menschengeist ist umgestoßen und mitten im Umguß zu neuer Gestalt. Wir*
> *schweben im Raum und kennen noch nicht die neue Ordnung* (Today the artist
> lives in a dogma-free time of dissolution. He stands spiritually alone. The
> old forms are shattered, the benumbed world becomes more flexible, the
> old human spirit is no longer valid and is in the midst of being recast. We
> are suspended in space and cannot yet know the new order).
>
> > GEORG WALTER ADOLF GROPIUS (1883–1969) in ARBEITSRAT FÜR KUNST (1919):
> > *Ja! Stimmen des Arbeitsrates für Kunst in Berlin* (Berlin: *bei der*
> > *Photographischen Gesellschaft in Charlottenburg*) §32

> Modern FOOLS...
> Renouncing all the *Rules* the ROMANS had,
> Are past reclaiming, obstinately mad.[1]
> ...modern Youth are taught to *sing* and *dance*,
> And learn the FOLLIES, and the *Modes* of *France*;
> Neglecting *Method*, *Order*, *Time*, or *Sense*,
> With all their JARGON, and their *Modes* dispense.
> ...Will they, or *not*, all Rules, all Modes deface.
> Invert all ORDER, and the Art *disgrace*?[2]
>
> > ROBERT MORRIS (1703–54): *The Art of Architecture, a Poem. In Imitation of*
> > *HORACE's Art of Poetry* (London: R. Dodsley 1742).

Introduction: Expressionist Interlude

The collapse of four great Empires, the Russian in 1917, the Austro-Hungarian and German in 1918, and the Ottoman in 1922,[3] heralded many changes, not least in the world of architecture and design. Much was to be jettisoned, however, thanks to the reductionist simplicities of Modernism in architecture, not least any consideration of beauty. But there was another glaring omission in the puritanical, humourless, desiccated programmes that eventually brought into being a monstrous, inhumane Dystopia, and that was eroticism. Like Aphrodite/Venus, Eros was expunged from the Modern Movement's new world: squalor and violent pornography replaced them.

Before the war, architects associated with Expressionism sought 'new' architectural idioms to encapsulate the German concept of the *Geist*, which included intellect, soul, and imagination, the opposite of the materialism of the contemporary world, and might be described as a search for a kind of spiritual Utopia. At the 1914 Cologne *Werkbund* Exhibition, supposedly 'organic' forms as in the theatre designed by van de Velde, and crystalline structures such as Taut's Glass pavilion were supposed to be attempts to invoke emotional and spiritual resonances, but the aphorisms on Taut's pavilion were really more to do with promoting the German glass industries. Scheerbart even argued for the removal of enclosure from inhabitable rooms, and the adoption of an architecture of glass which would create a 'new milieu', a 'new culture', until 'a paradise on earth' was allegedly attainable.[4]

Some quasi-religious and mystical beliefs were carried through into much later architecture, not inevitably with paradisean results. Revulsion against the whole system that had brought ruin on Germany led in some quarters to a yearning for a closer connection with the soil, with nature, and with handicrafts. Several groupings were formed. Behne and Taut founded *Arbeitsrat für Kunst* (work council for art) in the immediate aftermath of the armistice in 1918, and were joined by the architects Otto Bartning, Gropius, Paul Mebes, Erich Mendelsohn, Hans Poelzig, Paul Schmitthenner, and Max Taut, and numerous painters, sculptors, and patrons (including the aristocratic Mechtilde von Lichnowsky),[5] with the aim of fusing all the arts under the wing of architecture (the *Bauprojekt*) and unifying art and the people. This was a cherished and widespread belief of many hopeful idealists at the time, but one that has not been noticeably fruitful. The overtly 'left-wing' *Novembergruppe* was a union of radical creative artists representing largely pre-war Expressionism, again established in, and named after, the month in which the armistice ending hostilities with Germany came into force. It optimistically hoped to influence and demand participation in all activities of importance to the arts, especially in architecture as a public art, in order to 'change society'.

The Expressionist *Gläserne Kette* (glass chain) was founded by Bruno Taut (1919) to keep radical design-ideals alive during a period of economic and political instability. The last grouping included Hermann Finsterlin, Gropius, Hans and Wassili Luckhardt, and Hans Scharoun: it sought to promote forms derived from crystals, shells, and plants, using glass, steel, and concrete.

The Expressionist thread that ran through these movements and associations was really a continuation of the Nietzschean Dionysian, ecstatic element, and produced some extraordinary images, most of which remained on paper. But some projects were realized, including Poelzig's transformation (1919) of the *Zirkus Schumann* in Berlin as the enormous *Großes Schauspielhaus*, a 'great playhouse' 'for the people' under the direction of Max Reinhardt: with its stalactite vaults in the auditorium, it was one of the strangest creations of the period. Poelzig's unrealized designs for a *Festspielhaus* (festival theatre) in Salzburg (1920–2) were equally startling.[6] Erich Mendelsohn's Einstein tower, Potsdam (1919–24), suggests his free sketches of dynamic forms done during the war, and is regarded as a supreme example of Expressionism. Although it *seems* to have been moulded, and *looks* as though it is made of reinforced concrete (as was originally intended), it is in fact mostly of rendered brickwork, and so cannot be regarded as an 'honest' expression of structure. As for its stylistic aspects, the elegant plan owes a great deal to the Rococo heritage of German architecture.[7]

In the immediate aftermath of the 1914–18 war, under the aegis of organizations such as *Arbeitsrat für Kunst*, numerous architectural fantasies were exhibited. Gropius claimed that objects shaped by 'needs and utility' could never fulfil the longing for a new world of beauty (a view very much at variance with his later stances). There were many Utopian designs (including a 'crystal house' [Bruno Taut], a 'marble cathedral' [Max Taut], and other fantasies)[8] accompanied by fanciful claims for their 'spiritual' content. The key to understanding the various strands associated with the architectural mayhem of the time is the rejection of the past, with its associations with a discredited monarchical system that had brought Germany to defeat, humiliation, and penury. It should be remembered that many architects, including Gropius (who had been wounded), had served in the German army, and the psychological after-effects on them of Germany's ruin must have been considerable.

Talk of revolution was in the air, and the new Social-Democratic government did not enjoy universal support: street-fighting led to many deaths, and armed force was used to impose an uneasy order. In January 1919 the leaders of the Communist *Spartacusbund* movement, Karl Liebknecht and Rosa Luxemburg, were brutally killed, an event which seems to have had many repercussions in the artistic world. Miës van der Rohe was later to design a memorial to them, based on a steel frame, and erected (1926) in the *Friedrichsfelde Friedhof* (Frederick's field cemetery), Berlin (destroyed 1933): it had brick projecting and receding planes of brick on which the hammer and sickle were prominently displayed. It did not help its designer when he sought to ingratiate himself with the new Government of Germany after 1933.

Although Expressionist architecture in Germany was relatively short-lived, it was influenced by developments in The Netherlands, where J.M. van der Mey, M. de Klerk, and P.L. Kramer designed the *Scheepvaarthuis*, Amsterdam (1911–16), one of the first Expressionist buildings of the Amsterdam School. De Klerk's *Het Schip* housing complex for the *Eigen Haard* housing-association at *Spaarndammerplantsoen* (1913–20) (**Plate 3.1**), and de Klerk and Kramer's housing for the *De Dageraad* housing-association, Amsterdam South (1920–3), employed beautifully crafted brickwork and tiles with great flair and imagination.

Plate 3.1. Housing-block at the corner of *Zaanstraat* and *Spaarndammerplantsoen*, Amsterdam (1914–18), designed by Michel de Klerk

Behrens's *Ehrenhalle* (hall of honour, or memorial-hall) for the dyeworks of the I.G. Farben Company at Höchst-on-the-Main, west of Frankfurt, eschewed his pre-war simplified Classicism in favour of Expressionist coloured brickwork, used with crystalline skylights, to allude not only to Goethe's theory of colour, but to a gesture of expiation, tragedy, and hope (**Plate 3.2**). The *Ehrenhalle* was partly a war-memorial, and perhaps even a cenotaph, emphasized by the names of the six hundred or so employees of the Company who had died in the war inscribed on the roll of honour in front of which was an heroic bronze statue by Richard Scheibe.

Behrens intended this extraordinary work to be exalted, transcendental, and full of meaning. The huge reparations demanded of Germany under the Treaty of Versailles contributed, not only to national humiliation, but to catastrophic economic problems and social unrest that fostered a simmering resentment with far-reaching consequences. Germany began to experience hyper-inflation, and failure to pay reparations led to the occupation of the

Plate 3.2. *Ehrenhalle* at the dyeworks of the *I.G. Farbenindustrie* A.G., Höchst-am-Main (1920–4), by Peter Behrens

Ruhr by French and Belgian troops, something which did not come to an end until 1925. The *Ehrenhalle*, which was designed and built 1920–4, used Expressionist techniques to make several points not unconnected with defiance and protest as well as with commemoration and, perhaps, self-conscious mediaevalism in its suggestions of Gothic vaulting. The elegiac and commemorative aspects of this building have been missed by most architectural commentators.[9]

Behrens also designed a small polychrome brick pavilion for the *Kunstgewerbeschau* (Arts-and-Crafts exhibition) in Munich (1922). The geometries of its patterns of overlapping chevrons were carried upwards into the gables. Pyramidal corbels supported the main structure of the roof. Called the *Dombauhütte*, with reference to mediaeval masons' lodges associated with the building of cathedrals, the pavilion was intended to exhibit church furnishings (including a sarcophagus by Scheibe, stained glass by Alfred Partikel, a crucifix by Ludwig Gies [which aroused considerable controversy], and a triptych by Adolf Hölzel) in a suitable setting. Behrens saw his design as merely an exploration, perhaps 'in better times' capable of providing inspiration for others.

The *Bauhaus* at Weimar

Gropius had joined Behrens's office in 1908, and described himself as that architect's 'factotum': this is probably explained by his difficulty in using a pencil. All his life his draughtsmanship was less than competent, and he was obliged to redefine himself and his trajectory on several occasions. On leaving Behrens in 1910 he teamed up with Adolf Meyer, who appears to have been mostly responsible for getting designs down on paper. However, even in 1910, while still with Behrens, he presented a memorandum to the head of the *Allgemeine Elektrizitäts-Gesellschaft* (General Electricity Company) setting out his ideas for industrial housing, indicating that his interest in prefabricated processes in architecture was already fully formed.

There were many unpleasant sides to Gropius: he characterized Muthesius, Bruno Paul, and Poelzig as *Architekten-Hochstapler* (impostor-architects),[10] and there were other instances of disagreeable sayings or attitudes.[11] He seems to have joined virtually all the architectural groupings that emerged after the war, and had been a member of the *Deutscher Werkbund* since 1911. He associated himself with van de Velde's affirmation of belief in the significance of the individual creative spirit in contrast to Muthesius's arguments in favour of uniformity in the industrial arts.[12] He subsequently repudiated this association, but his later history suggests he went with the flow until he saw a possibility of controlling it himself.

In 1916 he composed a paper which he submitted to the authorities in Weimar[13] proposing a partnership between artists, industrialists, and technicians: in 1919 he was appointed head of the *Hochschule für Bildende Kunst* (Academy of Fine Art) by the new Republican administration, and received permission to amalgamate it with the *Kunstgewerbeschule* (school of Arts and Crafts). The new institution he named the *Staatliches Bauhaus*, an allusion to the mediaeval masons' lodge, especially the *Dombauhütte*. The German word *Bau* means 'building', 'composition', 'construction', or 'structure', but *bauen*, meaning 'build', 'construct', 'erect', also means 'cultivate', 'raise' (e.g. crops), or 'grow', so Gropius may have intended the name of the establishment to suggest the idea of sowing, nurturing, and harvesting talent.

Envisaging a new guild of craftsmen, without class distinctions between craftsman and artist, he called for the creative conception of the cathedral of the future,[14] encompassing everything in one form, architecture, sculpture, and painting: he stated that things shaped by utility and need cannot still the longing for a world of beauty built completely anew, for the rebirth of that spiritual unity which rose to the miracle of a Gothic cathedral.[15] In Weimar he imagined the building of a new estate with a centre of public buildings, theatres, a concert hall, and a structure used for 'religious' purposes. As a member of the 'leftist' *Arbeitsrat für Kunst*, he spoke of the dangerous worship of might and the machine which had led to a moral and economic abyss, and presumably he agreed with that organization's manifesto (written by Bruno Taut) which optimistically demanded that 'art and the people must form a unity', and declared that the true task of the Socialist State was to exterminate the evil demon of commercialism and to make the active spirit of construction bloom again among the people.

The *Dombauhütte* idea was further emphasized in the *Bauhaus* manifesto which Gropius published:[16] it was illustrated with a woodcut of the *Zukunftskathedrale*, a 'cathedral of the future', a cathedral of Socialism, a suggestion of a Gothic building (albeit with certain crystalline affinities), by the American-born Lyonel Feininger, appointed by Gropius to run the *Bauhaus* printmaking workshop. Curiously, the *Manifest* stated that the decoration of buildings was once the noblest function of the fine arts, and that the fine arts were essential to great architecture: this sounds Ruskinian but was the opposite of what emerged in the 'International Style' very soon after 1919 when all architectural embellishments were damned. Insisting that there was no essential difference between an artist and a craftsman, and that the artist was an 'exalted craftsman', Gropius declared that a foundation of handicraft is essential for every artist. He referred to a single form improbably rising towards the heavens from the hands of a million workers as the crystalline symbol of a new and coming faith.

In 1919, while Gropius was associating crystalline forms with renewal and 'spirituality', so also was Bruno Taut, who, taking his cue, perhaps, from the Socialist theories of Soviet Russia (notably those of Prince Peter Kropotkin), advocated breaking up cities and returning the populations to the land in order to promote agricultural- and handicraft-based rural communities.[17] Taut suggested a circular Utopian model for settlements with a residential core at the heart of which was a crystalline *Haus des Himmels* (house of heaven) for the governors of each area, an inevitably authoritarian notion that perhaps brings the uncomfortable association of *Blut und Boden* (blood and soil) later promoted by the National-*Socialist* German *Workers'* Party.[18] Some of Taut's more Utopian proposals included temples of glass on top of Alpine peaks.[19]

However, contrary to received opinion, and despite all the references to buildings and architecture, the *Bauhaus* had no department of architecture until 1927. 1919 was an unpromising time to try to establish anything in a Germany ruined by war and in a state of political flux, and it was not until 1920 that Weimar became the capital of the State of Thüringen (Thuringia): one of the ministries became responsible for the *Bauhaus*. Gropius abolished the title of 'professor' on the grounds that it was 'academic' and '*élitist*', and insisted that the teachers should be called 'masters' and students 'apprentices' and 'journeymen', emphasizing the supposedly craft-based nature of the institution, with workshops rather than studios at its core.

In the autumn of 1919, on the recommendation of his then wife,[20] Gropius appointed the Swiss painter and textile designer Johannes Itten as Master of Form at the *Bauhaus*: Itten (who had convinced himself that his views on the teaching of art were of world significance)[21] soon gained control of much of the instruction, and introduced a compulsory *Vorkurs* (preliminary course) which students had to pass before they were allowed to proceed to workshop training. He was a devotee of Mazdaznan, one of a great many mystical or quasi-religious cults that flourished in Germany at the time. It was related to the ancient Persian religion of Zoroastrianism, and therefore tentatively associated with Nietzsche's *Zarathustra* (though any connection with the philosopher's ideas was hopelessly corrupted). It held that the world was a warzone between good and evil, and that what is perceived as reality is really only a veil that hides a higher existence that can only be achieved by rigorous physical and mental exercises, a vegetarian diet (featuring huge doses of garlic), fasting, and regular enemas. Mazdaznan macrobiotic dishes became *de rigueur* in the *Bauhaus* canteen, and some students adopted Itten's garb (a loose robe) and shaved their heads.[22]

Some, of course, regarded him as a saintly figure, but many, probably more accurately, saw him as a charlatan. Itten would accept students on his 'intuitive judgement' without even looking at work or asking questions.[23] One of the many problems that emerged from this *régime* in malnourished, bankrupted, demoralized, defeated Germany, was that dishes like the garlic paste insisted upon by Itten caused students to look rather ill, with grey-green skin: furthermore, apart from the enemas, peculiar rituals such as 'purification of the body' involved pricking the skin and anointing it with oils, so that the pin-pricked areas began to suppurate: resultant infections caused illnesses.[24]

Itten's preliminary course was intended to 'liberate' students from their 'preconceptions' so that their 'latent' creative powers could be unleashed, but some critics, not without good reason, have perceived it as nothing less than brainwashing.[25] The *Vorkurs* itself involved studies of the qualities of different materials through paired contrasts: rough textures were compared with smooth; coarseness with that which was fine; and different materials were assembled in three dimensions to produce 'representational' objects. Exercises (usually preceded by physical limbering-up, breathing techniques, and so on)[26] included the making of collages from all sorts of materials, and Itten insisted this was education through play, an idea that had been promoted earlier by Cižek, Froebel, Montessori, and Pestalozzi. The cult Itten had embraced became closely interwoven with his pedagoguery, so much so that he acquired a devoted set of converts, whose shaven heads, prayers, fasting, limited diet, breath reeking of garlic, and monkish garb alienated many other students. It did not inspire much confidence outside the *Bauhaus*: Itten's bizarre behaviour and judgements began to grate, not least among the small businesses and hard-pressed craftsmen of Weimar trying to survive in extremely difficult times.[27]

For example, in the outcome of an exercise in which students were asked to draw 'war', the work of an army-veteran who had seen active service and who had been wounded was denounced as 'romantic' (a word often employed by Modernists as a term of abuse), whereas the efforts of those who had not served in the armed forces at all were praised for their expressions of personal experience.[28] Worse, not much work was produced in the workshops because of the dominance of Itten's *Vorkurs* (which seems to have been largely a talking-shop).

There were distinct rumblings outside the institution. Max Thedy, who had been acting director of the former academy of Fine Art, wrote to Gropius pointing out he was creating an artistic proletariat, and that after their supposed 'training' at the *Bauhaus* the young people would be incompetent in every way.[29] In 1920 a school of painting, established by Thedy and other artists who had taught at the former academy, split from the *Bauhaus*, and twenty-eight students left to join what became the State School of Fine Art. Thedy is described by some as 'conservative' and 'proficient in figure-painting';[30] but others have higher opinions of his *oeuvre*, finding it sensitive, beautifully observed, with a fine sense of colour and composition, and competently drawn, which is more than one could say about many of the products of the *Vorkurs*. Oskar Schlemmer, who taught at the *Bauhaus*, said of the years 1919 to 1923 that they reflected a period when a nation disintegrated.[31]

The former Grand Duchy (a *Freistaat* [Free State] in the new Republic), in the capital[32] of which the *Bauhaus* had been established, was economically and industrially underdeveloped, apart from the glass and optical works established by Otto Schott, Ernst Abbe, and Carl Zeiss in Jena: Zeiss's firm, which built up a world-renowned factory producing precision microscopes, was also to design and make ranges of celebrated cameras and binoculars. Most of the other industries were carried out by skilled craftsmen/tradesmen, who were quite numerous compared with other regions of the former German Empire, and many feared competition from mass-production in fully mechanized factories. Germany was not over-endowed with raw materials (though it did have plenty of timber), and was therefore dependent on its dedicated skilled craftsmen, labour forces, and industrial capacity to produce and market artefacts of high quality. There was therefore a considerable need to educate designers capable of inventing well-conceived objects that could be manufactured and exported by German entrepreneurs and industrialists.

Gropius, in the beginning, claimed to believe that a kind of Ruskinian/Morris-inspired Arts-and-Crafts ethos[33] would destroy the spectre of wicked

commercialization and revive a popular 'spirit of construction',[34] a stance
which bewildered Pevsner and Banham, both of whom appeared to have
had some sort of *idée fixe* concerning where Gropius actually stood (he did
not really stand anywhere, but adapted to circumstances). However, such
an ethos would have run contrary to what Germany needed; and anyway,
if Gropius had really believed in it, some of his appointments to the staff of
the *Bauhaus* would seem to have been inconsistent (to be charitable). His
avowed aim to keep the institution 'apolitical' was contradicted by the spiky
concrete 'Monument to the Victorious Proletariat'[35] erected to his design in
the main cemetery in Weimar to commemorate a group of strikers shot
dead in 1920 during the attempted Kapp-Lüttwitz *Putsch* (armed uprising).
Owing something to the crystalline shapes exploited by Expressionist architects, it was the antithesis of the approach Gropius and Meyer adopted at the
Fagus shoe-last factory and the 1914 *Werkbund* exhibition. The staggered
diagonal pointed elements were supposed by the newspaper of the trade-
union organization that had commissioned the monument to represent the
sharp-edged proletariat reacting with lightning speed to defend the Republic
against the forces of 'reaction'. However, Adolf Behne held that the monument could not be a Socialist image because it was too general a symbol of
uprising: it could just as easily have commemorated the Kapp-Lüttwitz
troops.[36] The structure suggests that Gropius was still very much influenced
by images associated with ideas prevalent among members of *Arbeitsrat für
Kunst*, the *Novembergruppe*, and the *Gläserne Kette*, connecting vague notions
about 'spiritual enlightenment', political 'liberty', and a striving towards
some sort of loosely defined Utopia. It was destroyed 1935–6 under National
Socialism, but reconstructed in modified form in 1946 when Communist
East Germany (later [1949–90] The German Democratic Republic [*Deutsche
Demokratische Republik*—DDR]) came into being.[37]

By 1920, opposition to the *Bauhaus* was growing, and came from several
sides. First of all there were the small businesses and local craftsmen who felt
threatened by the school's existence (not least because they were denounced
as members of the '*bourgeoisie*'); then there were those who believed (not
without reason) that the *Bauhaus* had Bolshevist sympathies; and staff members of the former academy of Fine Art (which had been amalgamated into
the *Bauhaus*) felt they were sidelined and their skills despised. The loss of the
Fine Artists removed an important element from Gropius's original vision,
yet of the nine members of staff he appointed as Masters of Form between
1919 and 1924, eight were painters. However, they were Modernists, unlikely

to be well-versed in the techniques of carpentry, metalwork, weaving, book-binding, or other crafts; theoretically they might evolve new systems of design owing nothing to historical precedent.

There was a problem, though: the Workshop Masters, well skilled in their own crafts, were supposed to impart knowledge to students to develop their manual skills and techniques, and the painters were entrusted with intellectual understanding and the encouragement of creativity. The Workshop Masters resented the airy-fairy 'arty' interference, as they saw it, of the Masters of Form, some of whom had no interest in the workshops: perhaps, despite their professed 'leftist' leanings, they took a superior attitude to handicrafts. There was definitely a cultural class-system, contrary to all protestations to the contrary, and the yawning divide between Arts and Crafts remained. Furthermore, policies regarding the running of the *Bauhaus* were decided upon by the Masters of Form and student representatives, and there was no obligation even to consult the Workshop Masters, who were discriminated against in other ways, such as length of summer vacations and prohibitions on their earning money outside the institution. In short, there was a consid-erable difference between the supposed aspirations of the *Bauhaus* and what was actually going on there: Schlemmer was not slow to point these out as early as 1921.[38] For this state of affairs Gropius was entirely responsible.

Adolf Meyer, Gropius's partner in his architectural practice, was brought in to teach architectural drawing and building technology, and there was an attempt to share instruction with the *Weimar Baugewerkenschule* (the building-trades school that trained stonemasons, bricklayers, plumbers, etc.). But after Meyer ceased teaching architectural drawing in 1922 and Paul Klopfer, director of the *Baugewerkenschule* from 1910 to 1922, also left, there does not appear to have been much, if any, architecturally relevant teaching at the *Bauhaus* at all, contrary to fondly-held Modernist mythology. Two of Gropius's appointments have been mentioned above (Itten and Feininger), but Adolf Meyer was a Theosophist, that is, associated with the Theosophical Society, re-founded by Madame Blavatsky and others in 1875. The *Bauhaus* attracted numerous followers of arcane sects, including the wandering mys-tic, gustav nagel, who felt capital letters were *élitist* (difficult in Germany, where every noun has to be a capital), so spelled his own name without them, and influenced later *Bauhaus* typography. Rudolf Steiner had once been involved with the Theosophical Society, but had fallen out with some of the personalities and founded Anthroposophy, which, in turn was to influence several people involved with the school.

Gerhard Marcks, a member of the *Werkbund*, was appointed (1919) Master of Form to the pottery-workshop, which was relocated at Dornburg some distance away from Weimar; this soon became something of a commercial success, not least because the design and manufacture of pottery for sale and use was mercifully free from 'theory' and meaningless abstractions. Marcks had had some experience of working with industry, and it showed. He also produced numerous woodcuts, and contributed to the *Bauhaus* in many ways. Nevertheless, there were criticisms of the *Bauhaus* as a whole, and of Gropius in particular, who was seen as having well-meaning Utopian ideas, according to Heinrich Basedow (who left the establishment in 1921). The problem was that, while it did plenty of sloganizing, the institution did not seem to many to make anything worthwhile.[39]

There was, however, one project that did result in a finished work of architecture: the timber merchant Adolf Sommerfeld commissioned Gropius and Meyer to design a villa for him in Berlin, and the result was a startling house constructed entirely of timber (1920-1—much later destroyed). The influence of Frank Lloyd Wright was apparent, overlaid on a traditional log- or block-house type of construction, but the carved geometrical decorations by the *Bauhaus* apprentice Joost Schmidt suggest Art-Deco and *De-Stijl* tendencies. Other apprentices, including Marcel Breuer (who designed furniture for the house) and Josef Albers (who was responsible for the abstract glass patterns), contributed, so that the collaborative efforts of several disciplines combined in a single building to achieve something of the Wagnerian[40] *Gesamtkunstwerk* (total work of art) aimed at in Gropius's philosophy.

When Gropius and Meyer obtained two more commissions for a villa and a domestic decorative scheme, the *Bauhaus* contributed again. However, the Masters of Form appointed by Gropius in 1920-1 were, curiously, three more painters: Schlemmer, Georg Muche, and Paul Klee. Schlemmer realized almost immediately that architectural work was only connected with Gropius's private practice, which did not seem to relate to the educational intentions of the workshops: he felt there was a fraudulent element in the whole set-up because the fact was always being concealed that the *Bauhaus* was just a school for Modern Art.

Schlemmer had had pre-war experience, designing murals for the 1914 Cologne *Werkbund* exhibition, but on his arrival at Weimar, he was shocked to find that the workshops had been denuded of fittings that had been sold during the war, and that for an institution that claimed to be teaching the crafts, the facilities were not there, so the students just played about. In 1923

Gropius appointed him Master of Form in the theatre-workshop, because theatre, being a public art, also involved various crafts. Schlemmer replaced Lothar Schreyer, whose beliefs were mystical and pseudo-religious, and some of whose creations for the theatre were incomprehensible, even to his *Bauhaus* colleagues.[41] Schlemmer's writings provide valuable information on the *Bauhaus*, its personalities, and its problems, yet even he seems to have had confused and confusing ideas about the aims of the place: instead of a 'cathedral' (of Socialism or anything else) he demanded that dreary old chestnut, 'the machine for living in',[42] yet was leery of industry and engineering, demanding that art as a metaphysical phenomenon should survive.[43]

Muche, who was supposed to support Itten, had himself some curiously mystical tendencies, took over the *Vorkurs* when Itten was away on retreat, and was Master of Form in the weaving-workshops until 1927. The 'left-wing' Klee's appointment was not welcomed by some of his colleagues: Schlemmer, for example, saw Klee's work as useless for craft purposes, but nevertheless Klee worked in the book-binding and stained-glass workshops, later moving to weaving. In 1922 Wassily Kandinsky arrived to teach, having left the Soviet Union somewhat disillusioned about the violent reactions against experimental Modernism there: he also brought certain metaphysical-transcendentalist attitudes with him (he had been influenced by Rudolf Steiner's Anthroposophy), which caused eyebrows as well as hackles to rise in some quarters of the *avant-garde*.[44]

Immediately after the seizure of power by the Bolsheviks in the former Russian Empire (October 1917), Kandinsky had been deeply engaged in the cultural politics of the infant state, and seems to have incorporated many of Gropius's ideas into the programme he prepared (1920) for the Moscow Institute of Art and Culture (INKhUK). While in the Soviet Union Kandinsky became familiar with the work of the Constructivist Vladimir Tatlin, the Suprematist Kazimir Malevich, and the Suprematist/Constructivist, El Lissitzky, all of whom were later to have some impact on developments at Gropius's institution. However, Kandinsky's teaching about colour, line, form, and so on embraced quasi-scientific analyses, encouraging abstraction, which appears to have influenced approaches to design at the *Bauhaus*. Both Klee and Kandinsky published their ideas:[45] Kandinsky, in particular, was influenced in his ideas about colour by the works of Goethe, Schoenmaekers (*see* pp. 105–6), and Steiner, but he was given to 'dogmatic assertion',[46] as were others connected with the school.

The magazine *De Stijl* published an explosive article in September 1922 denouncing the *Bauhaus* for wholly failing to unify the various disciplines it had claimed it would bring together at the beginning. The piece described Itten's works as superficial, pompous daubings; Gropius's *Märzgefallenen-Denkmal* in the Weimar cemetery as the 'result of a cheap literary idea' (it had pre-echoes of spikier tendencies within what was to become Decon-structivism, notably in the work of Libeskind, who, like his predecessors, seems to have obsessed about 'crystals'); and Klee's 'scribbles' as 'sickly dreams'.[47] The author was Vilmos Huszár, one of the founders of the Dutch periodical, but the *éminence grise* behind the attack was Theo van Doesburg, who first visited the *Bauhaus* in 1920. Later, in a series of lectures, Doesburg praised Gropius's initial *stated aims* about educational reform, but violently criticized the direction that the establishment's teaching had *actually* taken. Doesburg, like Itten, was dogmatic: sporting a black shirt, white tie, and monocle, he attracted Itten's (perhaps prophetic) comment that a man who wears a black shirt also has a black soul.[48] His outbursts, however, were *fortissimo*: he screamed, he shouted, he bullied, he harangued, and the louder he yelled the more he imagined his message supporting Constructivism and ideas embedded in the *De-Stijl* movement would be heard. It was.

Gropius's supposed intention that his school would accommodate many points of view was being dashed on the rocks of dogmatic intolerance, and Itten's influence at last began to be seen as malign. The idea of *Sachlichkeit* had been around for some time, but the Dutch term *nieuwe zakelijkheid* was used from *c.*1923 to suggest the end of Expressionism. That was the year in which Itten left the *Bauhaus* and Gropius shed his Utopian Socialism, aban-doning lip-service to Morris–Ruskin-inspired mediaevalism: it was also the beginning of *Neue Sachlichkeit* (usually translated as new objectivity; but new realism, new practicality, or new relevance might be more accurate to describe the new climate in which architecture and art were expected to evolve). Gropius replaced Itten with the Hungarian László Moholy-Nagy, who had left his native land after the short-lived but bloody Communist revolution (1919) led by Béla Kun. The last had been encouraged and indoc-trinated by Lenin, but his failure to begin social and cultural transformations led many, like Moholy-Nagy, to emigrate. Kun attempted one more Hungarian revolution in 1928, which failed, so he returned to the Soviet Union where he was 'liquidated' in the purges of 1936–7.

Moholy-Nagy was firmly within the van Doesburg/*De-Stijl* camp, and he followed Constructivist ideas as promoted by Tatlin and El Lissitzky: Tatlin's idea of an artist was somebody who made things, assembled parts, and was a sort of engineer, so Moholy-Nagy wore a type of boiler-suit to suggest he was a worker in some industrial concern. Versatile, he believed that any artist who confined himself to one medium did not deserve the name, and he was violently opposed to anything that was irrational, seeing the notions of 'spiritual revelation' espoused by some of the *Bauhäusler* as ridiculous, childish delusions. Klee, believing the purpose of art was to make the invisible visible, was therefore in the opposite camp to that of Moholy-Nagy, who felt that to be a painter when everybody should be concerned with survival (in extremely difficult political and financial times) was a mere indulgence that did nothing to improve the lot of the masses.[49]

Where other Masters dogmatically asserted, the Hungarian made clear, rational, sceptical statements; where those striving for 'spirituality' and the transcendent (like Kandinsky) loathed machines, Moholy-Nagy embraced them as the reality of the times, the tools of the proletariat, replacing any suspect 'transcendental spiritualism' of past eras.[50] When he took over the *Vorkurs* from Itten he eliminated all metaphysical speculations, meditation, devotion to the supposed benefits of garlic paste, breathing exercises, emotional responses to colour and form, enemas, and anything savouring of the irrational: instead, he taught technique, materials, rationality, and openness to new media.[51] With Christian Dell, the Workshop Master, he transformed the metal-workshop, introducing the design of artefacts such as electric light-fittings, tea-pots and -infusers, kettles, coffee-services, and so on, instead of the weirdly-shaped pots, 'intellectual door-knobs', 'spiritual samovars', and other absurdities encouraged under Itten's *régime*.[52]

Gropius indicated the fresh direction of the *Bauhaus* in a speech of 1923 in which he emphasized a supposed 'new unity' between art and technology: students were to be educated to design objects that could be manufactured using machines. Of course it should be remembered that the *Bauhaus* was expected to start to pay its way, and the only manner in which this could be achieved was to cooperate with industry, sell designs and patents, and so on.[53] The old idea of designing and making handcrafted artefacts for relatively well-off clients could not possibly give the institution anything like financial independence: there was resistance to this proposed industrialized direction, notably by those who looked down on engineers, imagining the 'artist' was somehow superior. But Gropius convinced doubters that earnings were essential if the school was to survive at all.[54] It was, and not for the first time, a complete *volte-face* on his part.

Moholy-Nagy was ably assisted by Josef Albers, who had studied at the *Bauhaus*, and who was asked by Gropius to stay on as Workshop Master for stained glass: Albers also taught on the *Vorkurs*, and was fascinated by the properties of materials and their uses, notably paper and card. With Moholy-Nagy and Gropius, Albers was an important figure in redirecting the institution, and the first effective manifestation of its change of course became overt in the major exhibition of 1923 for which Joost Schmidt designed an eye-catching poster. That the exhibition was imperative was obvious: the Thuringian government, exasperated by what appeared to be lack of progress, now demanded evidence of the school's effectiveness. Furthermore, the annual conference of the *Werkbund* was scheduled to take place in Weimar, so it was essential the *Bauhaus* should create a good impression. There were not only exhibits in plenty, but lectures, including one by Gropius himself on an alleged 'new unity' between art and technology, signalling changes of emphasis and direction; and the exhibition was widely advertised throughout Germany, helped by Gropius's contacts with the media and the impressively designed publicity material. When the exhibition was opened, many celebrities attended, including the Dutch architect, Oud (Rotterdam City Architect [1918–33], strongly under van Doesburg's influence, and member of *De Stijl*), the composers Busoni and Stravinsky (both of whom had impeccable Modernist credentials), and others. Oud and Kandinsky also gave lectures at that internationally acclaimed event.[55]

The summer and early autumn of 1923, when the exhibition was mounted, was a time of hyper-inflation, and there was a real possibility the German State would collapse into ungovernable chaos. Later that year, however, attempts were made to reform the currency, and the 'Dawes Plan' (named after the American statesman and financier) of 1924 made the actual transfer of war reparation payments conditional on the stability of the German exchange, and provided for a non-political and automatic means for determining Germany's ability to pay (which had been completely crippled not only by hyper-inflation, but by the partial occupation of Germany's industrial heartland by French and Belgian troops, causing widespread strikes, civil resistance, and industrial unrest). Foreign investment started to flow into Germany, and industry made a remarkable and rapid recovery, encouraging a demand for people capable of designing artefacts for mass production. The American industrialist Henry Ford established (1924) a German subsidiary in Cologne; other German industrialists followed suit, notably in the field of automobile-production, prompted further by the American advocate of Scientific Management, F.W.Taylor.

The prospect of mass-produced, well-designed goods, manufactured in Germany, and made possible by machinery, began to suggest a new society: a kind of industrialized Utopia, based on investment and capitalism, rather than the plethora of post-war, supposedly Socialist experiments that were associated with chaotic conditions, want, misery, and hyper-inflation; and, let it be said, with the *Bauhaus* Ittenites and other groupings embracing pseudo-religious cults to whom the machine was anathema. Machinery became a topic of enormous interest, and there were numerous publications aimed at the general public on aspects of technology.

Oud's involvement in the 1923 exhibition helped to establish closer links with The Netherlands, and especially with the *De-Stijl* movement. One of the new ventures carried out by the *Bauhaus* was the production of a very cheap experimental house, using modern materials, capable of being mass produced as a kit of standardized parts. Muthesius's pre-war ideas were starting to come to fruition with the genesis of this exhibit (although it is doubtful if he would have approved of the realized work), called *Haus Am Horn* after the Weimar street on which it was built.[56] Financed by Sommerfeld, it was designed by Muche (who earlier had been unsympathetic not only to the machine but to handicrafts as well): he was assisted by Adolf Meyer on the technical side. Gropius stressed the importance of function in every room, each of which had its own character appropriate to its use.[57] Moholy-Nagy designed the light-fittings (made in the *Bauhaus* workshops), and Marcel Breuer was responsible for the furniture and kitchen (apparently one of the very first with separate lower cupboards, upper cupboards fixed to the walls behind, a continuous work surface [all arrangements now ubiquitous], and ceramic containers for, e.g. sugar, designed in the *Bauhaus* and mass produced elsewhere).[58]

Some of the furniture, notably a dressing-table, was clearly influenced by the work of designers associated with *De Stijl*, especially Rietveld, and also by the paintings of Mondrian. Indeed, the Rietveld chairs (*see* **Figure 3.1**) and Breuer's *Am-Horn* dressing-table were examples of *Elementarism*, a term coined by van Doesburg to describe the constructive use of colour, line, plane, and volume as primary elements and as an end in itself: the concept seems to owe something to the publications of Heinrich Wölfflin, whose *Kunstgeschichtliche Grundbegriffe* (*Principles of Art History*, subtitled *the problem of the development of style in modern art*) had been published in 1915.[59] Stylistically,

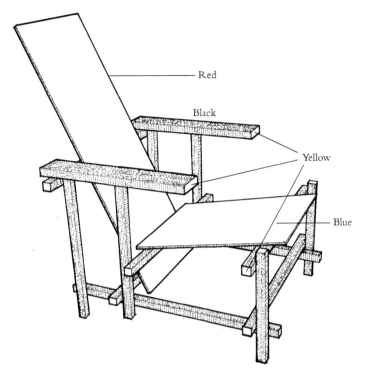

Red

Black

Yellow

Blue

Figure 3.1. 'Red-Blue' chair of *c*.1923, by Rietveld

the *Haus Am Horn* was stark, as was inevitable, given its construction consisting of a steel frame filled in with concrete: Gropius claimed the design aimed at the greatest comfort with the greatest economy. The living-room was placed in the centre of the house, lit by high-level windows, and the building had the obligatory 'flat' roof and absolutely plain window-openings devoid of any surrounding mouldings. Cills were simple metal drips rather than anything more substantial. This utilitarian structure was unlikely to age gracefully, and its external aesthetic was an ominous harbinger of what was to come.[60]

There was, however, a further connection with The Netherlands. The main influence on Mondrian was M.H.J. Schoenmaekers, Theosophist, who elaborated a theory of universal beauty by renouncing what he called the 'particulars of appearance' and embracing 'abstraction of form and colour' within the precision of geometries established by the straight line and 'clearly defined primary colour'.[61] Schoenmaekers specified rectilinear structures based on horizontals and verticals, and primary colours (red, yellow, and blue), to aid the quest for the Absolute: to him they had a cosmic signifi-cance, so the orthogonal image he connected to Divine Geometry, and thus should form the essential elements of an art that was cosmically pre-emi-nent, clarifying the mystical aspects of life and immortality, expressed in universal harmony.[62] This important influence on what was to be called the supposedly 'objective' 'International Style', and especially on figures such as Mondrian, Rietveld, and Le Corbusier, has not loomed large in the litera-ture, but there can be little doubt that a widespread adoption of harsh straight lines and primary colours by Modernism had a quasi-religious ori-gin that has been inconvenient for many writers who considered that style in purely materialist terms. Mondrian's painting, *Tableau 1 with Red, Black, Blue, and Yellow* (1921);[63] Rietveld's red, blue, yellow, and black armchair (*c.*1923—known as the 'Red-Blue chair' [**Figure 3.1**], originally designed [1918] without colour)[64] and Schröder-Schräder house, *Prins Hendriklaan* 50, Utrecht (1924–5) (**Figure 3.2**);[65] Theo van Doesburg and Cor van Eesteren's *Axonometric: Architecture from above* (1922–3);[66] and van Eesteren's design for a shopping-street in Den Haag, with housing above (1924)[67] are just a few examples of a direct influence from Schoenmaekers, and one that was embedded in Theosophical ideas, and not in any alleged 'scientific', 'rational', or 'functional' basis.

Reviews of the exhibition were, on the whole, positive: Behne wrote of the exceptional difficulties that had attended the first four years of the life of the *Bauhaus*, and apart from the Soviet Union, could not think of anywhere else in Europe where a similar experiment might have been undertaken.[68] Paul Westheim, however, felt there were too many repetitions of equilateral rectangles (squares) everywhere in Weimar, and that it was fortunate for the *Bauhaus* that Malevich, who had 'invented the square' in 1913, had not taken out a patent to protect it.[69] Westheim also worried that, influenced by Russian Constructivism, the *Bauhaus* might be modelling itself on industry and industrial art: he was uneasy about quasi-engineering Romanticism, and that the *Bauhäusler* might have deluded themselves into imagining they had created new forms in the square, triangle, circle, cube, etc., whereas those stereometrically pure shapes only had a point when they lay at the heart of a creative process. He feared that a new 'academicism' confined to the styliza-tion of the square and rectangle, relying on a rather unintelligent play of mechanistic forms, might be the unpleasant fruit of the new 'art school'.[70]

It was a perceptive comment, for what was to follow became a type of aesthetic straitjacket, limiting creation, and in the end failing to make a new

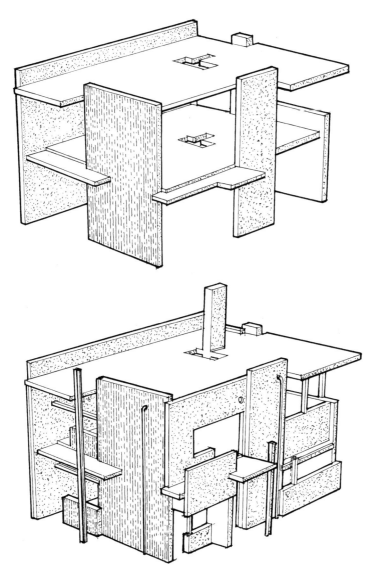

Figure 3.2. Exploded analytical drawings of the Elementarist house at *Prins Hendriklaan* 50, Utrecht (1924–5), by Rietveld and G.A. Schröder-Schräder, show-ing (*top*) the essential planes, with (*bottom*) the secondary elements added

world that was worth the effort. Westheim was not in the majority among those with *avant-garde* pretensions, however, for the *Bauhaus* was lauded widely among those unable to see where things might lead. The school was undoubtedly associated with the 'left', and there were too many links with the Soviet Union, with quasi-religious cults, and now with mechanization that threatened traditional craft-skills (despite Gropius's previously declared intentions), to be ignored.

There may also have been an unfortunate perceived association with the dire economic situation, for a *Bauhaus* 'apprentice', Herbert Bayer, was responsible for the design of banknotes issued (1923) by the Thuringian State Bank for denominations running not only into millions but billions of Marks: no matter how disconnected the two things might be, in straitened times persons tend to blame by making mental connections, and it seems something of the sort occurred. It should be remembered that the *Bauhaus* was suspected of being a waste of money, yet funded from public sources.

During the political unrest when hyper-inflation was hitting Thuringia very seriously and troops had to be stationed in Weimar to ensure some degree of public order, Gropius's apartment was searched by the military authorities because he was 'suspected of left-wing sympathies'.[71] Given that he had designed the *Märzgefallenen-Denkmal* and appointed members of staff who had connections with Soviet Constructivism and with the Béla Kun revolution in Hungary (and therefore, by association, with Lenin), such 'suspicions' were hardly surprising. But Gropius's changes of direction at various times suggest that he was at the very least a trimmer, capable, chameleon-like, of adapting to circumstances, and even of making dramatic political shifts, when he sensed a move would be advantageous to him. That he was an adept operator is clear.

Critical plaudits were one thing, but commercial success was another: if the *avant-garde* loved the exhibition, the connections with industry leading to financial security were modest. It is true that the *Bauhaus* managed to sell some of its products such as furniture and fabrics to members of the public before the exhibition, but firm connections with industry were few, and were mostly for pottery and metalwork. Some members of staff regretted the direction being taken: Muche felt that the great strengths of the pre-1923 *Bauhaus* were 'intuition and ignorance', and recalled meetings lasting for many hours to decide if doors should be numbered or lettered, and whether the numbers or letters should be coloured.[72] Furthermore, Gropius began to adopt a terminology that was quasi-scientific, referring to the workshops as 'laboratories' with 'instruments', and the need to 'train' a supposedly previously unknown type of person who commanded an equal knowledge of technique and form. His speeches and lectures contained many such references, contributing to the myth of 'scientific rationalism', 'objectivity', 'fit for function', and all the rest of it. The fact that this sort of stuff was swallowed whole in certain quarters says much for the collective state of intellectual comprehension. At this point it should be emphasized that none of the key players (including Gropius) in what became the Modern Movement or the 'new architecture' had even basic scientific training: all their limited knowledge came from their general schooling, and any science they did know was the strictly nineteenth-century mechanistic science of steam and rudimentary internal-combustion engines. Le Corbusier's obsessions with the primitive technology of automobiles, aeroplanes, and screw-driven ships were hardly 'modern' at all: indeed, those individuals who made portentous pronouncements about the 'scientific objectivity', etc., of Modern architecture had hardly any understanding of what real science was or what it involved.[73]

Although the exhibition impressed certain echelons of society, it did not endear the *Bauhaus* to Thuringian craftsmen or the tax-paying public, and in 1924 the State government became actively antagonistic to the institution.[74] An advertisement appeared in the public prints protesting at the continuing existence of the *Bauhaus*, and especially at State support for an institution under the direction of 'Herr Gropius with the teachers and Masters at present there'. In particular, it denounced the mechanical games, the arrangements of materials, the colour-effects, each distorted head and bizarre human body, all the schizoid scribblings and experiments in embarrassment, the decadent values theatrically inflated into suspect 'art' by the director and masters, the lack of true artistic creativity, the arrogance and pretensions of the institution that claimed the State was neglecting 'culture' if it withdrew its financial support. It questioned that the *Bauhaus* was a 'cultural institute' at all.[75] Schlemmer recorded that skilled craftsmen, impoverished and threatened local artists, the '*bourgeoisie*', and the Thuringian government were all up in arms against the *Bauhaus*, so leaflets hostile to the school were appearing in floods, counteracted by statements and notices from Gropius and posters designed and made by the students.[76]

Change was in the air.

The *Bauhaus* at Dessau

It became clear that the position had become untenable, so Gropius and his Council of Masters announced that the *Bauhaus* would close in March 1925. Feelers went out to several other places, but it was Dessau, capital of the former Duchy of Anhalt, which made the most positive proposals. Some members of staff left, including Adolf Meyer, who went to Frankfurt-am-Main with Christian Dell from the metal-workshop at Weimar, and the vacated buildings were occupied by a reconstituted school of arts and crafts under new management (some students and assistant teachers stayed on). Dessau had a pedigree going back to the days when its Princes (later Dukes) were devoted to the arts,[77] so was similar to Weimar in that respect. Otherwise it was different, being larger, with an industrial infrastructure (including aircraft-manufacture, engineering, and chemical-works), and its political make-up was Social Democratic. There was definitely a political decision connected with the Party that enabled the *Bauhaus* to relocate to Dessau,[78] but from the *Bauhaus* point of view there were other advantages, such as a speedy rail-connection with Berlin.

The *Bürgermeister* (mayor) of Dessau, Fritz Hesse, was the driving-force behind obtaining support, both moral and financial, and Gropius was credited with the design of a new complex of buildings which became a paradigm of the so-called 'International Style'. The original drawings clearly show the *Bauhaus* was designed in collaboration with Adolf Meyer, but, as noted previously, the persons mostly involved in the design were Carl Fieger and Ernst Neufert. It consisted of teaching and workshop areas, a theatre, a canteen with kitchen, a gymnasium, and studio apartments with roof-gardens on top. The architectural vocabulary included a huge curtain-wall (*see* **Figure 6.4**) illuminating the workshops, cantilevered balconies, and a 'flat' roof (an essential feature of what became known as 'The International Style', but it leaked, so had to be re-covered). The structure included a reinforced-concrete frame, and went up rapidly, though costs (unsurprisingly) greatly exceeded the original budget.

To *Bauhaus* was added *Hochschule für Gestaltung* (college for design); the 'masters' became 'professors'; craftsmen assisted in the workshops, but no longer had supposed equal status to that of the professors; students remained as 'apprentices' and 'journeymen' for a time; and the cumbersome so-called 'democracy' of Weimar was abandoned. Major decisions were to be taken by the director. Able former students were recruited to teach 'collaborators' who had mastered techniques and forms for industry, crafts, and building;[79] pottery and stained-glass workshops were no longer associated with the institution; cabinet-making and metal-workshops were merged to produce furniture and domestic equipment under Marcel Breuer's leadership; the printing-department under Bayer developed skills in design, typography, and especially advertising. Muche, assisted by a former student, a disciple of Itten, Gunta Stölzl, ran weaving; Schlemmer was in charge of the theatre-workshop; sculpture and mural decorations were supervised by Joost Schmidt and Hinnerk Scheper; Moholy-Nagy and Albers ran the *Vorkurs*; Kandinsky and Klee continued teaching Form; but Gropius abandoned teaching for administration and his architectural practice. In addition, space was created within the *Bauhaus* buildings for an innovation: this was the department of architecture, established in 1927.

Significantly, Sommerfeld financed a *Bauhaus* limited-liability company to market patents and designs. A journal was planned, and a series of books began to appear with distinctive typographical layouts. Despite the so-called 'machine-aesthetic' of the new buildings, Gropius professed to be still worried about poor attendance at classes and in workshops, and about the perceptions of the place as an 'art-school' establishment. He also published some statements of intent, claiming the *Bauhaus* would contribute to the development of housing, from domestic appliances and furniture to whole dwellings, in a manner that would be in 'harmony' with the 'spirit of the age',[80] a term which recurs with depressing frequency in the literature of the Modern Movement. There was talk of such appliances and furnishings relating to each other 'rationally',[81] and that systematic 'theoretical and practical research into formal, technical, and economic fields'[82] would be carried out in order to arrive at forms of objects from their 'natural functions and limitations'.[83]

Stating that 'modern man',[84] who wears 'modern not historical dress'[85] (one wonders how Itten's and nagel's modes of attire fitted in with the adjective 'modern'), also requires a 'modern dwelling...in harmony with himself and with the times in which he lives...equipped with all the modern objects in daily use',[86] Gropius went on to observe that before a container, chair, or house could 'function'[87] properly, its 'nature'[88] must be studied so that it would perfectly serve its purpose, function practically, and be cheap, durable, and 'beautiful'[89] (the word was placed in quotes, suggesting that already it was being regarded as 'relative'). Design was a matter of reason rather than passion, and machines would help to 'liberate'[90] individuals: there was no danger that standardization would deprive the individual of choice, he claimed. The *Bauhaus* workshops were essentially *laboratories*[91] in which prototypes suitable for mass-production 'and typical of their time'[92] were to be developed and 'constantly improved', and entirely new types of 'collaborators for industry and the crafts' with 'equal command of technology and design' were to be trained.[93]

Gropius continued with assertions that in order to fulfil all the economic and formal demands, rigorous selection of the best, most comprehensively trained minds, schooled in basic working methods and with precise knowledge of formal and mechanical design elements and the laws of their construction, would be essential. Crafts and industry, he claimed, were drawing closer, so that the crafts of the future would have a unity of labour in which they would be the medium of experimental work for industrial production. Nearly a century later one might be forgiven for questioning some of that. Under Albers, for example, everything known about an existing object would be questioned, and any answer also questioned: so the 'collaborators' strove to produce objects that were unlike anything that already existed, and the results were explained and laboriously discussed by the whole group. Exercises and classes led by Kandinsky and Klee augmented these activities. One can only imagine what resulted from interventions by the Russian Constructivist El Lissitzsky, the Dutch Modernist Mart Stam, the Russian Constructivist sculptor Naum Gabo, the Communist aesthetician Lu Märten, and the distinguished chemist, pacifist, and colour-theorist Wilhelm Ostwald. A seminar given by Ostwald ignited a pseudo-religious war between the disciples of his scientific theories of colour (which had influenced members of *De Stijl*, notably Piet Mondrian) and those who were wary of them.[94]

Several houses for the 'professors' were erected not far from the *Bauhaus* to designs allegedly by Gropius, although Fieger and others were also involved.[95] All had smooth white walls and 'flat' roofs: they were intended to shape the activities of life, yet the designs of the houses were at the same time to derive from the activities that took place inside them, and the overall shape of each house did not evolve arbitrarily, but as a result of its 'organism'[96] (what its 'organism' might have been was not explained). Despite these bold claims, the inhabitants of the houses became painfully aware of all too many design problems and failures which did not make for comfort: the Kandinsky house had an entrance-hall with a very large expanse of glazing enabling passers-by to see everything that went on inside, so Kandinsky painted the glass white in order to gain some privacy. Furthermore, Gropius did not favour coloured interiors, but Kandinsky 'appreciated' them, so duly painted the inside of his house.[97] As Osbert Lancaster observed, 'the conception of a house as *une machine à habiter* presupposes a barrenness of spirit to which, despite every indication of its ultimate achievement, we have not yet quite attained'.[98]

However, the new *Bauhaus* buildings themselves were assertions that old-fashioned crafts were 'out' and a new sort of industrial designer was being produced: furthermore, students recorded 'community spirit' as positive. 'Modernity' was proclaimed in the architecture itself.[99] It was also advertised in the work of one of the so-called Young Masters (former students who were taken on at the new *Bauhaus* as members of staff): Herbert Bayer, an Austrian, was adept at photography, typography, painting, graphics, and the design of packaging. Concerned with simplicity, clarity, and impact, he took nagel's ideas further, and created a typeface without serifs or capital letters, which, allied with bold rules and compositions that were asymmetrical, was obviously informed by *De Stijl* and by the work of Moholy-Nagy. German nouns require capitals for the first letter, and, given that much German printing at the time employed Gothic typefaces, Bayer's use of lower-case sans-serif alphabets only (on grounds of economy and clarity) was truly revolutionary. His designs have withstood the test of time.

Breuer was another former student who became a Young Master: of Hungarian birth, he was strongly influenced by *De Stijl* and especially by Rietveld, but by 1925 he was using bent tubular steel (said to have been suggested by chromium-plated bicycle handlebars) with leather, canvas, or other cloth supports for chairs, and he has been credited as one of the first to introduce chrome into the design of household goods, a material far-removed from traditional crafted furniture. His chairs (and their derivatives) have become as ubiquitous as Bayer's typography. Hinnerk Scheper was also influenced by *De-Stijl* designs, and revolutionized the application of colour to interiors, notably with areas of various matt colours for walls, ceilings, floors, etc. His wallpapers were successfully marketed, and he had a lasting effect on Modernist interior design. Joost Schmidt was important as an innovator in typography, and succeeded Bayer to run the printing-workshop from 1928. Stölzl was in charge of the weaving-workshops from 1926, and designed innumerable carpets, curtains, hangings, and runners, many for mass-production, and often of great complexity, with startling colour combinations arranged in abstract designs. The weaving side of the Dessau *Bauhaus* became one of its most commercially successful departments.

One of the first tasks of the Dessau *Bauhaus* was to work for Gropius on various projects, one of which was a housing-scheme at Törten, Dessau: erected 1926–8, it consisted of buildings to be put up using standardized systems, with concrete walls and other elements made *in situ*, so construction was rapid. The scheme was an attempt to show that houses could be built very cheaply and quickly, offering people the chance to own or rent properties with gardens: it included a co-operative shop and an apartment-block which featured architectural elements that were to become standard 'International-Style' *clichés*.

There was also an experimental steel house (1926–7) designed by Muche and Richard Paulick. After the 1939–45 war, Paulick rose rapidly to positions of influence in the Communist DDR, designing (from 1952) some of the massive blocks in the *Stalin-* (later *Karl-Marx-*) *Allee*, Berlin (a development ridiculed by Western Modernists who do not seem to have been aware of, or were in denial about, its links with the *Bauhaus*, but the *Allee* was greatly admired by luminaries such as Philip Johnson and Aldo Rossi), and laying out the centre of Dresden which largely obliterated the historic town plan. He wielded considerable power, and was partly responsible for directing East-German building construction towards industrialized prefabricated methods, which killed off what remained of craftsmanship.[100] The Törten steel house, which could be erected in just over a week, was hardly edifying as, or worthy of the name of, architecture, and the whole estate had from the start, and still has, a bleak, grim, hard, stark appearance that time has not softened, for such structures, by the nature of the materials used and their detailing (which turned its back on thousands of years of practice as to how buildings responded to the ravages of the elements), tend not to weather gracefully, and they leak.

Edmund Collein, who attended the *Bauhaus* 1927–30, made a photo-graphic record of Törten (on which he also worked), and spent much of his later life involved with industrialized building in the DDR, where he took part in many developments, notably that of the *Stalinallee*, Berlin, East Germany's showpiece. Neither Collein nor Paulick seems to have had a problem shifting from the sort of Modernist architectural language current at the Dessau *Bauhaus* towards the grandiose Party-approved Classically-inspired (though very stripped) style of the Stalinist era then *de rigueur* throughout the Soviet bloc after 1945, and stylistically not all that removed from Albert Speer's monumental designs for the North–South axis of Berlin, which were still being worked on well into the 1940s.[101]

Perhaps the most telling monument to German industrialized building methods and the legacy of those early experiments at the *Bauhaus* was the curiously named *Antifaschistischer Schutzwall* (anti-Fascist protective bar-rier), otherwise known as the Berlin Wall, a structure entirely formed of factory-made components, erected from 1961, not to keep Fascists out, but to prevent the population of the DDR from running away.[102]

A Department of Architecture at Dessau

In 1927 an architectural department was at last established at Dessau. Gropius had long stated that architectural problems could only be tackled after a student had acquired skills in crafts, theory, and design. For unexplained reasons, he changed his mind, so that after completing the *Vorkurs*, a student was free to move to the architectural department without having acquired any craft-skills or any knowledge whatsoever of traditional construction, design, or history. This pattern became the template of what would happen to architectural education throughout the West.[103]

It is also less than clear why Gropius decided to appoint as head of the new architectural department the former anthroposophist, the Swiss Hannes Meyer, who had adopted an aggressive communistic outlook to replace his earlier Steineresque beliefs. Given that Gropius was aware of the dangers of political activism, especially extreme 'leftist' commitment, in the increas-ingly unstable environment of the closing years of the Weimar Republic, his choice of Meyer seems more than bizarre. Nor is it clear why Meyer accepted the position of 'professor' at Dessau, as he was highly critical of work produced at the *Bauhaus*, and stated that the place had a reputation greatly exceeding its abilities to actually achieve anything:[104] even simple objects were subjected to time-wasting processes of analysis which tortured them into problematical shapes. He denounced 'incestuous theorising' that prevented every attempt to design in a manner that would enhance life, the 'psychological complexes' of female students, '*Bauhaus* snobs', and the deadly destruction of life by so-called 'art'.[105]

Meyer had visited England before the war to look at garden-cities and garden-suburbs, and to study aspects of the cooperative movement. He was of the view that architects should only design buildings that would enhance life, especially the life of the common man, but at Dessau his views on archi-tecture and society became more radical. He insisted that any question of aesthetics should be dropped entirely from any consideration of building, which had nothing to do with aesthetics but was a 'biological process', that it was only about social, technical, and economic organization, and that any continuation of tradition was 'Historicism' and should be stopped.[106] He also objected to the remark that a 'house is a machine for living in',[107] but was rather a kind of biological apparatus to satisfy physical and mental needs.[108]

Before he took up the post at Dessau in 1927, Meyer had published an article[109] full of praise for the modern world, lauding everything from light bulbs to the gramophone: but it was probably his demands for standardization and a collective approach to architecture, his insistence that building was not an aesthetic process, and that 'design' could be reduced to the pseudo-scientific formula *'function x economics'* that attracted Gropius, who was increasingly moving towards a supposedly 'rational', 'objective', and 'scientific' pose. Meyer was also gaining a reputation for uncompromising Modernism, producing, with his then partner, Hans Wittwer (who was also Swiss, and taught at the *Bauhaus* 1927–9), strenuously 'functional' designs that ignored context and natural features.

Hannes Meyer quickly managed to alienate many both inside and outside the *Bauhaus*. Moholy-Nagy, Kandinsky, and Klee quickly became his enemies, and Muche resigned in 1927. He was quickly followed by Gropius himself, who resigned as director in 1928 despite a contract which obliged him to stay on for a further couple of years: he went anyway, asserting that he intended to concentrate on his own architectural practice, but probably sensing troubled waters ahead. By that time his office had designed a few houses, including one of the earliest examples (1922–4) of *Neues Bauen*, planned on a module system of large building blocks (called *Baukasten im Großen*), for the scientist Felix Auerbach and his wife, the feminist Anna Silbergleit,[110] at 9 *Schaefferstraße*, Jena (**Plate 3.3**). Contemporary notices[111] credit the building to Gropius *and* Adolf Meyer.[112]

After Adolf Meyer had departed for Frankfurt to work with Ernst May in 1925, Gropius's office had designed two houses for the *Weißenhofsiedlung*, Stuttgart, using prefabricated techniques. The firm was to be responsible for several large public housing developments (*Dammerstock*, Karlsruhe [1928–9], *Am Lindenbaum*, Frankfurt-am-Main [1929–30], and the vast *Siemens-stadt*, Berlin [1929–30]). *Siemens-stadt*, with its long, parallel blocks, features as a model of the 'International Style', despite, or perhaps because of, its monotony and absence of any focus in either architectural or social terms.[113]

Plate 3.3. Auerbach house, 9 *Schaefferstraße*, Jena (1923–5), by Gropius & Adolf Meyer, one of the first realized examples of *Neues Bauen*. It was fully restored in 1995

Epilogue

In 1928 Gropius appointed Hannes Meyer as director of the entire *Bauhaus*, yet another seemingly irrational, eccentric, and damaging decision, made in the teeth of objections from other senior members of staff. Even the students objected to Meyer: they regarded his appointment as a disaster.[114] Moholy-Nagy, Breuer, and Bayer resigned, and the remaining members of staff registered their objections, saying that 'community spirit' was being replaced by 'individualist competition',[115] and that the old aim of unity between art and technology had come to a sudden stop when architecture became the dominant field of study.[116] It was an architecture of somewhat confined scope, mostly concerned with mass-housing and town-planning (perhaps those were the aspects which Gropius felt should be encouraged). Meyer brought in Ludwig Hilbersheimer to teach the last, and many other lecturers (including Stam) ensured that a heady brew of Marxist-Leninist theory, sociology, psychology, and elementary low-level physics would be on tap. Photography was also taught by Walter Peterhans, in order to strengthen knowledge of technique in advertising, display, and even journalism. A successful foray into wallpaper-design and -production was commercially profitable, and the workshops producing furniture, metal light-fittings, woven artefacts, and advertisement-designs all began to make money.

By 1925–8, the German economy had made strides towards recovery, and the country became a major producer and exporter of first-class electrical goods. However, all was not well at the *Bauhaus*, for the tendency towards the creation of student republics and Meyer's obsessions about 'sociological values' alarmed several members of staff: furthermore, political indoctrination, debate, and organization, heavily loaded towards communistic notions, reflected Meyer's views that all human actions were political, and the extreme 'left-wing' ethos of the institution could hardly be ignored.[117] The singing of communist-revolutionary songs by students, Meyer's open devotion to Marxism, and the growing opposition of some staff members (especially Kandinsky) created bad odour: enemies of the *Bauhaus* could claim, with some justification, that it was a breeding-ground for Bolshevism. Attacks in the press became vociferous: the behaviour of long-haired 'gangs' of *Bauhaus* students in Weimar, the city of Goethe, Schiller, and the *Aufklärung* (German Enlightenment), was deplored, as it had noisily introduced a 'Russian' flavour into the civilized calm of the old, aristocratic capital, and notions of salvation were peddled under innumerable labels, some quasi-religious, but all linked with the red star of Bolshevism.[118]

Matters came to a head in 1930 when the director of the Dessau *Gemäldegalerie* (picture gallery), the Modernist art-historian and architect Ludwig Grote (who had supported the mayor when he invited Gropius to Dessau in the first place, and who was a friend of Kandinsky), informed Hesse that under Meyer the *Bauhaus* had become a hotbed of 'left-wing' radicalism, and therefore the Swiss architect had to go. Other members of staff agreed (Schlemmer had departed in 1929, resulting in the closure of the theatre-workshop), apart from Klee (curiously) and Stölzl (unsurprisingly). It should also be remembered that there was growing tension between those with Marxist-Leninist tendencies 'sympathetic' to the Soviet Union (Gropius was one of them) and various uneasy groupings (e.g. Conservatives, Liberals, Monarchists, and the violently active *Nationalsozialistische Deutsche Arbeiterpartei* [NSDAP *or* National-Socialist German Worker's Party, under Adolf Hitler's leadership]). The Social Democrats were also inimical to the Bolshevists, who, in turn, despised the Social Democrats. Things became critical with the economic slump of 1929, and support for the National Socialists increased, not only because of the widespread distress caused by the economic depression, but because of the renewed controversies concerning the massive war-reparations payable by Germany due to come into force on 1 September 1930. The NSDAP violently objected to these reparations, thereby gaining backing from the electorate.

Meyer was obliged to resign in 1930,[119] and Communist students were expelled, some of them joining Meyer in the Soviet Union: there, supposedly, a true 'proletarian culture' was being 'forged'; there 'socialism' was being realized; and there the sort of society already existed for which Meyer and his followers had been 'struggling' (a favourite word of totalitarians) under Capitalism.[120] Gropius accused Meyer of having concealed his true political allegiances and of putting the future of the *Bauhaus* in jeopardy,[121] which is yet another indication of Gropius's shiftiness, for he cannot have been unaware of Meyer's views, which he had proclaimed loudly enough. Meyer's love-affair with the USSR did not last long: disillusioned, and perhaps uncomfortable with looming 'purges' and 'liquidations', he returned to Switzerland in 1936, although he still seems to have cherished a belief in a Communist Utopia. Gropius, who also peered at the USSR through deep-red spectacles, actually visited Leningrad in 1933, but left disappointed by the realities of his imagined Socialist ideal.[122]

Like many others on the 'left', Meyer seems to have believed that an organization such as the *Bauhaus* was impossible in a Capitalist state (even though the commercial successes of that institution in the late 1920s derived from a Capitalist system),[123] but, though under attack by then from various sides, the institution acquired a new director in 1930: Ludwig Miës van der Rohe.

IV

The International Style
1920s & 1930s

Introduction: The Transformation of Ludwig Mies; The Weißenhofsiedlung, *Stuttgart; The Strange Case of Erich Mendelsohn; Later History of the* Bauhaus *at Dessau & Berlin; Epilogue*

I have endeavoured to raise a definite issue between the Modernism which deliberately turns its back on the past, and Traditionalism which recognizes the past, and advances on technical lines which have hitherto been followed as a matter of course. Are we to accept that this Modernism is a step forward, or are we to regard it as a step downhill which, if unchecked, will end in...bankruptcy...? Since the war,[1] Modernism, or 'Modernismus', as it should be called on the German precedent, has invaded this country like an epidemic,...its attack is insidious and far-reaching, with the wholly fallacious prospect of a new heaven and earth which it dangles before the younger generation. My own concern is...with the 'New Architecture', and if I may seem to speak strongly, it is because, after long years of study and practice, I feel bound to do what I can to rescue a noble art from the degradation into which it seems to be sinking...the time has come to challenge this subversive movement all along the line.

Sir Reginald Theodore Blomfield (1856–1942): *Modernismus*
(London: Macmillian & Co. Ltd 1934) v–vi

Much that still is said and written about buildings is tainted by a doctrine that to architecture spells death. That doctrine, called 'functionalism',...may be regarded as a close architectural analogue of Puritanism, with its insistence upon moral values, its distaste for aesthetic values, its righteous slow-wittedness, and its abhorrence of gaiety. Like Puritanism it offered the consolations of assured virtue to those whom a naughty world might otherwise abash. It was built upon three major assumptions—that every requirement of structure or of use could be perfectly met in one certainly best way; that that way, being perceived as appropriate, was bound to please; and that a building thus pleasing came necessarily into the category of architecture.

Harry Stuart Goodhart-Rendel (1887–1959): *English Architecture since the Regency* (London: Constable & Co. Ltd 1953) 254–5

Introduction: The Transformation of Ludwig Mies

The appointment of Miës van der Rohe as director of the *Bauhaus* in 1930, was, yet again, Gropius's doing. We now have to retrace our steps in order to clarify certain matters.

Bruno Paul,[2] a member of the *Deutscher Werkbund*, was a pioneer in the design of machine-made furniture, the *Typen-Möbel*, and his achievements in standardization were to impress many, including Charles-Édouard Jeanneret-Gris (Le Corbusier). Paul was responsible for several interiors (including those of the German liners *Kronprinzessin Cecilie* [1907] and *Prinz Friedrich Wilhelm* [1908]). His beer-hall and restaurant for the Cologne *Werkbund* exhibition (1914) were admired, although they were ephemeral, and after the 1914–18 war his elegant designs for the interiors of the luxurious liner *Bremen* (1927) won him international renown.[3]

The young Ludwig Mies (as he then was), had no formal architectural education. He attended a local trade-school in Aachen (1900–2). His father was a master-mason and this building-trades background gave him a healthy respect for and understanding of how materials are used in buildings. After a couple of years spent as a draughtsman and designer for a firm that specialized in stucco decorations, he settled in Berlin (1905), where, wishing to improve his knowledge of timber-construction, he became apprenticed to Paul.[4] He was commissioned independently to design a house at No. 3, *Spitzwegstraße*, Berlin-Neubabelsberg (1906–7), for the philosopher Alois Adolf Riehl: with its steeply-pitched roof and tetrastyle verandah under one of the gabled ends, it was influenced by works of Muthesius,[5] Paul, and English Arts-and-Crafts houses (the eyebrow-dormers and interiors owe much to these).[6] This building brought Mies to the attention of Behrens, and Mies joined Behrens's office (1908–12), where he gained valuable experience, and supervised the erection and completion of the Imperial German embassy in St Petersburg, Russia (*see* **Plate 1.3**).[7] He also saw the important exhibition of work by Frank Lloyd Wright in Berlin (1910): Wasmuth's lavish publication of designs by Wright[8] made a huge impression in Germany, especially on Mies and his contemporaries, but any influence Wright may have exerted swiftly passed into oblivion as the rigid certainties of *Bauhaus*-inspired Modernism became not only accepted, but imposed.

In 1910 Mies prepared (unrealized) designs for a monument to Bismarck to be erected on the *Elisenhöhe* at Bingen-am-Rhein (**Figures 4.1*a* & *b***).

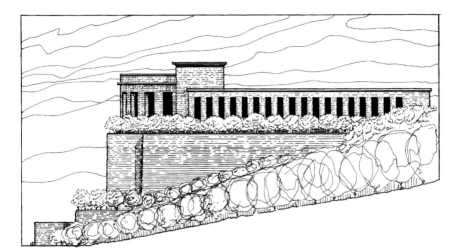

Figure 4.1a. Unrealized design (1910) by Ludwig Mies for a monument to Bismarck on the *Elisenhöhe*, Bingen-am-Rhein

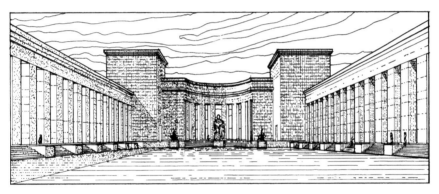

Figure 4.1b. Interior court of Mies's 1910 design for a monument to Bismarck at Bingen-am-Rhein

A symmetrical composition, its architectural language was a severe, stripped, Neo-Classicism, with a strong dose of Egyptianizing influences: it owed much to Karl Friedrich Schinkel's projects for the Athenian Acropolis (1834)[9] and *Schloß Orianda*, Crimea (1838),[10] and to Behrens's court (1910) for the *Ton-, Zement-, und Kalkindustrieauβtellung* (clay-, cement-, and lime-industry exhibition), Berlin-Treptow (*see* **Figure 1.6**);[11] it also looked forward to projects[12] by architects such as Wilhelm Kreis (**Plate 4.1**)[13] and Albert Speer.[14] It was labelled by Frampton as 'Boullée-like'[15] (although a study of designs by Étienne-Louis Boullée[16] will not reveal any such resemblance), and as 'the last significant project of his pre-war career'.[17]

Plate 4.1. Design by Wilhelm Kreis, One of numerous *Kriegerehrenmäler* (war memorials) designed by Wilhelm Kreis between 1941 and 1943 to commemorate the *Opfertod* (sacrificial death) of millions of German soldiers all over Europe. This one was to be erected in Norway, and its long ranges of columns are reminiscent of Mies' design (1910) for a monument to Bismarck (see **Figures 4.1***a* & *b*)

In those years Mies absorbed the influence of Behrens, mingled with a strong flavour of the Prussian Neo-Classicism of Schinkel, Behrens's hero. It should be remembered that Behrens was one of the most important architects of his time in that he not only designed buildings, but artefacts for manufacture by industrial processes, anticipating the theories of Gropius and others.[18] Mies also designed several more suburban villas, including the house at Nos. 14–15, *Hermannstraße*, Berlin-Zehlendorf (1911), for Hugo Perls, in which historical precedents were clear: this building was later (1926–8) extended for Eduard Fuchs, and with the extension the precedent of Schinkel's *Charlottenhof*, Potsdam (1826–7),[19] is present.[20]

Mies set up his own office in 1912, and in the same year was approached by Helene Kröller-Müller to design a house and gallery in The Netherlands for her collection of art.[21] The project (1912–13) was again stripped Neo-Classical, with a long portico similar to that proposed by Behrens for the Delstern columbarium (*see* **Figure 1.5**), with echoes of Schinkel's work at *Schloß Glienicke* (1824–32)[22] and some of Wright's designs he had seen in the Wasmuth publications;[23] but it was never realized. During a visit to The Netherlands associated with the Kröller-Müller project, Mies saw Berlage's

Koopmansbeurs in Amsterdam (1897–1903) with its robust detailing and clear expressions of structure, a building which he claimed had made a profound impression on him. Berlage himself was to later deplore the way architecture was going in the 1920s.[24] When Philip Johnson questioned Mies's supposed admiration for Berlage's great building, this act of *lèse majesté* made the German explode with anger.[25]

Other villas followed: the Ernst Werner house, Nos. 2/4, *Quermatenweg*, Berlin-Zehlendorf (1912–13), was again influenced by Muthesius; the Franz Urbig house, No. 9, *Luisenstraße*, Berlin-Neubabelsberg (1914–17), owed more to a severe Schinkelesque villa style, with its hipped roof and dormer-windows; the Kempner house, Nos. 5–7, *Sophienstraße*, Berlin-Charlottenburg (1919–22—demolished 1952), again owed debts to a simplified Schinkelesque domestic manner, a tendency also present in the Cuno Feldmann house, Nos. 10–12, *Erdenerstraße*, Berlin-Grünewald (1919–22—largely altered, almost beyond recognition); and the Georg Mosler house, Nos. 28–9, *Kaiserstraße*, Berlin-Neubabelsberg (1924–6). With the Georg Eichstaedt house, No. 30, *Dreilindenstraße*, Berlin-Nikolaßee (1919–22), the Muthesian influence once more was present,[26] but things began to change radically around this time.[27]

All the houses listed above were beautifully detailed, eloquent demonstrations of Mies's craft-based background, feeling for materials, and responses to the work of the gifted architects of the past. He was especially indebted to Schinkel (one of the unquestioned geniuses of the first half of the nineteenth century), whose influence on a far greater architect than Mies, Alexander 'Greek' Thomson,[28] was channelled through the Prussian's *Sammlung Architektonische Entwürfe*, which appeared in 1841–3.[29] Gropius, who had also worked in Behrens's office, organized (1919) an exhibition of architecture considered suitable for the new, republican, post-war era. Mies submitted his pre-war Kröller-Müller designs,[30] but Gropius (by then a convinced believer in starting again from scratch, although his appointments at the *Bauhaus* might suggest his thinking was somewhat inconsistent at that time) refused to accept them because of their clear links to historical precedent.[31]

The result was a partial transformation: although Mies designed the impressive private houses mentioned above, which were still being completed well into the 1920s, he emerged as a radical Modernist, and joined the *Novembergruppe* (directing its architectural division 1921–5). Despite this affiliation, he consistently argued that an association of Modernism with politics could well create major difficulties in the future: his connection with certain groupings after 1918 was eventually to lead to trouble for him, so his position was equivocal, to say the least.[32] Nevertheless, his involvement with the *Novembergruppe* also brought him into contact with other radical bodies, including *Arbeitsrat für Kunst* and *Gläserne Kette*, and produced a series of unrealized projects including *Glass Skyscraper* (1919), and the *Friedrichstraße* skyscraper (1921) published by Taut in *Frühlicht* (early light or dawn).[33] The architect's use of prismatic forms was not just to fit the triangular site, but by placing the glass walls at angles to each other he hoped to obtain a play of reflections: in a later (1922) version with curved plans,[34] the requirements were to obtain sufficient light within the building, to again exploit the play of reflections, and (from the angle of the street) to achieve a massing of the building which he found satisfactory. A study of the proposals today suggests that this last would have failed.

That transformation also involved a bit of self-invention, starting with the addition of an *Umlaut, tréma,* or *diaeresis* to the 'e' of his surname. *Mies* has connotations in German with what is seedy, poor, rotten, lousy, wretched, bad, awful, crummy, and out of sorts. A *Miesmacher* is a defeatist, a grouser, a killjoy, an alarmist, and a *Miesepeter* is a misery-guts, though its cuddly, pussycat (which would be *Miez, Mieze,* or *Miezekatze* in German, with the 'z' pronounced 'ts'), soothing sound in English appealed to Modernist enthusiasts when affectionately referring to the German architect. In 1921 Mies became *Ludwig Miës van der Rohe* (the pretentious *van der* sounds vaguely grand as well as reassuringly Dutch [*von der* would not have been possible because it was associated with ennoblement: also anything German, loosely connected with the old order, would not have gone down well at the time, so the Dutch was safer. Besides, in Dutch, *mies* means 'nasty, ugly, dismal, or vile',[35] so when the *e* is pronounced, a sound something like *mee-ess* results, which has no such associations in either Dutch or German]. *Rohe* [Mies's mother's maiden name], with suggestions of that which is crude, rough, raw, tough, unrefined, might suggest qualities more fashionable when the proletariat basked in the admiration of *avant-garde bourgeois* opinion, but the word also can be connected with that which is unpleasant, indecent, vulgar, coarse, and brutish).[36]

The new Miës van der Rohe then produced a design for a prophetic reinforced-concrete office-building with long horizontal strips of windows, possible because of the use of cantilevers throughout (1922–3): it heralded a change of direction (Erich Mendelsohn was to realize such a design in his *Columbushaus, Potsdamerplatz,* Berlin [1931–2]).[37] Now the predominant effect would be like a pile of sandwiches, an ominous and widely copied

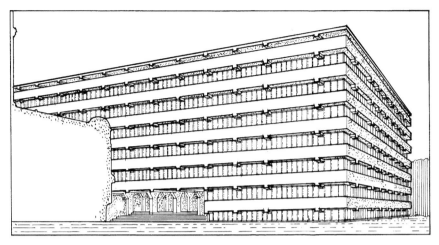

Figure 4.2. *Bürohaus* (office-block) design by Miës van der Rohe (1923), a type that became ubiquitous, to the great detriment of the appearance of countless towns and cities

type for the future, and one that has ignored the predominantly vertical rhythms of countless street-frontages (*see* **Figure 4.2 & Plate 1.2b**). Its creator wrote of it as a 'house of work... of organisation, of clarity, of economy', constructed of concrete, iron, and glass, with bright, wide undivided workrooms (easy to oversee), the 'maximim of effect with the minimum expenditure'. Form Follows Finance. A photomontage (1929) of how a competition-entry by Miës van der Rohe for an office-block on the *Friedrichstraße* would actually have looked in its context exists in the Mies van der Rohe Archive, Museum of Modern Art, New York.[38]

In 1923 there followed the unrealized design for a brick villa influenced by van Doesburg and Mondrian, with configurations of **L**- and **T**-shapes on plan, one of the first instances of walls being disposed according to the principles of *De-Stijl* composition (**Figure 4.3**).[39] With others, Miës formed *Der Ring*, which rapidly became a nationwide organization to reject all historical associations and to prepare the ground for an architecture of the 'new epoch', supposedly based (or to look as though it might be based) on new technology. Mention has already been made of his steel-framed (but looking like brick) monument to Liebknecht and Luxemburg in the *Friedrichsfelde Friedhof* (1926), a work that was not to endear him to the National Socialists.[40] He also exhibited (1923) at a show of *De-Stijl* work in Paris (his Dutch-sounding name would have eased things), made contact with protagonists of Russian Constructivism and Suprematism, and showed work in Berlin and

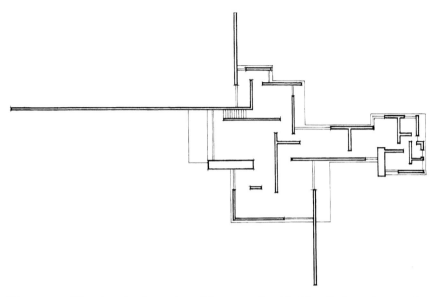

Figure 4.3. Plan (1923) of a projected but unrealized brick villa by Miës van der Rohe showing the configurations disposed according to the principles of *De Stijl*

Weimar. The invitation to exhibit at Weimar came from Gropius, who was clearly mollified by Miës's conversion to the Cause, despite the fact that Miës was still building Muthesian and Schinkelian villas in the Berlin suburbs.[41]

However, there were obvious changes of direction, even in villa-design, as can be seen from the Ryder house Miës and local architect Gerhard Severain designed at No. 20, *Zur schönen Außicht*, Wiesbaden (1923–8): it was Modernist in manner, with a symmetrical front and a 'flat' roof (the first of Miës's houses to have such a feature, but it was later [1980] hipped to enclose more accommodation).[42] Shortly afterwards, Miës designed and built a house (1925–7—destroyed) for Erich and Elisabeth Wolf at *Teichbornstraße*, Guben (now *ul. Piastowska*, Gubin, Poland): of brick, with blocky massing and 'flat' roofs, it clearly owed something to Dutch precedents, not least the *De-Stijl* movement and the precision of the beautifully crafted brickwork (although the expression of lintels and supports over openings was suppressed). The Josef Esters and Hermann Lange houses at Nos. 91 and 93, *Wilhelmshofallee*, Krefeld (1927–30—now museums),[43] were also of brick, again with 'flat' roofs, and Lilly Reich was involved in the design of the interiors.[44] The last (as far as is known) private house designed and realized by Miës in Germany was that for Karl and Martha Lemke at No. 60, *Oberseestraße*, Berlin (1930–3), a single-storey plain brick building with large windows and a 'flat' roof, restored 2000–2, and now a museum.[45]

The *Weißenhofsiedlung,* Stuttgart

It is strange, therefore, that an architect who had acquired his education from a crafts background, who had worked in one of the most progressive and competent architectural offices in Berlin, and who had produced several well-designed and beautifully-made private houses both before and after the 1914–18 war, should so radically have changed direction. The explanation must lie with Miës's assumption that he would be ignored or even ostracized by influential figures in German architecture (especially Gropius, who seems to have wielded considerable clout, and did not hesitate to use it) unless he conformed stylistically to Modernism, adopting 'flat' roofs, plain unadorned unmoulded surfaces, large windows, methods of framed construction, and so on that were becoming *de rigueur* in so-called 'progressive' circles.

It is also possible that, with his surname having unfortunate connotations in German, with his unacademic and craft backgrounds, and his relatively humble origins, he may have been somewhat cowed by the personality of Gropius, the Prussian officer, the well-educated privileged scion of a family of professionally eminent men, the socially well-connected architect who moved in exalted circles. So he had to reinvent himself as a Modernist with a new name, sounding rather grand, but avoiding any suggestion of taint with the old *régime*, and hinting at a Dutch background (Aachen, his birthplace, is not far from the border with The Netherlands).[46] However, in the following decade it became clear that he had ceased to think much of Gropius (whose credentials as an architect have been questioned, not only by Miës van der Rohe, but especially by Philip Johnson), and there are indications he eventually came to despise him.[47]

Miës also became active as a propagandist for the 'New Architecture', and was one of the founders of the magazine *G: Materialen zur Elementaren Gestaltung* (G: materials for elemental form-creation *or* structuring), published 1923–6,[48] which passionately promoted everything 'modern'. He also proved his credentials as an architect of working-class housing with his blocks of Modernist smooth-rendered, moulding-less, 'flat'-roofed apartments (1925–7) in *Afrikanischestraße*, Berlin-Wedding, an exercise in providing accommodation for those on what the Germans call *Existenzminimum* (subsistence level).[49] Thus, by 1923 a reinvented Miës van der Rohe had joined the Modernist Establishment, as proselytizer, practitioner, arbiter of taste, and then, as first vice-president of the *Deutscher Werkbund* from 1926, his was the driving-force behind what was to become a major paradigm for the future of architecture.[50]

Following the demise of a short-lived Expressionist tendency, and Gropius's speech in 1923 at the *Bauhaus* exhibition in Weimar, the *Werkbund* withdrew from the *Arbeitsgemeinschaft für Handwerkskultur* (Association *or* Co-operative for Handicrafts), severed its connection with the crafts lobby, and identified itself with so-called 'functionalism' and the *Neue Sachlichkeit*, concerned primarily with architecture and urban design. Under Miës's influence, the *Werkbund* was taken over by Modernist zealots, notably those (like Hilbersheimer, Adolf Rading, and Hugo Häring) connected with *Der Ring*, who contributed to the *Werkbund* journal, *Die Form*: this exercised a massive influence on the course architecture was to take between 1925 and 1930.[51]

Miës's most successful propaganda coup, however, was the creation of the housing exhibition at Stuttgart, the *Weißenhofsiedlung* (1927),[52] consisting of sixty housing-units in twenty-one buildings, constructed to a layout-plan by Miës, with contributions from sixteen architects (Victor Bourgeois from Belgium; Le Corbusier from France; Behrens, Richard Döcker, Gropius, Hilbersheimer, Miës himself, Poelzig, Rading, Scharoun, Adolf Schneck, Bruno and Max Taut from Germany; Oud and Stam from The Netherlands; and Josef Frank from Austria): with their 'flat' roofs, smooth white plain unmoulded walls, strip-windows, and concrete, steel, and glass construction, the buildings were a foretaste of the 'International Style' to be categorized and promoted by Barr, Hitchcock, and Johnson[53] (**Figures 4.4 & 4.5**).

However, the Stuttgart exhibition attracted opprobrium from several sides: the more extreme 'leftists' regarded it as *bourgeois* aesthetic indulgence; much Württemberg opinion objected to it as not only a threat to craftsmanship and stylistic freedom in terms of architectural design, but as alien, ignoring, and insulting local architects; and there were jokes about the development being an 'Arab Village', a 'Casbah', 'Casablanca in Stuttgart', and so on.[54] So, under Miës and his colleagues, the *Werkbund* had shifted ground from its mission to promote good industrial design and crafts to become a bullying pressure-group promoting the 'New Architecture', i.e., that approved by Miës, Gropius, and their circle: with the *Weißenhofsiedlung*, the image of the cult of International Modernism had been found.

Figure 4.4. Apartment-block by Miës van der Rohe at the *Weißenhofsiedlung*, Stuttgart (1927), showing the realized International Style of white-painted, smooth, rendered, unmoulded walls

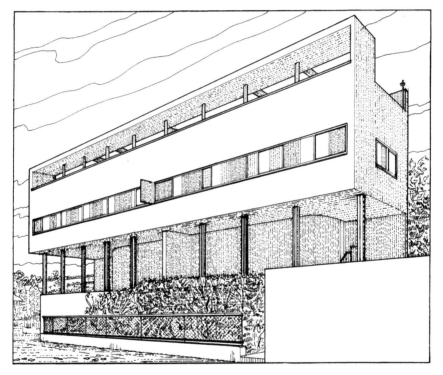

Figure 4.5. *Doppelwohnhaus* (double dwelling-house) by Le Corbusier and A.-A.-P. Jeanneret at the *Weißenhofsiedlung*, Stuttgart (1927)

When Kurt Schwitters visited the block of apartments designed by Miës at the *Die Wohnung* exhibition known as the *Weißenhofsiedlung*, he saw that the method of construction enabled the plan of each apartment to be free from any structural considerations, so partition-walls could be erected wherever they might be desired; but he wondered if this 'freedom' would be a problem for the residents, who might not be quite as mature and free as their own doors. He hoped, sarcastically, that the dwelling would ennoble its inhabitants.[55]

The notion of rearranging spaces around an idea of what life *should be* began to exercise the minds of many architects at the time, including that of Miës, who argued that standardization, while useful as a means, should never be the end of architecture; and in this respect his position differed from those who demanded industrialization and systems-building as an integral part of Modernist theory. Miës's thought embraced the idea of harmony and of creating suitable settings for new modes of living, and in this he was influenced by the writings of Hans Prinzhorn.[56]

One of the great problems was that Germany, bankrupted after 1918, faced a massive housing-shortage: it was argued that, by using technologies such as prefabrication and standardization, cheap accommodation could be provided, but this was not necessarily true. However, industrialization of the building-process, married to a powerful movement to improve urban hygiene, was seen as a means by which the *behaviour* of working-class residents might be altered for the better. Thus industrialized means of building began to be associated with social-engineering, a dangerous turn of events. Some architects (e.g. Fritz Block) went so far as to hold that buildings should be used to correct habits and morals towards what would be regarded as desirable lifestyles:[57] but others (e.g. Adolf Rading), while accepting what was thought to be the necessity of standardization, observed that it was not the job of architects to decide how people should live,[58] and that only arrogance or invincible ignorance could explain attempts to predict or even manufacture destiny.[59]

Miës has supposedly been influenced by several writers, including Siegfried Ebeling,[60] Rudolf Schwarz,[61] Romano Guardini,[62] and, especially, Hans Prinzhorn,[63] as he developed a more independent stance compared with that adopted by Gropius, Hannes Meyer, and others.[64] Through Ebeling, it has been claimed that influences from Nietzsche (such as the supreme importance of art)[65] and Raoul Francé were channelled to Miës; and Schwarz, active in the Roman Catholic youth-movement, emphasized the subordination of rationalization and technology to spiritual matters, querying the widespread belief in technical means as a path towards progress. Indeed, it seems to have been Schwarz who attempted to persuade Miës to distance himself from the purely materialistic apostles of Modernism. Through Guardini, Miës began to appreciate that life should be seen as a Nietzschean balancing-act between chaos and order; yet both chaos and order should be understood, not ignored.[66] Such perceptions were reinforced by Prinzhorn, who insisted upon the essential unity of body and soul, and whose own work drew upon that of Nietzsche, Carl Gustav Carus,[67] and Ludwig Klages.

However, there seems to be nothing in Miës's *work* from that time that suggests any influence whatsoever from Nietzsche (least of all Dionysian ecstasy), and if Ebeling, Guardini, and Prinzhorn managed to get any Dionysian allusions into Miës's architectural thinking, these never became overt in his realized designs. Nietzsche held that art was the most important thing in the world (more so than philosophy), and that art is with us in order that we do not perish from the truth.[68] Philip Johnson also believed that the hierarchy of important things in the world starts with art, 'not looking for truth, or science, or anything'.[69] Miës asserted that architecture was first of all an art: he had no patience with Gropius's insistence on the 'sociological importance of architecture'.[70] Johnson stated that since Gropius 'was not a great designer, he naturally stressed the sociological side',[71] and he also alleged that Miës was 'violently anti-intellectual', with hardly any books on his shelves, and the ones that were there had not been touched for years.[72]

To a certain extent one suspects that, despite perhaps somewhat over-stated claims about the impact of Nietzsche, Prinzhorn, Klages, *et al.*, on his thinking,[73] somewhere deep inside Miës's subconscious lurked the presence of that towering figure, *Doctor Communis* or *Doctor Angelicus*: St Thomas Aquinas, who recognized a kinship between all parts of reality, and sought to correlate all the sciences. In essence, Aquinas's teaching was based on a world ruled by purpose; he distinguished between the supernatural and the preternatural and miraculous; and his writings are suffused with considerations of faith and reason, which he did not perceive as either isolated from each other or confused. His all-embracing, non-compartmental thinking has echoes in Miës's approach, which, as Philip Johnson clearly saw, differed hugely from that of Gropius and his followers.[74] It is that mediaeval religious aspect that has been largely ignored by Modernist commentators, not least Pevsner,[75] who simply discounted it, something which explains his misinterpretation of Voysey and his attitudes towards creative Christian artists such as Dykes Bower[76] and Ninian Comper.[77] In the twenty-first century the power of religion should be obvious, not least in the various manifestations of Islam.[78]

Klages was associated with a group of anti-Modernists opposed to urbanization and industrialization, and concerned with the well-being of the *Geist*, or intellect, and *Seele*, or soul, recognizing that the authentic self lay in the subconscious.[79] Prinzhorn especially deplored the tendency present from around 1900 that emphasized the natural sciences as a means of quantifying and measuring the essence of life, and dismissing the soul. By insisting that humankind was a unity of soul and body and bound to nature in all its vagaries,[80] it is claimed he thereby influenced Miës, who more and more perceived that complex interdependencies were far more important than simplistic slogans (though he was not above issuing those when it suited him).[81] If any of the views of these men did really impinge on Miës, which is doubtful, it is surprising his later work became distressingly arid and ultimately meaningless, unlike his architectural designs before 1914.[82]

Klages was an anti-Semite,[83] and Prinzhorn moved close to National-Socialist positions in the 1930s,[84] despite having earlier been critical of political movements that sought to mould human beings into a prescribed type (as the National Socialists attempted). From *c.*1930 Prinzhorn abandoned the positions adopted in *Leib—Seele—Einheit* (Body—Soul—Unity)[85] as he began to express quite marked sympathies with National-Socialist ideologies: in this he was not alone, and there were plenty who sought to ingratiate themselves with the *régime* which came to power in January 1933. Among them were numerous architects.[86] Miës's own stance in relation to National Socialism deserves to be further investigated.[87]

It is not generally realized that when the *Werkbund* Stuttgart exhibition was first mooted, the architect Bonatz had prepared a plan for it which proposed buildings with pitched roofs, but after ferocious disputes, the Miësian solution won the day. Paul Bonatz[88] (whose *Hauptbahnhof* [main railway-station] at Stuttgart [1911–28], designed with Friedrich Eugen Scholer, was and is regarded as a masterwork,[89] with affinities to Saarinen's handsome railway-terminus in Helsinki [1904–14] and Behrens's celebrated AEG buildings in Berlin [1907–13]) and his colleagues, including Paul Schmitthenner, withdrew in protest. With other architects, including German Bestelmeyer and Paul Schultze-Naumburg, they formed (1928) *Der Block*,[90] a pressure-group to promote an architecture responsive to regional and national conditions, and suited to the tastes and needs of ordinary people, rather than the rigid ideologically-inspired cult imposed upon an unwilling populace by a supposedly 'leftist'-Modernist coterie.[91]

Both Bonatz and Schmitthenner were distinguished architects. The latter was responsible for the fine *Gartenstadt Staaken*, Berlin (1914–17),[92] built to house munitions workers, and designed in a pleasing, eclectic, traditional manner. Bonatz invited him to Stuttgart to teach at the *Technische Hochschule*, where, with the urban planner Heinz Wetzel, the school gained a reputation among German schools of architecture for encouraging sound, traditionally-based building-design, drawing on precedents and eschewing doctrinaire Modernism. Schmitthenner himself was to write several polemical works attacking International Modernism.[93]

Many versions of architectural 'history' hold that Modernism, as exemplified in the *Weißenhofsiedlung*,[94] was the only architecture produced during the Weimar Republic; that it reached heights of elegance with Miës's sparse Barcelona pavilion (1929)[95] (**Figure 4.6**) and his slightly later (and very luxurious) Tugendhat house, Brno (then Czechoslovakia) (1930),[96] which had some similar details; and that it was completely suppressed once the NSDAP came to power in 1933. It might be argued that this is untrue, and seems to be based on the emigration of certain personalities (e.g. Gropius, Hilbersheimer, *et al.*, sometimes erroneously labelled as 'refugees') shortly after the National Socialists gained control of Germany. Some, including Miës, stayed on well into the late 1930s, and many *Bauhäusler* had no obvious qualms about serving autocratic *régimes*. The National Socialists were ambivalent (to put it mildly) concerning architecture, and countless Modernist

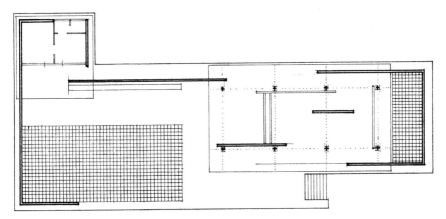

Figure 4.6. Plan of the German pavilion at the International Exposition, Barcelona (1929), by Miës van der Rohe

buildings were erected during the Third Reich, mostly for those housing industrial and technical facilities.

But Modernism was predominant in the design of works associated with transport, notably in the architecture of Herbert Rimpl (**Plate 4.2**).[97] The monthly magazine, *Moderne Bauformen*, published in Stuttgart, featured numerous examples of Modernist design, and did not confine itself geographically either, right up to 1944. That journal noted that there was a plurality of design under National Socialism rather than a rigid adherence to one style, and it published Modern architectural exemplars from countries other than Germany: indeed, *Moderne Bauformen* is an astonishingly rich record of what was really happening in architecture during the 1930s and 1940s, and is a salutary antidote to the bias in many accounts published in English dealing with the period.[98] The position of architecture in the Third Reich was highly complex, and not at all clear-cut. GEHAG (*Gemeinnützige Heimstätten Spar- und Bau-Aktien Gesellschaft*—which might be loosely translated as 'non-profit-making savings and building society', the National-Socialist organization) merely adopted (1935) Bruno Taut's designs for apartments at *Hartmannsweilerweg* 18–24, Berlin-Zehlendorf, in the development known as *Onkel Toms Hütte*; the only alteration was a pitched roof instead of a 'flat' one, which turned out to be a sensible change (**Plate 4.3**).[99]

Uproar over the 1927 exhibition led to greater caution when the *Werkbund* staged its next show (1929), entitled *Wohnung und Werkraum* (dwelling and workplace) in Breslau (now Wrocław, Poland): this time only architects and artists from Silesia exhibited, and work included buildings by Scharoun,

Plate 4.2. *Einflieghalle* (testing-hall) of the former Heinkel aircraft-factory, Oranienburg, Brandenburg (1936–8), designed by Herbert Rimpl and Josef Bernard in impeccably Modern-Movement style

Plate 4.3. Apartment-block at *Hartmannsweilerweg* 18–24, Berlin-Zehlendorf, based on designs by Bruno Taut, but with a pitched roof instead of a flat one. The statue of a German worker on the left does not suggest 'right-wing' public art

Moritz Hadda, Adolf Rading, and Heinrich Lauterbach, much of which was illustrated and described in *Der Baumeister* (the Architect—1929). It nevertheless followed the 'flat'-roofed-plain-white-walls aesthetic favoured earlier.

Disbanded in 1934, the *Deutscher Werkbund* was revived (1947) after the 1939–45 war, largely to promote Modernist ideology and oppose historical reconstruction of wrecked German cities: its motto was *das Einfache und das Gültige* (the simple and the valid); it published polemics, especially a monthly journal, *Werk und Zeit*, from 1952; and for the *Interbau* Exhibition (1957) in Berlin, several *Werkbund* architects designed modern public housing. It also encouraged local and regional initiatives, including the re-establishment of *Bauhaus* ideas at the *Hochschule für Gestaltung*, Ulm (1950), under Max Bill.

The Strange Case of Erich Mendelsohn

Following the disaster of 1914–18, many Germans were fascinated by the Soviet Union as well as by the United States of America. Strong cultural ties were formed between *avant-garde* artists in Weimar Germany and the Soviet Union: the Germans were particularly interested in ideas concerning the reformation of society and in the new art emanating from the East, notably the anti-aesthetic, anti-art, supposedly pro-technology (in that it favoured the use of man-made industrial materials and processes, e.g. welding), leftist movement known as Constructivism, which was promoted in the West, notably at the *Bauhaus*. Although that movement was never clearly defined, Constructivists insisted that architecture was simply the means of expressing a structure created by industrial processes from machine-made parts, with no hint of craftsmanship. They tended to stress utilitarian aspects, especially the function of elements of the building, such as lifts (elevators), services, etc. (*see* **Figures G.1, G.2, & G.3**). Its anti-environmental ethos, jagged overlapping diagonal forms, and deliberate rejection of craftsmanship and *bourgeois* values appealed to later Deconstructivists.[100]

The Soviet embrace of American technology, especially that of mass-production, and its promotion of what it claimed as 'rational' planning, led Germans to see the United States and the Soviet Union as offering complementary exemplars for their own development, a view consolidated by the publication of Henry Ford's autobiography in German in 1923.[101] As Kathleen James pointed out, 'German architects in particular were likely to have dual loyalties',[102] an obvious tendency among *Bauhäusler*, who were to flirt with both the Soviet Union and National-Socialist Germany, though many ended up in the United States for reasons far removed from ethical stances or political convictions.

Erich Mendelsohn, who visited the Soviet Union three times,[103] pointed out the chasm between the supposed 'modernity' admired by the German *avant-garde* and the actual social conditions, skills available, and buildings he saw there. Mendelsohn's discomfort with aspects of Constructivism's formalism (although he seems to have held both El Lissitzky and Tatlin's monument to the Third International in some esteem) was expressed in his book: he doubted if either the Soviet Union or the United States offered ways forward in respect of the absorption of new technology into architecture.[104] In particular, he was concerned that Soviet designers were airily unconcerned with the practicalities of real construction. Mendelsohn's work was interesting in that he transposed certain techniques of Soviet advertising on buildings (to promote the idea of the revolutionary state) to his own commercial architecture (the gigantic SCHOCKEN lettering on the department-stores he designed for that firm was an obvious example).

By the end of the 1920s Mendelsohn was defending what he regarded as the importance of emotional and spiritual values against the swelling tide of extreme anti-Humanist ideas promoted by men like Hannes Meyer, and he saw great dangers in the Soviet approach, in which deeply ingrained Russian mysticism and religiosity were being drowned in the ghastliness of a brutal, ugly, industrial Utopia which was rapidly becoming Dystopia. That so many Germans were adopting positions similar to that taken by Meyer deeply concerned Mendelsohn:[105] he tried to argue that what was needed was a marriage between American technological expertise and traditional Russian spiritual values by which the machine would be mastered and brought into play as a benign instrument for social unity.[106] During his visits to the Soviet Union Mendelsohn had seen numerous mediaeval buildings which impressed him by what he regarded as their orientalism, quite unlike Western Gothic or Romanesque. It is significant too that he, a Jew from East Prussia, described himself sometimes as an 'oriental'.[107]

Of course, there had been much talk of 'spiritual rebirth' and similar matters after Germany's defeat in 1918, notably among the Expressionists and especially in the work of Taut: but the Hannes Meyer emphasis on architecture as a means of industrialized production from which emotion, symbol, meaning, and metaphor had been expunged, rather than as a deeply-felt creative process, appalled Mendelsohn, and he was not alone in his reactions. He perceived the Soviets as more concerned with keeping alight a flame of revolution through force, incessant, mind-numbing propaganda, and dictatorship (rather than bettering the lives of the people). He saw that these preoccupations were crippling Russia, the former colossus.[108] Soviet architects, obsessed by abstractions and by paper-designs that wholly failed to take into account the primitive possibilities of the building industry as it actually existed then, came in for scathing criticism. Indeed, it is clear that Mendelsohn advocated the reform of architecture rather than the embrace of alien economic systems or of dehumanized architectural theory.

It was largely through liberal-minded German Jews (including the Mosses and the Schockens) that Mendelsohn built up his architectural practice. His various sketches, done when serving in the German army during the 1914–18 war, demonstrated his talent for arresting images, created at speed, suggesting a radical new architecture he was soon to realize in numerous buildings. In 1921–2 he proposed an office-building on the *Kemperplatz*, Berlin, featuring the long horizontal bands of window that were to become familiar elements in Modernist work for the next decades. But his masterpiece of 1921–3 was the *Mossehaus* renovation with additions on the corner of *Jerusalemer/ Schutzenstraße*, Berlin, designed in collaboration with Richard Neutra and Rudolf Paul Henning, slotted between the façades of the earlier building (1901–3) designed by Cremer & Wolffenstein. A brilliant solution, it incorporated Mendelsohnian devices which were to become typical,

Plate 4.4 Offices of Rudolf Mosse, corner of *Jerusalemer/Schutzenstraße*, Berlin, showing Mendelsohn's treatment of the corner (1921–3), slotted into the earlier building (1901–3) by Cremer & Wolffenstein. Neutra and Henning were also involved in the design of the corner

including the sweeping curved bands of window around the corner and the curving canopy over the corner entrance, giving the impression of a cornice that had slipped down the front (**Plate 4.4**). The Cremer/Wolffenstein design had suffered during the Spartacist revolt against the Republican government (the revolutionaries had occupied the building), and the new work by Mendelsohn cleverly suggested Modernism successfully married to tradition.

Mendelsohn had other agenda, however: he claimed that, just as mediaeval humankind needed the verticals of the cathedrals to find God above, so moderns could only find equilibrium in the 'tension-free horizontal'.[109] He also noted that the elimination of verticals and the stretching out of horizontals was how passengers travelling at high speeds in automobiles perceived the buildings they drove past, so Modern architecture should be an expression of speed. Like others, he saw the velocity of modern transport as providing catalysts for architectural design, and his own staff likened the additions to the *Mossehaus* to the docking of the Cunard Atlantic liner *Mauretania* in Berlin.[110] To Mendelsohn, a building was not an 'indifferent spectator' of the tides of traffic: his design for the curved corners responded to 'accelerated tendency to speed', and the use of materials produced an elegant, sophisticated work that responded well to the earlier fabric. Mendelsohn's store for the furriers, C.A. Herpich Söhne, *Leipzigerstraße*, Berlin (1924–5), had a façade of travertine, bronze, and glass (with predominantly horizontal bands of fenestration set over a ground floor almost entirely glazed); even so, the symmetrical elevation was terminated at either end by four-storey projections, each featuring curved glass at each of the outer corners, thereby balancing the horizontal and the vertical (**Plate 4.5**).

Some saw dangers in too much horizontal emphasis. Goodhart-Rendel, for example, wrote that in 'certain recent architecture abroad horizontality has been exaggerated, so as to produce buildings that can be described according to taste either as noble streamline compositions or as imitation railway accidents made of piled-up Pullman cars'.[111] Once the novelty had worn off, however, he described this 'exaggeration' as having 'descended into the bargain basement of novelties become fly-blown'.[112] There are exceptions, however, including Joseph Emberton's former Simpson's, at 203–6 Piccadilly, London (1935–6), where excellent materials, a welded-steel structure designed by Felix Samuely (who arrived in England in 1933), and curved glazing on the shopfront by E. Pollard & Co., combined in an elegant embrace of the new idiom that owed a huge amount to the work of Mendelsohn rather than to Gropius, Miës, the *Bauhäusler*, or any of the other denizens of the accepted Modernist Pantheon (**Plate 4.6**). The designs for the Herpich store had been opposed by Ludwig Hoffmann, *Stadtsbaurat* (director of planning and construction) of Berlin (1896–1924). Hoffmann and Peter Dybwad had collaborated as architects of the *Reichsgerichtsgebäude*

Plate 4.5. Store for the furriers, C.A. Herpich Söhne, *Leipzigerstraße*, Berlin (1924–5), by Mendelsohn, demonstrating how the horizontals are contained within verticals, thereby balancing the façade

(supreme-court building) in Leipzig (1885–95), and later worked with Messel on the design of the Pergamon museum, Berlin (1909–30), supervising its construction after Messel's death. Hoffmann was no mean architect, and was responsible for several very impressive buildings.

Arguments over the Herpich designs rumbled on, as Hoffmann believed the precedent of Alfred Messel's *Warenhaus Wertheim* building (1897–1904), with its series of verticals at the corner of *Leipzigerplatz* and *Leipzigerstraße*, Berlin (**Plate 4.7**),[113] should be followed, rather than the alien horizontals in Mendelsohn's designs. The *Wertheim* department-store buildings embraced many historical references, including late Gothic, and the top-lit hall which

Plate 4.6. The former Simpson's store, 203–6 Piccadilly, London (1935–6), by Joseph Emberton. Although the horizontals are contained, they are less successfully handled than in Mendelsohn's Herpich store, Berlin, of a decade earlier

was entered from the *Leipzigerstraße*, and presided over by an impressive bronze statue (1896) of *Die Arbeit* (work) by Ludwig Manzel,[114] owed a considerable debt to the splendid late-fourteenth-century *Rathaus* (town hall), Thorn (now *Ratusz*, Toruń, Poland):[115] commenced under the aegis of Konrad von Wallenrode, Grand Master (1391–3) of the Teutonic Order, it was a building that also fascinated Schinkel.[116]

However, twenty-three experts were called in and invited to sign a petition opposing the redesigning of the Herpich façade as a series of verticals: only one refused to sign, and that was Werner Hegemann, who clearly saw the dangers to urban design should the horizontal genie be approved. Indeed, the controversies over the design of the Herpich building prompted more support for *Neues Bauen*, and were certainly catalysts in the formation of the pressure-group known as *Der Ring*: this was vociferous in its backing for Modernism, and attacked the positions adopted by Hoffmann and his allies.

Plate 4.7. *Warenhaus Wertheim* at the corner of *Leipzigerplatz* and *Leipzigerstraße*, Berlin (1897–1904), designed by Alfred Messel

When Hoffmann was succeeded (1926) in his official post by the 'leftist' (and member of *Der Ring*) Martin Wagner (who had no interest in aesthetics, and saw himself as a kind of manager of a large industry), the balance of power shifted towards favouring the Modern Movement, and work by the older generation of German architects was dismissed or ignored. It was a taste of things to come.

There was another factor in this. The flagship *Warenhaus Wertheim*, by one of the *Kaiserreich*'s greatest architects, was extravagantly praised by numerous personalities, including the future Chancellor Gustav Stresemann and the Socialist leader Wilhelm Liebknecht[117] (who had written a sympathetic study of the British reformer and Socialist Robert Owen):[118] but the fact that bulk-purchasing and supply-chain mechanisms of department-stores enabled firms like Wertheim to undercut conventional retailers by as much as 30 per cent aroused considerable debate (not least one in the *Reichstag* itself in 1899), protest, and resentment. Department-stores, called by some 'temples of consumption', were perceived as un-German imports, for Paris had had such places some forty years earlier: that many (e.g. Schocken, Tietz, Wertheim) were owned by Jews also tended to fuel nascent anti-Semitism (National-Socialist propaganda frequently turned its venom on department-stores). However, the celebrated *Warenhaus Wertheim* designed by Messel was (architecturally) convincingly German, even alluding to the Teutonic Knights. Given the convoluted anxieties of the relatively new German Empire under the House of Hohenzollern (especially as the German Kaiser, Wilhelm II, was erratic and dangerously undiplomatic in his pronouncements),[119] it might be regarded as a symbol of successful Jewish assimilation.

Mendelsohn's *Columbushaus* (1931–2), however, erected on a site between *Bellevuestraße* and *Friedrich-Ebertstraße*, on *Potsdamerplatz*, was a ten-storey block of aggressive horizontals, as disruptive an element as could be imagined within the established grain of the urban fabric, and an obvious antecedent of countless exemplars erected in thousands of cities after 1945 (**Plate 4.8 and** *see* **Plate 1.2***b*). With the Rudolf Petersdorff store, at the corner of *Ohlauerstraße* (now *Oławska*) and *Schuhbrückstraße* (now *Szewska*), Breslau (1927–8—*now* Wrocław), Mendelsohn not only eroded the barrier between the pavement and the interior of the shop by means of plate-glass, but used horizontal strips of windows, and featured one of his favourite motifs, the rounded cantilevered glazed element at the corner (**Plate 4.9**). He was also

Plate 4.8. *Potsdamerplatz* with Mendelsohn's *Columbushaus* (1931–2), showing the disruptive effect of aggressive horizontal bands of windows. It was nevertheless the antecedent of countless later exemplars erected in thousands of towns and cities after 1945

Plate 4.9. *Kaufhaus* (department-store) Rudolf Petersdorff (1927–8), at the corner of *Schuhbrücke* (now *ulica Szewska*) and *Ohlauerstraße* (now *ulica Oławska*), Breslau (now Wrocław), by Mendelsohn, showing one of his favourite motifs, the rounded, cantilevered, glazed element at the corner

to employ curved glazed elements in other buildings, notably to contain stair-cases, as at the Schocken store, Stuttgart (1926–8), where elements of the design can be traced back to his wartime sketches, and huge letters spelling SCHOCKEN were set above the shopfront on the *Eberthardstraße* façade (**Plate 4.10**).

Of course, elegantly designed curved glazed elements also had been features of the Gropius/Meyer model factory at the *Werkbund* exhibition, Cologne (1914), but Mendelsohn employed them more dynamically. Adver-tising in the form of vertical signage on a radio-mast was added to the mix in Mendelsohn's Rudolf Mosse pavilion for the International Press exhibition (*PRESSA*), Cologne (1928), a brave attempt, organized under the aegis of the Mayor of Cologne, Konrad Adenauer, to show that Germany was once more a respectable part of the international community (**Plate 4.11**). Certain aspects of the pavilion design, especially the radio-mast and signage, were clearly influenced by Soviet architecture, but the structure, largely of steel

Plate 4.10. Schocken department-store, *Eberhardstraße* 28, Stuttgart (1926–8), by Mendelsohn

and glass, heralded a new kind of modernity, closely allied with modern technology, communications, advertising, and minimalist treatment, stripped of ornament, and with constructional elements as thin and elegant as could be possible, not least the spectacular cantilevers. Is it too fanciful to see Mendelsohn's Schocken stores and other works he designed in his stream-lined, horizontal manner as some sort of statement of apartness, the antithesis of the earlier 'assimilationist monumentality'[120] of the *Warenhaus Wertheim*? For, after all, he, like Salman Schocken, became a Zionist, and described himself as an outsider too.[121]

A couple of years earlier, when the *Werkbund* exhibition (originally called *Die Wohnung* [the dwelling]) was being planned for Stuttgart, Mendelsohn had refused an invitation to contribute a design for the *Weißenhofsiedlung*,[122] partly, it seems, because he did not trust Miës van der Rohe.[123] Richard Döcker (who was to become site manager for the exhibition) urged him to change his mind, but to no avail. However, Mendelsohn visited the exhibition,

Plate 4.11. Rudolf Mosse pavilion, International Press exhibition (*PRESSA*), Cologne, by Mendelsohn, 1928

probably on two occasions, and later was critical of Le Corbusier and Jeanneret's contribution (*see* **Figure 4.5**), observing that it had greatly exceeded the budget allowed for it, and finding it too arty for comfort. Certainly, the *Weißenhofsiedlung* buildings, with their thin, white surfaces (mostly smooth-painted rendering), horizontal fenestration, and 'flat' roofs, created the image that was to be enshrined as the 'International Style' a few years later by Hitchcock and Johnson,[124] and looked rather more insubstantial than Mendelsohn's robust, monumental, forceful, unashamedly commercial, and aggressively modern Schocken store being erected at the same time down in the city (*see* **Plate 4.10**).

There were those who could see that there were links between the two. Under the pseudonym Albert Sigrist, the architect and Communist Alexander Schwab published a book on the so-called 'New Building' in which he expressed grave doubts. To him, it was Janus-faced, both *bourgeois* and proletarian, Capitalist and Socialist, perhaps even authoritarian and supposedly democratic; but it was probably bogus because of this, and it was certainly not individualistic.[125] Mendelsohn's work, according to Schwab, straddled just about every aspect of those camps: he had worked for the Soviets, his clients included the Mosse dynasty, and he had designed buildings for the Schockens. In short, Schwab was one of the first to sense the shallow bases on which International Modernism was constructed, as well as its totalitarian nature masquerading as something else.[126]

However, the architect Bonatz had likened the *Weißenhofsiedlung* to a suburb of Jerusalem, and the prevailing architectural style of the exhibition was denounced by others as un-German and Bolshevist.[127] The dangers to Mendelsohn were further emphasized by opposition to department-stores, which were seen as 'internationalist' and a problem because most of them were owned by Jews.[128] However, it did not go unnoticed by enthusiasts of either so-called 'right' or 'left' that department-stores such as those bearing the Schocken name in very large *sans-serif* letters and the *Weißenhofsiedlung* exhibition were the results of close cooperation between German architects, designers, industrialists, managers, manufacturers, merchants, and workers: they were born of the same economic system and the same theories concerning 'rational' building.[129]

Mendelsohn's influence in the realm of private houses was limited: his own dwelling, a design in the *Weißenhof* aesthetic, called *Villa am Rupenhorn*, overlooking the Havel (1927–30), near Berlin, was luxurious, with much up-to-date gadgetry (like some of Miës's work, it had picture-windows that could be lowered into the basement), but less spatially adventurous than Miës's almost contemporary Tugendhat house, Brno. With his Herpich store in Berlin (1924–8), Schocken stores in Nuremberg (1925–6), Stuttgart (1926–8), and Chemnitz (1928–30—which was built on the *Brückenstraße* and had a long curved façade with several storeys of strip-windows across it [**Plate 4.12**]), Rudolf Petersdorff store, Breslau (1927–8), Universum cinema, Berlin (1926–8), Rudolf Mosse pavilion at the *PRESSA* exhibition, Cologne (1928), and *Columbushaus*, Berlin (1931–2), Mendelsohn had a huge impact on the design of offices, department-stores, cinemas, and other building-types promoted through lavish exhibitions (e.g. that of 1928 at the Neumann-Nierendorf gallery, Berlin) and handsome publications that made his *oeuvre* widely known.[130]

Hegemann became one of Mendelsohn's most enthusiastic supporters, having previously distanced himself, and by the early 1930s the German architect was being lauded as one of the most important prophets of Modern architecture. His designs certainly had a profound influence on British

Plate 4.12. Schocken department-store, *Brückenstraße*, Chemnitz (1928–30), by Mendelsohn

architecture in particular (the Berlei factory, Slough, Buckinghamshire, by O.R. Salvisberg, Sir John Brown, & A.E. Henson [1937—demolished];[131] Stockleigh Hall, Prince Albert Road, Regent's Park, London [1936–7], by A.F. B. Anderson and Robert Atkinson; Ibex House, Minories, London [1935–7], by Fuller, Hall, & Foulsham; and numerous cinemas, especially the series of *Odeons* designed for Oscar Deutsch by Harry Weedon, J.C. Clavering, and R.A. Bullivant. The *Odeon* at Scarborough, Yorkshire [1935–6], was an obvious exemplar [**Plate 4.13**]).[132]

Of all the German architects working in the 1920s and 1930s, Mendelsohn was, at the time, one of the most celebrated and successful. It is hard to see why he tended to be undervalued after 1933, and difficult to avoid the suspicion that anti-Semitism *outside* Germany had at the very least something to do with it. In 1932 he published a monograph on his own house, the *Villa am Rupenhorn*, hoping to attract commissions (the text was published in English, French, and German to attract as wide a readership as possible),[133] but reviews were muted, and some were hostile. Because it was a luxurious villa for one family, the design was attacked on ideological grounds, and

Plate 4.13. The former Odeon cinema, Scarborough, Yorkshire, designed by Cecil Clavering (1935–6) for Harry Weedon's office, heavily influenced by the work of Mendelsohn

Hegemann was particularly scathing about its lavishness, even sneering at it for its supposed descent from the luxuriousness of the *Kaiserreich*, a symptom of *Wilhelminismus*.[134] Mies's Tugendhat house at Brno was also damned for its extravagance and stratospheric costs, partly because it was irrelevant to the needs of the masses (and completed during a time of catastrophic economic collapse that ruined millions of ordinary people), but the fact that the Tugendhats were Jewish also proved to be a convenient weapon in anathematizing it.[135]

With growing anti-Semitism in Germany, Mendelsohn's position became threatened, and the National-Socialists' use of propaganda, aggressive advertising, and other modern techniques began to unnerve thinking people, who became uneasy about their earlier eagerness to embrace mass-culture as an essential element of fashionable Modernism. As *Neues Bauen* became transformed into the 'International Style', a shift prompted by the work of Barr, Hitchcock, and Johnson (*see* pp. 154ff.), Mendelsohn delivered a speech in Zürich in 1932[136] in which, among other things, he insisted that architecture once more spoke a basic language which the whole world understood: a statement that at the very least was questionable. The speech was published,[137] but Hegemann's response[138] was that it was naïve, ignored political and economic realities, and, by advocating a vague kind of inter-nationalism in cultural matters, cut across the views of those who saw the value of local, regional, and national styles in architecture, not least in coun-tries with which Hegemann had close ties, such as the USA and Britain. And of course, there was a growing reaction to Internationalism in Germany itself, where many publications began to laud vernacular architecture as well as other traditions that had been ignored or stifled by Modernism.[139]

After Hitler became Chancellor in January 1933, Mendelsohn, like many Jews, wholly underestimated the threat posed by National Socialism. He was not invited to participate in the 1933 *Reichsbank* competition, not because he was a celebrated Modernist, but because he was a Jew. (Miës *was* invited, and became one of the six finalists, at about the same time as his certificate of 'racial purity' was issued by the National-Socialist office of racial research.[140]) Mendelsohn soon realized that his own prospects for further work in Germany had evaporated, and two months after Hitler came to power, he left his native land for good. Five months later he was expelled from the Union of German Architects, and excluded from the Prussian Academy of Arts (a body from which Miës did not resign until 1937).[141]

Following an invitation from the RIBA, Mendelsohn travelled to London, where he formed a partnership (1933–6) with Serge Chermayeff: three buildings resulted (Shrub's Wood, a large house near Chalfont St Peter, Buckinghamshire [1933–5], the Cohen house, 64 Old Church Street, Chelsea [1935–6], and the De La Warr Pavilion, Bexhill-on-Sea, Sussex [1934–5—with impressive cantilevers and a curved glazed element containing the stair]) (**Plate 4.14**).[142] The Bexhill building rather turns its back on the street behind it, and displays the endemic Modernist problem of failure to respond with sensitivity to established context. One of the most interesting derivatives of the Bexhill job was the Rothesay Pavilion, Isle of Bute (1936–8), by the Ayr firm of J. & J.A. Carrick, 'perhaps the closest Scottish architecture came to the International Style'.[143]

Plate 4.14. The De La Warr Pavilion, Bexhill-on-Sea, front facing the sea

Mendelsohn's Zionist sympathies and his friendship with Chaim Weizmann (later [1948] first president of the provisional government of Israel, and in 1949 President of Israel) led to a commission to design a villa at Rehevot, near Tel Aviv, in what was then the British mandate of Palestine. His former client, Salman Schocken, who had also been obliged to leave Germany, and had settled in Palestine, managed to obtain several big commissions for the architect. But climatic, cultural, and physical influences greatly affected Mendelsohn's work, and there is virtually nothing of the character of his more celebrated buildings in Germany after the Bexhill Pavilion. Mendelsohn himself left Britain for Palestine in 1939, but when war broke out and commissions began to dry up, an invitation to the USA to teach in 1941 was all the more welcome, not least because of the threats posed by German forces in North Africa. Schocken also left for the USA around the same time.

Mendelsohn found that his German work was no longer regarded in high esteem in the United States. Much of his work there was for Jewish clients, including several synagogues and community centres, but the adulation accorded to Gropius, Miës, and the *Bauhäusler* put him in the shade, especially as Johnson had National-Socialist sympathies at that time as well as anti-Semitic tendencies.[144] Matters cannot have been helped when Mendelsohn put down the telephone on Johnson, who was asking him about his attitudes to Modernism during a visit to Germany in 1930.[145] Thereafter, Johnson marginalized Mendelsohn, whose expressionistic sculptural buildings did not sit comfortably with Barr and Johnson's preconceptions. The Americans rigorously excluded anything which did not conform to their idea of what the 'International Style' *ought* to be:[146] Russian Constructivists, the Dutch *De-Stijl* groupings, and German Expressionists were all omitted, as was noted at the fiftieth anniversary of the MoMA exhibition (1932) held at the Harvard Graduate School of Design in 1982 (Tom Wolfe compared that gathering with a 'convention of aging nudists').[147]

Barr, Hitchcock, and Johnson had sought to emphasize the aesthetic bases of Modern architecture rather than so-called 'functionalism'. Looking for a uniform image drawn from a narrow stylistic range of exemplars that would provide the model for *all* new architecture, they deliberately suppressed the stylistic diversity that actually existed in Europe.[148] In particular, they disapproved of those aspects of what was called 'dynamic functionalism' that included the curvilinear forms Mendelsohn so often employed, in favour of rigid rectangular boxes of which Miës was to become the most influential protagonist. For example, Thilo Schoder, a prolific and successful architect, who had been a pupil of van de Velde in Weimar, and whose work included the celebrated *Villa Stroß* (1923–5—a building much influenced by Mendelsohn [**Plate 4.15**]), *Husova 64*, Liberec (*formerly* Reichenberg),[149] and housing for the garden-city, Hermsdorf, Thuringia (**Plate 4.16**), has been largely ignored by Western commentators: their selective accounts of Modernism acknowledge only a favoured few, thanks to the early bias of Barr, Hitchcock, and Johnson. When the National Socialists came to power, Schoder emigrated to Norway.

In 1932 Barr had claimed the MoMA exhibition was an 'assertion that the confusion of the past 40 years, or rather the past century, may shortly

Plate 4.15. *Villa Stroß, Husova 64*, Liberec (*formerly* Reichenberg), now Czech Republic, of 1923–5, by Thilo Schoder

Plate 4.16. Housing in the garden-city of Hermsdorf, Thuringia, Germany (1925), by Thilo Schoder

come to an end',[150] and indeed that was the outcome he and Johnson had intended. Johnson admitted in 1982 that he and Barr were 'narrow' in their judgements, and had 'decided to sweep everything under the rug in order to make an effect'.[151] And they certainly did just that: the fact that in 1982 there was a conference of 'a stellar assortment of historians, critics, and architects' to 'celebrate' and discuss the 'nature' of an exhibition held half a century previously was testimony to its global influence.[152] The irony was that in 1982, in the very place where Gropius, Breuer, and *Bauhaus* principles had been replanted from Germany, the promise of that International Style and the wholesale rejection of the past were beginning to be recognized as questionable, and what Venturi called in 1966 'complexity and contradiction' were contributing to the dismantling of the Modern Movement's underlying basic assumptions. However, Venturi made it clear that new architecture should evolve out of Modernism, for architects and theorists who rejected all Modernism were following the 'excessive zeal' of the early Modernists who wanted to obliterate the past.[153] Mumford had protested about the 'restrictive definition'[154] of Modernism formulated as a result of the 1932 exhibition and the Hitchcock/Johnson book,[155] and R.A.M. Stern has said that Modern architecture is an inclusive term for something which has a single trunk, but many branches.[156] That is undoubtedly true.

Some of Mendelsohn's later writings convey his distress at perceiving himself increasingly cold-shouldered by promoters of 'The International Style', part of a movement of which he himself had been a founder. There can be little doubt that anti-Semitism was a contributing factor, not least in the attitudes of his non-Jewish former fellow-countrymen, but as he had neither exhibited at the *Weißenhofsiedlung* nor joined CIAM (*see* Select Glossary), he was refused membership of the Modern Architectural Research (MARS) Group (*see* Select Glossary) in London, a fact ingenuously excused by Wells Coates.[157] Gropius's attitude to Mendelsohn appears to have been less than friendly during their time in England. Gropius (who, like other *Bauhäusler*,[158] is recorded as having anti-Semitic views) had in 1934 received a communication from P. Morton Shand[159] questioning the inclusion of work by Mendelsohn in a London exhibition. One suspects that jealousy of Mendelsohn's phenomenal success in Weimar Germany combined with religious/racial prejudice (anti-Semitism was especially widespread in the 1930s, not only in Germany) in a toxic mix. Neither Gropius nor Miës opposed (in public at least)[160] the National-Socialist *régime*, and attempted to remain in Germany to work there until better offers reached them. Gropius was clearly a lesser architect than either Mendelsohn or Miës.[161] It was Miës who was to be in the vanguard of the 'International Style' after 1945: Mendelsohn's achievements became obscured, and as a true pioneer of Modernism he was eclipsed by the dogmatic (and ultimately sclerotic) certainties of International Modernism and some of its protagonists, notably Giedion, who referred (inaccurately) to 'concrete towers as flaccid as jellyfish' in a swipe at the Einstein observatory, Potsdam.[162]

Miës was to insist on architectural minimalism, summed up by the aphorism 'less is more'. Yet, when we consider the remark by Daniel Moynihan that ours 'is an age of great simplifiers', we must take into account the view of Jacob Burckhardt, who sagely observed that the 'essence of tyranny' is the 'denial of complexity'.[163] Given that in the late eighteenth century a multiplicity of styles in garden *fabriques* was seen as indicative of open-mindedness and enlightened views,[164] the rigid geometries of Miës and his disciples might be perceived as tyrannies that would brook no deviation: they gelled into what became known as the International Style.[165] Eventually, however, 'less' became not 'more', but a crashing 'bore',[166] as noted by Robert Venturi, who celebrated the messy vitality of ordinary, everyday familiar images, and a wide range of historical exemplars ignored by doctrinaire Modernists.[167]

Later History of the *Bauhaus* at Dessau & Berlin

The new director of the *Bauhaus* had quite a task on his hands, for he had to cleanse the establishment of its political taints (though he himself had well-documented 'form', associated with various 'left-wing' organizations, and his monument for Liebknecht and Luxemburg was unlikely to have been forgotten). 'Leftist' students opposed the appointment, regarding Miës as a 'formalist' (a chilling label that led to many 'purges', 'liquidations', or disgraces in the USSR during the 1930s): he was also suspect because he designed expensive houses for rich clients (many Jewish too) rather than affordable mass-housing for the 'workers' (though he had, in fact, produced designs for this building-type, erected in *Afrikanischestraße*, Berlin-Wedding). There were noisy meetings and near-riots, resulting in the police having to be called in, the institution cleared and closed, and new strategies evolved.[168]

Every student was interviewed by the director and informed that he or she would be expelled unless they obeyed the rules to be set down, which included non-involvement in political activities of any sort, satisfactory attendance of courses, not to waste time sitting for extended times in the canteen, to dress decently, and to behave in a dignified manner when out in town.[169] Some students refused to accept these conditions, and left the *Bauhaus* altogether. Miës gave even more emphasis to architectural training, and the workshops began to suffer, producing less and finally running out of steam. Hannes Meyer was to write that, horror of horrors, children of the 'upper classes' and of the dreaded '*bourgeoisie*' were admitted as students: 'exclusive' furniture was designed and then made from 'exclusive' (i.e. expensive) materials.[170]

Miës amalgamated the furniture, metal, and mural-painting workshops into one department of interior design, later (1932) combined with the hitherto successful weaving workshop under the overall directorship of his lover, Lilly Reich; she had long been a member of the *Werkbund* and had collaborated with Miës on such projects as the German pavilion for the Barcelona world exposition (1929), and the villa (1928–30) for Fritz and Grete Tugendhat (*née* Löw-Beer) outside Brno, then Czechoslovakia. The Tugendhats came of very distinguished German-Jewish families, which cannot have endeared Miës (or his architecture) to the National Socialists, then growing in strength in Anhalt: Meyer's dig at him may have referred obliquely to commissions such as that for the Tugendhats. The director demanded a ferocious work-ethic, and brought back to architectural studies something of the aesthetic awareness that had been submerged under Meyer. Klee left to take up an appointment in Düsseldorf (1931–3). Of the old guard only Kandinsky remained, although, since fine-art teaching had virtually ceased, he had little to do. National Socialism gained control of Dessau in 1931, and the *Bauhaus* came under fire.

Bolshevist tendencies had caused enormous damage. The 'flat' roofs of the *Bauhaus*, the Törten estate, and Miës's work (including the *Weißenhofsiedlung* and the Tugendhat villa) were linked with 'orientalism', and therefore with Jewishness (a connection strengthened by some of Miës's wealthy clients). Jewishness was also associated with Bolshevism (not least because Karl Marx had been Jewish). So, by a process of associationism and osmosis, spiced with simplistic and warped thinking, to certain minds the *Bauhaus* and the Modernism it peddled must be Jewish, Bolshevist, and non-German. Hitler himself does not appear to have thought that the *Bauhaus* had anything to do with a Jewish plot: in architecture, Hitler never came down emphatically for or against a blanket ban on 'functional' buildings at all.[171] The architect Julius Schulte-Frohlinde, however, declared that the *Neue Sachlichkeit* had contaminated architecture, and was indicative of a soulless international fashion invented by Jews and Marxists.[172] National-Socialist propaganda built up much support through an hysterical campaign equating Jewishness and Bolshevism, and that certainly had an effect on perceptions of architecture.

The Dessau authorities rescinded all grants to the *Bauhaus* and cut short staff contracts in 1932. National-Socialist thugs moved into the *Bauhaus* buildings, smashed the windows, and hurled furnishings and anything else they could find out of the gaping holes. The window- and -door-openings were blocked up, and so the *Bauhaus* remained, because the post-1945 East-German Communist line was that the teachings of that establishment had led to the 'destruction of architecture', that the courses taught had been designed for a 'capitalist' economy, and that the art taught was 'formalist': claims that only so-called 'right-wing' (a questionable label anyway, given the make-up of the bully-boys of National Socialism) movements were responsible for attacks on the *Bauhaus* are unconvincing: indeed, they are untrue.

Miës had ensured that all rights to *Bauhaus* products were retained by the school, and had not become the property of the city of Dessau. He rented a disused factory in *Birkbuschstraße* in the Berlin district of Steglitz,

and reopened the *Bauhaus* as a private establishment to be funded by
income from patents, fees from students, and support from sympathetic
individuals. It was a vain hope, for Hitler and the National Socialists came
to national power in January 1933, and a teaching institution associated with
'Jewish-Marxist' notions of art was an obvious target.[173] In April 1933 the
building was raided, and anyone without identity papers was taken away,
but many, including Miës, still hoped for a *rapprochement* with the new
régime.[174] Four months afterwards, the National Socialists indicated that
the *Bauhaus* might continue, provided Hilbersheimer, as a Social Democrat,
and Kandinsky, as a 'danger' with links to the USSR, were sacked.[175] Eugen
Hönig, President (1933–5) of the *Reichskammer der bildenden Künste* (*RdbK*),
a section of the *Reichskulturkammer* (*RKK*—the National-Socialist Reich
Culture Chamber, founded 1933), actually attempted to preserve something of the *Bauhaus* ethos.[176] However, this offer arrived after Miës,
Kandinsky, and the faculty had decided to close the place down: as a statement dated August 1933 from Miës explained, the reason was the 'difficult
economic situation' of the school. The National-Socialist Government did
not close down the *Bauhaus* (in fact, it was prepared to let it continue provided certain conditions were met): the decision was that of Miës and his
colleagues.[177]

Nor did Miës either encourage emigration or himself leave Germany: on
the contrary, he and many other *Bauhäusler* sought accommodation with
National Socialism.[178] Modernists like Miës hoped their 'progressive' ideas
would be eagerly accepted by the revolutionary New Order (and it must be
emphasized that the National Socialists were not 'conservative', 'right-wing',
'traditionalists' or any of those labels: their agenda were unquestionably
revolutionary).[179] So, like Gropius, Miës had no hesitation in joining the
appropriate section of the *RKK*,[180] the central and very powerful organization
responsible for the control and direction of German arts, embracing almost
the entire artistic life of the nation, including music and architecture.[181]
Both men submitted designs to the early architectural competitions organized
by the National Socialists. Miës himself was invited by the Party authorities
to enter the competition to design the German pavilion for the 1935 Brussels
Exposition Universelle et Internationale: sketches exist, demonstrating that the
very plan of the pavilion was a deconstructed Swastika (a motif that recurred
on the projecting walls and on the flags, although the detailed designs do not
appear to have survived the war) suggesting Miës was attempting to accommodate the taste of leading National Socialists.[182] Earlier (1933), he had also

submitted designs for the important *Reichsbank* architectural competition,[183] and there is plenty of evidence that he endeavoured to come to terms with the political realities of the times so that he could remain in Germany and practise architecture.[184]

For example, Miës signed (June 1933) a document supporting Hitler that had been circulated by Schultze-Naumburg, and joined the *Reichsluftschutzbund* in 1934, a National-Socialist organization for air-defence, and also the *National-Sozialistische Volkswohlfahrt* (*NSV*), devoted to the needs of the poor.[185] It is clear that Miës perceived the ambiguities of the National-Socialist architectural agenda as offering possibilities for him to continue his career in Germany.[186] Not knowing other languages would have made emigration difficult for him in any case, and to have to start again elsewhere would have been problematic, so it is perfectly understandable that he would have wanted to stay in the Fatherland.[187] After all, the National Socialists accepted Modernism for industrial architecture and motorway service stations (where ideological stances did not matter very much [*see* **Plates 4.2, 4.18–20**]),[188] and Miës's grasp of simplified Classicism, in which he had himself excelled in the earlier years of his career, and in which he had been influenced by his work with Behrens (*see* **Figures 4.1a & b**), could have ensured his future,[189] certainly in respect of the ambitious rebuilding of central Berlin desired by Hitler. The plans for this were overseen by Speer.[190] Challenged about working for the National Socialists and Goering's patronage, Miës declared this did not matter, for, after all, great artists such as Michelangelo, not noted for their religious convictions, had worked for the Pope.[191] Philip Johnson saw things very clearly in 1973: 'Nazis, schmatzis, ... Mies would have built for anyone'.[192]

One of the organizations active at that time, founded by Alfred Rosenberg in 1928 as the *Nationalsozialistische Gesellschaft für deutsche Kunst* (National-Socialist Society for German Culture), but renamed the more aggressive *Kampfbund für deutsche Kultur* (Fighting-League for German Culture, usually shortened to *KfdK*), was particularly effective for its bullying tactics and imposing its will in artistic matters. At a meeting of the *KfdK* in 1933, Christian Mergenthaler, newly appointed Minister of Culture and Education in Württemberg, stated that 'the revolution' (meaning the National-Socialist revolution) was 'above all cultural', and that there would be no freedom for anyone who would 'weaken and destroy' German art: throughout Germany intimidation, violence, and public ridicule were employed to enforce conformity with what might be acceptable to the new *régime*.[193]

It seemed for a time, however, that the National-Socialist German Students' Association (*Nationalsozialistische Deutsche Studentenbund* [*NSDStB*]) would be opposed to the racist interpretations of artistic nationalism as held by the *KfdK*: Miës and other leading figures from the Berlin cultural scene were invited to attend a rally in June 1933 at which student after student denounced the 'academicism' of the Wilhelmian *Kaiserreich*, regimentation of the arts, and the widespread use of the term 'cultural Bolshevism' to blacken anything of which the Party disapproved.[194] Furthermore, the young delegates, led by Otto Andreas Schreiber, an Expressionist painter, who praised the work of Miës, Tessenow, and others, proclaimed that National-Socialist students believed in the victory of quality and truth, and that the living element in all art was freedom.[195] Schreiber had been born in West Prussia, and his nationalism was undoubtedly coloured by the fact that he and his family had been driven out in 1919 when the lands from which he hailed became the 'Polish corridor'. He went on to castigate 'Historicism' as dogma, and stated that the National-Socialist student 'demanded' a 'revolutionary' view of art.[196]

To such as Miës, this kind of support must have sounded like heroic music,[197] but many were horrified, considering architects like Miës to be seditious, enemies of the new Germany.[198] Nevertheless, the outpourings of the *NSDStB* for a time sounded just like the slogans declaimed *fortissimo* by 'leftist' students in the aftermath of the 1914–18 war, demanding the *tabula rasa*, the dumping of academicism, the embrace of all that was modern, and much else asked for by their predecessors a decade earlier: for German Modernists it seemed there might be some hope, as opposition to the *KfdK* became overt, and sounded refreshingly like the sort of movement that had enabled Modernism to flourish in the 1920s. Many felt that their art might well be encouraged,[199] and even represent the revolutionary tendencies of the Third Reich.[200] Hitler himself demanded a crystal-clear 'functionalism' for some National-Socialist architecture.[201] Goebbels emphasized the *youthfulness* of the National-Socialist movement, whose adherents had nothing in common with the past: any artist who wished to give expression to his own time must not only be young but should create new forms.[202]

Such statements do not sound 'conservative', 'traditionalist', or 'reactionary'; on the contrary, they could easily have been key components of early-1920s 'leftist' revolutionary manifestos supporting Modernism and rejection of the past.[203] It was Goebbels who appointed the Expressionist painter Hans Weidemann to lead several cultural events of the Propaganda Ministry, and it was Weidemann who directed the exhibition planned for Berlin in the spring of 1934 entitled *Deutsches Volk—Deutsche Arbeit* (German people—German work). Weidemann lost no time in inviting Gropius, Miës, and Herbert Bayer to become involved. It was Miës who organized the architectural section of the *Außtellung* for which he designed the exhibition-hall. The aim of this exhibition was to explain National-Socialist doctrines of race and labour, warning the people of the dangers of 'racial degeneracy', and displaying how the *régime* proposed to correct matters.[204]

Robert Ley, who headed the *Deutsche Arbeitsfront* (*DAF*—German Labour-Front), sensed that Goebbels was identifying National Socialism with 'progressive' art and architecture, and requested that he should nominate a suitable person to lead the cultural wing of the *Nationalsozialistische Gemeinschaft Kraft durch Freude* (*KdF*—National-Socialist Strength-through-Joy Association): Goebbels suggested Weidemann, who in turn chose Schreiber to lead the Fine-Arts division of the *KdF*. These two youthful National Socialists, both artists themselves, determined to hold competitions to encourage architecture, literature, music, painting, and sculpture, the judges to include such world-renowned names as Ernst Barlach, Erich Heckel, Paul Hindemith, Miës van der Rohe, Emil Nolde, and Richard Strauss.[205]

It was no wonder that Miës returned to Berlin from Switzerland in the hope of obtaining significant commissions, for the young Expressionists, now in positions of some power, were members of a chorus praising his works as 'nationalistic', when once the same designs had been hailed as part of an 'International Style'.[206] To Miës, the important thing was to design buildings that would be erected, and in 1933–4 he felt confident that the new German *régime* would offer him scope to realize large schemes,[207] especially when Modernism seemed to have a real possibility of being accepted by the top brass in the Third Reich.[208]

Such anticipations, however, were short-lived, and rumours about Goebbels's 'adventurous' artistic tastes were soon discounted, as the *Führer* himself began to assert his own opinions, not least about personalities.[209] Weidemann fell from grace, and Goebbels, ever keen to do Hitler's bidding, withdrew his support. Rosenberg was placed in charge of the *Nationalsozialistische Kulturgemeinde* (National-Socialist Culture Community) in 1934, and the various jurors appointed by the young men were also removed from office, most falling foul of the Party to a lesser or greater degree. With the demotion of Weidemann and Schreiber, all hopes soon faded that Modernism, as understood by Gropius, Miës, *et al.*, would become in any way accepted for *official* architecture that presented National-Socialism's face to the world.

On the other hand, it would be used for industrial buildings and other structures not in the forefront of public view. It should be emphasized, though, that there was a considerable body of opinion among young, educated, artistic National Socialists that leaned towards a technology-inspired, forward-looking, modern aesthetic freed from both Wilhelmian bombast and Historicism, and which, for a time, looked as though it might become officially acceptable. During the short lifetime of the Third Reich, that view certainly did prevail, but only for selected building types.[210]

The bizarre structure of National-Socialist Germany, however, made it inevitable that the preferences of the *Führer*, expressed in violent terms, were sufficient to eliminate and submerge any other viewpoint: dissent was not permitted. Every Party *apparatchik*, no matter how lowly, absorbed the *Führer's* edicts on matters cultural, thus giving direction to all uncertain of taste in artistic matters, and the Party's attitudes were codified in the *Entartete 'Kunst'* (degenerate 'art') exhibition (1937);[211] yet in *architectural* terms Hitler's tastes were varied, and there was no consistency in them. When Paul Schultze-Naumburg, who directed (1930–42) the Weimar college that had been the *Bauhaus*, removed all Modernists from their posts, it did him little good, for Hitler described him as a mere *imitator* of the past; and he, a traditionalist architect, much influenced by Muthesius, received no significant commissions from 1933.

We know that in 1936 and 1937 Miës was offered posts in the USA to head architectural departments, but it was only when he realized that the taints of his 'leftist' connections and the *Bauhaus* were unlikely to be forgotten and forgiven by the National Socialists, and his name was anathema to Hitler, that in 1937 he accepted an offer in the USA and emigrated. One of his last acts in the Germany he was about to leave was to withdraw from the Prussian Academy of Arts (*Preussischen Akademie der Künste*); he concluded his letter of resignation (dated 19 July 1937, received by the Academy 21 July) with *Heil Hitler!* above his signature (**Plate 4.17**).[212]

Of course, the *Heil Hitler!* closure to letters had become common by then, replacing friendly greetings and other formalities, and obviously Miës would not have wished to further antagonize the National Socialists when he was planning to emigrate (and his path to do so seems to have been smoothed by his Party contacts). Nevertheless, it has become apparent that the myth of Miës's moral probity assiduously cultivated by Modernist apologists is somewhat coloured by rose-tinted spectacles.[213] Miës's ambiguous position is really typical of many architects' relations to Power,[214] a fact

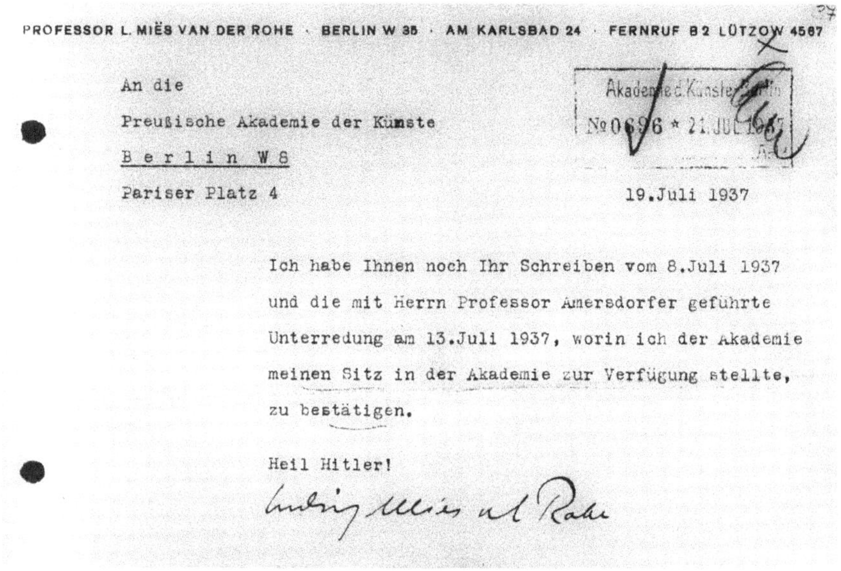

PROFESSOR L. MIËS VAN DER ROHE · BERLIN W 35 · AM KARLSBAD 24 · FERNRUF B 2 LÜTZOW 4567

An die

Preußische Akademie der Künste

B e r l i n W 8

Pariser Platz 4   19.Juli 1937

Ich habe Ihnen noch Ihr Schreiben vom 8.Juli 1937

und die mit Herrn Professor Amersdorfer geführte

Unterredung am 13.Juli 1937, worin ich der Akademie

meinen Sitz in der Akademie zur Verfügung stellte,

zu bestätigen.

Heil Hitler!

Plate 4.17. Letter from Miës van der Rohe from his address at *Am Karlsbad* 24, Berlin W 35, dated 19 July 1937, and addressed to the Prussian Academy of Arts, stating he puts his seat at the Academy at the Academy's disposal (an elliptical way of saying he is resigning). Note the *Heil Hitler!* immediately above his signature

that chroniclers of the Modern Movement have tended to circumvent,[215] although Philip Johnson was disarmingly honest in his own admissions concerning the obtaining of commissions, recognizing that they resembled those of Miës.[216]

Miës signed the pro-National-Socialist Proclamation of the Creative Artists (*Aufruf der Kulturschaffenden*) supporting Hitler's succession to Hindenburg in 1934, thereby giving him absolute dictatorial powers. The Proclamation included belief in the *Führer*, who had fulfilled the signatories' 'fervent wish for unity', a statement of trust and hope in Hitler's work, and a promise that none of the signatories would be missing when any future affirmation of trust might be needed. It was published in *Völkischer Beobachter*.[217] Hitler even insisted on choosing the designs for *Autobahn* service-stations, simple, 'flat'-roofed, functional buildings: two plans of these have been found that had been submitted by Miës himself (though rejected by Hitler because of the architect's previous associations rather than any aesthetic considerations),[218] but a spectacular realized example (*Heimatbahnhof des Reichsautozuges Deutschland*—service-station of the German state highways) with a huge cantilever designed by the team of Paul Hofer and Karl Johann Fischer,

Plate 4.18. *Heimatbahnhof* of the *Reichsautozuges Deutschland* (service-station for the German State Highways) by Paul Hofer & Karl Johann Fischer, an example of the Modernist architecture adopted by the National Socialists for the *Autobahn* system

was unquestionably as Modernist as any of the usually quoted exemplars (**Plate 4.18**).[219] Also Modernist, with cantilevered roofs, streamlined styling, and horizontal strips of window set in curved walls (reminiscent of the work of Mendelsohn), was the *Autobahn* service-station near Frankfurt-am-Main designed by Carl August Bembé.[220]

Miës's gnomic remark (typical of the pronouncements of over-inflated architectural egos of the time) that architecture is the 'will of the epoch translated into space' was repeated almost verbatim by Hitler in 1938.[221] Hitler also had no objection to factories built of steel frames with lots of glass, in the so-called 'functional' manner, and accepted that certain building-types, such as those associated with industrial processes, should not resemble great civic, government, or cultural edifices.[222] He particularly admired the Modernist buildings for the *Reichswerke Hermann Goering* (1937–45) designed by Herbert Rimpl.[223] The same architect's Heinkel aircraft-factory at Oranienburg (1935–9), designed with Josef Bernard, could easily pass for work by any of the *Bauhäusler* (*see* **Plates 4.2 & 4.19**).[224]

It would be tedious to list all the buildings designed and built during the Third Reich which have recognizably Modernist aesthetics, even though their architects subscribed more or less to the political realities of the National-Socialist State. They include the Opel works, Brandenburg-an-der-Havel (**Plate 4.20**), with long strips of horizontal glazing, erected

Plate 4.19. *Universalhalle* (assembly-hall) of the Heinkel *Flugzeugwerk* (aircraft-factory), Oranienburg, Brandenburg (1935–6), by Herbert Rimpl & Josef Bernard

Plate 4.20. Opel works, Brandenburg-an-der-Havel, built in 190 days to designs by Heinrich Bärsch in a Modernist style that belies conventional wisdom concerning National-Socialist attitudes to architecture

in 190 days in 1935 to designs by the otherwise obscure Heinrich Bärsch;[225] several very large works by Fritz Schupp and Martin Kremmer;[226] others by Hans Väth;[227] and the large complex of buildings for the *Deutsche Versuchsanstalt für Luftfahrt* (German Institute for Aviation), Adlershof, Berlin, by Hermann Brenner and Werner Deutschmann, which also included several extraordinary structures of reinforced concrete.[228] Speer himself, for one of his first Party commissions, the refurbishing of a villa in Grünewald (1931), chose *Bauhaus*-designed wallpaper,[229] so things were never as clearly defined as some have claimed. Speer is mostly remembered as an architect for his grandiose schemes for the replanning of Berlin,[230] for the Chancellery, and for the Party parade-gounds at Nuremberg, where the language used was a stripped Classicism not that far removed from that of Behrens or early Mies, with obvious Egyptianizing flavours. Some of his work was inflated in scale, owing debts to late-eighteenth-century French architecture,[231] but he also designed in a competent manner, drawing on German (Franconian) vernacular timber-framed architecture: an example is the accommodation for workers he designed and had erected at Nuremberg (**Plate 4.21**).

The architectural stylistic variety found in National-Socialist Germany and Fascist Italy compares favourably with the almost uniformly Modernist

Plate 4.21. *Arbeiter-Unterkünfte* (workers' hostels), *Regensburgerstraße*, Nuremberg (1939–40). Seven such structures were erected in the *Stil fränkischer Fachwerkhäuser* (Franconian half-timbered houses style) to designs by Albert Speer

architecture imposed on the West after the 1939–45 war from which little diversity was permissible.[232]

Epilogue

Alfred Rosenberg,[233] a Baltic German, leading ideologue of the National-Socialist movement, was himself an architect, and shared views with people like Gropius and other Modernists who rejected 'outmoded' styles, phoney decorations, and 'dishonest' architecture. He denounced 'pseudo-architecture', pompous monuments, Moresque railway-stations, and so on, demanding Germans should cease imitating foreign styles,[234] and that architecture might be the first of the arts to become 'honest' once more.[235] Hitler himself was uninterested in boring doctrinal disputes between architects, and particularly objected to Modernists' insistence that one style should be adopted for all building types.[236] But National-Socialist antipathy towards personalities associated with the International Style and the *Bauhaus* has been sufficient to ensure their and that institution's fame:[237] without National Socialism, the diaspora of *Bauhäusler* to, especially, the United States, and the various reverential hagiographies of the *dramatis personae*, it is unlikely that either the International Style or the *Bauhaus* would have been universally embraced after 1945.

Moholy-Nagy founded a 'New Bauhaus' in Chicago (1937), Gropius and Breuer promoted Modernism at Harvard (also from 1937), Albers revived workshops and courses based on *Bauhaus* principles at Black Mountain College, North Carolina, from 1933, and Miës van der Rohe settled in Chicago in 1938, directing the architectural and planning courses at what became the Illinois Institute of Technology, and dropping his by then unnecessary *Umlaut* as well. After the 1939-45 war, Max Bill revived (1950) a *Bauhaus* programme at the *Hochschule für Gestaltung*, Ulm. Thus the anti-Crafts, anti-Historicist, dogmatic stances that had evolved in Germany were disseminated throughout the world, not least through the 'compounds' described by Tom Wolfe,[238] who noted that from those 'compounds' poured manifestos treated like the Ten Commandments, spread by proselytizing evangelists, who ensured those Commandments were rigidly enforced.

That was not all. Former *Bauhaus* students were to rise to eminence in the DDR, not least Collein, who was one of the authors of the 'Sixteen Principles of Urbanism' agreed (1948) with Moscow as a radical alternative to the CIAM-Athens-Charter dogmas so widely accepted in the West after 1945.

Among the 'Principles' were the rejection of urban motorways cutting swathes through the fabric of towns and cities, the abandonment of zoning that was to play havoc in the West, and the re-establishment of the urban block and street (condemned by Le Corbusier) as essentials.[239] At the end of the 1960s, however, the East Germans began to promote the notion that the *Bauhaus* had been the German equivalent of experiments carried out in the Soviet Union in the early 1920s, that the school's 'socialist' ideals had been thwarted by the 'capitalist' climate, and that the institution had been all about social renewal, the community, and improving the lot of the proletariat. The results were startling: not only was there a flood of scholarly publications produced in the DDR, but archives, collections, and museums were set up dedicated to the place, and the Dessau buildings themselves were meticulously restored (with furnishings and fixtures) in the period 1975–7.[240]

Some *Bauhäusler* sought a future in the USSR, and many managed to rise to the top of the architectural profession in the DDR after 1945, finding no difficulty in adopting an acceptable stylistic language (that would have been anathema to Gropius, Meyer, *et al.*) to satisfy the Moscow-dominated *régime*. There was no shortage of educated, young, ambitious opportunists willing to serve any political system that would further their careers:[241] the extremes of 'right' and 'left' always manage to meet.[242] That perceptive architectural commentator, Osbert Lancaster, demonstrated[243] the connections between the buildings created under National Socialism and those produced under Stalinist Communism: 'we were told', he observed, 'that now we should see what the proletarian architect could accomplish when freed from the shackles of capitalistic patronage'. This new freedom 'would accomplish... a new and vital architecture cleanly expressive of its purpose... unencumbered with all those fripperies which the degraded taste of an outworn civilization had clung to as symbols of bourgeois taste'.

Unfortunately, the architecture which emerged in the Soviet Union was difficult to distinguish from that produced by the 'wage-slaves of capitalism' in the 'effete' social democracies. It was almost indistinguishable from the architecture of 'international fascism'. Soviet architects did away with capitals on 'ideological grounds', just as certain *Bauhäusler* abolished upper-case letters and found fault with serifs, doubtless as '*bourgeois*' affectations. They insisted that 'beauty is to be achieved by merely abolishing ornament', that 'political rhetoric is a sufficient substitute for genuine architectural inspiration', and that 'declamatory and didactic' idioms would bludgeon observers into acceptance.[244]

Reginald Blomfield put it succinctly when he wrote that Modernism had degenerated into frantic struggles for advertisement, and that only architects who shouted loudest and who were most talked about in the papers were likely to succeed.[245] He also wrote that 'the late war, instead of clearing the air, has let in a good deal of poison gas…it is time to make a stand…One runs some risk, because one is bound to run counter to fashionable criticisms, but art criticism…is not criticism so much as…journalism. An elaborate jargon has been devised…[246] it appears to be the aim of…professional art critics to make art unintelligible'.[247]

One of the *Bauhäusler*, *SS-Untersturmführer*[248] Friedrich Karl Ertl, who studied at Dessau 1928-31, went on to distinguish himself by working on buildings for the Auschwitz-Birkenau complex,[249] and he was not alone among those who went through the *Bauhaus* system and served one vile system or another. Ertl worked with *SS-Obersturmbahnführer*[250] Walther Dejaco under *SS-Sturmbahnführer*[251] Karl Bischoff, and together they adopted the Modernist maxim that everything depended on the marriage between function and economy, which would have been of no comfort to the unfortunate inmates. Ertl was to claim that the most important influences on him as an architect were the various *Bauhäusler* heroes of the Modern Movement.[252] These men created a Pandemonium, the capital of Hell in Milton's *Paradise Lost* (first printed 1667). If, however, the word 'pandemonium' is spelled with a lower-case 'p', it is a tumultuously noisy, disorderly place of unspeakable vileness: at Auschwitz-Birkenau the *apparatchiks* of National Socialism 'broke and sacrificed devils of their own making', a perverse realization of the Temple, with the Burnt Offerings of the crematoria terrible parodies of the daily sacrifices at the Temple in Jerusalem.[253]

On the other hand, Franz Joseph Ehrlich, who had studied (1927-30) at the *Bauhaus*, as a Communist, fell foul of the National Socialists, and spent two years (1937-9) in Buchenwald concentration-camp, near Weimar (of all places). While there he used *Bauhaus*-inspired lettering for the design of the inscription at the gates: *Jedem das Seine* (to each his own), reminiscent of the work of one of his teachers, Joost Schmidt. Ehrlich also designed furniture and camp buildings there, employed by the SS (*Schutzstaffel* or protection-squad) to do so.

Intolerant dogmatism, lip-service to 'scientific' principles without understanding what science is, and pretences to be 'objective' have begotten an inhumane world: they threaten to impose a global Dystopia on us all.[254]

V

The International Style
Truly International

Impresarios of the International Style; The Style Becomes Widely Accepted Outside Germany: Czechoslovakia, The Soviet Union, Hungary, Poland, Belgium, Brasil, Scandinavia, United States of America, Switzerland, The Netherlands, Austria; France & 'Le Corbusier'; Fascist Italy & The International Style: A Problem for Apologists; Early Modernism in England

Der moderne Mensch wird in der Klinik geboren und stirbt in der Klinik: also soll er auch wie in einer Klinik wohnen!—Diese Forderung hatte soeben ein führender Baukünstler aufgestellt, und ein anderer Reformer der Inneneinrichtung verlangte verschiebbare Wände der Wohnungen, mit der Begründung, daß der Mensch dem Menschen zusammenlebend vertrauen lernen müsse und nicht sich separatistisch abschließen dürfe. Es hatte damals gerade eine neue Zeit begonnen . . . , und eine neue Zeit braucht einen neuen Stil (Modern man is born in hospital and dies in hospital: consequently he should also live as if in a hospital!—This demand had just been formulated by a leading architect, and another, a reformer of interior design, demanded moveable partition-walls in apartments on the grounds that in living together a person must learn to trust others, and not be isolated in a spirit of separation. Just then a new epoch had begun . . . , and a new age requires a new style).

ROBERT MUSIL (1880–1942): *Der Mann ohne Eigenschaften* (The Man without Qualities) i (Berlin: Ernst Rowohlt 1930) v

The word *modern* means up to date; and to use the modern style means to take advantage of the technical achievements of our age. It means using the new materials and the new ways of construction that have been developed in recent years. It also means to study changes in our way of living and in our taste.

PHILIP CORTELYOU JOHNSON (1906–2005): *Arts and Decoration* **xvii**/4 (February 1935) 47

Impresarios of the International Style

This chapter will begin with a look at Philip Johnson, the American architect with an aloof disdain for the opinions of the masses: his immense inherited riches, independence of mind, flair for publicity, and political skills established him in a powerful position within the architectural world, both as designer and critic.[1] He was much later described as 'the doyen of architectural opportunists':[2] when puritanical Modernist austerity was 'an aesthetic cause', he was in the vanguard of that cause; when, after the Second World War, 'the business of American architecture' seemed to be just business, Johnson 'was its slickest salesman'. Later still, 'Postmodernism was partly of his making'; and when Deconstructivism 'hit New York, there was Johnson in his 80s in the thick of the theorists, networking, promoting favourites and talking, always talking'.[3] In short, Johnson was always ahead in the 'architectural game', although it has to be said that 'he never actually invented it'. His obituarist said that he, a 'second-class creative figure with a first-class brain and boundless wealth, charm and wit',[4] was the 'second to do everything'.[5]

What is of singular importance, however, is Johnson's part in the dissemination of International Modernism,[6] for it is arguable that without his energy, his enthusiasms, his impressive social contacts, his relationships with other influential figures, and, of course, the *Bauhäusler* immigrants and distorted perceptions of the artistic policies of the Third Reich, the 'International Style' would not have become ubiquitous.

Alfred Hamilton Barr Jr, first director of the Museum of Modern Art (MoMA) in New York, and Johnson, first Curator of Architecture there, were the evangelists, if not the apostles, of Modernism in North America. They were inspired by the *Bauhaus*, and by notions of merging architecture with the fine and applied arts, and by the proposition of a radical new aesthetic (supposedly rational, functional, machine-made, and ahistorical).[7] In June 1929 Barr first met Johnson, who was reading Philosophy at Harvard. Shortly afterwards, Barr was appointed first director of MoMA. That autumn, he invited Johnson to join him at the new museum in order to head the Department of Architecture and Design: although Johnson protested he knew nothing about architecture, Barr persisted, and Johnson arrived at the museum in 1930, specifically to help to prepare for a major architectural exhibition to reveal to North America what was going on in

Europe. Using the museum and their own apartments to promote new ideas in design, Barr regarded MoMA as a 'laboratory' (in the terminology of the *Bauhaus*) where the public would be invited to participate in its experiments.[8]

Barr had visited the *Bauhaus* in 1927, after it moved to Dessau. Johnson also travelled there several times between 1929 and 1933, and, gushingly enthusiastic in his hyperbole, described the Walter Gropius/Adolf Meyer/ Fieger/Neufelt/*et al. Bauhaus* as 'magnificent... the most beautiful building... having a majesty and simplicity which are unequaled':[9] the whole experience with people he regarded as 'geniuses' left him 'intoxicated, overwhelmed'.[10] Johnson went back to the *Bauhaus* in 1930 with Jan Ruhtenberg, an architect who had created an interior for his Berlin apartment in the manner of Miës and Lilly Reich. Johnson stayed there with Ruhtenberg, who designed a letterhead for his use when he made that address his base for travel in Germany (1930–1) to study the European *avant-garde*.[11] The apartment was later illustrated in *The International Style*, which Johnson co-authored with Henry-Russell Hitchcock.[12]

Barr and Johnson visited the Gropius-organized *Deutscher Werkbund* exhibition in Paris (1930): Barr considered German industrial design, thanks largely to the *Bauhaus*, to be 'years ahead of the rest of the world',[13] which, in many respects, it was. The results of all these travels were to lead, in 1932, to the first MoMA architectural show: *Modern Architecture: International Exhibition*,[14] curated by Johnson and Hitchcock.[15] The Department of Architecture had been officially created in that year with Johnson at its head: industrial design was added to that department, and more exhibitions followed that of *Modern Architecture*, including *Objects: 1900 and Today* (1933),[16] and *Machine Art* (1934).[17] Johnson had met Miës (who was then director of the *Bauhaus*) in 1930,[18] and commissioned him to design the interior of his New York apartment at 424 East 52 Street. The work was done in collaboration with Lilly Reich, so New York was introduced to monochromatic surfaces and minimal furnishings; and, particularly, to the Modernism espoused by Miës that to many had a refined sleekness others (including Gropius) could never match. Johnson was to design subsequent interiors for his own use using a Miës-Reich approach to spaces, details, materials, and furnishings. Miës[19] became a major influence on Johnson's thinking, and Johnson quickly realized that Miës's architecture was greatly superior to the supposed creations of Gropius. Barr, too, favoured a minimalist aesthetic.

Johnson made five or six visits to the *Bauhaus* over a four-year period, and began collecting works of art, including a drawing by Paul Klee. Like other homosexuals, he seems to have found his times in Weimar Germany liberating, enabling him to express not only his sexuality, but his personality: he grandly claimed he learned German by 'the horizontal method'[20] as well as acquainting himself with leading members of the *avant-garde* in architecture and art, notably *Bauhäusler*. He and Hitchcock travelled together in Germany, and formed a view at variance with received opinion in Europe: they regarded Modernist claims about 'social responsibility', 'functionalism', and so on as nonsense. What actually mattered was art and style: it was all a matter of aesthetics, and the more aesthetically appealing one could make architecture, especially by spending large amounts of money on it, the better.[21]

And it is certainly true that Modernism-on-the-cheap resulted in embarrassingly bad work: it was never a 'downmarket' style, and when it was used for 'downmarket' schemes (such as housing for the masses), not only did it not work, but was often hated (Goodhart-Rendel's sage remarks[22] about 'bargain-basements' and 'fly-blown novelties' were prescient). Barr and Johnson moved in influential New-York artistic circles and salons, and several *habitués* of those were to serve on MoMA's board and advisory committees. It was through wealthy contacts that fashionable Modernism, as promoted by Barr, Hitchcock, and Johnson, began to become accepted in the USA: it was not just accepted, but regarded as *chic* and the thing to embrace by those rich enough to do so. The problem was that the Modernism they promoted was of a very limited kind, and excluded an enormous amount of material which did not suit their agenda.[23]

For Barr and Johnson, the building that introduced the 'International Style' to North America was the Lovell health-house, Hollywood Hills, Los Angeles, of 1927–9, by Richard Neutra, Mendelsohn's former assistant, who had emigrated to the USA in 1923: it was described as 'stylistically the most advanced house built in North America since the War'.[24] It contained tubular-steel chairs also designed by Neutra, a type developed in the 1920s by designers such as Breuer and Miës. The *Modern Architecture: International Exhibition* display travelled to fourteen cities over two years, and *Machine Art* was taken to nineteen venues. Other Modernist exhibitions disseminated ideas in extensive tours,[25] and Barr's own exhibitions, including *Cubism and Abstract Art*[26] and *Fantastic Art, Dada, Surrealism* (both 1936),[27] helped to inform public taste in Modern art and design: but the really important impact of MoMA's campaigns was to convert the great, the good, and (especially) the very rich to the cause.

Johnson was listed as the American representative of the *Bauhaus* (by that time relocated to Berlin) in January 1933, a few months before it closed down.[28] Barr, who was in Germany at the time, was shocked by the atmosphere as National Socialism consolidated its power, and he witnessed its brutal political and cultural activities: he attempted to print articles on National-Socialist threats to art, culture, and society, but was only able to get one published by his friend, Lincoln Kirstein, in *The Hound and Horn*.[29] His other articles did not appear until after the war, such was the deference being paid to the New Germany,[30] and especially to its *Führer*, whose *Mein Kampf* (My Struggle) was greatly admired and published in many translations.[31] Barr saw the diaspora of *Bauhäusler* as potentially enriching the USA, and in due course those *émigrés* played a huge part in promoting Modernism in their adopted country, and, after 1945, throughout the whole world: a phenomenon that will be partly explained below.[32]

However, despite their evangelical enthusiasm, and the 1932 MoMA exhibition, Barr, Hitchcock, and Johnson were not the first to introduce the *Bauhaus* to the American public: for that, credit must go to Lincoln Kirstein. He organized an exhibition devoted exclusively to the school's work for the Harvard Society for Contemporary Art which opened in December 1930 and was also shown at the John Becker Gallery, New York (early 1931), and at the Chicago Arts Club (March 1931). Barr and Johnson helped Kirstein with the show, lent certain objects, and provided photographs (taken by Johnson) of various architectural works.[33] Even earlier, in 1926, the *Société Anonyme* had put on an exhibition (*International Exhibition of Modern Art*) at the Brooklyn Museum which included material on aspects of the *Bauhaus*, so American *cognoscenti* were already becoming familiar with German Modernism;[34] but the rôles of Barr and Johnson, through their influential and wealthy contacts in New York, cannot be overstated. They laid the foundations for the widespread acceptance of International Modernism in architecture after 1945.

Following the *International Style* exhibition (1932),[35] Johnson's next groundbreaking success was the *Machine Art* exhibition at MoMA, the culmination of his early collaboration with Barr. It was a critical success even before it opened, and established the museum's rôle as a design tastemaker. It also confirmed the view of Modernist critics that machines could no longer be ignored, and that it was time 'to calibrate attitudes to culture and industrial design'.[36] The exhibition was anti-craft and anti-styling, and with it MoMA was confirmed in its 'position of cultural leadership on design issues'.[37] Johnson was hailed in the *New York Sun* as the 'best showman, and possibly the world's best', with a 'genius for grouping things together and finding just the right background and the right light',[38] prescient remarks that might have described Johnson's future career as a successful impresario.

The use of quotations from Plato's *Philebus* in Classical Greek and English translations and from St Thomas Aquinas's *Summa Theologiae* (1266–73) in Latin and English created a 'genealogy for contemporary industrial design in the United States, which reached right back to "the Glory that was Greece and the Grandeur that was Rome"'. Modernists used this technique with conspicuous success to attempt to link their own time with the past (despite the vehement statements many Modernists issued about the total rejection of history). Not everyone was convinced: some found these quotations not only misleading, but superficial too, and one critic wondered if Plato himself might have been at all pleased by the exhibition.[39] Johnson was characteristically disarming in his honesty (he abhorred hypocrisy)[40] when he later admitted to his 'showmanship'; that he was just trying to 'fill up' the space in MoMA with 'a gorgeous installation'; and that he and Hitchcock were primarily interested in the 'style side of things—a word that everybody hated' (and still does).[41] Nevertheless, Johnson's intellect, culture, and breadth of understanding seemed to carry all before them. As a *Schauspieldirektor*, he was outstanding, an impresario of shameless virtuosity and energetic capability to pre-empt what the Germans called the *Zeitgeist* (spirit of the age): there were times when he, puckish, and with tongue in cheek, seemed almost to invent it.

Johnson then gave up his MoMA post (1934) to begin a short and inglorious career in politics (he, like many at the time, was anti-Semitic in certain attitudes),[42] assisting those opposed to Franklin Delano Roosevelt, thirty-second President of the USA 1933–45, backing Huey P. Long, after whose assassination (1935) he allied himself with an odious Detroit-based Roman Catholic priest of Irish extraction, Father Charles Edward Coughlin: anti-Semite, anti-Communist, anti-Capitalist, and anti-British, his National Union for Social Justice had much support, as did his radio broadcasts, which were followed by some 30 million people.[43] Coughlin's National Union Party, which backed William Frederick Lemke in the presidential elections, was ideologically allied with German National Socialism, though with an American flavour: for this party, also known as the 'Grey Shirts', Johnson designed its symbol, the flying wedge, a *Swastika* substitute. For Coughlin's newspaper, *Social Justice*, Johnson wrote diatribes which make unpleasant reading. Johnson had heard Hitler speak, and thereafter increasingly joined in the widespread adulation accorded to Nazi Germany (1933–45): according to one of his obituarists, he was 'titillated by the aesthetics and sexuality'[44] of National Socialism.[45]

Miës was supported by Johnson in attempts to get the National Socialists to embrace the 'International Style'. Recognizing the close connection between Power and Modernism, Johnson later held the view that Albert Speer would have made a great architect of skyscrapers.[46] Johnson attended one of the Nuremberg rallies in the late 1930s. He was apparently in Danzig (now Gdańsk) in 1939 when the Germans invaded, and thought the grey-green uniforms of the German army made the country look 'gay and happy'.[47] Notoriously anti-British,[48] he was contemptuous of British fellow-travellers of Modernism (especially those with pretensions to 'morality'), and later was to make fun of British critics who took themselves too seriously. He thought that National-Socialist Germany had many things in its favour, not least that its architecture would be monumental: instead of bath-houses, working-class *Siedlungen* (housing-estates), offices to house employment bureaux, and the like, there would be memorial-museums, splendid railway-stations, monuments a–plenty, and lots of impressively grand structures, because the *régime* wanted to leave a 'visible mark' of its greatness rather than provide 'sanitary equipment for workers'.[49]

Johnson's dalliance with politics and his absence from MoMA led to an unexpected change of direction at the museum. This was connected with the termination of Modernist influence on official public architecture in Germany, and its decline in France due to the economic situation, and with the succession of Johnson's assistant, Ernestine Fantl,[50] a former pupil of Barr, as MoMA's curator of architecture and industrial art. Hitchcock, an enthusiast for British architecture, seems to have been the 'principal motiva-tor'[51] for a special exhibition entitled *Modern Architecture in England* (Scotland, Wales, and Northern Ireland did not feature):[52] towards the end of 1936 Barr agreed it should be mounted at MoMA, and Fantl, guided by Hazen Sise, a Canadian member of the MARS Group (*see* Select Glossary) in London, was responsible for the selection of the exhibits as well as the organization of the show.

This very important demonstration of the vitality of English Modernism[53] has not been given the attention it merits, despite the handsome hardback catalogue with contributions from Hitchcock and Bauer which accompanied the exhibition.[54] What Hitchcock and Fantl actually did was to make a strong case for an English Modernism that was indigenous, yet much received opinion has over-egged its foreign or international aspects.[55] There is also strong evidence that, given the state of affairs in Continental Europe at the time, English developments had a much more profound impact on CIAM (*see* Select Glossary) through the MARS Group than has generally been accepted.[56] This was partly due to the 1932 *Exhibition 15: Modern Architecture: International Exhibition*[57] which had, largely through Johnson, emphasized the German contribution, and partly because although some *émigrés* had settled in London,[58] two of the biggest names went to the USA, and one of them was a very shrewd politician.

Thus MoMA's 1937 celebration of English Modernism was quickly over-shadowed. In the following year a major *Bauhaus* exhibition was mounted at MoMA (1938–9) organized by leading *Bauhäusler* who, helped by Barr, Johnson, and others, had recently arrived in the United States, where they were quickly established in various educational establishments to lead design programmes, training subsequent generations who spread the Modernist gospel. Among the earliest arrivals (1933) were Josef and Anni Albers, for whom Johnson secured teaching posts at the newly established Black Mountain College, North Carolina, where they were joined in 1936 by Alexander Schawinsky: for the MoMA *Bauhaus* exhibition, which was supervised by Gropius, Bayer designed the catalogue, assisted by Josef Albers and Schawinsky, and Barr wrote the foreword.[59] This exhibition had mixed and even negative reviews, however, largely because it focused on the Gropius era, but also because it was cluttered (some said it was like a jumble-sale or pot-pourri of dated Modernist 'isms'),[60] and even the book resembled 'a mail-order catalogue'.[61] Barr had found the whole thing exhausting and exasperating, and felt that some of the objects shown were mediocre or even worse.[62]

Gropius, secure in his high opinion of himself, was inclined to ignore the criticisms, and, despite these, the exhibition was well attended. Not all critics were hostile: Lewis Mumford, writing in the *New Yorker*, found it 'exciting' and full of 'gusto and high spirits';[63] and from that time onwards *Bauhaus*-centred programmes influenced other American museums. The exhibition itself was shown at four other venues (1939–40). The eclipse of the very considerable English contribution that had been clearly demonstrated in MoMA's *Exhibition 58* of 1937,[64] owed not a little to Johnson's antipathy towards England, but it should also be remembered that such hostility was endemic in much of American society, not least among those of German or Irish origin. An influx of *émigrés* claiming almost proprietorial rights over the Modern Movement would have tended to obscure and even discount the significance of England's Modernists.

Mumford,[65] the American theorist and critic, is of some interest to this study. Early in his life he was influenced by the writings of Ebenezer Howard, William Morris, and Patrick Geddes, and at one time was an advocate of developing an indigenous American style in architecture.[66] Envisaging town design that would embrace work and recreation, art and labour, and balance of urban and rural life in democratic organizations, the garden-city ideal loomed large in his philosophy.[67] Although he assisted Barr, Hitchcock, and Johnson in the organization of the 1932 MoMA exhibition in New York,[68] a decade later he had become highly critical of the International Style, and especially of that branch of Modernism influenced by Le Corbusier, deploring Miësian minimalism, and urging respect for local traditions, craft-techniques, design-themes, and materials, all of which had been jettisoned by Modernism. By the post-1945 period, Mumford had become an outspoken opponent of huge metropolitan conglomerations, which he referred to as '*megalopoleis*', and attacked the devastation of traditional city-centres and surrounding areas by high-rise buildings, road-construction to accommodate the motor-vehicle, and soulless 'dormitory suburbs'. He lamented the undermining of Western urban culture by technology, industrialization, and commercial greed. He considered the industrialized megalopolis corrosive of society but homogenizing in its tendencies: it destroyed agreeable urban spaces once used by the public and wrecked diversity.[69] Yet his position often shifted: his outspoken attack in the 1960s on Jane Jacobs is hard to explain, and his influence seems to have waned.

In the autumn of 1937 Breuer and Gropius settled in Cambridge, MA, to teach at Harvard (Barr was involved in the appointments).[70] Other *émigrés* included the son of Lyonel Feininger, T. Lux Feininger (1936), Moholy-Nagy and Miës van der Rohe (1937), and Herbert Bayer (1938). Miës had reluctantly accepted a post as director of the Department of Architecture at the Armour Institute, and was not best pleased when Gropius was appointed at Harvard.[71] He reorganized the entire curriculum in accordance with certain concepts he had inaugurated at the *Bauhaus*, and invited other *Bauhäusler* to join him, including Hilbersheimer and Peterhans. The Armour was renamed the Illinois Institute of Technology in 1940, and Mies (minus his *Umlaut*), designed the new campus, one of the largest architectural projects involving what had become known as the International Style at that time: it was the first of many important commissions he received in the USA.[72]

Numerous *Bauhäusler*, ably helped by Barr, Johnson, and many others, found their way into teaching, where they gained footholds almost everywhere that mattered: as a result they changed the entire direction of architecture in the United States, and thereby throughout the post-war world. Bayer revolutionized the field in visual communications through coordinated logos, graphics, typography, and so on for corporate imagery. 'Leftist' artists, many of whom had identified strongly with revolutionaries, with Marxism, and even with violence, began to serve big business and eventually multinational corporations.[73] The scene was set for a transformation: once the new German government's assessment of the *Bauhaus* placed it within the category of *Entartete 'Kunst'* (degenerate 'art') associated with Bolshevism and Jewry, the immense political and financial clout of the United States helped to begin the process of globally disseminating Modernism (and *Bauhaus* Modernism in particular).[74]

At MoMA, Johnson's rôle was that of critic and curator, not architect, and he realized he needed to do something about that. In the early 1940s, despite his championing of Mies, Johnson returned to Harvard to study architecture under Gropius and Breuer. Harvard was his *alma mater*, and the Armour Institute did not equal its prestige (social or otherwise), so there would have been a certain amount of snobbery in Johnson's decision (which did not please Mies, who seems never to have forgiven him).[75] By that time anyway, Johnson was finding Mies 'difficult', Chicago 'did not amuse'[76] him, and, besides, Boston 'was near enough'[77] to civilization. There was another problem: the first dean of Harvard's new Graduate School of Design, Joseph Hudnut,[78] had been advised by Johnson to invite Miës (as he then was) to head the school. But Barr said that two other names should be put forward, and proposed Gropius and Oud. When Miës found out that Hudnut was also approaching Gropius, he refused to have anything to do with a university that would even conceive that there would be an equivalence between him and the Prussian.[79] Johnson, then, not only admitted to the prickliness of Mies, but said that Le Corbusier was even worse.[80] After he had come to admire Mies's work, he formed a low opinion of Gropius, exacerbated by his contacts with the German at Harvard.[81]

The obvious question is, how did Johnson square his enthusiasm for the *Bauhaus* with that for National-Socialist Germany, when so many *Bauhäusler* had left that country? As some have pointed out, many converts to Modernism

chose to believe that those who abandoned the Fatherland 'were moral heroes who sacrificed life and limb in the pursuit of freedom'.[82] But in fact
there do not appear to have been many who left 'purely out of a sense of
moral indignation':[83] architects and artists who were wholly or partly Jewish
eventually realized that they *had* to get out *in order to survive*. Some exiles had
actually admired Hitler; others (like Pevsner) could even admit to 'National
Socialist feelings',[84] and Johnson disparagingly, even distastefully, referred to
'Sainted Sir Nikolaus' wanting 'to become an honorary Aryan and stay on'[85]
in Germany. Gropius wrote to Goebbels in 1934 claiming that the new
Modern architecture was 'Germanic',[86] derived from work by Schinkel,[87]
and even harked back to Gothic, a fanciful notion that does not survive
careful analysis. Others, imbued with their sense of being German and
ingrained authoritarianism, felt like fishes out of water in their adopted
homes. For Nikolaus Pevsner's reactions to National Socialism, for example,
Harries may be read with benefit.[88] It is difficult not to conclude that
Johnson's admiration for the certainties of Modernist evangelists was not
all that far removed from his essentially romantic image of National
Socialism: in the case of Miës van der Rohe, there is an obvious 'resemblance
of the motivating and dynamic forces that underlay his style (and, by implication, all of architectural modernism)'—its idealism, absolutism, arrogance,
and deprecation of empirical reality—'to the principles that supported the
Third Reich'.[89]

   Miës was often heard to refer to the 'Spirit of the Age' (*Zeitgeist*), and held
that it alone was what counted and defined the 'epoch': the true prophet
knew about it; the true 'leader' (*Führer*) was always talking about it; and
the real architect built it. The whole of life was 'perceived within a stern
hierarchy of values in which all was sublimated'[90] towards some higher goal:
for Miës, it was his architecture; for the National Socialists it was the State.
Individuals counted for very little: Miës himself had stated that the individual, in 1924, was losing significance, and that the individual's destiny was
no longer of any interest.[91] Less than a decade later, Goebbels was to utter
similar views when he mentioned the 'dethroning of the individual', whose
'destiny' was no concern of the new State under National Socialism.[92]
Neither Miës nor National Socialism was concerned with 'normal' values
and constraints of the everyday world: the former ignored both context and
the wishes of his clients; the latter jettisoned the restraints of empathy and a
long-established moral code based on Judaeo-Christian ethics and Roman
civilization.

This is a very unsettling similarity: given Miës's huge influence on the development of Modern architecture and the almost universal 'acceptance of the principles under which he operated',[93] it might be suggested that the looming problems of Miës's rigid, steely, unbending certainties, and the historical facts of the Third Reich, are not merely German and not only architectural issues. Careful study of the origins, progress, and almost universal acceptance of architectural Modernism reveals a strange similarity between the *élitism* of its protagonists and that thread of ruthlessness and sense of superiority that runs through National Socialism: there was a curious remoteness from any sense of reality; a rejection of the world as it existed and a desire to destroy it; and a fanatical adherence to aspirations of some 'radiant'[94] future world that only had its reality in minds from which all compassion had been eradicated.[95] If Pugin, Ruskin, and others had held to notions of morality in architecture,[96] the reality was that for men like Miës and Johnson, architecture as an art was all that mattered: morality had no place whatsoever in their work. It was no accident that *émigrés* such as Gropius and Miës were not keen to draw too much attention to their German origins (even though the latter architect's grasp of English was very poor when he first arrived in the USA), so they came to attempt a severance of the Modern Movement from its historical beginnings, its cultural, philosophical, and stylistic roots,[97] and its Teutonic context. A close examination of those beginnings, rather than a shallow grasp of a few stylistic *clichés* backed by simplistic slogans, induces a deep sense of unease: there can be no doubting the unfeeling authoritarianism, even totalitarianism, at the dark, irreligious heart of Modernism, something that generally has been ignored.

At Harvard, Johnson conceived a loathing for Gropius, who, in turn, detested him.[98] It should be remembered that before he returned to Harvard to study architecture, Johnson had had a sound grounding in philosophy and history:[99] although he was enthusiastic about interpreting Modernism for the American public, he had no qualms about disparaging its claims for so-called 'functionalism', 'social responsibility', and spurious 'morality' (which he opined were shallow, untrue, and pretentious nonsenses, and so set himself in opposition to Gropius). He made his position quite clear in later years.[100]

Johnson's wealth enabled him to design and erect ('for fun'[101]) a Modernist house in Ash Street, Cambridge, MA (1942), a small building screened behind a wall enclosing a rectangular outdoor space that was obviously influenced by the work of Mies. Johnson admitted he designed and built it 'as propaganda against Gropius', who was suitably 'annoyed' by the gesture.[102] However, Johnson was to acknowledge that the systems of *obligatory* prefabrication he used for the house cost about twice what ordinary conventional construction would have involved. Gropius started a prefabrication company at that time which 'went bust'[103] the next year. Prefabrication, of course, was one of the core beliefs of Modernists, even though it was 'the most expensive way you could possibly imagine building':[104] its adoption was not always concerned with the logic of costs of construction, but carried other associations not unconnected with social engineering. The 'mechanization takes command'[105] belief of Gropius *et al.* could only lead to 'madness', but Gropius 'never learned' because he was an ideologist with a frame of mind that was 'catching' and spread to all his students.[106]

At Harvard Johnson thought Breuer the 'best man . . . the only artist'[107] in the whole programme. Indeed, Johnson felt that the 'rejection of artistry' at Harvard was a major problem, and that that rejection was entirely because of Gropius's attitudes which stemmed from the fact that he (Gropius) was 'not an artist'[108] at all, unlike Breuer or Mies, who, according to Johnson, were. Johnson opined that if Gropius's buildings at Harvard were torn down, the architectural profession 'might applaud',[109] and voiced his bewilderment as to why Gropius had such a big reputation at Harvard and elsewhere.[110]

The Style Becomes Widely Accepted Outside Germany

Czechoslovakia

The *Deutscher Werkbund* inspired progeny in many other countries, notably in Czechoslovakia,[111] where several International-Style dwellings were erected at the Brno Exhibition (1928): examples included works by Hugo Foltýn, Bohuslav Fuchs, Jiří Kroha, Miroslav Putna, and Josef Štěpánek. A second Czechoslovak *Werkbund* Exhibition was organized at Baba Hill, Prague (1932), with a further array of International-Modernist dwellings designed by Josef Gočár, Antonín Heythum, Pavel Janák, Hana Kučerová-Záveská, Evžen Linhart, Oldřich Starý, and Ladislav Žák. Indeed International Modernism was enthusiastically embraced in that country, even more so than in Germany itself, as can be seen in works by, among others, Adolf Benš, Jaroslav Frágner, Josef Fuchs, Viktor Fürth, František Lydie Gahura, Josef Havlíček, Karel Honzík, Vladimír Karfík, Josef Kranz, Jaromír Krejcar,

Josef Kříž, Ludvík Kysela, Mojmír Kyselka, Heinrich Lauterbach, Ernst Mühlstein, Richard F. Podzemný, Josef Polášek, Kamil Roškot, Lubomír Šlapeta, and Oldřich Tyl.[112]

Many architects working in Czechoslovakia between the wars were of 'left-wing' persuasion, none more so than Karel Teige, who, with others, founded (1920) the anti-academic *Devětsil* group to aggressively promote Modernism and Constructivism. Opposed to aesthetic considerations predetermining construction, Teige believed that medical science should dictate layout, planning, and structure in the 'New Architecture'. He edited (1922–8) the *avant-garde* journal *Stavba* (Building), developed relations between Czechoslovak Modernists and leading figures of the Movement abroad (including Le Corbusier and Hannes Meyer), and promoted housing-schemes for the proletariat, advocating 'dwelling-cabins' for each individual grouped in 'dwelling-hives', also arguing for the abolition of family households (no living together of two persons in one unit would be possible) and for the complete socializing of childrens' education (1932). He prepared and edited the report *Die Wohnung für das Existenzminimum* for the third CIAM congress in Brussels, a document that can still chill the stoutest of hearts, and may be read in English as *The Minimum Dwelling*.[113] He chaired the Prague-based Left Front, arguing it was the Czechoslovak branch of CIAM, but its extremism caused dissent within Czechoslovakia and even among the true believers of CIAM itself: nevertheless, the 'left-wing' municipal authorities in Prague and Brno were determined for a time to construct working-class housing taking into account Teige's anti-family views.

The Soviet Union

Around 1935–6, as Czechoslovak architects became more and more isolated, not only because of the huge political changes in Germany, but because their outlandish attitudes became more unacceptable abroad, and because Teige's view of architecture as a branch of science was no longer in fashion (fashion had no small part to play in the course architecture took in the twentieth century), his influence waned. This was not least because of Stalin's attitude to architecture and the arts, which shifted the party line away from the '*bourgeois*' affectations of the International style and towards a 'true Socialist Architecture' (*also called* 'Socialist Classicism') that would not be 'inferior to the immortal works of the great ages of Greece, Rome, and the Italian Renaissance',[114] as observed by Aleksei Viktorovich Shchusev (architect of the stripped Neo-Classical-Egyptianizing mausoleum [1924–30] of Vladimir Ilyich Ulyanov [*known as* 'Lenin'] in Moscow). The heroic architecture that evolved in the USSR in the 1930s was also gigantic in scale: much that Piranesi could only dream was made reality under Stalin.[115]

There had indeed been a short-lived period when International Modernism had made an appearance in the Soviet Union, notably in the works of Boris M. Velikovsky (*Gostorg* Building, Moscow, 1925–7, with others), Moisei Y. Ginzburg (House of the People, Moscow, 1932, complete with very long strips of windows and *pilotis*), and the Vesnin Brothers (Aleksandr, Leonid, and Viktor).[116] These worked together on various projects when Constructivism was fashionable,[117] were leading lights in the OSA (acronym for *Obshchestvo Sovremenikh Arkhitektorov* [Society of Contemporary Architects]) Group (active 1925–30), an organization similar to the German *Der Ring* for promoting 'contemporary' architecture (which meant Modernism): Ginzburg and A. Vesnin edited the OSA journal, *Sovremennaya Arkhitektura* (Contemporary Architecture), which promoted the cause.[118] The Vesnins' Likhachev Cultural Palace, Moscow (1930–7—later called ZIL), looked to International Modernism, while the *Mostorg* Department Store, Krasnaya Presnya 2/48, Moscow (1926–8), demonstrated the crudities of Modernism in terms of not responding sensitively to its site and surroundings: it rose oafishly above its neighbours without subtlety, exposing blank walls on either side, ignored established geometries of existing buildings, and featured a large curtain-wall over most of its frontage. One of the Soviet projects truest to International Modernism was the All-Union Institute of Electrical Engineering, Moscow (1927–9), by a team led by Aleksandr Vasilyevich Kuznetsov.[119] However, 'Socialist Classicism' under Stalin was soon to make such experiments fall from favour.[120]

This discomfited the Modernists who had gone to the Soviet Union seeking the Promised Land, if not Paradise itself, and then found it prudent to leave in a hurry. Among them were Ernst May,[121] who settled in Africa before returning to Germany in 1953, and Hannes Meyer, who returned to Switzerland. Teige, whose influence had been very strong for some fifteen years or so,[122] fell from grace, and soon became a marginal figure until the early twenty-first century, when his authoritarian 'leftism' started to appeal to new generations.[123] That many Modernists became bitterly disappointed with the way architecture was moving in the USSR under Stalin is unquestionably true, and for some the experience was as traumatic as the loss of religious faith: yet others, knowing no other path to follow, persisted, tying themselves in knots to explain away what had happened, and remained disciples of the cult.[124]

Hungary

Hungary, like Bohemia and Moravia (which had become Czechoslovakia), had been part of the enormous Austro-Hungarian Empire. But after the 1914–18 war (during which it experienced huge casualties) it lost a significant part of its territory, suffered from economic stagnation, and had a violent Communist government for a short time in 1919 under the rigid, fanatical, doctrinaire Béla Kun: so conditions in the country did not permit architecture to flourish.

Nevertheless, as in Germany and Czechoslovakia, the desire to break with the past and with discredited political systems favoured Modernism. Even in the so-called 'Regency' of Admiral Horthy (1920–44—the monarchy did not officially end until 1946), Modernism made its mark with works by Bertalan Árkay, Virgil Birbauer, Károly Dávid, Ferenc Domány, József Fischer, Alfréd Forbát, Gedeon Gerlóczy, Dénes Györgyi, Béla Hofstätter, Gyula Kaesz, Nándor Kőrmendy, Lajos Kozma, László Králik, László Lauber, Pál Ligeti, Máté Major, Farkas Molnár, Aladár Münnich, István Nyiri, Aladár and Viktor Olgyay, Frigyes Pogány, Gábor Preisich, Gyula Rimanóczy, Oszkár Winkler, and others.

Poland

In Poland, national independence (1918) after well over a century of foreign domination and dismemberment did not mean a violent break with the architectural past, although some architects associated historical styles with Partition (between Prussia, Russia, and Austria), and advocated the embrace of the 'International Style' as the only way forward to express the renewal of nationhood. Some experimented with Expressionism, notably Jan Witkiewicz-Koszczyc, who also drew on the vernacular architecture of the Zakopane area and on a tough robust style with accentuated entasis on stumpy columns derived from his studies in Germany. Modernism tended to make an impact in Poland slightly later than in Germany, Czechoslovakia, or Hungary, mostly in the 1930s, although the *Werkbund* had a strong influence in those parts of Poland that were German between the wars. At the *Werkbund* Exhibition of 1929 in Breslau (now Wrocław), for example, Scharoun designed a hostel of undoubted International-Modernist lineage, and other exhibits designed by Adolf Rading and Heinrich Lauterbach made quite a stir at the time. An exhibition was held in Warsaw (1926) of Modernist architecture by Le Corbusier, Perret, Oud, Rietveld, Melnikov, and other 'names', but there were no really significant realizations immediately after that.

German exemplars began to have an effect in Poland itself in the 1930s, but the Polish national exhibition of 1929 in Poznań (clearly intended as a riposte to the German efforts at Breslau) can be regarded as a catalyst, although much of the architecture there was not overtly Modernist. There was a reason why the Poznań exhibition was important. The city of Posen (as it had been under Germany) was of huge national and emotional significance to Poles: in 1911 a big event, the *Ostdeutsche Auβtellung* (East-German exhibition),[125] had been held there, with as its centrepiece the huge Expressionist heptagonal water-tower and exhibition-building by Poelzig. This was a remarkable structure with panels of brick and glass fitting flush within a steel frame and an interior with exposed lattice steelwork (demolished).[126] It was therefore significant that a Polish national event should be celebrated there, as it was on a site not far from Poelzig's and other buildings left from the 1911 East-German exhibition: it undoubtedly played some part in debates about architecture that continued thereafter, notably in the journals *Blok* and *Praesens*.[127] Certainly the impact of Modernism on Poznań, especially after the heavy destruction in the 1939–45 war, was enormous,[128] even though the centre of the Old Town has been immaculately reconstructed.

Examples of the crisp International-Modernist style seem to have dated from as late as 1928: one of the first was the 'house for three families' in Warsaw by Bohdan Lachert and Josef Szanajca, which had long strips of windows, a 'flat' roof, party-walls expressed above the roofline, and even Corbusian *pilotis*. The work of Helena and Szymon Syrkus, especially for private houses, was often, within the limitations of the style, paradigmatic. Among 1930s Modernist Polish architects were Jan Bagieński, Henryk Blum, Barbara and Stanisław Brukalski, Jadwiga Dobrzyńska, Stanisław Hempel, Lucjan Korngold, Zygmunt Łoboda, Witold Minkiewicz, Edgar Norwerth, Wacław Nowakowski, Bohdan Pniewski, Witold Wardzała, Juliusz Żórawski, Zygmunt Zyberk-Plater, and others.[129]

Belgium

Belgium produced its fair share of 'International-Style' buildings: Hitchcock and Johnson singled out the work of De Koninck (Lenglet house, Uccle, near

Brussels [1926]),[130] but the same architect's Ley house, Prins van Oranjelaan, Uccle [1934] was perhaps a better example [though too late for the 1932 exhibition and book]). Other Belgian contributions are illustrated in numerous sources,[131] and mention might be made of Victor Bourgeois (holiday-homes, Sint-Idesbald [1929]); Joseph Diongre (NIR building, Elsene, Brussels [1933–9]); Gaston Eysselinck (houses in Vaderlandstraat, Gent [1930–1], and Peeters house, Antwerp [1932–3]); P.A. Michel (*Maison de Verre*, Uccle, Brussels [1935–6]); E. Goffay (house, Sint-Pieters-Woluwe, Brussels [1935]); L.E. Govaerts & A. van Vaerenbergh (Vanderborght store, Brussels [1932–5]); and M. Leborgne (Villa Deridder, Loverval [1928] and Queen Astrid maternity-hospital, Charleroi [1938]).

Brasil

Brasil did not feature in Hitchcock & Johnson (1932): but the work of Odessa-born Gregori I. Warchavchik, who became one of the leading Brasilian architects from 1923, designing several houses in the 'International Style' in São Paulo in the late 1920s, including that for Luiz da Silva Prado,[132] was both influential and, in its own terms, not without distinction. Works by Lúcio Costa, Oscar Niemeyer, and others, were realized in the later 1930s and after, so were too late for inclusion by Hitchcock and Johnson.

Scandinavia

Finland was represented in Hitchcock & Johnson by Alvar Aalto's *Turum Sanomat* building (1928–9),[133] though there were other works by him that might have been selected, not least the tuberculosis sanatorium, Paimio (1932); they also mentioned E.W. Bryggman's Finnish pavilion at the Antwerp exposition in Belgium (1930).[134] Denmark they cited not at all (Arne Jacobsen's *Bellavista* housing scheme, Klampenborg, Copenhagen [1932] probably was also too late for inclusion). Norway also missed the boat (the works of Arne Korsmo and Sverre Aasland were among the first 'International-Style' houses to be built in that country: the *Villa Stenersen*, Oslo [1937–8] demonstrated with its *pilotis* and other approved *clichés* that Corbusian influences had arrived in Norway, and several houses in Oslo by G. Blakstad & H. Munthe-Kaas conformed to the aesthetic of the *Weißenhofsiedlung*).

Sweden made it to *The International Style* with buildings by E.G. Asplund (pavilions at the Stockholm exposition [1930]),[135] S. Markelius & U. Åhrén (student union, *Kungliga Tekniska Högskola*, Stockholm [1928–30]),[136] and E. Sundahl (housing for the Swedish Co-operative Society, Hästholmen, near Stockholm [1930]).[137] Interestingly, Blomfield praised Sweden[138] and Denmark for developing modern architecture on much sounder lines than was apparent elsewhere, the best pursuing the even tenor of its way, and not losing touch with the splendid heritage of the past.[139] There were, however, sound reasons why this should have been so, including the fact that craft-traditions were still very much alive in Scandinavia.

United States of America

Hitchcock & Johnson's coverage of the German contributions to the 'International Style', unsurprisingly, was much greater than that of any other country, but they identified a limited number of architects in the United States of America of whose works they approved. These were the Standard Oil Company's filling-stations (1931), by German-born A. Clauss and G. Daub;[140] the Harrison house (also called the *Aluminaire house* because it was designed for mass-production, largely of metal), Syosset, Long Island (1931), by A.L. Kocher (a friend of Gropius) and Swiss-born A. Frey (who had worked in Le Corbusier's office);[141] the Philadelphia Saving Fund Society skyscraper (1929–32), by G. Howe and Swiss-born W.E. Lescaze;[142] the McGraw-Hill skyscraper, West Forty-Second Street, New York (1931), by R. Hood[143] and French-born J.-A. Fouilhoux;[144] the Lovell health-house, Hollywood Hills, Los Angeles (1927–9), by Austrian-born R.J. Neutra (who, as previously noted, had worked in Mendelsohn's office);[145] and the Sam T. Weyman memorial laboratory, Highlands Museum, North Carolina (1931), by Tucker, Howell, and German-born O.G. Stonorov (who had worked with Lurçat).[146]

Howe & Lescaze designed several other buildings that fitted within the 'International-Style' label, including the nursery building for the Oak Lane day-school, Philadelphia (1929), and the Field house, Connecticut (1932). When Hood died, Lescaze designed the headmaster's house, Dartington Hall, Totnes, Devon (England) (1930–2), the Churston estate-housing, Devon (1932–6), the Lescaze house, 211 East 48th Street, New York City (1933–4), and, with George Daub, houses at Harvey Cedars, New Jersey (1937). Neutra designed several other influential houses, including residential developments, Westwood, Los Angeles (1936–8), and villas, including the Barsha, North Hollywood, CA, and Mensendieck, Palm Springs, CA (both 1937).

Switzerland

Switzerland acquired its fair share of International-Modernist buildings too: among them the *Schule für Kunst und Handwerk*, Bern (1937–8), by Hans Brechbühler; Neubühl housing, Zürich (1932), by Werner Max Moser; the *La Chandoline* apartments, Lausanne (1933), by Henri Robert von der Mühll; the Doldertal apartments, Zürich (1935–6), by Alfred and Emil Roth, with Marcel Breuer—a CIAM commission through Giedion; the Morand-Pasteur studio-house, Saillon, Valais (1933–5), by Alberto Sartoris; several villas at Riehen, Basel (1927–30), by Paul Artaria and Hans Schmidt; a villa at Binningen, Basel (1936), by Otto Senn; a villa at Gerzensee, Bern (1935), by Otto and Walter Senn; and the *Zetthaus*, Zürich (1930–2), by Rudolf Steiger, Carl Hubacher, and Robert Winkler. The *Zetthaus* is set on the curve of a street, and has long bands of strip-windows, reminiscent of Mendelsohn's Schocken department store, Chemnitz (1928).

The Netherlands

The Netherlands in many respects led Modernism in that the 'International Style' was eagerly embraced by numerous Dutch architects, and movements such as *De Stijl* had a considerable impact on many Modernists, not least those associated with the *Bauhaus*. Rietveld and Schröder-Schräder's House, Utrecht (1921–4), with each element expressed, was very influential for a time (*see* **Figure 3.2**); but more immediate was the impact of works by Brinkman and van der Vlugt, including the Sonneveld house, Rotterdam (1933), the De Bruyn house, Schiedam (1930), the *Bergpolder* slab-block of flats, Rotterdam (1933–4—with Willem van Tijen), and the van Nelle tobacco-factory, Rotterdam (1926–30—with Mart Stam); by Johannes Duiker, including the open-air school, Amsterdam (1930), *Zonnestraal Sanatorium*, Hilversum (1926–8—with Bernard Bijvoet); and by J.J.P. Oud, including the residential developments at Hoek van Holland (1924–7) and *Kiefhoek*, Rotterdam (1925–9). Willem Marinus Dudok's beautifully composed and detailed town hall at Hilversum (1924–30) was greatly admired at the time, particularly in Britain; but it did not fall into the International-Modernist category, as its sources lay in the work of Frank Lloyd Wright and in the long tradition of well-crafted brickwork found in The Netherlands: so Dudok was largely passed over by Hitchcock and Johnson.[147]

Austria

International Modernism was indeed that, but it should be emphasized that *it only represented a very small proportion of the total amount of building that went on at the time.* What soon became apparent was that it required serious money to make it at all smart and respectable (as at Miës's Barcelona pavilion and the Tugendhat house): done on the cheap, with poor workmanship, which happened in the Soviet Union and elsewhere, it looked shoddy and performed badly, and that has been the case ever since (not least in the British Isles). Exhibitions, such as the *Werkbundsauβtellung* in Vienna (1932), showed smart houses with modern furnishings designed by architects including the Austrian Joseph F. Dex, the Frenchman André Lurçat, the Dutchman Gerrit Rietveld, and the Austrian Oskar Strnad. An employment-office in Vienna (1932) by Ernst A. Plischke demonstrated International-Modernist characteristics, as did his own summer-house on the Attersee (1933–4) using very simple means. The German-born O.E. Schweizer designed Vienna's stadium (1929–31) in which much concrete was cast *in situ*, and the impressions of the timber boards used in the shuttering of formwork left as features to the finished work. Bavaria-born Lois Welzenbacher favoured thin cantilevered balconies on several of his schemes (e.g. Pension 'Turm' at Hall-im-Tirol [1930–1], the Buchroithner house, Zell-am-See [1929–30], and the Treichl house, Innsbruck [1929]), the obvious influence being that of Mendelsohn. Welzenbacher returned to more traditional *Völkisch* forms after the National Socialists came to power.[148]

The 'International Style' in Austria, however, like all its manifestations in other countries, did not grow from earlier work. There have been attempts to connect the very beautiful creations of Otto Wagner and others working in Vienna early in the century with International Modernism. His *Moderne Architektur* first appeared in 1896,[149] with subsequent editions of 1898, 1902, and 1914. The last edition was renamed *Die Baukunst unserer Zeit* (The Architecture [or, literally, The Art of Building] of Our Time),[150] prompted by Hermann Muthesius's *Stilarchitektur und Baukunst* (Style-Architecture and The Art of Building).[151] Like Muthesius's publications, notably *Das englische Haus*,[152] it was hostile to *Art Nouveau* (and also to its German equivalent, *Jugendstil*), despite Wagner's brief association with the *Sezession* and the inclusion of various *Jugendstil* features in many of his buildings. A perusal of Wagner's beautiful book (particularly the 1902 edition) will reveal black-and-white illustrations of his designs (buildings, details, or furniture) flanked by decorative motifs printed in a light brown colour. Those motifs are rooted in Classicism, *fin-de-siècle* ornament, and even traces of *Jugendstil*, while the buildings themselves were clearly derived from numerous respectable historical sources, including the works of Schinkel and exemplars of Austrian Baroque.[153] Wagner, like Berlage, was a master in the art of combining an inventive architecture of traditional materials such as stone, with metal, notably in the brilliant and beautiful structures his office designed (1894–1901) for the Vienna *Stadtbahn* (municipal railway-system), where even Ionic capitals were transformed into machine-like elements, but nevertheless the architecture was clearly rooted in precedent and did not attempt to jettison everything of worth.

At his great church of St Leopold, *Am Steinhof*, Vienna (1903–7), aspects of *Jugendstil*, Neo-Classicism, and Baroque were combined in a masterly synthesized whole, and his *Postsparkasse*, Vienna (1903–12) has a façade clad in stone fixed to the structure behind with metal bolts, the heads of which are exposed, and the interior of the banking-hall is treated without any historical references in a fresh and confident manner, using metal and glass only. His second *Villa Wagner*, No. 28 *Hüttelbergstraße*, Vienna (1912–13), anticipated aspects of twentieth-century Neo-Classicism and even Art Deco. Despite all the claims for Wagner as yet another supposed 'pioneer' of Modernism, study of his extant buildings and extensively published designs[154] will not reveal anything that points to the Modern Movement or to the works of its famous protagonists such as Gropius or Miës van der Rohe. Indeed, virtually everything Wagner designed is closely identified with the fecund artistic milieu of late nineteenth- and early twentieth-century Vienna, Imperial and Royal capital of the vast Austro-Hungarian Empire, the architectural equivalent, perhaps, of the lush ripeness of Gustav Mahler's music. Wagner's celebrated pupils included architects Josef Hoffmann[155] and Jože Plečnik.[156] The former suffered from attacks against his 'outdated' Arts-and-Crafts mentality, and Giedion[157] did not do justice to his work 'because it would not fit easily into his polemically simplified version of architectural history'.[158] Plečnik's extraordinary and wonderfully inventive *oeuvre* was ignored (not least by Giedion, Hitchcock, Johnson, and Pevsner) until comparatively recently because it was steeped in an inconveniently fluent understanding of Classicism.

So why was Wagner mentioned so often by those promoting the Modern Movement? As is so often the case, this stems from his writings in which he did what many others had done in the nineteenth century: he fulminated against architectural styles, and called for an architecture suitable for 'modern living', with simplified expressions of structure and the materials used in such construction. But his architecture, both realized and on paper only, was part of a tradition: it was not a sundering, a break with what had gone before at all. Even the banking-hall of the celebrated *Postsparkasse*, Vienna, can be seen as a refinement of a type of iron-and-glass structure that had evolved from early nineteenth-century glass-houses and had further developed into building-types such as railway-termini, exhibition-halls, and shopping-arcades. Wagner's great schemes of town planning,[159] too, do not herald the demands of CIAM, Le Corbusier, or the Athens Charter: they are firmly within a Classical, even Baroque, tradition, influenced by earlier Viennese work of Gottfried Semper, Eduard van der Nüll, and August Siccard von Siccardsburg, and linked to the City Beautiful Movement in the USA (as promoted by C.M. Robinson, and culminating in the plan for Chicago [1906–9] by D.H. Burnham and E.H. Bennett), and also with the *Beaux-Arts* approach to urban layouts.

Perhaps Wagner's most telling influence was on his former pupil, Karl Ehn, whose massive *Karl-Marx-Hof*, Vienna (1927–30) was a fine example of the 'superblock' approach to municipal housing, and retained much of the clear geometry apparent in Wagner's town-planning schemes.[160]

France & 'Le Corbusier'

We now turn to France, and the Swiss-born Charles-Édouard Jeanneret, one of the most influential figures in twentieth-century architecture. He worked briefly with Auguste Perret in Paris (1908–9) before joining (again briefly) Behrens in Berlin (1910–11), an experience which gave him his admiration for German skills in organizational methods. In 1914–15 he evolved the *Dom-Ino* (from the Latin *domus* [house] and the *innovative* reinforced-concrete column grid that suggested the patterns of a domino piece). Essentially, columns supported floor-slabs, and the design offered a prototype for industrialized living-units, giving freedom in matters of room-arrangement and elevational treatment: non-structural partitions could be erected where desired, and elevations filled with any pattern of glazing and solid panels uninhibited by structural requirements because the columns were not placed around the edges of the slabs, but set back from the perimeters (**Figure 5.1**).

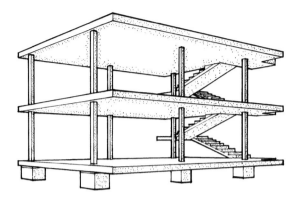

Figure 5.1. *Dom-Ino* skeleton by Le Corbusier showing floor-slabs supported on columns

He settled in Paris (1916), where he developed his considerable skills as a self-publicist,[161] and through Perret he met the painter, Amédée Ozenfant, with whom he founded *L'Esprit Nouveau* (1920–5), a journal devoted to the Modernist aesthetic in all its manifestations. C.-É. Jeanneret-Gris contributed polemics under a pseudonym, styling himself 'Le Corbusier-Saugnier', later shortened to 'Le Corbusier':[162] these were collected and published (1923) as *Vers une architecture* (Towards an Architecture), a heady brew of the latest technology, messianic slogans proclaiming the supposed moral and hygienic virtues of the architectural language (Corbusier was obsessed with hygiene), and debatable claims that ideas therein derived from Antiquity. The last attracted uncritical devotees.

It was not, however, a text that could be comfortably regarded as a serious book: rather it was a set of repetitive, simplistic slogans designed to act as a propaganda manual for destroying humane architecture and coherent, civilized urban structures. It set in motion an orgy of destruction, wrecking intricate and living urban organisms, ignoring complexity, and imposing deadly abstractions based on a confused misunderstanding that the superficial appearances of already outdated technical solutions such as motor-cars, primitive aeroplanes, and ocean-going liners were the same thing as real 'progress' and that their imagery could be applied to architecture to make it 'Modern'. Osbert Lancaster pithily noted that when

> Le Corbusier first propounded his theory of the house as *une machine à habiter* it was doubtful if he foresaw the exact form in which it would be translated into fact. That other well-known architectural authority, Herr Hitler, must claim the credit for recent compliance on the part of the insular British with the extreme dictates of the continental functionalists.[163]

Lancaster's comments accompanied a drawing of an 'Even More Functional' interior during the 1939–45 war.

After he assumed his pseudonym, Jeanneret carefully and comprehensively applied the eraser to his first thirty formative years (1887–1917), and thereafter there were two *personae*, as he himself explained in 1926:

> Le Corbusier creates architecture, recklessly. He pursues disinterested ideas; he does not wish to compromise himself in betrayals, in compromises. It is an entity free of the burdens of carnality. He must…never disappoint…Jeanneret is the embodied person who has endured the innumerably radiant or wretched episodes of an adventurous life….[164]

This piece of self-absorption was signed by both C.-É. Jeanneret and Le Corbusier.

Advocating that buildings should be as practically constructed as modern machines, with 'rational' planning, and capable of being erected quickly using mass-produced components, Corbusier seemed to offer something that might help to resolve the difficulties of housing large numbers of people quickly, efficiently, and cheaply. From 1921 he collaborated with his cousin, A.-A.-P. Jeanneret-Gris, and from their Parisian office flowed a torrent of Modernist polemics and designs for experimental housing in which simple forms and smooth walls were *de rigueur*. Then followed three well-publicized and influential designs, though not for cheap mass-housing at all: the first was the *Villa Stein*, Garches (1927–8); the second was for two houses at Miës's *Weißenhofsiedlung*, Stuttgart (1927); and the third the *Villa Savoie*, Poissy, Paris (1928–31).

The last was the definitive exemplar of Corbusier's *Five Points for a New Architecture*, and, with its formal, if limited, architectural language, *pilotis*, linkage of external and internal spaces, long strip-windows, and crisp, uncompromising lines, became a powerful paradigm for twentieth-century supposed 'Rationalism' (**Figure 5.2**). Its derivation from elements taken from ocean-going ships was evident (**Figure 5.3**). The *cinq points*, with other Commandments, were expounded in Alfred Roth's book[165] on houses by Corbusier and Jeanneret-Gris. They were, in essence:

> the use of *pilotis* as structural elements, lifting the building and leaving a space under it;
> columnar-and-slab construction enabling floor-plans to be left as free and as adaptable as possible, partitions (if required) not being structural;
> the creation of a roof-garden on the top, affording better light and air than on the ground;
> a mode of construction facilitating long continuous strips of windows;

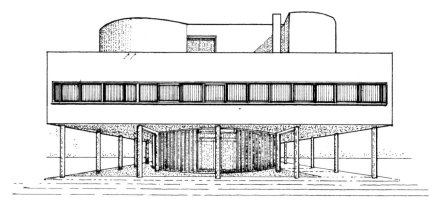

Figure 5.2. The *Villa Savoie*, Poissy, Paris (1928–31), by Le Corbusier, showing the *pilotis*, strip-windows derived from ships, and upperworks with a nautical flavour. It is striking how Le Corbusier's buildings never seem to grow naturally from, or are related in any way to, the ground: Nature is ignored

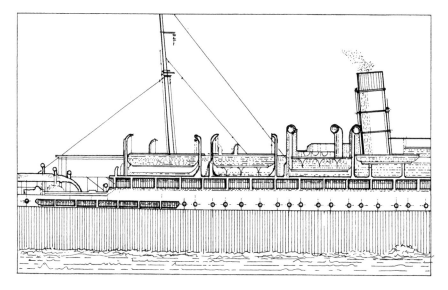

Figure 5.3. The ocean-going French liner, *Lamoricière*, built by Swan, Hunter, & Wigham Richardson Ltd., Wallsend, 1921, which sank in a storm off Cap Favàritx, north-east of Menorca, 1942. Le Corbusier used it as an exemplar, *ordering* architects to note the 'new architectural forms; elements both vast and intimate but on man's scale; freedom from the "styles" that stifle us; good contrast between the solids and voids; powerful masses and slender elements' (*see* Corbusier [1946] 93 [99 in the *c*.1930 edn.])

and

> complete freedom of façade-design.

Corbusier's staccato slogans, laced with his concerns with hygiene, included demands that:

> bathrooms face south and should be one of the largest rooms in the house, opening to a balcony for sun-bathing;
> adjoining should be a dressing-room because one should never (according to him) undress in a bedroom as that is not a clean thing to do and makes the room untidy;
> there should be bare walls in the bedroom, living-room, and dining-room;
> the kitchen should be on the top of the house to avoid smells;
> gramophones or the wireless give access to 'exact interpretations of first-rate music', so colds (as well as the embarrassing 'frenzy' of performers) could be avoided by *not* going to concert-halls;
> the maid's room [*sic*] should not be in an attic;

and

> 'servants' should not be 'parked' under the roof.

One should always bear in mind (without a hint of irony) economy in actions, household management, and thoughts, he instructed. Every modern man has, he claimed, the 'mechanical sense': feelings in regard to machinery are of respect, gratitude, and esteem, he asserted. Machinery included economy as an essential factor 'leading to minute selection', and there was a 'moral sentiment in the feeling for mechanics'. 'The man who is intelligent, cold and calm has grown wings to himself. Men—intelligent, cold and calm— are needed to build the house and to lay out the town.'[166]

At the *Exposition International des Arts-Décoratifs et Industriels Modernes*, Paris (1924–5), Corbusier and Jeanneret-Gris presented their *Pavillon de L'Esprit Nouveau*, a white box containing a model of the so-called *Plan Voisin* for Paris, an architectural and town-planning 'time-bomb',[167] proposing the complete destruction of part of Paris east of the Louvre, and between Montmartre and the Seine, and its replacement with eighteen gigantic skyscrapers. Corbusier's Utopian (really Dystopian) ideas for town planning, enshrined in his *Ville Contemporaine* (1922), *Urbanisme* (1925), and *Plan Voisin*, provided the imageries for redevelopment of existing cities and for new towns that were to be almost universally adopted, largely through the influence of CIAM and its effective secretary-general,

Sigfried Giedion,[168] although other forces were to help to propel them to pre-eminence.

Le Corbusier's deceptively mistitled book, *La Ville Radieuse* (1935), contains demands (the word is chosen with care) for a Utopian city in which only buildings conforming to his chosen aesthetic would be erected. Streets would be abolished, and cities would become part of the country. He himself would live under a pine-tree thirty miles outside the city, and his secretary would live thirty miles away from it too, in the opposite direction, under another pine-tree: both would have motor-cars, and would use up tyres, wear out road-surfaces, shred gears, and consume prodigious quantities of oil and petrol. Thus work would be created, enough for everybody. That sort of thing, viewed from the twenty-first century, suggests a fantasy-world very far removed from any reality, with no grasp whatsoever of any considerations of environmental damage, pollution, or much else. What it does suggest is a monstrous egotism, a destructive overweening conceit of staggering proportions, and an infatuation with unsustainable consumerism.[169]

In the 1930s, Le Corbusier and Jeanneret-Gris (whose contributions to the former's work are usually underestimated) were able to build the *Pavillon Suisse, Cité Universitaire*, Paris (1930–3), and the *Cité de Refuge* (a Salvation-Army hostel), Paris (1929–33): these paradigmatic slab-blocks of framed construction with large areas of glass caused difficulties with solar-heat-gain and -glare, as well as heat-loss, yet were to be progenitors of countless problematic slab-blocks thereafter solely because of image and pseudo-religious belief. Such a pretty pass can only be explained because of obsessions concerning glass (most probably derived from the slogans on buildings designed by people like Taut) as an indicator of 'modernity', 'progressiveness', and 'cleanliness': this excessive concern with hygiene-modernity-cleanliness-brightness (like Corbusier's horror of smells and undressing in bedrooms [no visual erethism there, then]) was symptomatic of a rigid, cold,[170] joyless puritanism that pervades much of Modernism. Corbusier's own background was that of Calvinism, which might explain a great deal.[171] The glass-industry, which had sponsored the Taut pavilion in 1914, had an interest in publicizing its products, so the aphorisms on the building drew on quasi-mysticism for commercial purposes.

Large-scale projects also occupied Le Corbusier from the late 1920s, including competition designs for the League of Nations Palace, Geneva (1926–7): his entries were among several to win a prize; only his proposal met the budget, yet there was resistance to realization of the designs, so he and Giedion orchestrated an international protest. When the job went to another architect, to be assisted by three other premiated[172] competitors, Corbusier accused the League of appropriating his plan, and attempted to sue for plagiarism. This created a furore: further uproar was ensured by a letter written to the 'world-*élite*', by several well-publicized exhibitions, and by a book,[173] all of which ensured that Corbusier was elevated as the great hero of International Modernism, and took a leading rôle in CIAM.[174] In the same year, after a preliminary limited competition, he was selected to design the headquarters of the Central Union of Consumer Operatives in Moscow, and, with Soviet disciples, he built (1928–36) the *Tsentrosoyuz* Building, Kirova (later Myasnitskaya) Street. However, while under construction, its purpose was altered to accommodation for the Ministry of Light Industry, in the process of which it lost both its air-conditioning system and the spaces celebrating the proletariat.

During this business, Corbusier seems to have caused something of a stir in architectural politics, and in 1931, with Gropius, Mendelsohn, Perret, and Poelzig, was invited to participate in the competition to design the Palace of the Soviets; but by that time the party line in the USSR was shifting, and in the event, after delaying tactics, two further competitions were held. In 1932 the Committee for the Construction of the Palace, chaired by Molotov (another pseudonym, associated with a Hammer—he was actually born Skryabin), fronting for Stalin, passed a resolution instructing architects to make use of 'both new designs and the best designs of classical architecture':[175] one can imagine the gnashing of teeth among the Corbusians and representatives of CIAM. In the event, Stalin chose a design by V.G. Gel'freikh, B.M. Iofan, and V.A. Shchuko that completely rejected the International-Modern 'style': it was to be a massive pile up of simplified Classical elements, the whole ensemble completed by a gigantic statue of Lenin plonked on top of it.[176] It had become absolutely clear that the extremely limited architectural language of International Modernism would not do to express the ambitions and aims of the Stalinist Soviet Union. Le Corbusier was to prepare other grandiose designs including the Ministry of Education and Health, Rio de Janeiro, Brasil (1936–45—executed by Lúcio Costa and a team of Corbusian disciples including Oscar Niemeyer and Affonso Reidy): the building influenced generations of Latin-American architects over the next three decades.

At the *Exposition Internationale des Arts et Techniques dans la Vie Moderne*, Paris (1937), the German (by Albert Speer) and USSR (by Iofan) pavilions glowered at each other across the main axis: the German pavilion was crowned by a massive eagle by Kurt Schmidt-Ehmen and flanked by heroic groups of figure by Josef Thorak: the USSR building had a colossal *Industrial Worker and Collective Farm Girl* by Vera Mukhina capping the front, gesturing energetically towards the German pavilion.[177] For the same exhibition, Corbusier and Jeanneret-Gris designed the *Pavillon des Temps Nouveaux* of steel, with a tent-like canvas roof, the whole derived from an image of the Jewish Tabernacle in the wilderness mixed with elements of aeroplane structures. The slogan over the rostrum evoked the Popular Front (an amalgam of Communist, Socialist, and Radical parties), and inside, like the Ten Commandments, were CIAM principles, some of which would be incorporated within the Athens Charter: a recipe for the destruction of urban fabric all over the world.

Thus, politically, Corbusier seemed to be allying himself with the 'left', but his position throughout the 1930s was ambivalent. Nevertheless, he was attacked for undermining Western society as part of a calculated programme of subversion organized under the aegis of the Comintern;[178] he was specifically identified as a malign influence by Gustave Umbdenstock;[179] and he was denounced by the French critic Camille Mauclair as a totalitarian, authoritarian vandal, intent on destroying regional, national, individual, and even racial characteristics[180] in his insistence of one style of architecture for the whole world. Le Corbusier responded, referring to the criticisms of himself and his works as a 'crusade'.[181] Significantly, his former Czech admirer, Karel Teige, charged him with empty monumentality and lofty speculation,[182] to which he provided a defence.[183]

Yet Le Corbusier was also involved with the Syndicalists (who started out as quasi-anarchists on the 'extreme left', but became transmogrified into an authoritarian organization on the 'extreme right' with similarities to Fascism:[184] they rejected '*bourgeois*' civilization, of course), and during the 1939–45 war, after the Fall of France, Le Corbusier toadied to the Vichy *régime*.[185] This affected his relationships with both Jeanneret-Gris and Charlotte Perriand, but his hero-worshipping disciples, oblivious to any possibility of their messiah having any faults, were always in denial. In 2015, however, the French architect Marc Perelman published a devastating critique of Le Corbusier, subtitled *une froide vision du monde* (a cold vision of the world), in which he firmly places the blame for the global wreckage meted out to towns and cities on this man.[186] Other recent studies should begin to persuade doubters that Le Corbusier was not above reproach,[187] and a hard-hitting article published in the journal *Quadrant* (2015) should serve to expose him for what he was, rather than as a figure far too many, even today, regard as a deity.[188] A careful, clear-headed reading *of what he himself wrote* should be enough to convince any reasonable person of Le Corbusier's unsuitability as a mentor whose programmes should be emulated or followed. The problem is that most people simply accept *what they are told he stood for* and obey commands to embrace his cult.

In 1921 Corbusier had met P.-A.-E. Winter, whose theories on hygiene clearly influenced his obsessions about the topic. Winter and Philippe Lamour formed (1928) a revolutionary Fascist party, and in 1931 both were involved with others of like mind in the founding of the short-lived *avant-garde* magazine *Plans: Revue Mensuelle*, backed financially by Jeanne Walter, wife of the architect Jean Walter, who also directed the journal. Others associated with it were F.-M.-J. M. de Pierrefeu (who was fascinated by the symbolism of numbers and shapes), Hubert Lagardelle (National Syndicalist, great admirer of Italian Fascism under Benito Mussolini, and future Minister of Labour [1942–3] under Pétain's Vichy *régime*), Le Corbusier, and Gropius. When *Plans* ceased publication in 1932, Corbusier, with Winter, Pierrefeu, and Lagardelle as co-editors, founded *Prélude* (1932–6); this had similar aims, not unconnected with promoting Corbusier's agendas, some of which were revealed in his *La Ville Radieuse* (1935), a publication advocating a reality that was anything but radiant. The book included a picture of a Fascist rally in Venice captioned 'little by little the world approaches its destiny'. In 'Moscow, in Berlin, in Rome...the masses gather around a strong idea', the 'strong idea' being kow-towing to an authoritarian *régime*, one capable of building a new age to fit in with Le Corbusier's ambitions. A perusal of *Plans, Prélude*, and *La Ville Radieuse* is sufficient to show that Le Corbusier had pronounced Fascist tendencies in the 1930s,[189] something one would never hear admitted in a British school of architecture. A salutary exercise might be to start by reading the editorials in *Plans*: fair-minded persons acquainted with the French language will find their tone repugnant.[190]

When France fell in 1940, Corbusier lost little time in attempting to ingratiate himself with the Vichy *régime*: notably with Bernard Marcel Peyrouton, Minister of the Interior and known anti-Semite, who, he hoped, would enable him to realize his authoritarian visions.[191] Soon he was to be rewarded: in 1941 he, Pierrefeu, and André Boll were appointed by the Vichy government to prepare a study on developing a national construction policy;[192] but the man in charge of planning, the technocrat François Lehidoux, found Le Corbusier's pretensions extremely irritating and impossible, so the whole thing was cancelled. Apart from being an unscrupulous bully, Corbusier had quite a history of antagonizing his enemies and exasperating his friends. Before the Vichy Government was established, Pierrefeu had worked with Le Corbusier and Jean Giraudoux on a study of housing; and in 1942 Pierrefeu and Le Corbusier published *La Maison des Hommes*.[193] This book was later translated by Clive Entwistle and Gordon Holt as *The Home of Man* (1948) with, significantly, Corbusier's name given before that of Pierrefeu, an indication of his almost deified status among British disciples.

Corbusier, autocratic himself, contemptuous of democracy and elections, and loving power, saw those who wielded it as potential clients or employers, no matter what their political colours. He was, like many other architects of that 'epoch', naturally attracted to authoritarian *régimes*, and, like many other supposedly 'leftist' architects of the period, prepared to serve anybody who would give him the means of realizing his ideas. He never acknowledged his links, least of all with the government of Marshal Pétain (1940–4), which was complicit in the deportation and therefore extermination of French Jewry,[194] but there is no doubt he was closely connected with several unsavoury individuals and groups.[195]

Absolutist tendencies in Corbusier may have been derived in part from the philosophy of Blaise Pascal,[196] who was also extremely rigid in his demands and ideas, holding that individuals should withdraw from society and meditate in solitude, away from the raucous company of the street. Admiration for Pascal's ideas may explain something of Corbusier's Dystopian designs for cities, and the blocks of apartments which would provide cell-like accommodation for purposes of self-exploration. Delvings into the unpleasant world of certain circles in pre-war and Vichy France suggest that Le Corbusier's flirtations with overtly Fascist or crypto-Fascist parties always left him disappointed, because they were not Fascist enough for his demanding, rigid, authoritarian, stentorian nature. He obviously had no idea what irony was or meant.

Other influential Modernists active in France between the wars included Pierre Chareau, whose house (designed 1928) in *Rue St-Guillaume*, Paris, had a steel-framed structure and employed glass-blocks (which pre-dated their more trumpeted use by Corbusier), giving the building the name *Maison de Verre*, completed (1932) in collaboration with the Dutchman Bernard Bijvoet. Another was the Armenian, Gabriel Guévrékian, whose *Villa Heim*, Neuilly, Paris (1927–8), had a garden broken up into small areas, including part on the roof. André Lurçat was a prolific polemicist, whose *École Karl-Marx*, Villejuif (1931–3), was an alleged attempt to associate architectural forms with the revolutionary workers' movement, and led to his invitation to Moscow (1934). He brought *Bauhaus* and CIAM dogmas with him, only to find that these did not fit within Stalinist Socialist Realism in which powerful, stripped Neo-Classicism loomed large: he accepted that form follows what is demanded during the Stalin era (1925–53), as his many buildings in St-Denis and Maubeuge (1946–50) tellingly demonstrate. Also worthy of note are Rob(ert) Mallet-Stevens, whose apartments, *Rue Mallet-Stevens*, Paris (1926–7), received the *imprimatur* of Modernists; and Georges-Henri Pingusson, whose *Style Paquebot* (as demonstrated in his *Hotel Latitude 43*, St Tropez [1931–2]) was a direct response to Corbusier's perceptions of passenger-ships as floating apartment-blocks:

> if we forget that a steamship is a machine for transport…we shall feel that we are facing an important manifestation of temerity, of discipline, of harmony, of a beauty that is calm, vital and strong…A serious-minded architect, looking at it as an architect (*i.e.* a creator of organisms), will find in a steamship his freedom from an age-long but contemptible enslavement to the past…the house of the earth-man is the expression of a circumscribed world. The steamship is the first stage in the realization of a world organised according to the new spirit.[197]

There is much more of the same in a book trumpeted in The Architectural Press's preface as having 'had as great an influence on English architectural thought as any one publication of the last fifty years',[198] a book, moreover, that was the 'first popular exposition in English of that "modern movement" in architecture' of which Le Corbusier was 'one of the principal prophets'.[199] That 'influence' explains much that is unacceptable in what is around us today.

Reginald Blomfield pithily commented on this sort of thing: he mentioned 'airship hangars, silos for cement, grain-elevators and refuse destructors as models admired by Modernists. Le Corbusier has much to say about the beauty of liners and motor-cars, and Golosov was so impressed with the beauty of a dynamo that he designed his building as a cog-wheel.'[200] By 'Golosov' Blomfield may have meant Ilya Aleksandrovich Golosov, but he could have confused Golosov with Mel'nikov, whose Rusakov Workers' Club, Moscow (1927–8), had auditoria and circulation-spaces expressed externally in strongly elemental forms resembling vast cogs (*see* **Figure G.2**). Mel'nikov did indeed design a project for the Commissariat of Heavy

Industry, Red Square, Moscow (1934, unrealized), where the cog-wheel was treated monumentally in a vast, almost Piranesian vision,[201] and it seems likely Blomfield simply made an error. The Architectural Press's claims about the influence of *Towards a New Architecture*, and about Corbusier as a 'prophet' were ominously true, but that prophet's influence, arguably, has been malign: *si monumentum requiris, circumspice.*[202]

What Blomfield complained of in the propaganda of Modernism was 'its confusion of thought, its persistent habit of begging the question, and of laying down as accepted principles what are, in fact, merely dogmatic assertions'. He protested strongly against the claim 'that buildings in which we live and work in are just "machines". Buildings... have a spiritual life of their own; it is possible to regard them with an affection that we should never bestow on a dynamo or a mowing-machine.'[203]

Miriam Wornum, American wife of the architect George Grey Wornum, raised questions about Le Corbusier and others, especially as they were 'too severe in their elimination of the past and all its ornaments and richness'. Instead, they gave us 'a plain box and ask us to believe it is the "last word" of the Spirit of the Age':[204] she did not believe a word of it. Amazed by the 'chorus of praise and admiration from architectural writers', she had heard from Le Corbusier's 'own lips that he deliberately ignores his clients' taste, and does not care what they do to the interior of his houses'. As a result, she saw builders 'putting into one of his houses old-fashioned plumbing discarded a decade ago'.[205] When I visited the *Villa Savoie* some years ago, I was amazed by the antiquated appearance of plumbing and fixtures of the same vintage as the *Titanic* (or even earlier). Wornum went on to state that by ignoring clients' needs and expressing just himself, Le Corbusier made 'bad art'. 'Why must I have... a bare, uncomfortable home designed by a man who doesn't care a jot about me and my personality?',[206] she asked.

Corbusier dogmatically asserted that ceilings of rooms should be low enough to be touched, something he justified by means of a mystical numerical system (always a dangerous path to follow). So floor-to-ceiling heights were to be fixed at 2.26 metres (*c.*7 feet 5 inches), but in recent years, fuelled by cost-cutting, oppressively even lower ceiling heights have often been adopted for housing, aided by industrialized design. Modernist theories were therefore drawn upon for commercial motives, and user-reactions based on human feelings were ignored.[207]

Some have asked why Corbusier is still 'rammed down' the 'throats'[208] of architectural students today? Lutyens, concerned about Le Corbusier's dismissiveness of the past, wrote that the 'experience of 3000 years of man's... creative work... cannot be disregarded unless we are prepared for disaster'.[209] He also felt Corbusier's proposals for a City of Towers were 'terrifying', and found 'mass-made cages suitable for machine-made men'[210] uncongenial. Even Martin Pawley said that Corbusier had a lot to answer for: his 'myopic vision'[211] was largely realized by his disciples, 'and the consequences have been disastrous'.[212] Yet, even when it had become clear that Corbusianity had done immense damage, a reverential exhibition at London's Hayward Gallery in 1987 drew 'admiring groups of architectural students' to pay homage to 'the architect of the century' who wanted to 'create a new type of human being'.[213] Architects should cease trying to mould humankind into what they want or deem appropriate, especially as they have no real scientific evidence to support their Utopian aims.

Corbusier's dogmatic assertions that the Romans knew nothing of the use of marble goes some way to explain why his disciples so admired raw, bare, crude concrete, seeing in it some sort of virtue: but the fact is that the Romans themselves never intended concrete walls to be seen at all, and covered them with up with marble and other finishes, including painted plaster.[214] So the Corbusians were just plain wrong, and had not understood that finishes get removed from walls, especially if they can be used for other purposes, such as marble burned to create quicklime for mortar in new building, or recycled for use as wall-coverings elsewhere. Plaster, subjected to damp and decay, tends to fall off walls, taking painted decorations with it. The result of such misconceptions was that raw concrete, uncovered, was promoted as 'Brutalism' and seen as 'moral', historically respectable, and 'honest', whereas 'discoloured concrete and rusted metal' actually proved a lot more offensive 'than mellowed brick and stone'.[215] And the disquieting fact is that, once again, in the twenty-first century, Brutalism is attracting new admirers who chronicle its supposed virtues, moral or whatever.[216]

Fascist Italy & The International Style: A Problem for Apologists

When it came to Italy, Modernists on the 'left' had a problem, for in terms of the language of the 'International Style' (such as it was), some of the better exemplars were in fact in that country, a Fascist dictatorship from 1925 under Mussolini (though the Fascists had actually come to power in 1922).

Although Hitchcock and Johnson only illustrated the Electrical House at the Monza Exposition (1930), by Luigi Figini and Gino Pollini,[217] the last exhibited an artist's studio-house at the *Triennale*, Milan (1933), while Figini's 'architect's house' in the 'Journalists' Village', Milan, complete with *pilotis* and long strips of openings cut in a crisp white box, was as perfect a model of International Modernism as could be desired. Those architects were members of *Gruppo 7* (founded 1926), an *avant-garde* association which announced the advent of Corbusian *esprit nouveau* in its manifesto, *La Rassegna Italiana* (1926–7), and laid the foundations for what became known as *Razionalismo*, in which the so-called 'machine aesthetic' was to be invoked: however, it also argued in favour of a sense of history and concerns for rhythm and Classical proportions, unlike Modernists in certain other countries who wished only for the *tabula rasa*. The manifesto claimed that the 'universal' achievements of the Modern Movement could be adapted to national characteristics, and indeed it clearly expressed a nationalist agenda that fitted within the cultural ambitions of the Fascist *régime*. Other important members of *Gruppo 7* included Ubaldo Castagnoli (soon replaced [1927] by Adalberto Libera), Guido Frette, Sebastiano Larco, Carlo Enrico Rava, and Giuseppe Terragni.

Gruppo 7 exhibited at the *Weißenhofsiedlung*, Stuttgart (1927), and the critical success of the Group's activities led to a major exhibition in Rome (1928), the *Esposizione dell'Architettura Razionale*; and soon a larger organization was formed, the *Movimento Italiano per l'Architettura Razionale* (MIAR). Of course, one of the most celebrated of these Italian 'Rationalists' was Terragni, with his *Novocomum* Apartments, Como (1927–8): but his *Casa del Fascio*, Como (1932–6), is regarded as his finest work, demonstrating successful Fascist patronage of Modern-Movement architecture. Most of his work in and around Como was designed with his brother, the underestimated and unsung Attilio, and included the *Kindergarten Antonio Sant'Elia* (after the celebrated Futurist) (1932–7), the apartment-block *Giuliani Frigerio* (1939–40), and the *Villa Bianca*, Seveso (1936–7), all in Como. With Antonio Carminati he also designed the *Casa del Fascio*, Lissone (1938–9). A convinced Fascist, like many other Italian Rationalists, his unrealized designs (1938) for the Dante memorial, museum, and study-centre, Rome, perhaps his finest achievements, with their stripped, bare, elemental monumentality and grave, dramatic impact, sum up the essence of architectural expression as favoured by the Fascist Party.[218] Terragni also collaborated with Pietro Lingeri: their joint efforts included the *Casa Rustici* and *Casa Lavezzari* apartment-blocks, Milan (1934–5). On his own account, Lingeri produced the *Amila* yacht-club, Tremezzo (1930); a studio-house on the island of Comacina (1935–6), both Lake Como; and a block of flats in Como itself (1935–6).

The work of Franco Albani made a considerable impression in the 1930s, and included the *Fabio Filzi* housing-project, Milan (1936–8—designed with Renato Càmus and Giancarlo Palanti): other architects managed to produce buildings of unquestionable International-Modern credentials, including the *Pietro Edouardo Crespi* Fascist headquarters in Milan (1938–9—by Gianni Angelini, Giuseppe 'Pepp.' Calderara, and Tito Varisco Bassanesi).

One of the most successful practices was BBPR Architectural Studio, established in Milan in 1932 by Gianluigi Banfi, Ludovico Barbiano di Belgiojoso, Enrico Peressutti, and Ernesto Nathan Rogers. Like many Italian Modernists, BBPR backed Fascism, hoping it would continue to favour 'progressive' architecture: indeed some of their buildings, e.g. the Heliotherapy Centre, Legnano (1937–8—destroyed 1956), were indubitably acceptable as 'Rationalist'. Nevertheless, Banfi perished in the infamous concentration-camp at Mauthausen, Austria, and Rogers, being of partly Jewish descent, prudently took refuge in Switzerland (1943–5). Then (1954–8) BBPR designed the *Torre Velasca*, Milan, with projecting upper storeys reminiscent of a mediaeval tower; by its allusive qualities, the firm signalled its rejection of the rigid dogmas of International Modernism, thereby arousing more than consternation among its adherents: indeed the violent reactions of the true believers were really indistinguishable from those of Fascists or of Stalin's servile creatures.[219]

Cesare Cattaneo, a friend of Terragni, also active in the Como region, was one of the more interesting of Italian Rationalists: his apartment-block in Cernobbio (1938–9) and the *Kindergarten Giuseppe Garbagnati*, Asagno (1935–7), were good examples of his work. Other architects of the period worthy of note in the context of International Modernism were Luigi Carlo Daneri (apartment-block in Genoa [1934–40] and the holiday-camp *Senatore Rinaldo Piaggio*, San Stefano d'Aveto [1938–9]); Augusto Magnaghi Delfino and Mario Terzaghi (apartment-block, Fino Mornasco, Como [1939]); Luciano Baldessari (Angeli Frua administration-building, Milan [1939—with Figini and Pollini]); Ignazio Gardella and Luigi Martini (Therapy-Centre, Alessandria [1935–8]); Gianluigi Giordani (Forlanini Airport, Linate, Milan [1938]); E.A. Griffini and C. Fratino (*Lino Redaelli* children's convalescent- home,

Cesenatico [1937–8]); and Mario Labò (*San Pietro* Restaurant [1937] and an apartment-block [1940], both in Genoa).

Giuseppe Pagano is a particularly interesting case, for he was a Rationalist-Fascist architect/polemicist, born Pogatschnig in what is now Croatia: his extension to the *Palazzo dell'Arte*, Milan (1936), was highly regarded at the time, and, with Gino Levi-Montalcini, he designed one of the first monuments of Italian Rationalism in Milan, the *Riccardo Gualino* office-block, *Corso Vittorio Emmanuele* (1928–9—destroyed). An influential editor of the journal *Casabella*, his writings, with those of Edoardo Persico, furthered the cause of *Razionalismo*. He was closely involved in the building of the *Città Universitaria*, the *Esposizione Universale di Roma*, and the ill-fated *E42* (*Esposizione Universale Roma*, to be the 1942 World's Fair to celebrate twenty-five years of Fascism, which had to be cancelled because of the war): all in Rome, and all showpieces of the Fascist era.

Persico saw that the identification of both Rationalists and Traditionalists with Fascism was potentially dangerous, and he was particularly scathing about certain aspects of the Modern Movement, not least its pretensions to be politically 'left-wing': architecture, he declared, was not a mere engineering solution to an architectural problem (as many Americans held), nor should its future direction be determined by the messianic dogmatic outpourings of Le Corbusier and his disciples, nor by the concerns of Bruno Taut and many others for linking architecture to social concerns. He sensibly regarded architecture as a means of liberating the human spirit, delighting the eye, and being what architecture had been about for aeons, with no doctrinaire overtones. He also wrote convincingly about the possibilities of architectural continuity, linking new architecture with the long tradition of Classicism in Italy: this was one of the reasons why much Italian Modernism was rather better than in those areas where all tradition, all of the past, had been jettisoned. Britain was to suffer enormously from this ejection of the baby with the bathwater, to its great cost. Probably Persico's best realized works were the two stores he designed in Milan (with Marcello Nizzoli) and the various displays he designed for international exhibitions. It is tragic he died so young, as his common-sense views might have helped to avoid what happened after 1945, the year in which Pagano died of pneumonia in the infirmary of Mauthausen concentration-camp.

Other Italian architects who produced Modernist designs under Fascism included Mario Cereghini (*Casa Madre* of the *Gioventù Italiana del Littorio* [Fascist Youth Movement], Milan [1934–5]); Gaetano Ciocca (prefabricated houses for farm-workers, Merone, Lecco [1939]); Agnoldomenico Pica (hostel for the *Gioventù Italiana del Littorio*, Narni [1937–9]); Mario Ridolfi (apartments in Rome [1936–7]); Giuseppe Vaccaro (holiday-camp for the AGIP Company, Cesenatico [1938]); and the Futurist, Enrico Prampolini (who designed the airport-building for the fifth Milan *Triennale* [1933], and was closely involved [with Libera] in the *Mostra della Rivoluzione Fascista*, Rome [1932–4], intended by Mussolini to promote a 'contemporary' style, very 'modern and audacious', avoiding 'melancholy references' to decorative styles of the past and without recourse to 'the dimensions of dinosaurs, the rhetoric of Spanish Baroque, or the formulae of Vitruvius').[220]

Prampolini knew numerous *Bauhäusler*, notably Kandinsky, and had contacts with members of the *Novembergruppe, Der Sturm*, and many other German and French *avant-garde* associations. Like not a few Modernists, he seems to have had little difficulty working with authoritarians, no matter what their supposed political colours might have been: the simple labels of 'right' or 'left' will not do.[221] Of course, designers such as Pier Luigi Nervi did not make it into the Hitchcock–Johnson pantheon, because his work did not accord with the *image* that was by then fixed.

Early Modernism in England

When it came to 'England', the only architect mentioned by Hitchcock and Johnson[222] was Joseph Emberton. His Royal Corinthian yacht-club, Burnham-on-Crouch, Essex (1930–1) was exhibited in New York, but it was mostly the work of George Fairweather. Emberton, as noted earlier, was also responsible for Simpson's department-store, Piccadilly, London (1935–6), which was regarded as progressive, in the new idiom, and handled with conviction. It has certainly worn well, and owes much to the designs of Mendelsohn (*see* **Plate 4.6**).

However, there were several Modernists who established successful practices in the British Isles, including the Tokyo-born son of a Canadian, Wells Coates, who, with Jack Pritchard of the Venesta Plywood Company, founded (1931) the Isokon Company to design houses, apartments, furniture and fittings. The Isokon flats at Lawn Road, Belsize Park, Hampstead, London (1932–4), was a pioneering development of twenty-two 'minimum dwellings' for tenants with few possessions: among early inhabitants were Breuer, Gropius, and Moholy-Nagy (**Plate 5.1**). Pevsner said (1952) of this building

Plate 5.1. Isokon 'minimum-existence' flats, intended for young professional people, Lawn Road, Belsize Park, Hampstead, Camden, London (1932–4), designed by Wells Coates for Jack Pritchard and his wife. The original colour of the concrete was a pale greyish-pink

that it 'put a forbidding face towards the street, with large unmitigated concrete surfaces, especially the long horizontals of heavy balcony parapets and the diagonals of staircase parapets. It is all in a spirit of revolution, unaccommodating and direct to the verge of brutality.'[223]

Wells Coates also designed Embassy Court, Hove, Brighton, Sussex (1934–6), a block of flats with strongly defined horizontal bands of windows and balconies, and a house ('Shipwrights') at 241 Benfleet Road, Hadleigh,

Essex (1934–6), very Corbusian, with *pilotis*, but for the latter, Patrick Gwynne was partly responsible. The team of Coates and Gwynne also designed 'The Homewood', Claremont, Surrey, again with Corbusian *pilotis* (1938–9).[224]

Others working in Britain who designed and built in the 'International Style' were New Zealand-born Amyas Connell, working from 1932 with Basil Ward and from 1933 with Colin Lucas: Connell was the architect for 'High & Over', Highover Park, Amersham-on-the-Hill, Buckinghamshire (1929–31), a pronouncedly Corbusian villa with a hexagonal centre and three radiating wings, producing a **Y**-plan: the projecting staircase is awkwardly done, and has clumsy junctions (H.S. Goodhart-Rendel mentioned this 'approved glass staircase functionally preserving the goings-up and the comings-down of its inhabitants from any shameful secrecy').[225] The structure was concrete frame, but the walls were of rendered brick (**Plate 5.2a**). Connell also designed smaller sun-houses at 4, 5, 6, and 8 Highover Park (1934) (**Plate 5.2b**). As Connell & Ward, the firm designed 'New Farm' (Goodhart-Rendel called it 'Pollard',[226] and it was later called 'Adling'), Grayswood, Haslemere, Surrey (1932), the second of their essays in Continental

Plate 5.2a. 'High & Over', Amersham Park, Amersham-on-the-Hill, Buckinghamshire (1929–31), designed by Amyas Connell, with walls of rendered brick

Plate 5.2*b*. Smaller sun-house at Highover Park, Buckinghamshire, by Connell-Ward, & Lucas (1934)

importations and deliberate rejection of native architecture: it was done, one feels, *pour épater les bourgeois*, and, with its 'bizarre juggling with concrete walls' and 'random windows', soon looked 'very dated'.[227]

After Lucas joined the partnership, other houses followed, including a very daring, heavily glazed one in Portnall Drive, Wentworth, Virginia Water, Surrey (1937), and No. 66 Frognal, Hampstead, London (1937). Not far from the latter building, in Frognal Way, is the sun-house (1934–6), by Maxwell Fry, whose *Miramonte*, Warren Rise, Kingston upon Thames, Surrey (1937), is in a similar idiom, where the influence of Miës's Tugendhat house is obvious. With Robert Atkinson, Elizabeth Denby, C.H. James, and Grey Wornum, Fry (described as 'executant architect')[228] designed Kensal House, Ladbroke Grove, London (1936–7), a Modern-Movement development of workers' flats, much publicized for its 'progressiveness' by Fry's clients, the Gas Light and Coke Company.[229] That accolade cannot have taken into account the unfunctional, tiny 'drying balconies', obviously added for stylistic rather than practical reasons (**Plate 5.3**).[230] Intended as an experiment in 'mass automatic fuel service to low-rental flats', the development was lauded in Modernist circles at the time, and included club-rooms for adult tenants and a nursery-school for children.[231]

Plate 5.3. Kensal House, Ladbroke Grove, North Kensington, London (1936–7), by Fry, Atkinson, Denby, James, and Wornum for the Gas Light and Coke Company through the agency of the Capitol Housing Association Ltd. The so-called 'drying balconies' are very small, and were obviously added for stylistic rather than practical reasons: the source of the design was clearly Bruno Taut (*compare* **Plate 4.3**)

Fry helped Gropius when he arrived in England (1934), and revised the German's designs for Impington Village College, Cambridgeshire (1936–7), supervising its construction.[232] He was active in the MARS Group, founded (1933) as a branch of CIAM to promote International Modernism in the United Kingdom. Taking its cue from Le Corbusier's *Plan Voisin* and other draconian ideas, it proposed (1942) widespread destruction and rebuilding of London on strictly Corbusian lines. Fry organized the MARS-Group exhibition (1938) to publicize its aims.[233]

Another architect involved in the introduction of International Modernism to Britain was the Australian-born Raymond McGrath, who, with Serge Chermayeff and Wells Coates, designed the interiors of BBC Broadcasting House, London (1930–3 [destroyed]): McGrath designed one of the more distinguished houses in that style (though it was also described as 'cold-hearted')[234] at St Ann's Hill, Chertsey, Surrey (1936–8), with a landscape designed by Canadian-born Christopher Tunnard.[235] At the Keene house, Carrygate, Gaulby, Leicestershire, McGrath combined International-Modern forms with materials including recycled bricks and natural elm weather-boarding (1938–42).[236]

Russian-born Chermayeff had settled in England in 1910, and with Mendelsohn (who arrived in England when the National Socialists came to power [1933]) designed the De La Warr Pavilion, Bexhill-on-Sea, Sussex (1933–5), with bands of windows and a streamlined curved-glass enclosure for the staircase (*see* **Plate 4.14**). These themes had already been explored at the Schocken store, Stuttgart (1926) (*see* **Plate 4.10**). Chermayeff's house, 'Bentley Wood', Halland, Sussex (1934–8), a finely detailed building of Jarrah wood (Eucalyptus) construction, again had a landscape designed by Tunnard. F. R.S.Yorke, too, was one of a handful of English architects devoted to the Modern Movement in the 1930s: among his works a house at Nast Hyde, Hatfield, Hertfordshire (1935—destroyed 1980s), conformed to the style. With Breuer, he also designed Sea Lane house, Angmering-on-Sea, East Preston, Sussex (1937), a rather crude effort on fat *pilotis*. Rather more successful was Thomas S. Tait's house, *Le Château*, at Silver End, near Braintree, Essex (1926–8), and the model village laid out from 1926 for the industrialist Francis Henry Crittall.[237]

Another immigrant, Berthold Lubetkin (supposedly born in Georgia, he may in fact have hailed from Warsaw), created several important buildings in the 'International Style'. Settling in London (1931), he became (1932) senior partner of Tecton, a firm composed of former students of the Architectural Association. Among his works were the Penguin Pool, London Zoo, with its spiral concrete ramps designed with the Anglo-Danish engineer Ove Arup (1934) and, also with Arup, Highpoint I, a block of apartments in Highgate, London (1933–5), was greeted with high praise, notably by Corbusier.[238] The Finsbury Health Centre, London (1935–8), was one of his most cele-brated buildings (although photographs cunningly exaggerated its scale, and the building in reality surprised by its miniature size).[239] Tecton also designed several slab-blocks for public housing at Priory Green (1937–51) and Spa Green (1938–46), London, that were early exemplars of the type in England. Of deeply held 'leftist' convictions, Lubetkin was active in the MARS Group and CIAM.

However, despite his credentials, his Highpoint II (1936–8), with elevations of brick, glass, and tile, suggested that Lubetkin realized the white-painted, plain, flat, unmoulded surfaces favoured by International Modernism were unsuited to London. Some saw the entrance canopy, supported by casts of *caryatides* from the Athenian *Erechtheion*, as a witty reference to Classicism, but others, of more puritanical dispositions, brooking no deviance from the Cause, saw this as either a vulgar manifestation of *Kitsch*, or as a betrayal of Modernism. This last earned him some opprobrium (*see* **Plate 2.12**), for no departure from orthodoxy was really permitted.[240]

The importance of English Modernism was revealed in the 1937 MoMA *Exhibition 58* referred to earlier,[241] although this was somewhat obscured by later adulation heaped on the *Bauhäusler*, largely through Gropius and the 1938–9 MoMA *Exhibition 82* on the *Bauhaus 1919–1928*. In addition, the very powerful influence the MARS Group[242] had on CIAM and the whole direction of Modernism in architecture has come under scrutiny: it could be argued that England, far from being a Modernist backwater, was actually in its vanguard.[243]

Yet so-called 'functionalism' was very much a minority obsession in the 1930s, for the vast majority of British people of all social classes refused to succumb to its limited charms. They did not want a 'machine for living' so much as a place where they could be comfortable, at ease with themselves, and even create their own familiar, pleasant spaces. There was an obvious reason why even educated patrons kept International Modernism at arm's length, and that was because the severe austerities of minimalist interiors were more about the coercive programmes of their designers than responses to clients' wishes. As Dorothy Todd and Raymond Mortimer put it in their *The New Interior Decoration* (1929), people needed 'fantasy, imagination, wit' in their houses … the interiors of buildings by Le Corbusier were 'as formal as the old French salon … we require our houses to be quieter, more informal, more personal'.[244]

VI

Universal Acceptance of the International Style

A Surprising Aftermath of 1945

The Style Established; Not All Were Convinced; The Situation from 1945; A Curious Shift; Transformation & Acceptance

Much concern has lately been expressed about the future of art in democracies. How can an aesthetically exacting popular art develop where majorities rule? Can democratic opinion which is by its nature diffuse be brought round to the saving grace of a Bauhaus style *without the application of force?*[1]

THE ARCHITECTURAL REVIEW **xcv**/565 (January 1944) 7

People having what used to be called 'advanced views' and no great sympathy with popular taste, built...houses that closely resembled what the illustrated papers shewed them were being built by people with advanced views abroad. Most of these houses had flat roofs, glass-walled staircases, heavy balconies, and enormous windows...Few of them looked as though they were built of brick, but almost all of them were...Flat roofs are more apt than any others to need constant attention, large, plain, wall-surfaces get shabby in no time and have to be recoloured, large areas of windows make heating bills enormous. On the Continent houses containing these elements became the height of fashion, but in England those who could afford to pay for them were usually not those who wanted them. Good specimens in this country are therefore few, although their more easily reproducible characteristics have been travestied over and over again in little mongrels of houses, half-conventional and half what their designers, ignorant of the meaning of words, have been pleased to describe as 'contemporary'.

HARRY STUART GOODHART-RENDEL (1887–1959): *English Architecture since the Regency*
(London: Constable & Co. Ltd 1953) 272–3

The Style Established

The first phase of the Modern Movement, as should be clear by now, consisted largely of theories and loud slogans publicized in manifestos, together with a limited range of realized projects. It ended in the early 1930s, and the next phase, identified as the 'International Style' which had evolved in the 1920s, was enshrined and codified in 1932 in the famous *Exhibition 15* at the Museum of Modern Art, New York.[2] It was organized under the aegis of Barr (who seems to have coined the label), and put together by Hitchcock and Johnson, whose book[3] of the same title also first appeared in 1932 and disseminated the style far and wide. Lewis Mumford also contributed to the exhibition.

In the 1930s the Modern Movement gained respectability through various exhibitions (not least those at MoMA), and the notion grew that the 'International Style' was the most appropriate one for the twentieth century, though purists objected to the use of the word 'style', claiming that any alleged 'style' should be avoided. It reached its apogee in the 1960s during orgies of destruction of town centres,[4] shaping urban skylines, obliterating streets and huge numbers of perfectly sound buildings that were capable of adaptation (but which, because of their unacceptable 'Historicism', were regarded as 'irrelevant' or worse), and creating Dystopia on a massive scale.[5] In Britain, the destruction of hundreds of thousands more houses than had been flattened during the war was partly due to Modernist theories about the 'clean slate', but there was also a visceral, blinkered desire to reject the past, perhaps a sense of shame about it, that worked in tandem with Modernists' agenda, and led to widespread unnecessary destruction and prodigious waste.[6] The 1950s and 1960s saw the universal adoption of a cheap, all-purpose, banal, badly-executed Modernism that not only obliterated local identities and memories, but led inexorably to Dystopias that were nevertheless lauded by their protagonists as 'excitingly modern',[7] but were hated by the uprooted people who had to live there.

In terms of its universal adoption, the International was probably the most successful architectural style of all time, but it did not create a beautiful Utopia, rather a world disturbingly reminiscent of the images in Fritz Lang's film, *Metropolis* (1926–7). The result, despite ferocious attempts to ridicule and suppress dissenting voices, was a growing opposition to what the Modern Movement had done to cities, to the environment generally (*see* **Figure Preface P.1**),[8] and to architecture, questioning the very essence of the Movement, and leading to popular campaigns for conservation, not least of resources which Modernism was visibly squandering as though they were limitless. In particular, Jane Jacobs and others led the attack in works including *The Death and Life of Great American Cities* (1961), a sustained assault on the policies promoted by Modernists that were killing the living organisms that were cities, and demanding a new respect for self-generating urban forces to create social and economic diversity and well-being.[9]

'Modernismus', as Reginald Blomfield cheerfully dubbed it in the 1930s (a dig at its indubitably Teutonic origins),[10] was a serious matter, and not something to be airily dismissed. Osbert Lancaster observed that

> a number of...architects came to the sad conclusion that architecture had died somewhere about the end of the first quarter of the nineteenth century and that therefore it was no longer any use continuing hopeless efforts at revival but that a completely new start must be made. Modern life, they argued, was governed by mechanical principles, and therefore the rules which held good for the construction of machines must now be applied to architecture.

He went on to say that 'this doctrine rests on a fallacy' and led to 'a ruthless abandonment of all ornamentation': thus 'the style which...emerged was one of the utmost austerity' in the search for 'fitness of purpose'; but although it might be appropriate for 'factories, airports, hospitals', and other 'utilitarian buildings, when the same principle was applied to domestic architecture, the success was not always so marked',[11] a wry understatement indeed.

Evelyn Waugh hilariously recorded something of *Modernismus*'s absurdities in *Decline and Fall*[12] in the person of 'Professor Otto Friedrich Silenus', who 'had first attracted...attention with the rejected design for a chewing-gum factory...reproduced in a progressive Hungarian quarterly'.[13] Silenus held that the 'problem of architecture...is the problem of all art—the elimination of the human element from the consideration of form. The only perfect building must be the factory, because that is built to house machines, not men.'[14] The good Professor also did not think it 'possible for domestic architecture to be beautiful', and that Man was never happy 'except when he becomes the channel for the distribution of mechanical forces'.[15] Waugh's prose was amusing, but was devastatingly accurate in its wry observations of dogmatic absurdities that became enshrined as belief which could never be questioned.

Although we may laugh at Silenus, there were actually real *émigrés*[16] who held views almost identical to those of Waugh's fictional Professor: that would not have mattered very much if they had not been taken seriously by the impressionable in the lands where they either ended up, passed through, or had their notions disseminated through journals or books. There were plenty of trendy young persons all too willing to accept slogans as truths if they were repeated often and loudly enough. John Summerson dryly observed that 'Le Corbusier repeats himself...he is not content to say a thing once, or twice, or a dozen times...in violent paragraphs...', and found *La Ville Radieuse* 'irritating,...with its flashy introduction, advertising the NEW AGE of the machine in the same terms as...advertising agencies use for new toothpastes and aperients'.[17]

Such methods, those of the commercial world,[18] impressed generations at the time: they were the ones who spread the new gospel. P. Morton Shand admitted that the Modernist found ocean-going liners, aircraft, transmission-poles, silos, and turbines 'infinitely more beautiful than traditional art forms':[19] if the proles did not care for those things or regard them as art at all, they could 'go hang',[20] for the Modernists would address themselves 'only to those capable of understanding',[21] as Maxwell Fry loftily put it. Fry added that he and his contemporaries were concerned 'not with architecture alone, but with society', as they were 'filled with a fervour as moral as it was aesthetic',[22] and also revealed his true colours by claiming 'the course of architecture and town planning...will rest...upon the capacity of the *common people*[23] to understand and to appreciate the quality of good things, and in doing so to place their confidence in those who can best help them to it'.[24] In the face of such assertions it is little wonder the 'common people' eventually turned violent and vandalized the 'good things' foisted on them by Modernists. The Victorian fallacy that art is useful when it promotes moral good had resurfaced, well-larded with superior attitudes assumed by wishful thinkers who embraced the fictional 'machine aesthetic'.

By 1927 International Modernism, or the 'International Style' (largely concerned with the *appearance* of buildings, with the emphasis on image or style), had arrived with a vengeance,[25] and the white rectilinear 'flat'-roofed building with strip-windows in metal frames (e.g. exhibits at the *Weißenhofsiedlung*, Stuttgart, and well-publicized designs by Le Corbusier, Gropius, and others) became the exemplary model of what Modern-Movement architecture should aim to be: no matter if the pristine white walls were actually painted, rendered blockwork (as they almost invariably were) rather than concrete or steel (*see* **Figures 2.1, 4.4**).

So the Movement that sought to abolish style had simply created a new one, albeit with a decidedly limited vocabulary (based on images that in the twenty-first century look very old-fashioned), backed by dubious 'moral' arguments, and insistence on conformity to demonstrate an alleged 'progressiveness' and adherence to what were optimistically thought to be 'left-leaning' agenda. Devoted to the destruction of academic architecture and institutions, it evolved its own theories, dogmas, and pedagogic establishment: the *Bauhaus* became the model for indoctrination from 1919; CIAM (*see* Select Glossary) set down agenda and laid down the creeds; and certain writers (e.g. Giedion[26] and Pevsner)[27] insisted on a continuous, logical, and inevitable development of Modernism from eighteenth- and nineteenth-century 'functional' buildings by alleged 'pioneers' of design to create the 'Grand Narrative' of Modernism. Architecture and architects who did not fit neatly into this seamless 'history' were ignored.

Hitchcock wrote in the foreword to the 1966 edition of *The International Style: Architecture since 1922*[28] that the 'style' had been universally recognized, and Barr, in his preface, that he believed that the 'International Style' was 'as original, as consistent, as logical, and as widely distributed as any in the past',[29] and that the conclusions reached by Hitchcock and Johnson seemed to him to be 'of extraordinary, perhaps of epoch-making, importance'.[30] The book claimed that 'a single new style has come into existence...this contemporary style...throughout the world, is unified and inclusive, not fragmentary and contradictory...it has produced sufficient monuments of distinction to display its validity and its vitality. It may fairly be compared in significance with the styles of the past.'[31] It then went on to state that in 'the handling of the problems of structure it is related to the Gothic, in the handling of the problems of design it is more akin to the Classical. In the preëminence given to the handling of function it is distinguished from both.'[32]

This demonstrates a lack of understanding of the very nature of the 'pointed style' of architecture, called inaccurately 'Gothic': anyone conversant with mediaeval architecture will realize immediately that the claim lacks substance. And insistence that the rich architectural language of Classicism, with its Orders, its amazing variety of mouldings, and its many associations, has any affinities whatsoever with the limited set of *clichés* displayed in International Modernism does not survive serious analysis.

Barr referred to Hannes Meyer as a 'fanatical functionalist',[33] and noted that 'Post-Functionalism' might be a more appropriate, precise, and 'genetically descriptive' label for the International Style. He always used a capital S for Style, something to which Hitchcock and Johnson objected. In 1932, Barr also stated that 'Mendelsohn, once the most conspicuous of the Expressionists', had 'gone over to the International Style',[34] which was very strange, as Mendelsohn had been working in that style with some success (both professionally and critically) for at least a decade. Hitchcock, in his foreword to the 1966 edition, written in the autumn of 1965, claimed that 'neither in gathering material for the exhibition on which the book was based nor in writing the book' had he and Johnson intended to provide a 'collection of recipes for success with the new style', and that it was 'contrary to' their intentions that what they had 'merely *described* was, to some extent, followed like a prescription since it offered a logical amalgam of the practice of three new leaders, Le Corbusier, Gropius and Miës, already generally accepted as such by the international avant-garde'.[35] Hitchcock also admitted at the time that the International Style was 'over', a 'generation after its heyday'.[36]

Barr could not accept it was a 'function' of a building to please the architect's client, as he looked down with patrician scorn on the 'architectural taste of real estate speculators, renting agents, and mortgage brokers.'[37] As for 'function' in another sense, however, it might be suggested that buildings which let in water, that look shabby in no time at all, that are subject to solar-heat gain making parts of them uninhabitable (and, conversely, leak energy), that have poor sound-insulation (really only possible with mass or with lots of insulating material that would make the so-called 'machine aesthetic' impossible), that generally perform badly, and that have to be demolished two decades or less after they are built at vast expense (and therefore represent a huge loss as the capital expended will never be recouped), can hardly be called 'functional'. Like much else concerned with Modernism, 'function' had very little to do with how a building performed, but was largely concerned with packaging for the sake of appearance in order to *suggest* the idea of 'function'.[38] The Modern Movement in architecture had its origins in Behrens's 'corporate branding' for AEG, and its subsequent history demonstrates it was intimately linked with commerce, with planned obsolescence, and with vast financial and industrial concerns,[39] without which it could never have been so universally embraced.

So what was regarded as 'functional' was *an appearance*, something that seems to have evolved from the aggressive and repetitive manifesto[40] produced by Le Corbusier, containing many photographs of motor-cars,[41] ocean-going liners of the *Aquitania* (built 1910–14), *Titanic* (built 1909–12), and *Lamoricière* (built 1921 [*see* **Figure 5.3**]) vintage,[42] aeroplanes,[43] and grain-silos.[44] The aesthetic of buildings such as the *Villa Savoie* (*see* **Figure 5.2**), which clearly owed much to the appearance of the promenade-decks of ships such as the *Aquitania* (now, in the second decade of the twenty-first century, more than a century old), was the way forward according to him, despite the inherent problems of using features of a steel-constructed liner as models for concrete, block, and rendered buildings. What is worse, the image he reproduced of 'Canadian Grain Stores and Elevators'[45] shows a large building with a 'flat' roof, but the photograph was doctored: the actual building had pitched roofs (**Figure 6.1**).[46] This has been aptly described as 'one of the most notorious falsifications in the history of modern architecture'.[47] That was not all: 'almost invariably' Corbusier 'transformed' photographs to suit his propaganda, removing them from context, erasing detail, and reframing them. Images were 'worked on, composed, constructed'.[48]

And if images of aeroplanes such as the Farman *Goliath* (**Figure 6.2**), the Triple Hydroplane (or Triplane Caproni), or Air Express are inspected, it

Figure 6.1. Le Corbusier published what purported to be a photograph of 'Canadian Grain Stores and Elevators' in *Towards a New Architecture* (*see* Corbusier [1946] 29 [27 in the *c.*1930 edn.]). He claimed 'the American grain elevators [were] FIRST-FRUITS of the new age', and that 'AMERICAN ENGINEERS OVERWHELM WITH THEIR CALCULATIONS OUR EXPIRING ARCHITECTURE' (Corbusier [1946] 31). He doctored the photograph, however: the buildings in question had pitched roofs (shown pecked in this drawing) so that he could further the Modernist aesthetic of the 'flat' roof by pretending the realized structure did not have pitched roofs

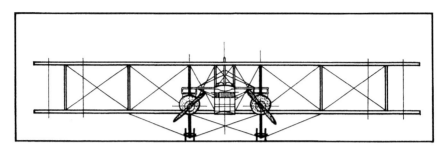

Figure 6.2. Front elevation of a Farman F.60 Goliath French bomber/airliner, designed 1918, produced from 1919. Le Corbusier stated that the 'airplane is indubitably one of the products of the most intense selection in the range of modern industry', and (questionably, at the very least) that it was conceived in the 'same spirit that built the Parthenon' (Corbusier [1946] 101). The elements between the wings suggested the ubiquitous *pilotis*

becomes clear that the uprights between the wings of those antiquated aircraft were the triggers for obligatory *pilotis* that recur in Corbusian buildings and in those of his myriad imitators (**Figure 6.3**). The many images of the Parthenon in Athens (447–438 BC) interspersed among the pictures of cars, planes, ships, and grain-silos in *Towards a New Architecture* are held up as the epitome of perfection. This is a device much favoured by Modernists in laying claim to some sort of respectable pedigree for their works: they fail to see the conflict between their invocation of Classical Antiquity and their demand for the *tabula rasa*. For all the imprecise language about the remains of the Parthenon (e.g. 'We shall be able to talk "Doric" when man, in nobility of aim and complete sacrifice of all that is accidental in Art, has reached the higher levels of the mind: austerity';[49] 'We are in the inexorable realm of the mechanical. There are no symbols attached to these forms:... Brutality, intensity, the utmost sweetness, delicacy and great strength';[50] the 'Doric state of mind and the Corinthian state of mind are two things. A moral fact creates a gulf between them';[51] and much more in the same vein), and later 'analyses' of the *Villa Savoie* as having certain themes drawn from the Athenian Acropolis, Corbusier missed certain botches at the corners of the Parthenon at high level. His gleaming white *Villa* with its *pilotis* owed far more to early ocean-going liners and biplanes than it did to the once *brightly coloured* temple.[52]

Le Corbusier, like Gropius, demanded that industrialized prefabrication was the way forward, yet the development of 'systems-building' has not brought the Promised Land to the world of architecture. Gropius claimed there had been a 'breach with the past', permitting a new architecture to evolve 'corresponding to the technical civilization of the age' and a return to 'honesty

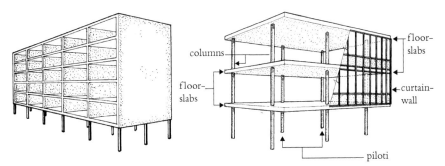

Figure 6.3–4. (*left*) Typical twentieth-century box-framed building, with structural walls at right angles to the façade, the whole set on *pilotis* (*right*) External non-loadbearing skin of metal and glass, known as a *curtain-wall*, fixed to a typical Modernist column-and-slab construction, the whole building raised up on *pilotis*. This formula was repeated, no matter where, so solar-heat gain in hot conditions and heat-loss in cold proved hugely problematic. The poverty of expression using such techniques has led to meaningless architecture

of thought and feeling',[53] a questionable statement at the very least. He did, however, state that 'modern' architecture became fashionable in certain countries, 'with the result that formalistic imitation and snobbery distorted' the 'fundamental truth and simplicity' of what he optimistically called a 'renascence'.[54] It is not clear what rebirth, exactly, he meant. He chillingly called for the Modern Movement to be 'purged from within' to save it from 'materialism and false slogans inspired by plagiarism or misconception. Catch-phrases like "functionalism" (*die neue Sachlichkeit*) and "fitness for purpose = beauty" have had the effect of deflecting appreciation of the New Architecture.'[55]

Then Gropius painted his Utopian view: with 'the development of air transport the architect will have to pay as much attention to the bird's-eye perspective of his houses as to their elevations. The utilisation of flat roofs as "grounds" offers us a means of re-acclimatizing' nature amidst 'the stony deserts of our great towns; for the plots from which she has been evicted to make room for buildings can be given back to her up aloft. Seen from the skies, the leafy house-tops of the cities of the future will look like endless chains of hanging gardens.'[56]

The twenty-first-century air traveller sees no such things: instead, vast sheds, urban wastelands, swathes of traffic-choked roads (grotesquely and wastefully overlit at night), and incoherent building-layouts replace the tight, confined regularity of the towns of yesteryear, and blight the vision. There are no 'endless chains of hanging gardens' in sight. Gropius went on to extol his vision of the *Bauhaus*, but deplored 'imitators who prostituted . . . fundamental precepts into modish trivialities': nevertheless, although he claimed he did not wish to propagate 'any "style", system, dogma, formula, or vogue'[57] that is exactly what he did. He wrote of the 'ethical necessity of the New Architecture', proven by the fact that in all countries 'Youth has been fired with its inspiration'.[58]

Not All Were Convinced

But untutored Youth, untouched by Wisdom, can be dangerous, as Blomfield pointed out. 'Our younger generation, trained exclusively in our architectural schools, are convinced they are introducing a new era in architecture',[59] he wrote, and, despite the efforts of Gropius and others to disdain 'style', the buildings that were actually realized were in the 'International Style', sanctified by Barr, Hitchcock, and Johnson. As early as 1925, Manning Durdin Robertson,[60] in his *Laymen and the New Architecture*,[61] stated that 'the new architecture is essentially "youthful; and strongly conscious of its origins"... it should aim "at the sensational and dramatic rather than the emotional and intellectual" and it should turn its back on all previous styles. "It is recognised [he did not say where, or by whom] that there should at present be only one style".'[62] Robertson, however, supposedly a 'serious critic and commentator on twentieth-century architecture and town planning',[63] claimed that the Four Courts (1776–1802) and Custom House (1780–91) in Dublin were 'excellent examples of the Wren School'.[64] Unfortunately, this is not so, as they were more clearly influenced by their architect's (James Gandon[65]) master, William Chambers,[66] who was born the year Wren died.

   Blomfield warmed to his theme concerning Youth: the

> post-war generation rather suggests...a lot of young hounds running loose and giving tongue vociferously without quite knowing what they are doing or where they are going. They have lost touch with the masterpieces of the past, or rather they have never put themselves to the trouble of acquainting themselves with those masterpieces... We have lost our sense of proportion, we have less understanding of the grace of life than our forefathers, less knowledge of how to make our surroundings comely and reasonable; and we shall not find the way to this by desperate attempts at making our art and our language modern. In doing so we only make it vulgar.[67]

Youth is easily swayed by slogans, and Blomfield picked up another unhealthy tendency: that of compulsion. He noted that the 'problem of the

"New Architecture", or "Modern Architecture" (as its advocates'[68] called it 'to the exclusion of about nine-tenths of the best contemporary work')[69] was that it was 'now widely advertised as the one and only gospel of artistic salvation'.[70] He saw that C.A. Barman regarded

> the issue between Modernism and Traditionalism as a crisis 'in which the future of a nation may be at stake' and stated that the Modernists were in the position of an army that must fight a battle or be slain, and that the outcome of this battle will affect 'the whole future of human life on earth'. Just think of it, unless we can live in houses designed by Le Corbusier and Mendelsohn ... the human race is doomed![71,72]

Although F.E. Towndrow[73] asserted 'with confidence' that the battle was already won,[74] Blomfield observed wryly that 'Herr Cohen-Portheim[75] wrote that there will be one style of architecture compulsory for the whole of Europe, and accepted by all countries as their own'.[76] Unfortunately, this turned out to be true, but it did not come to pass in the way its protagonists imagined.

As an antidote to this sort of thing, Blomfield suggested that it might be beneficial to read S.F. Wright.[77] 'Modernismus' has been a disaster for architecture, he declared, 'because for many years we shall have to endure its dreary and intolerable monotony'. Architecture 'will be standardised to the packing-case type; individuality will be wiped out; there will be no place for an architect at all'.[78] 'Modernismus' was 'sedulously advertised in most architectural journals by enthusiastic young writers with little or no experience of architecture, or knowledge of its past and its possibilities. It is easy to spin words in support of a prevailing fashion.'[79]

Even the French joined in the chorus of concern, referring to 'the deadly atmosphere of immeasurable dullness, the sterile materialism, and the desiccated commonplace vulgarities' that were infecting architecture in France. Félix Boutron complained of the 'lack of a research culture among architectural students impatient of the intellectual discipline which is the condition of all genuine attainment'.[80] Things have not improved since.

Blomfield perceived a real problem: 'Modernist architects' had 'tied themselves into such terrible knots that their efforts to go forward only land them deeper and deeper in impossible positions from which no amount of ingenious word-spinning will ever save them. The whole thing ... is pushed forward under a smoke-screen of German metaphysics and the jargon of current art criticism.'[81] Throughout his book, he rammed home the Modernist fallacies of 'honesty to materials':[82] from the first, Modernism had been 'a doctrinaire affair, mixed up with ethical and social considerations—the idea, for instance, that it is dishonest not to show the construction…'[83] Baillie Scott 'said rightly that "Modern architecture is wrong in its impudent claim to a monopoly of practical efficiency."'[84]

The Situation from 1945

After the 1939–45 war, the International Style became the only acceptable secular religion of the architectural establishment until it encountered new challenges from Modernist apostates (notably Philip Johnson),[85] advocates of 'contrast and contradiction',[86] the protagonists of Neo-Rationalist architecture (especially the Ticinese school),[87] New Classicism,[88] and New Urbanism,[89] and the critiques[90] of academics (some of whom have identified many strands within a 'movement' that has not been as logical, scientific, objective, intellectually sound, or homogeneous as its followers believed). Subsequent developments, such as Post-Modernism,[91] High-Tech,[92] Deconstructivism,[93] and Parametricism[94] have not proved to be panaceas, and the prognosis gives little cause for optimism or pleasure.

Obsessed with *images* of what was perceived to be 'Modern', many argued vociferously that mass-production and prefabrication had to be the agents through which the 'new architecture' could be made available cheaply and quickly (in practice, however, it was often neither cheap nor quick, as Philip Johnson pointed out).[95] Soon after the *Bauhaus* got going under Gropius, skilled artisans in Weimar realized that the institution was actually accelerating the elimination of traditional crafts,[96] despite its pretensions to unify all the arts.[97] Industrialization of building could enable architecture to reach the masses, it was claimed, but this would only become possible when the 'International Style' was universally adopted. And Modernism, associated from the very beginning with the 'left' and with 'progress',[98] was perceived by many believers as an inevitable historical process. All historical styles and well-tried, proven technologies and craft-skills had to be discarded, denounced as morally indefensible, or outmoded, or both, putting innumerable craftsmen and old-established firms out of business. This was the antithesis of the Morris-Ruskin-Arts-and-Crafts position (to which, nevertheless, certain Modernists claimed to adhere), yet, as Goodhart-Rendel correctly observed, the 'old ways of building still often are the cheapest and the most convenient',[99] but they were virtually obliterated by Modernism.

For the first time in the history of humankind, ornament and decoration were eschewed in architecture. Abstraction in art also eliminated all figurative elements, in search of 'pure' form, which was associated with 'truth'. This adoption of abstraction further damaged the potential for buildings to convey meanings through symbols. Geometrical abstractions were no substitute for decoration and enrichment to which people, especially the proletariat, could relate; but whether they wanted it or not, people were going to get Modernism from '*bourgeois*' architects pretending they were not themselves members of the despised '*bourgeoisie*'.[100] Modernism was also inimical to national/regional differences, so the same architectural style became *de rigueur*, no matter what the climatic conditions were: thus 'flat' roofs for sunbathing in rainy climes (deliciously caricatured by Osbert Lancaster),[101] and vast areas of glazing in hot tropical sunshine were compulsory (as with the slab-like buildings designed by Oscar Niemeyer, disciple of Le Corbusier, for Brasília), with impractical results (**Figure 6.4**).[102]

There can be no doubt that the internationalist stance of Modernism was partly prompted by the disasters of 1914–18. Many fondly (and naïvely) believed that an 'International Style' of architecture would encourage cultural interchanges and reduce the risks of wars between nations; but in their atheistical, anti-faith, anti-history, irrational cocoon, protagonists discounted religions, sectarianism, and much else.[103] The 'Perfectibility of Man', a notion inherited from the Enlightenment, proved to be a chimaera. The Modern Movement also had a strong evangelical streak, for it imagined it could transform untidy, philistine, disagreeable humankind by redesigning cities, and, through architecture and factory-made mass production of building components, change the outlooks and perceptions of whole populations.

Determinist ideas proposed that the masses would come to accept Modernist design as being the only one appropriate to the times. All other styles, including those manifested by old buildings, were not needed, and urban deserts were created through wholesale razings of existing fabric (*see* **Figure Preface P.1**).[104] Designs were claimed to be essential to the well-being and improvement of the masses, and the evangelical zeal of Modernist pronouncements makes uncomfortable reading: 'a great epoch has begun. There exists a new spirit… We must create the mass-production spirit. The spirit of living in mass-production houses… It is a question of building which is at the root of… social unrest…: architecture or revolution.'[105]

The tone is disquieting. Unsurprisingly, there were aspects of Modernism which resembled a fundamentalist religious cult, demanding total allegiance, conformity, and commitment. There was a totalitarian aspect to it all, for those who did not conform were either denounced or expunged from the record. The desire to employ industrialized processes to arrive at Utopian solutions, together with commitments to 'progress', internationalism, and totalitarian centralized planning infused with rigid dogma, created results that were to become devastatingly terrible, uninhabitable, noisy, dangerous, polluted Dystopias, manifestations of misconceived social engineering that have produced the opposite of civilization. The fundamental fallacy of Modernism was its assumption that it could improve society through 'design'; but 'design' is not 'moral', and in the belief that it was lay a fatal flaw.

There was another problem. The evangelical Modernists identified the 'proletariat' as the 'other', and recognized that it was incapable of forming judgements that accorded with their aims. Thus protagonists of the Modern Movement evolved a dictatorial determinism at odds with the tastes of the masses. Hubert de Cronin Hastings, the Modernist proprietor of the Architectural Press (which published the influential *Architectural Review* and *Architects' Journal*), thought that he and his team of editors *knew* what should be done about housing in Britain in 1967,[106] and would brook no dissent: the solutions he championed have not proved to be benign. An imposition of alien, minimalist taste on the home met with resistance from the very people for whom it was intended: the masses did not welcome being dictated to within their own living-spaces[107] or having their homes compulsorily purchased from them for a fraction of their real value.

This was already clear when the Austrian architect Josef Frank was denounced by doctrinaire Modernists for creating comfortable, '*bourgeois*', even 'feminine' interiors in the houses he designed for the *Weißenhof* housing-exhibition of 1927 in Stuttgart. In 1930, Frank warned of the dangers of discarding the lessons and traditions of history, demanded a deeper and more scientific understanding of the world than dogmatic posturing and sloganizing, and urged that room should be left for individualism and self-expression. In an outspoken attack on fundamentalist Modernist dogmas, he targeted the bullying attitudes emanating from the German *Bauhaus*, Communists in Czechoslovakia (especially the totalitarian Karel Teige), Le Corbusier, and the rigidities of CIAM.[108]

Frank was not the only one to question the Modernist orthodoxies of CIAM and certain individuals, but he was especially opposed to exaggerated forms and blind faith in industrialized techniques of building. There were public rows on many fronts,[109] and it would have been clear that

Modernism was well on the way to disintegrating in the 1930s,[110] had not opinions been politically polarized. A strange resurrection occurred thanks to its condemnation by the Stalinist Soviet Union as 'bourgeois formalism' created by 'reactionary jugglers' imbued with closet 'cosmopolitanism'.[111] The *régime* wanted to create and encourage a 'popular culture', and it was quickly realized that the art of the Western European *avant-garde*, created by a few 'bourgeois specialists'[112] (a judgement that was not far off the mark), was 'neither intelligible nor acceptable to the broad mass of the people'.[113] This statement was undoubtedly true, yet Modernists were in denial about it. Indeed, Trotsky had gone as far to say that there was no possibility of a strongly committed proletarian culture,[114] but Stalin, arguing against 'formalism', 'individualism', and 'negativism', urged that art, architecture, literature, poetry, and indeed culture generally should not only be accessible to, but understood by, the 'Workers and Peasants'.[115] Trends in the West, however, such as International Modernism and so-called 'abstract' painting, were not only perceived as foreign and cosmopolitan (suspect), but as *'bourgeois'* affectations, and therefore anti-proletarian, inimical to the new Soviet society then being built.[116]

The doctrine of 'Socialist Realism' promoted from 1934 was actually Party-approved art, intended to mould human souls using 'revolutionary romanticism' rooted in 'real life'. Although the objectives differed, the aura of compulsion had similarities to what had been going on in Weimar Germany and elsewhere in the West. Anyone who deviated from Party-approved attitudes to creativity in the arts was denounced as an 'enemy of the people', 'Trotskyist rabble', or a 'fascist agent', attempting to 'brake or hinder' the development of Soviet art, according to Comrade Nikolai Yezhov, 'People's Commissar', who was charged with creating an atmosphere of 'enthusiasm' among the 'entire mass of artists'.[117] Yezhov was actually General Commissar of State Security in the NKVD (1936–8), but he himself was 'purged': any creative person working in the Soviet Union at that time might suddenly have to apologize for 'mistakes' and develop a more 'positive' attitude to his or her art. Under the general canopy of Party activism, fellow-artists functioned as an aesthetic police-force, with powers to instruct, guide, denounce, and punish anyone who might be suspect. It does not take much imagination to realize that such a system was wide open to abuse, and created a permanent atmosphere of fear and hysteria: falling into line followed humiliation, but some individuals failed to appear sufficiently conformist, and were punished accordingly.[118]

Modernism was condemned by the Stalinist Soviet Union, which caused an uncertain fluttering in the concrete dovecotes of the 'left' in the West, where denial attempted to fudge the problem, further complicated by what was going on in Fascist Italy, where plenty of Modernist architecture, such as Giuseppe Terragni's *Casa del Fascio*, Como (1932–6), and *Casa del Fascio*, Lissone (1938–9—with Antonio Carminati), was realized, although 'leftist' critics find that inconvenient. Thanks to the polarization of European politics, however, other condemnations, especially those emanating from National-Socialist Germany and the *régimes* on the Iberian peninsula, were enough to ensure not only the survival of International Modernism and its universal adoption, but the 'automatic allegiance'[119] of the 'left' in the Western democracies.

The rigidities of the 'International Style' of architecture, as epitomized in works by Gropius (who objected to the label, preferring 'The New Architecture')[120] and Miës van der Rohe, promoted by Giedion,[121] Hitchcock, Johnson,[122] and Pevsner,[123] and disseminated by further enthusiasts, made the rectangle *de rigueur*, and ensured that any 'architect' ensnared in its dogma could no longer design buildings that could respond to their settings or turn corners (especially acute angles) with grace, thus leaving plenty of waste land (known as SLOAP [space left over after planning—*see* Select Glossary]) because the simple rectangular forms did not fill the spaces available: there were, almost inevitably, patches of unused and unusable land that did nothing for the street except help to destroy it. Exemplars are countless, disfiguring virtually every town and city. Those rigidities ushered in an age of visual horrors, urban incivility, and conspicuous waste. Matters were made worse when horizontal strips of glazing (for example, as found in works by Mendelsohn and Miës van der Rohe) cut against the established grain of street-façades, roofs became 'flat', and buildings were raised up on stilts rejoicing in the name of *pilotis*.

This sustained attack on the street (especially by Le Corbusier and his many disciples),[124] on the ordinary, on good manners in architecture, has given us what was inevitably entailed: not a 'radiant city', but an uninhabitable Dystopia.

A Curious Shift

One of the many puzzles concerning what happened to architecture after 1945 (not just in relatively small geographical areas such as the British Isles,

but throughout the Western world and beyond) cannot be solved by considering the dissemination of Modernist creeds through practitioners and
critics alone. Architectural journals and the somewhat loaded books by
Pevsner, aided by a perceived association of Modernism with 'progress' and
the 'left', undoubtedly helped, as did the denunciation of certain aspects of
Modernism by National-Socialist Germany (though Modernism was not by
any means dead under the Third Reich, either in architecture or in typography or propaganda),[125] and it flourished for much of the time Fascism
ruled in Italy. By a strange twist, everything seems to have been stood on its
head, and that could not have happened in such a short space of time without massive political, financial, and commercial support.

In the 1930s, public buildings in the USA, Britain, Germany, Italy,
Scandinavia, the Soviet Union, and indeed in many other countries, looked
very much the same, because they were all essentially based on the Classical
language of architecture: the conventions of Classicism were used to express
different ideologies, and not for the first time either. Classicism had many
advantages: it was recognizable, it was universal, it was flexible, and it could
mean different things to different people. Like a great language it was capable
of infinite variation, and it could rise above the provincial, the local, and a
restricted concept of symbolism.[126] Classical buildings were usually constructed of solid materials, and were sustainable, because they could last for
centuries, and could be well insulated: their floor-plans, too, were adaptable.
Most places in Europe (especially those that had been part of the Roman
Empire) had Classical architectural histories, and their colonies acquired
them as well. Such architecture suggested grandeur, order, power, and stability, linked to a great Graeco-Roman civilization on which much of Western
culture was based: the so-called 'International Style' completely failed to
suggest the same things, and so, for public architecture it simply did not rise
to the occasion.[127]

Authoritarian *régimes*, such as National-Socialist Germany, the Soviet
Union, or Fascist Italy, sought a monumentality that would be both very
modern and yet suggest permanence, and so Classicism played no small part
in their *public* architecture. In Germany, especially, a marriage between up-
to-date rational architecture and a Greek-inspired Neo-Classicism (as epitomized in the works of Karl Friedrich Schinkel) was sought, and numerous
examples of this union were realized.[128] That does not mean that Modernist
buildings were not erected in Germany during the Third Reich, for they
were, as a glance at some of the many lavish architectural publications of the

period will clearly show,[129] nor does it mean that buildings inspired by Classicism were not erected in the democracies.

Furthermore, inconveniently for Modernist admirers of the Soviet Union and fellow-travellers of Soviet Communism, Lenin had not condoned a rupture with the past in matters of art,[130] and Classicism became the favoured architectural language of 'Socialist Realism': streets were to have buildings on either side conceived as long, unified, Classically-inspired façades, such as the showpiece of Gorky (later Tverskaya) Street, Moscow (1937–9), by Arkady Mordvinov (incidentally a vociferous critic of Le Corbusier and other Western Modernists). In Communist East Germany, huge developments like the former *Stalinallee* (1952–8), designed by a team (which included several former *Bauhäusler*) led by Hermann Henselmann, employed a stripped Classical language for what was termed 'the first Socialist street' of East Berlin, and conformed to one of the *Sechzehn Grundsätze des Städtebaus* (Sixteen Principles of Urbanism);[131] this was the policy agreed with Moscow to reassert the primacy of the street and to *reject* destructive policies promoted by CIAM and Le Corbusier's 'Athens Charter' in the West (including the primacy of traffic, zoning, and just about everything that has contributed to the wreckage of urban fabric).

Those Sixteen Principles (1950) had a preamble stating that the planning and design of cities, which were to be models for construction throughout Germany, must express the social order of the German Democratic Republic as well as the progressive traditions and great goals of the German people. They also included several references to 'culture', a word rarely, if ever, found in British architectural and planning documents of the period. They were set out as follows:

> cities as forms of settlement did not arise by chance: the city is the richest economic and *cultural*[132] form of community settlement, proven over the centuries. The city is, in its structural and architectural design, an expression of political life and of civic and national consciousness;
>
> the goal of urban planning is the harmonious fulfilment of humankind's basic rights to employment, housing, *culture*, and recreation. Methodological principles of urban planning are based on the natural condition, on the social and economic foundations of the State, on the highest achievements of science, technology, and art, on the needs of the economy, and on the use of progressive elements within the *cultural heritage* of the people;
>
> cities, to a significant extent, are built by industry for industry, and their growth, their population, and their size are determined by industries, governing bodies, and *culture*, insofar as they have more than local significance. In the

capital, industry as an urbanising factor is of secondary importance to administrative organisations and *cultural sites*. The precise discernment and codification of city-forming factors is a matter determined by government;

city-growth must be subordinate to efficiency, and remain within certain limits. An overgrown city, its population, and its extent lead to difficulties in eliminating problems of infrastructure, organisation of *cultural life*, and daily well-being of the population, and create huge administrative complications, both in business and in the development of industry;

urban planning must be based on the principles of sound organisation, and the consideration of a city's *historical structure* in correcting that city's shortcomings;

the centre forms the true core of a city, and is the political, administrative, and *cultural heart* of a city. On the main squares and urban spaces of the centre are held popular celebrations on festive days. The centre should be composed of the most important and monumental buildings, dominating the architectural composition of the city plan and *determining the architectural silhouette or skyline*;

in cities that lie on a river, the river and its embankments shall be one of the main arteries and architectural axes of the city;

traffic-circulation should serve the city and its population: it should neither divide the city nor inconvenience the public. Through-traffic should be removed from the centre and central districts, and re-routed outside its borders or to an outer ring. Routes for the carriage of heavy goods, e.g. rail- and canal-ways, should be kept away from the central districts. Locations for main roads must take into account the coherence and tranquillity of residential districts, and in determining their widths it is important to note that these are not of crucial importance to urban transportation, but rather as an outlet for subsidiary roads in order to ease the demands of traffic-flow;

the image of the city (its individual artistic form) is defined by its squares, main streets, and prominent buildings in the centre, so squares and plazas shall serve as the structural bases for the planning of the city and for its overall architectural composition;

residential areas shall consist of housing districts with their own centres for necessary *cultural*, utility, and social services, and housing should be grouped with central parks, schools, *Kindergartens*, and nurseries to serve daily needs of the residents. Urban transport should not be allowed within closely-knit residential areas, but neither residential districts nor residential complexes should be isolated entities in and of themselves. Latent in their structure and design are the demands of the city as a whole. Housing structures themselves should function as a third most important element in the design of the city;

access to light and air are not the only determining factors for healthy and peaceful living conditions: density, orientation, and closeness to transport systems are also essential;

it is not possible to transform a city into a garden, but care must be taken to provide sufficient greenery without disrupting the fact that in cities one lives urbanistically, whereas in the outskirts of towns or in the country one lives rurally;

apartments in several storeys reflect urban character, and are more economical in the use of land than one-or two-storey dwellings;

urban planning is the basis of architectural design: central to urban planning and the architectural design of a city is the creation of an individual and unique character for that city. The architecture must embody both progressive tendencies and *historical traditions*;

for urban planning and architectural design there shall be no abstract schemes. Crucial are only essential architectural features and the demands of daily life;

simultaneously, and in accordance with work on a city plan, shall be completed designs for the planning and development of specific neighborhoods as well as plazas and main streets with neatly organised housing-blocks which will be constructed first.[133]

Throughout, then, *cultural* aspects were taken into consideration and given due weight.

Classicism for the official architecture of the Soviet Union and its satellites had a long life, and Western Modernism did not impinge much on the Soviet Union until after the death of Stalin, when official architectural policies changed, and the Communist world eagerly embraced failing Western fashions from 1955. The Western *riposte* to the *Stalinallee* in Berlin was the *Hansaviertel* (1957) to which various Modernist architects (including Gropius and Le Corbusier) contributed: its 'flat'-roofed skyscraper-blocks set in parkland and its incoherent layout were supposed to be 'paradigms' of design for the 'Free World'. It has not worn well, but neither has post-1955 industrialized building in the DDR, stripped of all historical allusions, as can be seen in the former *Stalinallee* between *Strausbergerplatz* and *Alexanderplatz*.

By the end of the 1939–45 war, it was clear that at no time in the past had such immense destruction of the built environment occurred in such a short period, but in the Western world no government would countenance any architecture that might in any way be associated with the defeated National-Socialist or Fascist *régimes*, despite the fact that a very similar architecture (albeit far more grandiose) had been favoured, and was still favoured, in the Soviet Union.[134] So, in the West, a break with so-called 'Historicist' architecture was assured, even though there were some in the Modernist camp (even, surprisingly, Giedion) who began to realize that there was a need for buildings that might provide more than mere 'functional' answers in order to satisfy the need for symbols connecting with deep-rooted cultural needs.[135] Such belated recognition, however, was too late: the damage had been done; the dogmas and demands had been set in tablets of stone; and real power was to pass elsewhere. Modernism, which in the guise of *Neues Bauen* had already begun to falter around 1930, before the National-Socialist takeover in 1933,[136] was to be adopted for political ends not envisaged by either its founders or its disciples, not least because of a perception that Modernism was somehow the antithesis of National Socialism, yet Modernism and Traditionalism were constantly present in Party ideology.[137]

The forms or social messages of the 'International Style', despite the trumpetings of MoMA, did not really catch on in the United States before the war. One of the reasons why it began to be accepted after hostilities had ceased must be attributed partly to the diaspora of Modernists from Germany, many of whom (including Gropius, Miës, and other *Bauhäusler*) ended up in the United States, often in positions of influence, and with the ears of people like Barr, Hitchcock, and Johnson. The United States suffered none of the massive destruction experienced in other parts of the world, especially Germany, Poland, Italy, France, Britain, Japan, China, and the Soviet Union. In the West, Modernist architectural ideas began to appear reasonable, not least the insistence on factory-made mass production of components, a desire to replace wrecked fabric with buildings and planning that would be better than what had existed before, and a notion of Utopia, a New World designed on new principles, owing nothing to a discredited past that was so full of horrors it had to be discarded completely, without any regrets or nostalgia.

In some countries, however, especially in Poland, destroyed urban fabric was painstakingly reconstructed, as it was recognized that a restoration of nationhood required more than simple-minded Modernist panaceas that turned out to be nothing of the sort. The triumphant rebuilding of the Old Town of Warsaw,[138] for example, much of which was carried out under the direction of Jan Zachwatowicz[139] and others,[140] including Stanisław Lorentz, was far, far more than just a scholarly exercise in what Modernists label 'pastiche': it was intimately connected with keeping alive a visible sense of national identity, threatened, as it had been, with complete obliteration under National-Socialist barbarism and Stalinist repression.[141] Warsaw's rebirth, and other wonderful works of what was called 'The Polish School of Conservation', including Gdańsk, Poznań, Toruń, and Wrocław, should be compared with what was done to war-damaged cities in the British Isles such as Belfast, Canterbury, Coventry, Liverpool, and London:[142] the Polish contribution wins hands down on every possible front. This is because it was recognized that a country without old buildings had similarities to a person without a memory, and that in order to keep national identity alive after several years of brutal attempts to destroy that identity, it was necessary to rebuild a visible reminder of a rich cultural past. Not only were large parts of historic town-centres painstakingly rebuilt to high standards of scholarship, craftsmanship, and detail, but badly-damaged urban fabric was restored, again with admirable skill. Poland, however, also acquired some particularly brutal examples of Modern 'architecture', notably at Nowa Huta, the satellite town outside the great historic city of Kraków, created from the late 1940s in opposition to the '*bourgeois*' inhabitants of Kraków who were not over-enamoured of the Communist government.

If much of the old social order had been changed by 1914–18, it was completely broken by 1945, and, in such a climate, Modernists, demanding recognition of what they regarded as an inevitable process, saw their aims made suddenly possible by the social, economic, and technological realities of the time. In this new world, there would be no choices as to how buildings would appear. They would have to conform to a new architectural language, even though it was an impoverished *patois* consisting of a few *clichés*; but it did have the supposed advantage, according to Pevsner, of being 'a genuine style' and 'totalitarian'.[143] Modernists insisted that what had been dubbed the 'International Style' had to be considered only on its own terms, supposedly 'rational', 'logical', definitely history-denying, intolerant of tradition or anything else that might get in its way, anti-Classical, inimical to monumentality, and supposedly capable of being realized very cheaply through mass-production. In fact, it was far more expensive than traditional methods of construction, put countless numbers of trained craftsmen on the scrapheap, ruined the economy of long-established building industries, and often failed technically very quickly, necessitating expensive remedial repairs or demolition long before the prime cost of construction had been paid off. It was also responsible for Dystopia, 'obliterating identity and memory'[144] as it cut swathes through long-established urban fabric.[145]

This embrace of what had not been a universally popular style by the West as part of a political agenda cannot be explained unless one looks beyond architectural polemics and the effusions of Modernist apologists. Why did architectural Modernism triumph so universally after 1945, and continue like some monstrous juggernaut to succeed, long after it had clearly failed to live up to the promises of its protagonists, and was proving to be a financial, social, environmental, and aesthetic disaster, with one huge development after another having to be dynamited, as fixing them could not be done?

Transformation & Acceptance

The answer appears to lie in that murky post-war world that existed in the late 1940s from the end of hostilities through the beginning of what became known as the Cold War. In the ruined, bankrupt, freezing aftermath of the 1939–45 war, there began an aggressive propaganda campaign launched by the Soviet Union. By the winter of 1947–8, relations between the erstwhile allies that had been ranged against the Axis powers were fracturing.[146] Western wartime propaganda building up the myth of a benevolent 'Uncle Joe Stalin' had worked all too well: it was not just the ordinary 'man in the street' who had swallowed this stuff, but a great many so-called 'Western intellectuals' blind to the realities of Soviet Communism.[147] The pro-Communist stance of so many in the West can be partly explained by a widespread obsession with Fascism in its various guises that excluded the so-called 'left' from any culpability for anything. Mythologies about the Bolshevik Revolution carefully contrived by the *Agitprop Apparat*[148] laid the ground for an adulation of Communism in the 1930s which might partly explain this phenomenon.[149]

The American writer Arthur Miller was somewhat disconcerted (he was not the only one) by the curiously shifting sands of the post-war world, when yesterday's ally became an enemy, and the erstwhile enemy became a friend.[150] He felt it 'ignoble', and that the transference of 'good' and 'evil' labels from one country to another was withering any idea of a 'world even theoretically moral'.[151] He recognized that something like Nihilism towards the concept of a 'moral imperative' came into being in the decade after Hitler's death, and that, 'even worse', that concept was treated more and more with 'yawning amusement' that augured ill for the future of civilization: he called it a 'wrenching shift'.[152]

The Soviets recognized that post-war Europe was very unstable, and profited by its instability to spread Soviet influence: those of us old enough can remember the fall of one country after another to Communism in the aftermath of 1945, and the real threat that Italy, France, and Greece might succumb to the Red advance at any moment. The Soviets were well-versed in the use of 'culture' as 'a tool of political persuasion',[153] and, lacking the economic clout of the United States, concentrated on the winning of minds, in which task they were rather successful. The so-called 'Cold War' was largely waged through propaganda, and much of that was cultural: when the Soviets opened their 'House of Culture' on *Unter den Linden*, Berlin, it put to shame the feeble efforts of the West, and the word *Kulturkampf* (Culture Struggle—originally the battle [*c.*1871–87] waged by the German Chancellor, Otto von Bismarck, to subject the Roman Catholic Church to State control) took on a newer and very serious meaning.[154]

The United States responded with the *Amerika-Häuser* to promote American culture in a Europe where both National Socialism and Soviet Communism had claimed such a thing did not exist.[155] American music, literature, theatre, and so on were enrolled to assist in promoting a counter-culture to that being flagged by the Soviets. Of course the widespread belief that the United States was a philistine, culturally barren, ignorant, gum-chewing, over-rich country of red-necked cowboys died hard, and it was not only Soviet propaganda that encouraged such notions: so did arrogantly 'superior' attitudes of 'intellectuals' (notably in France), who regarded Stalin as the guarantor of 'freedom' and denied the existence of the gulags.[156]

Moholy-Nagy's widow gave talks about the work of her late husband to the vanquished Germans, and the 'New Bauhaus' in Chicago was trumpeted.[157] There were lectures about Modern Art: the fracturing of European culture by the National Socialists was emphasized with references to such pre-war exhibitions as those showing so-called *Entartete 'Kunst'* (degenerate 'art'), so the astonishing change of climate was allied to a political agenda: Modernism was becoming associated with America, with democracy, with freedom, and with the antithesis of discredited National Socialism and Fascism. The 1938 Exhibition at MoMA (described, accurately, as the 'over-geared cartel of Modernism')[158] on the *Bauhaus: 1919–1928*[159] loaded matters in favour of Gropius's reign in Weimar and Dessau: and Barr, the 'authoritative tastemaker of his day',[160] claimed that Modernism was synonymous with democracy. He declared that Modernists' nonconformity and alleged love of freedom could never be tolerated within a monolithic tyranny. His proposition that Modern art was useless for any dictator's propaganda[161] seems rather dubious.

So we have the startling transformation of the German *émigrés*, the *Bauhäusler* who had been active in extreme 'left-wing' activities in the aftermath of

Germany's collapse in 1918, and whose pronouncements during the period 1918 to 1933 cannot be mistaken for anything other than revolutionary, messianic manifestos with strong 'leftist', even communistic, tendencies, being drawn into the Cold War as part of a riposte to the cultural pretensions of the Stalin-led Soviet Union. In 1947 the Communist information-bureau (*Cominform*) held its first meeting, and became a new weapon in ideological warfare replacing the *Comintern*. It claimed to represent all those in favour of 'democracy and peace' in opposition to the threat of 'reactionary and imperialist' aggression led by the United States, and would not tolerate the slightest deviation. Stalin himself was accorded adulation far surpassing that given in the past to the Tsars, glorified as the infallible leader of all peoples, the omniscient teacher, and arbiter of everything connected with the sciences or the arts. Even musicians lived in fear of some new composition being denounced for 'formalism' or worse, and thereby having to face life in the wilderness. Dmitri Shostakovich was one Soviet composer who found he had to tread very warily to avoid disaster.

Russian culture was lauded as superior to any other (shades of National-Socialist claims concerning German culture), and was closely woven into Leninist-Stalinist doctrines: unpleasant propaganda was turned against what was termed 'homeless cosmopolitanism' (a term suggesting the vicious anti-Jewish language used during the Third Reich), all of which sounds identical to the rantings of National Socialism. 'Formalism' in the arts was denounced,[162] together with anything that deviated from the Stalinist-dictated Party line, and an identification with an architectural language far-removed from the 'International Style' led to the widespread acceptance of that 'Style' in the democracies: though at first those democracies, as with their earlier brushes with National Socialism, were hamstrung by their beliefs in civil liberties and honourable dealings, and failed dismally to understand the essence of Communist doctrines and methods (or, indeed, the emptiness at the heart of Modernism itself). Something had to be done.[163]

Spurred on by Melvin Lasky, a brilliant Bronx-born Jew, a realization began to dawn in some quarters that the anti-democratic, anti-American, anti-'cosmopolitan', and anti-West formulae used by Goebbels were simply being reworked by the Soviets ('Uncle Sam', shown in cartoons as Shylock, was an unpleasant reminder of German National-Socialist propaganda), not least in denunciations of jazz and swing, incessant advertising, Hollywood 'inanities' (including what was termed 'cheese-cake' and 'leg-art'), 'warmongering', and 'hypocrisy' (notably on the racial front).[164] Lasky, an ex-Trotskyist, was one of the first of the American realists who understood that the main substance of the Cold War was cultural, and that it was on the cultural front that the Americans were weakest, for it was only through the winning of the educated and cultured classes (which eventually provide moral and political leadership) that the American cause could be put over.

Lasky insisted that every effort should be made to show that behind the representatives of America in Europe lay a 'great and progressive culture, with a richness of achievements in the arts, in literature, in philosophy, in all the aspects of culture which unite the free traditions of Europe and America.'[165] He proposed establishing a journal, provisionally entitled 'American Review', to demonstrate that the United States had major achievements in 'all the spheres of the human spirit common to both the Old and the New Worlds', and so persuade large numbers of the German intelligentsia away from the baleful influence of Communism. Warning voices had been raised that the material aspects of the Marshall Plan would not be enough: Jean Cocteau, for example, stated that the Western cause would not be rescued by weapons or cash, but by a 'thinking minority' capable of persuading what remained of civilized Europe to avoid its own extinction.[166] In the event, it was a close-run thing, but the resultant damage may be irreparable.

Thus was born (1948) *Der Monat* (The Month), a journal intended as a link between American and German intellectuals, edited (1948–71) by Lasky, financially backed first by the Marshall Plan and then by the Central Intelligence Agency (CIA).[167] The United States later supplied huge funds during the Cold War to cultural propaganda through the Congress for Cultural Freedom, run (1950–67) by the CIA *apparatchik* Michael Josselson, an American of Estonian-Russian extraction, with the aim of moving Western 'intellectuals' away from their sympathies for Marxism and Soviet Communism, aided by a growing (if reluctant) realization of the repressive totalitarianism of Stalin, towards a new *Pax Americana*.[168]

Many, however, were resistant to such blandishments: the totalitarian state demands an officially regulated intellectual orthodoxy that will not deviate from the approved party-line, and plenty fell into that position, especially those prejudiced against America in cultural terms. Much of the world was being forced to accept a Stalinist-approved idea of art and architecture,[169] and National-Socialist Germany under Hitler and Fascist Italy under Mussolini had centrally approved attitudes towards official, public architecture.[170] As an

antidote, the feeling grew in the post-war West that there should be no barriers to what anyone must write, say, do, design, or paint: but that, in turn,
had its drawbacks, for any criticism of anything claimed to be *avant-garde*
would be denounced as 'reactionary'.[171]

In 1952 an *Entartete 'Kunst'* exhibition in reverse was organized by
MoMA, New York, and shipped to Europe (1953–4) as part of a massive
effort to counter Soviet propaganda in the arts.[172] Entitled *Twelve Modern
American Painters and Sculptors*, it was intended to show that the best art of
the 'free world' consisted of anything totalitarians loved to hate, and the
message came out loud and clear: Modernism, and European Modernism
especially, owed its survival to America.[173] But not everyone was happy,
including many American artists who did not subscribe to what became
known as 'Abstract Expressionism', and who objected to MoMA's championing of non-objective art with deformation the essence, and painting just
a frivolous amusement manipulated by salesmen.[174] MoMA was seen as
the 'shrine' of abstract art by the editor (Sidney Finkelstein) of the Marxist
journal *Masses and Mainstream* (published 1948–63), who denounced Barr-
inspired art in an article entitled 'Abstract art today: Dollars, Doodles and
Death'.[175] Yet the political aspects of the sudden acceptance of Modernity
by America overcame such protests: the programme was set. Modernism
became firmly associated with 'democracy', no matter how historically
compromised it actually was, or how within it lurked coercive tendencies
no more admirable than those of totalitarian states.[176] It might even be suggested that in order to promote an acceptance of Modernism produced in
a democracy, the very democratic process 'had to be circumvented'.[177]

MoMA's relationship with a political programme therefore deserves
investigation. Nelson Rockefeller, who was closely involved with the
museum, chaired the 'Forty Committee' of the great and good to oversee
some of the CIA's activities.[178] In the United States, museums 'founded and
supported by the giants of industry and finance'[179] became significant forces
in the dissemination of Modernism. Governed 'largely by self-perpetuating
boards of trustees composed primarily of rich donors'[180] who also controlled banks and corporations, MoMA was always a 'Rockefeller-dominated
institution'.[181] Nelson Rockefeller became president of MoMA in 1939,
and was a major figure in the direction of the Museum's affairs throughout
the 1940s and '50s: the 'involvement' of MoMA in 'American foreign policy
became unmistakably clear during World War II'.[182] Indeed, after the war,
the museum was perceived as a 'weapon for national defense to "educate,

inspire, and strengthen the hearts and wills of free men in defense of their own freedom'".[183]

Thomas W. Braden had been MoMA's executive secretary (1948–9) before joining the CIA in 1950 to supervise its cultural activities, and was a key figure in the important rôle played by MoMA in the Cold War.[184] Modernism was promoted as the 'perfect contrast' to the 'regimented, traditional, and narrow' nature of 'Socialist Realism',[185] and when cultural propaganda played its part during the Cold War, the functions of both the CIA 'cultural apparatus' and MoMA's international programmes were 'similar and, in fact, mutually supportive'.[186] But as director of MoMA from its inception until 1944, Barr was 'the single most important man in shaping the Museum's artistic character and determining the success or failure of individual American artists and art movements'.[187] He had also been remarkably influential in the promotion of Modernism in the United States through MoMA ever since he became involved in the museum on its foundation. After 1945 his influence extended far beyond the boundaries of the United States, and he should be regarded as the *éminence grise* behind Johnson the impresario, the publicist, the advocate, the showman.

Funded by Rockefeller, the museum organized a travelling Exhibition:[188] *Modern Architecture for the Modern School*, first shown at MoMA 16–30 September 1942. It was influential, and determined the direction of school-architecture after the war.[189] 'Even after leaving' MoMA's directorship, 'Barr continued to serve as the Museum's reigning tastemaker'.[190] Barr denounced the art and architecture of National-Socialist Germany and of the Soviet Union, arguing that totalitarianism and realism were bedfellows, but that abstract art was feared and prohibited by such *régimes*, *ergo* the Modern Movement was on the side of democracy. This curiously warped notion proved very useful in the promotion of Modernism and its advocates. Intelligent Cold Warriors such as Braden realized that 'dissenting intellectuals' who believed themselves to be acting freely could become useful stooges in the international propaganda war.[191] Rich, powerful patrons, such as Rockefeller, also recognized the value of culture in political arenas. Thus in rejecting what they imagined to be '*bourgeois*' and 'materialistic' values, and fondly imagining they could function outside dominant cultures in some sort of bohemian enclave, Modernists failed to see that they were merely producing cultural commodities on demand, and, cocooned in their delusions, avoided responsibility for the uses to which their designs were put.[192]

By 1959, MoMA's championing of 'Abstract Expressionism' in painting meant that no other style would do, and any artist not conforming could not exhibit in New York: even critics who had the temerity to suggest that the 'monopolistic orgy'[193] had gone on long enough could find themselves threatened or suddenly out of a job. Such official backing had made the whole art scene an 'enormous business venture'[194] at the expense of real creativity,[195] and 'stylistic conformity',[196] as ordained by MoMA and its creatures, ensured that art became empty, meaningless, verged on *Kitsch*,[197] and commanded obscenely high prices. As big business bought canvases (the larger the better) to hang in its offices, few had the temerity to question anything, given the financial sums involved.[198] The parallels with architecture were obvious.

But there were some who began to perceive the Emperor was naked.[199]

VII

Descent to Deformity

Revolution in Architecture & Planning; Destructive & Unwholesome Events in Britain from 1945; Philip Johnson: 'Sourcerer' & Tastemaker

> Every bloodless abstraction, of left or right, will necessarily swell towards authoritarianism, and from the urge to control to the self-righteous justi-fication to kill is but a short step.
>
> ANGELO BARTLETT GIAMATTI (1938–89): Baccalaureate Address
to the Senior Class, Yale College (May 1982)

> In places where the argument wears particularly thin [Le Corbusier] does not disdain the use of sentimentality or gush or the purple patch of rhetoric ... worse than Ruskin! But a critic, already reduced to a state of languor by the sickly-sweet aroma of M. Le Corbusier's prose, falls into a swoon when ... he reads that 'Passion, fire, ardour, faith, rapture, animation, all lead to happiness'.
>
> ARTHUR TRYSTAN EDWARDS (1884–1973): 'The City of Tomorrow'
in *Concrete Way* ii (September 1929) 79–87

Revolution in Architecture & Planning

In architecture, the story is subtler, but nonetheless dramatic. From the 1920s, Barr and Johnson had been the most influential advocates of Modernism in America, and they crusaded to sustain and expand its accept-ance and influence. Barr, in his preface to the catalogue of the 1938 *Bauhaus: 1919–1928* exhibition at MoMA,[1] outlined eight foundation principles:

designers should focus on industry and mass-production;
design-school instructors should be leaders in their professions;
there should be no distinction between the fine and applied arts;
the task of designing a first-class chair is much harder than producing a second-rate painting (and is much more useful);

artists should be 'spiritual counterparts' to practical technicians, and should
work together;

experimental and practical instruction are essential to inculcate an understanding of materials;

technical studies of design should lead to a new, modern sense of what is
beauty;

and

designers should always look forward, not backwards.[2]

We have seen that several European, notably German, Modernists arrived
in the United States in the late 1930s, notably Gropius and Miës van der
Rohe, and yet more crossed the Atlantic in the years before the United
States entered the war in 1941. The immigration of *Bauhäusler* radically
transformed American design: indeed *Bauhaus* design, *Bauhaus* ideas, and
many *Bauhäusler* brought German Modernism to the United States and to
the rest of the world.[3] They can hardly have imagined their good fortune
when, after the war, those *émigrés* became the American artistic and architectural Establishment. And so the disastrous policies of the Athens Charter,
CIAM, and other Modernist orthodoxies (notably Corbusianity)[4] were
adopted, supposedly as evidence of freedom, democracy, anti-authoritarian-
ism, and much else: but in fact they were associated with widespread
destruction to create an environment free from any taint of the past, with
compulsion, with dogmatic, bullying attitudes, with closed minds, and with
the absolute conviction that if they were not adopted they would be
imposed by force.

And that is what happened, but it was not simply a matter of the Barr/
Hitchcock/Johnson/MoMA/*Bauhäusler émigrés*/CIAM/Pevsner/Giedion
influences. Without the massive clout of commerce it is doubtful if
Modernism would have been so universally acceptable in the West. The
obsessions of Le Corbusier and others with machines, especially fast cars,
ships, and aeroplanes, had resonances within the commercial world. By the
late 1920s huge American industrial concerns, such as General Motors,
had grasped that planned obsolescence would be necessary to sustain mass-
production, and industrial-strength propaganda was brought into play to
represent housing, clothing, food, and cars (the 'fourth American necessity')
as essentials, and, as the director of research for General Motors, C.F. Kettering,
observed, to make people dissatisfied with what they had.[5] Architectural
historians have tended to over-emphasize the rôles of architectural theorists

and historians, architects, critics, and government planners in making Modernism the orthodoxy in architecture and planning: tradition was purged from the practice of design, town planning, and architectural/planning education; and artists and craftsmen were put out of business.

But those groups and individuals alone could not have engineered such a massive transformation in such a short time: the part played by commerce and industry has been neglected until recently. Kettering and his associates realized that, in order to make the motor-car part of what would be perceived as basic human necessities, building roads between cities would not be enough: they would have to cut through the fabric of towns and cities, involving massive destruction, and permanently transforming them.[6] In other words, mass-production[7] coupled with effective publicity,[8] the overtly political programme of MoMA (with its close links to the CIA), and the influential figures of Barr 'the tastemaker'[9] and Johnson the persuader and charmer with the right social contacts, engineered the widespread acceptance of what became a global phenomenon. The theorists of and apologists for Modernism, including those with 'academic' pretensions, and several legendary *émigrés* from Europe, eventually became the agents (perhaps unwittingly, though it is difficult to accept that they were all blinkered or myopic) for military/industrial complexes and the promotion of what were called, optimistically but misleadingly, 'Western' 'democratic' values.

MoMA's 'International-Style' promotion of 1932[10] soon had a huge effect on an enormous industrial concern, the executives of which immediately recognized the possibilities inherent in Modernism to promote its products and make vast profits.[11] General Motors exhibited in numerous towns and cities, starting in Chicago's 'Century of Progress Exposition' (1933–4), and culminating in its 'Futurama' at the World's Fair, New York (1939), designed by the master of streamlining, Norman Bel Geddes: this included demands for new highways that were also attacks on America's cities and towns on behalf of the motor-industry, and resulted in various enactments that legalized comprehensive demolition of existing urban fabric, thus enabling motor-cars to pass through what once had been thriving town centres.

It was not only General Motors that argued for 'creative destruction' as supposed stimulants for the economy: obsolescence was embraced in real estate, finance, and city planning, all part of the consumerism that would condemn countless sound buildings and entire neighbourhoods to draconian change.[12] The idea took root in American industry that what had been created in the country so far was obsolete, and that the future required more

manufactured flashy goods and more speed. Le Corbusier's hatred of the
street was eagerly embraced: the automobile-industry promoted a modern,
high-tech, high-speed alternative to the 'obsolete' street with its pavements
('sidewalks') on which people once walked, and trumpeted that it had
joined with science and art to produce gleaming, streamlined, high-rise
megastructures between which were urban freeways on which motor-cars
could speed without hindrance in place of the old urban grids, with their
mixed uses, varied architectural styles, tram-cars, horse-drawn vehicles, and
early automobiles.

However, even Bel Geddes[13] was unhappy about superhighways penetrating existing cities, a position Robert Moses and automobile enthusiasts
denounced as 'bunk',[14] with the result that General Motors pursued the
more radical line promoted by Moses rather than the less destructive one
advocated by Bel Geddes. Kettering's 'Parade of Progress' travelling exhibition
of 1936–9, 1941–2 ('Our American Crossroads'), and updated version,
1953–6 ('Out of the Muddle'), depicted the changes from 1900 to a small
village called 'Pleasant Corners', once inhabited by very old and very bored
people. The unprepossessing settlement had dirt roads, a general store, black-
smith's shop, school-house, little church, and a scattering of nineteenth-
century farmhouses, all of which prompted mirth in two onlookers in a
film promoting the exhibit. The rapid transformation, with ever-increasing
traffic leading to Main Street becoming a four-lane highway on which
unimpeded motor-vehicles could speed, and all the humble vernacular
buildings replaced by Modernist structures, was shown as 'progressive'. Thus
'obsolescence' was overcome.

Later, even more radical exhibits in the 1950s proposed to resolve problems caused by the influx of large numbers of vehicles: car-parks were created on sites once occupied by old buildings, and one-way streets were
introduced. The resemblance to Lancaster's 'Drayneflete'[15] was striking (*see*
Figure Preface P.1), but there was little hint of irony in later manifestations
of 'Parade of Progress'. Eventually, what emerged was a place from which
the human being, walking on legs, had been evicted: now there was only an
inchoate sprawling subtopian landscape of dwellings and tower-blocks set in
forbiddingly manicured parks, where motor-cars would be essential for any
aspect of life. Propaganda techniques were brilliantly used in the travelling
exhibition, ridiculing the past and glorifying a mechanized Modernist
future: not only the content, but the psychological manipulation employed
led to its widespread success.[16]

What is clear is that the car-centric 'radiant city' of the future did not spring, fully accoutred, like Athene, from the head of one begetter. Corbusian theories, promoting the notions published in *The Athens Charter*[17] and other works,[18] conveniently dovetailed with the corporate-industrial-commercial plans of organizations such as General Motors,[19] and there can be little doubt that large business-concerns quickly saw the immense possibilities of financial gains and vast profits lurking among the turgid theories of Modernists, with their anti-urban, anti-street, anti-aesthetic, pro-automobile, and supposedly 'moral' programmes (in which industrialization, social engineering, and the destruction of all historical fabric loomed large). In fact, 'morals' and supposed 'leftist' agendas had virtually no part in the widespread destruction that followed the universal embrace of Modernism: the main attraction was the obvious one of huge financial killings.

In the decades following the 1939–45 war, partly as a response to the Cold War, governments throughout Western Europe established ambitious programmes for social welfare and the redistribution of wealth intended to improve the lives of their electorate. Many of these welfare-state programmes included the building of housing, schools, new towns, leisure centres, and so on, involving a new approach to architectural design and construction that was much debated and then adopted: Modernism became the official language of architecture and town planning, and its impact was profound and widespread. Architecture played a complex but very visible rôle in the formation and evolution of the welfare-state in both theory and practice: the built environments of Western welfare-states were the visible expression of political projects. There was a colonial dimension to it as well, for at the time several European countries still had colonies, notably France and the United Kingdom, and this resulted in welfare-state architecture and planning being exported to Africa and Asia, no matter what the climatic conditions were. Connected with this was the fact that welfare-state projects also promoted consumer culture and economic growth, and architects had considerable powers, for they determined what was built, what it looked like, and how it was constructed.[20]

Sociopolitical objectives and policies were expressed in built form, principally in housing, during the halcyon period of Modernism, 1945–75. The extent of the power and influence of architects at that time has been grossly underestimated: they were immense, especially in the United Kingdom and its territories. However, architects who tried to influence key decisions concerning welfare provision, in particular through CIAM and its successor in the UK, Team 10, fell victim to hubris and their self-regarding and self-aggrandizing propaganda when the realized results of their theories proved to be hated by those on whom their creations were imposed. Those architects, secure in the righteousness of their ill-founded beliefs, forced top–down solutions that did not work on an increasingly alienated and disenfranchised *clientèle* via an inefficient and incompetent bureaucracy.[21] It was a recipe for disaster.

Modernism became official, and no deviation was permitted: Classicism, with its vast, infinitely adaptable language, was besmirched by association with Fascism, National Socialism, and, during the Cold War, with Soviet (especially Stalinist) Communism. No matter that former *Bauhäusler* in East Germany had been behind the Sixteen Principles of Urbanism (which were not trumpeted in the West, and indeed were suppressed by being ignored), the control of traffic, the revival of the urban block: all were ditched in the West with catastrophic results. Worse, wholesale clearances of urban fabric to make empty spaces inevitably created conditions where unfortunate results might include local-authority corruption, possibilities of vast profits by developers and their architects, and the making of Dystopias in which anything like civilized urban life was impossible.[22]

The case of Robert Moses is just one of a great many instances when immense power held by one individual did not bring about a glorious, radiant, futuristic, change: his embrace of the kind of city promoted by General Motors, which was remarkably similar to that envisaged by Le Corbusier, CIAM, and many disciples of the Modern Movement, encapsulated just about everything that was wrong with Modernist interference with old-established urban fabric. A towering figure, a Modernist Pharaoh, he became the virtual dictator of public works in all five boroughs of New York and much of that city's suburbs from the early 1930s until the late 1960s, and endeavoured to impose an Americanized version of Le Corbusier's deadly urban vision on the city from which disorder, complexity, unpredictability, and mixed uses were all to be expunged.[23] Cars rather than pedestrians would be given priority, and empty, windswept plazas surrounded by glass towers replaced street life, the cohesion of neighbourhoods, and everything that makes a city agreeable as an environment for human beings.[24]

The environments Moses created became impossible to ignore by 1968, when he was removed from power, and his activities were among the prime catalysts for Jane Jacobs when attacking the essence of what he and others were doing and stood for.[25] Infatuated with cars and the relatively prosper-

ous people who drove them, Moses and his team were responsible for building extremely destructive roads (often in the wrong place, causing enormous
traffic-jams as well as blighting huge areas), laying out parks, erecting bridges,
creating playgrounds and beaches, and much else. But they also obliterated
whole neighbourhoods, flattened dwellings, and eliminated streets rich in
diversity (Le Corbusier, of course, loathed streets, so their destruction would
have had his *imprimatur*), replacing them with enclaves for the super-rich,
isolated impoverished ghettoes for the poor, and urban wastelands that were
menacing and dangerous. For example, his plans included the Cross-Bronx
expressway which drove an entire community (that had been living in lively
urban conditions for decades) out of the East Tremont district of New York,
with resultant social distress: and he was by no means the only agent for
such widespread damage.[26]

Yet people with similar agenda and powers (T. Dan Smith in England, for
example)[27] were often portrayed as 'progressives', 'champions of the people'
and so on, while in reality working hand-in-hand with big business, property tycoons, and their architectural/planning advisers to ruin the habitats
of those with insufficient power or money to mount effective resistance.[28]
There were parallels in other places, not least in Britain, where the possibilities
offered by the considerable powers given to local authorities wrecked town
after town, and city after city.[29] The wielders of such powers were responsible
for the creation of environments that have been failures in just about every
respect, and have not provided pleasant, safe places in which anyone could
live or even wish to do so.[30] Osbert Lancaster's 'Drayneflete', a settlement
that had gone through centuries of development, was obliterated by
Modernist town-planning dogma after the 1939–45 war,[31] yet a similar
vision had been promoted in Kettering's 'Parade of Progress' in its various
manifestations, ending with 'Out of the Muddle'.[32] Lancaster was profoundly
accurate in his diagnosis and prophetic visions.

This 'Croydonization' (Modernist almost complete destruction of existing urban fabric, so-called after Croydon, in Surrey, south of London, which
underwent drastic change in the post-war period, especially in the 1960s)
was not a fantasy or a joke, for something[33] horribly like Lancaster's drawing
(*see* **Figure Preface P.1**)[34] was proposed in 1965 by a team led by Leslie
Martin for the redevelopment of Whitehall, London, involving the demolition of almost every building south of Downing Street and Richmond
Terrace,[35] except for the original block of New Scotland Yard and Central
Hall:[36] the Palace of Westminster was 'graciously permitted to survive, as was

Westminster Abbey, but the Middlesex Guildhall in Parliament Square was to be replaced by a conference centre', as the late Gavin Stamp put it, with delicious understatement.[37]

There was hardly a squeak of objection from a populace cowed and browbeaten by Modernist rhetoric, although The Victorian Society went into action, pointing out in no uncertain terms that the decision-makers, including the then Minister of Public Building & Works,[38] had not noticed that Whitehall and the circumference of St James's Park, in the words of Christopher Hussey,[39] 'form the ceremonial scenic centre of one of the great capitals of the world', and that, seen 'from the park down the lake, the dramatic mass of... Portland stone enriched with countless statues composes one of the most grandly picturesque urban landscapes in the world'.[40] Despite such words of wisdom and sensitivity, in the end it was merely standard irresolute inaction and procrastination on the part of government (not unconnected with likely costs) that led to what was an appallingly destructive and insensitive scheme being dropped in 1970.[41] But it was a close-run thing: other places were not so lucky.[42]

In the aftermath of 1945, when Europe was in a state unknown since the Thirty Years War (1618–48), Britain, supposedly among the victors, was in severe economic difficulties,[43] and these persisted well into the 1950s and beyond.[44] Housing, a priority in the wake of wartime destruction and a post-war baby-boom, offered little that was inspiring, and indeed most of it was dull, architecturally and in layout:[45] there was nowhere any sense that policymakers had considered what might have been better possibilities. Radical enactments, such as those concerning New Towns (1946),[46] led to plans that were hardly urban at all, with very low densities, incredibly wasteful layouts, and a general ethos of uninspired suburbia, while the Town Development Act (1952),[47] enabling existing towns to receive 'overspill' populations from larger conurbations, managed to suck the lifeblood out of the 'donor' towns and cities only to radically alter the character of many a smaller market-town, usually involving destructive interventions in town-centres, so that there are very few old-established towns in Britain that have not been severely damaged.[48] Opinion, local and national, in Britain, corrupted by Ruskin *et al.*, seemed to be predominantly anti-city and pro-suburbia, not helped by the confusion, official and among the general public, between what was meant by 'suburban sprawl' and 'garden-cities'. A re-reading of a standard text on town and country planning of the period[49] suggests that a hostile attitude to large cities was official, a cherished belief that could not be dented, even though virtually everything connected with high culture had evolved in urban environments.[50]

Still, there were some who could see dangers ahead, especially when widespread cribbing of Modernist *clichés* began to become painfully apparent in schools of architecture, and was realized all over the country in countless schemes. There were warnings about using the distressingly limited, even poverty-stricken vocabulary of Modernism just for the sake of it: Corbusian *pilotis*, for example, employed 'parrot-wise, without understanding',[51] became common. Even the *external image* of a huge structure, like Le Corbusier's *Unité d'habitation* at Marseilles (1945–52—conceived as a massive development for 'autonomous living'),[52] was copied in a scaled-down form at the Alton West Estate, Roehampton Park, London. This was designed by the London County Council's Department of Architecture (built 1954–8),[53] and some contemporary commentators had the temerity to associate it with 'Palladian precedent of geometric forms in a picturesque landscape', though reluctantly admitting, with unintentionally comical disingenuousness, that it was difficult for twentieth-century architecture 'to provide satisfying counterparts'[54] (**Plate 7.1**).

This was yet another instance of an attempt to connect an arid Modernism *sans* wit, meaning, allusion, or coherent language, with respectable historical models, this time the splendid and celebrated Picturesque 'landskips' of Georgian England, with their fanciful and stylistically varied *fabriques*, glorious vistas with eye-catchers, and great Palladian houses.[55] Other *Unités* followed the Marseilles exemplar, at Nantes-Rezé (1952–5), Berlin-Charlottenburg (1956–8), Briey-en-Forêt (1957–9) (**Figure 7.1**), and Firminy-Vert (1959–67).[56] It usually escapes those who discuss the Marseilles *Unité* that not everybody thought it was 'breathtakingly heroic':[57] it was also assessed as 'an egocentric extravagance',[58] a 'terrible hunk',[59] 'a farce',[60] pointing to 'the destruction of the natural landscape and the decline of the sense of joy of life'.[61] These judgements demonstrated an understanding of numerous problems in the *design* of the building, which is 'conceptually flawed in numerous ways', with shortcomings in the heating-systems, sound-insulation, light- and heat-control, and much else.[62] Yet in architectural education, design through analysis was abandoned in favour of copying exclusively Modernist images, which partly explains how Corbusian progeny proliferated.[63]

Some brave souls even suggested that the mass-production and mechanization of the building-process, fundamental desiderata of Modernists, were fraught with dangers, and if employed unintelligently, would prove far more

Plate 7.1. Scaled-down versions of the *external appearance* of Le Corbusier's *Unités* at the Alton West estate, Roehampton Park, London, designed by the Department of Architecture, London County Council (built 1954–8). Some commentators attempted to argue this was 'Picturesque'

expensive than the traditional methods then under threat:[64] but their warnings were suppressed by interests connected with the multinationals. The universal adoption, without imagination or skill, of approved *clichés* illustrated in the architectural press, all derived from works supposedly fitting into the convenient label 'International Style', did cause some disquiet. In a talk[65] peppered with slogans such as 'Architecture wrote the history of the epochs', 'Architecture as a true symbol of our time', 'Architecture is the real battleground of the spirit', and so on, Mies van der Rohe did manage to say something very apt. Architecture, he observed, 'is not a playground for children, young or old'.[66] This hit the proverbial nail on the head, for the subject of architecture did become something like an infants' 'playground', where a 'cheap all-purpose' Modernism, conceived in a vacuum of banality, and poorly realized in execution,[67] was universally imposed.

Yet part of the campaign to establish Modernism through the educational system actually depended on conditioning through copying Modernist images rather than thinking analytically, and for this state of affairs Mies

Figure 7.1. *Unité d'Habitation,* Briey-en-Forêt (1957–9), by Le Corbusier, complete with massive *pilotis.* Its *external appearance* was cribbed in countless schemes, usually for public housing, with unfortunate results

himself must take part of the responsibility.[68] Standards of design sank lower and lower, and the executed results became all-too-obvious failures *as architecture*, although the profession itself as a whole remained in denial. Mies was not the only one who was worried: but, despite the fact that Modernism, by the early 1950s, was widely regarded as an essential part of 'progressive' ideas for the future, 'untainted' and uninformed by the past,[69] to be imposed on society by compulsion and bullying tactics if necessary,[70] some voiced their concerns, not least about the costs, social, cultural, and economic, of redeveloping cities according to the tenets of Modernism.[71]

Gordon Stephenson, for example, suggested that modern architecture had already reached several dead ends because it neglected to recognize 'truths established through the centuries',[72] and even Manning Robertson warned that no 'city can afford to disregard its history, and everything within reason should be done to preserve buildings or other features that help to keep that history alive'.[73] He also emphasized that it was not enough for a building to be a good work of architecture in itself: it must respect its neighbours so that the street, or the town taken as a whole, should not be damaged.[74] This lesson Modernists ignored: they disregarded everything that had gone before. A relatively small number of European architects and, perhaps more importantly, their unquestioningly fervent disciples, inflicted huge damage on the physical fabric of towns and cities, and therefore on human beings as well.

Many Modernists, for example, eagerly hoped that 'real architecture'[75] (meaning that which could be identified with Modernism) would everywhere triumph in Britain and elsewhere (as then looked more and more likely, once it had the backing of powerful forces and lavish funds flowing from the United States as a by-product of the Cold War).[76] They also unquestioningly accepted notions such as Le Corbusier's *Ville Radieuse* and images of his buildings from the 1930s to inform post-1945 planning-decisions, with disastrous results (**Figure 7.2**).[77] Peter Hall saw clearly what had happened: he equated Le Corbusier's malign influence over the architectural profession with that of Rasputin's over the Russian Imperial family.[78] In his outline of the relationship between politics and architecture in Britain, Jules Lubbock recognized that Le Corbusier had a major rôle in all this, largely through his English followers,[79] for a whole generation of British architect-planners exercised dictatorial control over developments,[80] yet were immune from criticism until the Poulson scandal of the early 1970s.[81] Thereafter, suspicions 'about high-level corruption and misallocation of

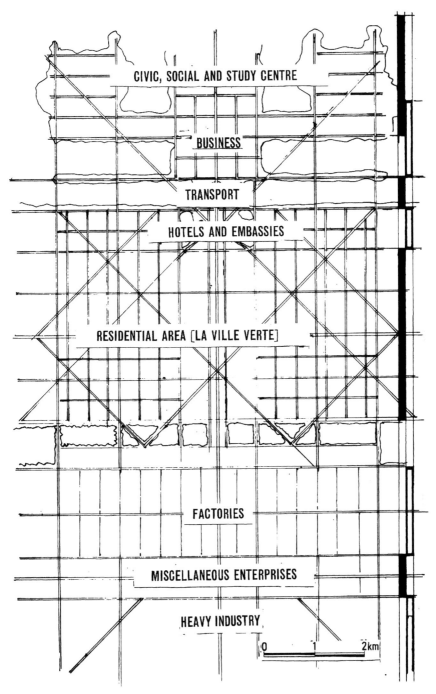

CIVIC, SOCIAL AND STUDY CENTRE

BUSINESS

TRANSPORT

HOTELS AND EMBASSIES

RESIDENTIAL AREA [LA VILLE VERTE]

FACTORIES

MISCELLANEOUS ENTERPRISES

HEAVY INDUSTRY

0   1   2km

Figure 7.2. Diagrammatic plan of *La Ville Radieuse* by Le Corbusier and A.-A.-P. Jeanneret (1931), showing the proposed zoning in rigid parallel bands, a recipe that has not proved beneficial to the life of cities

resources...would compound waves of growing concerns'[82] about how Modernists were transforming and had transformed cities. In a very short time, what has been termed 'a corrosive atmosphere of mistrust'[83] replaced the certainties that had guided developments from the 1950s.[84]

German towns and cities suffered massive destruction, especially in the closing stages of the 1939–45 war. That damage was far greater and more extensive than anything the *Luftwaffe* managed to inflict on the urban fabric of the United Kingdom, so it is perhaps worth considering why cities like Nürnberg (Nuremberg) and other ancient German towns manage to be much more agreeable *as urban experiences* than comparable reconstructions (e.g. Coventry and Exeter) in Britain. It seems that the Germans, like the Poles, realized that the *cultural* importance of old-established urban settlements somehow had to be rescued and preserved as part of a national identity under threat, and that the principles advocated by sensitive observers of urban design such as Karl Gruber,[85] Adolf Loos,[86] and Camillo Sitte[87] should be heeded. In particular, Gruber's studies of the morphology of mediaeval German urban fabric, and Sitte's well-observed analyses of urban compositions seem to have had a beneficial effect on post-war German planning, despite pressure from Modernists to obliterate the past, and despite reactions to the pre-war *Blut und Boden* tendency adopted by National Socialism. Loos too, although usually claimed as a 'pioneer' of the Modern Movement, greatly admired English Arts-and-Crafts work, especially the houses of the Domestic Revival.[88] He denounced the *fin-de-siècle* overblown architecture of Vienna's *Ringstraße*.[89] He held the work of K.F. Schinkel in high esteem (seeing in it lessons for contemporary design), and he rejected the self-conscious limited aesthetic of the *Bauhäusler*. He also argued for tact in slotting new buildings into urban fabric, deploring tendencies among architects to disregard context and be 'original'.[90]

Some of the architects involved in the enormous task of rebuilding German cities belonged to reconstruction bodies that had been established by Albert Speer, and their work was influential. Even systems of axes introduced during the Third Reich in cities including Düsseldorf and Wuppertal were retained after 1945, and attempts were made to harmonize new work with surviving fabric, notably in Münster and Nuremberg, where colossal bomb damage had been sustained.[91] Where Modernists succeeded in gaining a foothold, as in Rheydt, Alfons Leitl carried out major post-war planning, but the results were less harmonious, and have not worn well. In the former East Germany, anti-Modernist rules were proclaimed in 1950 under the leadership of Walter Ulbricht, so reconstruction tended to follow axial monumentality, as at the former *Stalinallee*, Berlin (from 1952), the *Roßplatz*, Magdeburg (1953–9), and the *Marktplatz*, Dresden (1953–7).

The importance of historical fabric to post-war towns in both Germany and Poland was recognized even to the extent of recreating it if it had been completely obliterated (as much of it had). Identity and historical memory were valued: the dangers of the Modernist goal of the *tabula rasa* were frequently resisted, but all too often they were ignored in the British Isles, where the dominant influence on town planning was the sort of commercial programme modelled on that backed by General Motors (although that would never be overtly acknowledged, so great was the obsession with Modernist theorists of architecture and planning, such as Le Corbusier. What was actually realized owed more to American commercially orientated ideas than most protagonists would ever be prepared to admit).

There were occasional apostates, but only after immense damage had been done. From the 1970s, for example, the Modernist South Africa-born British architect Theo Crosby,[92] influenced by Jane Jacobs and others, became a revisionist, questioning the sacred, strident texts of Modernism, placing a value on history, and, most surprising of all, insisting on the necessity of bringing back craftsmanship to a world where it had all but vanished. In 1987 he became one of a select group advising the Prince of Wales, whose interventions in opening up debate were to shake the architectural Establishment.

Destructive & Unwholesome Events in Britain from 1945

It has long been clear that architecture became one of the most politicized of all professions, and was taken over by 'left-wing' ideologues in the aftermath of the 1939–45 war, though some were in positions of power before hostilities commenced. One interesting case is that of Donald Gibson,[93] who, not yet thirty years old, was appointed to the new post of City Architect by the Labour Council of Coventry, Warwickshire, in 1938. From 1939 to 1940 he and his colleagues organized an exhibition which opened in May 1940, a propaganda exercise to soften up the public for what was actually to become 'comprehensive redevelopment'. Gibson's plan, which involved the demolition of, predictably, 'some fine buildings which very few people care about',[94] the creation of a ring-road that was far too near the centre, a pedestrianized shopping-area, and the retention of a few historic buildings left isolated without any context (Lancaster's vision of post-war 'Drayneflete' again springs to mind [*see* **Figure Preface P.1**]),[95] became possible to realize when the German air-force conveniently did the job of partially flattening the place for him between November 1940 and April 1941.

The essentials of the Gibson plan for Coventry (much influenced by the writings of Mumford)[96] thereafter became familiar in virtually all proposals for post-war British towns and cities, to their great detriment. Alternative plans were put forward by Coventry's City Engineer, Ernest Ford, and indeed there was considerable animosity between the established City Engineer's Department and the new City Architect:[97] such tensions were to be repeated all over the United Kingdom, not least when engineers pre-pared wasteful road layouts, and the architects failed to fill in those bits left over with any panache whatsoever, because they were so mesmerized by the rectangular boxy forms of the 'International Style' that they were no longer capable of designing anything except a simple rectangular block. This meant that they left useless patches of waste ground (SLOAP)[98] between the roads and their buildings.

The other enormously problematic aspects of the great amount of destruction and new building were not just the huge waste of resources, the disruption of communities, and the killing of the urban organism, but the mediocrity and incompetent detailing of the supposedly 'functional' archi-tecture which turned out to be nothing of the sort. The resultant environ-ment has proved to be uncivilized, aesthetically barren, and unsafe. In the summer of 1940, for example, 'The Coventry of Tomorrow' exhibition showed what was in store for the city *before* it was actually bombed, and a pretty awful example of mediocrity it was too, with timidly Modernist hints unimaginatively derived from Le Corbusier's propaganda and other sources.

The departure of so many architectural adherents of the Modern Movement from Germany fostered the legend that Modernism was *Verboten* (forbidden *or* prohibited) under National Socialism. A glance at the lavish architectural publications of the Third Reich[99] and later books on German architecture between the wars[100] will dispel this fondly-held delusion. This legend did Modernism a huge favour. Modernist *émigrés* such as Gropius, Miës van der Rohe, and other *Bauhäusler* began to be associated with every-thing National Socialism and Fascism were not, despite the prominence given to the Modern Movement in architecture in Italy, and despite the overt and very definite hostility to it within the Soviet Union, where several

Bauhäusler (e.g. Hannes Meyer)[101] had hoped to find acceptance, but were quickly disabused. Indeed the rather terrifyingly dogmatic stances taken under Stalin regarding Modernism caused confusion among adherents of the political so-called 'left'. Aesthetic positions and political attitudes were by no means as clear-cut as many seem to believe:[102] indeed, they were very contradictory and confused.[103] Some of those *émigrés* (including Gropius and Miës) had sought to ingratiate themselves with National Socialism, and others managed to make accommodation with authoritarian *régimes* as potential employers.

In 1945,[104] G.D.H. Cole (described[105] by his widow, M.I. Postgate, as a most 'Unsocial Socialist')[106] asked

> are we to plan? If so, what are we to plan, and what are the essential instruments for making our plans and for carrying them into effect? And, first and foremost, what is planning, and how much substance is there in the allegation that it is inconsistent with liberty...?...Would it mean less real and tangible freedom for ordinary people, or would it mean an enlargement of the kinds of freedom that most people want and value?[107]

Cole's questions engaged those with 'leftist' intellectual pretensions immediately after the war of 1939–45 had ended, and are among the subjects of an interesting tome, edited by and contributed to by Iain Boyd Whyte, dealing with the state of affairs in Britain as far as planning, education, and design were concerned.[108]

Whyte's book covered a very wide range of issues, and deserves to be read even now, several years after it was published. Jules Lubbock, in a telling chapter entitled '1947 and all that: why has the Act lasted so long?', outlined the origins and legacies of the Town and Country Planning Act;[109] Whyte gave us 'Otto Neurath and the sociology of happiness'; and Michiel Dehaene wrote on 'Surveying and comprehensive planning: the "co-ordination of knowledge"[110] in the wartime plans of Patrick Abercrombie[111] and Max Lock'.[112] Volker M. Welter's 'Everywhere at any time: post-Second World War genealogies of the city of the future' discussed some well-known texts by people such as Arthur Korn, Lewis Mumford, and Ludwig Hilbersheimer, who 'assembled in books extremely disparate selections of classical Greek and Roman towns, medieval northern European urban settlements, Renaissance towns, colonial cities in the Americas, and even the occasional Asian temple city. Together, these cities constituted a genealogy of human urban settlements that usually culminated in the authors' own designs for the city of tomorrow',[113] a mild and polite description of the realities of what those writers attempted.

The technique is familiar. By illustrating and describing mediaeval, Renaissance, and Classical towns and cities, a claim that Modernism was somehow connected with them was made by the protagonists. Korn, for example, utterly failed to make a convincing case for why *history* (as the alleged 'builder of towns') mattered one hoot to the Modernist planning schemes he described, promoted, and praised.[114] Hilbersheimer claimed that the modern city should be planned without *any* consideration for the past.[115] Welter showed that Hilbersheimer, Korn, and Mumford *preserved* historical cities in their books, but, metaphorically speaking, they *shattered* them by 'reducing them to mere sequences of images of past urban designs, which, furthermore', found their 'match in the city of the future, the teleological end-point of the genealogical surveys. Thus, the books achieved what, in reality, had for a long time been out of reach—the creation of a *tabula rasa*, a clean slate on which to start all over again'.[116] The MARS Group Plan for London (1942),[117] with which Korn[118] was closely involved, if implemented, would have done just that: almost the *entire* city would have been demolished, apart from a few historic buildings identified as of national significance:[119] it was a much enlarged version of Lancaster's 'Drayneflete' (*see* **Figure Preface P.1**),[120] and hugely destructive.[121]

Rhodri Windsor Liscombe, in his 'Perceptions in the conception of the Modernist urban environment: Canadian perspectives on the spatial theory of Jaqueline Tyrwhitt', demonstrated Tyrwhitt's influence on the formulation and transmission of Modern-Movement town planning during the post-war decades; Peter Larkham's 'Selling the future city: images in UK post-war reconstruction plans' dealt with the presentation of 'comprehensive development' plans throughout the UK; and Louise Campbell's 'Paper dream city/modern monument: Donald Gibson at Coventry' described the genesis and hatching of modern Coventry (Lewis Mumford optimistically described the Upper Precinct as the modern equivalent of a mediaeval Midland market square).[122] *The Buildings of England* volume on Warwickshire considered that the work of the Coventry City Architect's Department (under Gibson [1938–55] and Ling [1955–64]) at the Coventry two-level pedestrian shopping Precinct (originally planned 1941) 'cannot…be assessed in terms of aesthetics',[123] that the 'architectural quality' was 'indifferent',[124] and that the 'architecture as such can largely be overlooked',[125] which sums it up quite neatly (**Plate 7.2a–b**). The City Arcade (1960–2) in Coventry (**Plate 7.3a**) hardly rises to the architectural occasion compared

Plate 7.2a. Upper Pedestrian Precinct in Coventry, looking towards the handsome steeple (1370–1430s) of the cathedral destroyed in 1940: Pevsner noted that its survival was an 'untold boon', for the twentieth-century style had 'not been able to create anything anywhere both as elegant and as powerful', which sounds like a spectacular retreat from the position he had adopted earlier (Pevsner & Wedgwood [1966] 251)

with certain robust Victorian and Edwardian arcades, finished in hard-wearing and colourful, sensible materials, in cities like Leeds, Manchester, and Newcastle upon Tyne (**Plate 7.3***b*).

Coventry offered one example of a British architectural/planning response after war-damage (although, as noted above, comprehensive redevelopment had been planned before the destruction by German bombs); Canterbury in Kent was another, where the feeble work done under City Architect and Planning Officers Leslie Hugh Wilson (1945–56—who left to become Chief Architect and Planning Officer for Cumbernauld New Town [until 1962], and later, with Womersley, was responsible for the disastrous Hulme Crescents, Manchester), John Louis Berbiers (1957–65), and Donald Herbert Tomkinson (1966–72—an unquestioning devotee of Corbusianity),[126] all of whom embraced Modernism, should have been an object-lesson in how things should *not* have been done (**Plate 7.4***a* & *b*).

Then we had Keith D. Lilley on 'Conceptions and perceptions of urban futures in early post-war Britain: some everyday experiences of the rebuilding of Coventry, 1944–62', in which the reactions of many people (anything but

Plate 7.2b. View in the Precinct looking towards Mercia Tower, then (1966) under construction, as Ling wanted a 'vertical feature' at that point, but it compares unfavourably with the 'vertical feature' of St Michael's mediaeval steeple at the other end of the Precinct. Mercia Tower's original cladding was mosaic, which failed, so it was refurbished and re-clad just over forty years after it was completed in 1968

favourable to the brave new world created by Gibson and his team) were described; Elizabeth Darling, on' "Into the world of conscious expression":[127] Modernist revolutionaries at the Architectural Association, 1933–39', outlined how the principles and practices of Modernism began to take over in the educational establishments; and Clive B. Fenton gave us '*PLAN*: a student journal of ambition and anxiety'[128] in which the preoccupations of students in schools of architecture in the years immediately before the 1939–45 war were outlined. Simon Richards, in 'Destroy all humans!',

Plate 7.3a. City Arcade, Coventry (1960–2), demonstrating how ineffective aesthetic control of signage, combined with inferior materials, compares unfavourably with earlier designs of this type as shown in Plate 7.3b

enquired why it is that drawings of new development-schemes did not and do not include beggars, drunks, prostitutes, thieves, and 'cottagers':[129] Geoffrey Scott, arbiter of Taste, had drawn attention to this sort of thing much earlier, calling it the 'ethical fallacy'[130] of architecture, especially in relation to the critical attitudes of people like Ruskin and A.W.N. Pugin.[131] Richards effectively exposed the problems of high-rise living,[132] the inhumane, destructive simplicities of CIAM, and the snobbery concerning suburbia, among much else.[133] Then John McKean, in 'The English university of the 1960s: built community, model universe', outlined the building of post-war university campuses, contrasting them with the rather more subtle work of Giancarlo De Carlo for the Free University of Urbino. Finally, Miles Glendinning's 'The Tall Barracks artistically reconsidered:[134] Hyde Park Cavalry barracks and the total environment of modern military life' looked at reactions to Basil Spence's buildings.

Now all this is useful stuff,[135] but it could have done with some tough-minded examinations of the motives of ideologues who, having been seduced wholesale by figures such as Gropius and 'Le Corbusier', and by the supposed tenets of the *Bauhäusler*, did so much damage to our towns and

Plate 7.3*b*. Central Arcade, Newcastle upon Tyne (1906), clad in brown and yellow faïence, with pavement finished in vitreous mosaics by Rust of Battersea, designed by J. Oswald & Son, architects. This fine exemplar was mercifully spared the mass destruction of the city by T. Dan Smith *et al.*

cities, spawning appalling social problems and aesthetic atrocities. And in recent years an architectural trend has emerged, in which buildings are distorted, misshapen, and menacing.[136] Yet *Bauhaus*-inspired theories are still being taught in schools of architecture: there is a widespread denial that graduates of that institution were responsible, or even could be responsible, for creating an excremental Hell on earth in the form of places such as Auschwitz-Birkenau.[137]

Plate 7.4*a*. Post-war 'redevelopment' in war-damaged Canterbury, Kent, south of the great cathedral. The contrast between 'Bell Harry', the noble crossing tower (1494–1505) designed and built by John Wastell, an example of real architecture, and the feeble Modernist fabric in the foreground, is an eloquent statement of failure of nerve

As Whyte pointed out, the emotional and aesthetic contexts to post-war planning have been not only neglected, but ignored. When even Mumford, in 1942, began to question the CIAM stance, and pointed out serious flaws in the notion of the four functions of the city (dwelling, work, recreation, and transportation), alarm bells should have started to ring, audible even to the tone deaf. Mumford (who seems by then to have realized that his own writings may not have been entirely beneficial) asked where were the political, educational, and cultural functions of the city: he stated that he regarded the organs of political and cultural associations as the distinguishing marks of the city, that their omission was the chief defect of routine city planning, and that their absence from the programme of CIAM was 'inexplicable'.[138] One might suggest that this was anything but 'inexplicable', but quite deliberate. They were not omitted, however, from the Sixteen Principles of Urbanism of the DDR,[139] mentioned in Chapter VI.

During the World War of 1939–45, unlike the 1914–18 war,[140] many of the newer ideas concerning architecture proliferated, and, encouraged by

Plate 7.4*b*. All too often Modernist interventions, such as the driving of ring-roads around mediaeval city-walls, as at Canterbury, created visual squalor and Space Left Over After Planning (SLOAP). This eloquent exemplar should be compared with what was done around many Continental city- and town-walls, where delightful tree-lined promenades and other amenities were provided

adventurous publishers, such as Allen Lane's Penguin Books, intellectual debate flourished, with various exhibitions, periodicals, lectures, and the like acting as catalysts.[141] War-damage drew attention to schemes of reconstruction: a climate was created, largely by the 'left', favourable to wholesale redevelopment of many urban areas (not only those damaged by enemy action) through the evolution of 'comprehensive' planning and 'redevelopment' starting from scratch.[142]

So something very odd happened after 1945, when huge changes were made to the fabrics, layouts, and skylines of British towns and cities, involving massive destruction, social upheaval, and colossal waste of resources.[143] What prompted such a phenomenon, and why was aesthetically unedifying 'Modernism-on-the-cheap' universally adopted? 'Comprehensive redevelopment' plans were approved throughout the United Kingdom, despite the awkward fact that the nature and extent of war-damage was limited compared with what had occurred in Continental Europe and Japan: indeed, 'far more plans were produced than the number of seriously damaged towns would suggest'.[144] 'Comprehensive redevelopment' often foundered when it came up against the harsh realities of economics: tens of thousands of perfectly sound houses were compulsorily acquired, stripped of their roof coverings (to deter 'squatters'), boarded up, and left to rot, yet the 'developments' never happened.[145] Decent houses that could have been enhanced were either pulled down or blighted beyond redemption, impoverishing urban life, and representing a huge squandering of energy, capital, and scarce resources. This was all because of a quasi-religious belief in the tenets of the Modern Movement.

The facts were that the nation, supposedly victorious in war, was in severe economic difficulties, yet clung to the delusion that it was a world-power with an Empire *or* Commonwealth (which it could not afford, and had demonstrated it could not protect), yet decided to destroy as much as possible of existing urban fabric at home in order to realize the dream of that 'New Jerusalem'.[146] J.M. Keynes, in 1946, suggested that England, 'sticky' with self-pity, was 'not prepared to accept peacefully and wisely the fact that her position and her resources' were 'not what they once were'.[147] The distinguished diplomat, Sir Nicholas Henderson, noted in 1979 that the British had become 'poor and unproud', something that showed 'in the look of our towns, in our airports, in our hospitals', and that in many perceptions Britain was 'referred to as a model not to follow'. He warned that 'a considerable jolt' would be needed to resume 'mastery of our fate', but that this would only be possible if our 'national character' had not 'undergone some profound metamorphosis'.[148] Henderson was interested in architecture and in the environment, and his observations about the depressingly seedy appearance of so much of contemporary Britain rang true. Unfortunately, things have not improved since then.

However, Britain was in a far better condition than were many European countries such as ruined, divided, shrunken, and occupied Germany; battered Poland (which had not only shifted geographically but lost a large part of its population, and had much of its urban fabric utterly destroyed); or Italy (which had also suffered massive destruction as well as starvation). It was eclipsed, nevertheless, as a Great Power by the United States, and the indecent haste with which India was granted independence (and partitioned) finished its position as an Asian-Pacific Power (already badly damaged by defeats inflicted by the Empire of Japan [from 1941]). Given that war-damage to British towns and cities bore no comparison to that inflicted on, say, Germany or Poland, the decision to pull down massive amounts of substantially built urban fabric that could have been saved and sensitively brought up to date does not make any economic sense at all. There appear to have been two main reasons why such wasteful policies were pursued.[149] The first was widespread acceptance among architects and planners, working with politicians, of CIAM/MARS Group[150] dogmas, and the second, allied to the first, was a visceral hatred of the past,[151] part of the Modernist demand for the clean slate on which buildings of Modernist-approved appearance could be erected, but also part of a widespread and misplaced rejection of the Victorian age at a time when the very word 'Victorian' was a term of abuse.[152] In addition, American influences, outlined in Chapter VI, connected with 'planned obsolescence' and an obsession with the motor-car, cannot be ignored.

It never occurred to those who made the decisions that, rather than destroying sound houses which had no bathrooms, those and other amenities could be added, just as, if a human being had no teeth, he or she could be provided with dentures rather than be eliminated. The reason for such widespread destruction was not really all about 'slum-clearances' at all: it was about *image*, packaging, traffic, ambition, dismissal of the past,[153] and often greed, with not a word about aesthetics, culture, meaning, or symbolism to which people could relate, or what architecture used to signify.[154] It involved the obliteration of nineteenth-century or earlier fabric which did not look 'modern', which was unapologetically urban rather than comfortingly suburban, and quite unlike the gleaming promise revealed in seductive drawings of the clean, 'hygienic', over-glazed Utopia promoted by Modernists.

The consequences were overstretch, wholesale demolition, failure to modernize infrastructures and industry (especially the policy of propping up moribund industrial areas for political reasons and sentimentality). Marshall Aid was wasted on a 'New Jerusalem' which failed to materialize, and the universal adoption of the Modern Movement for developments cannot be explained in rational terms but only in relation to a widespread belief in the secular cult promoted through CIAM and other agencies, not least architectural journalism and texts by prominent Modernists and their supporters. Comprehensive 'planning' and development starting from scratch became articles of faith in this new cult: if the *Luftwaffe* had not destroyed a town- or city-centre, then the new architectural/town-planning Establishment would do so instead. If the cleared sites did not exist, and perfectly sound town- or city-centres had survived, then powers were sought and gained that would ensure the former came into being and the latter would be pulled down or damaged beyond recognition.[155] The flattening of St Ebbe's, Oxford, and the threats to destroy what remained of Listed historic

buildings in Charles Street there in the 1960s, was just one wretched episode[156] in a national orgy of destruction, not unconnected with dazzling
prospects of making a great deal of money.[157]

In the decades following, even more wrecking took place in British
towns and cities as municipal authorities devised and implemented radical
schemes to reshape and 'modernize' them to make them look disconcert-
ingly like the models promoted by General Motors in the 'Out of the
Muddle' exhibits of 1953–6.[158] In the process, councils wrecked far more
than enemy action managed to destroy: it was as though certain places
attempted to self-destruct. The case of Glasgow is particularly dramatic, for it
had suffered somewhat less from aerial bombardment than other comparable
British cities (**Plates** **7.5a** & *b*), yet its flattening of whole areas of substantial,
stone-built tenements possessing considerable architectural qualities was

Plate 7.5a. The unedifying Dystopian results of 'comprehensive redevelopment'
involving package deals in industrialized building (a Modernist obsession) offered
by contractors (1964–9) and resulting in twenty-storey slab-blocks built on the 'soda
wastes' of the St Rollox chemical works, an unpropitious site in itself. View from
Sighthill Cemetery (opened 1840), 225 Springburn Road, Glasgow

Plate 7.5*b*. Somewhat gloomy lodge in Romanesque-Revival style by Charles Wilson (1848) at the Southern Necropolis, Caledonia Road, Gorbals, Glasgow, completely overshadowed by four massive twenty-four-storey tower-blocks of the Area D Hutchesonstown 'comprehensive redevelopment' area by the Scottish Special Housing Association under Harold Ernest Buteux, built 1961–8. Two of these blocks were demolished in 2005–6 (another example of conspicuous waste of scarce resources) and the other two were refurbished. The great Glasgow architect Alexander 'Greek' Thomson was interred in the cemetery, and it says much about Glasgow that his original monument no longer exists

shocking.[159] Modernist high-rise replacements of the late-1950s and 1960s created huge problems, notably in the Gorbals, with the result that many new blocks soon had to be demolished, an eye-watering waste of money.[160] That was not 'planned obsolescence': it was a wrong-headed, ideology-inspired, monstrous piece of wilful vandalism.

Frank Worsdall accurately chronicled the fate of 'The City that Disappeared', lamenting that 'much of the architectural and historical heritage of the city' had been 'destroyed by people and institutions who should have known better. In the great majority of cases, the demolition was unnecessary and could have been avoided with a little foresight and imagination', qualities 'in remarkably short supply'.[161] Worsdall went on to state that architecture 'is a fine art. This simple fact seems to have almost totally escaped the attention of educationalists and others who influence our lives. It is an exceedingly strange state of affairs since architecture is the one art form which plays an important role in everyday existence.'[162] Worsdall compared Glasgow's sorry fate with the German and Polish cities which had been 'lovingly rebuilt according to the original designs' after enormous damage during the 1939–45 conflict:[163] Glasgow officials ensured this would not be possible in their virtually intact city, however, because they deliberately discarded 'many of the oldest architectural drawings in their possession just after the war',[164] and in 1972 the convenor of the Highways Committee, the body responsible for what Worsdall aptly labelled 'havoc in every quarter of the city,'[165] portentously announced that he did not wish the 'new Glasgow to be a museum piece for the delectation and delight of visiting professors of architecture',[166] a dig at the enthusiasm for the great historic buildings of Glasgow shown during the RIBA annual conference held in the city in 1964. Even Lord Esher, chairman of the RIBA's planning committee, when *en-route* to Glasgow for that conference, had wondered why he was scheduled to talk about preservation to 'people who, he understood, needed a completely new city', such was the badly-informed received opinion regarding not only Glasgow, but Victorian architecture in general. In twenty-four hours Esher realized Glasgow was a great stone-built city, far better than anything that could be built in 1964, and made an impassioned plea for its conservation that mostly fell on ears which did not wish to hear.

As a young man, I inspected many handsome, solidly-built, architecturally distinguished tenements in Glasgow (including a block designed by the great 'Greek' Thomson), all built of fine ashlar sandstone, and it was clear that they were capable of being sensitively updated, refurbished, fitted with modern amenities, and given new leases of life. That was not to be, however, as political decisions had been made to eliminate those splendid old buildings (which were real works of *architecture*, firmly rooted in the Classical tradition), replacing them with high-rise blocks in order to make the place look 'modern' and obliterate every vestige of the historic fabric. The staggering waste of resources and destruction of good architecture was unforgivable, especially as the badly-designed and poorly-constructed new towers and slabs did not stand the test of time, and rapidly became uninhabitable.[167]

There were some brave souls who did not subscribe to the new ortho-doxy: R.M.T. Tyler, for example, distrusted all theoreticians, especially those whose heads were stuffed with 'form follows function' and other empty slogans. As an architect, he deplored the lack of rigour of modern architec-tural training, and felt architects were unsuited to deal with the industrial-ized techniques of building that were increasingly favoured; their unsuitability soon became painfully obvious with one failure after another stacking up as a national disgrace.[168] That lack of rigour was and is endemic, and continued in many local-authority offices. In some establishments, political attitudin-izing took precedence over skills in architecture: in the London County Council, for example, the late Colin St John Wilson noted that the 'unargu-able existence of a prevalent Communist persuasion in high places'[169] (he meant the LCC) 'soon became manifested in the architectural "house-style" of, paradoxically, the mildest form grounded upon adherence to the works of the Swedish Housing Authority during the War' and tediously celebrated in the pages of *The Architectural Review* as 'The New Empiricism'.[170] However, the same journal had warned that the *Bauhäusler*, although allegedly possessed of 'boldness and architectural imagination', might well, 'like other revolutionaries, . . . destroy more than they can possibly create. They have no tolerance of accident.'[171]

As the anonymous author(s) of *The Architectural Review* correctly observed, *Sharawaggi* (or *Sharawadji*) was a word popularized in mid-eighteenth-century England to describe irregularity, asymmetry, and the Picturesque qualities of being surprising through graceful disorder, and so was applied to irregular gardens, known as 'Chinese', or as *les jardins anglo-chinois*: it was associated with the Whigs who created 'natural landskips' as expressions of *English freedom*, as opposed to the totalitarian gardens of France, with their insistence on regimented symmetry.[172] Local authorities, the *Review* asserted, were usually 'all out for Bankers' Georgian and road-widening',[173] so it urged that something rather drastic might have to be done to promote Modernism, tempered by 'inconsistency' and 'compromise', which it termed 'urban Sharawaggi'. The journal even suggested that the *Bauhaus* 'must accept Sharawaggi', as unlikely a scenario as might be imagined. *Sharawaggi* thus began to be used (somewhat pretentiously) in the 1940s to describe irregular, asymmetrical, informal layouts of housing-estates, a corruption of the word if ever there was one. But attempts to employ *Sharawaggi* or any other panaceas never stood a chance against the regimented dogmas of Corbusianity, CIAM, the MARS Group, and the Athens Charter, in unholy alliance with the kind of urban vision promoted by huge corporations in the United States.

However, the ideals of enlightened Whigs can hardly be compared with the views of the *Review* contributors, who went on to admit their article could be 'regarded by a sceptical reader . . . as a mere essay in casuistry. It is far from being that. On the contrary, it is in the nature of a profession of faith. It is a profession of aesthetic faith on the part of' *The Architectural Review.* 'There never was a profession of faith that did not antagonise its hearers, and this one may be no exception. There are times, however, when nothing else seems possible . . .'.[174] The quasi-religious tone of 'professions of faith' and inevitability of compulsion is further suggested in the acceptance of the notion that the *Bauhaus* 'style' had a 'saving grace', but that the problem was how to impose it without the 'application of force'.[175] That Gropius & Co., CIAM, members of the MARS Group (who by then exercised a considerable influence on CIAM),[176] or disciples of Corbusier would countenance anything like Enlightenment *Sharawadji*, especially that connected with English Whiggery, was wishful thinking indeed.

That so many accepted the staccato sloganizing of Corbusianity should have sufficed to warn of what was coming. Even Arthur Ling (who succeeded Gibson at Coventry in 1955), no 'right-winger' himself, spoke against the claims of the architectural profession to solve the problems of the world, and aimed some barbed criticisms at those who unthinkingly 'hero-worshipped Le Corbusier but only adopted the stylistic elements of his work':[177] images of the Alton Estate at Roehampton spring to mind (*see* **Plate 7.1**). Ling remarked that 'there was a fair amount of mediocrity around',[178] and that much of it was produced by the disciples of 'Le Corbusier'. His observation was devastatingly accurate, and in private conversation he was rather sharper in his condemnations.[179]

The 'New Humanists', associated with what has been called 'Humane Modernism' (influenced by Scandinavian Modernism), were regarded by British converts to Corbusianity as effete, and as 'unpardonably compromised and ingratiating'.[180] Nevertheless, whatever the flavour, most architects who identified themselves with Modernism remained fully convinced that it offered the 'right choices'[181] for future society, but that was a gross understatement: Modernism was believed to offer the *only choice* that was acceptable, and thus anything else was excluded by a sort of religious fiat. The entire Modernist approach was not one of *choice* at all, but the *imposition* of a single style and ideology. So no matter how dreadful the realities turned out to be (and unpleasant reality soon became apparent), Modernist supposed solutions were still enforced. It certainly involved cribbing from people like Le Corbusier, and there was also a great deal of copying from the works of 'Mies'. But the main reason why so many held on to Modernism was because it was a new pseudo-religious cult, and cults, being irrational, do not respond to logical argument: belief and attitudes are all.

When we are told that life 'at the LCC [London County Council] was great fun. We all did as we pleased, there was no discipline or central control. You just ignored the design briefs and got on with designing what you, as an architect, thought was best for people',[182] the immature arrogance is hard to miss. When it was suggested that some sort of evidence should be gathered about what people *actually wanted* when it came to housing, Hubert de Cronin Hastings of the Architectural Press (whose *ex cathedra* pronouncements were all too evident, especially in the pages of *The Architectural Review*), burst out with the dogmatic statement: 'but we *know* what should be done'.[183] The certainties of unswerving pseudo-religious belief have much to answer for.

The baleful influences of the simplistic totalitarianism of CIAM; the MARS Group (proposing widespread destruction and rebuilding of London);[184] Team X (which emerged from the CIAM X meeting in 1956, some of the members of which took themselves mightily seriously, and, in their own words, saw themselves as 'terrorists');[185] SPUR (Society for the Promotion of Urban Renewal—its tedious debates[186] disguised its real purpose, which was to destroy town-centres and provide access for traffic, thereby getting as much work as possible for Modernist architects such as themselves); and other pressure-groups, have been outlined in numerous publications,[187] most of which make depressing reading as monuments to the blinkered messianic messages of those whose efforts have done so much harm.

Among protagonists once given massive publicity, and treated as 'progressives', were the 'architect and criminal',[188] John Poulson, the 'local government leader and criminal',[189] T. Dan Smith (named as a 'Man of the Year for 1960' by *The Architects' Journal* in 1961),[190] and other enthusiasts for the disaster that has been post-1945 British architecture and town planning (it was not for nothing that the 1960s have been described as 'that high, dishonest decade').[191] Smith had 'enlisted in a succession of "left-wing" movements, including the Independent Labour Party and the Revolutionary Communist Party, before finally joining the Labour Party':[192] he was to declare that the 'democratic vote [was] no way to get the sort of changes we need in the North'.[193] He used intimidation, and could strike the fear of God into City Hall officials.[194]

Poulson started his career by being articled (1927) to Garside & Pennington (later Pennington,[195] Hustler, & Taylor), but when he decided to start up on his own (1932), one of the partners could not credit it, as Poulson could not draw and had little talent in design:[196] so his astonishing financial success says much about the state of Britain then. Poulson's repellent buildings included City House, an office-slab at Leeds Railway Station (1962), the International Swimming Pool, Leeds (1966–8—closed 2007, demolished 2009–10), and the Arndale Centre, Crossgates, Leeds (1965–6): they were typical of the short-term and destructive, aesthetically indefensible developments (then irresponsibly and fawningly lauded in the 'architectural' magazines as 'progressive' and 'modern'), none of which has worn well. Even in the City of London, Poulson ('of scandalous memory')[197] was responsible for the tawdry, dull,[198] and entirely unworthy curtain-walled office slab (**Plate 7.6a**) at Cannon Street Station (1961–6), all the more reprehensible for what it superseded (the war-damaged Italianate City Terminus Hotel by E.M. Barry of 1864–7 [**Plate 7.6b**—demolished 1960]), and for the methods by which the contract was obtained, including having a corrupt British Rail surveyor on Poulson's payroll. The dim Poulson building was demolished in 2007 and replaced by a new block (2007–11) designed by Foggo Associates and picking up themes established by Arup Associates' No. 80 Cannon Street (1972–6), sited at the corner of Bush Lane.

Smith was arrested in 1973 on a series of corruption charges arising from the Poulson affair, and served three years of a six-year sentence. Poulson's trial for corruption (he had greased palms in order to obtain lucrative contracts) in 1973 brought down some twenty-one people, including civil servants, members of parliament, and local-government officials (including Smith). Nevertheless, Poulson 'made a lasting impression on the faces of British towns, particularly in the north, where old civic centres were destroyed in the name of urban improvement but often in fact to line the pockets of Poulson and his associates'.[199] Poulson was lauded by Smith as the 'best architect Britain ever produced'[200] but also described as an 'ambitious, ruthless and friendless man whose object in life was to get as much money and work as he could by bribery and corruption'.[201] At its peak, his practice

Plate 7.6a. The building to the right, a dull curtain-walled office-slab (1961–6), at Cannon Street Station, City of London, was by the firm of the infamous Poulson (demolished 2007). To its left is No. 80 Cannon Street, London (1972–6), at the corner of Bush Lane, by Arup Associates: the stainless-steel lattice exoskeleton is filled with water, and takes the full weight of the floors, leaving the interior column-free. Compare with **Plate 7.6b** to see what has been lost

Plate 7.6b. The former City Terminus Hotel, Cannon Street Station (1864–7—demolished 1960), designed by E.M. Barry, shown in a wood-engraving from *Illustrated London News* (13 April 1867) drawn by L.H. Michael. A comparison with the banal Poulson slab (**see Plate 7.6a**) which replaced the Hotel's richness of façade detailing and complex skyline is an eloquent demonstration of how the built environment was impoverished once cheap Modernism became universally accepted

had 750 members of staff and offices in Beirut, Edinburgh, Lagos, London, Middlesbrough, Newcastle upon Tyne (Smith's fiefdom), and Pontefract: it was the largest in the country, though the work produced by the firm is not 'considered to have any lasting architectural merit',[202] a tactful understatement.

It had become obvious by the 1960s that architects, believing completely in their own absolute rightness (and righteousness), were more and more alienated from the public on whom they inflicted ever larger, uglier, more outrageously expensive, destructive, blighting failures that very soon had to be demolished. Their intellectual stature began to be questioned, and many of their utterances were greeted with contempt by those outside the 'compound'.[203] When architecture meant something, and really was *architecture*, philosophers could claim that it was 'really frozen music',[204] but such an aphorism could not be used in respect of work by the Poulsons of this world.[205] When a Modernist architect could claim a design was intended to 'reflect the culture of the 20th century',[206] it was pointed out that true culture was in a state of collapse, and such remarks were dismissed as 'sweeping nonsense' making 'the whole architectural profession seem sillier or more conceited than ever'.[207]

Few monuments of Modernism were more enthusiastically heralded by the architectural press than the centre of Cumbernauld, North Lanarkshire (historically Dunbartonshire),[208] in a drawing of which a gas-guzzling car with the registration-number GC 1963 was depicted. This example of self-absorption on the part of the architect, Geoffrey Copcutt, owed much to Le Corbusier's obsessions with automobiles and his own ego. That same centre, according to Copcutt 'a central infrastructure of highways and walkways, layers and ledges promising shelter, warmth and family freedom',[209] has 'fallen victim to an insidiously spreading process of dilapidation, fragmentation, redevelopment and demolition':[210] it became one of the most hated buildings in the country, and was partially demolished in 2004. As a failed symbol of Modernism and of 'progress', Cumbernauld centre was an excellent example, though once visited by hordes of architects, planners, officials, and students (10,000 official overseas visitors from sixty countries annually) in the 1960s.[211] A programme of tower-block demolition at Cumbernauld has begun, and other housing, for example Park 3 West, designed by Edinburgh University Housing Research Unit 1963–4, built 1967–70, was demolished in 2013,[212] another indictment of Modernism. Yet at the time such work was lauded in architectural circles, and could not be questioned: heretics were not tolerated, as is always the case with cults.

Even contributors to *The Architectural Review* began to be uneasy. In November 1967[213] an issue of that journal made a strong case for a reconsideration of 'comprehensive redevelopment', and argued for a more sensitive approach to townscape and to the visual relationships between old and new buildings. It also suggested that terrace-houses, rehabilitated, might prove to be better solutions than wholesale replacements. Solutions to public housing by architects who could usually do no wrong in the eyes of the *Review* were illustrated with pithy captions by Nicholas Taylor, highly critical of orthodox-progressive architectural opinion, of 'school-trained architects', and of the 'stupefying...disconnected twenty-story slabs' in Glasgow's Hutchesontown-Gorbals (elements within a 'veritable orgy' of system-built tower-blocks). The tone of the entire issue is often more angry than impressed.[214]

The same journal, in 2017, remarked that the

> vitriol of the editors was effective or at least prescient: the housing edition today reads like a catalogue of the demolished. In under fifty years, most of the projects featured in 1967—many on formerly terraced streets obliterated in slum clearances—are gone, having been subject to a second clearout. Spence's Hutchesontown C[215] ('human beings crushed by their own creation') was detonated in 1993, and the GLC's Chantry and Hermes Point towers on the Elgin Estate[216] came down in 1995. Stirling and Gowan's schemes at Preston[217] ('humiliating') and Runcorn[218] were also demolished. St Mary's in Oldham ('a chilling aesthetic')[219] was razed in 2007; Sam Bunton & Associates' Red Road flats in Glasgow,[220] and their 'dark, crowded, anonymous lift halls', followed suit in 2012…Proposals to demolish Hubert Bennett's Thamesmead were approved in November 2016.[221]

As Gillian Darley has observed, architects in Britain 'are scrutinised not only for the failed utopias of these postwar buildings but also for those conceived to replace them and their complicity in the "social cleansing" of tenancies…demolition is a pretext for a change of social mix, exchanging local authority housing with private flats'.[222] 'From an editorial perspective, the 1967 housing edition reads like a loss of faith…Exploration of…failed utopias is still central to criticism and fundamental in the search for a new architecture for housing and a renewed social purpose for architects.'[223]

Philip Johnson: 'Sourcerer' & Tastemaker

Mies van der Rohe had been very active from the time he first arrived in the United States, and designed the buildings for what became the Illinois Institute of Technology, Chicago (1939–58), in a structural aesthetic of steel and glass, something he was to repeat at the *Neue Nationalgalerie, Tiergarten*, Berlin (1962–8—an arid building set in an almost featureless area that deliberately ignored the historic grain and structure of the city).[224] When the Farnsworth House, Fox River, Plano, IL (1946–51) was built to his designs, with impeccable detailing also using steel and glass, a *frisson* ran through the architectural world. This paradigmatic work of International Modernism was widely praised, although Mies's relationship with his client, the nephrologist Edith Farnsworth, soon soured, largely due to the 'inordinate cost',[225] although there seem to have been other problems as well. Farnsworth claimed the building was uninhabitable, and filed a lawsuit against the architect. She lost the case, for she had, after all, approved the plans.[226]

Philip Johnson followed with his Glass House (for himself) at New Canaan, CT (designed in partnership [1946–51] with Landis Gores, completed 1949). The house was seen as a paradigm of Modernism at the time. It was constructed on a five-acre site, although now stands in some forty acres of grounds. Johnson thought the building was 'Miesian', but afterwards changed his mind, because the bathroom-fireplace core is held within a cylinder set off-centre, something that would have driven 'Mies up the wall'.[227] Johnson perversely claimed that, when designing the Glass House, he had been influenced by Le Corbusier, Ledoux, Malevich, Schinkel, and *De Stijl*, but then he was always mischievous.[228]

Soon afterwards, he was associated with Mies and others during the design of the Seagram Building, New York (1954–8), but once the 'International Style' he had energetically and effectively helped to promote (and label) became universally accepted in America, he turned away from it, and decided to stop designing in that style because he had become bored by it.[229] Yet he recognized it had lasted longer than had the Renaissance: once he had thought Barr, Hitchcock, and he had 'hit it'[230] in the 1930s, but by the 1950s he had begun to see through the shallowness of Modernist pretensions. His perspicacity he credited to his interest in and knowledge of history, something that orthodox Modernism and Modernists had deliberately discarded.

In 1953 Johnson's Abby Aldrich Rockefeller sculpture garden at MoMA, a mixture of architecture and landscape, with sculpture and water features, was laid out, something he was to describe as an 'urban room' with definite doorways and processionals, rather than as a garden. A decade later he produced the museum of pre-Columbian art, Dumbarton Oaks, Washington DC, an exquisitely detailed pavilion consisting of nine interconnecting domed spaces centred around a fountain, a building the architect Robert A.M. Stern (whose own works suggest a refreshing independence of mind) prophetically described as 'Post-Modern'.[231]

For the New York State Theater, Lincoln Center, New York (1962–4), at a time when raw concrete was the *de-rigueur* material, Johnson and his then partner, Richard Foster, not only introduced an opulence, with the use of travertine, gold leaf, and bronze that sent shock-waves through American architectural circles, but recognized that the form of the plaza around which, on three sides, were grouped the Metropolitan Opera House, the Avery Fisher Hall, and the State Theater, was suggested by Michelangelo's *Campidoglio* on the Capitoline Hill, Rome. This was an historical reference completely unacceptable to doctrinaire Modernists.[232] The architecture of the State Theater itself owed much to Classical symmetry and even to designs for Neo-Classical gaols,[233] but the genesis of the design lay in the best of earlier theatre designs, notably those of Charles Garnier at the Paris *Opéra* (1861–75) and of Gottfried Semper in Dresden (*Hoftheater* [1871–8]) and Vienna (*Burgtheater* [1872–86]). The clearance of the site for the Lincoln Center, incidentally, was made possible by Robert Moses.

Then, in partnership (1967–91) with John Burgee, came the extension (1964–73) to the Boston Public Library, that great building by McKim, Mead, and White (1887–8). Its façade was derived from Labrouste's *Bibliothèque Ste-Genéviève,* Paris [1838–50]). Johnson got the job because, he claimed, he was 'interested in history', and could talk 'learnedly' about McKim.[234] With its expensive finishes (which have worn well), monumentality, and large lunettes, the building attracted the opprobrium of the Gropius-cloned Harvard 'academics' who denounced the work as the worst they had ever seen.[235] However, it was praised by the formidable architectural critic Ada Louise Huxtable in the *New York Times*, thereby spiking some of the opposition pop-guns, and Johnson himself declared it was 'on the cusp' of Post-Modernism.[236] Nevertheless, the gnashing of critical teeth was audible on both sides of the Atlantic.[237]

More was to come. The American Telephone and Telegraph (AT&T) skyscraper, New York (1978–84—now the Sony Building), was a masonry-clad structure set on a stripped variation of a serliana-cum-triumphal-arch, and capped by a paraphrase of an open-topped pediment. Denunciations became hysterical (**Figure 7.3**): the building was supposed to be an 'inflated and simplistic reference to history', 'flippant', 'pseudo-classical', and much else, mostly pejorative. Reyner Banham excelled even himself in his denunciations,[238] which, of course, greatly amused Johnson, secure in his Olympian heights and confirmed in his views of the incurable dimness and conformity of British critics. Johnson's riposte was that it was designed out of 'sheer fatigue with the International Style'.[239] By pointing out that the monumental base was derived from a gigantic Hadrianic or Hellenistic triumphal-arch recalling the west front of a large Romanesque church, mingled with a paraphrase of a serliana (*also called* Palladian *or* Venetian window),[240] and reminiscences of the Pazzi Chapel portico façade in Florence (1472—supposedly by Brunelleschi, but probably by Giuliano da Maiano), he further infuriated his critics (**Plate 7.7**). Other works followed, sometimes in collaboration with different architects, and sometimes embracing quirky historical

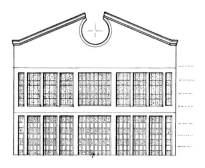

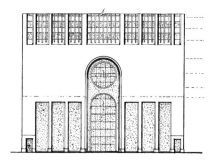

Figure 7.3. Upper and lower parts of the AT&T (later Sony) building, New York (1978–84), by Philip Johnson & John Henry Burgee. Pecked lines indicate floor-levels. The top of the structure is capped by a paraphrase of an open-topped pediment, and the base is a stripped variation on a serliana-cum-triumphal-arch with a nod to the portico of the fifteenth-century Pazzi Chapel, Florence (*see* Plate 7.7)

details dangerously verging on *Kitsch*, but there is no doubt that the *Kitsch* was intentional.[241]

A Ledoux-inspired basis of design was overt in the School of Architecture, University of Houston, TX (1983–6), but Johnson had not yet run out of ideas to shock and surprise. He confounded critics by returning to MoMA as guest-curator of the exhibition, *Deconstructivist Architecture* (1988), billed as 'development post-dating post-modernism', which he organized with Mark Wigley and Frederieke Taylor: featuring work by Peter D. Eisenman, Frank O. Gehry, Zaha M. Hadid, Rem Koolhaas, Daniel Libeskind, Bernard Tschumi, and Coop Himmelb(l)au (an Austrian firm established by Wolf Prix, R.M. Holzer, and H. Swiczinsky), it showed projects incorporating twisted volumes, warped planes, clashing lines, and intentional violation of the cubes, rectangles, and right angles of Modernism, challenging traditional

Plate 7.7. Portico of the Pazzi Chapel in the *chiostro* of *Santa Croce*, Florence, a variation on a Roman triumphal-arch and a possible prototype of the serliana or
Palladian window, supposedly designed (*c.*1423–4) by Brunelleschi, though it may
actually have been by Giuliano da Maiano, built 1472. Some have suggested the
chapel was erected under Bernardo Rossellino, who, however, was dead when
the front was put up (*compare with* **Figure 7.3**)

ideals of order and rationality, and undermining basic assumptions about
building.[242]

With this show, Johnson once again demonstrated his capabilities of
knowing and even creating 'celebrity culture'. He insisted that architecture is not about 'social engineering' or 'making life better', but should be
viewed as an aesthetic experience (even, perhaps, if it were an uncomfortable or unpleasant one), and his genius as a taste-former was once again
manifest.

He himself had earlier (1970) designed the sculpture-gallery at his
New Canaan estate, a jagged work that might be regarded as proto-
Deconstructivist,[243] but his *Da Monsta* gatehouse, also at New Canaan
(1994–5), a pavilion without any right angles, was his own homage to
Deconstructivism, and experimented with developing ideas drawn from

German Expressionism[244] (even a nod, perhaps, a tongue-in-cheek reference to Gropius's *Märzgefallenen-Denkmal*, Weimar).[245] It seems as though,
having shocked, Johnson went on to do something else, almost gleefully,
leaving critics floundering in his wake: he promoted, then subverted, the
International Style; did the same to Post-Modernism; then repeated the feat
with Deconstructivism, all of which adds up to quite a comment on the
times. He often described himself (and other architects) as a 'whore' (albeit
a well-paid one),[246] as he exposed pretence and exercised his influence as a
member of the American architectural Establishment with cynicism and a
puckish disregard for what others thought of his stance (this changed so
much anyway that nobody could actually pin him down, to the intense
annoyance of many critics, especially those on this side of the Atlantic).

Johnson admitted he was not a good architect, and indeed some of his
work might confirm his admission: it is often superficial, lacks depth, and
could be considered unusually brittle, suggesting he could not think architecturally (like Gropius, he was a poor draughtsman).[247] However, he was as
spectacularly successful in creating trends and forming opinions as he was in
deflating the pretensions of unthinking adherents to once-fashionable (and
frequently untenable) orthodoxies: his greatest achievement was to expose
the fake 'morality' of Modernism, and indeed the shallowness of major
trends in twentieth- and twenty-first-century architecture.[248]

Like Mies, Johnson believed in the *art* of architecture, whereas the group
around Gropius believed in its sociological importance (to its detriment).
Johnson held that because Gropius was not a great designer, 'he naturally
stressed the sociological side. This dichotomy is still present.'[249] The book he
wrote with Hitchcock on the International Style was written as a 'piece of
propaganda' against the sociological approach: the last sentence in that book
was 'We have an architecture still'.[250] He also dismissed schools of architecture as 'politically correct', declaring that architecture was lost in such attitudes.[251] He admitted cities were uglier than they were sixty years ago,[252]
and that 'Modern architecture is a flop'.[253]

Critics were uncomfortable with Johnson because of his chameleon-like
ability to change direction and because they could not damage him, secure
in his wealth, intelligence, and influence: but Johnson said of them that if
they started with the *parti pris* of being ideological about Modernism's 'correctness' (as was Giedion's position), nothing would ever change, and architecture would be stuck in a rut for ever. However, Barr, Johnson, and

Hitchcock came to architecture from history, and saw Modernism as a phase in a continuum, not as the end in itself its enthusiasts claimed.[254] Johnson paid tribute to the preservationist lobby, which, in his opinion, helped Post-Modernism to get off to such a big start. Johnson, as an historian, and Barr, as an academic, enjoyed looking at old buildings, and thought it foolish to dismiss them, not least as they were 'getting bored with the box'.[255] Mies and that generation thumbed their noses *at* history, but Johnson came to architecture *from* history, the opposite to the way most modern architects approach the subject.

Charles Jencks, always with the *bon mot* to hand, a felicitous pen, and a keen sense of humour, referred to Johnson, hilariously, as 'the candid King Midas of New York Camp', visualizing him in his 'cosmic fish-bowl...thinking out the next way' he could 'send up the Modern Movement, outrage the socially responsible, deny the underpinnings of Le Corbusier, Gropius, Fuller',[256] while English critics and defenders of the Modern Movement loved to catch Johnson playing at 'sourcery' and came 'in droves' to be 'deliciously outraged at his Camp sensibility'.[257] This is a masterly encapsulation of what Johnson was about, but then Jencks always has been a perceptive and enjoyable commentator.

The guesthouse at New Canaan (1952), with its domed ceilings, broke with Modernist 'structural honesty', and was described by its architect as representative of his 'High-Queen Period':[258] but the New Canaan 'pavilion' of a decade later, of precast concrete, a folly, with no 'social relevance' whatsoever, only six feet high, managed to drive English critics into frenzies of enraged disapproval of its 'decadence', 'trivial historicism' (the last a favourite word of abuse among Modernists, following Pevsner), and 'feeble' forms. Johnson responded by pointing out that the English, who were so 'good' about 'morals' and city planning, and had all their Councils and things they were so proud of, still managed to ruin London 'in the name of morality'—even worse than New York in its 'hopeless chaos'.[259] And London has been ruined: there is no doubt about that.[260]

Johnson took considerable pleasure in chiding those with anaemic pretensions to 'social purpose' in architecture, and was irrepressible in his concerted activities to deflate pomposity, *épater le Mouvement Moderne*, and make the 'shocking' claim that he would 'rather sleep in the nave of Chartres Cathedral with the nearest john two blocks down the street' than he would in a Gropius Harvard House 'with back-to-back bathrooms'.[261] Provocative, ruthless, heartless, and powerful, he rejected all claims that International Modernism was a social, cultural, and economic movement, and firmly labelled it for what it was: a style.[262] For a time (*c.*1929 to the late 1950s), he was the impresario of the 'International Style' before he began to twist its tail, sending up puritanical European Modernists and (especially) their unquestioning British disciples (his views on some of them were particularly scathing).[263] His biting lampoon on Ruskin, *The Seven Crutches of Modern Architecture*, suggests something of his impish tendency to disrupt, ridicule, and radically change directions.[264]

Johnson was unsparing, even in relation to his earlier heroes. He said of Mies that if the devil himself offered him a job, he would take it,[265] and was contemptuous of those protagonists who pretended to be 'rationalists', 'objective', or claimed 'social responsibility': he tore away veils to expose fraudulent 'morality', had no fears whatsoever in denouncing the hypocrisy of the architectural profession,[266] and enjoyed self-contradiction, paradox, and provocation, notably when, in Camp mode, he spoke of his 'ballet-school style'.[267]

After a century or so of getting on the nerves of the *bourgeoisie* (a species that has not been 'smashed' as yet), Modernist architects have found that few listen any more, that the 'synapses'[268] no longer jangle, and that they themselves are the only ones who can be bothered to engage in tedious arguments about what they assume might be 'architecture'. Johnson suggested that Modernism was the 'last religion of the Western intellectual', replacing both conventional religion and work with notions about 'creativity' and 'aesthetics'.[269]

Barr, Hitchcock, and Johnson institutionalized the International Style, which became established and no longer adversarial when it became the official American (and Western) style of architecture (not least as a by-product of the Cold War).[270] Post-Modernism started as a reaction against it, against the hegemony of the Modern Movement, against the whole MoMA ethos, and finally against the prevailing political consensus of American liberalism and its desiccated equivalents on this side of the Atlantic. And Deconstructivism, in its turn not a style, but a manner, was a reaction against the short-lived radicalism of Post-Modernism.

Johnson, the tastemaker, degraded International Modernism, Post-Modernism, and even, finally, Deconstructivism, having initially promoted all three: but most of all, he ridiculed the reductivist lies about 'social purpose' and 'morality' that had sustained the pretensions of Modernists ever since the end of the 1914–18 war. Jencks's amusing discussions with Johnson are recommended for their honesty, lack of obfuscation, and humour.[271]

When considering the convoluted explanations and advocacies of Deconstructivism[272] and Parametricism[273] today, one can imagine Johnson's wicked laughter echoing through the stratosphere.[274]

VIII

Dangerous Signals

Alleged Demise of Modern Architecture; Imposition, Packaging, Deformation, & Rejection; Deconstructivism & After; Cults, Compounds, & the Grand Narrative; A Religious Dimension; 9/11 & Other Uncomfortable Matters; Epilogue

> *Das war ein Vorspiel nur, dort wo man Bücher verbrennt,*
> *verbrennt man auch am Ende Menschen!*
>
> (That was only a prelude, where men burn books, in the end they will burn people!)
>
> HEINRICH HEINE (1797–1856): Almansor (1823) l. 2245

> Architecture is not a branch of information technology. It is not a con-structed text. Architecture is an art and as such is concerned with its own past and, just as importantly, the past of human beings. It is this concern for the human past that gives architecture its authority. As an art, architecture is not only a meditation of the present on the past but also a speculation of the present on the future.
>
> ROBERT ARTHUR MORTON STERN (1939–): Robert A. M. Stern Buildings
(New York: The Monacelli Press Inc. 1996) 15

Alleged Demise of Modern Architecture

Charles Jencks said that it was possible 'to date the death of Modern Architecture to a precise moment in time',[1] giving the year as 1972, 'having been flogged to death remorselessly by critics such as Jane Jacobs':[2] yet 'the fact that many so-called Modern architects' persisted in 'practising a trade as if it were alive' could be regarded as 'one of the great curiosities of our age' (like the survival of 'The Royal Company of Archers or The Extra Women of the Bedchamber' as part of the British Royal Establishment).[3]

Jencks was referring to the demolition of the huge Pruitt-Igoe slab-blocks, St Louis, MO, part of a housing complex (1951–6) of thirty-three eleven-storey blocks of flats, designed by Minoru Yamasaki, with George Francis Hellmuth and Joseph William Leinweber, following principles insisted upon by Le Corbusier and CIAM and almost universally adopted by the Western architectural Establishment after 1945.[4] Naturally, the designs (which conformed to contemporary doctrines, with their 'streets in the sky' free from motor-vehicles but not from crime, and the 'flat'-roofed external appearance demanded by protagonists of the International Style in the 1920s) received accolades from professional associations. But the people who inhabited the development felt no connection with the Corbusian open spaces, and did not 'interact' positively with each other in the increasingly grim public areas. Very soon the development suffered from appalling vandalism, defacement, arson, and violent crime on a terrifying scale. The lifts (elevators), designed to explore fads such as only stopping on the fourth, seventh, and tenth floors, soon became urine-soaked *pissoirs* that were admirably suited to aid muggings, criminal squalor, and general violence.

If ever proof were needed of the failure of Modernist architects to design housing that people might like to inhabit, this was it: a 'paradigm' of a realized CIAM-approved Corbusian housing development quickly became infamous (Yamasaki himself wished it was a job he had not done),[5] so only twenty years after this hugely expensive project started, it had to be dynamited (1972).[6] Every attempt to remedy the problems had failed to improve matters at all, and the buildings were violently attacked by their enraged inhabitants who simply could not relate to an alien, hard, unsympathetic environment conceived as an abstraction. They were not the only ones. On the eastern side of the Pond, architects employed by the Greater London Council (GLC) had designed the Canada estate at Bermondsey. This was a work in the then fashionable 'Brutalism', associated with *béton brut* (raw concrete, exposed after the formwork is struck, sometimes showing impressions of the timber boards of which formwork is constructed), derived from exemplars by Le Corbusier. Nicholas Taylor suggested that its unfortunate tenants expressed their hatred of the environment imposed on them by the GLC (successor to the LCC) by wrecking the place.[7]

One might ask what sort of economic sense that made? But even before Pruitt-Igoe was blown up, the Modernist juggernaut was questioned when the infamous Ronan Point twenty-three-storey tower-block of flats, Canning

Plate 8.1. Ronan Point, Canning Town, London Borough of Newham, demonstrating just one spectacular failure of Modernist obsessions concerning prefabricated industrialized systems of construction

Town, London Borough of Newham, constructed using the Larsen-Nielsen prefabricated system, partially collapsed in 1968 (**Plate 8.1**), and it was just one of a great many building failures associated with non-traditional methods of construction adopted without sufficient tests to ensure their long-term viability.[8] It should be noted that in Newham, 70 per cent of families were to be housed in flats, despite very public warnings in 1938 by Elizabeth Denby that flats were unsuitable for families (she advocated terrace-houses with small gardens instead, which would have been far cheaper and more satisfactory than high-rise blocks which had an absurdly short life).[9] To Taylor and his associates, there were few sights 'meaner and more pathetic than children of four or five finding what room they can in the upper lift halls as a playground'.[10]

The largest groups of people obliged to be housed in developments that embrace the Utopian (but in reality Dystopian) fantasies of architects who uncritically accepted the Modern Movement are those with no choice, and in the case of Pruitt-Igoe only violence and destruction succeeded in getting the disaster demolished. An 'icon of failure', however, it was only one of countless 'public policy blunders' the blame for which can be firmly laid at the door of those who subscribed to the cult of the Modern Movement.[11] Yet those who would never be able to accept that truth went on claiming well into the 1990s that the failure of Pruitt-Igoe had 'nothing to do with the Modern Movement',[12] which had for years revered the means of production, the so-called 'machine aesthetic', and slogans such as the 'house is a machine for living'. Miës had claimed (1924) that in industrialization lay the solution to the social, economic, technical, and artistic problems, a belief that has not turned out to be a 'solution' at all.[13] There can be no question that arrogance had elevated dogma above experience, logic, reason, or utility: it led architects to believe they knew better than their 'clients' how the latter should live, and this derives 'at least in part from attitudes which originated'[14] at the *Bauhaus*. But it was also generated by Le Corbusier's sloganizing in his odious publications,[15] and the pernicious doctrines of CIAM and the 'Athens Charter'. As a further exemplar of an obvious and expensive failure in social housing (though denied as such by Modernists), the gigantic Corviale project, Rome, built 1975–82 to designs by Mario Fiorentino *et al.*, can be cited.[16]

Imposition, Packaging, Deformation, & Rejection

The massive error at the very heart of Modernist dogma was to impose, on people who did not want them, alien 'flat' roofs, stark white walls, long strips of window, and other *clichés* that made houses look like unfinished industrial buildings or hospitals (themselves often copied from the Fagus shoe-last factory, an entirely inappropriate model for a building associated with healthcare), and certainly not like friendly homes.[17] One of the best examples of how inhabitants turned on the unacceptable aesthetic forced on them by a supremely arrogant architect was Le Corbusier's *Cité Fruges* development, Pessac, near Bordeaux (1925–6), with its vast windows, 'flat' roofs, terraces, and absence of any traditional symbolic signs. Those who actually lived in the houses converted terraces into extra rooms, made the windows smaller by blocking up much of the glazed areas or dividing them up by means of mullions and transoms, added window-boxes, mouldings, copings, and shutters, made the roofs pitched, and generally obliterated virtually everything of the architect's original Modern-Movement aesthetic with which they could not identify and for which they felt no affection. The authorities, however, undid such 'ill-informed' alterations to the sacred fabric, and reimposed a hard Corbusian aesthetic.

In 1975 Jencks criticized Mies's architecture for being 'the ultimate mechanistic metaphor of blankness and for not communicating with its users, either literally or metaphorically'.[18] But how, one might ask, can such an impoverished, limited language, as epitomized in Mies's designs for the glass-and-steel boxes that became his trademark, communicate much? If Mies's buildings (from 1940) for the Illinois Institute of Technology (IIT) are considered, it is clear that his minimalist architectural language made no distinction between the different functions of each structure: a building used for teaching looked like a factory, and a chapel looked like a workshop.[19] Modern architecture's major metaphor was indeed the factory: but why should dwellings or chapels or teaching-areas adopt the imagery of a factory (or a hospital, for that matter)[20] at all? No wonder Modern-Movement buildings alienated mere humankind which had to use them: buildings that give out false signals can put people off, to the extent that they might even begin to attract hatred and the urge to destroy them. There are countless instances where that is exactly what has happened.[21]

Lewis Mumford perceptively said that Mies completed the 'deformation of architectural modernism' by designing a type of building less like a machine and more like a 'package'. Mies's steel-and-glass aesthetic created buildings that were machine-forms without content, monuments to nothingness, with no relation to sites, climates, insulation, function, or internal activity: and that verdict is painfully obvious when considering the *Neue Nationalgalerie* in Berlin.[22] One might even perceive such buildings as cold, sterile, and, ultimately, aesthetic failures.[23]

Peter and Alison Smithson established themselves as leaders of the Modern Movement in Britain in the 1950s and 1960s, notably with their Miesian steel-framed school at Hunstanton, Norfolk (1949–54), which, with its exposed internal services and panels within the frame filled with brick and glass (**Plate 8.2**), was claimed in some quarters to be an 'honest' expression

Plate 8.2. Part of the Smithdon High School by the Smithsons, Hunstanton, Norfolk (1949–54), derived from the reduced detailing of Mies van der Rohe at the Illinois Institute of Technology, Chicago

of 'functionalism' and a paradigm of 'New Brutalism' (*see* Select Glossary). Its problems were many, including excessive solar heat-gain, lack of privacy, distortion of the steel frame through heat, breakage of glass due to that distortion, and much else, which might suggest to the detached observer that the building was actually failing to 'function' at all: indeed it seemed to ignore the needs of the children for whom it was supposed to have been erected. Furthermore, although the selection of the Smithsons' scheme was in an architectural competition, they appear not to have troubled to visit the site before the competition, and their building has 'bequeathed a maintenance headache in a class of its own'.[24] From the lofty heights of CIAM, of course, such matters would be of minor or no interest: all that mattered was the compliance of the architecture with the belief-system of the cult.[25]

With developments such as the rebarbative Robin Hood Gardens Estate, Tower Hamlets, London (1966–72—built on a horrible site flanked by two trunk roads or highways), the Smithsons expressed their notion of 'the building as street', and the rough precast and *in-situ* concrete aesthetic of Le Corbusier (**Plate 8.3***a* & *b*): but the scheme was 'ill-planned to the point of being inhumane', and the 'streets' were 'only decks cantilevered off the cross-walls of the reinforced-concrete box-frame, . . . with a grim aspect towards the traffic'. Furthermore, the 'tiny balconies' were 'too small to enjoy' and could be 'used only as fire escapes'.[26]

Like other Modernists, the Smithsons attempted to make spurious connections with earlier architecture, especially with the work of the Woods in the city of Bath. It is clear that they were very aware of how an architecture,

Plate 8.3a. Part of the eastern block, Robin Hood Gardens housing-scheme, Tower Hamlets, London (1966–72), by the Smithsons

with an extended, very rich vocabulary, coherence of architectural language, and harmonious geometries, could be created and understood by all. In other words they were actually aware of traditional symbols and how they could convey meaning.[27] This is extraordinary, because in their work they were opposed to tradition, took the usual anti-historical line, and although claiming at Robin Hood Gardens to provide a communal building

Plate 8.3*b.* Part of the east side of the eastern block, Robin Hood Gardens housing-scheme, showing some unattractive staining

on the scale of the great crescents and terraces of Bath, with an architectural language that would be familiar to many, this they singularly failed to do. Jencks perceptively observed that they had not succeeded in 'communicating the distinctions'[28] they had noted in Bath which provided so much of interest and meaning, 'for all developed languages must contain a degree of conventional usage, if only to make innovations and deviations from the norm more correctly understood'.[29] The Smithsons, observed Jencks, employed linguistic analogies 'based on machine production rather than on human usage'[30] or experience.

Thus there were massive contradictions between the stated aims of the Smithsons and the results of their work, but in this they were by no means alone: it was an endemic problem with the Modern Movement as a whole. Their Robin Hood Gardens scheme contained severe design-faults similar to those traced by Oscar Newman to a lack of defensible space.[31] Needless to say, the threat of demolition brought the architectural Establishment out in force to demand the scheme's retention, and the Twentieth Century Society published a book on the development.[32]

Many much-praised works of the Modern Movement in architecture were designed and built for clients who became multinational corporations. All the claims for 'social responsibility' in architecture trumpeted by Modernists in the 1920s lie uneasily with the realities of how architects of the Modern Movement served vast corporations and imposed huge CIAM- and Corbusier-inspired mass-housing blocks of the Pruitt-Igoe variety on the hapless 'proletariat'. Gropius's enormous PanAm Building (1958) added to the congestion of one of the busiest parts of New York: it might seem to be a contradiction of the aims of 'rational' Modernism.[33] On the other hand, true to form, he supported the demolition (1963–5) of Pennsylvania railway-terminus, New York, one of the greatest buildings designed by McKim, Mead, & White (1902–11). It had a gigantic hall based on the Baths of Caracalla (*known as* the *Thermae Antoninianae*, Rome [*begun c.*AD 211]). It was described as a design that dramatized 'the whole majestic symbolism of Classical Architecture', with a 'Roman theme', but resulting in a work that was 'splen-didly American'.[34] This superb building not only functioned rather better than anything Gropius claimed to have designed, but was one of the most Sublime works of architecture in the United States, a masterwork of ennobled architecture, engineering, and organization that put products of the Modern Movement to shame. This is probably why Gropius was keen for what he described as a 'monument to a particularly insignificant period in American architectural history,...a case of pseudotradition'[35] to be removed, because it showed up the shoddiness of much of Modernism to a painful degree. Its demolition was certainly a particularly low point in American cultural life.[36]

It is perhaps revealing that both Barr and Johnson were active in trying to save the station,[37] but that Gropius and his disciples were on the side of the destroyers. What Gropius and others like him failed to grasp was that the design and execution of so vast a scheme marked a high point in the ingenuity that had distinguished American enterprises for decades.[38] But it was far more than an engineering feat: it functioned superbly in utilitarian and symbolic rôles as a portal to the metropolis and as an impressive gateway out of the city to distant parts. One thing is certain: 'America is the poorer for its loss'.[39]

Embedded in Modernism was a conviction that architects could 'cure' what was regarded as '*bourgeois*' society by battering it to death with what the Soviets called 'social condensers', that is, breaking down hierarchies, based on the belief that architecture can influence social behaviour and therefore change the hated '*bourgeoisie*' into a more malleable breed capable of accepting the Modern Movement. This expensive experiment managed to produce a reality so unpleasant that a huge amount of it has had to be demolished.[40] Far from being 'paved with good intentions',[41] the road laid down for ideological reasons by Modernist zealots and disciples of Corbusianity to a supposed Utopia led to an environment 'as irrelevant to the needs of the people as to the visual structure of the town or city'.[42] A colossal crime has been committed against humanity and common sense: after all, 'half of Europe was destroyed due to the alliance of the Corb[43] dream of Mass Culture and greed. It was a triple alliance of power.'[44]

Bauhaus-Miesian-Corbusian Modernism was supposed to have died with Pruitt-Igoe. However, despite all the evidence that it was a disaster, it was still very much alive well into the twenty-first century. Le Corbusier and the proponents of the Modern Movement associated the simplistic design-forms which they favoured with concepts such as 'the moral' and 'social purity' (whatever that is), but why, when there were no logical reasons for this association, was it so universally accepted? The answer may lie in the nature of intuition as an involuntary, socially-induced perception rather than anything remotely connected with rationality.[45] Notions of 'efficiency' and 'rationalism', born of capitalist-backed enterprise and technology, seem to have been embraced by architects, mixed in with supposed aesthetics divorced from *any* rationale, and then spiced with pseudo-moral premises adopted by received opinion in order to force forward unpopular choices that were authoritarian and impractical: they ignored cultural or any other diversity, and relied on untested techniques that all too often failed.[46] It was all about assertion, acceptance of dogma, and a desire to be safe within the 'compound'[47] of a cult where reason, sensibility, and appreciation of beauty were entirely absent.

We have had Post-Modernism in its various guises, and a word or two about that will be in order here.[48] Essentially, Post-Modernism (known variously as *P-M*, *PoMo*, or *the Post*) was connected with a loss of faith in what were once regarded as certainties (that is, so-called 'progress', supposed 'rationality', and 'scientific' approaches to design, but in reality just a search for images to suggest all that), and with a growing acceptance of a bewilderingly large palette of logos, signs, and products promoted on a scale never before experienced in the history of the world, which some (for instance R.C. Venturi, who altered Mies's dictum 'less is more' to 'less is a bore') welcomed as offering 'complexity' and 'contradiction' in design.[49] Jane Jacobs and others advocated a new kind of urbanism based on the life-sciences and notions of organized complexity as a riposte to the dogmas of CIAM, Corbusianity, and the Athens Charter which were clearly destroying the living organisms of cities: yet, as more and more patients died, more of the same was prescribed with ever greater zeal.[50] Jacobs's views and Venturi's tended to overlap, and for a time 'complexity and contradiction' seemed to herald a change.

In the 1960s, also, 'Pop' architecture[51] began a tendency away from so-called 'rationalism' (the supposed 'scientific'[52] pretensions of which do not stand up to serious examination by anyone educated in the true spirit of enquiry embedded in real science) towards pluralism; and later architecture drew on elements that were not themselves archaeologically or historically accurate, but made vague references to once-familiar motifs such as the Orders of Classical architecture, cornices, pediments, etc., often brashly and crudely used. Post-Modernism seems to have heralded a major change in Western culture, even a new condition permeating every walk of life, involving cynicism, fragmentation, ill-digested eclecticism, and what some have called the 'cultural logic of late capitalism'.[53] The label has been loosely stuck to the work of various architects who moved away from the orthodoxies of the Modern Movement and so-called 'High Tech' (again, a style mostly concerned with image, sometimes even emphasizing the mechanical services, like hanging the tripes of a human being outside the body [**Plate 8.4**]), even though their responses differed widely from each other.

Some Post-Modern Classicists, such as Robert A.M. Stern, have produced work of a much higher order than the sort of commercial PoMo associated with the vulgarity of advertising and ill-informed nods towards a supposed Classicism which was nothing of the sort: such PoMo pseudo-Classicizing should be distinguished from the scholarly Classical architecture produced

Plate 8.4. *Centre Pompidou, Les Halles*, Paris, *aka Beaubourg* (1971–7), by Renzo Piano and Richard Rogers, in which the structure and services are exposed and emphasized. Nautical quotations promoted by Le Corbusier were continued in the ventilators

by a few practitioners. Some architects, e.g. Aldo Rossi, argued that as cities were organic works of art, their grain, history, and context must be responded to in any architectural intervention: this is the complete opposite of the International-Modernist position. Jencks has been the witty, amusing, and indefatigable chronicler of Post-Modernism in all its guises.

Deconstructivism & After

Following Johnson's championing of Deconstructivism, Jencks detected in it a 'change of heart, a new paradigm in architecture',[54] far more interesting and full of promise than the 'modern world' being left behind,[55] so a brief look at this comparatively recent phenomenon is necessary. Jencks believed that there was evidence of a beginning 'of a new way of constructing architecture and conceiving cities', that this change had 'grown out of the Post-Modern movement', and that it might 'produce' a 'more convivial, sensuous, and articulate environment', one 'more sustainable and urbane'.[56] After the sterility of International Modernism and the stripping of meaning from architecture, Jencks felt, given the 'stereotyping of most building, a shift in architecture is to be welcomed...a new movement is always exciting and full of hope and promise...its growth will...be helped by an appreciative and critical attitude.'[57]

But has this happened? How many more outrageously expensive, misshapen, fragmented, fractured, misnamed 'iconic' erections do we actually need? Has a sense of alienation not actually got worse? And where is there any suggestion of recognizable meaning? Is there one symbol visible anywhere that had resonances, that connects us to the architecture?

Instead of architectural students cribbing from images of designs by Le Corbusier or Mies, as they once did, in the early years of the twenty-first century they all wanted to be clones of Zaha Hadid. The phenomenon of Deconstructivism, whose midwife was undoubtedly that old magician Johnson, reflects a catastrophic deterioration of what Jencks has termed 'previous cultural formations. Christianity and Modernism, the two reigning worldviews that were supposedly celebrated at the Millennium are both, if architecture is any measure, just hanging on.'[58] They did, however, somewhat uncomfortably reveal 'disquiet and confusion over religious, spiritual, and public values... Architecture without a public content and spiritual direction loses its way.'[59]

Deconstructivist architecture claimed to be committed to pluralism, heterogeneity, and supposed 'fractal' forms,[60] rejecting Euclidian geometry in its blobs, crumples, clashing curves, folds, twistings, and scattered, unrelated, apparently random shapes. Many of these emerge from computers,[61] as to draw this sort of thing using traditional orthographic projections would be well-nigh impossible. The resultant disjointed 'iconic' structures (realized by engineers, of course) are even further removed from human experience and perceptions than the prim, mass-produced slabs of International Modernism.

Gehry's Guggenheim Museum, Bilbao, in the heart of the Basque country in Spain (1991–7), is often quoted as a prime exemplar of Deconstructivism ([**Figure 8.1**]—despite criticisms that it does not work very well to display art: it perhaps owes more to that celebrated Californian building-type, the roadside attraction, which some associate with *Kitsch*),[62] and its rapturous reception led to other municipalities funding 'iconic' architectural schemes to attract 'cultural tourism'.[63] Gehry was also responsible for the Biodiversity Museum, Amador Causeway, Panama City (1999–2014), a multicoloured pile-up, its siting emphasizing its anti-urban, anti-contextual, energy-profligate, stand-alone status as spectacle (**Figure 8.2**). The same architect's *Fondation Louis Vuitton* building, Paris (2006–14), resembling an inchoate mass of glass

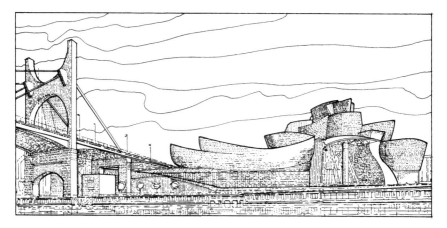

Figure 8.1. Guggenheim Museum, Bilbao, by Frank Gehry, designed from 1991, and built 1993–7. View from across the River Nervión, with the La Salve bridge on the left

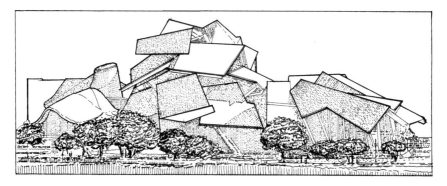

Figure 8.2. Biodiversity Museum, Amador Causeway, Panama City (1999–2014), by Frank Gehry. It is brightly treated in contrasting colours

sails, was photographed for several architectural journals in a crepuscular light: an eloquent comment on its qualities.[64] Buildings that shout for attention may be provocative, and fit the bill as supposedly 'iconic' exemplars of Parametricism (which succeeded Deconstructivism as the latest fad),[65] but they are not necessarily great architecture.[66]

Deconstructivism and Parametricism induce a sense of dislocation[67] both within buildings and between buildings and their contexts (which Deconstructivists and Parametricists pointedly ignore, taking things to even greater extremes than did earlier devotees of the Modern Movement). By breaking continuity, disturbing relationships between interior and exterior, and fracturing connections between exterior and context, they undermine harmony, unity, gravitational control, and perceived stability (which Coventry Patmore [one of the most perceptive architectural critics of the nineteenth century, infinitely more acute and sensible than Ruskin] identified as crucial to *any* successful architecture).[68] A particularly devastating example was the City Edge project, Berlin (1987), by Libeskind, which ripped through established geometries of urban fabric, responding to the ludicrously named *Antifaschistischer Schutzwall* (anti-Fascist protective barrier, otherwise known as the Berlin Wall [1961–89]) by slicing up territory. Libeskind, too, left his mark on the Royal Ontario Museum, Toronto, with his aggressively spiky Deconstructivist 'Michael Lee-Chin Crystal' extension (2002–7) (**Figure 8.3**). However, despite the pretensions of its apologists, Deconstructivism is hardly a new movement, nor is it a coherent style: rather it perhaps exposes the unfamiliar and the disturbing by means of deformity, distortion, fragmentation, and the awkward juxtapositioning of jarring, disparate grids, in opposition to established built fabric, therefore dismissing it and its historical evolution as irrelevant.

A further extreme example of clashing cacophony can be found in the *Musée des Confluences* (**Figure 8.4**), sited on a peninsula between the Rivers Rhône and Saône at Lyon, France (designed by Coop Himmelb(l)au from 2000, opened 2014, much over budget). A restless essay in sliced swoops of metal and glass, it was created with the stated aim to express turbulence and change. And have we not got enough tumult and violence as it is, without this 'lumbering cyborg dinosaur',[69] labelled a 'fatuous, pretentious, exorbitant wrapper' with 'all the lightness of a lump of lead', outrageous in its 'wasteful, harmful, ill-considered, overweening excess'?[70] The architect's job used to be to create order out of chaos: nowadays, the task seems to be to do the opposite. And what is the purpose of a museum? In this one, the

Figure 8.3. East Wing, Royal Ontario Museum, Toronto, Ontario, Canada (1932–2), by the distinguished Canadian architectural firm of Chapman & Oxley, in a late Byzantino-Romanesque Revival style, seemingly being gobbled up by the Deconstructivist 'Michael Lee-Chin Crystal' extension (2002–7), designed by Studio Daniel Libeskind, in collaboration with Canadian architects Bregman & Hamann (later B+H Architects). This expensive Deconstructivist addition was not entirely free from problems associated with the weather

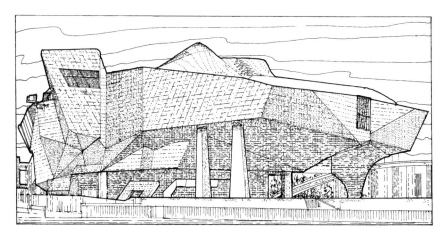

Figure 8.4. *Musée des Confluences*, Lyon (2001–14), designed by Coop Himmelb(l)au, sited on a peninsula between the Rivers Rhône and Saône: a somewhat restless, noisy 'iconic' statement, when seen approaching the city from the south

impact of the structure and spaces on the visitor appears to take precedence over the mere exhibits,[71] which, like the history to which those artefacts are connected, may no longer count. A calmer atmosphere might serve the exhibits in a museum rather better than does frenzied visual tumult achieved at huge expense, part, perhaps, of the quest for immediate impact, which, however, given the gestation period, already looks old-fashioned.

Then there was Maxxi (*Museo nazionale delle Arti del XXI secolo*), Rome (2000–10—by Hadid), supposedly an art gallery, made of an intermeshing of massive shapes, constructed at enormous expense, but imposing huge constraints for any curator (walls were not plumb, thus ensuring the architect's demand that no 'art' should be hung on them), and creating uneasy disorientation in the visitor. This building might seem to address its 'function' with something resembling disregard.[72]

For a short time another anti-urban, anti-contextual fashion of *Blobismus*, or Blobism,[73] involving buildings resembling large blobs with reptilian carapaces, became fashionable: those buildings may have scales, but they lack scale. Associated also with New Animal, Biomorphic, or Zoömorphic architecture, Blobism may involve forms based on non-geometrical naturally occurring phenomena, as in certain aspects of Organic architecture (sometimes defined as the opposite of rational, geometrical architecture, and probably associated with intuition, irregularity, and a blurring of the man-made artefact with what is natural). An example of Biomorphic architecture is Calatrava's Milwaukee Art Museum, WI (1994–2003), based on the wings of a bird in flight. In such architecture grids were replaced by blobs, and the rigid lines of International Modernism gave way to curving forms and undulating roofs. In some cases, critics detected allusions to specific creatures, e.g. the reptilian exterior of Future Systems' Selfridge's store at the Bull Ring, Birmingham (2001–3, which tries very hard to be as popularist as possible, so has been known as the 'Armadillo', the 'Blob', or the 'Digbeth Dalek', suggesting 'nostalgia for the' science-fiction 'thrills of 1960s adolescence'),[74] covered with anodized aluminium discs, rejecting the scale, materials, and geometries of surrounding buildings (**Plate 8.5**).[75] Martin Pawley, in his panegyric, thought the work of this firm might be 'The Story of Tomorrow': tomorrow, in 1994, has been and gone.[76] With its anti-urban contempt for context, it identifies with 'hedonistic consumer culture',[77] and is an 'appalling neighbour, because of its overwhelming bulk, looming over St Martin's'[78] church.[79]

Blobs, it seems, were just another fashion, one that quickly palled.

Plate 8.5. Reptilian exterior of Selfridge's department-store, the Bull Ring, Birmingham (2001–3), by Future Systems: it ignores context, its overwhelming bulk rendering insignificant the parish church of St Martin-in-the-Bull-Ring. The footbridge across Park Street adds to the reptilian allusions, as it resembles the long tongue of a chameleon

Cults, Compounds, & the Grand Narrative

Contrary to comfortable received opinion, 'religious' belief systems are by no means moribund as the twenty-first century nears its third decade,[80] and fanatically held beliefs are not confined to adherence to the supernatural. Cults, fundamentalist religions, political beliefs rooted in self-righteousness or envy, and dogmatic assumptions adopted wholesale without proper testing,[81] are inimical to that which exists: they are all destructive.

Here, I am not arguing for or against the adoption of any one system of religious belief: what is clear, however, is that in order to understand history, society, and indeed architecture, it is necessary to have a knowledge of the huge part religion played in all three of them. Before 1914, architecture and religion in the West were closely intertwined: any consideration of A.W.N. Pugin and the architects of the Gothic Revival without taking into account

Christianity and Ecclesiology, for example, would be pointless, and the passionate illusions of theatrical Baroque churches can only be explained within the context of the Counter Reformation and massive reconstruction in the aftermath of the ferocious Thirty Years War. Modernism substituted something in the place of religion, however, and that was a 'system phenomenon', a dangerous cult immune to whatever might change it into anything resembling a rational discipline: like other belief-systems, it is not founded on scientific experiment or rationalism, but is susceptible to complete collapse because it cannot tolerate change, so is kept alive within special 'compounds'[82] by those with a vested interest in perpetuating it.

Rather too many architects 'design' buildings based on fashion and passing 'concepts'.[83] The architectural Establishment, having jettisoned engineering, surveying, scholarship, precedent, history, and just about everything else, is left with empty husks, devoid of meaning. Modernism (in whatever guise) has had all the characteristics of a cult, but there were signs of unease, even in the pages of erstwhile supporters of that cult, as early as 1967.[84]

A dangerous cult may be defined as a kind of false religion, adoption of a system of belief based on mere assertions with no factual foundations, or as excessive, almost idolatrous, admiration for a person, persons, an idea, or even a fad. The adulation accorded to Le Corbusier, who was given almost the status of a deity in architectural circles, is just one example. It has certain characteristics which may be summarized as follows:

    it is destructive;
    it isolates its believers;
    it claims superior knowledge and morality;
    it *demands* subservience, conformity, and obedience;
    it is adept at brainwashing;
    it imposes its own assertions as dogma, and will not countenance
    any dissent;
    it is self-referential;

and

    it invents its own arcane language, incomprehensible to outsiders.[85]

Anyone unfamiliar with the workings within architectural schools who might feel the above overstates the case should attend a 'crit', read the architectural magazines published from the 1950s onwards, or glance at the staccato assertions in the publications of Le Corbusier[86] and the ecstatic reviews of those publications. If sitting in on a 'crit' is not practicable, a disturbing example may be viewed online.[87]

As Tom Wolfe noted in his *From Bauhaus to Our House*, in order to indoctrinate and further the aims of the cult, the 'compound' was invented,[88] the basis from which contemporary architectural 'education' evolved. Those entering the compound had to accept the tenets, the exclusive possession of the knowledge of what was best for the world, and no contrary arguments would be tolerated. Architecture, in such compounds, was seen as a means of promoting transcendental expression, freed from consideration of use or costs. The promoters of this cult had and have many of the instincts of mediaeval clergy, separated from ordinary people (denounced as the *bourgeoisie*, who neither understood or liked the products forced on them), and carried out proselytizing through the 'Manifesto',[89] a declaration, something similar to the Ten Commandments in that it could not be transgressed or questioned.

In turn, the Manifesto required the invention of a story, a supposed 'history', a 'Grand Narrative' that proposed a seamless flow of events, eschewing anything that might be inconvenient or divert that flow, and ignoring personalities or works that did not fit the *parti pris*. Certain figures were named as significant in the formation of the Narrative, claimed as 'pioneers' of the Modern Movement, even though they themselves, when alive and old, objected in the strongest terms to being described as such: Pevsner, author of one such Narrative, perhaps the most influential for some thirty years after its first appearance, did just that.[90] The Narrative was then larded with a dose of 'morality' to give it a flavour of redemption, and seasoned with questionable claims to be 'objective', 'rational', and even 'scientific': once concocted, it set in train a vast mechanism of 'research' to spread the gospel, and a sense of permanency and historical truth was established which quickly became ideological dogma, metamorphosing into tyranny, even though none of it had anything like sound foundations.

The vast 'literature' that forms the supposed 'history' of twentieth-century architecture is a stunning example of the Grand Narrative that has dominated the topic since the 1920s. Key personalities were identified, cleansed of anything that might not be convenient for a Narrative that showed the Modern Movement in architecture as the inevitable product of a continuous evolution, when it was nothing of the sort. It was actually a disruption, a fracturing, a devastating break with thousands of years of development.

In short, promoters of the Modern Movement either ignored or marginalized any architects who could not be slotted into the preconceived Narrative in order to give it credence. They also removed religion from the Narrative, despite protests from protagonists (such as Baillie Scott, Comper, Dykes Bower, and Voysey) who thought religion was important, even fundamental, to healthy creativity and that without it architecture was arid, cold, and alien, devoid of beauty.

A Religious Dimension

In Chapter II the religious factor was mentioned in relation to certain architects working in the nineteenth and twentieth centuries. That factor is noticeably absent from Grand Narratives of Modernism, although several early protagonists (such as Itten,[91] nagel,[92] and even Kandinsky, who had published [1911] an essay on the Spiritual in Art)[93] seem to have had a need to belong to some sort of belief-system, group, or sect. Was this a substitute for religion that had informed European culture for the best part of two millennia? Immediately before and after the 1914–18 war, many organizations flourished that were concerned with spiritual matters, or even with the occult, and numerous personalities connected with Weimar and the *Bauhaus* were involved with some of them.

The iconoclastic side of Modernism in architecture should therefore deserve some attention, for some sects, cults, and systems of belief can be destructively intolerant of anything not relevant to them, and can therefore be linked with the actions of other zealots at various times. If the Modern Movement had been *truly* scientific, rational, objective, and open-minded (as it claimed, but clearly was not), it would not have *demanded* a *tabula rasa* at all, and would have respected the great architectural achievements of the past rather than urged so much fanatically inspired demolition as though to obliterate all evidence of historical development.

In 2015 an exhibition was mounted in the British Museum which celebrated the depiction of the human body in Classical Greek sculpture:[94] many more exemplars would have survived from Antiquity had it not been for Christians and others inspired by religious enthusiasm who regarded such artefacts as pagan, idolatrous, and sinful. In the same year the self-styled Islamic State in Iraq and the Levant attacked Nimrud, destroying a huge legacy of historical artefacts. In its heyday (900–700 BC), Nimrud was one of the Assyrian Empire's largest and grandest cities. Other threatened sites, all, at different times, capitals of that Empire, included Nineveh. Many ancient sculptures in the Mosul museums were deliberately smashed as 'idolatrous'. In Mosul, too, since the spring of 2014, tens of thousands of books and manuscripts have been burned, and scholar-curators brutally murdered.

Books, packed with ideas and knowledge, of course, are prime targets for barbarians. In ancient times one can only guess at the immense losses when the library of the *Serapeion*, Alexandria, was obliterated under Theophilus (Patriarch of Alexandria 385–412), or, presumably egged on by St Paul and his followers, the valuable collections at Ephesus (where the great Hellenistic Ionic temple of Artemis, one of the Wonders of the Ancient World, also nearly fell victim)[95] were consigned to the fires.[96] There have been countless other infamous examples of book-burning, including the *Opernplatz* bonfire in Berlin (10 May 1933), when books disapproved of by the National-Socialist German Workers' Party went up in flames, and there have been sundry conflagrations prompted by zealous hatred both religious and secular. The *Opernplatz* obscenity in the *Forum Fredericianum* was all the more so as it occurred beside the 'Temple of Apollo' designed by Knobelsdorff for King Frederick the Great of Prussia, one of the most significant figures of Germany's *Aufklärung* (Enlightenment).

The ancient carved Buddhas at Bamiyan, Afghanistan, were blown up by the Taliban in 2001 after they were denounced as 'idols', and more recently substantial architectural remains dating from the Roman period at Palmyra have been destroyed by so-called ISIS. UNESCO's Director-General has pointed out that certain groups use the destruction of heritage as part of deliberate strategies to destabilize and manipulate populations in order to secure dominance. The damage inflicted by the Taliban and other groupings, such as 'ISIS', is not the result of 'mindless violence': it is deliberate.[97] Leaders of various *régimes* in history have realized that if evidence of the past is destroyed, the future can be controlled.[98] The Normans who invaded England in 1066 carried out a programme of massive destruction of the architecture of Anglo-Saxon times (including the great Royal Minster of Winchester, the excavated plan of which suggests it resembled the mighty Romanesque churches of the Rhineland) to impose their own *visible* dominance on the country through their new buildings (the Cathedral Church [begun 1093] of Christ, Blessed Mary the Virgin, and St Cuthbert of Durham is a potent statement of Norman Power that cannot be ignored), so surviving pre-Conquest architecture (apart from a handful of church towers, such as that at Earls Barton, Northamptonshire, a county which also boasts the spectacular All Saints, Brixworth) largely consists of fragments and details. There are numerous other examples of widespread destruction when one culture, group, or ideology conquers another. It is therefore important to grasp the simple fact that the *tabula rasa* demanded by Modernism has close links with manipulation, a programme of destruction, a fanatically held belief in a cult, and a burning desire to change the world. In that respect Modernism shared certain characteristics with other conquerors.

Given recent events, which have their parallels throughout history, it seems that destroyers are at their most destructive when fired up with self-righteousness, so it is not inappropriate to suggest that supposedly secular destructiveness is at its most effective when there is a religious or quasi-religious element at work. The German National Socialists, for example, undoubtedly used ceremonies and symbols that drew on religion,[99] and in this respect it might be suggested that commentators such as Hannah Arendt, who claimed that National Socialism owed 'nothing to any part of the Western tradition, be it... Catholic or Protestant',[100] were profoundly mistaken. Joseph Goebbels, for example, wrote of the 'struggle' (a favourite word employed by agitators of various political hues) between 'Christ and Marx', and saw Christ as perfection, the epitome of the anti-Capitalist,[101] discernible in the Sermon on the Mount;[102] which, if actually acted upon, would mean the end of Western Capitalism as we know it.

All monotheistic religions are essentially intolerant: one variety will be antipathetical to another, and the same is unquestionably true of branches of supposedly the same religion (e.g. Roman Catholic *versus* Greek Orthodox *or* Protestantism, or sects within, say, Protestantism, or Islam, holding what might seem to outsiders minor differences of speculative opinion). It is not possible to consider the 'Holocaust' or 'Shoah' as divorced from its theological origins (though many, unconvincingly, have tried):[103] the Jews as 'Christ-killers' have been convenient targets over the centuries, and horrific tracts, such as 'On the Jews and their Lies', of Martin Luther, sanctioned murder of Jews 'without mercy' by rulers who should 'cut, saw, and burn flesh, veins, bone, and marrow'.[104] Compared with such poisonous stuff, Richard Wagner's notorious *Das Judenthum in der Musik* (Jewishness in music),[105] though vile, is relatively mild in tone.

The importance of religion in the creation of great works of art, not least architecture, cannot be denied, yet it is curiously absent in official histories of Modernism, despite the unquestionable and well-documented links between certain revered figures of the Modern Movement with Theosophy and other groupings. The connections between the theories of M.H.J. Schoenmaekers and many celebrated Modernist architects (including Rietveld and Le Corbusier), especially in relation to the sole use of primary colours, for example, are known, yet the murkier recesses connected with mystical and quasi-spiritual groupings have been played down and submerged under claims for an 'objective', 'rational', 'scientific', 'functional' Modernism that have been greatly exaggerated.[106]

It is true that English readers tend to react to 'transcendental' notions with something akin to 'repugnance and suspicion',[107] and Patmore realized the problem when he wrote that anyone who might be afraid of being ridiculed 'by fools and knaves' should not attempt to define the relationship between art and religion.[108] That relationship has been denied or ignored by the supposedly learned.

9/11 & Other Uncomfortable Matters

Concern has been expressed as to how governing classes in some 'developing' countries have been influenced by the West, leading to a rejection of their own native architectural traditions. A manifestation of this phenomenon is an eruption of 'iconic' buildings erected at vast expense to show how 'up-to-date' such *élites* are: alien forms are imposed, sites are desecrated, and Western economic and financial dominance is encoded in yet another expensive work by a fashionable 'star' architect, lavishly illustrated and praised in glossy architectural magazines.[109] The architects, and their critical supporters, either do not understand or do not care about the consequences of the imposition of such forms on societies where cultural values and deep-seated beliefs are very different from those of the imposers. Even in China, in recent times, a halt has been called to the 'chaotic propagation of grandiose, West-worshipping and weird architecture';[110] and there were sharp intakes of breath when an academic at Tsinghua University, Beijing, had the temerity to remark that China had 'too many buildings designed by Zaha Hadid'.[111] Another prominent name, the ubiquitous Rem Koolhaas, with Ole Scheeren, of OMA,[112] designed the China Central Television headquarters in Beijing (2002–12): it was lampooned as 'The Big Underpants'[113] (**Figure 8.5**). There have been calls for new buildings to be less outrageously expensive, less wasteful of energy (i.e. more 'green'), more agreeable to look at,

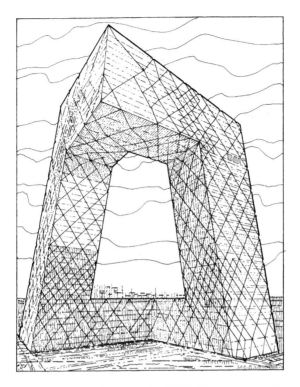

Figure 8.5. China Central Television (CCTV) Headquarters, East Third Ring Road, Guanghua Road, Beijing Central Business District (2002–12), designed by Koolhaas and Scheeren of Office for Metropolitan Architecture (OMA), known to irreverent Chinese as the 'Big Underpants'

and respecting and reflecting China's traditions; which might suggest that Western 'iconic buildings' have become at least a bore, and are possibly no longer welcome.[114] There is also the old problem of architects in the contemporary world working for oppressive *régimes*: criticism of this has been somewhat muted.

There are parallels, of course. When the *Beaux-Arts* school still inculcated its students with the principles that gave us Baron Georges-Eugène Haussmann's Paris, one of its graduates, Henri Prost, was appointed to oversee planning in Morocco: he conserved the old street patterns and *souks*, and designed new areas in a traditional 'Islamic' style, with control of heights so that minarets remained dominant features of the skyline.[115] Consequently, places like Fez and Marrakesh remained agreeable and beautiful. When the Ottoman Empire fell apart, however, and France acquired the mandate to govern Syria in 1923, the French influence was not beneficial at all: in 1935 a comprehensive plan for Damascus was prepared by René Danger which adopted the dreary destructive dogmas and toxic disconnectedness promoted by Le Corbusier and CIAM, with the unfortunate results that monuments were isolated, densely-packed urban fabric round those monuments was demolished, wide streets were driven through parts of the city judged insalubrious, rigid zoning was introduced to separate various functions, and Corbusian obsessions about hygiene spelled death to much of the historic city.[116] There was much uproar and objection, but the plans were implemented, and completed under the Ba'ath *régime* in the 1960s. Damascus became a Modernist city, and the subtle fabric which retained traces of four civilizations could no longer be read.[117]

Le Corbusier,[118] of course, wanted to demolish Paris and impose his simplistic vision on the corpse, but fortunately he did not prevail. He tried to do the same in Algiers, but fell out with the Vichy *régime*, so that, too, was not implemented. But the bacillus of his ideas[119] did not die, and infected much of the Middle East, feasting on the inferiority complexes of governing parties that sought to 'catch up'[120] with the West by erecting high-rise buildings, creating ill-designed open spaces, clearing away the humane clutter and cultural diversity of Ottoman cities, and ignoring the rural poor from the villages who flocked to the urban centres to just survive in unregulated, undesigned, unplanned shanty-towns that encrusted the outskirts.[121] It has been a recipe for disaster, and it suggests that Western town-planning dogma and Modernist buildings, worrying at the sores of indigenous senses of inferiority, might have played a part in the unrest that has bedevilled the Middle East.[122] Old-established settlements, humane in scale, were replaced by large Modernist blocks derived from images promoted by the *Bauhäusler* and their hangers-on: a hostile environment provoked hostility, and an explosion took place.[123]

A recent book sensitively relates how conflict has destroyed the city of Homs,[124] all the more interesting as it makes a convincing case that if the humane, serene, unflashy fabric of an ancient Levantine city is brutally wrecked, then the peace that once pervaded there is also threatened. Homs had narrow, twisting streets; mosques and churches coexisted within them, neither shouting nor indulging in any architectural triumphalism; and no significant building overdid itself in display.[125] There is 'a fine line', wrote the author,[126] 'between humility and indifference', but the people of Homs 'have now crossed that line aggressively'.[127] The author has no illusions about the contribution so-called 'architectural education' has made, when banalities are all-pervasive, and local traditions are parodied by pseudo-Islamic *clichés* affixed to thin walls.[128] 'Iconic' interventions in an ethical void should not happen.

Empty gestures are made closer to home as well. The Scottish Parliament-Building (1998–2004), by Enric Miralles Moya, sited at the foot of the Royal Mile, Edinburgh, opposite Holyrood Palace, with its almost unreadable allusions to upturned boats (why boats, upturned or otherwise, anyway?) and fatuous claims that its applied 'decorations' draw inspiration from the painting *The Reverend Robert Walker Skating on Duddingston Loch* (*c.*1784) by Sir Henry Raeburn, cannot be said to respond to its context. It has no connection whatsoever to indigenous Scottish architecture of any period, and ignores especially the great Classical architectural legacy that was such an integral part of Edinburgh. The stuck-on 'decorations' have no true symbolic meaning: and that is because architects no longer know what a symbol actually is. A symbol represents what it is; an allegory represents what it is not. But that is a distinction embedded in theology, and therefore not one that will be even vaguely familiar (or welcome) today.

The obliteration of history has always been high on the agenda of Modernist architects, and the Parliament building manages to ignore history, thereby conforming to the demands of the Modernist cult. This was clearly another instance of a country with a splendid and unique heritage of great architecture, turning its back on that heritage to acquire an 'iconic' building devoid of meaning and stuffed with banalities: all to be able to claim a spurious 'Modernity' and perhaps by so doing conceal a queasy sense of national disappointment.

One of the architects of the infamous Pruitt-Igoe scheme, mentioned earlier, Yamasaki (who, incidentally, was afraid of heights), was also responsible for the design, this time collaborating with Emery Roth & Sons, of the twin towers of the World Trade Center, New York (1964–74). The pilot who flew the hijacked aeroplane into the north tower in 2001 was an Egyptian-born architect, trained in Cairo and Hamburg. Mohamad Atta hated Western Modernist corporate office-blocks and hotels that were ubiquitous and were disfiguring city after city in the Middle East:[129] indeed his research at Hamburg Technical University was concerned with the clash between traditional architecture in the old town of Aleppo and Modernist Western buildings.[130] So the attack was connected with animosity towards Globalization, Westernization, and Modernism, and embedded within the reasons for that was a religious dimension, something completely discounted by the West, at its peril. The World Trade Center *represented* many things unwelcome to certain traditional societies, and it is that reality, a symbol, and not an allegory, that should be taken seriously, and not ignored. It was not just two towers: it was much more. (Events since 9/11, however, have hardly improved the fabric of Aleppo.)

Such vast developments were seen as expressions of Western dominance encoded in the abstracted fundamentalism of Modernism. This would be

Plate 8.6. *Centre Pompidou*, Paris (1971–7), showing the casings for the escalators, but signals indicating where the entrance might be are subdued in the architecture

something completely missed by the architects responsible. They have so lost all conception of the value of symbols that they have even discarded any signals that might inform mere humans where the entrances to their buildings might be: one has to look for a queue and where it leads, to find the entrance to, say, the *Centre Pompidou* (*aka Beaubourg*), Paris (1971–7—by Renzo Piano and Richard Rogers [**Plate 8.6**]), or the National Theatre, London (1967–76—by Denys Lasdun). Architects of the Modern Movement tended to avoid employing symbolic signs the meanings of which were established through conventional use, believing these were part of 'Historicism', and therefore had to be eschewed.[131] Even readable doorways, it seems, had become '*élitist*', following capitals into oblivion.[132]

Epilogue

Between 6 April and 23 July 2006 an exhibition entitled *Modernism: Designing a New World 1914–1939* was shown at the Victoria & Albert Museum, London, and a lavish publication, edited by Christopher Wilk (who also curated the exhibition), was produced to accompany it and provide an 'indispensable work of reference and an outstanding record of the defining movement of twentieth-century design'.[133] Simon Jenkins wrote that it was the 'most terrifying exhibition' he had ever seen, and that it was 'politics disguised as art'.[134] It opened with 'a word that says it all'—Utopia—and ended 'with an unspoken lie' that this Nihilist ideology became 'merely a style' and therefore was 'no longer a threat'. Jenkins observed that Modernists were the 'neocons of 20th-century art. They took a sound methodology—the questioning of conventional wisdom—and made it a dogma that brooked no opposition, even from reality. They turned a fad into a political programme' and bred 'a tradition of stylistic authority still alive today', they 'approached the past not as an aesthete does, respectfully building on it, but as an autocrat, destroying it and substituting his own values and rules.' And the 'worst offenders . . . were architects. When Gropius said a modern artist lived "in an era of dissolution without guidance",[135] he was declaring not a truth but narrowness of mind.'[136]

Jenkins awoke to the fact that the 'tawdriness' of so much Modernist architecture 'was deliberate': art was sacrificed just as history was rejected because it was '*bourgeois*', one of the most favoured labels of abuse used by the faithful. British Modernists, 'many of them refugees' (some were, notably

Jews, but others were nothing of the sort), gained a foothold 'when they won the ear of government' after the 1939–45 war: they claimed they could build the Socialist Utopia 'cheaper and faster than the free market' and many bought the old line that high-rise system building was 'urgently needed to rehouse the population'. The truth was that private builders (most of whom were equipped to work with traditional materials, using traditional, tried methods, in the architectural language derived from the Domestic Revival) could erect and sell popular semi-detached houses for around £500 a unit; yet the cheapest Modernist industrial housing 'cost £1,300 ex fac-tory... Today the system-built estates are crumbling, their concrete stained and rotting, while the despised "historicist" suburbs seem ready to last for ever.' Jenkins pointed out that Modernism rejected style because style requires 'hard work and talent'. Its apologists demanded 'straight lines and ball bearings, an insult to both culture and engineering' and it demanded a new 'ism': 'social authoritarianism'.[137]

One of the worst professional crimes ever inflicted on humanity was the application of Utopian Modernism to the public housing-stock in the 1950s, 1960s, and 1970s, which 'dehumanised communities', 'spoiled landscapes', and 'ruined lives', yet the architectural Establishment and the schools of architecture remained, and remain, in 'total denial'.[138] Thus Dystopia was imposed. The ditching of history has its consequences. In the 1970s Jenkins had witnessed the 'clearance' of the Hulme district of Manchester to make way for the Modernist Utopia designed by a team under Lewis Womersley: thousands of people 'who had survived Hitler's bombs... saw their homes destroyed by their home-grown' *Gauleiters* (area commanders),[139] and were then transported to new settlements elsewhere. 'The resulting slabs have since been demolished as uninhabitable.'[140]

The huge development at Hulme (completed 1971), one of the largest undertaken in England, had at its centre four quarter-mile long six-storey deck-access 'crescents' (**Plate 8.7**) designed by the Modernist firm (estab-lished 1964) of Wilson & Womersley (Hugh Wilson and J.L. Womersley): these were named after British architects of the Georgian, Regency, and early Victorian periods (Robert Adam, Charles Barry, William Kent, and John Nash), the usual shabby trick of Modernists claiming a wholly spuri-ous continuity with a respectable past (the philistine, uninformed press swallowed this nonsense whole, and raved about the new schemes as provid-ing 'Georgian elegance' worthy of 'Bloomsbury' and the best of 'Regency' England).[141] *The Buildings of England* volume dealing with *Lancashire:*

Plate 8.7. Modernist 'crescents', insultingly named after distinguished architects (Adam, Barry, Kent, and Nash), with unkempt 'landscape', designed by Wilson & Womersley, completed 1971. In less than a decade afterwards it had become 'one of the most dysfunctional housing estates in Europe' (Hartwell, Hyde, & Pevsner [2004] 455), though demolition did not begin until 1991

Manchester and the South (2004) called the crescents 'an act of hubris': an astonishing understatement to describe 'one of the most notoriously defective and dysfunctional housing estates in Europe', a 'spectacular failure', where problems 'were apparent from the beginning'.[142]

In the 1969 edition of *South Lancashire*, however, the Modernist received wisdom that tower-blocks and high-rise deck-access schemes were the answer to the nation's housing problems was clearly accepted as gospel: vast redevelopment schemes, both architecturally and socially, were the big story. Pevsner then said, approvingly, that Manchester was 'doing more perhaps than any other city in England...in the field of council housing', and trotted out the embarrassingly foolish justification for tower-blocks that architects 'understandably' wanted them to provide the 'necessary vertical accents' once found in 'church spires'.[143] Pevsner had been 'impressed by some of the schemes'[144] for public housing, when he should have demonstrated less confusion of mind and actually looked at the results through fewer Gropius-tinted spectacles. But the damage he did is beginning to be understood, though many still refuse to accept this. Wilson, it will be recalled, had been City Architect and Planning Officer at Canterbury (1945–56), where he imposed a stodgy Modernism, and subsequently presided over the planning of Cumbernauld New Town (1956–62), before setting up in private practice. His proposers for election (1960) as a Fellow of the Royal Institute of British Architects included, unsurprisingly, William Holford and Maxwell Fry: he himself became President of the Royal Institute of British Architects (1967–9), and was knighted in 1967.

At Hulme, Wilson & Womersley's redevelopment (1969–71) was later rightly termed 'a disaster',[145] leading to somewhat tardy demolition in the early 1990s: the same fate attended many blocks in other Manchester sub-urbs, such as those known as 'Fort Ardwick' and 'Fort Beswick', systems-built schemes that almost as soon as they were completed developed serious faults, and were denounced in the House of Commons in 1974. The life of these appalling Modernist exemplars was barely twenty years, hugely expensive failures that deserved far more than the very muted opprobrium reluctantly bestowed on them. As Jenkins said, wherever Modernists 'could find a sympathetic regime'—be it in Stalin's Union of Soviet Socialist Republics, Hitler's Third Reich, Grotewohl, Pieck, and Ulbricht's German Democratic Republic,[146] or Manchester City Council—they could perform; or, in Jenkins's words, they 'mimicked Albert Speer',[147] which, on reflection, is perhaps unfair to Speer, an architect Philip Johnson thought was much better than conditioned opinion could ever accept.

Jenkins noted that to Modernists 'necessity would have to defeat beauty'; that glass and steel were 'appropriate to achieve the communist expression of structure'; that the cruel 'Brutalism' of Le Corbusier's 'creations must have inspired more human misery than any in history' (actually, most of the damage was done by disciples of Le Corbusier, mere copyists incapable of thinking for themselves); that the Modernist 'cult' (the apposite word) 'took hold most firmly in countries that capitulated easily to dictatorship' (a view opposite to that of Barr); and that those who favour an art that gives 'pleasure, physical and intellectual comfort' and 'a sense of place' are regarded by Modernists as 'missing the point'.

He also stated that 'British architecture and its cheerleaders are stuck' in the Modernist 'time-warp, unable to handle historic reference in a building', and that the 'odious' Utopianism of Modernists deserves to be unequivocally rejected. Architectural schools, 'still ruled by nervous' Modernists, 'dare not teach' how to 'design streets or roofs or doors'.[148] A sobering fact is that this still holds good today: as we move further into the twenty-first century this dire situation has hardly altered.

Ever since the 1920s, architecture's divorce from science and history has become complete: it is a cult which has created a new Establishment, controlling architectural education, and even the architectural media. Remote now from high culture, it allies itself with technological gadgets and 'popular' culture, is self-referential, and has cut ties with reality outside its compound. That Establishment has a vested interest in prolonging and even extending the present system: but given its obvious and very visible failure, it is astonishing how it manages to hold on. There is something very wrong with any society that encourages impostors, for the viruses raised in Modernist 'laboratories' are infecting society as a whole, and show every sign of destroying it: yet the threat is being ignored. It is damaging all logical foundations of knowledge and reason, and, given its embrace of any new, fashionable 'ism', its aim is to ensure that destruction will be so complete no reconstruction will be possible. We are distracted by trivia, encouraged to be so by global media promoting a society of superficial spectacle, and fail to apply our advanced scientific knowledge to call a halt. It is clear that other, more traditional societies seem to sense something is going badly wrong, as they, too, are damaged by panaceas from the West that are beginning to be perceived as unbenign.[149] There are indications (largely missed by Western media) that their reactions could become cataclysmic.[150]

If things go on uncorrected, the end result will be the nightmarish Dystopian Nihilism[151] of Pornotopia.[152]

IX

Some Further Reflections

Something Was Missing; Measurable & Unmeasurable Aspects; High & Mass Culture;
A Pessimistic Future?; Royal Intervention; Coda

> *Nisi Dominus aedificaverit domum, in vanum laboraverunt qui aedificant eam.*
> *Nisi Dominus custodierit civitatem, frustra vigilat qui custodit eam.*
> (Unless the Lord has built the house, its builders have laboured in vain.
> Unless the Lord guards the city, the watchman watches in vain).
>
> VULGATE: Psalm 126 v.1

> And religion... [enjoins and sanctions]... the great aim of culture, [that] of
> setting ourselves to ascertain what perfection is and to make it prevail...
>
> MATTHEW ARNOLD (1822–88): Culture and Anarchy: An Essay in Political and
Social Criticism (London: Smith, Elder & Co., 1869) 12

Something Was Missing

Arthur Trystan Edwards had once pleaded for good manners in archi-tecture,[1] and he later tried to persuade that Modernism should be in partnership with Tradition, even though he admitted that the Modern Movement in architecture appeared to have rejected such a partnership, as it did not value 'traditional' architecture or even recognize it had any merits at all. Indeed, he noted that Modernists 'welcomed the demolition of old build-ings in the expectation that in their stead' room might be found 'for new buildings designed by themselves'.[2] It was actually worse than that, for in the wake of 1945 most authorities had planning-offices headed by Modernist architect-planners, who possessed considerable powers identified as replacing 'freedom, diversity, and individuality' with 'aesthetic dictatorship'[3] when tenants had no control over the environments into which those architect-planners put them.[4] Nicholas Taylor perceptively described such common-place conditions that were experienced by municipal tenants all over the country as 'municipal Fascism',[5] a remark that accords with the view expressed in this book that 'left' and 'right' labels are really meaningless. The designers and authorities responsible, however, were 'immune' from any criticism or effective objection, such was the widespread acceptance of Modernism dogma concerning housing, especially when most people seemed to want to live in low-rise, low-density suburbia.[6]

Although the mechanisms differed from country to country, the results of a widespread adoption of Modernism in architecture and planning were very similar. In the United States, Modernism impoverished American towns by promoting policies 'that destroyed age-old social arrangements and with them, urban life as a general proposition'.[7] It is curious that very early in the twentieth century, before the 1914–18 war, American innovations in con-struction, notably in high-rise buildings, influenced European architects who became interested in a new aesthetic made possible by steel-framed struc-tures and mass-production of building elements. European political upheavals led to many architects (often head-hunted by American institutions influ-enced by pressure from those connected with the Museum of Modern Art, especially Barr) crossing the Atlantic, thus reimporting American ideas, but transformed by theoretical fervour and evangelical zeal.

Notions embraced by CIAM and stiffened by MARS-Group enthusiasts[8] were promoted by the émigrés and devotees of Corbusianity,[9] and began to dominate urban planning. Seeing its abundant possibilities, it is no wonder property-developers, industrialists, vast corporations, financiers, architects, road-engineers, and politicians backed the Modernist Utopia, so high-rise buildings and super-highways became endemic, 'solutions' repeated over and over again, despite early evidence that they were not solutions at all but huge mistakes: however, more of the same was the order of the day, for hegemony existed very soon, and nobody could question Modernist ortho-doxy for fear of being denounced as 'conservative', 'reactionary', 'Fascist', or, even worse, '*bourgeois*'. The possibility that something had gone wrong was eventually, belatedly and reluctantly, recognized (after years of denial), but not before catastrophic destruction had been inflicted on urban fabric and urban civilization in countless instances.[10]

An insistence that utility alone could be beautiful was dogma partly derived from Pugin, but stripped of all its religious connotations: it is certainly true that something that is useful can be beautiful, but its beauty is accidental, uncertain, and dependent on other factors. Architecture is not just about service or utility: to be architecture at all it should have an effect on the human mind, spirit, and sensibilities.[11] Ideas of what might constitute beauty were twisted to fit a dubious technology, and the ancestry of the Modern Movement, like those improbable pedigrees of Renaissance Popes cooked up by Annius (Giovanni Nenni) of Viterbo,[12] lies in fantasy.

Utility and beauty do not lie easily in the same bed.

Measurable & Unmeasurable Aspects

The *Psalm* at the chapter-head is given in the Authorized Version as 'Except the Lord build the house: their labour is but lost that build it. Except the Lord keep the city: the watchman waketh but in vain.'[13] Sir Patrick Geddes paraphrased this, saying that unless the house is built with an ideal and the city also, the labour of creating them is all in vain.[14]

Much development since 1945 was based on measurable data, administrative expediency, the now questionable concepts of cost–benefit analysis,[15] space and light standards, projections of traffic (usually way off the mark), hygiene, and so on, all realized within the confines of a poverty-stricken Modernist design-vocabulary.[16] Lavatories, window areas, and cubic capacity are insufficient on their own to ensure an environment uplifting to the human spirit: that metaphysical extra capable of rising above the merely prosaic was always missing, for reasons outlined in previous chapters.[17]

To some, the city merely reflects organization: yet to others it may be an organism. At one level it might be likened to an anthill or a beehive, but the civilized city[18] offers cultural experiences and diversity far more complex than the purely functional mechanics of an anthill: cities are, or should be, far greater than massive urban concentrations of people.[19] At certain levels the city aspires to more than function, and a work of art is created, yet culture is something that has been absent in much official documentation and briefing concerning urban developments. Spiritual, uplifting aspects of life have been suppressed in welters of intentions, statistics, propaganda and advertising, political attitudinizing, and Modernist dogma, from all of which the transcendental, nobler aspirations of humanity have been expunged. The result, foreseen by many,[20] seems to be an ever more hideous Dystopia,[21] levelling, always downwards.

In French, the word *cité* can refer to a citizenry, a collection of citizens, or even the society itself, and means far more than a conurbation or a mass of people. Each city will have its own mythology. Such myths create in turn their own reality: the transcendent myths of Athens, Byzantium, Rome, and Vienna, to name but four, raise those great cities stratospherically above the Detroits, Essens, Pittsburghs, and Wolverhamptons of the world. In such mythologies human beings have an image of a model of some reality beyond the present, a truth of an ideal or myth infinitely potent, conveying a sense of significance, of spirituality, of human aspirations far higher than the level of empirical statistics: but that image has largely faded from a human consciousness bombarded by the fraudulent, encouragement to instant gratification, and cheap sensation. This is a problem, and, obviously, has a religious dimension.

The loss of cultural understanding of symbolic worth,[22] together with an inexorable rise in values based only on empirical data, have created enormous dangers. The empiricist, viewing a mediaeval *mappa mundi* for the first time, might be tempted to be amused: from his or her level of supposed superiority, the measurable and obvious faults in the drawings can be identified. But the symbolic and spiritual significance of such a document will be elusive, for it will not be seen in the same light as a representation of a labyrinth in a cathedral floor (*see* **Figures 1.1a & b**), an ideal-city plan (*see* **Figures 1.2, 1.4b, & c**),[23] or an Aztec vision of continents. The level of understanding is curtailed if only empirical faculties have been cultivated. It is true that there have been empirical aberrations in the past, including the society established *c.*540 BC by the Sage of Croton that was based on a system of numbers:[24] this Pythagorean curiosity was also associated with self-denial, something that has always possessed an attraction for certain individuals. But, as a result of depriving symbols of their reality and meaning,[25] the languages of art, of painting, of sculpture, of architecture, of city-building, of literature, of poetry, and of spiritual searchings became confused and impoverished. Only that which can be seen, which can be measured, which can be explained in 'real' phenomenal terms will have any use for a society that has jettisoned much of its historical and religious cultural inheritance. In this book I have attempted to identify some reasons why this has come about: the devaluation of the symbol,[26] and indeed its exclusion from architecture of the Modern Movement, has played an important part in what has turned out to be a disaster for the environment, and therefore for people too. The *tabula rasa* has, far too often, remained a desert, or has been

developed according to Modernist theories, then undone because the solution failed, and returned to a wasteland.[27]

The purely functional or empirical city will be a dreary place, unrelieved
by any of those finer, unquantifiable aspects that make life rise above the level
of the anthill. But since so much of contemporary society is ordered upon
the concept of easily measurable phenomena capable of being fed into a
databank, it is obvious that those things of the spirit, of the mind, of the finest
aspirations of humankind, being unmeasurable, will not be included in any
final analysis. People respond to beauty and to ideals: the terrifying growth
of vandalism, conjuring up images of blight, of smashed lifts, of broken
panes of glass, of painted or sprayed slogans, and of other unpleasant manifestations of a contemporary malaise is not inexplicable.[28] Uninformed alterations to existing buildings and the erosion of quality in the environment as
a direct result of the cult of Modernism are also aspects of vandalism.

There is much more to that phenomenon than in conventional notions
of what it is, for everywhere there are examples of official vandalism that are
more far-reaching and destructive than anything disaffected youth could
possibly achieve. The official destroyer has powerful agencies behind him or
her, including compulsory-purchase powers, redevelopment and planning-
machinery, the often meaningless predictions and statistics produced in
'surveys' to 'justify' the action taken, and many other weapons including
procrastination, tardiness, and inefficiency that help to cause planning-blight.[29]
However, destruction can also be prompted by the heartless predator, promoting programmes through various mechanisms of propaganda (the lecture, the article, the book, the conference, the slogan, the manifesto, the
internet, the polemic): in architectural circles, far too often, there are those
all too willing to become disciples of the promoters of any inhumane idea[30]
in times when culture has been so devalued as to be meaningless, and all that
remains is a void, an absence of intellect, a vast, empty confusion.[31]

This approach goes along with a mechanical conception of the world,
crudely measuring components and processes, one that was rooted in
Modernism, but which perhaps owed some of its origins to nineteenth-
century materialists, but otherwise was a complete break with all that went
before. Although techniques for such measurement became more sophisticated, the human being was largely ignored, or even treated like another
variable, so the whole methodology was badly distorted. More recent measurements of biological responses to the built environment, requiring greater
subtlety and care than crude mechanical techniques, show that human

physiology responds negatively to certain forms and spaces. Architects are not trained to read research-papers in biology, chemistry, or physics: they rely on architectural critics, theorists, and journalists to direct their views, and few, if any, of these have scientific backgrounds.[32] What they get instead ignores *real* science (which questions the whole Modernist-industrialist paradigm), promotes ephemeral fashion such as Parametricism or whatever will succeed that, and creates 'celebrity' architects who produce the next outrageously expensive 'iconic' structure which can only be realized with huge amounts of capital and a massive waste of resources.[33] The welfare of people is not considered, yet research has shown that buildings, the environment, and surroundings can have positive or negative effects on health.

For example, patient-recovery-times in hospital-rooms from which views of trees can be had, demonstrate that the body's healing-processes are influenced by sensory inputs that cannot be measured in the industrial sense of room dimensions.[34] Yet the architectural profession, focused on measurements of room-sizes, has largely ignored such findings. Schools of architecture train students in hospital-design based on formal, stylistic ideas of spaces and materials, despite the evidence accumulating towards a greater understanding of how human beings react physiologically to their surroundings.[35] This can even involve improvements in pain-relief in hospitals by viewing natural scenery.[36] In order to understand the effects of environments better, studies of higher mammals have been made that convincingly prove the psychological and social well-being of animals in zoos is greatly improved if they are given naturalistic habitats, and not kept cooped up in drab, bare, minimalist spaces, where neurotic, aberrant, and anti-social behaviour, never observed in the wild, is obvious.[37] It appears, too, that complexity and stimulation in the environment can lead to increased intelligence in a developing animal: this suggests that there are questions of grave culpability in creating habitats that ignore or minimize neurological matters.[38]

As the twentieth century drew to its inglorious close and the twenty-first looked like shaping up to be even more problematical, it became obvious that the very rich were getting even richer; that power was increasingly concentrated in vast multinational corporations; that huge tracts of the world were being despoiled; that much of the earth's population possessed no control whatever over its future and was deprived of basic human rights; and that so-called 'star' architects were making their fortunes by serving the very rich and the multinationals, ignoring environmental problems that were becoming increasingly worse.[39] There is little in all this that is new:

what *is* new is a total absence of political will to reverse or change direction. Yet voices have been raised in warning about the dangers to the welfare of humanity of globalization,[40] drawing attention to the very uneven geographical evolution of late twentieth-century capitalism, especially in respect of production and consumption, and still finding in the writings of Karl Marx much analysis and theory relevant to contemporary difficulties.[41] It has been suggested that what is needed is massive change in living and working environments, taking into account the micro-scale of the human body and its personal needs and the macro-scale of an increasingly global political economy. For centuries attempts have been made by Utopian movements to create more just societies.[42] Many did not succeed, yet some of the theories that lay behind such movements were not pie-in-the-sky but based on idealism, compassion, and observation, and so may offer bases for the future. What is missing from much debate about architecture today is empathy, respect for culture in the widest sense, understanding of history (including religion), recognition of the imperative of Nature as part of humankind's habitat, and understanding of the importance of expressions of gravity and stability in building design to induce calm and ease in those who have to live with the realized works of an architecture that denies gravity, that deliberately sets out to disturb, and that only respects itself.

David Harvey has drawn attention to the fact that private property has already been abolished for the majority of the population, as it is beyond reach and unaffordable. Free-market neoliberalism has virtually destroyed the barriers to the accumulation of capital by large corporations involving the rapid construction of built environments, transport infrastructures, and the like: in order to do this Modernist firms of architects have been essential enablers.[43] Harvey has been unsparing in his cold-eyed and devastatingly accurate descriptions of the existing urban environments, drawing on Baltimore, MD, as his case study: he has argued that we must insist on questioning the received opinion that 'there is no alternative'[44] to failed panaceas which were nothing of the sort, and indeed have all too obviously created, not Utopia,[45] but Dystopia.[46] Harvey's own Utopian vision insists on taking into account human qualities (rather than moulding human beings to fit a preconceived model dreamed up by authoritarian architects, a fatal flaw in the architectural Modern Movement);[47] respect for the essence of Nature, including its characteristics, capacities for recovery, and importance for humanity; and an appreciation of the dynamics of change, with all the dangers and opportunities inherent in change.[48]

There have been other studies that reappraised theories of urban planning and architectural design,[49] questioning the rôle of the architect-planner
in any intervention within the urban context. Moylan's work on Dystopia[50]
points to the idea of Dystopia as a critical tool for analysing and dissecting
modern urban developments, but it should also be read in conjunction with
works that have examined interactions between illusion and truth, power
and helplessness, and the problems which arise when sectors collide that
humankind can and cannot control. Henri Lefebvre insisted on the 'right'
of humankind to the city as the complete urbanization of society proceeded
apace: he perceptively saw that cities of the ancient world[51] could not be
understood as a mere agglomeration of people, and that their cultural climate was connected with the social production of spaces within the urban
fabric.[52] He was also highly critical of architects and planners of the Soviet
era who produced Modernist models of urban design[53] that were deficient
in understanding of what he described as social spaces. Similar problems,
however, were all too obvious in other non-Communist societies as well.[54]
Other studies have contrasted the gritty realities of modern urban life,
sometimes focusing on the conflict between so-called 'iconic' architecture
and what most people have to put up with in their immediate, alienating,
incompetently designed, and often squalid surroundings.[55] Urban space,
however, to be successful, according to some commentators, has to be a
collective work, socially produced, the opposite of mainstream Modernist
urban planning which has been largely based on abstracted knowledge and
non-participatory processes.[56] In other words, it does not work if merely
imposed as part of some design dogma, which was the endemic problem in
Modernist CIAM-inspired work, as revealed in critiques such as those of
Coleman,[57] Jacobs,[58] and others.[59]

Yet architecture depends on uncertainties and contingencies: what architecture is and what architects want it to be are often very different, for it has
duties to the world and to humanity, to the real world, something often
forgotten in the pursuit of abstractions that was and still is at the heart of
much of Modernism.[60] That is why the traditional street, the urban space,
the very fabric of towns and cities, in all its messy, varied uses, and disparate
elements, rarely survived draconian Modernist architectural interventions
which were too tidy and neat for the realities of use.[61] Jacobs[62] was undoubtedly correct in arguing for untidy, mixed-use places that could be lived in,
and Coleman's[63] dissection of what was wrong with Corbusier-inspired[64]
developments deserved attention: yet both were derided by the architectural

Establishment, which, in denial, refused to acknowledge the damage it had inflicted on vital urban organisms, many of which became seriously moribund as a result of Modernist interventions.[65]

Rejecting grand Utopian visions of 'total planning', 'total design', and other notions energetically promoted by CIAM, Corbusianity,[66] and sundry Modernist enthusiasts, an eclectic collage of architectural diversity[67] and mini-Utopias has been suggested as one possible approach. In *Collage City*[68] the authors attempted to describe the ideologies, philosophical origins, and manifestations of Modern architecture, touching upon their many flaws, by then (1980) painfully apparent. In essence, the book was concerned with architects who embraced ideas centred on the Ideal City.[69] It advocated a retreat from a single vision of Utopia to the making of forms of urban development drawing upon multiple sources, like a series of disparate overlays, overlaps, and, in effect, collages, taking on board many varied themes and ideas. For one of the authors, Colin Rowe, this was in itself a change of direction, for he had once made his name by exploring a supposed Classical continuity within Modernism, and embraced the commonly held view that International-Modern architecture of the 1920s offered paradigms for the second half of the twentieth century.[70] In short, he sought to invest International Modernism with an historical legitimacy by connecting it with Palladianism, just as Pevsner insisted Voysey and other unlikely candidates were 'pioneers' of the Modern Movement. By the end of his life, however, Rowe, like many others, appeared to regret his championship of Modernism, finding the study of Renaissance buildings 'gratifying and refreshing as the spectacle of Modern Architecture' became 'more depressing'.[71] Rowe advocated collage and a wide-ranging eclecticism, which he appeared to view as methods for using things and simultaneously disbelieving in them: in their manipulation lay a means of enjoyment without depth, for conviction and belief were no longer possible. Certainly, eighteenth- and early nineteenth-century eclecticism had been associated with open-mindedness,[72] but the Rowe-Koetter approach using collages was not quite the same thing, and seemed to be curiously devoid of roots in anything, least of all in a great cultural tradition. Rowe also sought to persuade that much Modernist intervention was done with the 'best intentions', but many would now dispute this.[73]

Watkin's books[74] attacking the positions of Pugin, Pevsner, and others undermined the supposed 'moral' pretensions of architecture, and Venturi questioned stylistic rigidity,[75] yet the undoubted importance of these volumes and others by Coleman,[76] Jacobs,[77] and Rowe[78] did not contribute convincingly to the improvement of architecture or the contemporary urban *milieu*, possibly because they all disregarded or underestimated the powerful influence of the market, and avoided the complex political aspects and machinations required if real transformation is to be achieved. Perhaps, therefore, many other sources should be noted, including Harvey,[79] but the malaise may well lie in the perilously confused, even seriously ill, state of what remains of a once-vibrant and healthy culture,[80] as well as in the deeply embedded infection of Modernist cant, aggressive assertion, and certainties that were not based on science, culture, religion, reason, tradition, historical continuity, or the long evolution of Western civilization. What happened after 1918 was a rupture, a sundering, a cultural catastrophe based on dissolution and unreason, an incitement to violence and vandalism, and an overweening conceit that convinced architects they could mould humanity in order to accept and inhabit the buildings and urban environments they provided and which replaced a legacy of thousands of years of cultural evolution.

The insensate modern city is in a great many ways a failure, and leaves its inhabitants feeling betrayed, and therefore without affection for their surroundings.[81] In this regard the writings of Fredric Jameson,[82] especially those influenced by Lefebvre[83] on the cultural logic of late Capitalism, Utopias, science-fiction, and the politics and ideologies of architectural and urban spaces, may be read with benefit. Lefebvre argued that the experience of everyday life was undervalued, even ignored, except in terms of how much it could consume. The sense of desperation that appears to exist in some sectors of society today is often directed at the environment. Some commentators have offered prescriptions for the disease, including the canalization of youthful energy, and the creation of an ideal Utopia[84] in which tasks are, in that ghastly phrase, 'socially meaningful'.

These are not cures, for the problem is the Dystopian environment that has been inflicted on humanity: it is that alien Dystopia which has to be changed, rather than its unfortunate inhabitants, who have little power to alter it by themselves except to attack it.

One of the inevitable results of an economy bent on over-production and ever-increasing gross national product is the need for periodic carnivals of destruction. If we suddenly find ourselves up to the ears in a sea of plastic gnomes, then it is reasonable to assume that something has gone wrong with the whole philosophy of production. It might be sensible to challenge official views that more production is ever necessary, as the obvious result would be the using up of national resources to the point where they become exhausted and we have a surfeit of expendable consumer goods.[85] We should, in short, be examining the real worth of what we produce; but that would raise awkward questions about the very nature of modern society. There are ultimate truths about the 'affluent society' (more properly the effluent society, as the state of the oceans might suggest).

Officially backed destruction is often carried out because of the alleged pressing needs of the many, or because of 'public good' or some other nebulous aim.[86] The public, however, is made up of individuals, no matter what governments, bureaucracies, party-machines, vested interests, vast international monopolies, urban-renewal enthusiasts, or advertising-men would prefer to the contrary. It is abundantly clear that much urban development created since 1945 is unsuited to the all-round needs of human beings, and the hatred expressed against a great deal of it has been manifest in violence, leading to widespread demolitions: yet those who created it have been rewarded rather than punished. Examples are legion.[87] Any environmental asset that we still possess must be conserved because of the genuine economic and psychological necessity of keeping it. Ancient settlements, old-established towns, and cathedral-cities have their *raison d'être*, but those that are still pleasant to visit, to inhabit, to enjoy, in which to work and live, are becoming fewer in number as more and more places fall victim to disastrous road proposals, blighting developments, buildings without meaning that ignore context, and urban spaces that are uninviting, dangerous, threatening, windswept, and alien. Squalid environments attract protests and violence: it is not difficult to see why.[88]

High & Mass Culture

That great English architect Sir John Soane, in his lectures at the Royal Academy, declared that architecture 'in particular, and the arts and sciences in general, for their great use and ornament in civilised society have in all ages been cultivated and cherished',[89] not least for their 'beneficial' influences. Indeed Soane, steeped in the 'ideals of the *Encyclopédistes* and the French Enlightenment',[90] also studied the 'sensationalist[91] and associational philosophy[92] of the Picturesque movement in Britain',[93] and his colossal library reflected his concerns with 'civic virtue and with the search for origins, whether those of language' (in Bonnot de Condillac); 'of society' (in Rousseau); 'of architecture' (in Laugier and Quatremère de Quincy); 'of religious or sexual symbolism' (in d'Hancarville and Payne Knight); 'of primitive customs, laws, and religions' (in Goguet and Lafiteau); 'of music' (in Rameau); and 'of plant forms' (in Goethe).[94] He castigated persons who claimed to be architects, but were ignorant of such matters, following the 'fashion of the day', the 'shadow and not the substance'.[95] Regrettably, fashion, shadows, and 'empty gestures'[96] seem to be followed at present by many connected with architecture, to judge from the contents of journals and the hagiographies of 'star' architects.[97]

Architecture, art, history, literature, music, philosophy, poetry, science, religion, embedded in the culture of the West, were once valued as essential to the enrichment, even the life, of the spirit and mind. Culture, which might be regarded as the intellectual part, even the essence, of a true civilization, permeating it through and through, used to inform university education: it was a kind of consciousness that continuously revived and acted as a catalyst to thought and understanding. In the second decade of the twenty-first century, not only is free speech threatened, but any airing of views which might be worthy of rational debate is increasingly prohibited,[98] and even 'culture' has become an offensive term. The very word has been largely discarded: Lionel Brett, Lord Esher, memorably remarked that when politicians and civil servants hear the word 'culture', they 'feel for their blue pencils',[99] a statement reminiscent of the rather more violent reaction recorded in Hanns Johst's play *Schlageter*, involving the release of the safety-catch of a Browning.[100] In addition, a further threat to culture may be detected in so-called 'no-platforming'. This not only stifles dissent: it curtails thought, abolishes honest debate, and destroys academic freedom.[101]

An essential element of education is to learn how to dispute and test ideas and differing points of view, and, to do that, those views and ideas have to be heard and argued. No longer, it seems, are we permitted to debate, to think, to express ideas, or, as Horace put it, *atque inter silvas Academi quaerere verum* (and seek for truth in the groves of *Academe*).[102] In the groves of the academy of the near future, as Edmund Burke observed of similar mentalities, eventually nothing will be seen at the end of every vista but the gallows[103] or worse. 'Those who attempt to level never equalize',[104] Burke reminded us in his *Reflections on the Revolution in France* (1790): 'under a false shew of liberty, but, in truth', aiming 'to exercise an unnatural inverted domination, tyrannically to exact . . . an abject submission to their occasional will, extinguishing thereby ... all moral principle, all sense of dignity, all use of judgment, and all consistency of character',[105] their 'tongue betrays them. Their language is in the *patois* of fraud ... in the cant and gibberish of hypocrisy.'[106] Burke asked 'what sort of a thing must be a nation of gross ... ferocious ... poor and sordid barbarians, destitute of religion, honour ...? Already there appears a poverty of conception, a coarseness and vulgarity in all the proceedings ... Their liberty is not liberal. Their science is presumptuous ignorance. Their humanity is savage and brutal.'[107]

Burke's powerfully-expressed views still merit attention. He might well have been describing disciples of Modernism who did so much to destroy, and then *imposed*, by bullying and violent assertion, their preferences, prejudices, and illogical certainties on humanity:[108] but his remarks could also be applied to those who support banning anyone with 'offensive' views from giving utterance to them.[109] Some demand the 'right' to close their minds against new ideas or anything else that 'threatens' them, including high culture. Illiberalism is no way to protect liberalism or liberty. Furthermore, research on support for restrictions on free speech[110] carried out by the Higher Education Policy Institute and published with the title *Keeping Schtum? What students think of free speech*, makes depressing reading.[111]

Perception of 'culture' as suspect is widespread, not least because it represents, as Sir John Soane realized, a vast inherited legacy of wisdom and beauty.[112] So-called 'popular' or 'mass culture' (which can be 'absorbed' without intellectual effort and does not require knowledge of the past)[113] is a mechanism of distraction providing easily accessed entertainment.[114] Some commentators have suggested that 'mass' or 'popular culture' might be a system of crowd-control,[115] consisting largely of deliberately manufactured illusions to hide truths. In this respect the superbly choreographed (that is, *designed*) mass-displays of regimented crowds, marching uniformed thousands, standards and flags, searchlights, and responses to shouted assertions in National-Socialist rallies at Nuremberg, or similar events in other totalitarian societies, can also be regarded as manufactured illusions, manipulated certainly, but creating an illusion that they represent the common will. There was an *architectural* input to those rallies too, not least in the buildings conceived as settings for them, but the movements of the masses of people were also *designed*: the manipulation of huge numbers of people through declamation, assertions that sound as though they are based in fact, and the need of human beings to *belong* to and be part of some sort of movement, has uncomfortable parallels with the ways in which Modernism was disseminated.

If such techniques of mass-culture could be used to put over simplistic notions, to whip up emotions (including hatred), to obtain approbation and confirmation of consolidation of power, to gain a perceived legitimacy, they could also be employed to advertise and sell mostly useless commercial products. High culture, true culture, on the other hand, which requires time, patience, intellectual effort, and a degree of receptive sensibility to acquire, is perceived as 'threatening', and it is easy for the demagogue to use his mastery over the crowd to have it shouted down. It would seem that the 'momentum of ignorance, rashness, presumption'[116] gathers speed: the age of the Enlightenment has long passed: that 'of sophisters, oeconomists, and calculators'[117] has succeeded.

No true culture (within which must be included real architecture, as it was perceived by Soane,[118] Vitruvius,[119] Wotton,[120] Wren,[121] and many others), it would appear, can develop except in relation to a knowledge of religion,[122] something that, if mediaeval Europe's achievements are considered, for example, would seem to be beyond question (although 'mediaeval' is another word that is increasingly used as a term of abuse).[123] A 'community of culture', as Eliot called it,[124] had nothing to do with secularism, ascetic retreatism, or cosmopolitanism (which sounds very much like the International Style in architecture), and held within it a realization that culture is that which actually makes life worth living.[125]

Popular 'culture', however, largely depends on *spectacle*, often veering towards the pornographic:[126] even that *soixante-huitard* guru, Guy Debord, produced a critique of the 'Society of the Spectacle',[127] while Lipovetsky and Serroy have demonstrated that the products churned out in modern consumerist societies have little to do with use, but are all about appearance, image, and sensation, advertised just long enough to attract purchasers in droves[128] until superseded by different illusions.[129] Indeed, Lipovetsky and Serroy have written of a 'disorientated society' and of a global non-culture dealing in representation, brand-names rather than objects, and seductive imagery concerned only with commercial gain.[130] And architecture, from which any understanding of history (an understanding which Soane deemed essential for any architect of worth)[131] and the importance of religion *in* history[132] has been abstracted, is hugely diminished by the phenomena of image, sensationalism, and the seeking after anything that could be described by that overused and foolish word, 'iconic'.

It is interesting that many of the recent, deeply-thought, and sensitive warnings about the destruction and corruption of values in society have come from Latin America, where some elements of an old culture or cultures still precariously survive, despite attempts to swamp them with consumerist bling. The Peruvian writer Mario Vargas Llosa amplified the work of T.S. Eliot as set out in the latter's *Notes Towards a Definition of Culture*, originally published in a post-war world not then defined by television or the internet.[133] Vargas Llosa[134] held that 'high culture' involves *judgements* that should equip humankind, confident and sure of where it stands, to discard what are merely fashionable 'popular' (but actually imposed on the public) ephemera in favour of those values that inform great art, and regretted that relativism, levelling, and the spectacle have replaced analytical thought. High culture is not just an 'epiphenomenon of social and domestic life, but an autonomous' *reality* in which 'ideas, aesthetic values, and works of art and literature' connect with the 'rest of social existence', and are not just 'reflections', but the very *sources* of economic, political, religious, and social phenomena.[135] The problem, as Vargas Llosa recognized, is that judgements themselves have become unacceptable: exhortations *not* to be 'judgemental' have become commonplace, presumably because they involve *discrimination*, and that is not allowed either. Humankind is becoming conditioned to accept without question what is advertised: the widespread acceptance of 'iconic' buildings by 'star' architects, promoted in glossy pufferies, is a prime example of this tendency.

Deliberate wrecking of the interaction between high culture and the rest of social existence is an almighty disaster that degrades the spirit and perhaps even humanity's capacity to understand itself. Without the ability to comprehend basic truths about morality and beauty, among the many aspects of life that have been corrupted or ignored (or both) by Modernism, working hand-in-glove with commerce and big business, humans are truly lost, adrift in a sea polluted with the flotsam and jetsam of discarded toys promoted by fashion, with nothing to which they can hold fast. High culture has been suppressed, even superseded, by advertising and the mass-media: cultural, intellectual, and political realities have been displaced, corrupted, pushed contemptuously aside. The vulgar spectacle of Pornotopia[136] dictates illusions of reality; and only the moment counts, the *now*, for what is past is consigned to oblivion, and the future is too frightening to be given a thought.

Vargas Llosa called as witness to his profoundly argued case Octavio Paz Lozano, the Mexican writer, with whom he shared a gloomy view of a dying culture, one that I completely share, though it gives me no pleasure so to do. Paz was suspicious, as well he might be, of 'The Spectacle', by which he appears to have meant something akin to the mass witness of pre-Columbian human sacrifice transmuted into public executions and later widespread use of media such as film, television, and the internet to watch extreme violence and killings. 'The Spectacle', therefore, is something intrinsically cruel, for 'spectators' who enjoy it have no memory, lack any conscience, and are incapable of feeling remorse. A society of voyeurs, which is clearly what has evolved in the West, lives for novelty of any sort, provided it is *new* (a little word constantly employed in advertisements): it views exponentially more violent scenes of death and destruction as 'entertainment'. If the society of 'The Spectacle' moves further and further towards lurid, violent, distorted ugliness, even murder, eventually, sated, it will be left with nothing but the boredom of a grotesque surfeit of idolatry: and idolatry, as we learn from a study of religion, is the Great Sin through which even the deities are finally lost to humankind,[137] but to judge from the current state of the West, the *Lares* and *Penates* were sent packing long ago, and our families, homes, and streets are watched over by them no more.

Robert Musil, indeed, suggested that if the human race could dream collectively, it would dream the murderer, Moosbrugger, who occupies a significant place in his gigantic novel, *Der Mann ohne Eigenschaften* (The Man without Qualities). Musil foresaw that what confronts society is what is good, true, and beautiful in reverse, or inverted. The absence of standards by which hideous crimes can be judged underscores that, increasingly, there are no measurements for crime on any scale, and so the evil, the false, and the hideous, universally imposed, become inevitable.[138] Humankind has been detached from the cultural and religious roots of its history,[139] quite deliberately, as those roots are not commercial, to be sold in the market-place: their value is incalculable, and therefore of no value to a society that, arguably, has lost its way. It may well be that the destruction of aesthetic, compassionate, educational, empathetic, ethical, and religious standards, parts of the agenda established in the manifestos of Modernism, has played no small part in the making of Dystopia.

In this context one might consider the 'star-architect' as effectively an idol: it should be remembered that a generation or two ago, and even today (as an article by Anthony Daniels in *Quadrant* eloquently points out),[140] Le Corbusier could do no wrong, and was virtually deified in Modernist architectural circles. Some critics of cultural fetishism warn against idolatry; not to bring us back within any conventional religious fold, but to celebrate those aspects of high culture (such as Classical or Gothic architecture and the formal architectural traditions of the rest of the world) that require serious effort, as Soane stressed in his lectures,[141] in order to understand them. Access to a world of thought, beauty, satisfying aesthetics, ideas, and breadth of knowledge cannot be had without hard work, and that involves analysis and study of the past, too:[142] in other words, the study of history (from which religion cannot be excised).[143] Study opens doors, and leads to further doors that swing open to reveal countless aspects of knowledge: 'popular culture' distracts, and the more ignorant human beings are of those things that make life beautiful, the easier they are to control.[144] There can be far more to life than being a spectator, with delusions that there is nothing else.[145]

Culture, Arnold noted, was about 'acquainting ourselves with the best that has been known and said in the world, and thus with the history of the human spirit'.[146] That history must involve too an understanding of the rôle of religion in history, without which the last two millennia, say, of European history make no sense at all.[147] Culture is certainly not about the Derrida-led 'deconstruction' of works in order to expose 'racist', 'sexist', 'homophobic', 'Eurocentric', and other labels, then writing about such unravelling in obfuscatory language that makes no sense, other than as a manifestation of a widespread repudiation of the spirit of free enquiry and the dethroning of reason, both once central to the Enlightenment.[148] The use of jargon, of course, in the rarefied 'compound' of '*Academe*', ensures the survival of that 'compound' as the habitat of those who set themselves apart, a kind of priesthood of Nihilism.[149] And that 'compound' was certainly set up from the 1920s, from which the high-priests of Modernism issued their manifestos, slogans, assertions, and demands from which reason was indeed dethroned and history and culture expunged.

High culture enshrines, in some aesthetically refined way, many centuries of humankind's experiences: its essence, as history shows, is steeped in religion.[150] One of the obvious problems of 'popular culture' is that it depends on spectacle and fantasy, on products churned out for the pleasure market, ever more outlandish, to distract from realities and truths, and obliterate what remains of any spiritual essence in everyday existence. That which nourishes the inner being has to be earned: it cannot be obtained on tick, or acquired online like a commercial commodity; it comes to console, if at all, through endeavour, humility, and penitence.[151] It also presupposes the acquisition of a basic vocabulary, a language, an understanding, all of which require patient, dedicated study and attention-spans of more than a few seconds: it needs to be understood in context, and that means in terms of history and religion.[152]

Soane emphasized these points at the beginning of the nineteenth century: his views are as relevant today as they were then, and are probably even more urgently necessary to heed.[153] For example, he unequivocally stated that it was essential 'to impress upon the mind of the student in architecture the necessity for close, unremitted, application, or deep, indefatigable, research, and that not a moment must be lost from study, even from earliest youth, by him who is desirous of attaining superior excellence in architecture'.[154] Soane warned that we must not be 'led astray by fashion and caprice, or by a vain and foolish pursuit after novelty and paltry conceits', for the results, often of 'great magnitude', 'objects of admiration at the time', and erected at enormous expense, 'are not subjects for imitation,... reflect no honour on those who raised them, nor will they ever be referred to as standards of taste',[155] remarks that could well be applied to much that is labelled 'iconic' today. Throughout his lectures, Soane refers to principles, appropriate precedents, the necessity of diligent study, and the importance of a coherent language of architecture, embedded in the culture of a healthy society. Architecture, he said, 'speaks a language of its own . . . and above all, a building, like an historical picture, must tell its own tale'.[156]

Communication, as Fanon pointed out, necessitates the use of a certain syntax, a grasp of the morphology of a language, but it requires, above all, a culture in order to support 'the weight of a civilisation'.[157] Unfortunately, the virus of Deconstruction has been highly successful in the dismantling of traditions in art, architecture, literature, and much else of cultural relevance: like a biological virus it partially destroys its host, avoiding complete obliteration, because, if that were to occur, further transmission would cease.[158]

The purpose of humankind is not merely eating, drinking, copulating, and looking for shelter: once material needs are met, other needs become apparent. These vary in each individual, and the more a society is civilized and cultured, the more will individuality be developed. This, of course, is the opposite of what happens in a corporate state or in systems where the individual is subsumed into an amorphous mass based on the questionable notion of the 'common good'. More and more, it seems that the modern State is becoming an exploiter and a robber, demoralizing, even terrorizing, its citizens. Tolstoy fully understood the dangers, and invoked moral and anthropocentric religious principles that could promise a more harmonious future for humankind: he instinctively comprehended that within real art lay paths to happiness and truth, but that political impositions and statutes were by their very nature untruthful.[159]

In Chapter I mention was made of the concept of the ideal city,[160] the longing for order, for harmony, for wholeness, for some sort of construct that might be conducive to a stable society within which culture and art could flourish to enhance the quality of life itself. It would be interesting to look at what might be conceived in terms of such an ideal today. In the past there were those geometrical images produced during the Middle Ages and in the Renaissance period (*see* **Figures 1.1a–1.4c**), but it is difficult to imagine a contemporary equivalent in times of increasing cultural and religious confusion and fragmentation, political correctness, and much else. In an ideal city humankind would be liberated to enhance its own culture and civilization; but if culture and civilization have been fractured and corrupted to such an extent that they no longer have any sense of continuity, and their roots have been grubbed up to create the desert of the *tabula rasa*, it is tricky to perceive how such aspirations might succeed.

Social identity and a healthy common culture give stability as well as the freedom to develop high culture to new plateaux within the social framework, but since there is always a dynamic and daemonic principle in civilization-culture (the Nietzschean Apollonian/Dionysian clash of opposites), there is always an element of risk, in that the stability of the structure could well be upset. Repressive *régimes* are well aware of this, and tend to stultify *or* exploit (within prescribed limits) creativity; but in the second decade of the twenty-first century, by substituting packaging and commercialized fashion for true creativity, the danger of real ideas erupting and threatening the modern state has been considerably minimized. By cheapening art and rendering it insignificant, the greatest enemy of the modern state has been rendered impotent: that has been part of the disastrous legacy of Modernism, the ally of repression, and itself repressive (though this is a contrary view to that expressed by Barr, which became part of Modernist orthodoxy disseminated through MoMA).

Historically, the ideal city gave meaning and sense to the appearance of things, providing inspiration for new ideals: in terms of religion, the ideal city combined the realities of this world and a more metaphysical context, so that the City of God became synonymous with Paradise. An ideal city could become an absolute reality, in essence a symbol of humankind's aspirations in the highest sense of cultural achievement, ordered existence, and moral stature, humane in the fullest sense, both in terms of aesthetics and social function: it might represent harmony and balance relating the whole of the cosmos to the realities of daily urban life. Through that balance and a lack of repressive restraint, it could even represent ethical perfection, the flowering of a whole civilization. Such a city, with its acropolis-forum-market place; its cloister-quiet-area-enclosed spaces; its cathedral-temple-spiritual centre, must, of course, be of a higher order than a mere conglomeration of a mass of people functioning as workers of some kind or another. An ideal city will not have 'slums'; but the answer is not necessarily to clear 'slums' (as the sound, stone-built, handsome Gorbals tenements in Glasgow were errone-ously perceived), but to cleanse them, as Patrick Geddes pointed out,[161] and as a recent rather wonderful book on Homs has reinforced.[162]

Geddes, too, was very much concerned with the beauty and aesthetics of cities in which a multiplicity of activities could flourish, and individuals could carry out many activities of a cultural nature within a harmoniously ordered city, rather like players in a first-class orchestra. Such a city is not stultified in its growth, and must be a living organism: as a living phenom-enon, aesthetic aspects come to the fore, for there is very little ugliness in Nature, where life and death are part of a logical sequence. Cities that are operated on too often, subjected to drastic surgery or constant interference in their natural functions based on theories such as those promoted by Corbusianity, CIAM, and the Athens Charter, will sicken and die, as Jane Jacobs courageously revealed.[163] Far too often, decisions on town and coun-try planning are taken by those who do not like towns: richnesses of the phenomena of town or city life terrify many. The bleeding-off of popula-tions from large urban centres to populate new towns, for example, brings in its wake new problems; but those theories and practices concerning new towns and 'overspill' populations owe much to the horror many founders of town-planning theories felt for large cities. All this is most peculiar since many of the founders of the new-towns movement were at least sympa-thetic to the aims of Socialism, and, according to Socialist theory, a city must provide the essentials for an ideal Communist community, centralized, standardized, and uniform in its social organization.[164]

Some have suggested that the patterns inherent in the layouts of ideal Socialist cities should reflect the unity of 'the people' as a whole and the classlessness of the society inhabiting them: indeed, the qualities of residen-tial areas, and the social composition of those areas, should be everywhere the same. Throughout Eastern Europe, we were told, thousands of hectares/ acres were covered in urban complexes to house people, and these were genuine new cities, constructed on previously virgin sites, representing the

Utopia of urban planning in socialist design.[165] If this had been the case, it should have been a compulsory requirement that every student of town planning should visit such Socialist Utopias: I did indeed see several of them, and came to the conclusion that they had many similar problems to those becoming all too apparent in the West, not least in the British Isles.

While there was a tendency among many to believe that political ideology was the essential factor in town planning, it is clear that the relationship between the ideal and its realization was only tenuous, and that what resulted was not only violently hated (thereby sparking outbreaks of extreme, but understandable, vandalism), but often had to be demolished long before costs of construction had been paid off.[166] Modernist-based experiments of the interwar years, and their widespread imposition after 1945 did not produce a glorious Utopia, nor can it be claimed that they transcended anything far worse than mediocrity. The annihilation of historic cities and whole districts, based on those intellectual dissolvents and vaporous outpourings of Modernism (that twilit world of abstractions, all about 'making humanity better', but actually driving it mad), was a crime against civilization, a policy of wanton destruction swallowed whole by adolescents of all ages.

It is submitted that at least part of the problem that led to this state of affairs was the gaping hole in the heart of a dogmatic and dictatorial Modernism: the jettisoning not only of rich and wonderful architectural languages capable of infinite variations of expression (a huge part of the culture of the West), but of any transcendental spiritual aspirations whatsoever.[167] The movement established a supposedly irrefutable orthodoxy from which no aspiring architect could deviate, and then stepped back, blamed everyone else for the awful consequences of the Dystopian reality for which it had been responsible, or even brazenly denied there was ever any problem at all. It could be argued that the one essential element Modernists could never adopt was freedom:[168] from the very start, the cult demanded total obedience and belief in a reductionist scheme of things from which beauty was for ever excluded.

Perhaps the Psalmist was right after all.[169]

A Pessimistic Future?

The combative journalist Martin Pawley[170] had an apocalyptic vision of an urban future that was arguably the inevitable outcome of the Modernism he had once so ardently espoused. Rejecting conservation, Post-Modernism, tradition, and deriding 'sustainable' architecture as 'utterly meaningless', he was impatient with those who did not eagerly embrace with evangelical fervour his limited concept of modern technology. He forecast a time when drugs, pornography (as opposed to eroticism), and 'virtual reality' would replace social intercourse; all public infrastructures lay in ruins; and the doped populace inhabited minimalist single-person pods with hologram interiors. He could be said to have laid claim to the mantle of Banham[171] by entitling one of his books *Theory and Design in the Second Machine Age*;[172] however, his vision of the future discarded Banham's misplaced optimism[173] and admiration for such publications as *Playboy*.[174] Yet what does it matter, it might be asked, when enormous numbers of people seem oblivious to their surroundings? They simply do not notice, and anyway are too absorbed with their mobile phones to bother with urban scenery. Their reality exists somewhere else. I think it does matter: ugliness, incessant noise, inhumane surroundings cut off from contact with Nature, a disagreeable and dangerous habitat, and a throwaway society based on advertising and spectacle are inimical to the human spirit, devaluing life and blunting sensibilities.

A very large part of the population appears to be disaffected, and that part does not inhabit pretty villages, charming market-towns, salubrious suburbs, or gracious Georgian streets and squares: it is stuck with what might be described as 'bog-standard Britain',[175] much of it created in the last seventy-odd years by devotees of the Modern Movement and of Corbusianity. We now have a huge problem of how to house the population in places where they would actually want to live, for disaffection will turn very ugly if something is not done soon. Edmund Burke, in his *Reflections on the Revolution in France*, observed that to 'make us love our country, our country ought to be lovely':[176] well, our country is increasingly ugly, and as Dystopia grows ever larger and less agreeable, nettles will have to be grasped, or something very unpleasant will occur. On a clear day, if one flies over parts of these islands, the experience can be depressing, for the amount of land taken by huge sheds and 'out-of-town shopping centres' is staggering. Huge car-parks and monstrous shelters in which goods are sold take up immense amounts of land, yet are devoid of any architectural qualities whatsoever; they blight the countryside; no attempt is made to soften their impact; and their deadly banality drags down the spirits of at least one observer into Stygian depths of profound gloom. However, many of these places are themselves becoming outdated as more and more people shop online, and that, in turn, will mean more dereliction, more Dystopian landscapes, more waste.

If vehicles, access-roads, and car-parks were placed underground, leaving the ground-level free for human beings, with access to shops, amenities, *and streets*, with housing over the shops arranged not as high-rise towers but as two- or three-storey constructions, land-wastage would be drastically reduced,[177] but such an approach, being expensive, would not suit those in search of the quickest short-term profit. However, short-termism and making money should not be the prime motivations for dealing with scarce resources, conspicuous waste, and a distressed environment. Furthermore, there are massive amounts of potential living-accommodation lying empty above existing business-premises, including shops, which, with a complete and sane overhaul of fiscal arrangements, could be brought into use as such. Wrecking yet more countryside should not be an option: what is needed is to make far more sensible use of that which is already wastefully developed or underused. In the past, it was possible to design and build agreeable streets, squares, alleys, towns, parks, and so on: if a failed, profligately wasteful Modernism based on false premises were to be abandoned, and in its place every effort made to create civilized environments that actually work as architecture and urban space, rather than wasting time, resources, and energy in the pursuit of a chimaera, this could be done again.[178]

Much ink has been spilled over 'Northern Power-Houses' and similar slogans, none of which carries great conviction, and all are flavoured with short-termism. However, a journey today along the Manchester Ship Canal (1885–94—designed by Sir Edward Leader Williams,[179] assisted by W.H. Hunter,[180] with James Abernethy[181] as consultant engineer) from the River Mersey near Birkenhead to Manchester reveals not only massive dereliction, but a huge wasted resource providing a great opportunity for imaginative development. The Canal (if deepened and widened) cries out to be considered as the spine of a vast linear city, linking Birkenhead and Manchester: the expanded waterway would be properly embanked and connected to a comprehensive linear public rapid-transport system. Short rib-like developments of self-contained neighbourhoods for housing would have all amenities, workshops, and places offering employment within walking distance of the transport-spine (the waterway would be used for transport as well as for recreation). This linear city (constructed rather like the spine of a fish with the ribs the connecting links from neighbourhoods to the main transport spine) would be about 300 metres wide on each side of the 'spine' (600 metres wide *in toto*), and about 36 miles (just over 57 kilometres) long. It would link Birkenhead, Bebington, Ellesmere Port, Runcorn, the Waltons near Warrington, Warburton, Partington, Irlam, Eccles, and Salford, and thereby connect with the great conurbations of Liverpool and Manchester, bringing new life to derelict lands, creating housing for huge numbers of people, providing employment for decades to come, and hugely improving the economies of a large swathe of the north-west of England. Arturo Soria y Mata proposed (1882) a *Ciudad Lineal*, a low-density linear city outside Madrid with as its 'spine' a tramway system.[182] The Ship-Canal proposal would be on a much larger scale, with high-density housing (which does *not* mean high-rise), each 'rib' being not a dormitory, but a proper neighbourhood, with shops, pubs, and other facilities (including employment), all within easy reach of the main transport 'spine' which would offer tracked fast transport as well as local tramways and water-transport. Segregated cycle-routes would also be provided. Scope for other places of employment, such as large storage-sheds, places for the manufacture of artefacts, warehouses, etc., would also be within easy access of the main 'spine'. There are sensitive architects who could realize that vision, if given the chance to do so, as part of a long-term project far-removed from the usual political short-termism which has been a familiar and disastrous factor in preventing real reforms from being made and solutions found.[183] To succeed, of course, the linear-canal city would require enlightened patronage to resist pressures from commercial developers and their architectural mercenaries.

It is difficult not to glimpse, in the adulation of obscenely expensive 'iconic' buildings that look deliberately unstable, yet another ugly facet of the violence, cruelty, and inhumanity of neoliberalism, the ideology of which seems to be intent on privatizing everything and selling anything that is publicly owned, widening the gap between the haves and the have-nots to an unbridgeable, unimaginable size, and imposing austerity on everyone who is an easy target. Architectural journals have long publicized the 'iconic' erections of so-called 'star' architects, but there are recent indications that some courageous writers are starting to express doubts.[184] Most people are not concerned with such hubristic structures: they experience everyday architecture (hospitals, housing, public spaces, schools—the sort of buildings and places, in short, where ordinary people spend most of their time), much of which is very poor in terms of design, detail, quality, and longevity. In 2016, however, an architect, enthusiast of Parametricism,[185] in a lecture, appears to have advocated building over 80 per cent of London's Hyde Park and moving all 'free-riding' social-housing tenants out from central areas to make way for 'more productive' residents, such as members of his staff, or foreign investors who, even though they might only live there for short periods, would bring with them 'multiplying events'. Such attitudes are common among the creators of flashy, expensive 'icons': they seem to only value wealth and success, to encourage the privatization of public spaces, and aim to push the poor out of sight. The yawning gap between their aspirations and those of the mass of humanity is not merely economic: it is a void empty of emotion, empathy, and basic human compassion. The social 'cleansing' of central London in order to sell it to the international *élite* is a betrayal of basic decency and of what used to be our national values.[186] It seems that the long-term needs of the people are being sold out to investors and grasping commercial developers, no matter where the money for such purchases originates. It is difficult not to regard architects who serve such investors and developers, not as the 'stars' they are misnamed by the media, but as opportunists thriving in an atmosphere of deeply-rooted ethical decay.

So what happened that architects turned away from the kind of social concerns with which they had been involved in the aftermath of the 1939–45 war? First of all, their record in providing architecture that worked as architecture was unconvincing, and far too many of their creations failed and had to be demolished: so the all-powerful local-authority architect's office was wound down, and privatization took over. Factional dissent on the political 'left' led to the disintegration of the consensus, and eventually to the fall from grace of much of the welfare-state in favour of increasing privatization. Now the inequalities between the ostentatiously very rich and the extremely poor are ever-wider, and housing for the masses is even more dire.[187] Political means have long existed, supposedly for the 'common good', to remove whole populations from thriving areas of cities in order to benefit the rich, commercial developers, and their tame architects, and further disadvantage the less well-off. All legislative interference in the market, however, has knock-on effects: the problem is, are those understood at the start? It would seem not.

When even the Governor of the Bank of England has acknowledged that globalization is 'associated with low wages, insecure employment, stateless corporations, and striking inequalities',[188] it is perhaps time to sit up and take notice. Much-vaunted free trade has undoubtedly hurt the poor, but it has also promoted rootless internationalism, not least in the promotion of 'iconic' works by 'star' architects. There is something very wrong with such

value-systems: they suggest that a destructive virus of relativism and
Deconstruction has infected rational thinking, endangering everything that
remains of high culture.[189]

As Economism assumes an ever greater role, architectural heritage, conservation areas, and the Green Belt (so successful in resisting the sprawl of
suburbia until now) are under threat, and even stretches of coastline are
surrendered to the sea. The conservation movement itself looks unlikely to
be able to resist what has been called the 'suck and drag'[190] of money, increasingly perceived as the only real virtue. When 'biodiversity', 'sustainable
development', 'ecosystems', and other terms have been adopted by interests
(selectively picking terms from science, paying lip-service to them, then
misapplying them) which discount 'beauty' (a word that seems to have vanished from official discourse), and bureaucrats and committees increasingly
avoid the awkward task of making aesthetic choices, being entirely at the
mercy of Economism and afraid of being 'judgemental', the fact that technical
solutions are not answers to cultural questions posits a grim future, one in
which Dystopia will triumph.[191]

There are, however, a few signs that the certainties of 'progress' towards a
completely Modernist future are at least being questioned by a few.[192]

Royal Intervention

By the early 1980s, the kind of language employed in architectural 'debate'
under Modernism became more arcane than ever, and the public, ever more
alienated, could not engage. Employed as a means of identifying with bodies
that award prestige and grants, obfuscatory jargon also sets groups apart
from ordinary people: it provides a useful shield from criticism and those
outside the 'compound', as Wolfe termed it.[193] It conceals that which is
empty and fraudulent. Someone in a privileged position, well-advised by
several thinkers (including Theo Crosby, a Modernist apostate who had
awakened to his earlier errors),[194] perceived this, grasped its import, and
acted upon it.

H.R.H. The Prince of Wales greatly increased public awareness of the built
environment, and his interventions and pronouncements,[195] though deeply
resented by the architectural Establishment and others, stimulated public
debate about the character of buildings and cities (something Modernists
discouraged by means of the twin weapons of arcane language and dogmatic

assertion). His pleas for humanity in architecture began to strike chords, and he led by example through a series of pioneering initiatives, such as his School of Traditional Crafts in East London, and the Poundbury development outside Dorchester in Dorset. He has carefully outlined ten principles for sustainable urban growth that value and take into account the best aspects of tradition in architecture, planning, responses to context (including Nature), and materials used in buildings.
These are:

the need for developments to respect the land and the landscape, responding to the setting rather than destroying it;
    the recognition that architecture, to mean anything, has to have a coherent language, avoiding dissonance and confusion (Deconstructivism and Parametricism would not fit the bill here);
    the scale of buildings should relate to human beings and to the scale of buildings and other elements in the context of where they are to be erected;
    new work should be harmonious, diverse, yet coherent, with great attention to sensitive detailing;
    enclosures should be well designed, perhaps surrounded by fine architecture (as in, say, the Georgian square);[196]
    local building-materials and regional details should be used in new work;

    excessive confusing signage, overhead wires, and other clutter should be discouraged;
    human beings as pedestrians should be at the centre of the design process, and streets should be diverse and interesting, reclaimed from the motor-car;
    densities should be high, but not high-rise, for many places developed by the Georgians and early Victorians have very high population-densities and great diversity, yet are desirable places to live, architecturally interesting, and in parts very beautiful;

and finally

the rigidities of planning should be avoided, especially the destructive demands of road-engineers, and flexibility should be all, for there are many ways of doing things without applying one blanket solution.[197]

These not unreasonable objectives are the antitheses of just about everything advocated by the gloomy apparatchiks of CIAM, the MARS Group, the Athens Charter, Corbusianity's myriad brainwashed disciples, and Modernist orthodoxy. The Prince's concerns were not to repeat the mistakes of the past, but to look to the future. Aware of the fact that, barring a cataclysm, by the middle of the twenty-first century there will be another three billion people on the planet needing to be housed, fed, schooled, etc., humankind must create truly sustainable urban environments that respect human scale, that do not waste land with the usual profligacy, that use low-carbon materials, and that are not dependent on the private motor-car. The last things needed are Deconstructivist or Parametricist 'icons'.

Much of the architecture in the Prince's brave experiment at Poundbury has been denounced as 'pastiche'.[198] In no sense was the term pejorative until Modernists imagined it was: it actually suggests compositions incorporating allusions to many things, often handled with considerable originality. Philip Johnson even described himself as a *pasticheur*,[199] another barb which annoyed Modernist critics. Thus Poundbury follows a long and honourable tradition in architecture, one followed during the Hellenistic period, in Imperial Roman times (take the *Villa Adriana* at Tivoli as just one of many examples),[200] during the Renaissance, and especially when eighteenth-century Picturesque eclecticism became widespread, notably in the *jardin anglo-chinois*, where a huge variety of themes and motifs was drawn upon, suggesting open-mindedness and freedom from stylistic restraint, neither of which was a characteristic of the puritanical Modern Movement. The English landscape garden, embellished with *fabriques* in a variety of architectural styles, including Chinese,[201] Greek, 'Gothick',[202] 'Hindoo',[203] Moresque, Mughal, Primitive, Roman, 'Rustick',[204] and much else, was hugely influential all over Europe, and was a source of delight. Its richness triggered ideas, memories, allusions, feelings, thoughts, and those who experienced it were both spectators and themselves added to the composition as they explored its meanings:[205] it was filled with pleasures, which is more than can be said for the bleak, Dystopian, wasteful failures of the Hulmes and Cumbernaulds (to name just two disasters) of Modernism.

The Prince has stressed the need to reconnect with those traditions that have shaped lives, landscapes, and societies over the centuries: in other words he has made pleas to create surroundings with which people can positively connect and with which they can feel comfortable,[206] rather than Modernist Dystopias they hate and attack with violent protest. He has also insisted, like many before him, that we can learn much from Nature through its cycles, processes, and patterns, and that our disconnection from Nature posits very real dangers. Through architecture, human beings can connect with cultural, ecological, and social forces that can actually have an impact on lives: visitors are attracted to great cities like Bath, Kraków, Prague, Venice, and Vienna by the beauties of their architecture.[207]

His Royal Highness noted the coherence of the natural world and the highest achievements of humankind in not only responding to that world, but enhancing it through sensitive design to create beautiful, humane architecture and pleasant, enchanting landscapes. Thus he was able to see clearly the poverty-stricken, inhuman, and alienating aspects of Modernist architecture and planning. One of the main problems is that most architects do not have the background or training to grasp these matters, and fail to see the crucial link with humanity, without which architecture cannot succeed. All that many of them are concerned with is style, which actually means the latest fashion, and that grows ever more remote from human experience.

Government 'initiatives', on the other hand, almost inevitably pay lip-service to the nineteenth century, but display no understanding at all of history. There has been glib talk of new 'Garden Cities' which do not appear to have anything to do with the visions of Ebenezer Howard, because, as far as can be judged, proposals were just for more car-reliant dormitory-suburbs built by the private sector.[208] Another proposal has referred to the Crystal Palace, but it seems to have little to do with Paxton's original; and there are other instances in which nods to worthy Victorian schemes disguise the realities of shoddy, commercial examples of short-termism that will lead to yet more problems in the future. There appears to be no real grasp of the immensity of the difficulties facing the nation or the world, not least that an enormous number of errors will have to be undone and made good: all that appears to matter is flurries of fraudulent activity to create the illusion that something is on the cards before the next election. A long-term official vision for anything connected with the making of agreeable environments and a civilized, humane future for towns and cities does not appear to exist.

The Prince of Wales, however, has attempted to argue[209] for another way forward, and has actually put his own resources into the experiment. As he rightly observed, 'we have to be mindful of the long-term consequences of what we construct in the public realm and, in its design, reclaim our humanity and our connection with Nature'.[210] And our relationship with Nature should be taken seriously, because it is irresponsible to ignore something which gives us so much, and with which we used to be intimately connected. So-called 'star' architects,[211] whose 'iconic' but flaccid erections are becoming more bizarre with each passing year, depend on ever-increasing commercialism to fund their self-indulgent solipsisms, and are as far-removed from Nature as can be imagined.[212] It should not be forgotten that global finance uses the so-called 'star' architects, not least as statements of power and for advertising purposes: those 'iconic' erections are concerned with sensation and fashion, both of which pall quickly. They are light-years away from what is needed to improve the quality of life for everybody.

Coda

So what should be done to improve matters? Schools of architecture should be redeemed by massive restructuring starting from basic principles. Parametricism,[213] Deconstructivism, and reliance on computers to generate ever more bizarre shapes should be ditched, together with all the destructive legacies and dubious claims of the Modern Movement and its apologists. Learning how to really look at buildings by drawing and measuring them, then producing accurate surveys to scale, would not only encourage an understanding of sound building, but would enable students to gain a feeling for how structures are put together with real materials (and how those materials function): such in-depth studies would also begin to inculcate an appreciation of the qualities of real architecture, provided that suitably fine exemplars were selected for measured drawings. The creation of the 'compounds' mentioned earlier has severed students from crafts (as the Modern Movement intended), so they no longer have any sensitivity towards how materials are actually used: concrete, metal, plastics, and glass are universally employed without understanding, on a global scale, with no respect for indigenous traditions or climatic conditions, and tend to look seedy and fail very soon after a building goes up.

   The character of local buildings should be studied, especially in relation to how readily available materials in the area were used in their construction, and that would involve an understanding of craft-skills as well. This would also encourage a realization that existing buildings can be used and adapted for modern use, but this process requires expertise and sensitive responses to surviving fabric, so much more could be done to teach students the value of conserving resources rather than destroying them in order to create the *tabula rasa* that was the goal of Modernists. There should also be fiscal reforms to encourage the reuse and bringing back to life of old buildings, because present tax-systems are actually geared to destroying them, which is yet another demonstration of how the entire structures of legislation and finance are biased in favour of destruction and redevelopment, in other words, in line with Modernist aims.

Design should be based on sound precedents, which is what architecture used to be all about in the past: such precedents should have stood the test of time. The vast resource of pattern-books could provide budding architects with plenty of precedents as well as the basis to understand architectural languages, but it must be emphasized that a knowledge of how materials perform and how they are used is essential to any successful design. That suggests students should actually work with materials and structures in order to understand how buildings are put together and respond to conditions of weather and so on (this was supposed to be a prime concern of the *Bauhaus*, but nothing remotely like it actually occurred). A study of history is essential, as more often than not, new architecture is realized within a context of existing urban fabric or in an established landscape, both of which can be either damaged or enhanced by new building, so an understanding of context is of huge importance to ensure a sensitive response to it. Tendencies to so-called 'originality' involving frenetic 'design' should be discouraged: the lessons of what makes a pleasing townscape or architectural composition should be learned, and that will involve study of established urban fabric, even that which has been damaged by ill-considered changes. Good manners and reticence in design can often prove far more successful than flashy interlopers in an established street.

There are welcome signs among certain students (those unmesmerized by 'star' architects and who are becoming aware of the perils of blindly following fashion) that they are beginning to question orthodoxies, are starting to think outside the confines of the 'compound', and are longing to acquire coherent architectural languages and an understanding of appropriate materials (and how such materials are put together). Unfortunately, they often find themselves being pushed or forced by their tutors into adopting attitudes with which they are not in sympathy, so are obliged to work on their chosen paths in a clandestine manner to acquire the skills needed. In these islands, if they wish to graduate or 'qualify', they have to pretend to adhere to certain Modernist tenets but pursue their real interests in congenial offices, and consult sympathetic professionals as their teachers.[214] Practitioners of what has been called the 'New Urbanism'[215] promote the design of traditional urban blocks, mixed uses, and a coherent, literate architectural language as antidotes to unpleasant, inhumane, threatening, and jangling environments that were the direct result of the work of devotees of CIAM, Le Corbusier,[216] the Athens Charter,[217] and the Modern Movement. Thousands of years of urban history demonstrate that the complex relationships of streets (hated by disciples of Corbusianity), squares, parks, monuments, buildings, etc., not only form means of communication, but help identification and orientation, giving the urban fabric a sense of character and place: the Modern Movement jettisoned all that.

The New Urbanists, including Robert Adam,[218] Andrés Duany,[219] Léon Krier,[220] Elizabeth Plater-Zyberk,[221] Demetri Porphyrios,[222] Aldo Rossi,[223] John Simpson,[224] Gabriele Tagliaventi,[225] and many others, have honourably endeavoured to recover a coherent architectural language in the teeth of Modernist opposition, and have shown that civilized environments can still be created, with care, scholarship, and sensitivity. Their works have been denounced as 'escapist', 'historicist', and 'irrelevant': some would argue that if this is the case, then we need more escapism, historicism, and irrelevancy. If students were trained in the offices of the New Urbanists, perhaps in a modern version of the apprenticeship system, or as 'articled pupils' (which is how architectural training used to function), rather than in the restrictive 'compounds' where so much dangerous brainwashing has resulted in dysfunctional, inhumane, alien Dystopias, there could be some hope for the future.

In the aftermath of the catastrophic fire at the Grenfell tower-block,[226] Kensington & Chelsea (2017), which killed many of those who had lived there, one of the main supporters and indeed promoters of a scheme (1962–9) to erect a late design for an office-tower designed by Mies van der Rohe beside the Mansion House, City of London (a proposal that was not shelved until 1985), Peter (later Lord) Palumbo wrote a powerful letter stating that the 'deficiencies' of the tower-block model 'for lower-income housing go far beyond the problems of cladding. The original planners and architects had good intentions[227] but the road they took has led to a hell of atomised communities and crime-ridden dystopias.' He went on to say 'it is time to revert to a model that is known to work: to terraces and squares whose inhabitants are connected to the ground, to greenery, to life and to other people'.[228] This is a heartening admission from a man who was an ardent supporter of Modernism, and his realization that a blanket CIAM-inspired solution to all architecture and planning has been a great error is both encouraging and brave. In the case of the Grenfell Tower, one of the problems seems to have been the addition of highly flammable cosmetic cladding to the exterior to make what was never beautiful more visually acceptable, with dreadful consequences: the cheap Modernism adopted for public housing was problematic from the very start, and not all the cosmetic cladding in the world can save what has turned out to be a massive error of judgement.

Like it or not, the architecture of insolence realized as buildings has profound effects on its users, and eventually has pitiless moral consequences for those who produce it.[229] Without a complete change of direction in architectural education, those consequences will be inevitable.

X

Epilogue

> In many of the great works in architecture there is a sublimity of thought, a fertility of invention, and a boldness of design, which exalted minds alone could produce...The student...should not only reflect on what he has read in his study but he must, from actual mensurations taken by himself, make finished sketches of such structures as are most valuable; he must closely meditate upon the original purposes for which they were raised; he must consider how far situation and materials influenced the architects of these structures. The mouldings, the ornaments, the most minute details, must not escape his observation...
>
> Sir John Soane (1753–1837): Royal Academy Lectures I and XII, quoted in David John Watkin (1941–): Sir John Soane: Enlightenment Thought and the Royal Academy Lectures (Cambridge: Cambridge University Press in assn. with Sir John Soane's Museum & The Bank of England, 1996) 492, 661–2

> Composition, silhouette, and proportion are disregarded. The great masters of the past felt that something more than this was required of them.
>
> Sir Reginald Theodore Blomfield (1856–1942): Modernismus (London: Macmillan & Co. Ltd, 1934) 11

Loss of Meaning

There is a massive problem connected with the Modernist elimination of information encoded even in the design of surfaces. The insistence on the removal of meaning from the built environment left human beings incapable of relating to it. By banishing ornament, by adopting the fundamentalism of smooth surfaces and simple geometries, the Modern Movement and its authoritarian practitioners[1] affronted many religions by severing the possibilities of individuals to connect with spiritual realms through colour, ornament, calligraphy, and beautiful architecture, thus denying sensory connections.[2] A religious building can convey meaning through just about everything the Modern Movement discarded: Le Corbusier's repetitive published remarks[3] about historical architecture (e.g. Greek Doric temples and Gothic cathedrals)[4] reveal a shallowness of understanding that deserved harsher criticism than the muted objections actually meted out to them, but in recent times some powerful attacks have been mounted against Le Corbusier in particular, not least by Anthony Daniels,[5] and even by some Francophone authors,[6] one of whom has actually had the temerity to spell out *un fascisme Français*,[7] something Corbusian partisans have attempted, with some success, to conceal, but which is now starting to emerge, despite howls of rage from disciples and many Modernists in various states of denial.[8]

Glances at the colour, geometrical patterns, and calligraphy in the great masterpieces of Islamic architecture;[9] at the exquisite sculptures of ancient Greek temples;[10] at the overwhelming beauties of mediaeval ecclesiastical architecture and decoration;[11] at the theatrical, swirling, joyous delirium of the Rococo pilgrimage-churches of South Germany;[12] or at the muscular and inventive detail of the best Victorian Gothic-Revival interiors (Christ the Consoler, Skelton-on-Ure [1871–6],[13] by William Burges,[14] would suffice), will be sufficient to understand that all were connected with religion, and express everything Modernists hated and outlawed. They are linked in various ways with long histories of humankind's nobler aspirations and achievements, and they did not occur by spontaneous combustion, but evolved: they can only be truly appreciated through study and understanding of culture, styles, and history, and that has to include religion for obvious reasons.

Yet Modernist architects adhere fanatically to a fundamentalism that will not permit any expression other than its own. This suggests belief in something other than mere architectural style. All cults are intolerant of any departure from their core orthodoxies. J.M. Richards referred to the 'gospel' of Modernism having its 'prophets' on both sides of the Atlantic once the *Bauhäusler émigrés* gained control of the architectural Establishment in the United States, and deplored the post-war tendencies in Italy for architects to make 'wilful departures from orthodoxy' and 'failure' to give building programmes 'much relationship to social priorities'. With such language Richards admitted the quasi-religious and dogmatic tone of early Modernism.[15]

However, the fundamentalism of Modernism can be seen as akin to religious fundamentalism in many ways, not least in how it reacts to the catastrophic disasters for which it has been responsible: it is impossible not to observe what effect the imposition of CIAM- and Modernist-inspired schemes has had on human society, alienating people from the built environment and severing them from their history and traditions. One might think this would give cause for a rethink, but such a stranglehold the cult of Modernist fundamentalism has had on architecture that the only solution is more of the same, but applied with even greater ferocity. Other writers have seen that the Modern Movement has been a 'religion as irrational as all others...Like all religious cultists, the members of the sect treat their critics with patient condescension: those...who don't know what's good for them; but the cultist, to whom the Truth has been revealed, does know, and...will ram it down the non-believers' throats even if it chokes them.'[16]

The universal embrace of the International Style after 1945 by the Western industrialized countries was held to be an indication of modernity, prosperity, democracy, and, with its pretensions to be rational, 'scientific', and suitable for mass-production, was forced upon more traditional cultures, destroying traditions, and threatening the very fabric of vast areas of the earth. The result is something like a massive reaction, manifested by the embrace of religious fundamentalisms, tribalisms, and suicidal hatred. Lewis Mumford saw the problem clearly in 1962: he wrote that an 'age that worships the machine and seeks only those goods that the machine provides, in ever larger amounts, at ever rising profits, actually has lost contact with reality; and in the next moment or the next generation may translate its general denial of life into one last savage gesture of...extermination.'[17] Mumford, in fact, despite some of his curiously ambivalent, even contradictory, stances, was highly critical of advanced industrial societies, and, thirty years after his involvement in the MoMA exhibition, said that architectural Modernism had disintegrated into sects and mannerisms because architects had adopted a belief in mechanical progress as an end in itself. In this respect he had Le Corbusier firmly in his sights.[18] Much of what Barr, Hitchcock, and Johnson had labelled the 'International Style' was a superficial aesthetic that sought to make buildings *look* as if they respected the machine, no matter what the materials or methods of construction actually were. However, it proclaimed its indifference to actual mechanical or biological functions and, indeed, to human needs. The problem, to Mumford, was that architects of the Modern

Movement had no philosophy that did justice to organic functions, or responded to what human beings actually do or how they live.[19]

Fundamentalist Modernism, far from being the supposed Utopian language of social progress, is increasingly seen in terms of how it affects the host society and as a symbol of huge economic and military power. Much contemporary architecture and interference with established towns under the label of 'renewal' or 'planning' is actually a massive assault on urban fabric, organized established societies, and traditional ways of life. And many manifestations of such phenomena are made possible through vast corporations and business-industrial complexes, but, increasingly, as such corporations and complexes claim to be associated with 'progress' and are inimical to individuals and groups (labelled, of course, anti-progressive, Luddite, or backward) that oppose their aims, so the educational processes that give rise to such alleged 'progress' should be subjected to critical assessment.

The Failure of Architectural Education

In 1934, Sir Reginald Blomfield observed a great truth. His remarks are worth repeating here:

> the less one's mind is stored with knowledge of antiquity, the better the prospects of the New Architecture. Thus a mind quite empty of such knowledge will be all the more ready to accept any form that presents itself...the mind of the designer...will have to be passive and receptive, waiting for the impress of purely external conditions....architecture will be a very easy affair, because the design will come of itself, and the long years of critical study...will be dispensed with as a mischievous waste of time....thoughtless and badly trained students are already adopting this ridiculous view as a convenient short-cut to the practice of Modernist architecture.[20]

By jettisoning 'long years of critical study', together with any knowledge of historical architecture, Modernist pedagogues held up the possibility of instant gratification (without having to acquire any knowledge or skills)[21] to new recruits attracted by fairy-stories concerning the 'creative genius' of the almighty architect. Students were indoctrinated, and instead of studying and absorbing the treasure of a huge reservoir of knowledge concerning buildings, structural techniques, materials, and architecture, they had to bow to, and swear allegiance to, the new cult of Modernist 'architecture'.[22] A core belief of Modernism was and is the destruction of all old buildings apart from a handful deemed to be worthy of retention, usually for questionable reasons. Conservation of resources had no place in Modernist theory.

Friedensreich Hundertwasser had no doubts where the fault lay in creating cities which were 'the concretisation of the hare-brained ideas of criminal architects'... 'without feelings or emotions, dictatorial, heartless, aggressive, flat, sterile, unadorned, cold and unromantic, anonymous and yawning emptiness', all an 'hallucination of functionality':[23] he laid the blame very firmly on doctrinaire Modernists. The *Bauhaus* mentality, he wrote, 'destroyed the world we dwell in',[24] yet its 'soulless dogma' was still being taught in architectural schools, 'against reason, beauty, nature',[25] and humankind. He pointed out that humans are 'misused' for 'perverse, dogmatic, educational, architectural experiments... Young architects who still have dreams of a more beautiful and better world in their heads', get those dreams 'taken away from them by force' or else they do not receive their qualifications.[26] 'Thus, only architects who have been brought into line become certified and so have the right to build.'[27] He was to add that 'today's architecture is criminally sterile' and that the 'architect as we know him today is only entitled to construct uninhabitable architecture'.[28]

Indoctrination started with damaging a student's self-esteem and confidence: humiliation was used, notably at 'crits' (criticisms and grading by tutors and guest architects of work displayed by students in sessions attended by fellow-students),[29] when anyone even hinting at the sensual possibilities of colour, ornament, surface treatments, and forms[30] was criticized for committing 'a criminal act',[31] because the deified prophet, Le Corbusier, had proclaimed that decoration was 'of a sensorial and elementary order, as is colour, and is suited to simple races, peasants and savages... the peasant loves ornament and decorates his walls... decoration is the essential overplus, the quantum of the peasant'.[32] So any suggestion of decoration, colour, ornament, or delight had to be eschewed:[33] to conform to and accept without question Modernist positions became compulsory; feelings of guilt were sown in the minds of those who questioned such orthodoxy;[34] and then solutions were offered to assuage that guilt.[35]

Those 'solutions' included prodding students to use alien forms and employ crude surfaces (like raw concrete, which ordinary members of the public hated, but adherents of the cult insisted was 'honest' and 'true', and therefore somehow 'pure', 'untainted', and 'moral'),[36] and of course 'study' (i.e. look at the pictures of) buildings by Corbusier, Mies, and other deities acceptable to the cult. Today, the generation of Modernists that rose to prominence in the 1920s is being eclipsed by later fashionable figures, all of whom claim to be Modernists taking the approved anti-Historicist line. Attending a 'crit' nowadays can be as alarmingly dispiriting as it ever was, for projects far too often seem to have no connection with the real world at all: context, people, places, and scale are all ignored as students retreat into fantasies where distorted forms are *de rigueur*, and spider-webs of mechanically drawn lines serve to create a pea-souper of a fog that hides the uncomfortable suspicion that the visuals are there to conceal an absence of thought.

In Chapter II dealing with the *Bauhaus*, it was pointed out that new students arriving at that establishment were indoctrinated to reinvent the wheel,[37] for every design had to start from scratch, and psychological conditioning was used to destroy every preconception.[38] Salingaros put it very well when he described this process as a rewiring of 'the students' neuronal circuits'.[39] Furthermore, students' 'projects', produced in 'studios', were largely graded on the basis of how closely they resembled whatever 'architecture' illustrated in the magazines was currently fashionable. Despite the supposed abolition of 'style', students who did not conform to stylistic dogma were cast into outer darkness.[40] I can confirm this, for my own time in schools of architecture was a revelation: it left me wholly unprepared for the real world, designing real buildings. That experience was by no means unique, for others have come to similar conclusions concerning their own inadequate 'education' and the tactics used by tutors (often reinforced by their fellow-students anxious to ingratiate themselves with the tutors) to enforce conformity on pain of rejection and ultimate failure.[41] Any real knowledge of what architecture actually was and can be was painfully acquired by a process of self-education.

In architectural education when Modernism was embraced, a 'class of critics... offered initiation into' the Modernist cult,[42] and began to promote 'the incomprehensible and the outrageous',[43] repudiating beauty and discarding any chance of redemption by acts of wilful desecration. This is the antithesis of what certain Modernists, such as T.S. Eliot or Arnold Schönberg, saw as their task: not to *break* with tradition, but to *renew* it, linking it with a long *cultural history* of creativity.[44] A break, they saw, would lead to empty, mechanical, repetitious *clichés* (which is exactly what International-Modern architecture actually became), and sought to protect a battered aesthetic ideal from the corrosive influence of 'popular' culture, conserving it as an essential element of the spiritual side of human aspirations.[45] To Eliot,

Schönberg, and other genuinely creative people, beauty was held to be a manifestation of transcendent values, and hence had a religious dimension denied by so many advocates of architectural Modernism, who not only ignored, but fled from any attempt to consider what might be beautiful, and indeed set out to despoil it in terrible acts of aesthetic iconoclasm. Beauty could not be discerned among the scenes of desecration created by Modernist practitioners in the aesthetically indefensible housing-estates denounced by *The Architectural Review* in 1967,[46] for beauty, that rare and tender thing, whispers humility, and entreats us to respect the world and the best endeavours of humankind.[47]

In the curious 'compound' of Modern architecture, however, critics and certain practitioners became adept at using a rarefied, somewhat cloudy language, which many confused with profundity, but then cults invent their own liturgies, ambitious claims, and opaque language, designed to veil rather than illuminate, or perhaps, by obfuscation, to suggest a depth of meaning that in truth is absent. The crabbed texts of Modernism deserve to be analysed and unpicked: readers with telluric tastes are capable of doing so. One could wish that critiques of Modernism could delve deeper and hit a few targets squarely where deserved, but at least they have started to appear,[48] even if rather more restrained in their approaches than one might have wished. Relativism can be unhealthy. However, as noted earlier, in 2011 *The Architectural Review* launched a new series entitled 'The Big Rethink', which began to question the works of so-called 'star-architects' and their expensive 'iconic' buildings, and indeed to look at the whole sorry mess that architecture had become, including architectural education, the discarding of history, and much else. It was not before time, but it should be remembered that the *Review* had promoted Modernism in the past, and so this represented a complete *volte-face*. It was a belated admission that something had gone seriously awry, and the beginnings of an attempt to explore possible remedies for a problem that had been avoided for far too long.

The warnings were there, long before the 1939–45 war. Blomfield observed that the 'young lions' in architectural schools imagined they were 'starting a new manner of their own', and kept 'assuring each other and the public' that this was so, 'in order... to prevent any misgivings in themselves'. They considered that 'the past' had 'no meaning for them', so students looked to 'contemporary work as illustrated' in the journals 'for their inspiration: armed with the time-honoured ruling... that "knowledge hampers originality" they' started on their 'architectural careers, unimpeded by any knowledge of the past',[49] so that their aim was to be purveyors of 'thrills for the onlooker'.[50] What impressed Blomfield most in these 'struggles for something new' was 'not their originality' at all, 'but their immodesty',[51] and he went on to observe that the 'deliberate search after originality is utterly futile',[52] something Loos had said earlier, and he was not the only one. T.S. Eliot noted that the 'poem which is absolutely original is absolutely bad; it is, in the bad sense, "subjective" with no relation to the world to which it appeals'.[53]

There was a time when students of architecture were required to survey buildings of quality and prepare measured drawings based on the surveys. Structures selected for such investigations were usually (but not always) Classical (either eighteenth- or early nineteenth-century exemplars) or mediaeval Gothic (usually churches, but sometimes collegiate or domestic survivals), and drawings and notes were subjected to close scrutiny, criticized, and then graded. This discipline proved invaluable, instilling a healthy respect for the complexities, subtleties, and qualities of historical architecture: it obliged students to look at buildings with care, and understand them and the materials of which they were made. It was only by such close examination that detailed knowledge could be acquired of proportional systems, relationships of parts, axial planning, mouldings, how junctions are formed in a satisfactory manner, and, above all, how materials were used and put together in a building, especially dressings around openings such as windows or doors, where the materials often differed from those used in expanses of wall.

Such study revealed how a moulded skirting stopped at a block above which an architrave rose; how a band of mouldings joined another band at right angles to it; how the features of a room (e.g. fire-surrounds, windows, doors, and bays) related to each other by means of main and subsidiary axes; how subtle, recessed bands or planted beads could not only disguise joints, but helped objects to look pleasing by their logical positioning and the resulting subdivision of planes; how plinths, pedestals, rails, and cornices divided and finished the designs of walls; how pilasters, *antae*, or buttresses could break up a long wall into a series of parts and relate to the design of entablatures, ceiling-compartments, and the geometries of floor-finishes; how to treat a corner (inside and out); how the structural aspects of holes in walls such as those required for windows and doors are expressed in design, and how the treatment of a doorway might signal its significance and meaning; and a great deal more.[54] In other words, an understanding of the ways in which a building was constructed was encouraged by such detailed hands-on study at close proximity to the fabric, reinforced by having to draw it to scale with accuracy and sensitivity.[55]

The student would discover a rich alphabet to start with, then a vocabulary, and then a whole language capable of infinitely adaptable use, enabling him or her to look at buildings with informed eyes, and making visits to fine cities, towns, and works of architecture all the more enjoyable and instructive. Furthermore, armed with such a language, an architect did not have to stick pedantically to dull copyism. Skilled designers such as Karl Friedrich Schinkel, Leo von Klenze, Sir John Soane, or Alexander 'Greek' Thomson (all of whom were thoroughly immersed in architectural languages [and fluent in their uses too]) could employ them as springboards for adaptability, invention, and creativity, all in the service of making architecture that uplifted, delighted, and worked, not just 'functionally', but as architecture with profound resonances and meanings, which is what real architecture is about. Those languages with which they were acquainted gave them the means by which they could actually design with fecund invention and skill, drawing on true expertise and deep learning, to make buildings that were actually fresh, truly original, and which really functioned as architecture.

From the 1940s and 1950s, however, architectural students were required to 'design' in the manner that had become *de rigueur* after 1945: this eschewed all 'historical' references, although it was perfectly all right, indeed encouraged, to crib bits from cunningly composed illustrations of works by Le Corbusier, Mies van der Rohe, Walter Gropius, and others currently fashionable. Students were required to produce drawings that complied with talk of 'building for our own time', the 'poetry of concrete', the 'honest expression of structure', and other doleful matters.[56]

Yet not only was the favoured style promoted in schools of architecture arguably not architecture at all, because it had no vocabulary, grammar, syntax, serenity, repose, quality, or beauty, but it was extraordinarily easy to produce, and required the minimum of effort in terms of thought, analysis, or draughtsmanship. Classical, Gothic, Romanesque, Arts-and-Crafts, and all other exemplars provided by historical architecture of all periods and cultures (including local vernacular buildings around the world) required patient study, practice, understanding, knowledge of sources, familiarity with how materials were put together and how they functioned, scholarship, and thought. It was far too difficult for people who wanted the easy way out, who did not care for the environment or about the past, or how human beings adapted their buildings to that environment.[57]

When I was an undergraduate, it was fashionable among those of an iconoclastic disposition (that is, those who had absorbed uncritically the tenets of Modernism) to express the desire to destroy all old buildings, especially cathedrals, churches, museums, country-houses, and all works of architecture with Classical porticoes because they were either 'irrelevant' or 'intimidating'. Capitals on columns, pilasters, and piers, of course, were '*élitist*' and had to be eschewed.[58] The iconoclasts preferred to copy the latest *clichés* from pictures in one of the 'architectural' magazines to expending any effort on learning about what real architecture might possibly be.[59] Thus high culture was betrayed.

A great language capable of infinite variety of expression, a mighty and expansive vocabulary, a vast resource based on two and a half millennia or more of civilization (codified and made available in hundreds of admirably illustrated pattern-books that enabled ordinary builders and architects of only moderate talent to create streets and buildings that harmonized with each other), was superseded by a series of monosyllabic grunts, foisted on the populace with a totalitarian disregard for the opinions of those who had not been drilled to conform. Vitruvius, Alberti, Palladio, and all the other distinguished architectural writers were jettisoned, backed by spurious claims of 'rationality', 'scientific methodology', and 'objectivity', none of which was discernible in most realized Modernist architecture.[60] The quality of the buildings created as a result of the fashions of the 1940s through to the present is on view virtually everywhere: it has been weighed, and for the most part, has been found wanting (*see* **jacket illustration and Frontispiece**). Some very large and outrageously expensive structures, 'designed' without the slightest regard for quality or how they would actually perform, and hated by those forced to inhabit them or look at them, have been demolished, long before their construction costs were paid off, while others have been unconvincingly dressed up in different garb (some of which has proved to be lethally inflammable, as certain events in Kensington and Chelsea demonstrated in 2017) in vain attempts to make them more visually acceptable.[61]

In contrast, the Georgian street or square was not only an economical use of land but provided an environment greatly superior to anything produced in recent times. There is confusion, however, about whether or not society actually likes towns or cities (another unattractive legacy of the Morris–Ruskin axis and their hangers-on), yet most people actually live in them.

Much contemporary 'architecture' seems to be conceived on the premiss that it has no neighbours, and 'designed' in a vacuum, as though in a desert, or somewhere where there is an infinite amount of spare land, which is patently not the case. Fitting in, designing with sensitivity to surroundings, 'keeping in keeping',[62] if not actively discouraged, are clearly not high on the agenda in schools of architecture, where Modernists have always oafishly *insisted* that any addition to existing fabric should be 'frankly of our day and age'.[63] The Georgian street and square were composed of harmonious units, not shouting for 'originality',[64] but conforming to certain patterns, proportions, use of materials, and a coherent architectural language. Such exemplars were greatly superior to the kind of thing produced after architectural education became a supposedly 'academic' subject, with degrees given to mark each hurdle jumped. Another problem is the attempt to pretend, as Modernists most certainly did, that architecture is a 'rational', 'scientific' subject: by adopting jargon and aping the sciences without any understanding of true scientific thinking, architectural education has actually rejected real scientific models.[65] Architecture, as Philip Johnson and many others have pointed out in no uncertain terms, is an art.[66]

Blomfield, perceptive as always, identified some glaring difficulties. He knew that the 'New Architecture' had become a 'stunt': the movement was 'based on a confusion of the functions of the architect and engineer, and on a narrow formula' of the fulfilment of purpose in architecture which 'excluded that aesthetic gratification that had been one of its essential qualities since the earliest dawn of civilisation. Moreover, owing to the deliberate neglect of the study of the past, the range of imagination and inventive ability' in the 'New Architecture' was 'extremely restricted...in some...architectural schools the fatal mistake' was made of 'discouraging the study of any but contemporary architecture...Students were thrown headlong into the *mêlée* without any independent standard of judgment', and 'with a wholly inadequate architectural vocabulary'. He compared this sorry state of affairs with the plight of someone 'set to write a serious book with only the most rudimentary knowledge of the resources of the language'[67] he had to use, and cited the concerns of the Classical scholar John William Mackail, expressed in his celebrated lecture on Virgil: Mackail held that in times of rapid and chaotic change it was essential to have a standard of quality.[68] That need is more pressing than ever today.

So there were criticisms of architectural education long before the 1939–45 war; but in 1958 the outcome of the RIBA Oxford Conference of Architectural Education was that the subject was 'intellectually underdeveloped'[69] compared with other professions, and that this, according to protagonists such as Richard Llewellyn Davies, could only be remedied by interdisciplinary systematic research and a supposedly rationalist 'scientific' Modernism. This argument, 'a typical fantasy of the rationalist, scientific version'[70] of Modernism, 'of which Llewellyn Davies was one of the high priests',[71] soon gained credence within 'government circles',[72] and Llewellyn Davies's was a leading voice in the transformation of architectural education from a *Beaux-Arts* approach to one derived from the model 'developed' by Gropius at the *Bauhaus* in the 1920s and later established by German *émigrés* in well-funded American universities. The results have not been universally admired. Llewellyn Davies's 'interdisciplinary research', embrace of a supposedly 'scientific' Modernism (its connection with real science was, at the very best, only tenuous), and jettisoning of history ensured a narrowness and shallowness of education that did architecture a huge disservice. His own limited view ensured that what was actually built as a result of his influence lacked any 'clear aesthetic' whatsoever:[73] as his obituarist wryly noted, in an inversion of the famous inscription[74] on Sir Christopher Wren's memorial in St Paul's Cathedral, London, 'if one looks around there are few monuments in which to seek him'.[75]

'Architectural education' for far too long has been hermetically sealed from reality, a form of navel-gazing, irrelevant to the real world outside. It has stagnated for half a century, and is the misbegotten child of the 1958 Oxford Conference. Cribbing from Le Corbusier *et al.* in the aftermath of 1939–45 led to the making of an alienating, dangerous, and ultimately uninhabitable Dystopia. Obsessions about large expanses of glass have not proved to be beneficial in times of war or when buildings are attacked by 'terrorists' or other discontented groups, a point made by Osbert Lancaster: after the first air raid 'much of that enthusiasm for vast areas of plate glass, which has been so marked a feature' of the Modern Movement, might be dissipated.[76] One might also compare the ways in which the Pentagon, Arlington County, VA, near Washington, DC (1941–3—designed by George Bergstrom) stood up to the attack of 9/11 compared with the heavily-glazed World Trade Center twin towers, New York, totally destroyed on the same day. Vast areas of glazing, essential elements of the International Style, did not prove helpful in hot climates either, where the areas behind such glazing were uninhabitable when the sun shone (which was often). The universal application of glass could hardly be described as 'functional', 'rational', or 'scientific': it was just packaging, an illusion of 'Modernity'.

architectural practice in reality). So much of the problem in architectural education lies in the profession itself: architectural design in a vacuum makes little sense without a contextual and historical anchor, something early critics of Modernism realized.[86]

Teachers in schools of architecture need to recognize that 'didactic' (as in 'didactic teaching') is not a dirty word. Young people do not absorb skills by a kind of osmosis in the studio, as some seem to imagine.[87] It is no more possible to design a building without understanding the language of architecture than it is to write meaningful prose without a developed vocabulary, an understanding of syntax and grammar, and of course a little inspiration and soul.[88] So the second reform might be a recognition of the need for the delivery and development of basic skills (really looking [which means understanding by means of detailed note-taking and sketches], drawing, critical reading, critical writing) in schools of architecture.

An architect needs to understand and be informed by both geography and history, and by the fundamental interrelationship of the two. There is much talk of the *genius loci* (spirit of the place, for every place has its own unique qualities, not only in terms of its physical make-up, but of how it is perceived, so it ought to be [but far too often is not] the responsibility of the architect to be sensitive to those qualities, to enhance rather than to destroy them), without any concern for what that might mean, how an understanding of it might be arrived at, and, most importantly, how a design might respond to it.

Students often struggle to properly understand a site selected for them to prepare their designs both at a macro- and micro-scale: they carry out a huge of amount of analysis which is either of no help in arriving at a solution or is carefully filed away and forgotten once 'designing' begins. So a third reform could be to make the analysis, understanding, and response to place an explicit continuum. Uncoupling architecture from place leads to meaningless ephemeral architecture that is here today, and, sadly, not gone tomorrow.[89]

Sixty per cent of undergraduates who read for a degree in architecture do not go on to practise as architects. That is not failure. People who study law do not all become lawyers, and people who study English do not all become writers, but they should be intellectually enriched by their university education. Schools of architecture often see their rôle exclusively as preparing students for practice, which may be true at Master's level, but is only true for the minority at undergraduate level. Schools of architecture can serve all

their students best by providing a good, general, arts and humanities education with an understanding of real science, technology, and management.
Graduates should leave university seeing the world in a different way from
that they perceived when they entered, and with an appreciation of what
makes 'culture' in the widest sense of the word, and that would include history and the importance of religious history as well.

The cost and value of an architectural education need to be reviewed.
A five-year course at university adds up to a very expensive business, exacerbated by probably not being the best preparation for a life in architectural
practice. Some combination (particularly at Master's level) of university and
practice-based pupillage or apprenticeship would allow students to 'learn
and earn': this would have the added advantage of widening access to architecture as a profession for those excluded by inability to pay. There is also an
argument in favour of undergraduates working in practices for a year *before*
they commence their studies. Offices would thus make a contribution to
their low-paid labour. Universities seem unable to accept the idea that only
students intending to qualify as architects should enter departments to study:
a year working in offices should help students to concentrate minds and
enable the non-committed to drop out. Students wishing to proceed would
also start full-time at universities with some savings.

Finally, there is the issue of 'style'. Schools of architecture see architectural
expression in a particular way (often a reheating of the tutors' own architectural education served up in new[ish] containers). Style is about much more
than appearance and surface decoration (or an absence of the latter): in any
case, the long history of architectural 'decoration' was concerned with symbolism,[90] meaning, emphasis, and much more. Its expulsion by Modernism
demonstrated a complete misunderstanding of its origins, history, and
purpose. Walt Whitman, in his *Song for Occupations*, observed that:

> All architecture is what you do to it when you look upon it,
> (Did you think it was in the white or gray stone? or the lines of the arches
>   and cornices?)
> All music is what awakes from you when you are reminded by the instruments,
> It is not the violins and the cornets, it is not the oboe nor the beating drums,
>   nor the score of the baritone singer singing his sweet romanza, nor that
>   of the men's chorus, nor that of the women's chorus,
> It is nearer and farther than they.[91]

Students must be taught that what they do as architects will awaken *some-thing* in those who look upon it (even those who pass it by in distraction and even those not yet born), and better it be joy than horror. The design of buildings and the shaping of the urban fabric to which they contribute (or from which they detract) are awesome, onerous responsibilities (it is hard to imagine greater), not to be taken lightly or arrogantly imposed from some dogmatic stance adopted from a manifesto. Students should therefore be set exercises to study existing towns, cities, and streets: how they were planned, developed, and damaged; how materials were used; how buildings relate to each other (or not); how the grain, texture, and geometries of a street are formed of different buildings in juxtaposition; and how to develop a respect for the contexts into which new buildings are slotted. Those who aspire to be architects should leave university in no doubt that this is the burden (and the joy) they bear, and therefore realize they must exercise their 'craft or sullen art'[92] with the greatest care, attention, and sensitivity, nurtured by immersion in an historical understanding of the wider meanings of culture.[93]

Architectural education, therefore, should commence with studies of existing historic buildings of quality and several different styles, involving detailed surveys and the production of finely-crafted measured drawings. Such studies should embrace how materials are used, how details work, and how features such as mouldings help buildings to weather gracefully (or not). These exercises should be accompanied by a programme of reading about historical architecture and writing essays on selected topics to encourage techniques of historical research and the ability to write clear, unambiguous, properly referenced English. At present students are expected to work in a kind of vacuum, insulated from history, culture in its widest sense, and an understanding of the contexts within which buildings were designed and erected.

Unfortunately, many of their tutors are also products of a system from which much that is essential has been omitted, so architects with a knowledge of history and steeped in wider culture should be encouraged and actively recruited in order to fill *lacunae*. It might be necessary to establish some sort of national network of talks and lectures for trainees, aimed to set architecture within a wider culture, and not merely treated within its own 'box'.

There is some hope that brighter, more sensitive students are becoming aware of the need to take account of old buildings: a certain enthusiasm for entering work to bodies such as the Society for the Protection of Ancient Buildings (SPAB) is detectable among them. Part II students, for example, have entered schemes for the SPAB Philip Webb Award, intended to encourage sympathetic reuse of old buildings and sensitive design in an historical context. There could well be more of a rôle for the national amenity societies in encouraging measured surveys of old buildings, and promoting the work of those persons who carry out such valuable recording of historical architecture.[94]

Some other matters might be reconsidered. Schools of architecture could be better off as departments within art-schools rather than universities (which used to be the case in many instances). The problem seems to have originated with the 1958 Oxford Conference, which did a great deal of damage. On the European Continent, especially in Germany, there has been a long tradition of the teaching of architecture within technical-institutions that have the same kudos as universities: the switch to expansion of universities in the UK seems to have been based on a kind of snobbery, looking down on technical-colleges as somehow inferior, which could be perceived as a huge error of judgement. Society actually needs technical and professional proficiency, and the old technical-colleges provided much of that. There has also been a long tradition that established architects were encouraged to become regular part-time lecturers or tutors, as is still the case in several European countries: many university bureaucracies are opposed to this, as they do not understand it, and it does not fit neatly within an increasingly box-ticking culture. However, that tradition also presents problems, because practitioners themselves, in a great many instances, will remain as unreconstructed Modernists, with ingrained attitudes unhelpful if genuine reforms have any chance of being implemented.

An overall educational programme might look something like this:

Year 1: a student works as an apprentice or pupil in an architect's office;

Year 2: student enrols in a school of architecture where essential parts of the course would be architectural history (understood as part of a wider culture), studies of how materials are put together to form buildings, taught by drawing actual exemplars, carrying out measured surveys, and studying urban structure, including streets and spaces. This would put architecture in context, encourage students to use their eyes, and analyse how traditional structures take shape, as one cannot 'design' something without having studied how elements of it actually work and are employed to create an artefact;

Years 3 & 4: history and design projects, with real sites in real contexts, involving study of the context, the history of the site and developments on that site, surveys, and careful development schemes for those sites, responding to them with sensitivity and scholarship, not ignoring them. At the end of Year 4 graduation.

Year 5: return to architectural practice, remaining there until qualification at the end of year 7;

OR

Years 6 & 7: two-year postgraduate course offering specializations in planning, masterplanning, historic building conservation (this might be combined with time in a specialist conservation practice), or even history of architecture.

These draft proposals are intended as skeletal outlines to suggest some possible ways forward, to address what is clearly a problem, and to stimulate debate.[95]

Hubris: The End of Architecture?

Pronouncements by 'star' architects often project self-images as liberal-minded, socially concerned, 'left'-leaning goodies, yet the same people have careers devoted to serving wealth and celebrity, and some have seemed ruthless when discarding friends, colleagues, and even ethical positions.[96] The public, too, is not permitted to judge the work of such architects: those who do not worship the personalities and works of these deified creatures are judged blind, stupid, or reactionary. However, the public, which has to look at the built fabric and use it, not only has a right to judge its qualities, but has the only right so to do.

The *Hubris* of 'star' architects leads only one way: the grand-daughter of Chaos (*Χάος*) and Phanes (*Φάνης*), and daughter of Night (*Νύξ*) and Oceanus (*Ὠκεανός*) is a formidable force. Her name is Nemesis (*Νέμεσις*), Goddess of retribution and all just revenge, punisher of extraordinary crimes, and merciless destroyer of those who think themselves superior and inflict violence on others. She comes, without fail, after *Hubris*.

Much architecture in the West, regrettably, has become empty, uncouth, trashy, ill-mannered (in that it pays no respect to its context), often threatening, and in artistic terms, worthless.[97] Practitioners, mouthing cant about affordability, ethical regeneration, sustainability, and which ever fashionable aims float in the polluted air at the time, behave like Philip Johnson's 'whores',[98] slavering at the sight of the money-bags of anyone with eye-watering off-shore 'investments'. With interests a-plenty in places like China and the Middle East as well, they seem oblivious to the truth that the world in which they bask is stratospherically distant, light-years away from the humdrum, deadly

lives of the unfortunates trying to scratch a living or keep afloat in an increasingly unpleasant environment, who are affected and bludgeoned daily by
monuments to the cupidity of monstrous egos untouched by spiritual or
compassionate values. And, alarmingly, what seems to have escaped many is
that Modernism is essentially Westernization.

Yet the West took a long time to modernize, and managed it up to a
point, but now cultures that are not Western are attempting to rush to *be*
Western or are having Westernization *imposed* upon them far too quickly.
As this happens, massive damage is caused, and those cultures are destroyed
or at the very least badly weakened, stressed, and corrupted, creating huge
problems that never seem to have concerned Western commentators, and
still do not.[99] Overwhelmingly dangerous resentments are being generated,
and this will lead inevitably to a West that has discarded its culture, history,
and values being out-produced and out-reproduced. There are already signs
of extreme hatreds against the West, backed by fanatical religious fundamentalism that seems incomprehensible to Western pundits who myopically and
arrogantly discounted religion decades ago.[100] Every overbearing piece of
whatever is the current Western architectural fashion that is realized in non-
Western cultures is an aggressive statement. Theodore von Laue's great book,
The World Revolution of Westernization,[101] lucidly sets out the arguments,
backed by impeccable scholarship and perceptive insights.

London, a global city, attracts migrants, rich and poor, and serious money,
no matter where it comes from: money flows through it, but its land and its
built fabric seem increasingly to be regarded as mere commodities, sold to
the highest bidder, with no thought given to its ordinary inhabitants, discounted, no doubt, as *bourgeois* or as 'free-riding' inhabitants of social housing.[102] With its inventions of Green Belts;[103] public housing;[104] sewers, water
supplies, and cemeteries;[105] Clean Air Act;[106] and many other innovations
that helped to potty-train Urban Man,[107] London changed in the course of
the nineteenth and twentieth centuries, solving a great many of the problems experienced in earlier times. In the twenty-first century, however, it
appears that government of a great city has become enfeebled, reactive, and
not able to deal coherently with the built environment that affects everyone.[108] It seems that, in order to be visibly, acceptably 'modern', large new
developments in London have to dwarf their neighbours and pierce the
skyline with ever-more 'empty gestures':[109] images of these proposals, pouring
out of computers and backed by slick 'sales speak' to make inflated claims
digestible, bear little resemblance to what will actually be the reality on the

ground.[110] One might question the wisdom (or lack of it) in not only allowing, but mendaciously encouraging, the property bubble to expand exponentially, thereby wrecking what remains of social order in the capital.[111]

In the City of London itself, the fantasies of Gropius about high-level
'roof gardens' and so-called 'public' terraces have been wheeled out in support of more and more developments when the 'public' will never have
access to them, even if they are realized; or, if access is permitted, it will
involve tickets, queues, and (probably) charges.[112] In addition, those areas
squeezed between the feet of high-rise buildings, supposedly for human
access, recreation, amenity, and so on, usually turn out to be miserable, boring little gaps, with no amenities whatsoever, and almost inevitably inimical
to humans because of the wind-tunnels resulting from tall buildings designed
with no consideration at all for how they will perform at ground level. In
short, the quality of London at ground level is being eroded at a frightening
rate, and 'amenity-spaces' are often gloomy, dark, overshadowed, windy
holes where nobody would like to linger. Fine old buildings, often part of
the context of monstrous modern developments, are ignored, often to their
detriment, easing the path for their destruction. And many architects (with
some honourable exceptions), trained in the hothouses of schools of architecture, are conditioned to ignore context, see their 'iconic'[113] creations as
though there were no buildings adjoining them at all (not likely in an over-
crowded, heavily urbanized island), and pursue fame in the glossy journals
and fortune in the marketplace, with not a thought about what their interventions will inevitably do not only to established, historic urban fabric, but
to the quality of the lives of those who live and work in cities.[114] Such a
state of affairs is not Subtopia, which the architectural press used to deplore,
but Dystopia of the worst kind.[115]

This is not only a problem facing the English capital: it is one that is
increasingly and obviously global. At the present accelerating rate of change,
every great city on earth will have similar problems and present the same
ill-favoured image to the world. All local, regional, and national character
will be lost, and 'International Style' will no longer mean the architecture
that became ubiquitous after the *Weißenhofsiedlung* in 1927, the MoMA
exhibition a few years later,[116] and the influential book entitled *The
International Style*.[117] It will suggest something infinitely worse, hinted at in
Laue's seminal work.[118]

Anthony Burgess set his *A Clockwork Orange*[119] in a Dystopian London,
and when Stanley Kubrick made it into a film (1971) he chose the Modernist

setting of Thamesmead in Woolwich for some of the nastier scenes. Thamesmead was planned in 1965–6 by the Greater London Council with a comprehensive upper-level pedestrian network that quickly became vandalized and unsafe, while the buildings soon showed signs of major problems, including water penetration and generally unsound design. Kubrick did not have to build a film set: architects and planners obligingly provided everything he needed, and the scenes in that film sum up the failure of the Modern Movement. *The Buildings of England* volume timidly records that 'Thamesmead...bears but little resemblance to the ideal community visualized by its begetters', that 'hardly any of the advantages worked in practice', that the 'spine block does not incorporate the different activities that one might expect in a traditional urban street', that the 'point blocks' appear 'dour and oppressive', and that by 1976 the 'industrialized system' chosen 'was given up altogether' (**Plate 10.1**).[120]

It was far too late, however: the damage had been done, and J.G. Ballard in his writings painted a future which looks more than prophetic.[121] For a sane and angry analysis of what Modernism has done to London, Rowan

Plate 10.1. Typical unappetizing structures of the phase 1967–72 at Coralline Walk off Harrow Manor Way in South Thamesmead, in which industrialized building-systems were employed

Moore may be read with profit.[122] 'Proposals to demolish most of Hubert Bennett's Thamesmead were approved in November 2016'.[123]

This sort of comprehensive failure was repeated again and again and again in the making of Dystopia, and again and again it was claimed that the deserts made of urban fabric came into being with the 'best of intentions'[124] and because of pinched 'financial resources'.[125] That is patently untrue, not least because many developments had to be demolished less than two decades after they were expensively designed and erected: the only 'intention' was to do what the cult demanded, to continue to create environments which did not house people in decent conditions, in leak-proof, well-planned and -detailed buildings, in settings that lifted the spirits rather than depressed and frightened them. No wonder the unfortunate tenants used violence against what had been imposed on them, and that violence has been widespread:[126] that there will be a lot more violence can hardly be doubted.

Shelter, in the form of dwelling-places, fuelled by mortgages (which only inflate prices, as was pointed out in the middle of the nineteenth century by the housing reformer Henry Roberts),[127] is now treated like currency, and the whole ethos of an ethical-religious-based philosophy of providing housing for the 'labouring classes' has been jettisoned. Roberts, among whose sensible principles was the insistence that no family should pay out more than *a fifth of its income* on housing itself, would be horrified by the situation today. His solid achievements in the design of philanthropic housing, soundly constructed, taking into account the need for privacy, decent hygiene (his model designs of 1851 even had internal lavatories, revolutionary for that time), dignity, and affordability, were not to be surpassed in his own century, and only at the end of that century did some designs for working-class housing begin to reach the point where Roberts had left off.[128]

Compared with Roberts's very real contributions, grounded in his evangelical Christian conscience,[129] the record of public housing designed on Modernist principles, such as the huge blocks at Pruitt-Igoe, or at Hulme, Manchester, is weighed in the balance, and found seriously wanting. And we should make no mistake about where models for such abysmal failures originated. Inflated egos, self-interest, and unthinking belief in fake 'science', in false 'rationality', and in an inhumane cult that has informed far too much non-architecture, have made Dystopia. Commercial and political interests, too, played more than minor rôles.[130]

Afterword: Nemesis

It is difficult, when considering the psychotic process that passes for 'architecture' today, not to form the opinion that the courses architecture and town planning have taken almost universally since 1945 have been deranged. Panaceas have proved not to be anything of the sort, yet, despite early evidence of failure, they were still applied. The 'scientific', supposedly 'rational' bases of the Modern Movement in architecture were neither. Inclusion of the works of many designers in books about what is supposed to be great architecture is mistaken. Challenges to the orthodoxies of Modernism which have created an inhuman world are denounced by those who just want more of the same because they have vested interests in continuing the ruinous policies that have virtually destroyed all vestiges of civilized living. Worship of 'star' architects is idolatry, with everything that idolatry brings as Nemesis: Western heroes of architecture are simply self-interested servants of big business, vast corporations, or repressive *régimes* abroad. There is ample evidence, however, that there is a mighty reaction to what 'celebrity' architects are doing in other countries,[131] where the main ways of making buildings and designing settlements over the centuries were wholly unlike existing 'paradigms'.[132] Critical voices are already starting to be audible, even in the cowed West itself.[133]

What Western architects, producing yet more blobs or wildly expensive Parametricist fantasies that might amuse for a short time but are not fit for purpose, and will cost billions to maintain, do not seem to begin to understand is that there is a huge reaction to what they are doing in traditional societies where spiritual values survive, rather than the vulgar commercial 'celebrity' ones that conspire to make them 'stars' among themselves, among sensation-seekers, and among those of all ages in thrall to advertising.[134] This is a fatal weakness at the very heart of the West.[135]

In 1965 the *avant-garde* magazine *Bau* featured a photograph of the launchpads for rockets at the American base of Cape Canaveral, labelling it 'cathedrals of a new worldview'; and in the same year Reyner Banham claimed that in 'Gizmos' (which he defined as any mass-produced gadget, such as a cordless shaver or a transistor radio), representing popular technology, could be found the true essence of contemporary architecture.[136] In 1968 the Austrian architect Hans Hollein suggested that everything, including lipstick, pill-capsules, spacesuits, and even those ubiquitous photographs of 'Che' Guevara so prized by adolescents, was 'architecture',[137] a view which might arouse some doubts, even serious misgivings, for if what Banham and Hollein *decided* was architecture *really was* architecture, then the rest of us might decide we did not want it.[138]

Soon afterward the *soixante-huitards* had their 'revolution' in Paris, and many artefacts, including plaster-casts of Classical architectural details held in academies,[139] were smashed. Some architects and visionaries loosely associated with the 1968 upheavals took part in a conference about design at Aspen, Colorado, including François Dallegret, who had collaborated with Banham on 'A Home is not a House' in 1965.[140] That conference was held near the end of an era in which it was widely and naïvely supposed that technological progress would lead inevitably to a far more enlightened, prosperous, and 'liberal' society, and on a global scale too: a piece of wishful thinking that has turned out to be founded on quicksands, and that signalled the beginning of the end of a time when Modernists believed technological advances and social development went hand-in-hand, mutually interdependent.[141] The unswerving belief of those *avant-garde* techno-utopians was pure *Hubris*: the future did not lie in the 'High-Tech' of the *Centre Pompidou*, any more than it did with a Modernist insistence that architects had to reinvent society through new ways of living or face decline and disintegration. Indeed, it looks as though architectural interference with the urban fabric has not saved it at all, but is successfully killing it.

Many in architectural circles fondly imagined that design involving major rôles for computers would resolve the aesthetic confusions of Post-Modernism. Practitioners of Parametric design[142] also believed that Parametricism would respond to social/political pressures, but all it seems to have done is to create extravagant interlopers that respect nothing except themselves. Both represent yet another catastrophic, wasteful failure, based on *Hubris* and attitudes masquerading as 'scientific' when they are nothing of the sort. They 'exacerbate rather than solve the main failings' of Modern architecture, 'and not only because they are energy-profligate, anti-urban, stand-alone buildings that fail to define urban space and defy relationship with other buildings and humans'.[143] Parametricism, indeed, has been identified as a 'perfect example of...a sunset effect, an exaggerated caricature of now obsolete characteristics of a waning era'.[144]

In the 1920s and 1930s speed and fast motor-cars were very much admired, and the commercial/manufacturing interests promoting them hugely influenced the destruction of urban fabric and the creating of an environment dominated by highways from the 1950s onwards.[145] Indeed, places with primitive roads and without fast cars were objects of mirth and contempt, while open roads and shiny machines were associated with Modernity and glamour. Later, some entrepreneurs succeeded in associating sex with 'upward mobility' in campaigns for hedonistic utilitarianism in the magazine *Playboy*,[146] predictably praised by Reyner Banham, who, trendy as ever, claimed he only read it for its architectural/design content. Indeed, scattered among the ample bosoms, bottoms, salacious cartoons, and lavishly composed suggestive 'centrefolds' were laudatory hagiographies of the deified heroes of Modernism: architectural and sexual revolutions were thereby inextricably intertwined, as revealed in an amusing volume entitled *Pornotopia*.[147]

It is possible that our times will be viewed with astonishment in the future because of our inability to exercise intelligent critical judgement concerning what passes as 'architecture' (much of which is irrelevant in relation to pressing contemporary problems), but which is often only empty show, ignoring context, gobbling up money, and possessing no meaning other than as an assertion of overweening self-importance (*see* **Figures 8.1–5**). 'The flaws in all this stuff... are so obvious', Peter Buchanan has written, that 'future generations will be aghast it was ever taken seriously, let alone mistaken' for harbingers of what was to come.[148] Conspicuous Deconstructivism or its misshapen offspring, Parametricism,[149] are no substitutes for real architecture, and belong in the realms of extravagance, passing fashion, showing off, and superfluous bling, which a rich *élite* and international corporations feel entitled to inflict on everybody else.[150] A reaction may come sooner than some predict, and it may not be containable: 'increasingly unequal times' may provoke an upheaval against an 'anti-democratic neoliberal ethos' that imposes its monuments to egotism on the world.[151]

Only a few disciplines have any chance at all of counteracting the worst aspects of architectural Modernism: these are history (including the history of religion); true science; hands-on study of how materials are used in building and how they fit together (brickwork, for example); and detailed studies of old buildings and established urban contexts with the intention of developing conservation techniques and methods of slotting in where appropriate new designs that respect existing grain and character (from all of which the cult deliberately distanced itself over the last century).

There have been warnings, including the pioneering work of 1959 by Henry Hope Reed,[152] who argued that contemporary architecture was fraudulent, empty of intellectual content, ugly, and illiterate. His influence on brave, pioneering practitioners associated with New Urbanism and New

Classicism has been profound. Initially, Hope Reed's work was largely ignored, but it has certainly made a profound impact in parts of the United States, as can be seen in the distinguished work of T.H. Beeby, Allan Greenberg, R.A.M. Stern, and many others, some of whom have been mentioned above. In the creations of those architects who have rejected the Modernist stranglehold, perhaps, there lie some glimmerings of hope.[153]

At the School of Architecture, University of Notre Dame,[154] South Bend, Indiana, USA (the only one that teaches young student architects the *practice*, as opposed to merely the *history*, of traditional and Classical architecture), the competition to design the Walsh Family Hall at that school was won (2014) by the English architect John Simpson, with a scheme embedded in Classicism. It includes the Institute for the Study of Classical Architecture and Urbanism,[155] a foundation that would be unthinkable without the early work of Hope Reed. Some perceptive young men and women are beginning to see and understand some of the dangers in blind acceptance of Modernism (a few former students have worked in joiners' workshops and learned the basics of some building trades, such as how to lay bricks, because they realized they could not 'design' brick buildings without knowing how the materials were put together to create something structurally sound and aesthetically pleasing), but the damage is so widespread, on a global scale, that it will be extremely difficult to begin to repair, especially as tidal waves of adulation and pufferies are confined to 'star' architects and their 'iconic' works.

Apart from the Dystopias it has created, Modernism has left another legacy: the rash of private 'estates' (especially in the south-east of England but visible almost everywhere to a greater or lesser degree) demonstrates that formal architecture has been largely abandoned, forgotten, and rejected. It is little wonder the contemporary housing market is dominated by speculative builders who have no problems giving the public architecturally illiterate parodies of 'Georgian', 'Tudor',[156] and other styles bearing no resemblance to the originals, because most of today's architects have neither the skills nor the wit to break out of their constricting stylistic straitjacket, nor does their school-of-architecture 'training' equip them with the scholarship and knowledge to be able to produce correct 'period' detailing. The public as a whole, indeed, never embraced what Modernists insisted on giving them: large numbers of working-class people, however, had crude Modernism forced upon them.

Those still able to afford to buy dwellings reject mass callisthenics and refuse to do what they are told by architectural bullies whose failures are legion.

This is a sorry state of affairs compared with late-Georgian times when pattern-books were widely available, resulting in agreeable buildings that did not assault the sensibilities.

That, as Jenkins sagely observed, is Modernism's true Nemesis (**Plate 10.2**).[157]

Plate 10.2. *Knell for a Past, and Vision of a Barbarous Present and Future: with respectful apologies to Alfred Rethel.* The author, exhausted by his efforts to alert humanity against architectural barbarism leading to Dystopia, has expired in his chair, but Death comes as a friend to continue ringing the warning bell: outside, exemplars of the International Style, Deconstructivism, Blobism, Brutalism, and Corbusier-inspired structures are seen against a sky filled with the flames of widespread destruction

Notes

You will find it a very good practice always to verify…references…

MARTIN JOSEPH ROUTH (1755–1854) in JOHN WILLIAM BURGON (1813–88):
Lives of Twelve Good Men (London: John Murray 1888–9) i 73

PROLEGOMENON, PREFACE, & ACKNOWLEDGEMENTS I–XXXVIII

1. Mertins (2014) 155–61.
2. *See* Arts Council of Great Britain (1979).
3. Hyman (2001) 108–9.
4. https://www.youtube.com/watch?v=IQFEaAUrfAk
5. Richard Boyle, 3rd Earl of Burlington and 4th Earl of Cork, to whom Morris's poem was dedicated.
6. Morris (1742) 5.
7. For many years authorship of this work was erroneously attributed to John Gwynn.
8. Wilk (ed.) (2006) 12.
9. Given as 'flat' because they had to have slight falls otherwise the water would just remain there and not drain away.
10. Quotes from Wilk (ed.) (2006) 12.
11. Hitchcock, Johnson, & Mumford (1932).
12. Mehaffy & Salingaros (2013).
13. Nathaniel Robert Walker (2016).
14. Lancaster (2015).
15. Lancaster (2015*a*).
16. Lancaster (2015) xi.
17. *See* Wolfe (1981).
18. Rosemary Hill (2016): 'Bypass Variegated' *London Review of Books* **xxxviii**/2 (21 January) 32. *See also* Boston (1989).
19. Lancaster (2015*b*).
20. *Ibid.* 46–7.
21. Curl & Wilson (2015) 578.
22. Adam (2017) ix.
23. *See* Sklair (2017).
24. Jencks (2002) for example.
25. Stamp (2009).
26. Costa's influence led to massive destruction of Brasilian historic buildings.
27. Corbusier (1943).

28. *See* Jane S. Turner (ed.) (1998) **iv** 679, **viii** 6–8, and **xxiii** 117–20 for articles on the place and its designers.

29. For the phenomenon of giving the car pride of place, *see* Nathaniel Robert Walker (2016).

30. Schumacher (ed.) (2016).

31. *Ibid.*

32. *Ibid.* for 136 pages of this sort of stuff.

33. There is nothing new in this, as Mehaffy & Salingaros (2013) have explained.

34. Even *The Architectural Review*, which championed Modernism in its various manifestations for many years, began to have second thoughts in 1967 (*see The Architectural Review* **cxlii**/849 [November 1967]), and in 2011 began publishing a series of issues containing essays on a new campaign it entitled 'The Big Rethink'.

35. *See* Curl & Wilson (2015).

36. Jacobs (1961).

37. For Mumford's architectural writings *see* Wojtowicz (1998).

38. *New Yorker* **xxxviii** (1 December 1962) 148–79.

39. Mumford (1922).

40. Mumford (1924).

41. Donald L. Miller (ed.) (1986) reproduces this 1962 article.

42. Sudjic (1992) 23.

43. Watkin (1977).

44. *Apollo* **cvi**/188 (October 1977) 260–1.

45. *TLS* (17 February 1978) 191–2.

46. Harries (2011) 788.

47. *Ibid.*

48. *The Independent* (8 June 2001).

49. 13 January 1978.

50. *See* Harries (2011) 785.

51. *The Sunday Times* (10 April 1977) article on 'Sacred Cows'.

52. Muthesius (1908–11), for example.

53. Corbusier (1946) on the Athenian Parthenon is a prime example of this.

54. For a recent example *see* David Cole (2015).

55. Pevsner (1936) 158, or (2005) 133.

56. Brittain-Catlin (2008) 78–9 and *passim*.

57. Hanks (ed.) (2015); Howard (2016).

58. Nathaniel Robert Walker (2016).

59. Saunders (2013).

60. Mehaffy & Salingaros (2013) 4.

61. *Ibid.*

62. *Ibid.*

63. *See* The architect has no clothes (http://onthecommons.org/magazine/architect-has-no-clothes).

64. Mehaffy & Salingaros (2013) *passim*.

65. Buchanan (2015) is scathing on some of these matters.

66. Hillman (2016) should be studied.

67. Watkin (2016).
68. Adam (2017).
69. Stern (1996) 15.
70. *Ibid*. American Classicism was exceedingly impressive in the hands of great architects: the Modernists dismissed it.
71. *Ibid*. 16.
72. *Africa* ix 455–7.
73. Bufano (ed.) (1975) 1070 (9.453ff.).
74. Adam (2017) 42.
75. Crook (2003).
76. Curl & Wilson (2015) 560.
77. Nathaniel Robert Walker (2016).
78. Mehaffy & Salingaros (2013).
79. *See* Geelhaar, Christiane, *et al.* (eds) (1999–2004); Wolbert (ed.) (2004).
80. Kempter (2007) *passim*.
81. *See Proceedings of the British Academy* **lxxvi** (1990) 171–201.

CHAPTER I: ORIGINS OF A CATASTROPHE 1–48

1. 1914–18.
2. More (1516). *See also* Miller (tr.) (2001).
3. *The Revelation of St John the Divine*, especially Chapter 21.
4. Curl (2011) 49–52.
5. Carver (1962) 31.
6. Rosenau (1983) *passim*, but *see* Eaton (2001) for a detailed study.
7. Huxley (1932).
8. Orwell (1949).
9. *The Listener* (5 January 1967) 22.
10. *New Scientist* (11 July 1968) 96/3.
11. For recent works on Utopia/Newtopia *see* Wakeman (2016) and Reece (2016).
12. Greenhalgh (ed.) (1990) 1.
13. Wattjes (1927).
14. 1896, 1898, 1902 (especially), and 1904. *See* Wagner (1988).
15. Hegemann (1929).
16. Hegemann & Peets (1922).
17. *See* Pevsner & Richards (eds) (1973).
18. *See* Curl & Wilson (2015) 49, 643.
19. Curl (2007) 221–2, 428 and *passim*; Curl & Wilson (2015) 41.
20. Duncan (1994) 7.
21. Hitchcock, Johnson, & Mumford (1932); Hitchcock & Johnson (1966).
22. Curl (2005).
23. Cherry & Pevsner (1991) 191.
24. Curl & Wilson (2015) 490.
25. Wilk (ed.) (2006) *passim*.
26. Curl (2007) *passim*.

27. Britt (ed.) (1995) *passim.*
28. Images of these occur in some profusion in Corbusier (1946) *passim.*
29. Leuthäuser & Gössel (eds) (1990).
30. Pevsner (2005) *passim.*
31. Coe & Reading (1981) *passim.*
32. Greenhalgh (ed.) (1990) 9.
33. Pugin (1853) 1 and *passim. See also* Pugin (1843); Hill (2007).
34. I am grateful to the mathematician, Nikos Salingaros, for this observation.
35. Paul Waterhouse in *RIBA Journal* 3rd Series **viii** (1901) 49–51.
36. Crook (2003) 157.
37. Kugler (1856–9).
38. Crook (2003) 154.
39. *See* Wainwright (2013) on this.
40. Mehaffy & Salingaros (2013) note this point too.
41. Alain de Botton (2005): 'The special and the ordinary' in *RIBA Journal* **cxii**/2 (February) 26–7.
42. This campaign is brilliantly described by Nathaniel Robert Walker (2016).
43. Hitchcock, Johnson, & Mumford (1932); Hitchcock & Johnson (1966).
44. Pevsner (1960) 661.
45. *Ibid.*
46. *Ibid.*
47. *Ibid.*
48. Lancaster (2015*a*) 66.
49. Gropius (1956) 25.
50. Curl (2011) 175–245.
51. Mehaffy & Salingaros (2013).
52. Vautel (1921) *passim.*
53. Blomfield (1934) 135.
54. *Ibid.* 169.
55. *Ibid.* 64.
56. For more on this *see* Banham (1971) 64.
57. Blomfield (1934) 165.
58. Koch (ed.) (1897–1932).
59. Essay on Vernacular Art by Loos. *See* Safran *et al.* (1985) 113.
60. Sir Roger Scruton in Adam (2017) ix.
61. Curl (2011*a*).
62. Pugin (1843) 1–2.
63. Curl (2007) 91–113.
64. Pugin (1853) 1.
65. *Ibid.*
66. *Ibid.*
67. *Ibid.*
68. *Ibid.*
69. Wotton (1624) part i.

70. For words in square brackets *see* Vitruvius Pollio (1999) 26, although he was referring to the principles *of* those, so the words appear in the genitive in his original.
71. Vitruvius Pollio: *De Architectura* **i** 3 sect. 2.
72. Wren (1942) 126. *See also* S. Wren (ed.) (1750).
73. Pugin (1853) 3.
74. Curl (2007) Ch. 2, and 91–5.
75. Pugin (1853) 2–3.
76. Corbusier (1946) 185–207.
77. *Ibid.* 201.
78. Curl (2003) 17–24, 188–9.
79. Watkin (2001) 24–5.
80. Pugin (1853) 38.
81. Pugin (1843) 1.
82. *Ibid.* 5.
83. For example, George Basevi, Decimus Burton, George Dance, William Donthorn, the Inwoods, John Nash, George Stanley Repton, Sir Robert Smirke, Sir John Soane, William Wilkins, James Wyatt.
84. Pugin (1843) 3.
85. *See* Lancaster (2015) 32.
86. Curl (2011*a*) *passim.*
87. Curl (2007) 61–5, 91–5, 96–145.
88. Ruskin (1849) *The Lamp of Obedience* IV.
89. *Ode on a Grecian Urn* (1820) st. 5.
90. Lancaster (2015) 40.
91. *Ibid.*
92. Landow (1971) 218; Pevsner (1936) 42; Swenarton (1989) 197.
93. Scruton (2009) is revealing on this topic.
94. Pugin (1843) 39; Pugin's italics.
95. Alison (1790). *See also Proceedings of the British Academy* **lxxvi** (1990) 171–201.
96. Blomfield (1934) 67–8.
97. Including Pevsner.
98. Blomfield (1934) 149–50.
99. Lancaster (2015) xii.
100. All these quotations *ibid.*
101. Trevelyan (1944) Ch. xvii.
102. Stamp (ed.) (1999) 111.
103. *Ibid.* 111–23.
104. Eastlake (1970) 269–70.
105. *Ibid.* 270.
106. Crook (2003) 154.
107. *Ibid.* 197 n.203.
108. *Builder* **lxxviii**/2973 (27 January 1900) 73–4.
109. *Ibid.*
110. Crook (1987) 299 quoting Blomfield in *Builder* **lxi** (1891) 57–8.

111. More than a century now.
112. *RIBA Journal* **xxxix** 3rd Series (20 February 1932) 293–302; *The Architectural Review* **xi**/65 (April 1902) 107–12.
113. Pevsner (1960) 7.
114. *RIBA Journal* **xii** 3rd Series (25 February 1905) 237–45.
115. *Builder* **cv**/3692 (7 November 1913) 482–4.
116. Kerr called Ruskin a 'vaporer': *see* Fergusson (1891) 123; Summerson (1970) 11.
117. *ODNB* **xlviii** (2004) 173–93.
118. Summerson (1970s) 1–18.
119. Almost six centuries now.
120. *Journal of Design* **ii** (1849–50) 72.
121. Barnett (1995) 123–64; Tombs (2014) Ch. 18.
122. *See* Pevsner (1960).
123. *See* Pevsner (2005).
124. Pevsner (1968*a*) ii 39, 46, 48, 58, 63–4, 68–9, 80, 104–7, 129, 126, 133.
125. *Ibid.* 104.
126. *Technischer Attaché.*
127. Karl Alexander August Johann (b. 1818).
128. Grand-Ducal Saxon Art School Weimar.
129. Grand-Ducal Saxon High School for Fine Art.
130. Dohme (1888).
131. Sharp (ed.) (2007) xxv.
132. Muthesius **i** (1908) III: *eines sogenannten modernen Stils.*
133. *Ibid.: Verblüffenden Außtellungsleistungen.*
134. *Ibid.: Gott sei Dank ist von Jugendstil keine Spur zu finden.*
135. Muthesius (1908–11).
136. *See* Cumming & Kaplan (2004); Livingstone & Parry (eds) (2005).
137. *See* Muthesius **i** (1908) *passim.*
138. Sharp (ed.) (2007) **i** 153.
139. *Ibid.* 154.
140. Nairn & Pevsner (1971) 307.
141. Sharp (ed.) (2007) **i** 162.
142. *Ibid.* 162–3.
143. For excellent reproductions in colour of several Voysey drawings, *see* David Cole (2015), although his subtitle, claiming Voysey as an 'English Pioneer Modernist Architect and Designer', is fanciful when the contents of the book are examined.
144. Sharp (ed.) (2007) **ii** 128, 131; Muthesius (1912) 149–64; Valinsky (2014) *passim.*
145. Posener (2004) *passim.*
146. *See* Muthesius (1908–11) for bibliographical details.
147. Sharp (ed.) (1987) ix.
148. But *see*, for example, Stevenson (1880); Turner & Parker (1851–9).
149. Sharp (ed.) (1987) ix.

150. Pevsner (2005) 86, repeated in Frampton (2007) 98. Samuel Otto Bing was actually Siegfried's brother: confusion seems to have arisen because both Bings died in 1905.

151. Geelhaar *et al.* (eds) (1999–2004); Wolbert (ed.) (2004).

152. Brothel.

153. Easton (2002) 94.

154. *Ibid.* 95–6.

155. Duncan (1994) 40–1.

156. Crawford (1995) 31–41; Easton (2002) *passim*; Easton (ed. & tr.) (2011) *passim*; Gössel & Leuthäuser (2005) 75; Whitford (1984) 43.

157. Easton (ed. & tr.) (2011) 573.

158. Nerdinger & Mai (eds) (1994) *passim*.

159. Associated with the Nietzsche proposals were the Austrian poet Hugo von Hofmannsthal and the German composer Richard Strauss (whose tone-poem, *Also sprach Zarathustra* [1895–6, Opus 30], was a celebration of Nietzsche's work). Kessler was also involved in the creation of the scenario that became von Hofmannsthal's libretto for the wildly successful opera *Der Rosenkavalier*, with music by Strauss (Opus 59), first given in Dresden in 1911. In the following year he provided the outline for a ballet, *Josephs Legende*, with music again by Strauss (composed 1913–14, Opus 63). It was first performed in Paris in 1914 just before the outbreak of hostilities, a factor that led to its neglect thereafter (Curl [2005] 373).

160. Easton (2002) 92.

161. For Expressionism in architecture, *see* Sharp (1966) esp. 145–64, an excellent compendium.

162. For a perceptive study *see* Kater (2014).

163. Denis (1957) 109.

164. Easton (2002) 165.

165. Nostitz (1979) 100–4.

166. Kater (2014).

167. *See* Robert E. Lerner (2016) for Kantorowicz.

168. Kantorowicz (1927).

169. Muthesius (1902) *passim*.

170. *See* Stamp (2015).

171. H.S. Goodhart-Rendel, quoted in Stamp (2015).

172. For further observations on style, *see* Rybczynski (2001).

173. Hitchcock, Johnson, & Mumford (1932).

174. Rybczynski (2001).

175. *See* Cornforth (1988) *passim* for further observations on style.

176. For *Art Nouveau* in detail *see* Greenhalgh (ed.) (2000).

177. Pevsner & Richards (eds) (1973).

178. Muthesius (ed.) (1907).

179. Jane S. Turner (ed.) (1998) **viii** 824–7.

180. Anderson (2000); Geelhaar *et al.* (eds) (1999–2004); Windsor (1981); Wolbert (ed.) (2004).
181. Nerdinger (1988).
182. Frank (ed.) (1994).
183. Michelis (1991); Wangerin & Weiss (1976).
184. Campbell (1977) for further details.
185. 1912.
186. 1913.
187. 1914.
188. Mehaffy & Salingaros (2013); and 'How Modernism got square' (http://www.metropolismag.com/Point-of-View/April-2013/Toward-Resilient-Architectures-3-How-Modernism-Got-Square/) in Metropolis magazine, accessed 1 February 2017.
189. Howard (2016) 250.
190. Sons of Zeus, whose characteristic mode of action was the Epiphany at a moment of crisis.
191. Curl (2005) 371–2; Pehnt (1987) 153.
192. Curl (2005) 372; Hoeber (1913); Pehnt (1987) 154; Windsor (1981) 137–8.
193. I am glad to have this confirmed by two German-born friends.
194. Sharp (1966) 28.
195. Scheerbart (1914).
196. Haag-Bletter (1975); Sharp (ed.) (1972) *passim*.
197. For something of the flavour of the Second Reich, *see* Kurtz (1970) and Röhl (2004, 2014).
198. Kühnemann (ed.) (1896/7). *See also* Curl (2005) 371–3; Pehnt (1987) 154.
199. Curl (2005) 372.
200. For insights into van de Velde's career and time at Weimar, *see* Schirmer (ed.) (2011) and Velde (1986).
201. Sharp (1966) 42.
202. For Wrocław buildings *see* Eysymontt *et al.* (2014).
203. *Wendingen* **xi** (1919) 10ff.
204. Wren **xix** (1942) 126.
205. Ruskin (1849) *The Lamp of Memory* §10.
206. Posener (1992) for details.
207. *Wendingen* **xi** (1919) 10ff.
208. A glance at some of his earlier solo works in Isaacs **i** (1983) will bear this out.

CHAPTER II: MAKERS OF MYTHOLOGIES & FALSE ANALOGIES 49–86

1. Read (1933) 59.
2. Sharp (ed.) (1987) x.
3. Although regrettably, several captions do not relate to the images they purport to describe.
4. Sharp (ed.) (2007) ix.

5. Muthesius (1908–11).

6. Sharp (ed.) (2007) 51.

7. For pithy comments on the horrific way in which Mackintosh's building has been treated, *see Private Eye* **1382** (20 December–8 January 2015) 18.

8. For Mackintosh *see* Crawford (1995), Howarth (1977), Macaulay (2010), Steele (1994).

9. Pevsner (2005) 135.

10. *See* MacGibbon & Ross (1887–92) and Maxwell-Irving (2000, 2014) for a feast of Scots historic buildings.

11. *The Architectural Review* **lxxvii**/451 (January 1935) 23–6.

12. Pevsner (2005) 133, and in the 1936 edn. 158.

13. Pevsner (2005) 134.

14. *See* Curl & Wilson (2015) 578.

15. Pevsner (2005) 134.

16. Cumming & Kaplan (2004) 7.

17. *See* the 1936 edn. and compare with that of 2005.

18. Gradidge (1980) xvi.

19. *RIBA Journal* 3rd Series **lxiii**/6 (April 1956) 228–31.

20. *The Observer* (6 July 1969).

21. Harries (2011) 206.

22. *See* Isaacs **i** (1983) 71–3, 109, 116–17, 120.

23. Lewis & O'Connor (1994) 24.

24. Harries (2011) 221.

25. Some (e.g. Harries [2011] 221) seem to have interpreted this as Hannes Meyer, but it was actually Adolf Meyer.

26. *See* Engelmann & Schädlich (1991) *passim*.

27. Barth & Topfstedt (eds) (2000) *passim*.

28. Hahn (1995) *passim*.

29. Neufert (1936).

30. Without acknowledgement. Information gathered by the author when in the DDR 1986–7.

31. Prigge (ed.) (1999) *passim*.

32. Pevsner (1968*a*) **ii** 242–59.

33. Harries (2011) 220.

34. *Ibid.*

35. *The Burlington Magazine* **cli**/1278 (September 2009) 617–19.

36. Harries (2011) 221.

37. Pevsner (2005) 163.

38. *Ibid.*

39. Pevsner (1936) 206.

40. Pevsner (2005) 162.

41. *See* Hilmes (2015).

42. Gold (2013) for much on this.

43. *Ibid.* 259.

44. *See* Brandreth (2006) 77; Richards (1980) 123.

45. *See* Isaacs **ii** (1983–4) 674 and note 6 referring to a communication dated 17 February 1934: this is acknowledged in a letter from Gropius to Shand dated 28 February 1934. James (1997) 246 seems to misinterpret this: she says the 17 February letter was *from* Gropius, but it was actually *from* Shand *to* Gropius. Shand's original 17 February letter appears to be missing from the *Bauhaus-Archiv*, Berlin: I have seen a copy of it, however. I am grateful to Nina Schönig of the *Archiv* for information.

46. For some revelations *see* Weber (2009) *passim.*

47. *Ibid.* 39, 48, 228–32, and *passim.*

48. James (1997) 5.

49. Harries (2011) 47.

50. *Ibid. passim.*

51. Muthesius (1908) **i** 181–4.

52. Hitchmough (1995) 110–13.

53. Pevsner (1968a) **ii** 148.

54. Pevsner (1960) 645.

55. *Ibid.* 646.

56. Dated May 1940, the article reappeared in Pevsner (1968a) **ii** 141–51.

57. Pevsner (1968a) **ii** 143: my emphasis.

58. Yorke (1946) 45.

59. *ODNB* **lvi** (2004) 610.

60. Allibone (1991) 136.

61. *See* David Cole (2015) for one of the latest books making such claims.

62. Curl (2007) 272–3 and *passim.*

63. *See The Ecclesiologist* **xi** (1850) 227–33; **xiii** (1852) 247–62; **xiv** (1853) 70–80.

64. Turner & Parker (1851–9).

65. Cumming & Kaplan (2004) 32–3. *See also* Allibone (1991) *passim.*

66. *The British Architect* (18 December 1891) 456.

67. *See* Hitchmough (1995) 41–2, 164, 168.

68. *Ibid.* 95–6, 112.

69. Pevsner (1968a) **ii** 141.

70. Allibone (1991) was a good start, but much more could be said about Devey.

71. *See* 'Charles Francis Annesley Voysey, the architect of individualism' in *The Architectural Review* **lxx**/419 (October 1931) 93–6.

72. Betjeman (1933).

73. *The Architect & Building News* **cxvii** (21 January 1927) 133 and other issues of the period.

74. Brandon-Jones (1957).

75. In a personal comment to me.

76. *RIBA Journal* **xxxv**/2 (26 November 1927) 52–3.

77. Later Sir James Maude Richards.

78. Brandon-Jones joined Cowles Voysey in 1933, later becoming a partner.

79. Simpson (1979) Preface.

80. *See* Richards (1940).

81. *RIBA Journal* **xli**/9 (10 March 1934) 479. Report of a lecture by Voysey given to The Bartlett School of Architecture Architectural Society (21 February 1934), written by Reginald W. Cave, Hon. Secretary of the Society.

82. Mackmurdo (1883) title page.

83. Pevsner (1968*a*) **ii** 135.

84. Curl (2002) 47; Curl (2007) 221–2, 428, and *passim*; Curl & Wilson (2015) 41.

85. Sheppard (ed.) (1973) 354. For Mackmurdo *see* Pevsner (1968*a*) **ii** 133–9.

86. Hitchmough (1995) contains abundant evidence of this.

87. *The Magazine of Art* **ii** (1904) 211–12.

88. Hitchmough (1995) 222.

89. *Ibid.*

90. *See*, for these matters, Zatlin (1990, 2016).

91. Muthesius **i** (1908) III.

92. *Ibid.* 186–7.

93. Greenhalgh (ed.) (2000) 138 and *passim*.

94. Pevsner (1968*a*) **ii** 151.

95. Giedion (1941).

96. Korn (1953).

97. Fry (1944) Ch. 4; Korn (1953) plates 81–2.

98. Korn (1953) plates 83–4.

99. *Ibid.* plates 87–8.

100. *Ibid.* plates 108–9.

101. *Ibid.* 101.

102. *See* Pevsner (2005) for details of 1975 edn.

103. Howard (2016) demonstrated how Wright was cold-shouldered by Modernists.

104. A perusal of the two volumes of Graf (1994) will be sufficient to demonstrate the falsehood of claims for that great master, Wagner, as remotely connected with the Modern Movement.

105. Pevsner (2005) wrapper blurb.

106. David Cole (2015).

107. Pevsner (2005).

108. Harries (ed.) (2015) 62.

109. *Ibid.*

110. Ashbee (1911) 4; Ashbee (1917) 3.

111. Pevsner (2005) 18 (28 in 1936 edn.).

112. Harries (ed.) (2015) 67.

113. Crawford (1985) 420.

114. Harries (ed.) (2015) 68.

115. Pevsner (2005) 15 (23 in 1936 edn.).

116. Harries (ed.) (2015) 68.

117. *ODNB* (2004) **xxx** 353–4; Jane S. Turner (ed.) (1998) **xvii** 624–5.

118. Child *et al.* (1986) 35.

119. Pevsner (1968*a*) 190–209, originally published in *The Architectural Review* **xcii**/548 (August 1942) 31–4.

120. Pevsner (1968*a*) 210–25, originally published in *The Architectural Review* cxxxii/790 (December 1962) 421–8.
121. Pevsner (1968*a*) 226–41, originally published in *DIA Yearbook* (1964–5).
122. Harries (ed.) (2015) 64.
123. *Ibid.* 69.
124. Comino (1980) 42, 45.
125. Pevsner (2005) 128 (148 in 1936 edn.).
126. *Ibid.*
127. Harries (ed.) (2015) 70.
128. *Ibid.*
129. *Ibid.*
130. Singelenberg (1972) 177, 228 n.42.
131. Muthesius (1908–11) **i** 176–7, 181–4; **iii** 91.
132. Geelhaar, Christiane, *et al.* (eds) (2000–4) *passim*.
133. Pevsner (1968) 127, 140, 142.
134. Kornwolf (1972) 187–8, 520.
135. *Ibid.* 188.
136. *Ibid.*
137. Wilk (ed.) (2006) 82–3, 100, 347.
138. Gradidge (1980) 189.
139. *Ibid.* 187–95 is very perceptive on Baillie Scott.
140. For George, *see* Grainger (2011).
141. For Shaw, *see* Saint (1976).
142. Curtis (1996) 172 has illustrations, as has Wilk (ed.) (2006) 82.
143. Gradidge (1980) 189.
144. Scott & Beresford (1933) 71.
145. *Ibid.*
146. *Ibid.* 74.
147. *Ibid.* 77.
148. *Ibid.* 76.
149. *Ibid.* 4.
150. *Ibid.* 5.
151. *Ibid.*
152. *Ibid.* 7.
153. *Ibid.* 10.
154. In several letters to me he aired these views.
155. Scott & Beresford (1933) 10.
156. *The Architectural Review* cxvi/695 (November 1954) 303.
157. *RIBA Journal* 3rd Series lxiv/8 (June 1957) 307–13.
158. Charlton *et al.* (eds) (2007) 102.
159. Gropius (1956).
160. Dykes Bower often commented on these matters in conversations with me during our long acquaintance from the 1960s until his death.
161. *The Architectural Review* cix/651 (March 1951) 138–40.

162. An aim shared by the Russian composer Sergey Prokofiev, when he chose the title 'Classical' for his first Symphony. *See New Statesman* (3 February 2003): 'Terrorism: the price we pay for poverty'.
163. *Focus* ii (Winter 1938) 76–9.
164. *RIBA Journal* 3rd Series **clxxiv** (June 1967) 232.
165. Nathaniel Robert Walker (2016).
166. Saunders (2013).
167. Goodhart-Rendel (1953) 17, 165–76; *Architectural Association Journal* **lii** (1937) 63; *RIBA Journal* 3rd Series **xxxv**/15 (9 June 1928) 515–16.
168. Charlton *et al.* (eds) (2007) 16–38.
169. *Ibid.*; *see* Blauert *et al.* (eds) (2009).
170. Scott & Beresford (1933) 77.
171. Mehaffy & Salingaros (2013, 2015); Salingaros *et al.* (2004).
172. However, there is a curious feature about the 1995 edition (Scott [1995]) of Scott's 1906 book of the same title: first of all, *Arts and Crafts Interiors* was added as a subtitle; and, secondly, in the new foreword by Simon Houfe, C.R. Mackintosh was described as 'the father of the modern movement' (Scott [1995] 9). Coming from the heir of Sir Albert Richardson, some of whose work Pevsner described as 'almost grotesquely reactionary' (he was referring to Nos. 25–35 Grosvenor Place, Belgravia [1956–8], despite the fact that it stood the test of time, which is more than can be said of much over-praised Modernist exemplars, the failures of which have been painfully [and expensively] obvious), that claim is extraordinary, and shows how wrong-headed utterances can become sacrosanct beliefs of received opinion. *See* Bradley & Pevsner (2003) 752.
173. Pevsner (2005) 132.
174. Scott & Beresford (1933) 4.
175. *Ibid.* 5.
176. *Ibid.* 8.
177. *Ibid.* 9.
178. Scott (1995) *passim.*
179. Scott & Beresford (1933) 66.
180. Not with absolute accuracy.
181. Kipling (1913): '*Envoi*' to *Life's Handicap*, clearly a Masonic allusion. The poem originally appeared in 1892.
182. Scott & Beresford (1933) 7.
183. Hitchmough (1995) 143.
184. *Ibid.* 57.
185. *Ibid.*
186. Voysey (1915) sets out much of his religious belief.
187. Pevsner (1968a) ii 108–17.
188. *ODNB* **xxxix** (2004) 317–24.
189. William Morris (1910–15) **xxii** 92, 101, etc.
190. *Ibid.* 11.
191. May Morris (1936) i 266.

192. *Ibid.* 285.
193. William Morris (1910–15) **xxii** 318.
194. For Voysey's designs *see* Livingstone, Donnelly, & Parry (2016).
195. Korn (1953) 65, 79, 81, 88, 96.
196. Lancaster (2015*a*) 50.
197. *See* Hill (2007).
198. *See* Willis (1996) *passim*.
199. *The Times* (17 April 2015) 35. *See also* Chaslin (2015), Millais (2015, 2017), and Jarcy (2015) which should be enough to disabuse the most convinced disciples of their deity's feet of clay.
200. Lloyd & Pevsner (2006) 216.
201. Pevsner (2005) 94–5.
202. *See* Pevsner & Richards (eds) (1973).
203. *See* Reynolds (2016).
204. *ODNB* **xii** (2004) 875.
205. Comper (1933) 32.
206. In the 1974 edition of *The Buildings of England* volume on *Suffolk*, the stupendous restoration of the screen (1923–5) in the church of Sts Peter and Paul, Eye, was not even attributed to Comper, though matters were remedied in the 2015 edition (Bettley & Pevsner [2015] 212).
207. Symondson & Bucknall (2006) 196–7. I am indebted to Fr Symondson of The Society of Jesus for discussing these matters with me in depth.
208. Pevsner (1960) 665.
209. Pevsner (2005) 135.
210. Berlage (1996).
211. Viollet-le-Duc (1863–72).
212. Frampton (2007) 72.
213. *Ibid.* 72. 'Epoch' was a favourite word of many Modernists and totalitarians, who invariably 'demanded' what they asserted was the only way forward.
214. Especially Giedion (1941, 1948).
215. Singelenberg (1972) 177, 228 n.42.
216. Simpson (1979) Preface.
217. Symondson (2011) *passim*.
218. O'Hear (1999) 166.
219. Reid (ed.) (1996) 55.
220. In *Cambridgeshire* in the *Buildings of England* Series (1970): the latest revision (2014—by Simon Bradley) avoids any judgements at all.
221. His model of his proposals for the Erasmus Building at Queens' College (from 1955) was stolen, apparently by students at the Cambridge school of architecture. This episode caused him to resign. Dictatorial and unscrupulous tactics used to get a Modernist solution for the site in question were typical of the Modern Movement: they reflect no credit, and the building that was actually erected (1959–60) to designs by Basil Spence is scarcely a triumph (Symondson [2011] 85).

222. He bitterly recalled his feelings to me about such repugnant bullying in our conversations and correspondence.

223. Symondson (2011) 146.

CHAPTER III: MODERNISM IN GERMANY IN THE AFTERMATH OF THE 1914–18 WAR 87–120

1. Robert Morris (1742) 26.
2. *Ibid*. 27–8.
3. An armistice with the Ottoman Empire was concluded in October 1918, but the Empire did not officially end until 1922. A truncated part became the Republic of Turkey in 1923.
4. Scheerbart (1914). *See also* Conrads (ed.) (1970) for a translation of Scheerbart, and *see* Benson (ed.) (2001) 127.
5. Wife of Prince Karl Max Lichnowsky, Anglophile Imperial German Ambassador to the Court of St James, 1912–14.
6. *See* Sharp (1966) 39–58.
7. James (1997) 28–47.
8. Many are illustrated in Sharp (1966).
9. Windsor (1981) 149–56 is an honourable exception.
10. Joan Campbell (1977) 130.
11. Hesse-Frielingshaus *et al.* (1971) 472–3; Isaacs (1983–4); Weber (2009) 5–94.
12. Jane S. Turner (ed.) (1998) **xxxi** 877.
13. Much concerning the *Bauhaus* in this Chapter is indebted to Frank Whitford's excellent study (*see* Whitford [1984]).
14. Franciscono (1971) 15.
15. *Ibid*.
16. Gropius (1919); Wingler (1978).
17. Taut (1920).
18. *Socialist* and *Workers* are here given in italics to emphasize the dubiousness of calling that Party 'right-wing'.
19. Taut (1919*a*, 1920). *See also* Sharp (1966) 85–96.
20. Alma (*née* Schindler), widow of Gustav Mahler, was Gropius's wife 1915–20.
21. Schreyer (1966) 142.
22. Jane S. Turner (ed.) (1998) **xvi** 789; Whitford (1984) 53–4.
23. Scheidig & Beyer (1967) 18.
24. Whitford (1984) 55.
25. *Ibid*.
26. Göppinger Galerie (1964) 39 and *passim*.
27. Whitford (1984) 151 and *passim*.
28. *Ibid*. 59.
29. *Ibid*. 44.
30. *Ibid*. 29.
31. Christian Geelhaar (1973) 12.
32. The capital of Thuringia is now Erfurt.

33. See *The Architectural Review* **cxxxiii**/793 (March 1963) 165–8; Banham (1960) 277–8.
34. See Schädlich (1989) for revealing correspondence.
35. For this monument *see* Winkler & Bergeijk (2004).
36. Nerdinger (1985) 46–7.
37. Wilk (ed.) (2006) 63–4.
38. Schlemmer (ed.) (1977) 96 and *passim*.
39. Basedow (1973) 60–1.
40. Referring to the composer, Richard Wagner.
41. Whitford (1984) 85.
42. Schlemmer (ed.) (1977) 59.
43. Hüter (1976) 142.
44. Whitford (1984) 95.
45. Kandinsky (1979); Klee (1968); Weber (2009) 204–58.
46. Whitford (1984) 97.
47. Wick (1982) 35. For Klee *see* Weber (2009) 95–203.
48. Whitford (1984) 117.
49. Jane S. Turner (ed.) (1998) **xxi** 792–6; Waetzold *et al.* (eds) (1977) 1/92.
50. Schreyer (1966) 138 and *passim*.
51. Moholy-Nagy (1950) 19, 35–9.
52. Farmer & Weiss (1971) 50. The contrast is clear in Whitford (1984) 130–1.
53. Neumann (ed.) (1970) 180–1.
54. Herzogenrath (ed.) (1968) 75.
55. Kater (2014) *passim*; Weber (2009) 62–75, 80, 143, 146, 480.
56. Whitford (1984) 70.
57. *Ibid.* 143–5.
58. *Ibid.* 150; Weber (2009) 66, 70–1, 74.
59. Wölfflin (1915).
60. Weber (2009) 70 and Whitford (1984) 144 for an illustration.
61. Jane S. Turner (ed.) (1998) i 74–5.
62. See Hilton Kramer (1995): 'My Long Search is Over' in *New Criterion* **xiv**/1 4–14. https://www.newcriterion.com/issues/1995/9/mondrian-mysticism-ldquomy-long-search-is-overrdquo accessed 4 January 2018.
63. Wilk (ed.) (2006) 30.
64. Jane S. Turner (ed.) (1998) **xxvi** 378.
65. Wilk (ed.) (2006) 55.
66. *Ibid.* 39.
67. *Ibid.* 148.
68. *Wissenschaftliche Zeitschrift der Hochschule für Architektur und Bauwesen* **xxvi**/4/5 (Weimar: 1979) 302. *See also* Weber (2009) 62–75, 80, 143, 146, 480.
69. Wingler (1978) 69.
70. *L'Esprit Nouveau* **xx** (January/February 1924); *Wissenschaftliche Zeitschrift der Hochschule für Architektur und Bauwesen* **xxvi**/4/5 (Weimar: 1979) 329.
71. Whitford (1984) 148.

72. Muche (1965) 153.

73. Personal communication from Professor Salingaros (18 February 2017).

74. *See* Kater (2014) and *London Review of Books* **xxxviii**/10 (19 May 2016) 31–2.

75. *Weimarische Zeitung* (6 July 1924); Hüter (1976) doc.93.

76. Schlemmer (ed.) (1977) letter to Otto Meyer-Amden (20 May 1924).

77. Curl (2011) 204–14.

78. Schwitters (1975) 93.

79. *Form+Zweck: Fachzeitschrift für industrielle Formgestaltung* **viii**/6 (1976) 4.

80. Note by Gropius on the Dessau *Bauhaus* (Dessau: 1926), quoted in Whitford (1984) 205–6.

81. *Ibid.*

82. *Ibid.*

83. *Ibid.*

84. *Ibid.*

85. *Ibid.*

86. *Ibid.*

87. *Ibid.*

88. *Ibid.*

89. *Ibid.*

90. *Ibid.*

91. My italics.

92. Whitford (1984) 206.

93. All the above from Whitford (1984) 205–6.

94. *Form+Zweck: Fachzeitschrift für industrielle Formgestaltung* **xi**/3 (1979) 66.

95. *See* Engelmann & Schädlich (1991); Schmitt (2006) S. 94–101.

96. Bauhaus-Archiv, Museum für Gestaltung (ed.) (1981) 184.

97. Kandinsky & Kruger (1976) 118.

98. Lancaster (2015) 80. *See also* Weber (2009) 84–8, 178–9, 239–43, 398.

99. Eckardt (1961) 73.

100. *Architektur der DDR* **xxxii**/10 (October 1983) 618–22; Müller (1975).

101. *See* Krier (ed.) (1985).

102. I am indebted to architectural colleagues in Berlin who discussed this with me during the organization of an exhibition there to celebrate the 750th anniversary of the founding of the city in 1987.

103. *See* Pontikis & Rofè (eds) (2016) 30–49; Salingaros & Masden II (2008) for observations on architectural education.

104. Meyer (1980) 42. *See also* Weber (2009) 90–2, 187, 197, 251–2, 401–3, 439–42.

105. *Form+Zweck: Fachzeitschrift für industrielle Formgestaltung* **viii**/6 (1976) 36.

106. Schmidt (1966) 47.

107. Corbusier (1946) 89, but first published by him in 1923.

108. *Bauhaus: Zeitschrift für Bau und Gestaltung* **ii**/4 (1928) 12–13; Meyer (1980) 47–9.

109. *Werk* **xiii**/7 (1926) 205–24; Meyer (1980) 27–32.

110. Both committed suicide in February 1933 after Hitler came to power.

111. Wattjes (ed.) (1927) 105.
112. Happe & Fischer (2003).
113. Jane S. Turner (ed.) (1998) **xiii** 688.
114. *Form+Zweck: Fachzeitschrift für industrielle Formgestaltung* **viii**/6 (1976) 35.
115. Moholy-Nagy (1950) 46.
116. Farmer & Weiss (1971) 30.
117. Schlemmer (ed.) (1977) 113.
118. The Dessau newspaper, *Anhalter Anzeiger*, which had earlier supported the *Bauhaus*, started to attack the institution, and by 1930 was overtly hostile (*see*, for example, the issue of 7 May 1930).
119. Meyer (1980) 69.
120. Schmidt (1966) 51.
121. Jane S. Turner (ed.) (1998) **xxi** 408.
122. *Ibid.* **xiii** 688.
123. Hermand & Trommler (1978) 414 and *passim*.

CHAPTER IV: THE INTERNATIONAL
STYLE 1920S & 1930S 121–70

1. 1914–18.
2. *Stadt* **xxix**/10 (1982) whole issue; Ziffer & Drebusch (eds) (1992) *passim*.
3. *Ibid.*; Jane S. Turner (ed.) (1998) **xxiv** 279.
4. For Mies's career *see* Schulze & Windhorst (2014).
5. Muthesius (1912). *See also* Muthesius (ed.) (1907).
6. Hochman (1989) 33–5, 43, n.321; Muthesius (1908–11); Jane S. Turner (ed.) (1998) **xxi** 490.
7. Frampton (2007) 161; Hochman (1989) 38; Jane S. Turner (ed.) (1998) **xxi** 490; Windsor (1981) 121–4.
8. Frank Lloyd Wright (1910–11).
9. Bergdoll (1994) 218–21; Börsch-Supan & Grisebach (1981) 203–5, 206–9; Zukowsky (ed.) (1994) 108, 138.
10. Bergdoll (1994) 210, 217, 222–5; Zukowsky (ed.) (1994) 109–10, 138.
11. Hoeber (1913); Pehnt (1987) 154; Windsor (1981) 137–8.
12. *See* Wolschke-Bulmahn (ed.) (2001).
13. *See* Nerdinger & Mai (eds) (1994).
14. Speer (ed.) (1941); Troost (ed.) (1942–3).
15. Frampton (2007) 162.
16. *See* Rosenau (ed.) (1953); Rosenau (1976).
17. Frampton (2007) 162.
18. Buddensieg *et al.* (1984) *passim*; Jane S. Turner (ed.) (1998) **iii** 511–14; Windsor (1981) 81, 93, 123.
19. James Stevens Curl (1991): 'Charlottenhof, Potsdam' in *The Architects' Journal* **cxciv**/4&5 (24 & 31 July) 22–39.
20. Schinkel (1989) 48 & plates 109–12.

21. Hochman (1989) 43; Jane S. Turner (ed.) (1998) **xxi** 490; Windsor (1981) 117.
22. Schinkel (1989) 51 & plates 137–9.
23. F.L. Wright (1910–11).
24. Berlage (1996) *passim.*
25. Hochman (1989) 23; Windsor (1981) 124.
26. Muthesius (1908–11, 1912); Muthesius (ed.) (1907).
27. Hochman (1989) *passim.*
28. *See* McFadzean (1979) 14–15, 30, 57–8, 79, 82, 141, 196, 216–20, 284–5; Stamp & McKinstry (eds) (1994) 3, 23, 32, 40–3, 174, 189–95, 212, 214, 232–3.
29. *See* Schinkel (1989) for a modern version.
30. Curtis (1996) 142.
31. Curl & Wilson (2015) 483–5; Schulze & Windhorst (2014) *passim;* Zukowsky (ed.) (1986) *passim.*
32. Hochman (1989) 49.
33. Curtis (1996) 189.
34. *Ibid.* 189–90.
35. Bastiaansen *et al.* (eds) (2008) i 1141.
36. In German *roh* is raw, unrefined, unwrought, crude, etc., and *Roheit* means rawness, crudeness, rudeness, roughness, brutality, etc. *See* Betteridge (ed.) (1978) 498.
37. James (1997) 127.
38. Reproduced in James (1997) 197.
39. Curtis (1996) 191–2; Hochman (1989) 12.
40. Illustrated in Curtis (1996) 192 and Hochman (1989) 53. Given his antipathy to mixing politics with architecture, designing this was a curious act on his part, and one that was to cause him difficulties after 1933.
41. Schulze & Windhorst (2014) for a comprehensive account.
42. *Architectura—Zeitschrift für Geschichte der Baukunst* **xxxvi**/2 (January 2006) 199–220.
43. The Lange house was illustrated in Hitchcock & Johnson (1966) 185.
44. Zukowsky (ed.) (1994) 108–9.
45. *Ibid.* 52–3.
46. Hochman (1989) 13–31.
47. Hochman (1989) 41; Lewis & O'Connor (1994) 23 and *passim.*
48. Mertins & Jennings (eds) (2011) *passim.*
49. Riley & Bergdoll *et al.* (2002) 206.
50. Hochman (1989) *passim;* J.S. Turner (ed.) (1998) 490–4.
51. Schulze & Windhorst (2014) *passim.*
52. Mies van der Rohe *et al.* (eds) (1927).
53. *See* Hitchcock, Johnson, & Mumford (1932); Hitchcock & Johnson (1966).
54. Kitchen (2015) 30.
55. *Internationale Revue* i (1927) 348.
56. *See* Mertins (2014) 206–7, 217; Mertins & Jennings (eds) (2011) 89–90, 154–6; Neumeyer (1991) 21; Poppelreuter (2007) 127, 143; Poppelreuter (2016) *passim;* Schulze & Windhorst (2014) 45, 89, 91.

57. *See Wohnungswirtschaft* **vi** (1929) 281–2; *Technisches Gemeindeblatt* **xxxi**/2 (1928) 155; Neubert (1926) 24–6; *Die Form* **ii**/2 (1927) 40–6.

58. *Die Form* **ii**/2 (1927) 47–9.

59. Deutscher Werkbund (ed.) (1927) 103.

60. Ebeling (1926, 1947).

61. Pehnt & Strohl (1997) *passim*.

62. Guardini (1925).

63. Prinzhorn (1922).

64. Meyer *et al.* (1925); Nerdinger (ed.) (1993); Neubert (1926); Quiring *et al.* (eds) (2011).

65. Neumeyer (1991) 51–61.

66. *Ibid.* 200.

67. Carus (1846).

68. This was in his *Attempt at a Self-Criticism* added to the 1886 edn. of *The Birth of Tragedy: or, Hellenism and Pessimism*.

69. Lewis & O'Connor (1994) 175.

70. *Ibid.* 156.

71. *Ibid.*

72. Cook & Klotz (1973). *See also Architecture Plus* **i**/8 (September 1973) 80.

73. *See* Poppelreuter (2007, 2016).

74. Jencks (1990) 139–69; Lewis & O'Connor (1994) *passim*.

75. For Pevsner's attitudes towards religion *see* Harries (2011) 47–8, 162–3, 400, 541–2, 784.

76. Symondson (2011) *passim*.

77. Symondson & Bucknall (2006) 196–7.

78. The literature on this is vast, and would be impossible to include here. *See*, however, Tombs (2014) for interesting confirmation of the potency of religion that was underrated almost entirely in the second half of the twentieth century, and especially *see* Wood (2016) and Douglas Murray (2017) for perceptive remarks on how the West has failed to grasp truths.

79. Botar & Wünsche (eds) (2011) 16ff.; Lebovic (2013) *passim*.

80. Poppelreuter (2016) 258.

81. Neumeyer (1991) 252.

82. This was especially true of his work at the Illinois Institute of Technology. *See* Millais (2009) 49–50, 238–41, 264.

83. Falter (2003); Lebovic (2013); Phelan (ed.) (1985) 80.

84. Brodersen & Fuchs (eds) (2002) 34.

85. Prinzhorn (1927).

86. For ramifications of philosophy and other matters supposedly influencing Miës, *see* Brodersen & Fuchs (eds) (2002), Ebeling (1926, 1947), Guardini (1925), Hellpach (1917), Klages (1926, 1981), Mertins (2014), Mertins & Jennings (eds) (2011), Neumeyer (1991), Pöldinger (ed.) 1992), Poppelreuter (2007, 2016), Prinzhorn (1922, 1927), Schulze & Windhorst (2014).

87. But *see* Hochman (1989).

88. Bongartz *et al.* (1977).
89. It also had Egyptianizing influences: *see* Pehnt (1987) 156.
90. *See* Teut (ed.) (1967) 29.
91. Kirsch (1987).
92. Kiem (1997).
93. Schmitthenner (1932).
94. Kirsch (1987).
95. Mertins (2014) 180; Hitchcock & Johnson (1966) 182–4.
96. For criticisms of the Tugendhat house, *see Die Form* **vi**/9 (September 1931) 76, **vi**/10 (October 1931) 392–3, **vi**/11 (November 1931) 437–8. *See also* Mertins (2014) 175; Hitchcock & Johnson (1966) 186–90.
97. For further information *see* the useful accounts of Peter Adam (1992), Lane (1968), Spotts (2002), R.R. Taylor (1974), and, especially, Zukowsky (ed.) (1994*a*).
98. For further interesting insights *see* Nerdinger (ed.) (1993); Speer (1970); Speer (ed.) (1941); Troost (ed.) (1942–3).
99. Zukowsky (ed.) (1994*a*) 12–13, 26. The building was published in *Monatshefte für Baukunst und Städtebau* (June 1939).
100. Curl & Wilson (2015) 192–3. *See also* Gray (2012) 97, 109, 167, 185, 196, 200–2, 204, 226, 235, 239, 245–76, 280.
101. Ford (1923) *passim.*
102. James (1997) 70.
103. *Ibid.* 71.
104. Mendelsohn (1929) *passim.*
105. *Ibid.* 5, 214, 217.
106. *Ibid.* 16, 171, 185, 217.
107. *Ibid.* 37–112; James (1997) 73.
108. James (1997) 75.
109. *Ibid.* 93.
110. *Ibid.*
111. Goodhart-Rendel (1953) 267.
112. *Ibid.*
113. Blauert *et al.* (eds) (2009) 10–15, 56–63, 138–57.
114. *Ibid.* 152–3.
115. Anuszewski *et al.* (2011).
116. Also known as *Der deutsche Orden, Deutsche Ritter*, or Teutonic Knights of St Mary's hospital at Jerusalem.
117. Father of Karl Liebknecht.
118. Liebknecht (1892).
119. *See* Röhl (2004, 2014).
120. Paul Reitter in *Times Literary Supplement* (18 March 2016) 28.
121. For Jews and German department-stores, *see* Lerner (2015).
122. James (1997) 202–3.
123. *Ibid.* 203.

124. Hitchcock, Johnson, & Mumford (1932); Hitchcock & Johnson (1966).

125. Sigrist (1930) 65.

126. *Ibid. passim.*

127. *See* Lane (1968) 125–45.

128. *See* Strohmeyer (1980) 153–8, and *see especially* Buchner (1931) *passim.*

129. James (1997) 208.

130. *See especially* Mendelsohn (1924, 1930) and Scheffauer (tr.) (1924).

131. Brown & Henson also designed the Black & White Milk Bar, Gray's Inn Road, London (1937—destroyed), a very Mendelsohnian essay, with lettering reminiscent of that in the cash-register area of the Schocken store in Stuttgart.

132. *See* Charlton, Harwood, & Powers (eds) (2007) 16–38.

133. Mendelsohn (1932).

134. 'Mendelsohn-Haus und Goethe-Haus' in *Wasmuths Monatshefte für Baukunst* **xvi** (1932) 548.

135. Neumeyer (1986) 244 and *see also* the translation (Neumeyer [1991]) and Schulze & Windhorst (2014) *passim.*

136. To the *Kongreß des Internationale Verbandes für kulturelle Zusammenarbeit.*

137. Mendelsohn (1932a).

138. As note 134 above.

139. *See*, for example, Gustav Wolf (1940); Heymanns Verlag (1936); Troost (ed.) (1942–3).

140. Hochman (1989) 158.

141. James (1997) 235; Hochman (1989) 304–5.

142. James (1997) 239; *Architectural History* **xxxiii** (1990) 135–66; *The Architects' Journal* **lxxix** (8 February 1934) 205–23.

143. Walker (2000) 86, 621.

144. 'Jencks on Johnson' in *Building Design* (4 February 2005) 9; *The Times* (28 January 2005) 69–70; Saint (2005); *RIBA Journal* (3 March 2005) xix.

145. James (1997) 245.

146. Hitchcock, Johnson, & Mumford (1932); Hitchcock & Johnson (1966).

147. Schulze (1994) 73; *see also* Forgey (1982) 1–2.

148. James (1997) 245.

149. Wattjes (1927) 132–3; Šlapeta *et al.* (eds) 2010) *passim.*

150. Forgey (1982) 1.

151. *Ibid.* 5.

152. *Ibid.*

153. *Ibid.* 2.

154. *Ibid.*

155. Hitchcock & Johnson (1966), but referring to the original 1932 edn.

156. Forgey (1982) 4.

157. Gold (2013) 258–9.

158. Weber (2009) 39, 48, 228–32, and *passim.*

159. Brandreth (2006) 77; Richards (1980) 123.

160. *See* Nerdinger (ed.) (1993) 153–65; Pommer & Otto (1991) 96–145.

161. Johnson was scathing about Gropius's abilities and work: *see* Lewis & O'Connor (1994) 23–4, 88–9, 156 and *passim*; Jencks (1990) 144.

162. Giedion (1941) 394.

163. Quoted in McFadden & Smith (2004) 241.

164. *See*, for example, Curl (2011, 2011*a*) for these matters.

165. Hitchcock, Johnson, & Mumford (1932); Hitchcock & Johnson (1966).

166. Venturi (1966) ch. ii.

167. Jane S. Turner (ed.) (1998) **xxxii** 234–6.

168. Hochman (1989) *passim*; Whitford (1984) 192–201.

169. Kandinsky & Kruger (1976) 144.

170. Meyer (1980) 79.

171. R. R. Taylor (1974) 44, 54.

172. *Bauten der Bewegung* (1939) **i** iv.

173. Schmidt (1966) 7.

174. Neumann (ed.) (1970) 229.

175. Kandinsky & Kruger (1976) 150.

176. Gaber (1966) 126.

177. On the closing of the *Bauhaus*, *see* Teut (ed.) (1967) 138–42; Wingler (1978) 11, 181–9, 558–65; *Journal of the Society of Architectural Historians* **xxiv**/1 (1965) 24f., and **xxiv**/3 (1965) 254–6.

178. Hochman (1989) 150–1, 156, 173–4, 247–8, 256–7, 282–3; Lane (1968) *passim*; Millais (2009) 239.

179. Dwork & van Pelt (1996); Holborn (ed.) 1972); Kershaw (1998, 2000); Spotts (2002); R. R. Taylor (1974).

180. Spotts (2002) 340.

181. Peter Adam (1992) 52.

182. Illustrated in *Wissenschaftliche Zeitschrift der Hochschule für Architektur und Bauwesen Weimar* **xxxix**/1/2 (1993) 106–7; Riley, Bergdoll, *et al.* (2002) 284–7.

183. *Wissenschaftliche Zeitschrift der Hochschule für Architektur und Bauwesen Weimar* **xxxix**/1/2 (1993) 104–5; Riley, Bergdoll, *et al.* (2002) 63–4; Wilk (ed.) (2006) 361.

184. Hochman (1989) is revealing on this.

185. *Ibid.* 225.

186. *Ibid.* 173–4, 247–8, 256–7, 282–3.

187. *Ibid.*

188. Troost (ed.) (1942) **i** 103–14.

189. Hochman (1989) *passim*.

190. Krier (ed.) (1985).

191. Hochman (1989) 283.

192. *Ibid.* 283, 349 n.4.

193. *The Magazine of Art* (October 1945) 211–30.

194. Hochman (1989) 81, 133, 165, 172, 330 n.25.

195. *Ibid.* 169, 173.

196. Holborn (ed.) (1972) 400.

197. Brenner (1963) 68; Hochman (1989) 166.

198. Hochman (1989) 166–7.
199. Brenner (1963) 68 and *passim*.
200. Holborn (ed.) (1972) *passim*.
201. Teut (ed.) (1967) 90–1.
202. Lane (1968) 176.
203. *See* Hochman (1989) *passim*.
204. *Ibid.* 168, 170–4, 202–5, 209–10.
205. *Ibid.* 173.
206. *Ibid.*
207. Neumann (ed.) (1970) 231.
208. Hochman (1989) 173, 336 n.34.
209. For Hitler's tastes *see* Stratigakos (2015).
210. Spotts (2002) is illuminating on these matters, but *see also* Troost (ed.) (1942–3).
211. *See* Peter Adam (1992) *passim*.
212. Brenner (ed.) (1972) 145; *see also* Hochman (1989) *passim*. The architect's name is spelled 'Miës' on the headed paper held in the *Archiv der Preussischen Akademie der Künste*, and his address is given as Berlin W 35, *Am Karlsbad* 24. It is also the case that 'Miës' with *Umlaut* is the form used consistently by Hitchcock & Johnson (1966) *passim*, and, lately, by Howard (2016).
213. *See* Hochman (1989) *passim*.
214. Britt (ed.) (1995) is illuminating on this. *See also* R.R. Taylor (1974).
215. *Wissenschaftliche Zeitschrift der Hochschule für Architektur und Bauwesen Weimar* **xxxix**/1/2 (1993) 103.
216. Hochman (1989) 283, 349 n.6.
217. 18 August 1934.
218. Spotts (2002) 392.
219. Troost (ed.) (1942–3) i 103. *See also* Petsch (1976) 183.
220. Zukowsky (ed.) (1994a) 16–17.
221. Spotts (2002) 341.
222. Lane (1968) 204.
223. Kitchen (2015) 34; Petsch (1976) 183.
224. Troost (ed.) (1942–3) ii 73–5.
225. *Ibid.* i 113.
226. *Ibid.* i 108–11; ii 66–8.
227. *Ibid.* i 114; ii 69–70.
228. *Ibid.* i 103–5.
229. Kitchen (2015) 25. *See also* Petsch (1976) *passim* for an excellent overview of the period.
230. Larsson (1983).
231. Krier (ed.) (1985).
232. Jenkins (2006). But *see* Stevenson (2018) *passim*.
233. For aspects of Rosenberg *see* Matthäus & Bajohr (2015); Wittman & Kinney (2016).
234. Rosenberg (1934) 6.

235. *Ibid.* 386. For more information on architecture in National Socialist ideology *see* R.R. Taylor (1974).

236. Spotts (2002) 311–402.

237. *See* 'Mies, Politics, and the Bauhaus Closure' in *Proceedings* of the 85th annual meeting and technology conference of the Association of Collegiate Schools of Architecture (1997) 617–22.

238. Wolfe (1981) 18–19. For Albers's destructive activities *see* Lending (2017).

239. Curl & Wilson (2015) 709.

240. Piltz (1982) 246.

241. McDonough (2015) *passim.*

242. *The Times Saturday Review* (8 August 2015) 13.

243. Lancaster (2015) 76–9.

244. Lancaster (2015) 78.

245. Blomfield (1934) 134.

246. *Ibid.* 140.

247. *Ibid.* 141.

248. Junior Storm Leader (i.e. Lieutenant): he was promoted *SS-Hauptsturmführer* (equivalent to Captain) while at Auschwitz. His SS number was 417.971.

249. For the inglorious career of this *Bauhaus*-trained architect, *see* Seeger (2013).

250. Senior Assault (*or* Storm) Leader, equivalent to First Lieutenant.

251. Storm Unit Leader, equivalent to Major.

252. Curl (2011) 96. *See also* Seeger (2013) for an excellent analysis. I am also indebted to Robert Jan van Pelt for interesting insights.

253. Charney (1991) 35–53; Curl (2011) 93–6; Dwork & van Pelt (1996) 197–235; Pelt (1984).

254. *See* Ballard (1975).

CHAPTER V: THE INTERNATIONAL STYLE TRULY
INTERNATIONAL 171–216

1. Howard (2016) *passim.*

2. Saint (2005).

3. *Ibid.*

4. *Ibid.*

5. *Ibid.*

6. Forgey (1982).

7. Hanks (ed.) (2015) 14.

8. *Ibid.* 15.

9. *Ibid.* 33.

10. Somol (ed.) (1997) 44.

11. Hanks (ed.) (2015) 33 and notes 27–8.

12. Hitchcock & Johnson (1966) 205.

13. Bayer *et al.* (eds) (1938) 5.

14. Exhibition 15.

15. Hitchcock, Johnson, & Mumford (1932).
16. Exhibition 27.
17. Exhibition 34.
18. Hanks (ed.) (2015) 33.
19. Miës is given thus throughout Hitchcock & Johnson (1966) *passim*.
20. Saint (2005).
21. Howard (2016) *passim*; Franz Schulze (1994) *passim*.
22. Goodhart-Rendel (1953) 267.
23. Forgey (1982). *See* Stevenson (2018) *passim*.
24. Hitchcock, Johnson, & Mumford (1932) 158.
25. Hanks (ed.) (2015) 25.
26. Exhibition 46.
27. Exhibition 55.
28. *Architectural Forum* lviii (January 1933) 20.
29. *The Hound and Horn* vii/2 (January–March 1934) 278–83.
30. 'Art in the Third Reich—Preview 1933' in *The Magazine of Art* xxxviii/6 (October 1945) 212–22.
31. Hitler (1933, 2008).
32. Colomina (1998) is illuminating on this.
33. Kentgens-Craig (1999) 233–7 reproduces the Chicago catalogue.
34. *Ibid.* 70–1.
35. Hitchcock, Johnson, & Mumford (1932).
36. Hanks (ed.) (2015) 150–1.
37. *Ibid.* 151.
38. *New York Sun* (10 March 1934).
39. *Parnassus* vi/5 (October 1934) 27; *Parnassus* vii/2 (February 1935) 6–8; *The Art Digest* viii/12 (15 March 1934) 10; *The American Magazine of Art* xxvii/5 (May 1934) 267.
40. As did Frank Lloyd Wright, who preferred 'honest arrogance' to 'hypocritical humility': Johnson had similar preferences. *See* Howard (2016) 244 and *passim*.
41. For these, and other matters, *see* Staniszewski (1998) 158 and *passim*, and Hanks (ed.) (2015) *passim*.
42. Saint (2005).
43. Howard (2016) 145.
44. Saint (2005).
45. For art and architecture under National Socialism, *see* Adam (1992), Braungart (ed.) (2002), Britt (ed.) (1995), Kitchen (2015), Spotts (2002), R.R. Taylor (1974).
46. Jencks (1990) 150.
47. Saint (2005), also quoted in Howard (2016) 147 and Schulze (1994) 139.
48. Howard (2016) 147.
49. Jencks (1990) 147.
50. *ODNB* x (2004) 345–6.

51. Powers (2013) 277.
52. Hitchcock & Bauer (1937).
53. The hardback catalogue came out in an English co-edition from George Allen & Unwin.
54. Hitchcock & Bauer (1937).
55. *RIBA Journal* **xliv** (22 May 1937) 746–7.
56. Gold (2013) is a useful paper on this matter.
57. Hitchcock, Johnson, & Mumford (1932).
58. Powers (2013) has interesting things to say on this.
59. Bayer *et al.* (eds) (1938) 6. But *see* Lending (2017) for iconoclasm.
60. *See* Staniszewski (1998) 142–52.
61. *New York Times* (11 December 1938).
62. Hanks (ed.) (2015) 37.
63. *New Yorker* **xiv**/46 (31 December 1938) 40.
64. Hitchcock & Bauer (1937); Powers (2013).
65. Jane S. Turner (ed.) (1998) **xxii** 282–3.
66. Mumford (1924).
67. Mumford (1938).
68. Hitchcock, Johnson, & Mumford (1932).
69. Mumford (1961).
70. Hanks (ed.) (2015) 217 n.59.
71. Lewis & O'Connor (1994) 23.
72. Hanks (ed.) (2015) 40.
73. *See* Mehaffy & Salingaros (2013).
74. Bayer *et al.* (eds) (1938) 5–6 and Hanks (ed.) (2015) *passim*.
75. Lewis & O'Connor (1994) 23.
76. *Ibid*.
77. *Ibid*.
78. Pearlman (2007) *passim*.
79. Lewis & O'Connor (1994) 23.
80. *Ibid*.
81. *Ibid*. 23–4; 'Jencks on Johnson' in *Building Design* (4 February 2005) 9.
82. Hochman (1989) xv.
83. *Ibid*.
84. Harries (2011) 165.
85. Jencks (1990) 149. But *see Architectural Association Quarterly* (*AAQ*) **vi**/2 (1974) 58. Pevsner, not unnaturally, strongly objected to this.
86. Jencks (1990) 149.
87. Lane (1968) 181 and *passim*.
88. Harries (2011) 81, 110–14, 116–19, 123–4, 127, 148–50, 165–8, 190, 233, 259, 284, 306.
89. Hochman (1989) 315.
90. *Ibid*. 316.
91. *Der Querschnitt* **iii** (1924) quoted in Johnson (1978) 186.

92. *Journal of the Society of Architectural Historians* **xxiv** (October 1965) 256.

93. Hochman (1989) 316.

94. *See* Corbusier (1935) for what he had in store for us.

95. *See* Arendt (2004); Hochman (1989) 311–16.

96. Watkin (1977).

97. Hochman (1989) 318.

98. 'Jencks on Johnson' in *Building Design* (4 February 2005) 9.

99. Howard (2016) *passim*.

100. 'Jencks on Johnson' in *Building Design* (4 February 2005) 9.

101. Lewis & O'Connor (1994) 23.

102. *Ibid.* 24.

103. *Ibid.*

104. *Ibid.*

105. Title of book by Sigfried Giedion: *see* Giedion (1948).

106. Lewis & O'Connor (1994) 24.

107. *Ibid.* 19.

108. *Ibid.* 23.

109. *Ibid.*

110. For these matters *see* Pearlman (2007), a generally uncritical study.

111. For a useful overview of Modernist architecture in Czechoslovakia, *see* Anděl (2006).

112. For Czechoslovak architects *see* Anděl (2006); Leśnikowski (ed.) (1996) 37–109; Leuthäuser & Gössel (eds) (1990) 335–61.

113. *See* Teige (2002).

114. *Arkhitekturnaya gazeta* (23 March 1935).

115. *Stroitel'stvo Moskvy* **iv** (1935) 36.

116. Jane S. Turner (ed.) (1008) 381–3.

117. Kopp (1986).

118. Khan-Magomedov (1986).

119. *See* Kopp (1970).

120. *See* Britt (ed.) (1995) 186–256.

121. *See* Dreysse (2001) for May's work in Frankfurt.

122. *See* Anděl (2006) and Leśnikowski (1996).

123. For Teige *see* Dluhosch & Švácha (eds) (1999).

124. For architecture under the dictators, *see* Britt (ed.) (1995).

125. *Zeitschrift für Kommunalwirtschaft und Kommunalpolitik* **ix**/10 (1911) 386.

126. Sharp (1966) 40–6.

127. Wachowiak (ed.) **ii** (1930) 3–163.

128. Cichy (1974).

129. Leuthäuser & Gössel (eds) (1990) 276–85; Leśnikowski (ed.) (1996) 181–95.

130. Hitchcock & Johnson (1966) 164–5.

131. Loo (ed.) (2003) *passim*; Leuthäuser & Gössel (eds) (1990) 39–49.

132. Leuthäuser & Gössel (eds) (1990) 50–3.

133. Hitchcock & Johnson (1966) 97.

134. *Ibid.* 111.
135. *Ibid.* 102–3.
136. *Ibid.* 174–5.
137. *Ibid.* 220–1.
138. Elmlund & Mårtelius (eds) (2015).
139. Blomfield (1934) 61–2.
140. Hitchcock & Johnson (1966) 112–13.
141. *Ibid.* 162–3.
142. *Ibid.* 158–9.
143. *See* Kilham (1973) for Hood.
144. Hitchcock & Johnson (1966) 156–7.
145. *Ibid.* 192–3. According to Philip Johnson, Neutra wished that 'Hitler would give him a job' (*see* Jencks [1990] 149).
146. Hitchcock & Johnson (1966) 222–3.
147. For a recent study of Wright and Johnson *see* Howard (2016) *passim*.
148. *Prologomena* **xiii**/1 (1984) special issue.
149. Published in Vienna by Anton Schroll.
150. *Ibid.*
151. Muthesius (1902).
152. Muthesius (1908–11).
153. Wagner (1988).
154. Geretsegger *et al.* (1983); Graf (1994); Pintarić (1989).
155. Sekler (1985); Jane S. Turner (ed.) (1998) **xiv** 627–31.
156. Prelovšek (1997).
157. Giedion (1941) 240, 243, 388, 407, 423.
158. Jane S. Turner (ed.) (1998) **xiv** 631.
159. *See* the comprehensive two-volume Graf (1994).
160. Hautmann & Hautmann (1980).
161. The Modern Movement was largely disseminated by the mass media, aided by huge financial and political backing. *See*, for example, Colomina (1998) and Nathaniel Robert Walker (2016).
162. Supposedly derived from the name of a relative on his mother's side called Lecorbésier *or* Le Corbésier, but seemingly connected with *corbeau*, meaning 'crow' *or* 'raven'. It is perhaps worth noting that other authoritarian figures also adopted pseudonyms: in the case of Joseph Vissarionovich Dzhugashvili, the name assumed was 'Stalin' (Man of Steel).
163. Lancaster (2015a) 68. Salingaros *et al.* (2006) 182 also sees similarities, in that within both Hitler's and Le Corbusier's books lurk recipes for destruction. *See also* Millais (2009) 93, and Millais (2017) *passim*.
164. Birksted (2009) 10.
165. Roth (1927). *See also* Roth (ed.) (1946).
166. Corbusier (1946) 114–19.
167. Watkin (2005) 609.
168. For example, Giedion (1941).

169. Quoted from Corbusier (1935) in Mehaffy & Salingaros (2013).

170. Perelman (2015).

171. Even odder, some of his other connections are expounded in Birksted (2009).

172. Awarded a prize. 'Premiated' was the term usually given to prize-winning designs in architectural competitions from the nineteenth century onwards.

173. Jeanneret-Gris (1928).

174. Jane S. Turner (ed.) (1998) **xix** 43.

175. *Sovetskoye iskusstvo* **iii** (March 1932).

176. Britt (ed.) (1995) 51.

177. *Ibid. passim.*

178. Senger (1928, 1931).

179. Jane S. Turner (ed.) (1998) **xix** 52; Umbdenstock (1932, 1933–4).

180. *Ibid.*

181. Corbusier (1933). The term has resonances in the Islamic world, connecting Western Modernism with something hated.

182. Jane S. Turner (ed.) (1998) **xix** 52.

183. Reprinted in *Oppositions* iv.

184. Jarcy (2015); Millais (2017) *passim.*

185. Noted in Jencks (1990) 149. *See also* Chaslin (2015); Jarcy (2015); Millais (2017).

186. Perelman (2015).

187. *Ibid.*; Chaslin (2015); Fishman (1982) 180, 237; Jarcy (2015); Millais (2017).

188. Anthony Daniels (2015): 'The Cult of Le Corbusier' in *Quadrant* **lix**/9 (September) 38–42. *See* https://quadrant.org.au/magazine/2015/09/cult-le-corbusier/ and https://architecturehereandthere.com/2017/02/25/corbusier-fascist-drivel/. *See also* Millais (2015, 2017).

189. Chaslin (2015); Jarcy (2015); Perelman (2015).

190. *The Times* (17 April 2015) 35.

191. *See* Chaslin (2015); Fishman (1982); Jencks (1987, 1990); Jarcy (2015); Perelman (2015).

192. Fishman (1982) 245.

193. Pierrefeu & Le Corbusier (1942).

194. For Corbusier and Vichy *see* Fishman (1982) 243–52.

195. *See* note 188 above.

196. *See* Simon Richards (2003).

197. Corbusier (1946) 96–7.

198. *Ibid.* 5.

199. *Ibid.*

200. Blomfield (1934) 71.

201. Britt (ed.) (1995) 201.

202. 'If you seek a monument, look around' (inscription at the place of entombment in St Paul's Cathedral, London, of Sir Christopher Wren, its architect, attributed to his son, also Christopher).

203. Blomfield (1934) 162–3.

204. Murray & Osley (eds) (2009) 39.

205. *Ibid.* 43.

206. *Ibid.*

207. http://www.metropolismag.com/Point-of-View/December-2015/Why-Do-Some-People-Choose-Oppressive-Environments/

208. Murray & Osley (eds) (2009) 263.

209. *Ibid.* 36. *See The Observer* (29 January 1928).

210. Murray & Osley (eds) (2009) 37–8.

211. *Ibid.* 261.

212. *Ibid.* 262.

213. *Ibid.* 294–7.

214. *See*, for example, David Hemsoll (1989): 'Reconstructing the octagonal dining room of Nero's Golden House' in *Architectural History* **xxxii** 1–17.

215. Murray & Osley (eds) (2009) 74.

216. *See*, for example, Beanland (2016), Calder (2016), and Harwood (2015).

217. Hitchcock & Johnson (1966) 138–9.

218. Etlin (1991).

219. For a taste of these matters *see* Newman (ed.) (1961) *passim.*

220. *Casabella* **lxxiii** (January 1934); Britt (ed.) (1995) 120–83.

221. Work by the Italians listed here is illustrated in Leuthäuser & Gössel (eds) (1990) 166–227.

222. Hitchcock & Johnson (1966) 136–7.

223. Quoted in Cherry & Pevsner (1998) 243.

224. Leuthäuser & Gössel (eds) (1990) 137–41.

225. Goodhart-Rendel (1953) 258.

226. *Ibid.* 274.

227. Nairn & Pevsner (1971) 262.

228. Sheppard (ed.) (1973) 334.

229. Fry (1944) 32.

230. Cherry & Pevsner (1991) 531.

231. Sheppard (ed.) (1973) n.334.

232. Fry (1944) 77–9 & plates 21–2.

233. *Ibid.* Ch. 4.

234. Nairn & Pevsner (1971) 152.

235. Leuthäuser & Gössel (1990) 154–5.

236. For McGrath *see The Architectural Review* **clxii**/695 (July 1977) 58–64; *Thirties Society Journal* **iii** (1982) 2–11.

237. *Thirties Society Journal* **iii** (1982) 36–42.

238. *The Architectural Review* **lxxix**/470 (January 1936) 10.

239. Coe & Reading (1981).

240. An overview of 'International-Style' houses can be gained from Yorke (1946) *passim.*

241. Hitchcock & Bauer (1937); Powers (2013).

242. Gold (2013).

243. For insights regarding the powerful Modernist forces unleased in the 1950s, *see* Stamp (2013*a*).

244. Stevenson (2018) *passim*; Todd & Mortimer (1929) 28.

CHAPTER VI: UNIVERSAL ACCEPTANCE OF THE INTERNATIONAL
STYLE 217–46

1. My italics.
2. Hitchcock, Johnson, & Mumford (1932).
3. Hitchcock & Johnson (1966). *See also* Hanks (ed.) (2015) *passim*.
4. *London Review of Books* **xxxviii**/6 (17 March 2016) 25–8.
5. *See*, for example, Caro (2015).
6. *See* Stamp (2009, 2010, 2013) for an eloquent account of this, and also Colls (2002) 344–7.
7. Tombs (2014) 765.
8. *See* Lancaster (2015*b*) 46–7.
9. Jacobs (1961) *passim*.
10. Blomfield (1934).
11. All quotes from Lancaster (2015) 80.
12. Waugh (1928).
13. Waugh (1947) 135.
14. *Ibid.* 136.
15. *Ibid.*
16. I knew some of them personally, and, when young, observed their insistence on their own rightness.
17. *Architect & Building News* **cxlv** (10 January 1936) 56–7.
18. Colomina (1998) *passim*. *See also* http://www.academia.edu/5074196/Geometrical_fundamentalism, accessed 1 February 2017
19. *The Architectural Review* **lxv**/386 (January 1929) 17–31.
20. Esher (1981) 85.
21. *Ibid.* But *see* Stevenson (2018) *passim*.
22. Fry (1975) 147.
23. My italics.
24. Fry (1944) 2.
25. Hitchcock & Johnson (1966); Leuthäuser & Gössel (eds) (1990).
26. Giedion (1941).
27. Pevsner (1960, 2005).
28. Hitchcock & Johnson (1966) vii.
29. *Ibid.* 11.
30. *Ibid.*
31. *Ibid.* 19–20.
32. *Ibid.* 20.
33. *Ibid.* 14.
34. *Ibid.* 15.
35. *Ibid.* x.
36. *Ibid.* xi.
37. *Ibid.* 14.
38. *See* Buchanan (2015) 32; Millais (2009) *passim*.
39. Mehaffy & Salingaros (2013).

40. Corbusier (1946).
41. *Ibid.* 121–38.
42. *Ibid.* 81–97.
43. *Ibid.* 99–119.
44. *Ibid.* 25–33.
45. *Ibid.* 29.
46. Millais (2009) 95.
47. Jean-Louis Cohen in Corbusier (2008) 8.
48. Colomina (1998) 124. Cohen in Corbusier (2008) also makes these points.
49. Corbusier (1946) 188.
50. *Ibid.* 195.
51. *Ibid.* 198.
52. Le Corbusier does not appear to have realized (or he ignored) the fact that Greek temples were coloured, and were not left as bare white marble.
53. Gropius (1935) 19.
54. *Ibid.* 20–1.
55. *Ibid.* 23.
56. *Ibid.* 30.
57. *Ibid.* 92.
58. *Ibid.* 112.
59. Blomfield (1934) 4.
60. *Dictionary of Irish Biography* **viii** (2009) 528–9.
61. Robertson (1925) *passim.*
62. Blomfield (1934) 4. *See* Stevenson (2018) *passim.*
63. *Dictionary of Irish Biography* **viii** (2009) 528.
64. Blomfield (1934) 4.
65. *See* Curl (2011*a*) 181–2.
66. *See* Duffy (1999).
67. Blomfield (1934) 81.
68. *Ibid.* 51.
69. *Ibid.*
70. *Ibid.*
71. Barman (1926).
72. Blomfield (1934) 162–4.
73. Towndrow (1933) *passim.*
74. Blomfield (1934) 164.
75. Cohen-Portheim (1933).
76. Blomfield (1934) 170.
77. S.F. Wright (1932).
78. Blomfield (1934) 173–4.
79. *Ibid.* 175.
80. Umbdenstock (1932, 1933–4). *See also* Blomfield (1934) 177–8 and Boutron (1931).
81. Blomfield (1934) 136.

82. *Ibid.* 71.
83. *Ibid.* 79.
84. *Ibid.*
85. *See* Lewis & O'Connor (1994) *passim.*
86. Venturi (1966).
87. Botta (1991); Frampton (2007) 294–7, 306, 322, 338–9; Grassi (1982); Gregotti (1993); Krier & Pavan (eds) (1978); Melvin (2005); Porphyrios (ed.) (1993); Rossi (1982).
88. Jencks (1987*a*); Papadakis & Watson (eds) (1990).
89. Curl & Wilson (2015) 524; Gregotti (1993); Katz (1994); Kelbaugh (2002); Krier & Pavan (1980).
90. *See* Colquhoun (2002); Curl & Wilson (2015) 520–2; Frampton (2007); Salingaros *et al.* (2004); Watkin (1977); Woodham (1997).
91. Jencks (1987*a*).
92. Daniels (1998); Jane S. Turner (ed.) (1998) **xiv** 520–2.
93. Salingaros *et al.* (2004).
94. Schumacher (ed.) (2016).
95. His prefabricated house in Ash Street, Cambridge, MA (1942), cost twice as much as it would have cost if built in a traditional manner (Lewis & O'Connor [1994] 24).
96. Kater (2014).
97. *See* Gropius (1935) and Whitford (1984).
98. A doctrine 'of idlers and Belgians', according to Charles Baudelaire: *La Croyance au progrès est une doctrine de paresseux, une doctrine de Belges (Journaux Intimes* [1887] IX).
99. Goodhart-Rendel (1953) 282.
100. *See* Mehaffy & Salingaros (2013).
101. Lancaster (2015) 80–1.
102. Philippou (2008).
103. Wood (2016) should be read for contemporary myopic reactions to the forces of religion.
104. *See* Lancaster (2015*b*) 46–7.
105. Corbusier (1946) 12, 14.
106. Gold (2007) 273–6.
107. Lancaster (2015*a*) 50, 68. *See also* Todd & Mortimer (1929) *passim.*
108. Jane S. Turner (ed.) (1998) **xi** 727–8.
109. *Ibid.* **vii** 292–6; 343–4.
110. Steinmann (ed.) (1979).
111. Britt (ed.) (1995) 187.
112. *Ibid.* 186.
113. *Ibid.*
114. Trotsky (1960).
115. For such matters *see* Elliott (1986).
116. Britt (ed.) (1995) 187.

117. Golomstock (1990), esp. 112–13.
118. For useful insights *see* Bown (1991); London (1937).
119. Wilk (ed.) (2006) 173.
120. Gropius (1935); Gropius (1956) 13, 21, and *passim*.
121. Giedion (1941).
122. Hitchcock & Johnson (1966).
123. Pevsner (1960, 1968, 1968*a*, 2005).
124. For an excellent exposure of Le Corbusier *see* Anthony Daniels (2015): 'The Cult of Le Corbusier' in *Quadrant* **lix**/9 (September) 38–42. *See* https://quadrant.org.au/magazine/2015/09/cult-le-corbusier/ and https://architecture-hereandthere.com/2017/02/25/corbusier-fascist-drivel/
125. *See*, for example, Troost (ed.) (1942–3).
126. Gabriel (2004).
127. Britt (ed.) (1995) 258–69.
128. *See* Britt (ed.) (1995); Troost (ed.) (1942–3); Zukowsky (ed.) (1994).
129. March & Rohrbach (1936); Troost (ed.) (1942–3); and especially Zukowsky (ed.) (1994).
130. Britt (ed.) (1995) 186.
131. Bolz (1951); Curl & Wilson (2015) 709; Glabau (2010); Kostof (1995) 723.
132. My italics in all instances within the Sixteen Principles.
133. *See* Bolz (1951); Glabau (2010).
134. Wilk (ed.) (2006) 173.
135. Kostof (1995) 719.
136. Teut (ed.) (1967) 10.
137. For these matters *see* Bessel (ed.) (2001).
138. Curl & Wilson (2015) 864.
139. *See* Zachwatowicz *et al.* (1952).
140. *Kwartalnik Archiektury i Urbanistykí Teoria i Historia* (1994) **xxxviii**/3–5.
141. Personal information from Pani Katarzyna Zachwatowicz-Jasiénka.
142. For a flavour of appalling destruction, *see* Stamp (2009, 2010, 2013).
143. Pevsner (1936) 206.
144. Tombs (2014) 765.
145. For a taste of what has been lost, *see* Stamp (2009, 2010, 2013).
146. Saunders (2013) 10.
147. Many even refused to accept the irrefutable evidence of the massacre of Polish nationals at Katyń, near Smolensk, Russia, by the Soviets in 1940.
148. For such matters *see* Nabokov (1975).
149. It certainly puzzled some, including Nicolas Nabokov, cousin of Vladimir: for Nicolas Nabokov *see* Giroud (2015).
150. Saunders (2013) 15.
151. *Ibid.* 14–15.
152. Miller (1988) *passim*.
153. Saunders (2013) 15.
154. *Ibid.* 16.

155. *Ibid.* 17.
156. Miller (1988) is useful on this. *See also* Saunders (2013) 59.
157. Saunders (2013) 20.
158. *Ibid.* 231.
159. Bayer *et al.* (1938).
160. Saunders (2013) 223.
161. In *The New York Times Magazine* (14 December 1952). *See also* Saunders (2013) 226.
162. Britt (ed.) (1995) 187. 191ff.
163. For the above *see* Saunders (2013) 7–26; Britt (ed.) (1995) 195–248.
164. Saunders (2013) 25.
165. *Ibid.* and 364.
166. Guilbaut (ed.) (1990) for this and much more.
167. Saunders (2013) 26.
168. *Ibid.*
169. Britt (ed.) (1995).
170. *Ibid.* and Peter Adam (1992). Modern, industrialized, 'functional' architecture, however, contrary to widely held belief, was not prohibited either in the Third Reich or in the Soviet Union for factories, service stations, etc.
171. Saunders (2013) *passim*, esp. 216.
172. Miller (1952) and Barr started the ball rolling with *15 Americans*. The travelling exhibition was organized by the International Council of MoMA.
173. *The Bulletin of the Museum of Modern Art* **xxi**/3–4 (Summer 1954) 3–30.
174. Saunders (2013) 382 n.33.
175. Finkelstein (ed.) (1952).
176. Saunders (2013) 212–34.
177. *Ibid.* 216.
178. Abscher *et al.* (2012) 390. *See also* Saunders (2013) 216–17, 219, 221, 223, and *passim*.
179. Eva Cockcroft: 'Abstract Expressionism: Weapon of the Cold War' in Frascina (ed.) (1985) 125, originally published in *Artforum* **xii** (June 1974) 39–41.
180. *Ibid.* 125–6.
181. *Ibid.* 126.
182. *Ibid.*
183. Lynes (1973) 233.
184. Frascina (ed.) (1985) 128.
185. *Ibid.* 129.
186. *Ibid.*
187. *Ibid.* 131.
188. Number 194.
189. *See* https://www.moma.org/calendar/exhibitions/2302?locale=en and https://www.moma.org/learn/resources/archives/EAD/CEf.html
190. Frascina (ed.) (1985) 131.
191. *Ibid.* 132.
192. *Ibid.* 125.

193. Saunders (2013) 231.
194. *Ibid.*
195. *Ibid.* 230–1, 384.
196. *Ibid.* 231.
197. Braungart (ed.) (2002) *passim.*
198. Saunders (2013) *passim.*
199. *Ibid.* 384 n.65.

CHAPTER VII: DESCENT TO DEFORMITY 247–92

1. MoMA Exhibition 82.
2. Bayer *et al.* (eds) (1938) 6; Hanks (ed.) (2015) 31.
3. Bayer *et al.* (eds) (1938) 5–6.
4. Anthony Daniels (2015): 'The Cult of Le Corbusier' in *Quadrant* **lix**/9 (September) 38–42. *See* https://quadrant.org.au/magazine/2015/09/cult-le-corbusier/ and https://architecturehereandthere.com/2017/02/25/corbusier-fascist-drivel/
5. Nathaniel Robert Walker (2016) for a devastating critique.
6. *See* https://architecturehereandthere.com/2017/01/31/general-motors-walker-parade-of-progress/
7. Nathaniel Robert Walker (2016).
8. Colomina (1998).
9. Frascina (ed.) (1985) 131.
10. Hitchcock, Johnson, & Mumford (1932); Hitchcock & Johnson (1966).
11. Nathaniel Robert Walker (2016) for an excellent account.
12. Colomina (1998).
13. Norman Bel Geddes (1940).
14. *See* https://architecturehereandthere.com/2017/01/31/general-motors-walker-parade-of-progress/
15. Lancaster (2015*b*).
16. *See* https://architecturehereandthere.com/2017/01/31/general-motors-walker-parade-of-progress/
17. Corbusier (1943). Giraudoux, who wrote the Foreword, was not untainted with the sickly odour of Vichy.
18. Corbusier (1935).
19. Nathaniel Robert Walker (2016) *passim*, a scholarly and devastating *exposé*.
20. Swenarton *et al.* (eds) (2015) for a useful series of essays on these matters.
21. Nicholas Taylor (1973), esp. 19, 100, 108–11.
22. Fitzwalter & Taylor (1981) *passim*.
23. *London Review of Books* **xxxviii**/6 (17 March 2016) 25.
24. For an unrelenting account *see* Caro (2015).
25. *See* Jacobs (1961).
26. Caro (2015), a long book, but an *exposé* that should cure the blinkered of wishful thinking.

27. *See*, for this unedifying story, Fitzwalter & Taylor (1981); *ODNB* **li** (2004) 347–8; and, esp. *North East Labour History Bulletin* **xxviii** (1994), articles by D. Byrne, R. Challinor, and A. Potts.
28. *The Times* (14 November 2015) 13.
29. There is an excellent and sober factual account of urban transformation in Gold (1997, 2007). *See* Tombs (2014) 765 and *passim*.
30. *See* Millais (2009) for a relentless account of this unhappy state of affairs.
31. Lancaster (2015*b*) 43–7, 63–9.
32. Nathaniel Robert Walker (2016) *passim*: an excellent review.
33. Stamp called it 'megalomaniac conception' (Stamp [2013] 22).
34. Lancaster (2015*b*) 46–7.
35. *See* Martin *et al.* (1965).
36. A photograph of the model of this proposal is reproduced in Stamp (2013) 23.
37. Stamp (2013) 22–3.
38. Geoffrey Rippon.
39. *ODNB* **xxviii** (2004) 982–3.
40. *The Victorian Society Report 1963–1964* 8, quoted in Stamp (2013) 22, 188 n.39.
41. *London Review of Books* **xxxviii**/2 (21 January 2016) 32.
42. Jones & Matthews (2016) have exposed crass, low-quality redevelopment schemes in nine cities, emphasizing national failure to respect and learn from existing urban patterns.
43. *See* Tombs (2014) 751ff.
44. Gold (2007) 2.
45. Tombs (2014) 765.
46. 9&10 Geo.VI c.68.
47. 15&16 Geo.VI & 1 Eliz.II c.54.
48. If only the contents of Gruber (1977) and other sensitive studies had informed those responsible things might have been different.
49. Keeble (1952) 215 is revealing in this respect.
50. High culture, however, was never very high on the agenda of the political classes in Britain.
51. Dannatt (ed.) (1953) 7.
52. But *see* Millais (2015).
53. Compare other LCC blocks of the same period, e.g. those at Bentham Road, Hackney, London (*see* Cherry & Pevsner [1998] 503).
54. Cherry & Pevsner (1983) 691.
55. On this, *see* Pevsner (1959).
56. For a history of the origins of these, and accurate critical appraisals, *see* Millais (2015).
57. Frampton (2001) 164.
58. Lewis Mumford (1963) 81.
59. Blake (1977) 33.
60. *Ibid.*
61. Tzonis (2001) 160–3.

62. Chronicled intelligently in Millais (2015, 2017).
63. Anthony Daniels (2015): 'The Cult of Le Corbusier' in *Quadrant* **lix**/9 (September) 38–42. *See* https://quadrant.org.au/magazine/2015/09/cult-le-corbusier/ and https://architecturehereandthere.com/2017/02/25/corbusier-fascist-drivel/
64. *Architectural Design* **xxiii** (December 1953) 330ff.
65. 17 April 1950.
66. *Architectural Design* **xxiii** (December 1953) 331–2.
67. For building failures *see* Scott (1976) *passim.*
68. Salingaros & Masden II (2008) goes into this matter in some detail.
69. Gold (2007) 10.
70. For a wryly grim account of various unsavoury incidents *see* Stamp (2013*a*).
71. *Ibid.* 12.
72. *The Architects' Journal* **cxix**/3073 (21 January 1954) 69.
73. Robertson & Robertson (1948) 158.
74. *Ibid.* 157.
75. *The Architect's Journal* **cxix**/3073 (21 January 1954) 72–3.
76. Saunders (2013) is illuminating on this topic.
77. Ravetz (1980) 54.
78. Hall (1988) 5.
79. *See* Gold (2013) for the impact through the MARS Group.
80. Lubbock (1995) 299.
81. Fitzwalter & Taylor (1981).
82. Gold (2007) 12.
83. *Ibid.*
84. Witemeyer (ed.) (1997) 2 and *passim.*
85. Gruber (1977).
86. Safran *et al.* (1985) 113. I am grateful to Jules Lubbock for reminding me of Loos's continuing influence.
87. Sitte (1889).
88. For which *see* Muthesius (1908–11).
89. *Ver Sacrum* **vii** (1898) contains Loos's views on the *Ringstraße.*
90. Safran *et al.* (1985) 113.
91. Jane S. Turner (ed.) (1998) **xii** 379.
92. Jules Lubbock jogged my memory here, recalling to mind conversations I once had with Crosby.
93. For Gibson *see ODNB* **xxii** (2004) 667–8.
94. Whyte (ed.) (2007) 121–44.
95. Lancaster (2015*b*) 46–7.
96. Especially Mumford (1938).
97. *ODNB* **xxii** (2004) 67.
98. *See* Select Glossary.
99. For example, Troost (ed.) (1942–3).
100. Zukowsky (ed.) (1994).

101. Jane S. Turner (ed.) (1998) **xxi** 408; Whitford (1984) 191.
102. Among believers were legions of youthful British middle-class architects from whose tweed jackets sprouted *The New Statesman and Nation* to advertise their anti-*bourgeois* credentials. They were to do so much damage in the decades to come.
103. *See*, for a flavour of this, Britt (ed.) (1995) *passim*.
104. G.D.H. Cole (1945).
105. M. Cole (1971).
106. *ODNB* **xii** (2004) 509.
107. G.D.H. Cole (1945) 38.
108. Whyte (ed.) (2007).
109. 10 & 11 Geo.VI *c.* 53.
110. Geddes (1924).
111. Town planner and theorist.
112. Architect and town planner, attended the Architectural Association 1926–31 and subsequently (1937–9) became a Unit Master there.
113. Whyte (ed.) (2007) 59.
114. Korn (1953) *passim*.
115. Hilbersheimer (1944) 17.
116. Whyte (ed.) (2007) 74–5.
117. *See* Gold (2013) on the influence of the MARS Group, not least on CIAM.
118. For high-handed, even discourteous sides of Korn, *see* Gold (1997) 220.
119. *The Architectural Review* **xci** (1942) 143–50; Fry (1944) Ch. 4; Gold (1997) 156–63.
120. Lancaster (2015*b*) 46–7.
121. For damage to London *see* Stamp (2009).
122. Lewis Mumford (1962).
123. Pevsner & Wedgwood (1966) 49.
124. *Ibid.*
125. *Ibid.* 272.
126. Personal knowledge.
127. 'The AA Story, 1936–1939' in *Focus* **iii** (1939) 82.
128. *PLAN: Journal of the Architectural Students Association* (Liverpool, Cheadle, London, etc., various dates from 1942).
129. For a take on this, *see* Huw Lemmey (2017): 'Outrage' in *The Architectural Review* **ccxli**/1439 (March) 12–14.
130. Scott (1914) 123.
131. For Ruskin and Pugin *see* Curl (2007) *passim*.
132. For a prophetic vision of high-rise living *see* Ballard (1975).
133. For more positive views on suburbia *see* Nicholas Taylor (1973).
134. Compare with Sullivan (1896).
135. *See* Curl (2009).
136. *See* Salingaros *et al.* (2004) *passim*.

137. One latrine hut for 7,000 inmates, for example, and the crematoria were of the 'triple muffle' type (i.e. with three openings for corpses) in single furnaces, both exemplars of heartless so-called 'functionalism', perhaps. *See* Dwork & Pelt (1996) *passim*.

138. E.P. Mumford (2000) 9–10.

139. Bolz (1951); Glabau (2010).

140. In both these conflicts, hostilities and mayhem went on for several years after 1918 and 1945.

141. *See*, for example, Sharp (1940).

142. *See* Bullock (2002) for a useful outline.

143. Colls (2002) 344–7; Tombs (2014) 765.

144. Whyte (ed.) (2007) 99.

145. Gold (1997) x–xi.

146. Barnett (1995) provides a useful summary of all that.

147. Clarke & Trebilcock (eds) (1997) 149.

148. Parris & Bryson (2010) 205–13.

149. Gold (1997, 2007) is excellent on these matters.

150. Gold (2013).

151. Colls (2002) 344–7.

152. Curl (2007) 10–12 and *passim*; Stamp (2009, 2010, 2013).

153. Colls (2002) 344–7.

154. A scan of documents of the period produced to justify clearances and 'redevelopment' will be sufficient to show this was indeed so.

155. *See* Stamp (2009, 2010, 2013).

156. Chronicled in Curl (1977) 107–31.

157. *See*, for a witty take on what went on, Sturdy (1972).

158. Nathaniel Robert Walker (2016).

159. Worsdall (1981).

160. Gold (2007), drawing on a a vast range or primary documentation, drily chronicles this whole sorry tale.

161. Worsdall (1981) 9.

162. *Ibid.*

163. *Ibid.* 17.

164. *Ibid.*

165. *Ibid.* 16.

166. *Ibid.*

167. For an excellent study of the Glasgow tenement *see* Worsdall (1991).

168. Obituary in *The Times* (6 February 2009) 75.

169. Gold (2007) 26.

170. Lancaster (2015*a*) 70 for a dig at this.

171. *The Architectural Review* **xcv**/565 (January 1944) 7.

172. *See* Curl & Wilson (2015) 699–700; Curl (2011) 175–245; Curl (2011*a*) 25–90.

173. *Ibid.*

174. *The Architectural Review* **xcv**/565 (January 1944) 7.

175. *Ibid.*
176. Gold (2013).
177. Ling in 1987, quoted in Gold (2007) 11.
178. *Ibid.*
179. Ling made pithy observations on the matter to me many years ago.
180. Gold (2007) 26.
181. *Ibid.* 11.
182. Quoted in Gold (2007) 45.
183. Taylor (1973) 79. *See also* Gold (2007) 274–6; Curl (2009a).
184. Fry (1944) Ch. 4.
185. Peter Carter, a disciple of Mies, quoted in Gold (2007) 236.
186. Catatonically boring exercises in cupidity, in which the lack of rigour of which Tyler spoke was all too obvious.
187. *See* the Bibliography of this book.
188. *ODNB* **xlv** (2004) 48.
189. *Ibid.* **li** (2004) 347.
190. *The Architects' Journal* **cxxxiii**/3431 (19 January 1961) 78–89. *See also* Fitzwalter & Taylor (1981) 24. Gillard & Tomkinson (1980) 60 appears to be mistaken with the date of the nomination.
191. Collard (2016).
192. *ODNB* **li** (2004) 347.
193. *The Observer* (21 February 1965).
194. *Newcastle Journal* (28 July 1993).
195. George Farquhar Pennington was a gifted architect and artist.
196. Hackney (1990) 48.
197. Bradley & Pevsner (1997) 290.
198. *Ibid.*
199. *ODNB* **xlv** (2004) 49; *The Independent* (4 February 1993).
200. *The Independent* (31 July 1993).
201. *Ibid.* (4 February 1993).
202. *ODNB* **xlv** (2004) 48.
203. Wolfe (1981) *passim.*
204. *Die Architektur überhaupt die erstarrte Musik ist.* Schelling **iii** (1927) 244.
205. In my experience few architects have much interest in music.
206. *The Architect* **ii** (April 1972) 35.
207. *Ibid.*
208. Designed by a team led by Geoffrey Copcutt.
209. Close, Gifford, & Walker (2016) 237.
210. *Ibid.* 236.
211. *Ibid.* 234.
212. *Ibid.* 246, plate 114.
213. *The Architectural Review* **cxlii**/849 (November 1967).
214. Nicholas Taylor on 'The Failure of Housing' in *The Architectural Review* **cxlii**/849 (November 1967) 341–2, 359.

215. In Glasgow.
216. In London.
217. Avenham Lane, Preston, Lancashire, of 1957–61.
218. Southgate, Runcorn, Cheshire (1968–78), actually designed by James Stirling, Michael Wilford, & Associates, demolished 1990. A hated development with fenestration that was likened to the doors of washing machines. *See* Hartwell *et al.* (2011) 76, 565.
219. Built 1960s using the Jespersen prefabricated ststem. By 1971 it was clear there were already major problems, and soon anti-social behaviour, burglaries, dampness, and high energy bills demonstrated the development was yet another Modernist disaster.
220. At Springburn, 1962–70.
221. Gillian Darley on 'Home' in *The Architectural Review* **ccxl**/1437 (December 2016/January 2017) 34.
222. *Ibid.* 35.
223. *Ibid.*
224. Jane S. Turner (ed.) (1998) **xxi** 490–4.
225. Frampton (2007) 235.
226. *See* Schulze & Windhorst (2014) for this and other matters.
227. Lewis & O'Connor (1994) 33.
228. Howard (2016) *passim.*
229. Lewis & O'Connor (1994) 36.
230. *Ibid.*
231. Howard (2016) 52.
232. Lewis & O'Connor (1994) 74–83.
233. A connection pointed out by Virgil Thomson, the musicologist and composer.
234. Lewis & O'Connor (1994) 91.
235. *Ibid.*
236. *Ibid.*
237. Reviews were generally negative and often vitriolic.
238. *The Architectural Review* **clxxvi**/1050 (August 1984) 22–7.
239. Lewis & O'Connor (1994) 104.
240. Curl & Wilson (2015) 695–6.
241. For *Kitsch see* Braungart (ed.) (2002) *passim.*
242. Johnson & Wigley (1988) *passim.*
243. Jencks (1990) 154.
244. Winkler & Bergeijk (2004).
245. Personal observation.
246. *Building Design* (4 February 2005) 9. Johnson used this word on many occasions to describe himself and other architects (*see* Howard [2016] 276). However, he and they were 'high-class whores' (*RIBA Journal* **iii** [March 2005] xix).
247. Saint (2005).
248. Curl & Wilson (2015) 398–9.

249. Lewis & O'Connor (1994) 156.
250. Hitchcock & Johnson (1966) 95.
251. Lewis & O'Connor (1994) 156.
252. *RIBA Journal* **iii** (March 2005) xix.
253. *Ibid.*
254. Lewis & O'Connor (1994) 159.
255. *Ibid.*
256. Richard Buckminster Fuller, whose breathless writings were once admired.
257. Jencks (1990) 139.
258. *Ibid.* 140.
259. *Ibid.* 142.
260. *See* Moore (2016) for a devastating critique. *See also* Stamp (2009).
261. Jencks (1990) 144.
262. Saint (2005).
263. *Building Design* (4 February 2005) 9.
264. *Perspecta* **iii** (1955) 40–5.
265. Jencks (1990) 149.
266. *The Times* (28 January 2005) 69–70; *RIBA Journal* (3 March 2005) xix; *The Architectural Review* **ccxvii**/1297 (March 2005) 30–3; Curl & Wilson (2015) 397–9.
267. Saint (2005).
268. As Jencks called them.
269. Jencks (1990) 153.
270. Saunders (2013) *passim.*
271. Jencks (2002) 138–69.
272. Johnson & Wigley (1988); Jane S. Turner (ed.) (1998) 609–10.
273. Schumacher (ed.) (2016).
274. For further insights *see* Howard (2016) *passim.*

CHAPTER VIII: DANGEROUS SIGNALS 293–326

1. Jencks (2002) 9.
2. *See* Jacobs (1961).
3. Jencks (2002) 9.
4. Millais (2009) 51, 260–2, 264.
5. *Ibid.* 262.
6. *Ibid.* 260.
7. *The Architectural Review* **cxlii**/849 (November 1967) 341.
8. Scott (1976) *passim.*
9. *ODNB* **xv** (2004) 762–3.
10. *The Architectural Review* **ccxl**/1437 (December 2016/January 2017) 34, quoting from the same journal **cclii**/849 (November 1967).
11. *St Louis News* (1 June 2005).

12. Sudjic (1992) 181.

13. For this *see* Conrads (ed.) (1970) 81.

14. Whitford (1984) 200.

15. Notably Corbusier (1946).

16. http://www.metropolismag.com/Point-of-View/November-2011/Frontiers-of-Design-Science-Evidence-based-Design/ reprinted in Mehaffy & Salingaros (2015).

17. *See* quotation at the head of Chapter 5. *See also* Stevenson (2018) *passim*.

18. Jencks (2002) 6.

19. *Ibid.* 12–15.

20. Musil (1930) v.

21. *See* special issue of *The Architectural Review* entitled *Housing and the Environment* cxlv/849 (November 1967) 334, 341, and *passim*. *See also* Gold (2007) 273–89.

22. *Architectural Record* cxxxi (April 1962) 155–62; Hughes & Hughes (eds) (1990) esp. the paper by Leo Marx on Mumford; Donald L. Miller (ed.) (1986) reproduces Mumford's 1962 article.

23. On the *Neue Nationalgalerie see* http://www.metropolismag.com/Point-of-View/January-2012/Frontiers-of-Design-Science-Computational-Irreducibility/ accessed 1 February 2017, and Mehaffy & Salingaros (2015).

24. Pevsner & Wilson (1999) 444.

25. Millais (2009) 250–1.

26. Cherry, O'Brien, & Pevsner (2005) 647–8.

27. *Architectural Design* xxxix/10 (October 1969) 554–64.

28. Jencks (2002) 17.

29. *Ibid.*

30. *Ibid.*

31. Newman (1973, 1996).

32. Powers (ed.) (2010).

33. Jencks (2002) 21.

34. Richardson & Corfiato (1952) 163, 230.

35. Salingaros *et al.* (2006) 186.

36. Watkin (2005) 530. For more, *see* Semes (2009) *passim*.

37. Lewis & O'Connor (1994) 14, 159.

38. Cruickshank (ed.) (1996) 1486.

39. Drexler (ed.) (1977) 484.

40. *The Architectural Review* ccxl/1437 (December 2016/January 2017) 33–4.

41. Sixteenth-century Proverb. *See* Smith (1975) 366–7 and Rowe (1994) *passim*.

42. *The Architectural Review* cxlii/849 (November 1967) backed away from previous self-congratulation and support for Modernism, and became comprehensively critical of what had clearly become a catastrophe. The damage, however, had been done.

43. 'Corb' or 'Corbu' were used by enthusiasts as shorthand for Le Corbusier.

44. Jencks (1990) 250.

45. Brolin (1976) *passim. See also* Murray & Osley (eds) (2009) 293; and a useful contribution by Nikos A. Salingaros in http://zeta.math.utsa.edu/%7eyxk833/cognitivedissonance.pdf which analyses this phenomenon.

46. *Ibid.*

47. Wolfe (1981) *passim.*

48. The term is said to have originated with R.A.M. Stern (Lewis & O'Connor [1994] 159).

49. Venturi (1966).

50. Jacobs (1961).

51. John A. Walker (1992) 517.

52. *See especially* Salingaros *et al.* (2006) for a dissection of such pretensions.

53. Fredric Jameson (1993, 2009).

54. *See* Jencks (2002) 1.

55. *Ibid.* 264.

56. *Ibid.* 1.

57. *Ibid.* Those 'celebrations', mistakenly held at the end of 1999, were a year too early anyway, as the inglorious twentieth century did not expire until midnight on 31 December 2000.

58. Jencks (2002) 1.

59. *Ibid.*

60. But *see* Salingaros *et al.* (2004) on the use and misuse of this word.

61. Jencks (2002) 1.

62. Braungart (ed.) (2002) and Brinks *et al.* (eds) (2005).

63. *The New York Review of Books* **lxii**/1 (8 January–5 February 2015) 36.

64. Buchanan (2015) for a powerful critique.

65. Schumacher (ed.) (2016).

66. For Gehry *see* Goldberger (2015); *see also The New York Review of Books* **lxiii**/5 (4 March–6 April 2016) 40–2.

67. Salingaros *et al.* (2004) *passim*: an excellent analysis that might have benefited from illustrations and an index.

68. Crook (2003).

69. *The Architectural Review* **ccxxxvii**/1423 (September 2015) 9.

70. *Ibid.*

71. *RIBA Journal* **cxxii**/2 (February 2015) 16–22.

72. Racana & Janssens (2010).

73. Waters (2003) *passim.*

74. Foster *et al.* (2005) 87.

75. *The Times* (19 January 2009) 52.

76. Pawley (1994).

77. Foster *et al.* (2005) 88.

78. *Ibid.*

79. St Martin-in-the-Bull Ring, the ancient parish church of Birmingham, much rebuilt (1872–5) to designs by Julius Alfred Chatwin, repaired after war damage by Philip Boughton Chatwin and Anthony Chatwin.

80. *See* Wood (2016) and Douglas Murray (2017) for refreshingly informed critiques of the myopia of Western politicians and commentators in this regard.

81. *See* Salingaros *et al.* (2004) for this.

82. As Wolfe (1981) described them.

83. *See,* for example, Schumacher (ed.) (2016).

84. *The Architectural Review* **cxlii**/849 (November 1967).

85. *See* Salingaros *et al.* (2004) 103–4.

86. Corbusier (1946) is a prime example.

87. *See* https://www.youtube.com/watch?v=IQFEaAUrfAk for an unpleasant demonstration of what might be regarded as bullying discourtesy.

88. Wolfe (1981) 16.

89. *Ibid.* 18.

90. Pevsner (1960; 1968*a*; 2005, and earlier edns. of 1936 and 1976).

91. Jane S. Turner (ed.) (1998) **xvi** 788–9; Whitford (1984) 30, 51–9, 62, 68, 70, 80, 82, 85, 89–90, 103–10, 112, 115, 119–21, 123, 128, 133, 136, 175, 184.

92. Whitford (1984) 52.

93. Kandinsky (2006).

94. For a mischievous interpretation *see* Wilenski (1932).

95. *Acts of the Apostles* **xix** 27.

96. *Ibid.* 19.

97. *See* Wood (2016) for a sober analysis and corrective.

98. *The Times* (7 March 2015) 24.

99. *See* Adam (1992); Jencks (1969); Lane (1968); Spotts (2002), Steigmann-Gall (2003); Taylor (1974).

100. *Partisan Review* **xii** (1945) 96.

101. Goebbels (1987) 66.

102. *Matthew* **v–vii.**

103. Steiner (1996) 336. The essay, 'Through the Glass Darkly' deserves repeated reading.

104. Luther (1971) 267, 289, 292.

105. Originally published under a pseudonym in the *Neue Zeitschrift für Musik* (September 1850), it was subsequently expanded and appeared under Wagner's own name. *See* Wagner (1869).

106. H. Kramer (1995): 'My Long Search is Over' in *New Criterion* **xiv**/1 4–14. *See* https://www.newcriterion.com/issues/1995/9/mondrian-mysticism-ldquomy-long-search-is-overrdquo

107. *Edinburgh Review* **xcv** (1852) 402.

108. *British Quarterly Review* **x** (1849) 441.

109. Salingaros *et al.* (2006) 177.

110. Jonathan Morrison in *The Times* (25 February 2016) 18.

111. *Ibid.*

112. Office for Metropolitan Architecture, founded 1975.

113. Jonathan Morrison in *The Times* (25 February 2016) 18.

114. *The Times* (26 September 2015) 29.

115. Roger Scruton in *The Times* (9 April 2016) 24.
116. *Ibid.*
117. *Ibid.*
118. Corbusier (1935).
119. For some glimpses of Corbusian Dystopia, see Corbusier (1929).
120. Roger Scruton in *The Times* (9 April 2016) 24.
121. *Ibid.*
122. *Ibid.*
123. https://www.opendemocracy.net/conflict-us911/article_173.jsp
124. al-Sabouni (2016) *passim.*
125. Roger Scruton in *The Times* (9 April 2016) 24.
126. A young female architect.
127. al-Sabouni (2016) *passim.*
128. Roger Scruton in *The Times* (9 April 2016) 24.
129. Crawford (2015); *The Times* (7 November 2015) 16.
130. *Times Literary Supplement* (20 May 2016) 12–13.
131. Jencks (2002) 35.
132. *See* Lancaster (2015) 78.
133. Wilk (ed.) (2006) wrapper.
134. Jenkins (2006).
135. Lane (1968) 45; Weitz (2007) 194.
136. Jenkins (2006).
137. *Ibid.*
138. Simon Jenkins in *The Sunday Times* (7 January 2007) 42. *See also* Jenkins (2006).
139. A National-Socialist title.
140. Jenkins (2006).
141. Samples of this of sort of infantile, uninformed stuff may be read in, e.g., *The Guardian* (24 October 1966, 22 April 1968) and the *Manchester Evening News* (17 March 1969), and there are many such paeans of praise, although tunes would change quite soon when such ludicrous comparisons were ditched for rumblings about 'Colditz' (which is actually a very handsome and important historic building), 'Bunkers', and other sour notes.
142. Hartwell *et al.* (2004) 455.
143. Pevsner (1969) 53.
144. Hartwell *et al.* (2004) 89.
145. *Ibid.*
146. It was, of course, hardly German, as it took orders from Moscow; it was certainly not Democratic; and as a Republic it would hardly pass the criteria for such a label.
147. Jenkins (2006).
148. Simon Jenkins in *The Sunday Times* (7 January 2007) 42. *See also* Jenkins (2006).
149. al-Sabouni (2016) *passim.*
150. Douglas Murray (2017) *passim.*
151. Salingaros *et al.* (2004) 107.
152. Preciado (2014).

CHAPTER IX: SOME FURTHER REFLECTIONS 327–60

1. Edwards (1968) 9–17.
2. *Ibid.* 128.
3. Nicholas Taylor (1973) 108–11.
4. *Ibid.* 19.
5. *Ibid.* 100.
6. *See* Kuchta (2010) 198 and *passim* for an excellent discussion of these weighty matters.
7. Kunstler (1993) 59–84.
8. Gold (2013).
9. Anthony Daniels (2015): 'The Cult of Le Corbusier' in *Quadrant* **lix**/9 (September) 38–42.
10. Kunstler (1993) 59–84. *See also* Semes (2009) *passim*.
11. Ruskin (1849) I Aphorism 4, but *see also* Edwards (1968) 129–32.
12. Curl (2005) 86–8, 130.
13. Psalm 127 v.1.
14. *See* Patrick Geddes (1998).
15. For this *see* Lichfield & Whitbread (1972).
16. *See* Wakeman (2016) on the New Towns Movement.
17. *See* Mumford (1922, 1938, 1961).
18. Mumford (1938, 1961) and Wycherley (1962).
19. *See* Gruber (1977); Sitte (1889).
20. Some early warnings are reprinted in Murray & Osley (eds) (2009).
21. Claeys (2017) on Dystopias contains many observations of interest.
22. Becker (1994); Cassou (1984); Heller (1971); Hiscock (2007).
23. Eaton (2001); Rosenau (1983).
24. Douglas (1915) 309–13.
25. Hiscock (2007).
26. Heller (1971) is illuminating on this.
27. Gold (1997, 2007) soberly provides useful material on these matters, expressed clearly and backed by sound research.
28. *The Architectural Review* **cxlii**/849 (November 1967) 341–2, 359.
29. *See* Gold (1997, 2007) for excellent studies of the experience and practice of Modernism.
30. Anthony Daniels (2015).
31. All the above is based on a lecture I gave in the early 1970s at the Architectural Association, London.
32. Nikos Salingaros, in a personal communication.
33. Buchanan (2015).
34. Ulrich (1984, 2000).
35. Frumkin (2001).
36. Tse *et al.* (2002).
37. Heerwagen (2005).

38. Squire & Kandel (1999) 200.
39. Moore (2016) *passim.*
40. Laue (1987).
41. Harvey (2002) *passim.*
42. Griffin & Moylan (eds) (2015).
43. Mehaffy & Salingaros (2013) have raised some useful matters.
44. A favourite saying of the late Margaret Thatcher.
45. *See* Reece (2016); Wakeman (2016).
46. Harvey (2002) *passim.*
47. Anthony Daniels (2015).
48. I am indebted to Nikos Salingaros for insights here.
49. Wakeman (2016).
50. *See,* for example, Moylan (2000); Griffin & Moylan (eds) (2015).
51. *See,* for example, Wycherley (1962).
52. For some interesting observations *see The Architectural Review* **ccxli**/1439 (March 2017) 6–29.
53. Korn (1953) praised them.
54. *See* Lefebvre (1968, 1972, 1991).
55. Lehtovuori (2010).
56. *Ibid. passim.*
57. Coleman (1990).
58. Jacobs (1961).
59. http://www.city-journal.org
60. On these matters *see* Till (2009).
61. *See* al-Sabouni (2016) for a most interesting take on this; *see also* Roger Scruton in *The Times* (9 April 2016) 24.
62. Jacobs (1961).
63. Coleman (1990).
64. Corbusier (1929, 1935, 1946); Jeanneret-Gris (1928).
65. *See* for this damage, Coleman (1990), Jacobs (1961).
66. *See* Anthony Daniels (2015) for a devastatingly accurate critique.
67. *See* Venturi (1966).
68. Rowe & Koetter (1980).
69. Eaton (2001); Rosenau (1983).
70. *The Architectural Review* **ccxl**/1437 (December 2016/January 2017) 35–8, where the article is reprinted.
71. *The Architectural Review* **ccxiv**/1278 (August 2003) 88.
72. Curl (2011) 175–245.
73. Rowe (1994).
74. Watkin (1977, 2001).
75. Venturi (1966).
76. Coleman (1990).
77. Jacobs (1961).
78. Rowe & Koetter (1980).

79. Harvey (2002).
80. Salingaros *et al.* (2005).
81. *See* Lewis Mumford (1938, 1961).
82. Jameson (1993, 2009).
83. Lefebvre (1968, 1972, 1991).
84. *See* Griffin & Moylan (eds) (2015).
85. Nathaniel Robert Walker (2016) has drawn attention to aspects of this.
86. *See* Swenarton *et al.* (2015) for a useful overview.
87. *See* Hatherley (2011).
88. *The Architectural Review* **cxlii**/849 (November 1967) was prescient regarding these matters.
89. Watkin (1996) 490.
90. *Ibid.* 1.
91. Not in the common modern usage, but suggesting perception by means of the senses.
92. Curl (2011*a*) 13–17.
93. Watkin (1996) 1.
94. All quotes from Watkin (1996) 1.
95. Sir John Soane's Museum archives 1/212.
96. Buchanan (2015), a deeply thought and passionate article, full of wisdom and common sense.
97. Mehaffy & Salingaros (2013) is interesting in this respect.
98. *See*, for example, reports of this phenomenon in *The Times* (18 January 2016) 1, 9.
99. Speech in the House of Lords (2 March 1960).
100. *Wenn ich Kultur höre…entsichere ich meinen Browning* (Johst [1933] Act 1 Sc. 1). Albert Leo Schlageter, former soldier, member of the *Freikorps*, who took part in the Kapp *Putsch*, carried out sabotage operations against French forces occupying the Ruhr, and was executed by a French firing squad (1923). He became a hero of National Socialism.
101. Hillman (2016).
102. Horace (2014) *Epistulae* **ii**/2 line 45.
103. *See* Burke (1823) **v** 151.
104. *Ibid.* 103.
105. *Ibid.* 178.
106. *Ibid.* 195.
107. *Ibid.* 154–5.
108. For a key figure in this, *see* Anthony Daniels (2015): 'The Cult of Le Corbusier' in *Quadrant* **lix**/9 (September) 38–42. *See also* Millais (2017).
109. David Aaronovitch in *The Times* (5 November 2015) 31; Nicola Woolcock in *The Times* (6 November 2015) 5.
110. Valentine Low in *The Times* (23 May 2016) 6.
111. Hillman (2016) *passim*.
112. Watkin (1996) *passim*.

113. Scruton (2015*a*).
114. *See* Eliot (1948) on this.
115. Theodor Adorno *et al.* (2010), for example, and *see* Scruton (2015*a*).
116. Burke (1823) **v** 99.
117. *Ibid.* 148.
118. Watkin (1996) 489–667.
119. Vitruvius Pollio (1999) **i** iii 2.
120. Wotton (1624) pl. i.
121. Wren (1942) 126. *See also* Stephen Wren (ed.) (1750).
122. Eliot (1948) 27.
123. *See*, for interesting remarks on the longevity and power of religion, Hurd (2015), Reiss (2016), and Spencer (2016).
124. Eliot (1948) 50.
125. *Ibid.* 27.
126. *See* Preciado (2014) for an interesting interpretation.
127. Debord (2013).
128. Nathaniel Robert Walker (2016).
129. *See* Serroy & Lipovetsky (2008); Lipovetsky & Serroy (2013).
130. Scruton (2015*a*).
131. Watkin (1996) 491 and *passim*.
132. Spencer (2016) should be read on this.
133. Scruton (2015*a*).
134. Vargas Llosa (2015).
135. Quoted in *The New York Review of Books* **lxiii**/9 (26 May–8 June 2016) 46.
136. Preciado (2014) *passim*. Pornography must not be confused with eroticism.
137. Scruton (2015*a*).
138. Musil (1979) xviii.
139. Yet *see* Spencer (2016) for how Christianity has shaped values in the West.
140. Anthony Daniels (2015).
141. *See* Watkin (1996) 489–667.
142. *Ibid.* 491.
143. Hurd (2015), Spencer (2016).
144. Scruton (2015*a*).
145. Vargas Llosa (2015) is splendid on this.
146. Arnold (1873) xiii.
147. Spencer (2016).
148. Scruton (2015) 82.
149. Salingaros *et al.* (2014) Part 7.
150. Spencer (2016).
151. *See* Vargas Llosa (2015) *passim*.
152. *See* Hurd (2015) and Spencer (2016) for the global importance of religion and how it has shaped values.
153. *See* Watkin (1996) 489–667.
154. *Ibid.* 609.

155. *Ibid.*

156. Soane Museum Archives 1.259 fol. [7].

157. Fanon (1967) 17–18.

158. For these matters, *see* Salingaros *et al.* (2004) *passim.*

159. Tolstoy (1933) *passim.*

160. Eaton (2001); Rosenau (1983).

161. For this and other matters *see* Geddes (1998).

162. al-Sabouni (2016), a volume which deserves to be read by everyone connected in any way with architecture and planning.

163. Jacobs (1961).

164. *See* Fisher (1962).

165. *Ibid.*, and *see also* Korn (1953).

166. *The Architectural Review* ccxl/1437 (December 2016/January 2017) 33–4.

167. *See* Cullmann (1961); Fisher (1962); Geddes (1998); Mannheim (1968); Mead (1966); Rosenau (1983).

168. There are perceptive comments on such matters in Drexler (1977) 6–59.

169. *Psalm* 126 v.1.

170. *The Architectural Review* ccxxiii/1334 (April 2008) 37; Obituary in *The Times* (28 March 2008) 71.

171. *See* Banham (1960).

172. Pawley (1990).

173. *See*, for example, Banham (1969).

174. *London Review of Books* xxxviii/8 (21 April 2016) 27.

175. Clive Aslet in *The Times* (20 October 2015) 28.

176. Burke (1823) 152.

177. Clive Aslet in *The Times* (20 October 2015) 28 and (16 August 2016) 26.

178. *See* Adam (2017), Economakis (ed.) (1993), Porphyrios (ed.) (1993), Porphyrios (2016), and Watkin (2016) for examples of what can be done.

179. Cross-Rudkin *et al.* (eds) (2008) 841–5.

180. Chrimes *et al.* (eds) (2014) 308–9.

181. Cross-Rudkin *et al.* (eds) (2008) 3–6.

182. Pereira (1998).

183. Clive Aslet in *The Times* (16 August 2016) 26.

184. *The Architects' Journal* 1423 (September 2015) 8–9 and Buchanan (2015) are just two instances where serious questions have been asked.

185. Schumacher (2011–12); Schumacher (ed.) (2016).

186. For a powerful denunciation of what she termed the 'pimping-out' of London, *see* Libby Purves: 'Don't let the stinking rich purge the poor' in *The Times* (28 November 2016) 31.

187. *Ibid.*

188. Philip Aldrick: 'UK suffers its first lost decade in 150 years' in *The Times* (6 December 2016) 41.

189. *The Times* (9 July 2016) 26.

190. *Apollo* clxxxiv/644 (July/August 2016) 110.

191. Reynolds (2016) *passim*.
192. Mehaffy & Salingaros (2013).
193. Wolfe (1981) *passim*.
194. I acknowledge Theo Crosby's conversations years ago as having influenced my own thoughts.
195. Papadakis (ed.) (1993); Wales (1989).
196. For an overview of the Georgian achievement *see* Curl (2011*a*).
197. *The Architectural Review* **ccxxxvii**/1415 (January 2015) 103.
198. *See*, for example, *RIBA Journal* **cxxii**/2 (February 2015) 52.
199. Howard (2016) 276.
200. *Interdisciplinary Science Reviews* **xxv**/2 (Summer 2000) 123–35.
201. *See* 'Chinoiserie' entry in Curl & Wilson (2015) 167–9.
202. Curl & Wilson (2015) 323.
203. Papworth (ed.) (1852–92) **iv** 58. The term is not pejorative.
204. Curl & Wilson (2015) 662.
205. Curl (2011) 199–245.
206. Papadakis (ed.) (1993); Wales (1989).
207. *See also* the Prince's Foreword in Watkin (2016) 13.
208. *RIBA Journal* **cxxi**/11 (November 2014) 36–8.
209. For the Prince's views *see The Architectural Review* **ccxxxvii**/1415 (January 2015) whole issue.
210. *Ibid.* 98.
211. *The New York Review of Books* **lxi**/9 (22 May–4 June 2014) 12–15.
212. For a robust and spirited denunciation, Buchanan (2015) on 'Empty Gestures' should be read.
213. Schumacher (2011–12); Schumacher (ed.) (2016).
214. I have been obliged to help several young men and women by recommending them to suitable practices, and by teaching them myself, while reluctantly advising them to give their official tutors what they want in order to jump through the required hoops. Fortunately, what those tutors require does not need a great deal of effort, so most energies can then be expended on studying real problems, real architecture, real urban difficulties, and acquiring a real understanding of the complexities of what is a vast subject.
215. Curl & Wilson (2015) 520–2, 524.
216. Corbusier (1929, 1935, 1946). *See* Anthony Daniels (2015) for an opposite view.
217. *Ibid.* (1943).
218. *See* Adam (2017).
219. *See* Duany *et al.* (2003).
220. *See* Economakis (ed.) (1992).
221. *See* Duany *et al.* (2003).
222. *See* Economakis (ed.) (1993) and Porphyrios (2016).
223. *See* Rossi (1982, 1983, 1996).
224. *See* Watkin (2016).
225. *See* Tagliaventi & O'Connor (eds) (1992); Tagliaventi (ed.) (1996).

226. Built 1972–4 to designs by Clifford Wearden & Associates, who were not responsible for the later cladding.
227. A dubious claim: *see* Rowe (1994) *passim*.
228. *The Times* (20 June 2017) 32.
229. Moore (2012) *passim*.

CHAPTER X: EPILOGUE 361–88

1. Corbusier (1946) 133.
2. Salingaros *et al.* (2006) 174.
3. *See* Corbusier (1946) *passim*.
4. *See* Murray & Osley (eds) (2009) for some of those, esp. 35–8 (Lutyens) and 39–43 (Miriam Wornum).
5. Anthony Daniels (2015): 'The Cult of Le Corbusier' in *Quadrant* **lix**/9 (September) 38–42.
6. Chaslin (2015).
7. Jarcy (2015).
8. *See* https://quadrant.org.au/magazine/2015/09/cult-le-corbusier/ and https://architecturehereandthere.com/2017/02/25/corbusier-fascist-drivel/
9. Blair & Bloom (1995).
10. Dinsmoor (1950).
11. Toman (ed.) (1999).
12. Hitchcock (1968).
13. Curl (2002) 98–9 and Plate VIII; Crook (1981) 85, 99, 225, 229–39, and Plates 44–50, 105, 107, 137, 143.
14. Crook (1981) *passim*.
15. Norwich (1978) 233, 242.
16. Blake (1977) 149.
17. Donald L. Miller (ed.) (1986) 82.
18. *See also* Anthony Daniels (2015).
19. *Architectural Record* **cxxxi** (April 1962) 155–62.
20. Blomfield (1934) 70.
21. *Ibid.* made the same point.
22. Salingaros *et al.* (2004) 105.
23. Taschen (ed.) (1997) 69.
24. *Ibid*.
25. Salingaros *et al.* (2004) 3.
26. *Ibid*.
27. All quotes from Salingaros *et al.* (2004) 3.
28. Taschen (ed.) (1997) 49 and *passim*.
29. *See* https://www.youtube.com/watch?v=IQFEaAUrfAk
30. For a fierce condemnation of this sort of thing, *see* Taschen (ed.) (1997) *passim*.
31. *Ibid.* 106.
32. Corbusier (1946) 133.

33. Taschen (ed.) (1997) 62–6.
34. Salingaros *et al.* (2004) 106.
35. *Ibid.*
36. Raw concrete finishes appear to be in fashion again with the younger generation. *See* Beanland (2016); Calder (2016).
37. Whitford (1984) *passim* for a relentless description of such goings-on.
38. Wolfe (1981) 13–14 touches on this matter.
39. Salingaros *et al.* (2004) 106.
40. *Ibid.*
41. Anyone doubting that bad manners and bullying are used in architectural 'education' should study the unedifying https://www.youtube.com/watch?v=IQFEaAUrfAk
42. Scruton (2000) Ch. 12.
43. *Ibid.*
44. Scruton (2009) 172–4.
45. *Ibid.*
46. *The Architectural Review* cxlii/849 (November 1967) 341–2, 359, and *passim*. *See also The Architectural Review* ccxl/1437 (December 2016/January 2017) 33–4.
47. Scruton (2009) 174.
48. *See*, for example, the hard-hitting Hatherley (2011) and Buchanan (2015).
49. Blomfield (1934) 9.
50. *Ibid.* 6.
51. *Ibid.* 14.
52. *Ibid.* 50.
53. Davis & Jenkins (eds) (2007) 55.
54. Curl (2003) 9.
55. For a good modern exposition, *see* Saumarez Smith (2013).
56. Curl (2003) 9–10.
57. *Ibid.* 10.
58. This point was also made in Lancaster (2015) 78–9.
59. Curl (2003) 10. Some survivors from those days have realized their error, and have made contact to admit them.
60. *Ibid.*
61. *The Architectural Review* ccxl/1437 (December 2016/January 2017) 33–4.
62. Edwards (1944) *passim*; Gavin Stamp, in his obituary of Roderick Gradidge, *ODNB* xxiii (2004) 164; Scheer & Preiser (eds) (1994) 58.
63. *ODNB* xxiii (2004) 164.
64. Safran *et al.* (1985) 113 for observations on 'originality'. On 'false originality' and fraudulent claims *see RIBA Journal* 3rd Series xli/9 (10 March 1934) 479 (note by Reginald W. Cave, Hon. Secretary of the Bartlett School of Architecture Architectural Society, describing a paper given to the Society by Voysey on 21 February 1934). *See The Antiquaries Journal* xcvi (2016) 477–8.
65. Salingaros *et al.* (2004) 3 and *passim*. *See also* Salingaros *et al.* (2005, 2006) *passim*.

66. Lewis & O'Connor (1994) 14, 156, 174, 192.
67. Blomfield (1934) 80, for all quotes in this paragraph.
68. Mackail (1931).
69. *ODNB* **xv** (2004) 397.
70. *Ibid.*
71. *Ibid.*
72. *Ibid.*
73. *Ibid.*
74. *Si monumentum requiris, circumspice* (if you seek his monument, look around you).
75. *ODNB* **xv** (2004) 397.
76. Lancaster (2015*a*) 68.
77. But *see* Janice Turner in *The Times* (26 September 2015) 29.
78. Schumacher (ed.) (2016).
79. *See* Wainwright (2013).
80. I am indebted to Andrew Saint for this acute observation.
81. Blomfield (1934) 176.
82. http://www.bdonline.co.uk/riba-agrees-biggest-shake-up-in-architectural-education-for-50-years/5074559.article
83. Dr Brittain-Catlin, in a personal communication.
84. *Ibid.*
85. *See* Sklair (2017) on this.
86. For further thoughts on these matters *see* Mehaffy & Salingaros (2013).
87. Peter Walker, in a personal communication.
88. *Ibid.*
89. *Ibid.*
90. Cassou (1984); Hiscock (2007).
91. Whitman (1980) 90, lines 93ff.
92. Dylan Thomas (1946): *In My Craft or Sullen Art*.
93. I am indebted to Peter Walker for his observations, some of which are encapsulated above.
94. Information from Timothy Brittain-Catlin, who generously shared his view with me.
95. I am indebted to Timothy Brittain-Catlin, Peter Walker, and many others for sharing their thoughts on these matters with me.
96. Ingrid D. Rowland in *The New York Review of Books* **lxiii**/5 (4 March–6 April 2016) 40–2 for a keenly observed view.
97. *See* Buchanan (2015) for a penetrating analysis of recent architectural trends.
98. *See* Howard (2016) 276; Lewis & O'Connor (1994); Jencks (1990) 139–69.
99. But for sobering insights *see* al-Sabouni (2016) and Rotbard (2015).
100. Wood (2016).
101. Laue (1987).
102. Moore (2016).
103. 10&11 Geo.VI c.53 (1947).

104. 53&54 Vict. c.70 (1890).
105. Curl (2004, 2015).
106. 4&5 Eliz. II c.52 (1956).
107. Curl (2007) 443–83.
108. Moore (2016).
109. Buchanan (2015).
110. Meades (2016).
111. For the terrible damage inflicted on London and other parts of Britain, *see* Stamp (2009, 2010, 2013) and Dyckhoff (2017).
112. *Times Literary Supplement* **5906** (10 June 2016) 16.
113. *See* Sklair (2017) *passim* on this.
114. *See* Gillian Darley's perceptive comments in *Apollo* **clxxxiii**/642 (May 2016) 23.
115. *See* Claeys (2016) for Dystopias galore.
116. Hitchcock, Johnson, & Mumford (1932).
117. Hitchcock & Johnson (1966).
118. Laue (1987).
119. Burgess (1962).
120. Cherry & Pevsner (1983) 294–300.
121. *See*, for example, Ballard (1975).
122. Moore (2016). *See also* Jonathan Meades (2016): 'Capital Gains' in *The Literary Review* **440** (March) 18–19 for comments that excoriate 'star architects' and their benighted works.
123. Gillian Darley in *The Architectural Review* **ccxl**/1437 (December 2016/January 2017) 34.
124. Rowe (1994) *passim*.
125. *See* Swenarton *et al.* (2015) for a useful outline.
126. *The Architectural Review* **cxlii**/849 (November 1967) whole issue.
127. Roberts (1867) and Curl (1983).
128. Curl (1983) 87–110.
129. *Ibid.* 11–61 and *passim*.
130. Nathaniel Robert Walker (2016).
131. *The Times* (25 February 2016) 18.
132. al-Sabouni (2016) *passim*.
133. Anthony Daniels (2015).
134. *See* Dyckhoff (2017) for an interesting take.
135. al-Sabouni (2016) is revealing on these matters. *See also* Douglas Murray (2017).
136. The article on Gizmos was reproduced in Banham (1981) 108–14.
137. 'Alles ist Architektur' in *Bau: Zeitschrift für Architektur und Städtebau* **i**/2 (1968) 1–32.
138. *See also* Liane Lefaivre (2003): 'Everything is Architecture' in *Harvard Design Magazine* **xviii** (Summer) 1–5.
139. One was illustrated in Corbusier (1946) 199. *See* Lending (2017) *passim*.
140. 'A Home is not a House' in *Art in America* **ii** (April 1965) 70–9.

141. *The Architectural Review* **ccxxxviii**/1423 (September 2015) 18–20.
142. Schumacher (ed.) (2016) for a depressing read.
143. Buchanan (2015) 32.
144. *Ibid.*
145. Nathaniel Robert Walker (2016) is illuminating on this.
146. *London Review of Books* **xxxviii**/8 (21 April 2016) 27–8.
147. Preciado (2014). If pornography is ubiquitous, true eroticism is in short supply.
148. Buchanan (2015) 32–5, an excellent critique.
149. *See* Schumacher (2011–12) and Schumacher (ed.) (2016).
150. Buchanan (2015) 34.
151. *Ibid.*
152. Reed (1959).
153. *See* Watkin (2016) 50–61 for recent developments.
154. A Roman Catholic foundation.
155. Watkin (2016) 50–61. However, at Kingston University, Surrey, the *application* of the Classical language of architecture is now taught.
156. A vast gulf separates these architectural travesties from scholarly designs of the New Urbanists and the architects who have worked on experiments such as Poundbury.
157. For all the above, *see* Jenkins (2006).

Select Glossary

To make dictionaries is dull work.

SAMUEL JOHNSON (1709–84): *A Dictionary of the English Language* (1755), definition no. 8 of 'dull'.

To include every architectural and planning term would not be possible here: readers are therefore referred to James Stevens Curl & Susan Wilson (2015): *The Oxford Dictionary of Architecture* (Oxford: Oxford University Press). However, attempts have been made to define a few words that recur in the text of this book for purposes of clarification and convenience.

Athens Charter *See* **CIAM**

Brutalism Term somewhat loosely used, it could mean almost anything to those employing it. However, its main meaning signified an architecture which emphasized exposed rough concrete finishes and chunky, blocky forms, especially in works influenced by Le Corbusier from 1945 (i.e. where *béton brut* [raw concrete] was treated particularly uncompromisingly, with the formwork [temporary timber *shuttering* constructed as the mould into which the concrete is poured] patterns of the boards used not only visible, but deliberately emphasized, as in Corbusier's *Unité d'Habitation de Grandeur Conforme*, Marseilles [1948–54]). Corbusier erroneously believed that in Roman architecture bare concrete was exposed, and because of this belief his disciples followed suit without questioning the facts, so in the second half of the twentieth century this type of finish became almost compulsory, despite the fact that we know that, in ancient times, the Romans used sheets of coloured marbles, mosaics, and painted plaster to cover bare concrete. Banham noted that the 'ultimate disgrace' of Brutalism is to be seen in the 'innumerable blocks of flats built throughout the world that use...*béton brut* as an excuse for low-cost surface treatments': those have often been covered with 'cladding' (to hide stained, ugly concrete), some of which has proved to be dangerous, as in the disastrous Grenfell Tower fire in the Royal Borough of Kensington and Chelsea in 2017.

The Smithsons' Smithdon High School, Hunstanton, Norfolk (1949–54), a steel-framed building much influenced by the work of Mies van der Rohe in Chicago, was hailed, confusingly, as an exemplar of **New Brutalism** (*see* **Plate 8.2**). The last, perhaps, was a label of self-regard, which in this case had nothing to do with *béton brut*, but was derived from the first four letters of P.D. Smithson's nickname, 'Brutus', mingled with the first three letters of Alison Smithson's first name and the first two of her surname. Described by the Smithsons as an 'ethic', not an 'aesthetic' (echoes of Puginian-Ruskinian 'moral' stances), New Brutalism was a term referring to supposed rigour, the expression and exposure of structure and services, but it has a shaky pedigree, mostly based on a claim that one of the Smithsons' unexecuted designs, a house featuring brick, timber, and exposed concrete, leaving the structure entirely revealed, without any internal finishes, would have been the first example of New Brutalism in England, so, by a process of what appears to have been osmosis and association, the Hunstanton school was hailed as an example of *New Brutalism*, because of what its creators *might have done*, had their work been realized.

    The Architects' Journal cxliv/26 (28 December 1966) 1590–1; *Architectural Design* xxiii (December 1953) 342; *The Architectural Review* cxviii/708 (December 1955) 355–8; Banham (1966); Curl & Wilson (2015) 121–2; Smithson (ed.) (1965); Jane S. Turner (ed.) (1998) v 55–7, xxviii 889–90

CIAM The *Congrès Internationaux d'Architecture Moderne* was founded in 1928, instigated by Madame Hélène de Mandrot, Le Corbusier, and Sigfried Giedion. Its aim was to coordinate international forces in the interests of its approved versions of the Modern Movement in architecture and planning. The first meeting, attended by other leading Modernists, including El Lissitzky, Rietveld, and Stam, took place at de Mandrot's home, the *Château La Sarraz* in Switzerland, and established the Modern Movement in architecture as an organized body, with its inevitable manifesto, statutes, an elected committee called *Comité International pour la Résolution des Problèmes de l'Architecture Contemporaine* (**CIRPAC**), and an address in Zürich which was actually Giedion's, CIAM's Secretary-General. Karl Moser, became first President (1928–30), and quickly CIAM became the arbiter and disseminator of the dogmas of International Modernism until its dissolution (1959), promoting **Functionalism**, standardization, and supposed 'rationalization', dominated first by the Germans, and then by Le Corbusier. The fourth meeting of CIAM (1933) set down the primary functions and principles of Modernist urban planning, including rigid functional zones with green belts between, high-rise apartment blocks for housing, provision for traffic, wholesale destruction of existing urban fabric, and space for recreation. These became enshrined in Le Corbusier's *Athens Charter* (*La Charte d'Athènes*, 1943), a document that treated the functions of cities simplistically and crudely, yet its pernicious assertions were widely accepted, leading to great damage inflicted globally on countless towns and cities, and indeed in many instances heralded the end of civilized urban living. Brasília, by Costa, Niemeyer, *et al.* was to be the realization of CIAM's aims, but the reality, as in the cases of many other instances where CIAM orthodoxies were imposed, has not been happy aesthetically, functionally, socially, nor in any other ways. Furthermore, insistence on the rigid rectangular structures of International Modernism resulted in plenty of wasteful **SLOAP** (*see* entry below). After 1954, several younger members of CIAM, including the Smithsons, rejected the mechanical functionalism of the Athens Charter, emphasizing instead the primacy of human association in urban planning, but the damage had already been done, and the questioning of dogma led to the end of the organization as an effective body.

Corbusier (1943); J. Jacobs (1961); Lampugnani (gen.ed.) (1988); E.P. Mumford (2000); A.M. Smithson (ed.) (1965); Smithson & Smithson (1991); Steinmann (ed.) (1979); Jane S. Turner (ed.) (1998) **vii** 292–6, 343–4

CIRPAC *Comité International pour la Résolution des Problèmes de l'Architecture Contemporaine*. *See* **CIAM**. Essentially the executive organ of CIAM, it organized and administered the CIAM members of each country, liaised with headquarters in Zürich through Giedion, publicized the aims of CIAM through exhibitions and the media, recruited new members, carried through resolutions passed by CIAM and prepared new ones, organized congresses, and energetically proselytized in favour of the versions of the Modern Movement approved of by the parent body.

Jane S. Turner (ed.) (1998) **vii** 343–4

Constructivism Anti-aesthetic, supposedly pro-technology (in that it favoured the use of man-made industrial materials such as metal, glass, etc., and processes, e.g. welding, to produce abstract sculptures, rather than modelling or carving), 'leftist' tendency that evolved from just before the 1914–18 war, and blossomed in the USSR from *c.* 1920, associated with the notion of the machine and heavy industry and supposed to represent the aspirations of the working class. The machine was said to be a metaphor for the new culture of Communism and was therefore the means by which the economy could be rebuilt and '*bourgeois*' distinctions between art (considered as just another aspect of manufacture) and industry abolished. It was largely disseminated in the West through the *Bauhaus* and the Dutch *De-Stijl* movement. Constructivists insisted that architecture was simply the means of expressing a structure made using industrial processes and machine-made parts, with no hint of craftsmanship, and stressed utilitarian aspects, especially the function of elements of the building. Architectural exemplars include Tatlin's enormous monument to the Third International (1920), a distorted frustum in the form of a diminishing spiral (**Figure G.1**); Mel'nikov's Rusakov Workers' Club, Moscow (1927–8), with cantilevered concrete lecture-halls expressed (**Figure G.2**); and Vesnin's project for the *Leningradskaya Pravda* building, Moscow (1923–4), with advertising signs, clocks, loudspeakers, lifts (elevators), and a searchlight all incorporated as integral elements of the design (**Figure G.3**). A key figure of Constructivism was El Lissitzky, who was the link between Russian Constructivism and Western Europeans such as the German Gropius, the Swiss Hannes Meyer, and the Dutchman Mart Stam. Constructivism gave rise to many sub-theories and factions, some more extreme than others, and its anti-environmentalist aspects, jagged overlapping diagonal forms, aggressive expressions of mechanical elements (such as services, lifts, etc.), have proved to be potent precedents for so-called 'High-Tech' architecture (e.g. the *Centre Georges Pompidou*, Paris [1971–7], designed by Piano & Rogers), and later for the protagonists of **Deconstructivism**.

Curl & Wilson (2015) 192–3; Ingberman (1994); Khan-Magomedov (1986); Lodder (1983); Milner (1983); Jane S. Turner (ed.) (1998) **vii** 767–72; Wilk (ed.) (2006)

Corbusianity Quasi-religious cult, the most characteristic aspect of which was uncritical adulation of the works and personality of Swiss-born architect Charles-Édouard Jeanneret-Gris, *called from* 1920 'Le Corbusier', a major figure in CIAM, whose advocacy for wholesale destruction of urban fabric and traditional streets and squares, to be replaced by motorways and high-rise build-

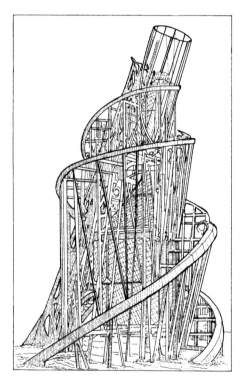

Figure G.1. Design (1919–20) for a monument to the Third International Communist Congress, Moscow (1921), by Tatlin. Taller than the Eiffel Tower in Paris, this structure was intended to have suspended within it glazed volumes (housing legislative assemblies, executive committees, and information offices for the international proletariat), each of which would rotate on axes: one, a cube, would take a year to revolve the full 360°; another, a pyramid, would need a month to do this; and the last, a cylinder, would need only a day. Intended to express a revolutionary society constantly on the move, this work of Russian Constructivism might also be regarded as a form of kinetic architecture

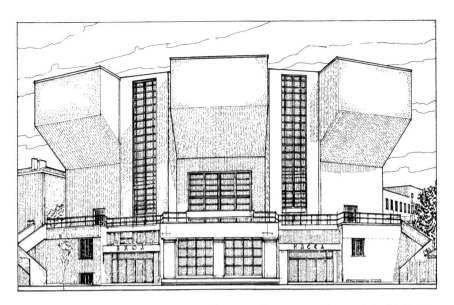

Figure G.2. The Rusakov Workers' Club, Stranynka, Moscow (1927–8), by Mel'nikov, with the cantilevered lecture-halls expressed externally

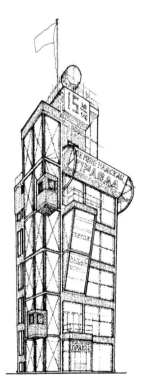

Figure G.3. V. & L. Vesnin's unexecuted project (1923–4) for the *Leningradskaya Pravda* building, Moscow, with the elevators (lifts), signboards, searchlight, advertisements, clocks, loudspeakers, radio masts, and framed structure clearly expressed

ings constructed of raw, exposed concrete, was responsible for widespread dystopias on a global scale.

    Corbusier (1929, 1933, 1935, 1943, 1946, 2008); Jeanneret-Gris (1928); Millais
(2009, 2015, 2017); Salingaros *et al.* (2004); Weber (2008); Wilk (ed.) (2006)

Dada Short-lived (*c.*1916–*c.*1922) international movement in art and literature that
repudiated traditional conventions including naturalism, perspective, all forms
of representation, and reason, and deliberately set out to scandalize and outrage.
Its protagonists claimed it was free from prejudice and all academic conventions,
so a climate would be created in which new ideas and new forms would supposedly develop by means of inventive spontaneity. Leading figures were Hans
Arp, Hugo Ball (who chose the name *Dada*, which means 'hobby horse' in
French), Emmy Hennings, Richard Huelsenbeck, Marcel Janco, and Tristan
Tzara, who edited the review *Dada* (1917–22). For a time Dada was centred on
the *Cabaret Voltaire*, Zürich, where Hennings sang, but was introduced to Berlin
by Huelsenbeck (1917–22). Arp brought its influences to Kandinsky and Klee,
and therefore to the *Bauhäusler*, and also helped to promote it in Berlin, Cologne,
Hanover, and other German cities, as well as in The Netherlands, Constructivist
groups, and those associated with *De Stijl*, notably van Doesburg. Tzara spread
its tendencies in Paris: his *manifest dada 1918*, issue 3 of *Dada*, advocated chaos,
the mixing of genres, and laid the foundations or 'revolutionary art'. In 1920
Tzara joined Francis Picabia, and for a brief period influenced such luminaries
as Louis Aragon, André Breton, and Philippe Soupault, whose journal, *Littérature*
(1919–24), promoted Dada and Surrealism. Dadaism was therefore closely connected with 'revolutionary' movements totally opposed to the epoch in which
they existed. Perhaps the most celebrated exemplar of Dadaism's disdain for
tradition was Duchamp's exhibit (1917) entitled *Fountain*, a urinal signed 'R.
Mutt'. Dadaism created what might be described as 'a metaphysic of banality
by discovering the plastic vitality that emanates from nameless or unnoticed
things': its protagonists denied that good sense, clarity, and humour played any
part in real artistic endeavour. Many of its attitudes permeated the Modern
Movement in architecture, not least its total rejection of the past, and the
humourless earnestness of its protagonists.

    Giedion-Welcker (1956) xiv; *Times Literary Supplement* (2 September 1920)
569/3; Jane S. Turner (ed.) (1998) **viii** 433–40

Deconstructivism *and* **Deconstructionism** Late-twentieth-century tendencies in
architecture having certain formal similarities to aspects of Russian Constructivism,
such as diagonal overlappings of rectangular or trapezoidal elements, and the
frequent use of warped planes, as in works by Lissitzky, Malevich, and Tatlin (*see*
Figure G.1), although some have denied those similarities. Deconstructivist
architecture has been held to embrace works by Eisenman, Gehry, Hadid,
Johnson (his gatehouse at New Canaan [1994–5]), Libeskind, and Tschumi,
among others (though not all would wish to be associated with this label).
Eisenman, in particular, designed from 1968 some deliberately dysfunctional

houses that aimed to realize a kind of aesthetically autonomous, self-referential architecture freed from all surviving conventional Modernist sociocultural values, including human context or function. An example is his House VI (the Frank House), Cornwall, CT (1972), which featured a door too narrow to be entered without turning sideways (provided one was slim), and a staircase that could not be climbed.

If **Deconstructivism** took aspects of Russian Constructivism as its starting point, **Deconstructionism** was closely linked to and influenced by the writings of Derrida. Instead of aiming for unified forms in their architecture, figures such as Eisenman and Tschumi took an eclectic approach, drawing on other traditions, e.g. Modernism, and incorporated them into designs that altered their usual functions and confused their meanings, attempting a deconstruction of the components of architecture similar to Derrida's approach to texts, therefore treating buildings rather like texts. Derrida's *Glas* suggests the model for deconstructing places experienced in everyday life. However, Deconstructionists ran into difficulties: if it were presupposed that architecture is a language, capable of communicating meaning, it would be capable of being treated using methods of linguistic philosophy. This raises profound problems, as it is arguable if late-twentieth- and early-twenty-first-century architecture possesses claims to any vocabulary, let alone a language. Nevertheless, some, including Jencks, hailed Deconstructivism as a 'new paradigm', but others demurred (Christopher Alexander called it 'nonsensical'), aware of the disruptive impact it has on the built environment: it has been justly perceived as fundamentally destructive because of its rejection of everything that went before and its failure to provide clear values as replacements. **Deconstructivism** and **Parametricism** (*see* Preface & Chapter VIII) can be construed as intentional attacks on human sensibilities so as to arouse anxiety and discomfort, all at outrageous expense, and extremely far removed from the enormous and very real problems that beset contemporary towns and cities. They are really deformed manifestations of the Modern Movement (although rejection of the past was always a key feature of Modernism from its very beginning), 'grand gestures of built nihilism' (*see* Salingaros *et al.* [2004] 198). They also confuse the *meaning* of architecture, deliberately blurring the 'readability' of buildings to make their function unclear. If this is a new paradigm, then it must give cause for the deepest concern. *See also* **Chapter VIII**.

Abram *et al.* (1999); Amsoneit (1994); *Architectural Design* **xlvii**/5 (1977) *Profile* 5, 315–27, & **lx**/9–10 (1990) 32–49; Broadbent (1991); Brunette & Wills (eds) (1994); Curtis (1996); Derrida (1986); Jencks (2002); Jodidio (1995); Johnson & Wigley (1988); Lampugnani (gen. ed.) (1988); Norris (1987); Norris & Benjamin (1996); Richter (2001); Salingaros *et al.* (2004) 194, 198; Schumacher (2011–12); Schumacher (ed.) (2016); Jane S. Turner (ed.) (1998) **viii** 609–10, **x** 120–1, **xxv** 358–60

Elementarism *See Stijl, De*

Functionalism Theory that good design results from or is identical with functional efficiency, i.e., architecture should be determined by function alone. Viollet-le-Duc and other nineteenth-century architects promoted it before Louis Sullivan coined his 'form follows function' slogan (1896). It was used by Giedion, Pevsner, *et al.*, to justify International Modernism, a style believed to suggest it, even though that style was no more 'functional' than any other, and in many ways less so. Indeed Functionalism discarded much that made buildings aesthetically pleasing, interesting, or successful as architecture, thus contributing in no small part to the making of Dystopia.

Banham (1960); J.M. Richards (1958); Sartoris (1936); Jane S. Turner (ed.) (1998) **xi** 839–42; Zurko (1957)

Futurism Italian architectural movement founded (1909) by Marinetti, with the usual Modernist aims of rejecting the past, revolutionizing culture, and embracing, with a near-religious belief in science and technology, an imagined advanced future owing nothing whatsoever to history. It exploited images derived from industrial buildings (dams, hydroelectric schemes, silos, etc.), skyscrapers, multi-level highways, airports, and factories, and it glorified machines, speed, violence, and war. Its main architectural exponents were Sant'Elia and Chiattone, who produced visions of the metropolis of the future, with forms that anticipated work by certain architects, e.g. Mendelsohn. Futurism became closely associated with Fascism, and many of its ideas and slogans were absorbed by the so-called *avant-garde*, notably Russian Constructivists, Le Corbusier, and later groups.

Banham (1960); Caramel & Longatti (1988); Curl & Wilson (2015) 298; Hulten (1987); Marianne W. Martin (1977); E.D.C. Meyer (1995); Jane S. Turner (ed.) (1998) **xi** 862–9; Tisdall & Bozzolla (1977)

Machine Aesthetic Giedion, Mumford, Pevsner, *et al.* claimed to find the origins of the Modern Movement in some of the great achievements of the nineteenth century in engineering and the applied arts, often citing the Crystal Palace, designed by Paxton for the Great Exhibition of 1851 in London as a paradigm. The machine began to be regarded as a source of beauty, and Corbusier's dictum that a house is a 'machine for living' established an architectural aesthetic supposed to be analagous to the qualities found in successful engineering works. Such architecture *suggested* something machine-made, acknowledging industrialization, mass production, and the logic of engineering by copying elements of metal structures (ships, aeroplanes, automobiles, etc.) in an eclectic fashion, more a matter of arriving at an *appearance* rather than of actually *being* what it seemed, a fact that contradicted demands for 'honesty' and 'truth' in architecture, and denied the logic of structural principles. For example, International Modernism favoured smooth wall finishes and long strips of metal-framed windows suggested by ocean-going liners of the *Titanic* vintage, but the walls were almost invariably of rendered brick or blockwork. Later, the **Machine Aesthetic** led to the so-called 'High-Tech' style, epitomized in the *Centre Georges Pompidou*, Paris (1971–7), designed by Piano & Rogers (*see* **Plates 8.4 & 8.6**), where the structure and services are not only exposed, but emphasized, something influenced by aspects of Russian **Constructivism** (*see* **Figure G.3**).

The Architectural Review **lxxviii** (December 1935) 211–18; Banham (1960); Curl & Wilson (2015) 457; Giedion (1941, 1948); Pevsner (1960, 2005); Jane S. Turner (ed.) (1998) **xix** 896–7

MARS (Modern Architectural Research) Group Organization of British and *émigré* architects, designers, engineers, and journalists (incuding John Betjeman, Wells Coates, Maxwell Fry, H. De Cronin Hastings, Arthur Korn, Berthold Lubetkin, J.M. Richards, Philip Morton Shand, and others), formed in 1933 to promote International Modernism in the United Kingdom, and disbanded in 1957. It was the UK branch of CIAM, and its efforts culminated in the 1938 London exhibition entitled *New Architecture*, the layout of which was by L. Moholy-Nagy (just before his departure for the USA), and the co-ordinating designer was Russian-born Misha Black. Taking its cues from Le Corbusier's *Plan Voisin* and other theoretical notions, in 1942 it proposed widespread destruction and rebuilding of London in a master-plan which was based largely on a traffic network, with the urban fabric broken down into 'neighbourhood units' of fixed sizes: if implemented, it would have resembled a monstrously enlarged version of Osbert Lancaster's 'Drayneflete', and London would have been successfully killed off.

Louise Campbell (1985); Fry (1971); Gold (2013); Korn (1953); Lasdun (1957); MARS Group (1938); Reading (1986); Jane S. Turner (ed.) (1998) **xx** 475.

Minimalism Term employed to describe a tendency in design that emerged in the 1920s characterized by impersonal austerity, simplicity, plain, geometrical configurations, and industrially produced materials and elements, producing clean, uncluttered architecture, especially interiors. The work of Miës van der Rohe and Lilly Reich in the 1930s could be classed as Minimalist, but Minimalism again became fashionable in the 1980s, influenced by some impressively austere Japanese exemplars. Minimalism was preferred for exclusive shop interiors in the latter part of the twentieth century: it was used to intimidate by announcing exclusiveness and suggesting wares that could only be acquired at vast expense.

Blueprint **i** (October 1983) 14–15; Tate & Smith (1986); Jane S. Turner (ed.) (1998) **xxi** 645–7; John A. Walker (1992) 412–13

Modernism *See* the first section of **Chapter I**

Neo-Classicism Dominant style in European and American architecture in the late eighteenth and early nineteenth centuries, essentially a return to a Classicism of Antiquity as the Italian Renaissance began to be perceived as offering architectural paradigms that were untrue to the architecture of Ancient Greece and Rome. Taste also turned away from the exuberance of Baroque and Rococo, and moved towards simplicity and a greater appreciation of the importance of archaeology and scholarship to arrive at an architecture that was more true to the spirit of Antiquity. Bodies such as The Society of Dilettanti of London began to sponsor expeditions and surveys leading to accurate publications to record ancient architecture, of which *The Antiquities of Athens* (from 1762) was one of the most important, and a major catalyst of that branch of Neo-Classicism known as the Greek Revival. Comprehensive excavations prompted a huge number of publications dealing not only with the surviving architectural fabric in Greece and Rome, but with important Roman sites at Herculaneum and Pompeii, leading to the so-called Etruscan style, and contributing in no small measure to the treatment of interior design popularized by the Adam Brothers in Britain and the *Empire* style in France. The primitive and the severe began to be appreciated, especially the baseless Doric Order of Ancient-Greek architecture, and, promoted by Winckelmann, Greek architecture began to be taken seriously, first in studies of the temples at Paestum and Sicily, and then in Greece itself, which led to the Doric Revival and the use of bold, primitive forms in architectural composition. Theorists such as Laugier argued for a return to simplicity, to rational design freed from clutter and unnecessary ornament, and confinement of the use of the Orders of architecture for structural rather than decorative purposes, enabling volumes, parts of buildings, and elements to be clearly seen and understood. While certain aspects of Neo-Classicism involved scholarly reproductions of Antique buildings and elements, as in the Greek-Revival works of Smirke and Wilkins, the movement as a whole was not confined to copying (though accurate quotation was an integral part of it), but favoured clarity, stereometrical purity of form, and a lack of superfluous ornament, as can be seen in works by Boullée, Ledoux, Schinkel, and Soane. The publication of accurate surveys of Ancient-Egyptian buildings from 1802 brought further elements into the vocabulary of architects seeking stark, tough forms. Neo-Classicism reached peaks of refinement in the hands of French *Empire* designers and architecture by von Klenze, Schinkel, and James Wyatt, and also enjoyed a twentieth-century Revival as a reaction to Neo-Baroque and *Art-Nouveau* styles, often in a very stripped, simplified form, such as in certain works by Behrens, Poelzig, and Speer.

Council of Europe (1972); Crook (1972); Curl (2003, 2005, 2011*a*); Curl & Wilson (2015, 2016) 515; Stuart & Revett (1762–1816); Toman (ed.) (2000)

Neo-Plasticism Associated with Mondrian's austere abstractions after 1919, the term suggests art freed from any naturalistic tendencies or influences, confined to designs featuring straight vertical and horizontal black lines forming grids, filled with blocks of primary colours, with black, grey, and white, reducing three-dimensional forms to simplified, elemental plans. Developed from the theories of Schoenmaekers, it was adopted as an aesthetic, notably by Rietveld, and greatly influenced *De Stijl*, having a profound effect on Modernist architectural plans of the 1920s.

Boekraad *et al.* (eds) (1983); Chilvers *et al.* (eds) (1988); Mondrian (1920); Overy (1969); Jane S. Turner (ed.) (1998) **xxii** 749

New Brutalism *See* **Brutalism**

Parametricism Promoted from 2008 by Patrik Schumacher (then in partnership with Hadid) as a 'mature style', a new paradigm, the legitimate successor to the 'transitional episodes' of **Modernism**, **Post-Modernism**, **Deconstructivism**, and **Minimalism**. Permeating all aspects of architecture, urbanism, interior design, the world of products, and even tectonic detail, it is dependent on advanced computer-design technologies rooted in digital animation techniques. Its protagonists insist that there are no more landmarks to hold onto, no more boundaries to cross, and that there is no 'axis' to follow, which sounds like the *tabula rasa* set within a landscape of nihilism. They insist that contemporary architecture aims to construct new logics—the logics of fields—that gear up to organize and articulate the new level of dynamism and complexity of contemporary society, thus it might be suggested that this latest 'paradigm' seals architects and architecture even more hermetically within their 'compounds', far removed from any comprehension by or relevance to mere mortal human beings.

P. Schumacher (2011–12); P. Schumacher (ed.) (2016)

Pluralism *See* **Post-Modernism**

Post-Modernism Style or styles in architecture and the decorative arts that was or were a reaction to the International Modern Movement and the dogmas developed especially at the *Bauhaus*. Some hold it began in 1972 when Yamasaki's monstrous Pruitt-Igoe housing, St Louis, MO, was dynamited after all attempts to make it inhabitable had failed. **PoMo** has been connected with a loss of faith in what were once regarded as certainties (e.g. 'progress', 'rationality', and so-called 'scientific' approaches to design [in reality the adoption of a limited selection of *clichés* adding up to a kind of packaging to suggest these]) and with a new acceptance of a large palette of images, signs, and products promoted on a scale never experienced before, which some (e.g. Venturi) welcomed as offering 'complexity' and 'contradiction' in design. One of the characteristics of Post-Modernism was Pluralism, signifying a situation in which several different styles might coexist in one work of architecture. In fact, Post-Modern architecture inverted many of the sacred principles of Modernism: the latter was opposed to ornament, so Post-Modernism embraced it; Modernism objected to any style, let alone mixing styles, pretending that International Modernism, for example, as epitomized in the work of Miës van der Rohe, was not a style, when it patently was, albeit with a very limited vocabulary, so Post-Modernism favoured stylistic eclecticism; Modernism made a radical break with the past in an attempt to create the *tabula rasa*, so Post-Modernism began to include historicist allusions, mixing old and new, sometimes clumsily, with a demonstrable lack of expertise in how to handle historical architecture; Modernism paid lip service to **Functionalism** (sometimes only suggested in packaging), but Post-Modernism recognized the importance of metaphor and signs to make a building acceptable; Modernism was deadly earnest, puritanical, and intolerant of anything of which it did not approve, while Post-Modernism revelled in humour, light-heartedness, a certain vulgarity, whimsicality, and *pastiche*; Modernism was exclusive, so Post-Modernism was inclusive; and Modernism (with certain exceptions, notably the primary colourings of *De Stijl*) was white, grey, or black, yet Post-Modernism revelled in colour, often to a garish extent. Some Post-Modern architecture drew on elements that were not themselves archaeologically or historically accurate, but made vague, often illiterate references to once-familiar motifs such as the Classical Orders (Doric, Ionic, Corinthian, Composite, and their variations), often brashly and crudely used. **PoMo** seems to have heralded a change in Western culture, even a new condition permeating every walk of life, involving cynicism, fragmentation, ill-digested eclecticism, and what Jameson called the 'cultural logic of late capitalism'. The label is rather too comprehensive to have much meaning other than to refer to architecture from the last quarter of the twentieth century that rejected the certainties of the International Modern style and the straitjackets imposed by CIAM and its *apparatchiks*.

Appignanesi (ed.) (1986); Jameson (1993, 2009); Jencks (1987*a*, 1990, 2002, 2015); M.S. Larson (1993); Lyotard (1984); Jane S. Turner (ed.) (1998) **xxv** 358–60; Venturi (1966); John A. Walker (1992) 517, 526–9

Prussian Neo-Classicism Under King Friedrich Wilhelm II, Neo-Classicism in a remarkably refined and elegant form became almost the official Prussian State architectural style from the death of Friedrich II ('the Great') in 1786, starting with the internal works for the palaces in Berlin and Potsdam by Erdmannsdorff in 1787, a complete contrast to the Rococo favoured by the late King. Friedrich Wilhelm II summoned (1788) Erdmannsdorff, David Gilly, and Carl Gotthard Langhans to Berlin to establish a new style of architecture that did not reflect the Francophilia of his predecessor. Gilly founded the Building School (*Bauschule*) in Berlin, re-established 1799 as the *Bauakedemie*, which became one of the most important architectural schools in Europe, numbering Friedrich Gilly, Leo von Klenze, Schinkel, and other illustrious Neo-Classical architects among its students. David Gilly founded *Sammlung nützlicher Aufsätze und Nachrichten die Baukunst betreffend* (collection of useful articles and news concerning architecture) one of the first German illustrated architectural journals, published in Berlin 1797–1806, and designed several important buildings in and near Berlin. Langhans was responsible for that great pioneering monument of Neo-Classicism, the Brandenburg Gate, Berlin (1789–94), one of the first buildings of the eighteenth century to be based on the Athenian *Propylaea*, and an examplar that proved to be profoundly influential. However, Prussia's most celebrated architect, Schinkel, administrator of the State building-service, architect to the royal family, and teacher, gave his name to a period in Prussian culture known as the *Schinkelzeit* (Schinkel Time *or* Age) during the reigns of Kings Friedrich Wilhelm III (1797–1840) and IV (1840–61), when an administrative class created a new Prussia, governed by a self-perpetuating body of highly intelligent enlightened civil servants advising the hereditary Hohenzollern monarchy. Schinkel's designs never descended to mere pedantry: on the other hand, he created some of the greatest exemplars of Neo-Classical architecture in Berlin, treated with imagination and scholarship, including the *Neue Wache*, *Unter den Linden* (1816–18), the *Schauspielhaus, Gendarmenmarkt* (1818–21), the new (now Old) Museum, *Lustgarten* (1824–30), and the New Pavilion, *Schloß Charlottenburg* (1824–5). He also designed the *Casino* (1824–5), the *Schloß* (1824–32), and the exquisite *Große Neugierde* (New Curiosity, 1835–7), all at Glienecke, and several buildings at Potsdam, including *Charlottenhof* (1826–7), the Court Gardener's House (1829–33), the 'Roman Baths' (1830), and the noble, stereometrically pure *Nikolaikirche* (1830–7). In the wake of the post-Napoleonic reorganization of Europe, Schinkel was involved as restorer, architect, and assessor throughout the Prussian lands, extending from the Rhineland in the West and well into what is now Poland in the East. It should be remembered that Neo-Classicism was uncluttered with associations, unlike Baroque (which was inseparable from Absolutism and the Counter Reformation), so it was free from any such taints, and was therefore thought suitable for a growing, high-minded, victorious nation, expressing the desire of King Friedrich Wilhelm III that Prussia should be strong in intellectual might, so Neo-Classicism was an expression of that aim. The King gathered together an enviable constellation of politicians, philosophers, scientists, writers, and artists who contributed to the evolution of what was to become the most powerful state in Germany. Schinkel's work has never fallen into disfavour, and so he influenced later generations of German architects, not least Behrens, Miës van der Rohe, and Speer, as well as non-Germans, including Krier, Philip Johnson, Porphyrios, and Stirling.

Bergdoll (1994); Curl & Wilson (2015, 2016) 678–80; Leuthäuser & Feierabend (eds) (1996); Snodin (ed.) (1991); Streidt & Feierabend (eds) (1999); Toman (ed.) (2000); Watkin & Mellinghoff (1987); Zadow (2001); Zukowsky (ed.) (1986); Zukowsky (ed.) (1994)

Rationalism Term meaning different things at different times used by various groups in the history of twentieth-century architecture, but mostly (and inappropriately) applied to mean the so-called principles behind the International-Modern Movement led by Gropius, Miës van der Rohe, *et al.*, subscribing to the **Machine Aesthetic** and to alleged **Functionalism**. However, the word has been so loosely used that some expanded explanations are necessary.

Classical and Renaissance architectural treatises argued that architecture was a science with principles that could be understood on a *rational* basis. Eighteenth- and nineteenth-century theorists, notably J.-N.-L. Durand, Viollet-le-Duc, Semper, and others also argued for *reasoned* approaches to design derived from the culture of the European Enlightenment, building on what had gone before. However, those arguing for twentieth-century supposed 'Rationalism' were iconoclastic, making assumptions that architectural and urban problems could be solved primarily through an abandonment of what they pejoratively called 'Historicism' and of movements such as the Arts-and-Crafts (despite lip-service to William Morris), *Art Nouveau*, and Expressionism (which they regarded as dead ends), thus creating a *tabula rasa* on which to start again from scratch. They were messianic in their desire for a 'new world', 'better' architecture, and 'leftist' political systems: they held quasi-religious beliefs in the inherent rightness of their cause, drawing on the '**Machine Aesthetic**' to achieve *images* appropriate to their arguments. Their position, therefore, was wholly unlike that of nineteenth-century theorists, but was based on spurious analogies, false, twisted reasoning, and a jettisoning of all intellectual rigour. They evolved certain principles by which their aims were to be met. First, architecture, industrial design, and planning could be used for social-engineering and conditioning purposes, and design was accorded supposedly 'moral' meanings (a notion partly derived from the writings of A.W.N. Pugin and Ruskin, both of whom, however, would have been horrified by the inhumane results). Second, strict economy, cheap industrialized building methods, prefabrication, and mass-production at all levels were to be employed in the making of a new environment to achieve a minimum standard for everyone's habitation, but, even if traditional methods of construction (much cheaper than the supposed 'rational' industrialized varieties) were used (bricks, after all, are mass-produced, standardized, prefabricated building components), architecture should *look* machine-made in its pristine state (so brickwork and blockwork were disguised by being covered with smooth render). All ornament, of course, was eschewed. Third, wholesale clearances, demolitions, and the total destruction of urban fabric were held to be essential to create the *tabula rasa* and eliminate anything with which modern structures could be compared. Fourth, form itself should be evolved for constructional, economic, functional, political, and social reasons, and so was not (in theory) subject to individual fancy (but in fact was largely determined by a few predetermined paradigms).

In practice, Rationalism promoted an approved International style from which all historical and decorative elements were expunged, drawing on influences from, e.g. **Constructivism** and *De Stijl*, and no deviations from it would be tolerated. Among key buildings were the *Bauhaus*, Dessau (1925–6), the *Maison Stein*, Garches (1927), and houses at the *Weißenhofsiedlung*, Stuttgart (1927) (*see* **Figures 4.4, 4.5**), while theoretical and unifying bases were provided by **CIAM** and certain writers, notably Giedion. After the 1939–45 war, that style became *de rigueur* throughout Western Europe and America. Looked at objectively, it was just another style, drawing its motifs from a limited range of features approved in the late 1920s and early 1930s, owing nothing to true Rationalism at all, but more to *images* thought to be appropriate for the times, and that, in any case, were only *metaphors* of mass production, 'modernity', and industrialization.

Rationalism, in another sense, flourished in Italy under Benito Mussolini's Fascist *régime* (1922–43), and International Modernism was also called *Razionalismo* by *Gruppo 7*, the association of Italian architects, members of which were mostly associated with Fascism, and who attempted to balance the Classical heritage of Italy with the '**Machine Aesthetic**'. Terragni's architecture was perhaps the most distinguished of works associated with Italian Rationalism.

Behne (1926); Brolin (1976); Etlin (1991); Giedion (1941, 1948); Gropius (1919, 1923, 1935, 1952, 1956); Koulermos (1995); Lampugnani (ed.) (1988); Mantero (ed.) 1969); Mantero (1984); Millais (2009, 2017); Pevsner (1960, 2005); Pevsner & Richards (eds) (1973); Thomas Schumacher (1991); Jane S. Turner (ed.) 1998) **xxvi** 12–16; Watkin (1977); Wolfe (1981)

SLOAP (Space Left Over After Planning) Useless patches of ground left between roads and the rigidly rectilinear International-Style Modernist buildings which rarely respected traditional established street or urban patterns, so considerable waste of land ensued, contributing to the desolation and ugliness now resignedly and universally accepted as normal.

Curl & Wilson (2015) 711; Schofield (ed.) (2016) 63–5

Stijl, De Literally 'The Style'. Dutch artistic movement and name of a journal founded by van Doesburg, and published in Leiden 1917–32. Other members included van 't Hoff, Mondrian, Oud, and Rietveld. Influenced by Cubism, by **Neo-Plasticism**, and by a Calvinistic concern with supposed objectivity, simplicity, and truth, it was, like many twentieth-century movements in art, antihistorical and antagonistic to tradition. Its protagonists proposed an abstracted clarity of expression, wholly divorced from Nature, and advocated straight lines, pure planes, right angles, primary colours (here the influence of Schoenmaekers was paramount), and decomposed cubes: it was one of the most powerful influences on architecture between 1918 and 1939, especially through the *Bauhaus* and International Modernism. The paradigms of *De-Stijl*-inspired design were Rietveld's 'Red-Blue' chair (an unpainted version was made in 1918, but the coloured variation dated from between 1920 and 1923) and the house at *Prins Hendriklaan* 50, Utrecht (1921–4), designed with and for Truus Schröder-Schräder (*see* **Figure 3.2**). The house is built up of grey and white horizontal and vertical slabs, combined with secondary horizontal and vertical elements painted in primary colours and black (another instance of the potent influence of Schoenmaekers): the subdivision between external and internal spaces was blurred, and the clarity of expression of the planes and forms was a development of the design technique displayed in the Red-Blue chair (*see* **Figure 3.1**), known as Elementarism (*see* Chapter III).

Friedman (ed.) (1982); Jaffé (1956); Overy (1969); Overy *et al.* (1988); Padovan (2002). Petersen (ed.) (1968); Sezon Bijutsukan (1998); Troy (1983); Jane S. Turner (ed.) (1998) **xxi** 850–7, **xxvi** 378–80, **xxix** 660–1; Warncke (1994); Zevi (1974)

Suprematism Term coined in 1915 by Malevich for a 'new system' of art that claimed, like most other *avant-garde* groups and movements of the time, superiority over all the art of the past, to be supposedly purely aesthetic, and divorced from any political or social relevance. It was concerned with the purity of shape, especially the square, rectangle, circle, cross, and triangle, and used a very narrow range of colour. Malevich's *White Square on a White Ground* (1918) was regarded as the paradigm of Suprematism, influencing **Constructivism**, Kandinsky,

Lissitzky, Moholy-Nagy, the *Bauhäusler*, the **De-Stijl** group in the Netherlands, and therefore the evolution of the International-Modern style. Paul Westheim observed of the acceptance of Malevich's ideas by the *Bauhäusler* that it was fortunate the Russian[1] had not taken out a patent to protect the square,[2] but he feared that adherence to Suprematist notions would lead to a type of aesthetic straitjacket, limiting creativity, and ultimately becoming only an unintelligent play on a very limited range of simple geometrical forms, which is largely what happened. Although Suprematism was largely *passé* by 1919, its influence was perpetuated in the Lomonosov porcelain factory in Leningrad, especially through Malevich's followers, Chashnik and Suetin, and indeed in the International style of architecture after that.

Chilvers, Osborne, & Farr (eds) (1988) 307, 482; Malevich (1927); Jane S. Turner (ed.) (1998) **xx** 192–6, **xxx** 6–9; *Wissenschaftliche Zeitschrift der Hochschule für Architektur und Bauwesen* **xxvi**/4/5 (Weimar: 1979) 329; Zhadova (1982)

Traditionalism 1. In theological terms, a system of philosophy which gained status in the Roman Catholic Church around 1840, according to which all human knowledge, especially knowledge of religious and moral truth, is derived by traditional instruction from original Divine Revelation. **2.** In architecture, the word suggested acceptance of the handing down, through many generations, of trusted and tried methods of building that informed design, notably in the Arts-and-Crafts movement as influenced by William Morris. Traditionalist architects, notably George Devey and Blunden Shadbolt, drew on the huge legacy of vernacular buildings to inform their work, especially in the field of domestic design, and much fine work of what we now call the Domestic Revival was recorded by Hermann Muthesius in his monumental study before the catastrophe of 1914–18. It therefore follows that traditionalist architects rejected the siren calls of the Modern Movement, and so their buildings were consequently ignored. 'Traditionalist' architecture began to be applied to anything that did not conform to Modernism, and so the term was increasingly used as one of abuse.

Allibone (1991); Cumming & Kaplan (2004); Gradidge (1980); Muthesius (1908–11)

1. Though of Ukrainian birth.   2. Wingler (1978) 69.

Bibliography

Books are sepulchres of thought.

HENRY WADSWORTH LONGFELLOW (1807–82): 'The Wind over the Chimney' in
Tales of a Wayside Inn (Boston, MA: Ticknor & Fields, 1863) 8

This lists items cited in the References and also includes suggestions for further reading.

Abram, Joseph, *et al.* (1999): *Tschumi Le Fresnoy Architecture In/Between* (New York: Monacelli Press).

Abscher, Kenneth Michael, *et al.* (2012): *Privileged and Confidential: The Secret History of the President's Intelligence Advisory Board* (Lexington, KY: The University Press of Kentucky).

Adam, Peter (1992): *The Arts of the Third Reich* (London: Thames & Hudson Ltd).

Adam, Robert (2017): *Classic Columns: 40 Years of Writing about Architecture*, Clive Aslet (ed.) with a Foreword by Sir Roger Scruton (London: Cumulus).

Adorno, Theodor W., *et al.* (2010): *Aesthetics and Politics* (London: Verso).

al-Sabouni, Marwa (2016): *The Battle for Home: The Vision of a Young Architect in Syria* (London: Thames & Hudson).

Alberti, Leone Battista (1755, 1758): *The Architecture of Leon Batista Alberti, In Ten Books, . . .* etc. James Leoni (tr.) (London: Edward Owen for Robert Alfray).

Alexander, Christopher, *et al.* (1977): *A Pattern Language: Towns, Buildings, Construction* (New York: Simon & Schuster).

Alison, Archibald (1790): *Essay on the History and Nature of Taste* (Edinburgh: Robinson; London: Bell & Bradfute).

Allibone, Jill (1988): *Anthony Salvin, 1799–1881* (Cambridge: Lutterworth Press).

Allibone, Jill (1991): *George Devey, Architect, 1820–1886* (Cambridge: Lutterworth Press).

Amsoneit, Wolfgang (1994): *Contemporary European Architects* i (Cologne: Taschen).

Anděl, Jaroslav (2006): *The New Vision for the New Architecture: Czechoslovakia 1918–1938* (Zürich: Scalo Verlag AG).

Anderson, Stanford (2000): *Peter Behrens and a New Architecture for the Twentieth Century* (Cambridge, MA & London: Massachusetts Institute of Technology Press).

Andreae, Johannes Valentinus (1619): *Reipublicae Christianopolitanae descriptio* (Argentorati [Strassburg]: Haeredes Lazari Zetzneri). *See also* Held, Felix Emil (tr.) (1916): *Christianopolis: An Ideal State of the Seventeenth Century* (Oxford: Oxford University Press).

Anuszewski, Artur Stefan, *et al.* (2011): *Toruń* (Toruń: Wydawnictwo Orient Artur Anuszewski).

Appignanesi, L. (ed.) (1986): *Post-Modernism* (London: Institute of Contemporary Arts).

Arbeitsrat für Kunst (1919): *Ja! Stimmen des Arbeitsrates für Kunst in Berlin* (Berlin: bei der Photographischen Gesellschaft in Charlottenburg).

Arendt, Hannah (2004): *The Origins of Totalitarianism*, with Introduction by Samantha Power (New York: Schocken Books).

Arnold, Matthew (1869): *Culture and Anarchy: An Essay in Political and Social Criticism* (London: Smith, Elder, & Co.).

Arnold, Matthew (1873): *Literature & Dogma* (London: Smith, Elder, & Co.).

Arthur, Donald (tr.) (2015): *see* Hilmes, Oliver.

Arts Council of Great Britain, The (1979): *Thirties: British Art and Design before the War: an exhibition organised by the Arts Council of Great Britain in collaboration with the Victoria & Albert Museum, Hayward Gallery, 25 October 1979–13 January 1980* (London: The Arts Council of Great Britain).

Ashbee, Charles Robert (1911): *Should we Stop Teaching Art?* (London: B.T. Batsford).

Ashbee, Charles Robert (1917): *Where the Great City Stands: A Study in the New Civics* (London: Essex House Press; Batsfords).

Aslet, Clive (ed.) (2017): *see* Adam, Robert.

Bacon, Mardges (2001): *Le Corbusier in America: Travels in the Land of the Timid* (Cambridge MA: MIT Press).

Bajohr, Frank (2015): *see* Matthäus, Jürgen.

Ballantyne, Andrew (ed.) (2004): *Architectures: Modernism and After* (Oxford: Blackwell Publishing Ltd).

Ballard, James Graham (1975): *High-Rise* (London: Jonathan Cape).

Banham, Reyner (1960): *Theory and Design in the First Machine Age* (London: Architectural Press).

Banham, Reyner (1966): *The New Brutalism: Ethic or Aesthetic?* (London: Architectural Press).

Banham, Reyner (1969): *The Architecture of the Well-Tempered Environment* (London: Architectural Press).

Banham, Reyner (1971): *Los Angeles: The Architecture of Four Ecologies* (London: Allen Lane).

Banham, Reyner (1981): *Design by Choice*, Penny Sparke (ed.) (London: Academy Editions).

Barman, Christian Augustus (1926): *Balbus, or, The Future of Architecture* (London: Paul, Trench, Trubner, & Co. Ltd).

Barnett, Correlli (1995): *The Lost Victory: British Dreams, British Realities, 1945–1950* (London: Macmillan).

Barr, Alfred H., Jr (1932): *see* Hitchcock, Henry-Russell.

Barth, Holger, & Topfstedt, Thomas (eds) (2000): *Vom Baukünstler zum Komplex-projektanten: Architekten in der DDR* (Erkner: Institut für Regionalentwicklung und Strukturplanung).

Basedow, Heinrich (1973): *Meine Lebenserinnerungen* Heinz Müller (ed.) (Hamburg: Heinz Müller).

Bastiaansen, Cora, *et al.* (eds) (2008): *Groot woordenboek Nederlands-Engels* (Utrecht & Antwerp: van Dale).

Bauer, Catherine K. (1937): *see* Hitchcock, Henry-Russell.

Bauhaus-Archiv, Museum für Gestaltung (ed.) (1981): *Sammlungs-Katalog (Auswahl) Architektur, Design, Malerei, Graphik, Kunstpädagogik* (Berlin: Gebr. Mann).

Baumhoff, Anja, & Droste, Magdalena (eds) (2009): *Mythos Bauhaus. Zwischen Selbsterfindung und Enthistorisierung* (Berlin: Reimer Verlag).

Bayer, Herbert, *et al.* (eds) (1938): *Bauhaus 1919–1938* (New York: Museum of Modern Art).

Beanland, Christopher (2016): *Concrete Concept: Brutalist Buildings Around the World* (London: Frances Lincoln).

Becker, Udo (1994): *The Continuum Encyclopedia of Symbols*, Lance W. Gardner (tr.) (New York & London: Continuum).

Bednorz, Achim (photographer) (1999): *see* Toman, Rolf (ed.).

Behne, Adolf (1926): *Der Moderne Zweckbau* (Munich: Drei Masken).

Bellaigue, Sheila de (tr.) (2004, 2014): *see* Röhl, John C.G.

Benjamin, Andrew (1996): *see* Norris, Christopher.

Bensinger, Eric Sigmund (tr.) (1937): *see* London, Kurt.

Benson, Timothy O. (ed.) (2001): *Expressionist Utopias: Paradise, Metropolis, Architectural Fantasy* (Berkeley, CA & London: University of California Press).

Beresford, Arthur Edgar (1933): *see* Scott, Mackay Hugh Baillie.

Bergdoll, Barry (tr.) (1988): *see* Lampugnani, Vittorio Magnano (gen. ed.).

Bergdoll, Barry (1994): *Karl Friedrich Schinkel: An Architecture for Prussia*, with photographs by Erich Lessing (New York: Rizzoli International Publications Inc.).

Bergdoll, Barry (2000): *European Architecture 1750–1890* (Oxford: Oxford University Press).

Bergdoll, Barry (2002): *see* Riley, Terence, *et al.*

Bergeijk, Herman van (2004): *see* Winkler, Klaus-Jürgen.

Berlage, Hendrik Petrus (1996): *Thoughts on Style 1886–1909*, Iain Boyd Whyte & Wim de Wit (trs) (Santa Monica, CA: The Getty Center for the History of Art and the Humanities).

Berman, Marshall (1982): *All that is Solid Melts into Air: The Experience of Modernity* (New York: Simon & Schuster). *See also* 1983 (London: Verso) and subsequent edns.

Bessel, Richard (ed.) (2001): *Life in the Third Reich* (Oxford: Oxford University Press).

Betjeman, John (1933): *Ghastly Good Taste: Or, a Depressing Story of the Rise and Fall of English Architecture* (London: Chapman & Hall Ltd). *See also* the 1986 edn. (London: Century Hutchinson Ltd in assn. with The National Trust).

Betteridge, Harold T. (ed.) (1978): *Cassell's German–English English–German Dictionary* (London: Cassell Ltd; New York: Macmillan Publishing Co. Inc.).

Bettley, James, & Pevsner, Nikolaus (2015): *Suffolk: East* (New Haven & London: Yale University Press).

Beyer, Klaus G. (1967): *see* Scheidig, Walther.

Birksted, J.K. (2009): *Le Corbusier and the Occult* (Cambridge, MA & London: Massachusetts Institute of Technology Press).

Blair, Sheila S., & Bloom, Jonathan M. (1995): *The Art and Architecture of Islam 1250–1800* (New Haven & London: Yale University Press).

Blake, Peter (1977): *Form Follows Fiasco: Why Modern Architecture Hasn't Worked* (Boston MA: Little, Brown).

Blauert, Elke, *et al.* (eds) (2009): *Alfred Messel 1853–1909: Visionär der Großstadt* (Munich: Edition Minerva).

Blomfield, Sir Reginald Theodore (1934): *Modernismus* (London: Macmillan & Co. Ltd).

Bloom, Jonathan M. (1995): *see* Blair, Sheila S.

Blower, Jonathan (tr.) (2015): *see* Wölfflin, Heinrich.

Boekraad, Cees, *et al.* (eds) (1983): *Het Nieuwe bouwen: de nieuwe beeldung in de architectuur* (Delft: Delft University Press; Den Haag: Haags Gemeentemuseum).

Bolz, Lothar (1951): *Von deutschem Bauen: Reden und Aufsätze* (Berlin: Verlag der Nation).

Bongartz, Norbert, *et al.* (1977): *Paul Bonatz 1877–1956* (Stuttgart: Krämer).

Börsch-Supan, Helmut, & Grisebach, Lucius (1981): *Karl Friedrich Schinkel: Architektur Malerei Kunstgewerbe* (Berlin: Staatlichen Schlösser und Gärten und National Galerie Berlin Staatliche Museen Preußischer Kulturbesitz).

Boston, Richard (1989): *Osbert: A Portrait of Osbert Lancaster* (London: Collins).

Botar, Oliver Arpad Istvan, & Wünsche, Isabel (eds) (2011): *Biocentrism and Modernism* (Farnham & Burlington, VT: Ashgate).

Botta, Mario (1991): *Mario Botta 1980–1990* (Zürich: Verlag für Architektur).

Boutron, Félix (1931): 'Le Salon de 1931' in *L'Architecture xliv*/6 181–210.

Bowe, Nicola Gordon (ed.) (1993): *Art and the National Dream* (Dublin: Irish Academic Press).

Bown, Matthew Cullerne (1991): *Art under Stalin* (Oxford: Phaidon).

Bozzolla, Angelo (1977): *see* Tisdall, Caroline.

Bradley, Sculley (ed.) (1980): *see* Whitman, Walt.

Bradley, Simon, & Pevsner, Nikolaus (1997): *London 1: The City of London* in *The Buildings of England* series (London: Penguin Group).

Bradley, Simon, & Pevsner, Nikolaus (2003): *London 6: Westminster* (New Haven & London: Yale University Press).

Brandon-Jones, John (1957): *C.F.A. Voysey: A Memoir* (London: Architectural Association).

Brandreth, Gyles Daubeny (2006): *Charles & Camilla: Portrait of a Love Affair* (London: Arrow Books).

Braungart, Wolfgang (ed.) (2002): *Kitsch: Faszination und Herausforderung des Banalen und Trivialen* (Tübingen: Niemeyer).

Brenner, Hildegard (1963): *Die Kunstpolitik des Nationalsozialismus* (Reinbek-bei-Hamburg: Rowohlt Taschenbuch Verlag).

Brenner, Hildegard (ed.) (1972): *Ende einer bürgerlichen Kunst-Institution. Die politische Formierung der Preussischen Akademie der Künste ab 1933* (Stuttgart: Deutsche Verlags-Anstalt).

Bridge, Roy (tr.) (2014): *see* Röhl, John C.G.

Brinks, Jan Herman, *et al.* (eds) (2005): *National Myths and Modern Media: Cultural Identity in the Age of Globalisation* (London: I.B. Tauris).

Britt, David (ed.) (1995): *Art and Power: Europe under the Dictators 1930–45* (London: Hayward Gallery).

Brittain-Catlin, Timothy (2008): *The English Parsonage in the Early Nineteenth Century* (Reading: Spire Books Ltd).

Brittain-Catlin, Timothy (2014): *Bleak Houses: Disappointment and Failure in Architecture* (Cambridge, MA & London: The MIT Press).

Broadbent, Geoffrey (1991): *Deconstruction: A Student Guide* (London: Academy Editions).

Brodersen, Kai, & Fuchs, Thomas (eds) (2002): *Wahn Welt Bild: die Sammlung Prinzhorn* (Heidelberg: Universitäts-Gesellschaft).

Brolin, Brent C. (1976): *The Failure of Modern Architecture* (London: Studio Vista).

Brooks, Michael W. (1989): *John Ruskin and Victorian Architecture* (London: Thames & Hudson Ltd).

Brunette, Peter, & Wills, David (eds) (1994): *Deconstruction and the Visual Arts: Art, Media, Architecture* (Cambridge: Cambridge University Press).

Bryson, Andrew (ed.) (2010): *see* Parris, Matthew (ed.).

Buchanan, Peter (2015): 'Empty Gestures' in *The Architectural Review* **ccxxxvii**/1417 (March) 30–5.

Buchner, Hans (1931): *Warenhauspolitik und Nationalsozialismus* (Munich: F. Eher).

Bucknall, Benjamin (tr.) (1959): *see* Viollet-le-Duc, Eugène-Emmanuel.

Bucknall, Stephen Arthur (2006): *see* Symondson, Anthony.

Buddensieg, Tilmann, *et al.* (1984): *Industriekultur: Peter Behrens and the AEG, 1907–1914*, Iain Boyd Whyte (tr.) (Cambridge MA: MIT Press).

Budny, Mildred (1985): *see* Safran, Yehuda, *et al.*

Bufano, Antonietta (ed.) (1975): *Opere latine di Francesco Petrarca* (Turin: Unione Tipografico-Editrice Torinese).

Bullock, Michael (tr.) (1997): *see* Conrads, Ulrich.

Bullock, Nicholas (2002): *Building the Post-War World: Modern Architecture and Reconstruction in Britain* (London: Routledge).

Burgess, Anthony (1962): *A Clockwork Orange* (London: Heinemann).

Burgon, John William (1888-9): *Lives of Twelve Good Men* (London: John Murray).

Burke, Edmund (1823): *The Works of Edmund Burke,* **v**: *Reflections on the Revolution in France* (London: Thomas M'Lean).

Burton, Thomas E. (tr.) (1970): *see* Kopp, Anatole.

Calder, Barnabas (2016): *Raw Concrete: The Beauty of Brutalism* (London: William Heinemann Ltd).

Campbell, Colen (1715–25): *Vitruvius Britannicus, or the British Architect,* etc. (London: The Author).

Campbell, Joan (1977): *The German Werkbund: The Politics of Reform in the Applied Arts* (Princeton, NJ: Princeton University Press).

Campbell, Louise (1985): 'The MARS Group, 1933–1939' in *Transactions* of the RIBA **iv**/2 68–79.

Caramel, Luciano, & Longatti, Alberto (1988): *Antonio Sant'Elia: The Complete Works* (New York: Rizzoli).

Caro, Robert Allan (2015): *The Power Broker: Robert Moses and the Fall of New York* (London: Bodley Head).

Carus, Carl Gustav (1846): *Zur Entwicklungsgeschichte der Seele* (Pforzheim: Flammer & Hoffmann).

Carver, Humphrey (1962): *Cities in the Suburbs* (Toronto: University of Toronto Press).

Cassou, Jean (1984): *The Concise Encyclopedia of Symbolism* (Ware: Omega Books Ltd).

Chadwick, Peter (2016): *This Brutal World* (London: Phaidon Press).

Chambers, William (1759): *A Treatise on Civil Architecture, in which the Principles of that Art are laid down, . . .* etc. (London: J. Haberkorn for The Author).

Chandler, Robert (tr.) (1990): *see* Golomstock, Igor.

Charles, Martin (2007): *see* Grainger, Hilary J.

Charlton, Susannah, Harwood, Elain, & Powers, Alan (eds) (2007): *British Modern: Architecture and Design in the 1930s* (London: Twentieth Century Society).

Charney, Melvin (1991): *Parables and Other Allegories: The Work of Melvin Charney* (Montréal: Centre Canadien d'Architecture; Cambridge, MA & London: MIT Press).

Chaslin, François (2015): *Un Corbusier* (Paris: Fiction & Cie).

Cherry, Bridget (1971): *see* Nairn, Ian, & Pevsner, Nikolaus.

Cherry, Bridget & Pevsner, Nikolaus (1983): *London 2: South* in *The Buildings of England* Series (Harmondsworth: Penguin Books Ltd).

Cherry, Bridget & Pevsner, Nikolaus (1991): *London 3: North West* in *The Buildings of England* Series (London: Penguin Group).

Cherry, Bridget & Pevsner, Nikolaus (1998): *London 4: North* in *The Buildings of England* Series (London: Penguin Group).

Cherry, Bridget, O'Brien, Charles, & Pevsner, Nikolaus (2005): *London 5: East* in *The Buildings of England* Series (New Haven & London: Yale University Press).

Child, Heather, *et al.* (1986): *More than Fine Writing: Irene Wellington: Calligrapher (1904–84)* (London: Pelham).

Chilvers, Ian, Osborne, Harold, & Farr, Dennis (eds) (1988): *The Oxford Dictionary of Art* (Oxford: Oxford University Press).

Chrimes, M.M., *et al.* (eds) (2014): *Biographical Dictionary of Civil Engineers in Great Britain and Ireland* iii: 1890–1920 (London: ICE & Thomas Telford Ltd).

Christian, Margareta Ingrid (tr.) (2011): *see* Mertins, Detlef.

Cichy, Adam (1974): *Poznań* (Poznań: Wydawnictwo Poznańskie).

Claeys, Gregory (2017): *Dystopia: A Natural History* (Oxford: Oxford University Press).

Clarke, Peter, & Trebilcock, Clive (eds) (1997): *Understanding Decline: Perceptions and Realities of British Economic Performance* (Cambridge: Cambridge University Press).

Close, Rob, Gifford, John, & Walker, Frank Arneil (2016): *Lanarkshire & Renfrewshire* in *The Buildings of Scotland* Series (New Haven & London: Yale University Press).

Coe, Peter, & Reading, Malcolm (1981): *Lubetkin and Tecton: Architecture and Social Commitment* (London: Arts Council of Great Britain; Bristol: University of Bristol).

Cohen, Jean-Louis (2008): *see* Corbusier, Le.

Cohen-Portheim, Paul (1933): *The Spirit of France*, Alan Harris (tr.) (London: Duckworth).

Cole, David (2015): *The Art and Architecture of C.F.A. Voysey: English Pioneer Modernist Architect and Designer* (Mulgrave, Victoria: Images Publishing Group Ltd).

Cole, George Douglas Howard (1945): *Building and Planning* (London: Cassell).

Cole, Margaret (1971): *The Life of G.D.H. Cole* (London: Macmillan).

Coleman, Alice (1990): *Utopia on Trial: Vision and Reality in Planned Housing* (London: Hilary Shipman).

Collard, David (2016): 'Rubber and Acid' in *Times Literary Supplement* (18 March) 13.

Collins, Christiane Craseman (tr.) (1965): *see* Sitte, Camillo.

Collins, George R. (tr.) (1965): *see* Sitte, Camillo.

Colls, Robert (2002): *The Identity of England* (Oxford: Oxford University Press).

Colomina, Beatriz (1998): *Privacy and Publicity: Modern Architecture as Mass Media* (Cambridge, MA: MIT Press).

Colquhoun, Alan (2002): *Modern Architecture* (Oxford: Oxford University Press).

Comino, Mary (1980): *Gimson and the Barnsleys: 'Wonderful Furniture of a Commonplace Kind'* (London: Evans Bros.).

Comper, John Ninian (1933): 'Further Thoughts on the English Altar, or practical considerations on the planning of a modern church 1932' in *Transactions of the St Paul's Ecclesiological Society* x/2 (London: W. Heffer).

Conrads, Ulrich (ed.) (1970): *Programmes and Manifestoes on 20th-Century Architecture*, Michael Bullock (tr.) (London: Lund Humphries).

Cook, John Wesley, & Klotz, Heinrich (1973): *Conversations with Architects* (London: Lund Humphries).

Corbusier, Le (1928): *see* Jeanneret-Gris, Charles-Édouard.

Corbusier, Le (1929): *The City of To-morrow and its Planning*, Frederick Etchells (tr.) (London: John Rodker).

Corbusier, Le (1933): *Le Croisade ou le crépuscule des académies* (Paris: Les Editions G. Crès & Cie.).

Corbusier, Le (1935): *La Ville radieuse, éléments d'une doctrine d'urbanisme pour l'équipement de la civilisation machiniste* (Boulogne: éditions de l'architecture d'aujourd'hui).

Corbusier, Le (1942): *see* Pierrefeu, François de.

Corbusier, Le (1943): *Urbanisme de CIAM: La Charte d'Athènes: avec un discours liminaire de Jean Giraudoux* (Paris: Plon). *See also* (1973): *The Athens Charter*, Anthony Eardley (tr.) (New York: Grossman Publishers).

Corbusier, Le (1946): *Towards a New Architecture*, Frederick Etchells (tr.) (London: The Architectural Press). First published in England (1927). *See also* the (*c.*1930) edn. (New York: Brewer, Warren, & Putnam).

Corbusier, Le (1950): *L'Unité d'habitation de Marseille* (Souillac: Mulhouse).

Corbusier, Le (2008): *Toward an Architecture*, John Goodman (tr.) with new Introduction by Jean-Louis Cohen (London: Frances Lincoln).

Corfiato, Hector Othon (1952): *see* Richardson, Albert Edward.

Cornforth, John (1988): *The Search for a Style:* Country Life *and Architecture 1897–1935* (London: Andre Deutsch in assn. with *Country Life*).

Council of Europe (1972): *The Age of Neo-Classicism* (London: Arts Council of Great Britain).

Crawford, Alan (1985): *C.R. Ashbee: Architect, Designer and Romantic Socialist* (New Haven & London: Yale University Press).

Crawford, Alan (1995): *Charles Rennie Mackintosh* (London: Thames & Hudson Ltd).

Crawford, James (2015): *Fallen Glory: The Lives and Deaths of Twenty Lost Buildings* (London: Old Street Publishing).

Crook, Joseph Mordaunt (ed.) (1970): *see* Eastlake, Charles L.

Crook, Joseph Mordaunt (1972): *The Greek Revival: Neo-Classical Attitudes in British Architecture 1760–1870* (London: John Murray).

Crook, Joseph Mordaunt (1981): *William Burges and the High Victorian Dream* (London: John Murray).

Crook, Joseph Mordaunt (1987): *The Dilemma of Style: Architectural Ideas from the Picturesque to the Post-Modern* (London: John Murray [Publishers] Ltd).

Crook, Joseph Mordaunt (2003): *The Architect's Secret: Victorian Critics and the Image of Gravity* (London: John Murray [Publishers] Ltd).

Cross-Rudkin, P.S.M., *et al.* (eds) (2008): *Biographical Dictionary of Civil Engineers in Great Britain and Ireland* ii: 1830–1890 (London: Thomas Telford Publishing for The Institution of Civil Engineers).

Cruickshank, Dan (ed.) (1996): *Sir Banister Fletcher's A History of Architecture* (Oxford: Architectural Press).

Cullmann, Oscar (1961): *Der Staat im Neuen Testament* (Tübingen: Mohr).

Cumming, Elizabeth, & Kaplan, Wendy (2004): *The Arts and Crafts Movement* (London: Thames & Hudson Ltd).

Curjel, Hans (ed.) (1986): *see* Velde, Henry van de.

Curl, James Stevens (1971): 'The Erosion of Canterbury' in *Town and Country Planning* **xxxix**/11 (November) 494–9.

Curl, James Stevens (1977): *The Erosion of Oxford* (Oxford: Oxford Illustrated Press Ltd).

Curl, James Stevens (1983): *The Life and Work of Henry Roberts, 1803–1876, Architect: The Evangelical Conscience and the Campaign for Model Housing and Healthy Nations* (Chichester: Phillimore & Co. Ltd).

Curl, James Stevens (1997–8): Review of Curtis (1996) in *Environments by Design* ii/1 (Winter) 113–16.

Curl, James Stevens (1998): Review of Gold (1997) in *Journal of Urban Design* iii/3 (August) 382–3.

Curl, James Stevens (2002): *Piety Proclaimed: An Introduction to Places of Worship in Victorian England* (London: Historical Publications Ltd).

Curl, James Stevens (2003): *Classical Architecture: An Introduction to its Vocabulary and Essentials, with a Select Glossary of Terms* (New York & London: W.W. Norton & Co.).

Curl, James Stevens (2004): *The Victorian Celebration of Death* (Thrupp, Stroud: Sutton Publishing Ltd).

Curl, James Stevens (2005): *The Egyptian Revival: Ancient Egypt as the Inspiration for Design Motifs in the West* (Abingdon & New York: Routledge).

Curl, James Stevens (2007): *Victorian Architecture: Diversity & Invention* (Reading: Spire Books Ltd).

Curl, James Stevens (2009): Review of Whyte (tr.) (2007) in *Journal of Urban Design* **xiv**/1 (February) 121–5.

Curl, James Stevens (2009*a*): Review of Gold (2007) in *Journal of Urban Design* **xiv**/3 (August) 399–402.

Curl, James Stevens (2011): *Freemasonry & the Enlightenment: Architecture, Symbols, & Influences* (London: Historical Publications Ltd).

Curl, James Stevens (2011*a*): *Georgian Architecture in the British Isles 1714–1830* (Swindon: English Heritage).

Curl, James Stevens (2015): *The Victorian Celebration of Death: An Introduction to Nineteenth-Century Thanatopsis* (Harlech: Heritage Ebooks).

Curl, James Stevens, & Wilson, Susan (2015): *The Oxford Dictionary of Architecture* (Oxford: Oxford University Press). Also published in paperback (2016).

Curtis, William J.R. (1996): *Modern Architecture since 1900* (London: Phaidon Press Ltd).

Czech, Hermann (ed.) (2005): *see* Frank, Josef.

Dakin, J.A. (tr.) (1946): *see* Roth, Alfred (ed.).

Dal Co, Francesco (1986): *see* Tafuri, Manfredo.

Daniels, Anthony (2015): 'The Cult of Le Corbusier' in *Quadrant* **lix**/9 (September) 38–42. *See* https://quadrant.org.au/magazine/2015/09/cult-le-corbusier/ and https://architecturehereandthere.com/2017/02/25/corbusier-fascist-drivel/

Daniels, Klaus (1998): *Low-Tech, Light-Tech, High-Tech: Building in the Information Age* (Basel: Birkhäuser Verlag).

Dannatt, Trevor (ed.) (1953): *Architects' Year Book 5* (London: Elek).

Davis, Alex, & Jenkins, Lee M. (eds) (2007): *The Cambridge Companion to Modernist Poetry* (Cambridge: Cambridge University Press).

Deastyne, Howard (tr.) (1979): *see* Kandinsky, Wassily.

Debord, Guy (2013): *Society of the Spectacle* (London: Notting Hill).

Denis, Maurice (1957): *Journal* **ii** *1905–20* (Paris: La Colombe).

Derrida, Jacques (1986): *Glas*, John P. Leavey, Jr, & Richard Rand (trs) (Lincoln, NE: University of Nebraska Press).

Deutscher Werkbund (ed.) (1927): *Bau und Wohnung: die Bauten der Weißenhofsiedlung in Stuttgart* (Stuttgart: F. Wedekind).

DIB: see Dictionary of Irish Biography

Dictionary of Irish Biography from the Earliest Times to the Year 2002 (*DIB*) (2009): James McGuire & James Quinn (eds) (Cambridge: Cambridge University Press for The Royal Irish Academy).

Dinsmoor, William Bell (1950): *The Architecture of Ancient Greece: An Account of its Historic Development* (London: B.T. Batsford Ltd).

Dluhosch, Eric, & Švácha, Rostislav (eds) (1999): *Karel Teige / 1900–1951: L'enfant terrible of the Czech Modernist Avant-Garde* (Cambridge, MA: Massachusetts Institute of Technology Press).

Dohme, Robert (1888): *Das englische Haus: Eine kultur- und baugeschichtliche Skizze* (Braunschweig: Georg Westermann).

Donnelly, Max (2016): *see* Livingstone, Karen.

Douglas, Norman (1915): *Old Calabria* (London: Martin Secker).

Drebusch, Thomas (ed.) (1992): *see* Ziffer, Alfred.

Drexler, Arthur (ed.) (1977): *The Architecture of the École des Beaux-Arts* (London: Martin Secker & Warburg Ltd).

Dreyer, Ernst Adolf (ed.) (1934): *Deutsche Kultur im neuen Reich. Wesen, Aufgabe und Ziel der Reichskulturkammer* (Berlin: Schlieffen-Verlag).

Dreysse, Dietrich W. (2001): *May-Siedlungen: Architekturführer durch Acht Siedlungen des neuen Frankfurt 1926–1930* (Cologne: Verlag der Buchhandlung Walther König).

Droste, Magdalena (ed.) (2009): *see* Baumhoff, Anja (ed.).

Duany, Andrés, *et al.* (2003): *The New Civic Art: Elements of Town Planning* (New York: Rizzoli).

Duffy, Hugo (1999): *James Gandon and His Times* (Kinsale: Gandon Editions).

Duncan, Alastair (1994): *Art Nouveau* (London: Thames & Hudson Ltd).

Dwork, Debórah, & Pelt, Robert Jan van (1996): *Auschwitz: 1270 to the Present* (New York: W. W. Norton).

Dyckhoff, Tom (2017): *The Age of Spectacle: Adventures in Architecture and the 21st-Century City* (London: Random House).

Eardley, Anthony (tr.) (1973): *see* Corbusier, Le (1943).

Eastlake, Charles L. (1970): *A History of the Gothic Revival*, Joseph Mordaunt Crook (ed.) (Leicester: Leicester University Press; New York: Humanities Press).

Easton, Laird M. (2002): *The Red Count: The Life and Times of Harry Kessler* (Berkeley & Los Angeles, CA & London: University of California Press).

Easton, Laird M. (ed. & tr.) (2011): *Journey to the Abyss. The Diaries of Count Harry Kessler, 1880–1918* (New York: Alfred A. Knopf).

Eaton, Ruth (2001): *Ideal Cities: Utopianism and the (Un) Built Environment* (Antwerp: Mercatorfonds).

Ebeling, Siegfried (1926): *Der Raum als Membran* (Dessau: C. Dünnhaupt Verlag).

Ebeling, Siegfried (1947): *Extra Muros: Einleitung in d. Theorie d. freien Hauses* (Hamburg: Phönix-Verlag).

Eckardt, Wolf Von (1961): 'The Bauhaus' in *Horizon* **iv**/2 58–75.

Economakis, Richard (ed.) (1992): *Léon Krier: Architecture and Urban Design 1967–1992* (London: Academy Editions).

Economakis, Richard (ed.) (1993): *Building Classical: A Vision of Europe and America* with an introduction by Demetri Porphyrios (London & New York: Academy Editions).

Eden, William Arthur (1942): *The Process of Architectural Tradition* (London: Macmillan & Co. Ltd).

Edwards, Arthur Trystan (1929): 'The City of Tomorrow' in *Concrete Way* **ii** (September) 79–87.

Edwards, Arthur Trystan (1944): *Good and Bad Manners in Architecture* (London: J. Tiranti Ltd).

Edwards, Arthur Trystan (1968): *Towards Tomorrow's Architecture: The Triple Approach* (London: Phoenix House).

Eliot, Thomas Stearns (1948): *Notes Towards the Definition of Culture* (London: Faber & Faber Ltd).

Elliott, David (1986): *New Worlds: Russian Art and Society 1900–1937* (New York: Rizzoli).

Elmlund, Peter, & Mårtelius, Johan (eds) (2015): *Swedish Grace: The Forgotten Modern* (Stockholm: Axon Johnson Foundation).

Engelmann, Christine, & Schädlich, Christian (1991): *Die Bauhausbauten in Dessau* (Berlin: Verlag für Bauwesen).

Entwistle, Clive (1948): *see* Pierrefeu, François de.

Esher, Lionel Gordon Baliol Brett, Viscount (1981): *A Broken Wave: The Rebuilding of England, 1940–1980* (London: Allen Lane).

Etchells, Frederick (tr.) (1946): *see* Corbusier, Le.

Etlin, Richard (1991): *Modernism in Italian Architecture, 1890–1940* (Cambridge, MA: MIT Press).

Evans, Edwin (tr.) (1910): *see* Wagner, Richard (1869).

Eysymontt, Rafał, Ziątkowski, Leszek, & Klimek, Stanisław (2014): *A Guide to Wrocław* (Wrocław: Via Nova).

Fairclough, H. Rushton (tr.) (2014): *see* Horace.

Falter, Reinhard (2003): *Ludwig Klages. Lebensphilosophie als Zivilisationskritik* (Munich: Telesma-Verlag).

Fanon, Frantz (1967): *Black Skin, White Masks*, Charles Lam Markmann (tr.) (New York: Grove Press; London: MacGibbon & Kee [1968]), first published (1952) as *Peau noire, masques blancs* (Paris: Éditions du Seuil).

Farmer, John David, & Weiss, Geraldine (1971): *Concepts of the Bauhaus; the Busch-Reisinger Museum Collection* (Cambridge, MA: Harvard University Press).

Farr, Dennis (ed.) (1988): *see* Chilvers, Ian.

Feierabend, Peter (ed.) (1996): *see* Leuthäuser, Gabriele (ed.).

Feierabend, Peter (1999): *see* Streidt, Gert (ed.).

Fergusson, James (1891): *History of the Modern Styles of Architecture* (London: John Murray).

Filler, Martin (2014): 'The Insolence of Architecture' in *The New York Review of Books* **lxi**/10 (5–18 June) 12–16.

Finkelstein, Sidney (1952): 'Abstract Art Today: Dollars, Doodles and Death' in *Masses and Mainstream* **v**/2 (September) 22–31.

Fischer, Martin S. (2003): *see* Happe, Barbara.

Fisher, Jack Carrington (1962): 'Planning the Cities of Socialist Man' in *Journal of the American Institute of Planners* **xxviii** 251–68.

Fishman, Robert (1982): *Urban Utopias in the Twentieth Century: Ebenezer Howard, Frank Lloyd Wright, Le Corbusier* (Cambridge, MA: MIT Press).

Fitzwalter, Raymond, & Taylor, David (1981): *Web of Corruption: The Story of John Poulson and T. Dan Smith* (St Alban's: Granada Publishing).

Ford, Henry (1923): *Mein Leben und Werk* (Leipzig: P. List).

Forgey, Benjamin (1982): 'The International Revisited' in *The Washington Post* (19 April) 1–5: https://www.washingtonpost.com/archive/lifestyle/1982/04/19/the-international-revisited accessed 31 January 2017.

Form + Zweck: Fachzeitschrift für Industrielle Formgestaltung (Various Years): (Berlin: Amt für industrielle Formgestaltung).

Foster, Andy, *et al.* (2005): *Birmingham* in the *Pevsner Architectural Guides* Series (New Haven & London: Yale University Press).

Frampton, Kenneth (2001): *Le Corbusier: Architect and Visionary* (London: Thames & Hudson).

Frampton, Kenneth (2007): *Modern Architecture: A Critical History* (London: Thames & Hudson Ltd).

Franciscono, Marcel (1971): *Walter Gropius and the Creation of the Bauhaus in Weimar: The Ideals and Artistic Theories of its Founding Years* (Urbana, IL & London: University of Illinois Press).

Frank, Hartmut (ed.) (1994): *Fritz Schumacher: Reformkultur und Moderne* (Stuttgart: Hatje).

Frank, Josef (2005): *Architektur als Symbol: Elemente deutschen neuen Bauens*, Hermann Czech (ed.) (Vienna: Löcker Verlag).

Frascina, Francis (ed.) (1985): *Pollock and After: The Critical Debate* (New York: Harper & Row).

Friedman, Mildred (ed.) (1982): *De Stijl: 1917–1931. Visions of Utopia* (Oxford: Phaidon).

Frumkin, Howard (2001): 'Beyond Toxicity: Human Health and the Natural Environment' in *American Journal of Preventive Medicine* **xx** 234–40.

Fry, Maxwell (1944): *Fine Building* (London: Faber & Faber Ltd).

Fry, Maxwell (1971): 'The MARS Plan of London' in *Perspecta* **xiii** 162–73.

Fry, Maxwell (1975): *Autobiographical Sketches* (London: Elek).

Fuchs, Thomas (ed.) (2002): *see* Brodersen, Kai (ed.).

Gaber, Bernard (1966): *Die Entwicklung des Berufsstandes der freischaffenden der dargestellt an der Geschicht des Bundes Deutscher Architekten* (Essen: R. Bacht).

Gabriel, J. François (2004): *Classical Architecture for the Twenty-First Century. An Introduction to Design* (New York & London: W.W. Norton & Co. in assn. with The Institute of Classical Architecture and Classical America).

Gardner, Lance W. (tr.) (1994): *see* Becker, Udo.

Geddes, Norman Bel (1940): *Magic Motorways* (New York: Random House).

Geddes, Patrick (1924): 'A Proposed Co-ordination of the Social Sciences' in *The Sociological Review* **xvi**/1 54–65.

Geddes, Patrick (1998): *Cities in Evolution* (London: Routledge/Thoemmes Press).

Geelhaar, Christian (1973): *Paul Klee and the Bauhaus* (Bath: Adams & Dart).

Geelhaar, Christiane, *et al.* (eds) (1999–2004): *Mathildenhöhe Darmstadt: 100 Jahre Planen und Bauen für die Stadtkrone* (Darmstadt: Justus von Liebig Verlag & Die Stadt Darmstadt).

Geretsegger, Heinz, *et al.* (1983): *Otto Wagner 1841–1918* (Salzburg & Vienna: Residenz Verlag).

Giedion, Sigfried (1941): *Space, Time, & Architecture: The Growth of a New Tradition* (Cambridge, MA: Harvard University Press; London: H. Milford for Oxford University Press).

Giedion, Sigfried (1948): *Mechanization Takes Command: A Contribution to Anonymous History* (Oxford: Oxford University Press).

Giedion-Welcker, Carola (1956): *Contemporary Sculpture: An Evolution in Volume and Space*, Mary Hottinger-Mackie & Sonja Marjasch (trs) (London: Faber & Faber).

Gifford, John (2016): *see* Close, Rob.

Gilbert, Basil (tr.) (1978): *see* Wingler, Hans Maria.

Gillard, Michael, & Tomkinson, Martin (1980): *Nothing to Declare: The Political Corruptions of John Poulson* (London: John Calder).

Giroud, Vincent (2015): *Nicolas Nabokov: A Life in Freedom and Music* (Oxford: Oxford University Press).

Glabau, Leonie (2010): *Plätze in einem geteilten Land: Stadtplatzgestaltungen in der Bundesrepublik Deutschland und der Deutschen Demokratischen Republik von 1945 bis 1990* (Frankfurt-am-Main: Verlag Peter Lang).

Goebbels, Joseph (1987): *Michael: A Novel*, Joachim Neugroschel (tr.) (New York: Amok Press). Originally published (1929) in Munich as *Michael: ein deutsches Schicksal in Tagebuchblättern*.

Gold, John R. (1997): *The Experience of Modernism: Modern Architects and the Future City, 1928–53* (London: E. & F.N. Spon: Thomson Professional).

Gold, John R. (2007): *The Practice of Modernism: Modern Architects and Urban Transformation, 1954–1972* (Abingdon & New York: Routledge: Taylor & Francis Group).

Gold, John R. (2013): '"A Very Serious Responsibility"? The MARS Group, Internationality and Relations with CIAM, 1933–39' in *Architectural History* lvi 249–75.

Goldberger, Paul (2015): *Building Art: The Life and Work of Frank Gehry* (New York: Alfred A. Knopf).

Golomstock, Igor (1990): *Totalitarian Art in the Soviet Union, the Third Reich, Fascist Italy, and the People's Republic of China*, Robert Chandler (tr.) (London: Collins Harvill).

Goodhart-Rendel, Harry Stuart (1953): *English Architecture since the Regency: An Interpretation* (London: Constable & Co. Ltd).

Goodman, John (tr.) (2008): *see* Corbusier, Le.

Göppinger Galerie (1964): *Bauhaus: Idee, Form, Zweck, Zeit: Dokumente und Äußerungen* (Frankfurt-am-Main: Göppinger Galerie).

Gössel, Peter, & Leuthäuser, Gabriele (2005): *Architecture in the 20th Century* (Cologne: Taschen GmbH).

Gradidge, Roderick (1980): *Dream Houses: The Edwardian Ideal* (London: Constable & Co. Ltd).

Graf, Otto Antonia (1994): *Otto Wagner: Das Werk des Architekten* (Vienna: Böhlau Verlag).

Grainger, Hilary J. (2011): *The Architecture of Sir Ernest George* with photographs by Martin Charles (Reading: Spire Books Ltd).

Grassi, Giorgio (1982): *Progetti e Disegni 1965–1980* (Mantua: Exhibition Centre).

Grawe, Gabriele Diana (2000): *see* Wick, Rainer K.

Gray, Camilla (2012): *The Russian Experiment in Art 1863–1922* (London: Thames & Hudson Ltd).

Greenhalgh, Paul (ed.) (1990): *Modernism in Design* (London: Reaktion Books Ltd).

Greenhalgh, Paul (1993): *Quotations and Sources on Design and the Decorative Arts* (Manchester: Manchester University Press)

Greenhalgh, Paul (2000): *Art Nouveau 1890–1914* (London: V&A Publications).

Gregotti, Vittorio (1993): *La Città Visibile* (Turin: Einaudi).

Griffin, Michael J., & Moylan, Tom (eds) (2015): *Exploring the Utopian Impulse: Essays on Utopian Thought and Practice* (Oxford: Peter Lang).

Grisebach, Lucius (1981): *see* Börsch-Supan, Helmut.

Gropius, Walter (1919): *Manifest und Programm des Staatlichen Bauhauses in Weimar* (Weimar: Bauhaus).

Gropius, Walter (1923): *Staatliches Bauhaus in Weimar* (Weimar: Bauhausverlag).

Gropius, Walter (1935): *The New Architecture and the Bauhaus*, P. Morton Shand (tr.) with an Introduction by Frank Pick (London: Faber & Faber Ltd).

Gropius, Walter (1952): *Architecture and Design in the Age of Science* (New York: Spiral).

Gropius, Walter (1956): *Scope of Total Architecture* (London: George Allen & Unwin).

Grospierre, Nicolas (2016): *A Subjective Atlas of 20th-Century Architecture*, Alona Pardo & Elias Redstone (eds) (Munich: Prestel).

Gruber, Karl (1977): *Die Gestalt der Deutschen Kunst* (Munich: Verlag Georg D.W. Callwey).

Guardini, Romano (1925): *Der Gegensatz. Versuche zu einer Philosophie des Lebendig-Konkreten* (Mainz: Werkkreis im Matthias-Grünewald-Verlag).

Guilbaut, Serge (ed.) (1990): *Reconstructing Modernism: Art in New York, Paris, and Montreal, 1945–1964* (Cambridge, MA: MIT Press).

Haag-Bletter, Rosemarie (1975): 'Paul Scheerbart's Architectural Fantasies' in *Journal of the Society of Architectural Historians* **xxxiv**/2 83–97.

Hackney, Rod (1990): *The Good, the Bad and the Ugly* (London: F. Muller).

Hahn, Peter (1995): *Bauhaus in Berlin: Bauten und Projekte* (Berlin: Bauhaus-Archiv).

Halbertsma, Marlite (1992): *Wilhelm Pinder und die deutsche Kunstgeschichte* (Worms: Wernersche Verlagsgesellschaft).

Halbertsma, Marlite (1993): 'Nikolaus Pevsner and the End of a Tradition' in *Apollo* **cxxxvii**/371 (February) 107–9.

Hall, Peter Geoffrey (1988): *Cities of Tomorrow: An Intellectual History of Urban Planning and Design in the Twentieth Century* (Oxford: Basil Blackwell).

Handlin, David P. (1985): *American Architecture* (London: Thames & Hudson Ltd).

Hanks, David A. (ed.) (2015): *Partners in Design: Alfred H. Barr Jr. and Philip Johnson* (New York: The Monacelli Press).

Happe, Barbara, & Fischer, Martin S. (2003): *Haus Auerbach: von Walter Gropius mit Adolf Meyer* (Tübingen: Wasmuth).

Harries, Susie (2011): *Nikolaus Pevsner: The Life* (London: Chatto & Windus).

Harries, Susie (ed.) (2015): *Pevsner and Victorian Architecture*: vol. v of *Studies in Victorian Architecture and Design* (London: The Victorian Society).

Harris, Alan (tr.) (1933): *see* Cohen-Portheim, Paul.

Harten, Ulrike (ed.) (2000): *Karl Friedrich Schinkel; Lebenswerk* (Munich: Deutscher Kunstverlag).

Hartwell, Clare, Hyde, Matthew, Hubbard, Edward, & Pevsner, Nikolaus (2011): *Cheshire* in *The Buildings of England* Series (New Haven & London: Yale University Press).

Hartwell, Clare, Hyde, Matthew, & Pevsner, Nikolaus (2004): *Lancashire: Manchester and the South-East* in *The Buildings of England* Series (New Haven & London: Yale University Press).

Harvey, David (2002): *Spaces of Hope* (Edinburgh: Edinburgh University Press).

Harwood, Elain (ed.) (2007): *see* Charlton, Susannah (ed.).

Harwood, Elain (2015): *Space, Hope and Brutalism: English Architecture 1845–1975* (New Haven & London: Yale University Press in assn. with Historic England for The Paul Mellon Centre for Studies in British Art).

Hatherley, Owen (2011): *A Guide to the New Ruins of Great Britain* (London & New York: Verso).

Hatherley, Owen (2015): Review of Rotbard (2015) in *The Guardian* (24 January) 8.

Hatje, Gerd (gen. ed.) (1963): *see* Lampugnani, Vittorio Magnano (gen. ed.) (1988).

Hautmann, Hans, & Hautmann, Rudolf (1980): *Die Gemeindegebauten des Roten Wien, 1919–1934* (Vienna: Schönbrunn).

Hazlett, Kenneth S. (ed.) (1989): *see* Schinkel, Karl Friedrich.

Heard, Charles, *et al.* (trs) (2011): *see* Quiring, Claudia, *et al.* (eds).

Heerwagen, Judith H. (2005): 'Psychological Value of Space' in *Whole Building Design Guide* http://www.wbdg.org/design/psychspace_value.php.

Hegemann, Werner (1929): *Façades of Buildings: Fronts of Old and Modern Business and Dwelling Houses* (London: Ernest Benn Ltd).

Hegemann, Werner, & Peets, Elbert (1922): *The American Vitruvius: An Architects' Handbook of Civic Art* (New York: The Architectural Book Publishing Co.; Paul Wenzel & Maurice Krakow).

Held, Felix Emil (tr.) (1916): *see* Andreae, Johannes Valentinus.

Heller, Erich (1971): *The Disinherited Mind: Essays in Modern German Literature and Thought* (London: Bowes & Bowes).

Hellpach, Willy Hugo (1917): *Die geopsychischen Erscheinungen. Wetter, Klima, und Landschaft in ihrem Einfluss auf das Seelenleben* (Leipzig: W. Engelmann).

Herder, Johann Gottfried (1778): *Plastik: einzige Wahrnehmungen über Form und Gestalt aus Pygmalions bildendem Traume* (Riga: Johann Friedrich Hartknoch).

Hermand, Jost, & Trommler, Frank (1978): *Die Kultur in der Weimarer Republik* (Munich: Nymphenburger Verlagshandlung).

Herzogenrath, Wulf (ed.) (1968): *50 Years Bauhaus* (London: Royal Academy of Arts).

Hesse-Frielingshaus, Herta, *et al.* (1971): *Karl-Ernst Osthaus: Leben und Werk* (Recklingshausen: Bongers).

Heymanns Verlag, Carl (1936): *Das Handwerkerhaus an den Preussischen Höheren Technischen Staatslehranstalten für Hoch- und Tiefbau* (Berlin: Carl Heymanns Verlag).

Hilbersheimer, Ludwig Karl (1925): *Großtadt Architektur* (Hanover: Apos).

Hilbersheimer, Ludwig Karl (1927): *Internationale Neue Baukunst* (Stuttgart: Hoffmann).

Hilbersheimer, Ludwig Karl (1944): *The New City: Principles of Planning* (Chicago: Paul Theobald).

Hill, Richard (1999): *Designs and their Consequences: Architecture and Aesthetics* (New Haven & London: Yale University Press).

Hill, Rosemary (2007): *God's Architect: Pugin and the Building of Romantic Britain* (London: Allen Lane).

Hillman, Nick (2016): *Keeping Schtum? What Students Think of Free Speech* (Oxford: Higher Education Policy Institute).

Hilmes, Oliver (2015): *Malevolent Muse: The Life of Alma Mahler*, Donald Arthur (tr.) (Boston: Northeastern University Press).

Hiscock, Nigel (2007): *The Symbol at Your Door: Number and Geometry in Religious Architecture of the Greek and Latin Middle Ages* (Aldershot: Ashgate).

Hitchcock, Henry-Russell (1968): *Rococo Architecture in Southern Germany* (London: Phaidon Press Ltd).

Hitchcock, Henry-Russell, & Bauer, Catherine K. (1937): *Modern Architecture in England* (New York: Museum of Modern Art).

Hitchcock, Henry-Russell, & Johnson, Philip (1966): *The International Style* with a new Foreword and Appendix by Henry-Russell Hitchcock (New York & London: W.W. Norton & Co.), originally published (1932) as *The International Style. Architecture since 1922* (New York: W.W. Norton & Co.).

Hitchcock, Henry-Russell, Johnson, Philip, & Mumford, Lewis, With Foreword By Alfred H. Barr Jr (1932): *Modern Architecture: International Exhibition: New York Feb. 10 to March 23 1932, Museum of Modern Art* (New York: Museum of Modern Art).

Hitchmough, Wendy (1995): *C.F.A. Voysey* (London: Phaidon Press Ltd).

Hitler, Adolf (1933): *My Struggle* (London: Hurst & Blackett). *See also* the 2008 edn. entitled *Mein Kampf*, James Vincent Murphy (tr.) (New York: Fredonia Classics).

Hochman, Elaine S. (1989): *Architects of Fortune: Mies van der Rohe and the Third Reich* (New York & London: Weidenfeld & Nicolson).

Hoeber, Fritz (1913): *Peter Behrens* (Munich: G. Müller & E. Rentsch).

Holborn, Hajo (ed.) (1972): *Republic to Reich: The Making of the Nazi Revolution: Ten Essays*, Ralph Manheim (tr.) (New York: Pantheon Books).

Holt, Gordon (tr.) (1948): *see* Pierrefeu, François de.

Horace (Quintus Horatius Flaccus) (2014): *Satires; Epistles; The Art of Poetry* H. Rushton Fairclough (tr.) (Cambridge, MA: Harvard University Press).

Hottinger-Mackie, Mary (tr.) (1956): *see* Giedion-Welcker, Carola.

Howard, Hugh (2016): *Architecture's Odd Couple: Frank Lloyd Wright and Philip Johnson* (London: Bloomsbury Press).

Howarth, Thomas (1977): *Charles Rennie Mackintosh and the Modern Movement* (London: Routledge, Kegan, Paul).

Howe, Thomas Noble (commentary & illus.) (1999): *see* Vitruvius Pollio, Marcus.

Hubbard, Edward (2011): *see* Hartwell, Clare.

Hubbard, William (1980): *Complicity and Conviction: Steps toward an Architecture of Convention* (Cambridge, MA & London: The MIT Press).

Hughes, Robert (1980): *The Shock of the New: Art and the Century of Change* (London: BBC).

Hughes, Thomas Parke, & Hughes, Agatha C. (eds) (1990): *Lewis Mumford: Public Intellectual* (New York: Oxford University Press).

Hulten, Pontus (1987): *Futurism and Futurisms* (London: Thames & Hudson).

Hurd, Elizabeth Shakman (2015): *Beyond Religious Freedom: The New Global Politics of Religion* (Princeton, NJ: Princeton University Press).

Hüter, Karl-Heinz (1976): *Das Bauhaus in Weimar: Studie zur gesellschaftspolitischen Geschichte einer deutsche Kunstschule* (Berlin: Akademie-Verlag).

Huxley, Aldous Leonard (1932): *Brave New World* (London: Chatto & Windus).

Hyde, Matthew (2004, 2011): *see* Hartwell, Clare.

Hyman, Isabelle (2001): *Marcel Breuer, Architect: The Career and the Buildings* (New York: Harry N. Abrams Inc.).

Ingberman, Sima (1994): *ABC: International Constructivist Architecture, 1922–1939* (Cambridge, MA & London: Massachusetts Institute of Technology Press).

Isaacs, Reginald R. (1983–4): *Walter Gropius: der Mensch und sein Werk* (Berlin: Gebr. Mann).

Jabs, Wolfgard (tr.) (1978): *see* Wingler, Hans Maria.

Jacobs, Jane (1961): *The Death and Life of Great American Cities* (New York: Random House).

Jaeggi, Annemarie (1994): *Adolf Meyer, der zweite Mann: ein Architekt im Schatten von Walter Gropius* (Berlin: Argon-Verlag).

Jaffé, Hans Ludwig Cohn (1956): *De Stijl 1917–1931: The Dutch Contribution to Modern Art* (Amsterdam: J.M. Meulenhoff).

James, Kathleen (1997): *Erich Mendelsohn and the Architecture of German Modernism* (Cambridge: Cambridge University Press).

Jameson, Fredric (1993): *Postmodernism: Or, the Cultural Logic of Late Capitalism* (Cambridge: Cambridge University Press).

Jameson, Fredric (2009): *The Cultural Turn: Selected Writings on the Postmodern, 1983–1998* (London: Verso).

Janssens, Manon (2010): *see* Racana, Gianluca.

Jarcy, Xavier de (2015): *Le Corbusier: un fascisme Français* (Paris: Albin-Michel).

Jarzombek, Mark (tr.) (1991): *see* Neumeyer, Fritz.

Jaskot, Paul B. (2000): *The Architecture of Oppression. The SS, Forced Labour and the Nazi Monumental Building Economy* (London & New York: Routledge).

Jeanneret-Gris, Charles-Édouard ('Le Corbusier') (1928): *Une maison—un palais: à la recherche d'une unité architectural* (Paris: G. Crès & Co.).

Jencks, Charles (1969): 'The Silent Zone': review of Lane (1968) in *Architectural Association Quarterly* **i**/2 (April) 81–2.

Jencks, Charles (1987): *Le Corbusier and the Tragic View of Architecture* (Harmondsworth: Penguin Books).

Jencks, Charles (1987a): *Post-Modernism: The New Classicism in Art and Architecture* (London: Academy Editions).

Jencks, Charles (1990): *The New Moderns: from Late to Neo-Modernism* (London: Academy Editions).

Jencks, Charles (2002): *The New Paradigm in Architecture: The Language of Post-Modernism* (New Haven & London: Yale University Press).

Jencks, Charles (2015): 'In What Style Shall We Build?' in *Architectural Review* **ccxxxvii**/1417 (March) 90–101.

Jenkins, Lee M. (ed.) (2007): *see* Davis, Alex (ed.).

Jenkins, Simon (2006): 'For a real exhibition of modernism, skip the V&A and go to Manchester' in *The Guardian* (7 April) 24: http://www.theguardian.com/commentisfree/2006/apr/07/comment.society accessed 1 February 2017.

Jennings, Michael William (ed.) (2011): *see* Mertins, Detlef.

Jodidio, Philip (1995): *Contemporary European Architects* **iii** (Cologne: Taschen).

Johnson, Philip (1932): *see* Hitchcock, Henry-Russell.

Johnson, Philip (1966): *see* Hitchcock, Henry-Russell.

Johnson, Philip (1978): *Mies van der Rohe* (New York: Museum of Modern Art).

Johnson, Philip (1989): *see* Schinkel, Karl Friedrich.

Johnson, Philip, & Wigley, Mark (1988): *Deconstructivist Architecture* (New York: Museum of Modern Art).

Johst, Hanns (1933): *Schlageter: Schauspiel* (Munich: A. Langen/G. Müller).

Jones, Adrian, & Matthews, Chris (2016): *Cities of the North* (Nottingham: Five Leaves Publications).

Kaiser, Ernst (tr.) (1979): *see* Musil, Robert.

Kandel, Eric R (1999): *see* Squire, Larry R.

Kandinsky, Nina, *with* Kruger, Werner (1976): *Kandinsky und Ich* (Munich: Kindler Verlag).

Kandinsky, Wassily (1979): *Point and Line to Plane*, Howard Deastyne & Hilla Rebay (trs) (New York: Dover Publications).

Kandinsky, Wassily (2006): *On the Spiritual in Art*, Michael Thomas Harvey Sadleir (tr.) (Boston, MA: MFA Publications).

Kantorowicz, Ernst Hartwig (1927): *Kaiser Friedrich der Zweite* (Berlin: G. Bondi).

Kaplan, Wendy (2004): *see* Cumming, Elizabeth.

Kater, Michael Hans (2014): *Weimar: From Enlightenment to the Present* (New Haven & London: Yale University Press).

Katz, Peter (1994): *New Urbanism* (New York: McGraw-Hill).

Keeble, Lewis Bingham (1952): *Principles and Practice of Town and Country Planning* (London: Estates Gazette).

Keith-Smith, Brian (ed.) (2002): *see* Schreyer, Lothar.

Kelbaugh, Douglas S. (2002): *Repairing the American Metropolis* (Seattle: University of Washington Press).

Kellert, Stephen R., *et al.* (eds) (2008): *Biophilic Design: The Theory, Science, and Practice of Bringing Buildings to Life* (New York: John Wiley).

Kempter, Georg Friedrich (2007): *Die Säule* (Winterbach: Gesellschaft für Natur und Kunst).

Kentgens-Craig, Margaret (1999): *The Bauhaus and America: First Contacts, 1919–1936* (Cambridge, MA & London: The MIT Press).

Kershaw, Ian (1998): *Hitler 1889–1936: Hubris* (London: Penguin Books).

Kershaw, Ian (2000): *Hitler 1936–1945: Nemesis* (London: Penguin Books).

Khan-Magomedov, Selim Omarovich (1986): *Alexandr Vesnin and Russian Constructivism* (London: Lund Humphries).

Kiem, Karl (1997): *Die Gartenstadt Staaken (1914–1917): Typen, Gruppen, Varianten* (Berlin: Gebr. Mann).

Kilham, Walter H. (1973): *Raymond Hood, Architect: Form Through Function in the American Skyscraper* (New York: Architectural Book Publishing Co. Inc.).

King, John (tr.) (2015): *see* Vargas Llosa, Mario.

Kinney, David (2016): *see* Wittman, Robert King.

Kipling, Rudyard (1913): *Songs from Books* (London: Macmillan).

Kirsch, Karin (1987): *Die Weißenhofsiedlung: Werkbundausstellung 'Die Wohnung', Stuttgart, 1927* (Stuttgart: Deutsche Verlags-Anstalt).

Kitchen, Martin (2015): *Speer: Hitler's Architect* (New Haven & London: Yale University Press).

Klages, Ludwig (1926): *Die psychologischen Errungenschaften Nietzsches* (Leipzig: Johann Ambrosius Barth).

Klages, Ludwig (1981): *Der Geist als Widersacher der Seele* (Bonn: Bouvier Verlag Herbert Grundmann).

Klee, Paul (1968): *Pedagogical Sketchbook*, Sibyl Moholy-Nagy (tr.) (London: Faber & Faber).

Klimek, Stanisław (2014): *see* Eysymontt, Rafał.

Klotz, Heinrich (1973): *see* Cook, John W.

Koch, Alexander (ed.) (1897–1932): *Deutsche Kunst und Dekoration; Illustrierte Monatshefte für moderne . . . Architektur . . . etc.* (Darmstadt: A. Koch).

Koch, Alexander (1913): *Die Margarethen-Höhe bei Essen* (Darmstadt: A. Koch).

Koetter, Fred (1980): *see* Rowe, Colin.

Kopp, Anatole (1970): *Town and Revolution: Soviet Architecture and City Planning, 1917–1935*, Thomas E. Burton (tr.) (London: Thames & Hudson).

Kopp, Anatole (1986): *Constructivist Architecture in the USSR*, Sheila de Vallée (tr.) (London: Academy Editions).

Korn, Arthur (1929): *Glas im Bau und als Gebrauchsgegenstand* (Berlin-Charlottenburg: Ernst Pollak Verlag).

Korn, Arthur (1953): *History Builds the Town* (London: Lund Humphries).

Kornwolf, James David (1972): *M.H. Baillie Scott and the Arts and Crafts Movement: Pioneers of Modern Design* (Baltimore, MD: Johns Hopkins University Press).

Kostof, Spiro (1995): *A History of Architecture: Settings and Rituals* (Oxford: Oxford University Press).

Koulermos, Panos (1995): *Twentieth Century European Rationalism*, James Steele (ed.) (London: Academy Editions).

Kramer, H. (1995): 'My Long Search is Over' in *New Criterion* **xiv**/1 4–14. See https://www.newcriterion.com/issues/1995/9/mondrian-mysticism-ldquomy-long-search-is-overrdquo accessed 4 January 2018.

Krier, Léon (1980): *Léon Krier: La ricostruzione della città europea* (Venice: Cluva).

Krier, Léon (ed.) (1985): *Albert Speer: Architecture 1932–1942* (Brussels: Archives d'Architecture Moderne).

Krier, Léon, & Pavan, Vincenzo (ed.) (1978): *Rational Architecture* (Brussels: Archives d'Architecture Moderne).

Kruger, Werner (1976): *see* Kandinsky, Nina.

Kuchta, Todd (2010): *Semi-Detached Empire: Suburbia and the Colonization of Britain, 1880 to the Present* (Charlottesville, VA: University of Virginia Press).

Kugler, Franz Theodor (1856–9): *Geschichte der Baukunst* (Stuttgart: Ebner & Seubert).

Kühnemann, Albert (ed.) (1896/7): *Groß-Berlin: Bilder von der Ausstellungsstadt* (Berlin: Verlag von W. Pauli's Nachf. [H. Jerosch]).

Kunstler, James Howard (1993): *The Geography of Nowhere: The Rise and Decline of America's Man-Made Landscape* (New York: Simon & Schuster).

Kurtz, Harold (1970): *The Second Reich: Kaiser Wilhelm II and his Germany* (London & New York: Macdonald Unit 75).

Lampugnani, Vittorio Magnano (gen. ed.) (1988): *The Thames and Hudson Encyclopaedia of 20th Century Architecture*, Barry Bergdoll (tr.) (London: Thames & Hudson Ltd; New York: Harry N. Abrams Inc.). Originally published (1963) as *Encyclopaedia of Modern Architecture*, Gerd Hatje (gen. ed.) (London: Thames & Hudson Ltd).

Lancaster, Osbert (2015): *Pillar to Post: English Architecture without Tears* (London: Pimpernel Press Ltd, orig. pub. London: John Murray 1938).

Lancaster, Osbert (2015a): *Homes Sweet Homes* (London: Pimpernel Press Ltd, orig. pub. London: John Murray 1939).

Lancaster, Osbert (2015b): *Drayneflete Revealed* (London: Pimpernel Press Ltd, orig. pub. London: John Murray 1949).

Landow, George P. (1971): *The Aesthetic and Critical Theories of John Ruskin* (Princeton, NJ: Princeton University Press).

Lane, Barbara Miller (1968): *Architecture and Politics in Germany 1918–45* (Cambridge, MA & London: Oxford University Press).

Larson, Magali Sarfatti (1993): *Behind the Post-Modern Façade: Architectural Change in Late Twentieth-Century America* (Berkeley, CA & London: University of California Press).

Larsson, Lars Olof (1983): *Albert Speer: Le Plan de Berlin 1937–1943* (Brussels: Archives d'Architecture Moderne).

Lasdun, Denys (1957): 'MARS Group, 1953–57' in *Architect's Yearbook* **viii** 57–61.

Laue, Theodore Hermann (1987): *The World Revolution of Westernization: The Twentieth Century in Global Perspective* (Oxford: Oxford University Press).

Leavey, John P. (tr.) (1986): *see* Derrida, Jacques.

Lebovic, Nitzan (2013): *The Philosophy of Life and Death. Ludwig Klages and the Rise of a Nazi Biopolitics* (London & New York: Palgrave Macmillan).

Lefebvre, Henri (1968): *Le Droit à la ville* (Paris: Anthropos).

Lefebvre, Henri (1972): *Espace et Politique* (Paris: Anthropos).

Lefebvre, Henri (1991): *The Production of Space*, Donald Nicholson-Smith (tr.) (Oxford & Cambridge, MA: Blackwell).

Lehmann, Helmut T. (gen. ed.) (1971): *see* Luther, Martin.

Lehtovuori, Panu (2010): *Experience and Conflict: The Production of Urban Space* (Farnham: Ashgate).

Lending, Mari (2017): *Plaster Monuments: Architecture and the Power of Reproduction* (Princeton, NJ & Woodstock, Oxon: Princeton University Press).

Lerner, Paul Frederick (2015): *The Consuming Temple: Jews, Department Stores, and the Consumer revolution in Germany, 1880–1940* (Ithaca, NY: Cornell University Press).

Lerner, Robert E. (2016): *Ernst Kantorowicz: A Life* (Princeton, NJ: Princeton University Press).

Leśnikowski, Wojciech (ed.) (1996): *East European Modernism: Architecture in Czechoslovakia, Hungary & Poland Between the Wars* (London: Thames & Hudson Ltd).

Lessing, Erich (1994): *see* Bergdoll, Barry.

Lessing, Gotthold Ephraim (1766): *Laokoon, oder, Über die Grenzen der Mahlerei und Poesie* (Berlin: C.F. Voss).

Leuthäuser, Gabriele, & Feierabend, Peter (eds) (1996): *Potsdam: Palaces and Gardens of the Hohenzollern* (Cologne: Könemann).

Leuthäuser, Gabriele, & Gössel, Peter (eds) (1990): *Functional Architecture: The International Style 1925–1940* (Cologne: Benedikt Taschen).

Leuthäuser, Gabriele (2005): *see* Gössel, Peter.

Lewis, Hilary, & O'Connor, John (1994): *Philip Johnson: The Architect in His Own Words* (New York: Rizzoli International Publications Inc.).

Lichfield, Nathaniel, & Whitbread, Michael (1972): *The Use of Cost–Benefit Analysis for Plan Evaluation: A Rationale* (London: University College London).

Liebknecht, Wilhelm (1892): *Robert Owen: sein Leben und sozialpolitisches Wirken* (Nuremberg: Wörlein).

Lieven, Alexander (tr.) (1982): *see* Zhadova, Larissa A.

Lindberg, Steven (tr.) (2011): *see* Mertins, Detlef.

Lipovetsky, Gilles (2013): *L'Esthétisation du monde: vivre à l'âge du capitalisme artiste* (Paris: Éditions Gallimard).

Lipovetsky, Gilles, & Serroy, Jean (2008): *see* Serroy, Jean.

Livingstone, Karen, Donnelly, Max, & Parry, Linda (2016): *C.F.A. Voysey: Arts & Crafts Designer* (London: V&A Publications).

Livingstone, Karen, & Parry, Linda (eds) (2005): *International Arts and Crafts* (London: V&A Publications).

Lloyd, David, & Pevsner, Nikolaus (2006): *The Isle of Wight* in *The Buildings of England* Series (New Haven & London: Yale University Press).

Lodder, Christina (1983): *Russian Constructivism* (New Haven & London: Yale University Press).

London, Kurt (1937): *The Seven Soviet Arts*, Eric Sigmund Bensinger (tr.) (London: Faber & Faber).

Longatti, Alberto (1988): *see* Caramel, Luciano.

Loo, Anne van (ed.) (2003): *Repertorium van de Architectuur in België van 1830 tot heden* (Antwerp: Mercatorfonds).

Loos, Adolf (1998): *Ornament and Crime: Selected Essays*, Michael Mitchell (tr.) (Riverside, CA: Ariadne Press).

Lorman, Alba (tr.) (1970): *see* Neumann, Eckhard (ed.).

Lubbock, Jules (1995): *The Tyranny of Taste: The Politics of Architecture and Design in Britain, 1550–1960* (New Haven & London: Yale University Press for The Paul Mellon Centre for Studies in British Art).

Luther, Martin (1971): *Luther's Works* **xlvii**, Helmut T. Lehmann (gen. ed.), Franklin Sherman (ed.) (Philadelphia: Fortress Press).

Lynes, Russell (1973): *Good Old Modern: An Intimate Portrait of the Museum of Modern Art* (New York: Atheneum).

Lyotard, J.-F. (1984): *The Post-Modern Condition* (Manchester: Manchester University Press).

Maass, John (tr.) (1985): *see* Sekler, Eduard Franz.

Macaulay, James (2010): *Charles Rennie Mackintosh* (New York & London: W.W. Norton & Co.).

McDonough, Francis (Frank) Xavier (2015): *The Gestapo: The Myth and Reality of Hitler's Secret Police* (London: Hodder & Stoughton General Division/Coronet).

McFadden, Anna Hicks, & Smith, Penny (2004): *The Social Construction of Educational Leadership* (New York, etc.: Peter Lang).

McFadzean, Ronald (1979): *The Life and Work of Alexander Thomson* (London, Boston, & Henley: Routledge & Kegan Paul).

MacGibbon, David, & Ross, Thomas (1887–92): *The Castellated and Domestic Architecture of Scotland from the Twelfth to the Eighteenth Century* (Edinburgh: David Douglas).

McGuire, James (ed.) (2009): *see Dictionary of Irish Biography*.

Mackail, John William (1931): *Virgil: Annual Lecture on a Master Mind* (London: Humphrey Milford).

McKinstry, Sam (ed.) (1994): *see* Stamp, Gavin (ed.).

Mackmurdo, Arthur Heygate (1883): *Wrens [sic] City Churches* (Orpington: G. Allen).

Mai, Ekkehard (ed.) (1994): *see* Nerdinger, Winfried.

Malevich, Kazimir Severinovich (1927): *Die Gegenstandlose Welt. Bauhausbücher 11* (Munich: Albert Langen).

Mallgrave, Harry Francis (tr.) (1988): *see* Wagner, Otto.

Manheim, Ralph (tr.) (1972): *see* Holborn, Hajo (ed.).

Mannheim, Karl (1968): *Ideology and Utopia: An Introduction to the Sociology of Knowledge* (London: Routledge & Kegan Paul).

Mantero, Enrico (ed.) (1969): *Giuseppe Terragni e la città del razionalismo italiano* (Bari: Dedalo).

Mantero, Enrico (1984): *Il Razionalismo Italiano* (Bologna: Zanichelli).

March, Werner, & Rohrbach, Charlotte (1936): *Bauwerk Reichssportfeld* (Berlin: Deutscher Kunstverlag).

Marjasch, Sonja (tr.) (1956): *see* Giedion-Welcker, Carola.

Markmann, Charles Lam (tr.) (1967, 1968): *see* Fanon, Frantz.

MARS Group (1938): *New Architecture: An Exhibition of the Elements of Modern Architecture Organized by the MARS (Modern Architectural Research) Group, New Burlington Galleries, January 11–29, 1938*, with an Introduction by George Bernard Shaw (London: MARS).

Mårtelius, Johan (ed.) (2015): *see* Elmlund, Peter (ed.).

Martin, Leslie, *et al.* (1965): *Whitehall: A Plan for the National and Government Centre* (London: HMSO).

Martin, Marianne W. (1977): *Futurist Art and Theory* (New York: Hacker Art Books).

Masden II, Kenneth G. (2008): *see* Salingaros, Nikos A.

Matthäus, Jürgen, & Bajohr, Frank (2015): *The Political Diary of Alfred Rosenberg and the Onset of the Holocaust* (Lanham, MD: Rowman & Littlefield).

Matthews, Chris (2016): *see* Jones, Adrian.

Maude, Aylmer (tr.) (1933): *see* Tolstoy, Leo.

Maxwell-Irving, Alastair M. T. (2000): *The Border Towers of Scotland: Their History and Architecture* i, *The West March (Dumfriesshire & Eastern Galloway)* (Blairlogie, Stirling: The Author).

Maxwell-Irving, Alastair M. T. (2014): *The Border Towers of Scotland: Their Evolution and Architecture* ii (Blairlogie, Stirling: The Author).

Mead, Margaret (1966): *New Lives for Old: Cultural Transformation—Manus, 1928–1953* (New York: William Morrow & Co.).

Meades, Jonathan (2016): 'Capital Gains' in *The Literary Review* **440** (March) 18–19.

Mehaffy, Michael W. (2002): *see* Salingaros, Nikos A.

Mehaffy, Michael W., & Salingaros, Nikos A. (2013): *A Vision for Architecture as More Than the Sum of Its Parts: How Modernist Fundamentalism Degrades the Human and Natural Environment'. See* http://www.onthecommons.org/magazine/vision-architecture-more-sum-its-parts accessed 1 February 2017.

Mehaffy, Michael W., & Salingaros, Nikos A. (2015): *Design for a Living Planet* (Portland, OR: Sustasis Press).

Mellinghoff, Tilman (1987): *see* Watkin, David John.

Melvin, Jeremy (2005): *Isms: Understanding Architectural Styles* (London & New York: Herbert Press & Universe).

Mendelsohn, Erich (1924): *Bauten und Skizzen* (Berlin: E. Wasmuth).

Mendelsohn, Erich (1929): *Russland-Europa-Amerika—ein architektonischer Querschnitt* (Berlin: Rudolf Mosse Buchverlag).

Mendelsohn, Erich (1930): *Das Gesamtschaffen des Architekten: Skizzen, Entwürfe, Bauten* (Berlin: Rudolf Mosse Buchverlag).

Mendelsohn, Erich (1932): *Neues Haus, neue Welt* (Berlin: Rudolf Mosse Buchverlag).

Mendelsohn, Erich (1932a): *Der schöpferische Sinn der Krise* (Berlin: Bruno Cassirer).

Mertins, Detlef (2014): *Mies* (London: Phaidon Press Ltd).

Mertins, Detlef, & Jennings, Michael William (eds) (2011): *G: An Avant-Garde Journal of Art, Architecture, Design, and Film, 1923–1926*, Steven Lindberg & Margareta Ingrid Christian (trs) (London: Tate Publications in assn. with the Getty Research Institute).

Meyer, Adolf, *et al.* (1925): *Ein Versuchshaus des Bauhauses in Weimar* (Munich: Albert Langen Verlag).

Meyer, Esther Da Costa (1995): *The Work of Antonio Sant'Elia: Retreat into the Future* (New Haven & London: Yale University Press).

Meyer, Hannes (1980): *Bauen und Gesellschaft: Schriften, Briefe, Projekte*, Lena Meyer-Bergner (ed.) (Dresden: VEB Verlag der Kunst).

Meyer-Bergner, Lena (ed.) (1980): *see* Meyer, Hannes.

Michaelis-Jena, Ruth (tr.) (1967): *see* Scheidig, Walther.

Michelis, Marco D. (1991): *Heinrich Tessenow 1876–1950* (Milan: Electa).

Miës van der Rohe, Ludwig, *et al.* (1927): *Die Wohnung: Amtlicher Katalog der Werkbundaustellung* (Stuttgart: Tagblatt Buchdruckerei).

Millais, Malcolm Gordon William (2009): *Exploding the Myths of Modern Architecture* (London: Frances Lincoln Publishers).

Millais, Malcolm Gordon William (2015): 'A Critical Appraisal of the Design, Construction, and Influence of the Unité d'Habitation, Marseilles, France' in *Journal of Architecture and Urbanism* **xxxix**/2 103–15. See http://dx.doi.org/10.3846/20297955.2015.1062636

Millais, Malcolm Gordon William (2017): *Le Corbusier: The Dishonest Architect* (Newcastle upon Tyne: Cambridge Scholars Publishing).

Miller, Arthur (1988): *Timebends: A Life* (London: Methuen).

Miller, Clarence H. (tr.) (2001): *Utopia* (New Haven & London: Yale University Press).

Miller, Donald L. (ed.) (1986): *The Lewis Mumford Reader* (New York: Pantheon Books).

Miller, Dorothy Canning (1952): *15 Americans* (New York: Museum of Modern Art).

Milner, John (1983): *Vladimir Tatlin and the Russian Avant-Garde* (New Haven & London: Yale University Press).

Mitchell, Michael (tr.) (1998): *see* Loos, Adolf.

Moholy-Nagy, Sibyl (1950): *Moholy-Nagy: Experiment in Totality. A Biography* (New York: Harper & Brothers).

Moholy-Nagy, Sibyl (tr.) (1968): *see* Klee, Paul.

Mondrian, Piet (1920): *Néo-plasticisme: principe général de l'équivalence plastique* (Paris: Éditions de l'effort moderne, Léonce Rosenberg).

Moore, Rowan (2012): *Why We Build* (London: Picador).

Moore, Rowan (2016): *Slow Burn City: London in the Twenty-First Century* (London: Picador).

More, Sir Thomas (1516): *Libellus vere aureus…de nova insula Vtopia…cura M. Petri Aegidii Antuerpiesis…* etc. (Louvain: Arte Theodorici Martini). *See also* Miller, Clarence H. (tr.) (2001).

Morris, Eleanor Smith (1997): *British Town Planning and Urban Design. Principles and Policies* (Harlow: Addison Wesley Longman Ltd).

Morris, May (1910–15): *see* Morris, William.

Morris, May (1936): *William Morris: Artist, Writer, Socialist* (Oxford: Basil Blackwell).

Morris, Robert (1742): *The Art of Architecture, a Poem. In Imitation of Horace's Art of Poetry* (London: R. Dodsley).

Morris, William (1910–15): *Collected Works* with Introductions by May Morris (London: Longmans Green & Co.).

Mortimer, Raymond (1929): *see* Todd, Dorothy.

Mowl, Timothy (2000): *Stylistic Cold Wars: Betjeman versus Pevsner* (London: John Murray [Publishers] Ltd).

Moylan, Tom (2000): *Scraps of the Untainted Sky: Science Fiction, Utopia, Dystopia* (Boulder, CO: Westview Press).

Moylan, Tom (ed.) (2015): *see* Griffin, Michael J. (ed.).

Muche, Georg (1965): *Blickpunkt: Sturm, Dada, Bauhaus, Gegenwart* (Tübingen: Wasmuth).

Müller, Heinz (ed.) (1973): *see* Basedow, Heinrich.

Müller, Manfred (1975): *Das Leben eines Architekten: Porträt Richard Paulick* (Halle: Mitteldeutscher Verlag).

Mumford, Eric Paul (2000): *The CIAM Discourse on Urbanism, 1928–1960* (Cambridge, MA: MIT Press).

Mumford, Lewis (1922): *The Story of Utopias* (New York: Boni & Liveright).

Mumford, Lewis (1924): *Sticks and Stones: A Study of American Architecture and Civilization* (New York: Boni & Liveright).

Mumford, Lewis (1932): *see* Hitchcock, Henry-Russell.

Mumford, Lewis (1938): *The Culture of Cities* (New York: Harcourt, Brace, & Co.).

Mumford, Lewis (1961): *The City in History: Its Origins, its Transformations, and its Prospects* (New York: Harcourt, Brace, & World, Inc.).

Mumford, Lewis (1962): 'Lady Godiva's Town' in *The New Yorker* (10 March).

Mumford, Lewis (1963): *The Highway and the City* (New York: Harcourt Brace).

Murphy, James Vincent (tr.) (1933): *see* Hitler, Adolf.

Murray, Douglas (2017): *The Strange Death of Europe: Immigration, Identity, Islam* (London: Bloomsbury).

Murray, Irena, & Osley, Julian (eds) (2009): *Le Corbusier and Britain: An Anthology* (Abingdon & New York: Routledge).

Murray, Patrick (tr.) (1967): *see* Scheidig, Walther.

Musil, Robert (1930): *Der Mann ohne Eigenschaften* i (Berlin: Ernst Rowohly).

Musil, Robert (1979): *The Man Without Qualities* i, Eithne Wilkins & Ernst Kaiser (trs.) (London: Secker & Warburg).

Muthesius, Hermann (1902): *Stilarchitektur und Baukunst: Wandlungen der Architektur im XIX. Jahrhundert und ihr heutiger Standpunkt* (Mülheim-Ruhr: Verlag von K. Schimmelpfeng).

Muthesius, Hermann (ed.) (1907): *Landhaus und Garten. Beispiele Neuzeitlicher Landhäuser nebst Grundrissen, Innenräumen und Gärten* (Munich: Verlagsanstalt F. Bruckmann A.-G.).

Muthesius, Hermann (1908–11): *Das englische Haus: Entwicklung, Bedingungen, Anlage, Aufbau, Einrichtung und Innenraum* (Berlin: Ernst Wasmuth). *See also* Sharp, Dennis (ed.), Seligmann, Janet, & Spencer, Stewart (trs) (2007): *The English House* (London: Frances Lincoln Ltd). An earlier, abridged version (1979), also edited by Sharp and translated by Seligmann, was published (London: Crosby Lockwood Staples), and (1987) in paperback (Oxford: Blackwell Scientific Publications).

Muthesius, Hermann (1912): *Landhäuser von Hermann Muthesius* (Munich: F. Bruckmann AG). *See also* the excellent facsimile edn. (Berlin: Gebr. Mann Verlag 2001).

Nabokov, Nicolas (1975): *Bagázh: Memoirs of a Russian Cosmopolitan* (London: Secker & Warburg).

Nairn, Ian (2014): *Nairn's London* with Afterword by Gavin Stamp (London: Penguin Group).

Nairn, Ian, & Pevsner, Nikolaus (1971): *Surrey* in *The Buildings of England* Series revised by Bridget Cherry (Harmondsworth: Penguin Books Ltd).

Nerdinger, Winfried (1985): *Walter Gropius* (Berlin: Gebr. Mann).

Nerdinger, Winfried (1988): *Theodor Fischer: Architekt und Städtebauer* (Berlin: Ernst).

Nerdinger, Winfried (ed.) (1993): *Bauhaus-Moderne im Nationalsozialismus, zwischen Anbiederung und Verfolgung* (Munich: Prestel).

Nerdinger, Winfried, & Mai, Ekkehard (eds) (1994): *Wilhelm Kreis: Architekt zwischen Kaiserreich und Demokratie 1873–1955* (Munich: Klinkhardt & Biermann).

Neubert, Rudolf (1926): *Der Mensch und die Wohnung* (Dresden: Deutscher Verlag für Volkswohlfahrt).

Neufert, Ernst (1936): *Bau-Entwurfslehre: Handbuch für den Baufachmann, Bauherrn, Lehrenden und Lernenden* (Berlin: Bauwelt-Verlag).

Neugroschel, Joachim (tr.) (1987): *see* Goebbels, Joseph.

Neumann, Eckhard (ed.) (1970): *Bauhaus and Bauhaus People: Personal Opinions and Recollections of Former Bauhaus Members and their Contemporaries*, Eva Richter & Alba Lorman (trs) (New York: van Nostrand Reinhold Co.).

Neumeyer, Fritz (1986): *Mies van der Rohe: Das kunstlose Wort-Gedanken zur Baukunst* (Berlin: Siedler-Verlag).

Neumeyer, Fritz (1991): *The Artless Word: Mies van der Rohe on the Building Art*, Mark Jarzombek (tr.) (Cambridge, MA: MIT Press).

Newman, Oscar (ed.) (1961): *New Frontiers in Architecture: CIAM '59 in Otterlo* (New York: Universe Books).

Newman, Oscar (1973): *Defensible Space: Crime Prevention through Urban Design* (New York: Macmillan).

Newman, Oscar (1996): *Creating Defensible Space* (Washington, DC: US Dept. of Housing and Urban Development, Office of Policy Development and Research).

Nicholson-Smith, Donald (tr.) (1991): *see* Lefebvre, Henri.

Norberg-Schulz, Christian (2000): *Principles of Modern Architecture* (London: Andreas Papadakis Publisher).

Norris, Christopher (1987): *Deconstruction* (London: Methuen).

Norris, Christopher, & Benjamin, Andrew (1996): *What is Deconstruction?* (London: Academy Editions).

Norwich, John Julius (ed.) (1978): *Great Architecture of the World* (New York: Bonanza Books).

Nostitz, Helene Von (1979): *Aus dem alten Europa: Menschen und Städte*, Oswalt Von Nostitz (ed.) (Frankfurt-am-Main: Insel Verlag).

Nostitz, Oswalt Von (ed.) (1979): *see* Nostitz, Helene Von.

Nudel, Ernst (ed.) (1975): *see* Schwitters, Kurt.

Nuttgens, Bridget (1988): *see* Nuttgens, Patrick.

Nuttgens, Patrick, & Nuttgens, Bridget (1988): *Understanding Modern Architecture* (London: Unwin Hyman Ltd).

O'Brien, Charles (2005): *see* Cherry, Bridget.

O'Connor, John (1994): *see* Lewis, Hilary.

O'Connor, Liam (ed.) (1992): *see* Tagliaventi, Gabriele (ed.).

O'Hear, Anthony (1999): *After Progress: Finding the Old Way Forward* (London: Bloomsbury).

O'Malley, Stephen (ed.) (1989): *see* Schinkel, Karl Friedrich.

O'Regan, John, *et al.* (eds) (1983): *see* Rossi, Aldo.

Orwell, George (1949): *Nineteen Eighty-Four: A Novel* (London: Secker & Warburg).

Osborne, Harold (ed.) (1988): *see* Chilvers, Ian.

Osley, Julian (ed.) (2009): *see* Murray, Irena (ed.).

Otto, Christian F. (1991): *see* Pommer, Richard.

Overy, Paul (1969): *De Stijl* (London: Studio Vista).

Overy, Paul, *et al.* (1988): *The Rietveld-Schröder House* (Cambridge, MA: Massachusetts Institute of Technology Press).

Padovan, Richard (2002): *Towards Universality: Le Corbusier, Mies, and De Stijl* (London: Routledge).

Palmer, Shirley (tr.) (1972): *see* Sharp, Dennis.

Palmes, James (tr.) (1972): *see* Sharp, Dennis.

Papadakis, Andreas C. (ed.) (1993): *Architecture & the Environment: The Prince of Wales and the Earth in Balance* (London: Academy Editions).

Papadakis, Andreas C., & Watson, Harriet (eds) (1990): *New Classicism* (London: Academy Editions).

Papworth, Wyatt Angelicus van Sandau (ed.) (1852–92): *The Dictionary of Architecture* (London: The Architectural Publication Society, **i-vi** printed Thomas Richards, **vii** [1887] & **viii** [1892] printed Whiting & Co.).

Pardo, Alona (ed.) (2016): *see* Grospierre, Nicolas.

Parker, John Henry (1851–9): *see* Turner, Thomas Hudson.

Parris, Matthew, & Bryson, Andrew (eds) (2010): *Parting Shots* (London: Viking).

Parry, Linda (ed.) (2005): *see* Livingstone, Karen (ed.).

Parry, Linda (2016): *see* Livingstone, Karen.

Pavan, Vincenzo (1980): *see* Krier, Léon.

Pawley, Martin (1990): *Theory and Design in the Second Machine Age* (Oxford: Blackwell Scientific Publications).

Pawley, Martin (1994): *Future Systems: The Story of Tomorrow* (London: Phaidon Press Ltd).

Pearlman, Jill E. (2007): *Inventing American Modernism: Joseph Hudnut, Walter Gropius, and the Bauhaus Legacy at Harvard* (Charlottesville, VA: University of Virginia Press).

Peets, Elbert (1922): *see* Hegemann, Werner.

Pehnt, Wolfgang (1987): 'Altes Ägypten und neue Architektur' in *Bruckmanns Pantheon: Internationale Jahreszeitschrift für Kunst* **xlv** 154.

Pehnt, Wolfgang, & Strohl, Hilde (1997): *Rudolf Schwarz 1897–1961: Architekt einer anderen Moderne* (Ostfildern: Gerd Hatje).

Pelt, Robert Jan van (1984): *Tempel van de wereld: de kosmische symboliek van de tempel van Salomo* (Utrecht: HES).

Pelt, Robert Jan van (1996): *see* Dwork, Debórah.

Pereira, José Ramón Alonso (1998): *La Ciudad Lineal de Madrid* (Barcelona: Fundación Caja de Arquitectos).

Perelman, Marc (2015): *Le Corbusier: une froide vision du monde* (Paris: Michalon Éditeur).

Perrault, Claude (1673): *Les Dix Livres d'Architecture de Vitruve* (Paris: J.-B. Coignard).

Petersen, Ad (ed.) (1968): *De Stijl* (Amsterdam: Athenaeum).

Petropoulos, Jonathan (2014): *Artists under Hitler: Collaboration and Survival under Hitler* (New Haven & London: Yale University Press).

Petsch, Joachim (1976): *Baukunst und Stadtplanung im Dritten Reich: Herleitung/Bestandsaufnahme/Entwicklung/Nachfolge* (Munich: C. Hansler).

Pevsner, Nikolaus (1959): 'Roehampton, Housing, and the Picturesque Tradition' in *The Architectural Review* **cxxvi**/750 (July) 21–35.

Pevsner, Nikolaus (1960): *An Outline of European Architecture* (Harmondsworth: Penguin Books Ltd).

Pevsner, Nikolaus (1968): *The Sources of Modern Architecture and Design* (London: Thames & Hudson Ltd).

Pevsner, Nikolaus (1968a): *Studies in Art, Architecture and Design* (London: Thames & Hudson Ltd).

Pevsner, Nikolaus (1969): *South Lancashire* in *The Buildings of England* Series (Harmondsworth: Penguin Books Ltd).

Pevsner, Nikolaus (1971): *see* Nairn, Ian.

Pevsner, Nikolaus (1983, 1991, 2005): *see* Cherry, Bridget.

Pevsner, Nikolaus (1997): *see* Bradley, Simon.

Pevsner, Nikolaus (2003): *see* Bradley, Simon.

Pevsner, Nikolaus (2004): *see* Hartwell, Clare.

Pevsner, Nikolaus (2005): *Pioneers of Modern Design: from William Morris to Walter Gropius* with an Introduction by Richard Weston (New Haven & London: Yale University Press). The first edn. (1936) was entitled *Pioneers of the Modern Movement from William Morris to Walter Gropius* (London: Faber & Faber). *See also* 1975 edn. of *Pioneers of Modern Design: from William Morris to Walter Gropius* (Harmondsworth: Penguin Books Ltd).

Pevsner, Nikolaus (2006): *see* Lloyd, David.

Pevsner, Nikolaus (2011): *see* Hartwell, Clare.

Pevsner, Nikolaus (2015): *see* Bettley, James.

Pevsner, Nikolaus, & Richards, James Maude (eds) (1973): *The Anti-Rationalists* (London: Architectural Press).

Pevsner, Nikolaus, & Wedgwood, Alexandra (1966): *Warwickshire* in *The Buildings of England* Series (Harmondsworth: Penguin Books Ltd).

Pevsner, Nikolaus, & Wilson, Bill (1999): *Norfolk 2: North-West and South* in *The Buildings of England* Series (London: Penguin Group).

Phelan, Anthony (ed.) (1985): *The Weimar Dilemma: Intellectuals and the Weimar Republic* (Manchester: Manchester University Press).

Philippou, Styliane (2008): *Oscar Niemeyer: Curves of Irreverence* (New Haven: Yale University Press).

Pick, Frank (1935): *see* Gropius, Walter.

Pierrefeu, François de, & Corbusier, Le (1942): *La Maison des Hommes* (Paris: Plon). It was published (1948) in an English translation by Clive Ernest Entwistle & Gordon Holt under the title *The Home of Man* (London: Architectural Press), and Corbusier's name was placed before that of Pierrefeu.

Piltz, Georg (1982): *Kunstführer durch die DDR* (Leipzig, Jena, Berlin: Urania-Verlag).

Pintarić, V. Horvat (1989): *Vienna 1900: The Architecture of Otto Wagner* (London: Studio Editions).

Pöldinger, Walter (ed.) (1992): *Kulturelle Psychologie und Psychiatrie* (Karlsruhe: Braun).

Pommer, Richard, & Otto, Christian F. (1991): *Weissenhof 1927 and the Modern Movement in Architecture* (Chicago & London: University of Chicago Press).

Pontikis, Kyrianos, & Rofè, Yodan (eds) (2016): *In Pursuit of a Living Architecture: Continuing Christopher Alexander's Quest for a Humane and Sustainable Building Culture* (Champaign, IL: Common Ground Publishing).

Poppelreuter, Tanja (2007): *Das Neue Bauen für den Neuen Menschen: zur Wandlung und Wirkung des Menschenbildes in der Architektur der 1920er Jahre in Deutschland* (Hildesheim & New York: Georg Olms).

Poppelreuter, Tanja (2016): 'Spaces for the Elevated Personal Life: Ludwig Mies van der Rohe's Concept of the Dweller, 1926–1930' in *The Journal of Architecture* **xxi**/2 244–70.

Porphyrios, Demetri (1993): *see* Economakis, Richard (ed.).

Porphyrios, Demetri (2016): *Porphyrios Associates: The Allure of the Classical* with a Foreword by Vincent Scully and Essays by Kenneth Powell & Ellis Woodman (New York, London, etc.: Rizzoli International).

Posener, Julius (1992): *Hans Poelzig: Reflections on his Life and Work* (New York, Cambridge, MA, & London: Architectural History Foundation; MIT Press).

Posener, Julius (2004): *Heimliche Erinnerungen In Deutschland 1904 bis 1933* (Munich: Siedler).

Powell, Kenneth (2016): *see* Porphyrios, Demetri.

Power, Samantha (2004): *see* Arendt, Hannah.

Powers, Alan (ed.) (2007): *see* Charlton, Susannah (ed.).

Powers, Alan (ed.) (2010): *Robin Hood Gardens Re-Visions* (London: The Twentieth Century Society).

Powers, Alan (2013): '*Exhibition 58*: Modern Architecture in England, *Museum of Modern Art, 1937*' in *Architectural History* **lvi** 277–98.

Powers, Alan (2014): 'British Architecture after the Great War' in *Architectural Review* **ccvvvvi**/1414 (December) 98–101.

Preciado, Paul Beatriz (2014): *Pornotopia: An Essay on Playboy's Architecture and Biopolitics* (New York: Zone Books).

Preiser, Wolfgang F.E. (ed.) (1994): *see* Scheer, Brenda Case (ed.).

Prelovšek, Damjan (1997): *Jože Plečnik* (New Haven & London: Yale University Press).

Preziosi, Donald (ed.) (2009): *The Art of Art History: A Critical Anthology* (Oxford: Oxford University Press).

Prigge, Walter (ed.) (1999): *Ernst Neufert. Normiert Baukultur im 20. Jahrhundert* (Frankfurt-am-Main: Campus).

Prinzhorn, Hans (1922): *Bildnerei der Geisteskranken. Ein Beitrag zur Psychologie und Psychopathologie der Gestaltung* (Berlin: Julius Springer).

Prinzhorn, Hans (1927): *Leib—Seele—Einheit: Ein Kernproblem der neuen Psychologie* (Potsdam: Müller & Kiepenhauer Verlag).

Prost, Henri (1960): *L'oeuvre de Henri Prost* (Paris: Académie de l'architecture).

Pugin, Augustus Welby Northmore (1843): *An Apology for the Revival of Christian Architecture in England* (London: John Weale).

Pugin, Augustus Welby Northmore (1853): *The True Principles of Pointed or Christian Architecture* (London: Henry G. Bohn).

Pundt, Hermann G. (1989): *see* Schinkel, Karl Friedrich.

Quinn, James (ed.) (2009): *see Dictionary of Irish Biography.*

Quiring, Claudia, *et al.* (eds) (2011): *Ernst May, 1886–1970*, Charles Heard *et al.* (trs) (Munich & London: Prestel).

Racana, Gianluca, & Janssens, Manon (2010): *Maxxi* (New York: Skira Rizzoli).

Rand, Richard (tr.) (1986): *see* Derrida, Jacques.

Ravetz, Alison (1980): *Remaking Cities: Contradictions of the Recent Urban Environment* (London: Croom Helm).

Read, Herbert Edward (1933): *Art Now: An Introduction to the Theory of Modern Painting and Sculpture* (London: Faber & Faber).

Reading, Malcolm (1981): *see* Coe, Peter.

Reading, Malcolm (1986): 'A History of the MARS Group, 1933–45' (Dissertation: University of Bristol).

Rebay, Hilla (tr.) (1979): *see* Kandinsky, Wassily.

Redstone, Elias (ed.) (2016): *see* Grospierre, Nicolas.

Reece, Erik (2016): *Utopia Drive: A Road Trip through America's Most Radical Idea* (New York: Farrar, Straus, & Giroux).

Reed, Henry Hope (1959): *The Golden City* (Garden Cities, NY: Doubleday).

Reid, Scott M.P. (ed.) (1996): *A Bitter Trial: Evelyn Waugh and John Carmel Heenan on the Liturgical Changes* (Curdridge: Saint Austin Press).

Reiss, Robert (2016): *Sceptical Christianity: Exploring Credible Belief* (London: Jessica Kingsley Publishers).

Revett, Nicholas (1762–1816): *see* Stuart, James.

Reynolds, Fiona (2016): *The Fight for Beauty: Our Path to a Better Future* (London: Oneworld Publications).

Richards, James Maude (1940): *An Introduction to Modern Architecture* (Harmondsworth: Penguin).

Richards, James Maude (1958): *The Functionalist Tradition in Early Industrial Buildings* (London: Architectural Press).

Richards, James Maude (ed.) (1973): *see* Pevsner, Nikolaus (ed.).

Richards, James Maude (1980): *Memoirs of an Unjust Fella* (London: Weidenfeld & Nicolson).

Richards, Simon (2003): *Le Corbusier and the Concept of Self* (New Haven & London: Yale University Press).

Richardson, Albert Edward, & Corfiato, Hector Othon (1952): *The Art of Architecture* (London: English Universities Press Ltd).

Richardson, George (1787): *A Treatise on the Five Orders of Architecture in which the Principles of that Art are Illustrated* (London: G. Nicol for The Author).

Richardson, Sara (1989): *Bernard Tschumi: A Bibliography* (Monticello, IL: Vance).

Richter, Eva (tr.) (1970): *see* Neumann, Eckhard (ed.).

Richter, Klaus (2001): *Architecture: From Art Nouveau to Deconstructivism* (Munich: Prestel).

Riley, Terence, Bergdoll, Barry, *et al.* (2002): *Mies in Berlin* (New York: Museum of Modern Art; London: Thames & Hudson).

Roberts, Henry (1867): *The Dwellings of the Labouring Classes, their Arrangement and Construction, &c.* (London: Society for Improving the Condition of the Labouring Classes). This fascinating and important book, first published in 1850, went into several editions, and was translated into several European languages.

Robertson, Manning Durdin (1925): *Laymen and the New Architecture* (London: John Murray).

Robertson, Manning Durdin, & Robertson, Nora K. (1948): *Approach to Architecture* (London: Edward Arnold & Co.).

Robertson, Nora K. (1948): *see* Robertson, Manning Durdin.

Rofè, Yodan (ed.) (2016): *see* Pontikis, Kyriakos (ed.).

Röhl, John C.G. (2004): *Wilhelm II: The Kaiser's Personal Monarchy, 1888–1900*, Sheila de Bellaigue (tr.) (Cambridge: Cambridge University Press).

Röhl, John C.G. (2014): *Wilhelm II: Into the Abyss of War and Exile 1900–1941*, Sheila de Bellaigue & Roy Bridge (trs) (Cambridge: Cambridge University Press).

Rohrbach, Charlotte (1936): *see* March, Werner.

Rosenau, Helen (ed.) (1953): *Boullée's Treaty on Architecture* (London: Tiranti).

Rosenau, Helen (1976): *Boullée and his Visionary Architecture* (London: Academy Editions).

Rosenau, Helen (1983): *The Ideal City: Its Architectural Evolution in Europe* (London & New York: Methuen & Co. Ltd).

Rosenberg, Alfred (1934): *Revolution in der bildenden Kunst* (Munich: Zentralverlag der NSDAP, Eher).

Rosenberg, Alfred (1936): *Der Mythus des 20. Jahrhunderts: Eine Wertung der seelisch-geistigen Gestaltenkämpfen unserer Zeit* (Munich: Hoheneichen).

Ross, Thomas (1887–92): *see* MacGibbon, David.

Rossi, Aldo (1982): *The Architecture of the City* (Cambridge, MA: MIT Press).

Rossi, Aldo (1983): *Selected Writings and Projects*, John O'Regan *et al.* (eds) (London: Architectural Design).

Rossi, Aldo (1996): *Opera Completa* (Milan: Electa).

Rotbard, Sharon (2015): *White City Black City: Architecture and War in Tel Aviv and Jaffa* (London: Pluto Press).

Roth, Alfred (1927): *Zwei Wohnhäuser von Le Corbusier und Pierre Jeanneret* (Stuttgart: F. Wedekind & Co.).

Roth, Alfred (ed.) (1946): *The New Architecture*, J.A. Dakin (tr.) (Erlenbach-Zürich: Les Éditions d'Architecture).

Rowe, Colin (1994): *The Architecture of Good Intentions: Towards a Possible Retrospect* (London: Academy Editions).

Rowe, Colin, & Koetter, Fred (1980): *Collage City* (Cambridge, MA & London: MIT Press).

Rowland, Ingrid D. (tr.) (1999): *see* Vitruvius Pollio, Marcus.

Rudolph, Christopher (ed.) (1989): *see* Schinkel, Karl Friedrich.

Ruskin, John (1849): *The Seven Lamps of Architecture* (London: Smith, Elder, & Co.).

Rybczynski, Witold (2001): *The Look of Architecture* (New York: Oxford University Press).

Sadleir, Michael Thomas Harvey (tr.) (2006): *see* Kandinsky, Wassily.

Safran, Yehuda, Wang, Wilfried, & Budny, Mildred (1985): *The Architecture of Adolf Loos* (London: Arts Council of Great Britain).

Saint, Andrew (1976): *Richard Norman Shaw* (New Haven & London: Yale University Press).

Saint, Andrew (2005): Obituary of Philip Johnson in *The Guardian* (29 January 2005) http://www.theguardian.com/news/2005/jan/29/guardianobituaries. artsobituaries1 accessed 31 January 2017.

Salingaros, Nikos Angelos (2005): *Principles of Urban Structure* (Amsterdam: Techne Press).

Salingaros, Nikos Angelos (2006): *A Theory of Architecture* (Solingen: Umbau-Verlag).

Salingaros, Nikos Angelos (2013): *see* Mehaffy, Michael W.

Salingaros, Nikos Angelos (2015): *see* Mehaffy, Michael W.

Salingaros, Nikos Angelos, & Masden II, Kenneth G. (2008): 'Intelligence-Based Design: A Sustainable Foundation for Worldwide Architectural Education' in *International Journal of Architectural Research* **ii**/1 (March) 129–88.

Salingaros, Nikos Angelos, & Mehaffy, Michael W. (2002): https://www.opendemocracy.net/conflict-us911/article_173.jsp accessed 10 February 2017.

Salingaros, Nikos Angelos, *et al.* (2004): *Anti-Architecture and Deconstruction* (Solingen: Umbau-Verlag). *See also* the revised edn., https://www.amazon.com/Anti-Architecture-Deconstruction-Nihilism-Nikos-Salingaros/dp/0989346927

Salmon, Frank (ed.) (2008): *The Persistence of the Classical: Essays on Architecture Presented to David Watkin* (London: Philip Wilson Publishers Ltd).

Samber, Robert (1723): *Roma Illustrata: or, a Description on the most Beautiful Pieces of Painting, Sculpture, and Architecture, Antique and Modern, at and near Rome* (London: Daniel Browne & S. Chapman).

Sánchez Vidiella, Àlex (2011): *Sourcebook of Contemporary Architecture* (New York: Harper Design).

Sartoris, Alberto (1936): *Gli Elementi dell'architettura funzionale* (Milan: Hoepli).

Saumarez Smith, George (2013): *A Treatise on Modern Architecture in Five Books* (Cumnor, Oxford: The Bardwell Press).

Saunders, Frances Stonor (2013): *The Cultural Cold War: The CIA The World of Art and Letters* (New York & London: New Press).

Sayer, Phil (photographer) (1992): *see* Sudjic, Deyan.

Schädlich, Christian (1989): *Bauhaus Weimar 1919–1925* (Weimar: Ständige Kommission Kultur der Stadtverordnetenversammlung).

Schädlich, Christian (1991): *see* Engelmann, Christiane.

Scheer, Brenda Case, & Preiser, Wolfgang F.E. (eds) (1994): *Design Review: Challenging Urban Aesthetic Control* (London: Chapman & Hall).

Scheerbart, Paul (1914): *Glasarchitektur* (Berlin: Verlag der Sturm).

Scheffauer, Herman George (tr.) (1924): *Erich Mendelsohn: Structures and Sketches* (Berlin: E. Wasmuth).

Scheidig, Walther, & Beyer, Klaus G. (1967): *Weimar Crafts of the Bauhaus 1919–1924: An Early Experiment in Industrial Design*, Ruth Michaelis-Jena & Patrick Murray (trs) (London: Studio Vista).

Schelling, Friedrich Wilhelm Joseph Von (1927): *Werke*, Manfred Schröter (ed.) (Munich: C.H. Beck).

Schinkel, Karl Friedrich (1989): *Collection of Architectural Designs including designs which have been executed and objects whose execution was intended*, Kenneth S. Hazlett, Stephen O'Malley, & Christopher Rudolph (eds) with an *Introduction* by Philip Johnson and Prefatory Essay by Hermann G. Pundt (Guildford: Butterworth Architecture).

Schirmer, Heidemarie (ed.) (2011): *Van de Veldes Kunstgewerbeschule in Weimar: Geschichte & Instandsetzung* (Weimar: Bauhaus Universität Weimar Verlag).

Schlemmer, Tut (ed.) (1977): *Oskar Schlemmer: Briefe und Tagebücher* (Stuttgart: Gerd Hatje).

Schlösser, Manfred (ed.) (1980): *Arbeitsrat für Kunst Berlin, 1918–1921* (Berlin: Akademie der Künste).

Schmidt, Diether (1966): *Bauhaus: Weimar 1919 bis 1925, Dessau 1925 bis 1932, Berlin 1932 bis 1933* (Dresden: VEB Verlag der Kunst).

Schmitt, Uta Karin (2006): *Architektur und Natur: ein Einheit* in *Dessauer Kalendar* 50 S.94–101.

Schmitthenner, Paul (1932): *Baugestaltung: Das deutsche Wohnhaus* (Stuttgart: Konrad Wittwer Verlag).

Schmitthenner, Paul (1934): *Die Baukunst im neuen Reich* (Munich: Callwey).

Schofield, John (ed.) (2016): *Who Needs Experts? Counter-mapping Cultural Heritage* (Abingdon: Routledge).

Schreyer, Lothar (1966): *Erinnerungen an Sturm und Bauhaus: was ist des Menschen Bild?* (Munich: List). *See also* new edn. (2002): Brian Keith-Smith (ed.) (Lampeter: Edwin Mellen Press).

Schröter, Manfred (ed.) (1927): *see* Schelling, Friedrich Wilhelm Joseph Von.

Schulze, Franz (1994): *Philip Johnson: Life and Work* (New York: Alfred A. Knopf).

Schulze, Franz, & Windhorst, Edward (2014): *Mies van der Rohe: A Critical Biography* (Chicago & London: University of Chicago Press).

Schulze, Konrad Werner (1929): *Glas in der Architektur der Gegenwart* (Stuttgart: Zaugg).

Schumacher, Patrik (2011–12): *The Autopoeisis of Architecture* (Chichester: Wiley).

Schumacher, Patrik (ed.) (2016): *Parametricism 2.0: Rethinking Architecture's Agenda for the 21st Century AD* (Hoboken, NJ: John Wiley & Sons Inc.).

Schumacher, Thomas L. (1991): *Surface and Symbol: Giuseppe Terragni and the Architecture of Italian Rationalism* (New York: Princeton Architectural Press).

Schwitters, Kurt (1975): *Wir spielen, bis uns der Tod abholt: Briefe aus fünf Jahrzehnten*, Ernst Nudel (ed.) (Frankfurt-am-Main: Ullstein).

Scott, Geoff (1976): *Building Disasters and Failures: A Practical Report* (Hornby, Lancaster: The Construction Press Ltd).

Scott, Geoffrey (1914): *The Architecture of Humanism: A Study in the History of Taste* (London: Constable). *See also* the 1980 edn. (London: Architectural Press).

Scott, Mackay Hugh Baillie (1995): *Houses and Gardens. Arts and Crafts Interiors* (Woodbridge: Antique Collectors' Club Ltd). New edn. of the book first published 1906 (London: George Newnes Ltd).

Scott, Mackay Hugh Baillie, & Beresford, Arthur Edgar (1933): *Houses and Gardens* (London: Architecture Illustrated).

Scruton, Roger (2000): *An Intelligent Person's Guide to Modern Culture* (South Bend, IN: St Augustine's Press).

Scruton, Roger (2009): *Beauty* (Oxford: Oxford University Press).

Scruton, Roger (2015): *How to be a Conservative* (London: Bloomsbury Continuum).

Scruton, Roger (2015a): 'After Sacred Mystery, the Great Yawn' in *Times Literary Supplement* (6 November) 15.

Scruton, Roger (2017): *see* Adam, Robert.

Scully, Vincent (2016): *see* Porphyrios, Demetri.

Seeger, Adina Hulda Ingeborg (2013): *Vom Bauhaus nach Auschwitz* (University of Vienna Historisch-Kulturwissenschaftliche Fakultät: Mag. phil. Dissertation).

Sekler, Eduard Franz (1985): *Josef Hoffmann: The Architectural Work*, John Maass (tr.) (Princeton, NJ: Princeton University Press).

Seligmann, Janet (tr.) (2007): *see* Muthesius, Hermann.

Semes, Steven W. (2009): *The Future of the Past* (New York & London: W.W. Norton & Co.).

Senger, Alexander von (1928): *Krisis der Architektur* (Zürich: Rascher & Cie.).

Senger, Alexander von (1931): *Le Cheval de Troie du Bolchévisme* (Bienne: Éditions du Chandelier).

Sennott, R. Stephen (ed.) (2004): *Encyclopedia of 20th-Century Architecture* (New York & London: Fitzroy Dearborn).

Serroy, Jean, & Lipovetsky, Gilles (2008): *La Culture-Monde: réponse à une société désorientée* (Paris: O. Jacob). *See also* Lipovetsky, Gilles.

Sezon Bijutsukan (1998): *De Stijl 1917–1932: Art and Environment of Neoplasticism* (Tokyo: Kawade Shobo Shinsha).

Shand, P. Morton (tr.) (1935): *see* Gropius, Walter.

Sharp, Dennis (1966): *Modern Architecture and Expressionism* (London: Longmans, Green, & Co. Ltd).

Sharp, Dennis (ed.) (1972): *Glass Architecture by Paul Scheerbart and Alpine Architecture by Bruno Taut*, James Palmes & Shirley Palmer (trs) (London: Praeger Publishing).

Sharp, Dennis (ed.) (1987): *The English House* (Oxford: BSP Professional Books). *See* Muthesius, Hermann (1908–11).

Sharp, Dennis (2007): *The English House* (London: Frances Lincoln Ltd). *See* Muthesius, Hermann (1908–11).

Sharp, Thomas Wilfrid (1940): *Town Planning* (Harmondsworth: Penguin).

Shaw, George Bernard (1938): *see* MARS Group.

Sheppard, Francis H.W. (ed.) (1973): *Survey of London* **xxxvii**, *Northern Kensington* (London: Athlone Press for the Greater London Council).

Sherman, Franklin (ed.) (1971): *see* Luther, Martin.

Sigrist, Albert (1930): *Das Buch vom Bauen* (Berlin: Verlag der Bücherkreis).

Sim, Stuart (ed.) (2001): *The Routledge Companion to Postmodernism* (London: Routledge).

Simpson, Duncan (1979): *C.F.A. Voysey: An Architect of Individuality* (London: Lund Humphries).

Singelenberg, Pieter (1972): *H.P. Berlage, Idea and Style: The Quest for Modern Architecture* (Utrecht: Haentjens, Dekker, & Gumbert).

Sitte, Camillo (1889): *Der Städte-Bau nach seinen künstlerischen Grundsätzen* (Vienna: C. Graeser). *See also* George R. Collins & Christiane Craseman Collins (trs) (1965): *City Planning According to Artistic Principles* (London: Phaidon Press Ltd).

Sklair, Leslie (2017): *The Icon Project: Architecture, Cities, and Capitalist Globalization* (New York & Oxford: Oxford University Press).

Šlapeta, Vladimir, *et al.* (eds) (2010): *Great Villas of Bohemia, Moravia, and Silesia* (Prague: Foibos).

Smith, C. Ray (1986): *see* Tate, A.

Smith, Penny (2004): *see* McFadden, Anna Hicks.

Smith, Peter F. (1979): *Architecture and the Human Dimension* (London: George Godwin Ltd).

Smith, William George (1975): *The Oxford Dictionary of English Proverbs*, F.P. Wilson (ed.) (Newton Abbot: Readers Union).

Smithson, Alison Margaret (ed.) (1965): *Team 10 Primer* (London: Standard Catalogue Company).

Smithson, Alison Margaret, & Smithson, Peter (1991): *Team 10 Meetings: 1953–1984* (New York: Rizzoli).

Snodin, Michael (ed.) (1991): *Karl Friedrich Schinkel: A Universal Man* (New Haven & London: Yale University Press in assn. with The Victoria and Albert Museum).

Somol, Robert E. (ed.) (1997): *Autonomy and Ideology: Positioning an Architectural Avant-Garde in America 1923–49* (New York: Monacelli Press).

Sparke, Penny (ed.) (1981): *see* Banham, Reyner.

Speer, Albert (ed.) (1941): *Neue Deutsche Baukunst* (Berlin: Volk & Reich).

Speer, Albert (1970): *Inside the Third Reich: Memoirs*, Richard & Clara Winston (trs) (London: Weidenfeld & Nicolson).

Spencer, Nick (2016): *The Evolution of the West: How Christianity has Shaped Our Values* (London: SPCK Publishing).

Spencer, Stewart (tr.) (2007): *see* Muthesius, Hermann.

Spotts, Frederic (2002): *Hitler and the Power of Aesthetics* (London: Hutchinson).

Squire, Larry R., & Kandel, Eric R. (1999): *Memory: From Mind to Molecules* (New York: Scientific American Library).

Stamp, Gavin (ed.) (1999): *The Light of Truth and Beauty: The Lectures of Alexander 'Greek' Thomson* (Glasgow: The Alexander Thomson Society).

Stamp, Gavin (2009): 'Lost London: for its history of architectural vandalism, our capital is very hard to beat' in *Country Life* cciii/40 (7 October) 68–71.

Stamp, Gavin (2010): *Britain's Lost Cities* (London: Aurum Press Ltd).

Stamp, Gavin (2013): *Lost Victorian Britain: How the Twentieth Century Destroyed the Nineteenth Century's Architectural Masterpieces* (London: Aurum Press Ltd).

Stamp, Gavin (2013a): *Anti-Ugly: Excursions in English Architecture and Design* (London: Aurum Press).

Stamp, Gavin (2014): *see* Nairn, Ian.

Stamp, Gavin (2015): 'What's in a Style?' in *Country Life* ccix/29 (15 July 2015) 46. *See also* the same issue 90.

Stamp, Gavin, & McKinstry, Sam (eds) (1994): *'Greek' Thomson* (Edinburgh: Edinburgh University Press).

Staniszewski, Mary Anne (1998): *The Power of Display: A History of Exhibition Installations at the Museum of Modern Art* (Cambridge, MA: MIT Press).

Steele, James (1994): *Charles Rennie Mackintosh: Synthesis in Form* (London: Academy Editions).

Steele, James (ed.) (1995): *see* Koulermos, Panos.

Steigmann-Gall, Richard (2003): *The Holy Reich: Nazi Conceptions of Christianity, 1919–1945* (Cambridge: Cambridge University Press).

Stein, Joseph (ed.) (1978): *see* Wingler, Hans Maria.

Steiner, George (1996): *No Passion Spent: Essays 1978–1996* (London: Faber & Faber Ltd).

Steinmann, Martin (ed.) (1979): *CIAM: Dokumente 1928–1939* (Basel: Birkhäuser).

Stern, Robert Arthur Morton (1996): *Buildings* (New York: Monacelli Press).

Stevenson, Jane (2018): *Baroque Between the Wars: Alternative style in the arts, 1918–1939* (Oxford: Oxford University Press).

Stevenson, John James (1880): *House Architecture* (London: Macmillan & Co.).

Strange, Edward Fairbrother (1896): *Alphabets: A Handbook of Lettering for the Use of Students* (London & New York: George Bell & Sons).

Stratigakos, Despina (2015): *Hitler at Home* (New Haven & London: Yale University Press).

Streidt, Gert, & Feierabend, Peter (eds) (1999): *Prussia: Art and Architecture* (Cologne: Könemann).

Strohl, Hilde (1997): *see* Pehnt, Wolfgang.

Strohmeyer, Klaus (1980): *Warenhäuser: Geschichte, Blüte, und Untergang im Warenmeer* (Berlin: Wagenbach).

Strunsky, Rose (tr.) (1960): *see* Trotsky, Lev Davidovich.

Stuart, James, & Revett, Nicholas (1762–1816): *The Antiquities of Athens* (London: Haberkorn, etc.).

Sturdy, David (1972): *How to pull a town down: a handbook for local councils…illustrated chiefly from Oxford, Westminster, Liverpool, Abingdon, and other famous places* (London: Ram's Head).

Sudjic, Deyan (1992): *The 100 Mile City* with photographs by Phil Sayer (New York & San Diego, CA: Harcourt Brace).

Sullivan, Louis Henri (1896): 'The Tall Office Building Artistically Considered' in *Lippincott's Magazine* **lvii** (March) 403–9.

Summerson, John (1970): *Victorian Architecture: Four Studies in Evaluation* (New York & London: Columbia University Press).

Švácha, Rostislav (ed.) (1999): *see* Dluhosch, Eric (ed.).

Swenarton, Mark (1989): *Artisans and Architects: The Ruskinian Tradition in Architectural Thought* (Basingstoke: The Macmillan Press Ltd).

Swenarton, Mark, *et al.* (eds) (2015): *Architecture and the Welfare State* (New York: Routledge, Taylor & Francis Group).

Symondson, Anthony (2011): *Stephen Dykes Bower* (London: RIBA Publishing).

Symondson, Anthony, & Bucknall, Stephen Arthur (2006): *Sir Ninian Comper: An Introduction to his Life and Work with Complete Gazetteer* (Reading: Spire Books Ltd in assn. with The Ecclesiological Society).

Tafuri, Manfredo, & Dal Co, Francesco (1986): *Modern Architecture*, Robert Erich Wolf (tr.) (London: Faber & Faber Ltd).

Tagliaventi, Gabriele (ed.) (1996): *A Vision of Europe: Rinascimento Urbano=Urban Renaissance* (Bologna: Grafis).

Tagliaventi, Gabriele, & O'Connor, Liam (eds) (1992): *A Vision of Europe: Architecture and Urbanism for the European City* (Florence: Alinea).

Taschen, Angelika (ed.) (1997): *Hundertwasser Architecture: For a More Human Architecture in Harmony with Nature* (Cologne: Taschen).

Tate, Allen, & Smith, C. Ray (1986): *Interior Design in the Twentieth Century* (New York: Harper & Row).

Taut, Bruno (1919): *Die Stadtkrone* (Jena: E. Diedrichs).

Taut, Bruno (1919*a*): *Alpine Architektur in 5 Teilen und 30 Zeichnungen* (Hagen-i-W.: Folkwang-Verlag).

Taut, Bruno (1920): *Die Auflösung der Städte; oder Die Erde eine gute Wohnung; oder auch: Der Weg zur Alpinen Architektur; in 30 Zeichnungen* (Hagen-i-W.: Erschienen im Folkwang).

Taylor, David (1981): *see* Fitzwalter, Raymond.

Taylor, Nicholas (1973): *The Village in the City: Towards a New Society* (London: Maurice Temple Smith in assn. with New Society).

Taylor, Robert R. (1974): *The Word in Stone: The Role of Architecture in the National Socialist Ideology* (Berkeley & Los Angeles, CA & London: University of California Press).

Teige, Karel (2002): *The Minimum Dwelling* (Cambridge, MA & London: Massachusetts Institute of Technology Press).

Teut, Anna (ed.) (1967): *Architektur im Dritten Reich, 1933–1945* (Berlin: Ullstein).

Thomson, Alexander 'Greek' (1999): *see* Stamp, Gavin (ed.).

Till, Jeremy (2009): *Architecture Depends* (Cambridge, MA: MIT Press).

Tisdall, Caroline, & Bozzolla, Angelo (1977): *Futurism* (London: Thames & Hudson).

Todd, Dorothy, & Mortimer, Raymond (1929); *The New Interior Decoration: An Introduction to its Principles, and an International Survey of its Methods* (London: B.T. Batsford Ltd.).

Tolstoy, Leo (1933): *A Confession, the Gospel in Brief, and What I Believe*, Aylmer Maude (tr.) (London: Humphrey Milford at Oxford University Press for The Tolstoy Society).

Toman, Rolf (ed.) (1999): *The Art of Gothic: Architecture, Sculpture, Painting*, with photographs by Achim Bednorz (Cologne: Könemann).

Toman, Rolf (ed.) (2000): *Neoclassicism and Romanticism: Architecture, Sculpture, Painting, Drawings, 1750–1848* (Cologne: Könemann).

Tombs, Robert (2014): *The English and their History* (London: Allen Lane).

Tomkinson, Martin (1980): *see* Gillard, Michael.

Topfstedt, Thomas (ed.) (2000): *see* Barth, Holger.

Towndrow, Frederic Edward (1933): *Architecture in the Balance: An Approach to the Art of Scientific Humanism* (London: Chatto & Windus).

Trebilcock, Clive (ed.) (1997): *see* Clarke, Peter (ed.).

Trevelyan, George Macaulay (1944): *English Social History* (London: Longmans, Green).

Trommler, Frank (1978): *see* Hermand, Jost.

Troost, Gerdy (ed.) (1942–3): *Das Bauen im Neuen Reich* (Bayreuth: Gauverlag Bayerische Ostmark).

Trotsky, Lev Davidovich (1960): *Literature and Revolution*, Rose Strunsky (tr.) (Ann Arbor: University of Michigan Press).

Troy, Nancy J. (1983): *The De Stijl Environment* (Cambridge, MA: Massachusetts Institute of Technology Press).

Tse, Mimi M.Y., *et al.* (2002): 'The Effect of Visual Stimuli on Pain Threshold and Tolerance' in *Journal of Clinical Nursing* **xi** 462–9.

Turner, Jane Shoaf (ed.) (1998): *The Dictionary of Art* (London: Macmillan Publishers Ltd).

Turner, Thomas Hudson, & Parker, John Henry (1851–9): *Some Account of Domestic Architecture in England, from The Conquest to Henry VIII* (Oxford & London: John Henry & James Parker).

Tzonis, Alexander (2001): *Le Corbusier: The Poetics of Machine and Metaphor* (London: Thames & Hudson).

Ulrich, Roger S. (1984): 'View Through Window May Influence Recovery from Surgery' in *Science* **ccxxiv** 420–1.

Ulrich, Roger S. (2000): 'Evidence Based Environmental Design for Improving Medical Outcomes' in *Healing By Design: Building for Health Care in the 21st Century* (Montreal: McGill University Health Center).

Umbdenstock, Gustave (1932): 'La Défense des métiers de main des artistes et artisans français' in *L'Architecture* **xlv** 134–8.

Umbdenstock, Gustave (1933–4): 'La Défense de nos traditions artistiques dans le domain architectural' in *Art National* (Dec. 1933) 25–6. *See also Art National* (Jan. 1934) 5–6, (Feb. 1934) 9–10, (March 1934) 9–10, and (June 1934) 25–7.

Valinsky, David A. (2014): *An Architect Speaks: The Writings and Buildings of Edward Schröder Prior* (S.I.: David Valinsky for Shaun Tyas Press).

Vallée, Sheila de (tr.) (1986): *see* Kopp, Anatole.

Vargas Llosa, Mario (2015): *Notes on the Death of Culture: Essays on Spectacle and Society*, John King (tr.) (London: Faber & Faber Ltd).

Vautel, Clément (1921): *Les Folies Bourgeoises* (Paris: Albin Michel).

Velde, Henry van de (1986): *Geschichte meines Lebens*, Hans Curjel (ed.) (Munich: Piper).

Venturi, Robert Charles (1966): *Complexity and Contradiction in Architecture* (New York: Museum of Modern Art).

Viollet-le-Duc, Eugène-Emmanuel (1863–72): *Entretiens sur l'Architecture* (Paris: A. Morel & Cie). *See also* the English version, Benjamin Bucknall (tr.) (1959): *Discourses in Architecture* (London: Allen & Unwin).

Vitruvius Pollio, Marcus (1999): *Ten Books on Architecture*, Ingrid D. Rowland (tr.) & Thomas Noble Howe (commentary and illus.) (Cambridge: Cambridge University Press).

Voysey, Charles Francis Annesley (1915): *Individuality* (London: Chapman & Hall).

Wachowiak, Stanisław (ed.) (1930): *Powszechna Wystawa Krajowa w Poznaniu w roku 1929* (Poznań: Nakł. Powszechnej Wystawy Krajowej).

Waetzold, Stephan, *et al.* (eds) (1977): *Tendenzen der Zwanziger Jahre. 15. Europäische Außtellung Berlin 1977* (Berlin: Dietrich Reimer Verlag).

Wagner, Otto (1988): *Modern Architecture*, Harry Francis Mallgrave (tr.) (Santa Monica, CA: The Getty Center for the History of Art and the Humanities). The book was originally published in Vienna in 1896, 1898, 1902, and 1914, all by Anton Schroll: the 1914 edition was entitled *Die Baukunst unserer Zeit*.

Wagner, Richard (1869): *Das Judenthum in der Musik* (Leipzig: J.J. Weber) *See also* the English version (1910): *Judaism in Music*, Edwin Evans (tr.) (London: William Reeves).

Wainwright, Oliver (2013): 'Towering folly: why architectural education in Britain is in need of repair' in *The Guardian Architecture and Design Blog* (30 May) https://www.theguardian.com/artanddesign/architecture-design-blog/2013/may/30/architectural-education-professional-courses

Wakeman, Rosemary (2016): *Practicing Utopia: An Intellectual History of the New Town Movement* (Chicago & London: University of Chicago Press).

Wales, Charles, H.R.H. The Prince of (1989): *A Vision of Britain: A Personal View of Architecture* (London & New York: Doubleday).

Walker, Frank Arneil (2000): *Argyll & Bute* in *The Buildings of Scotland* Series (London: Penguin Group in assn. with The Buildings of Scotland Trust).

Walker, Frank Arneil (2016): *see* Close, Rob.

Walker, John A. (1992): *Glossary of Art, Architecture and Design since 1945* (London: Library Association Publishing).

Walker, Nathaniel Robert (2016): 'American Crossroads: General Motors' Midcentury Campaign to Promote Modernist Urban Design in Hometown USA' in *Buildings & Landscapes: Journal of the Vernacular Architecture Forum* **xxiii**/2 (Fall) 89–115 http://www.jstor.org/stable/10.5749/buildland.23.2.0089 accessed 1 February 2017.

Wang, Wilfried (1985): *see* Safran, Yehuda, *et al.*

Wangerin, Gerda, & Weiss, Gerhard (1976): *Heinrich Tessenow: Ein Baumeister 1876–1950* (Essen: Bacht).

Warncke, Carsten-Peter (1994): *De Stijl 1917–1931: The Ideal as Art* (Cologne: Taschen).

Waters, John K. (2003): *Blobitecture: Waveform Architecture and Digital Design* (Hove: Rockport).

Watkin, David John (1977): *Morality and Architecture: Development of a Theme in Architectural History and Theory from the Gothic Revival to the Modern Movement* (Oxford: Clarendon Press).

Watkin, David John (1992): 'Sir Nikolaus Pevsner: a Study in "Historicism"' in *Apollo* **cxxxvi**/367 (September) 160–72.

Watkin, David John (1996): *Sir John Soane: Enlightenment Thought and the Royal Academy Lectures* (Cambridge & New York: Cambridge University Press in assn. with Sir John Soane's Museum & The Bank of England).

Watkin, David John (2001): *Morality and Architecture Revisited* (Chicago: University of Chicago Press).

Watkin, David John (2005): *A History of Western Architecture* (London: Laurence King Publishing).

Watkin, David John (2016): *The Architecture of John Simpson: The Timeless Language of Classicism* (New York: Rizzoli International Publications Inc.).

Watkin, David John, & Mellinghoff, Tilman (1987): *German Architecture and the Classical Ideal 1740–1840* (London: Thames & Hudson).

Watson, Harriet (ed.) (1990): *see* Papadakis, Andreas C. (ed.)

Wattjes, Jannes Gerhardus (1927): *Moderne Architectuur* (Amsterdam: Uitgevers-Maatschappij 'Kosmos').

Waugh, Evelyn (1928): *Decline and Fall: An Illustrated Novelette* (London: Chapman & Hall). *See also* the Uniform Edition of Chapman & Hall (1947).

Weale, John (ed.) (1844–5): *Quarterly Papers on Architecture* (London: John Weale).

Weber, Nicholas Fox (2008): *Le Corbusier: A Life* (New York: Alfred A. Knopf).

Weber, Nicholas Fox (2009): *The Bauhaus Group: Six Masters of Modernism* (New York: Alfred A. Knopf).

Wedgwood, Alexandra (1966): *see* Pevsner, Nikolaus.

Weiss, Geraldine (1971): *see* Farmer, John David.

Weiss, Gerhard (1976): *see* Wangerin, Gerda.

Weitz, Eric D. (2007): *Weimar Germany* (Princeton, NJ: Princeton University Press).

Weston, Richard (2005): *see* Pevsner, Nikolaus.

Whitbread, Michael (1972): *see* Lichfield, Nathaniel.

Whitford, Frank (1984): *Bauhaus* (London: Thames & Hudson Ltd).

Whitman, Walt (1980): *Leaves of Grass: A Textual Variation of the Printed Poems*, Sculley Bradley *et al.* (eds) (New York: New York University Press).

Whittick, Arnold (1974): *European Architecture in the Twentieth Century* (London: Leonard Hill Books).

Whyte, Iain Boyd (tr.) (1984): *see* Buddensieg, Tilmann, *et al.*

Whyte, Iain Boyd (tr.) (1996): *see* Berlage, Hendrik Petrus.

Whyte, Iain Boyd (ed.) (2007): *Man-Made Future: Planning, Education, and Design in Mid-Twentieth-Century* (Abingdon & New York: Routledge: Taylor & Francis Group).

Wick, Rainer K. (1982): *Bauhaus-Pädagogik* (Cologne: DuMont). But *see also* the version entitled *Teaching at the Bauhaus* (2000) with text by Gabriele Diana Grawe (Ostfildern-Ruit: Hatje Cantz Verlag).

Wigley, Mark (1988): *see* Johnson, Philip.

Wilenski, Reginald Howard (1932): *The Meaning of Modern Sculpture: an essay on some original sculpture of the present day together with some account of the methods of professional disseminators of the notion that certain sculptors in ancient Greece were the first and the last to achieve perfection in sculpture* (London: Faber & Faber).

Wilk, Christopher (ed.) (2006): *Modernism 1914–1939: Designing a New World* (London: V&A Publications).

Wilkins, Eithne (tr.) (1979): *see* Musil, Robert.

Willis, Peter (1996): *Dom Paul Bellot, Architect and Monk* (Newcastle upon Tyne: Elysium Press).

Wilson, Bill (1999): *see* Pevsner, Nikolaus.

Wilson, F.P. (ed.) (1975): *see* Smith, William George.

Wilson, Susan (2015): *see* Curl, James Stevens.

Windhorst, Edward (2012): *see* Schulze, Franz.

Windsor, Alan (1981): *Peter Behrens: Architect and Designer* (London: The Architectural Press).

Wingler, Hans Maria (1978): *The Bauhaus: Weimar, Dessau, Berlin, Chicago*, Joseph Stein (ed.) Wolfgang Jabs & Basil Gilbert (trs) (Cambridge, MA & London: MIT Press).

Winkler, Klaus-Jürgen, & Bergeijk, Herman van (2004): *Das Märzgefallenen-Denkmal in Weimar* (Weimar: Bauhaus-Universtitätsverlag).

Winston, Richard & Clara (trs) (1970): *see* Speer, Albert.

Wit, Wim de (tr.) (1996): *see* Berlage, Hendrik Petrus.

Witemeyer, Hugh (ed.) (1997): *The Future of Modernism* (Ann Arbor: University of Michigan Press).

Wittman, Robert King, & Kinney, David (2016): *The Devil's Diary: Alfred Rosenberg and the Stolen Secrets of the Third Reich* (London: HarperCollins).

Wojtowicz, Robert (1998): *Lewis Mumford and American Modernism: Eutopian Theories for Architecture and Urban Planning* (Cambridge: Cambridge University Press).

Wolbert, Klaus (ed.) (2004): *Künstlerkolonie Mathildenhöhe Darmstadt 1899–1914* (Darmstadt: Institut Mathildenhöhe Darmstadt).

Wolf, Gustav (1940): *Haus und Straße im Vorort* (Munich: Georg D.W. Callwey).

Wolf, Robert Erich (tr.) (1986): *see* Tafuri, Manfredo, & Dal Co, Francesco.

Wolfe, Tom (1981): *From Bauhaus to Our House* (New York: Picador/Farrar, Straus, & Giroux). Later edn. 2009.

Wölfflin, Heinrich (1915): *Kunstgeschichtliche Grundbegriffe: das Problem de Stilentwicklung in der neueren Kunst* (Munich: Hugo Brockman). See also (2015): *Principles of Art History: The Problem of the Development of Style in Early Modern Art*, Jonathan Blower (tr.) (Los Angeles, CA: Getty Research Institute).

Wolschke-Bulmahn, Joachim (ed.) (2001): *Places of Commemoration: Search for Identity and Landscape Design* (Washington, DC: Dumbarton Oaks Research Library and Collection).

Wood, Graeme (2016): *The Way of the Strangers: Encounters with the Islamic State* (London: Allen Lane).

Woodham, Jonathan M. (1997): *Twentieth-Century Design* (Oxford: Oxford University Press).

Woodman, Ellis (2016): *see* Porphyrios, Demetri.

Worsdall, Frank (1981): *The City that Disappeared: Glasgow's Demolished Architecture* (Glasgow: Richard Drew Publishing Ltd).

Worsdall, Frank (1991): *The Glasgow Tenement: A Way of Life. A Social, Historical, and Architectural Study* (Edinburgh: Chambers).

Wotton, Sir Henry (1624): *The Elements of Architecture, Collected from the Best Authors and Examples* (London: I. Bill).

Wren, Sir Christopher (1942): *The City Churches . . . , etc., . . . and the Five Tracts on Architecture* in *Publications of The Wren Society* **xix** (Oxford: Oxford University Press for The Wren Society).

Wren, Stephen (ed.) (1750): *Parentalia: or, Memoirs of the Family of the Wrens* (London: S. Wren & J. Ames).

Wright, Frank Lloyd (1910–11): *Ausgeführte Bauten und Entwürfe von Frank Lloyd Wright* (Berlin: Ernst Wasmuth).

Wright, Sydney Fowler (1932): *The New Gods Lead* (London: Jarrolds).

Wünsche, Isabel (ed.) (2011): *see* Botar, Oliver Arpad Istvan (ed.).

Wycherley, Richard Ernest (1962): *How the Greeks Built Cities* (London: Macmillan & Co.).

Yorke, Francis Reginald Stevens (1946): *The Modern House* (London: The Architectural Press, 5th edn.).

Zachwatowicz, Jan, et al. (1952): *Architektura Polska* (Warsaw: Pánstwowe Wydawnictwo Naukowe).

Zadow, Mario Alexander (2001): *Karl Friedrich Schinkel: ein Sohn der Spätaufklärung* (Stuttgart & London: Menges).

Zatlin, Linda Gertner (1990): *Aubrey Beardsley and Victorian Sexual Politics* (Oxford: Oxford University Press).

Zatlin, Linda Gertner (2016): *Aubrey Beardsley: A Catalogue Raisonné* (New Haven & London: Yale University Press for The Paul Mellon Centre for Studies in British Art).

Zevi, Bruno (1974): *Poetica dell'architettura neo-plastica* (Milan: Einaudi).

Zhadova, Larissa A. (1982): *Malevich: Suprematism and Revolution in Russian Art, 1910–1930* Alexander Lieven (tr.) (London: Thames & Hudson).

Ziątkowski, Leszek (2014): *see* Eysymontt, Rafał.

Ziffer, Alfred, & Drebusch, Thomas (eds) (1992): *Bruno Paul: Deutsche Raumkunst und Architektur zwischen Jugendstil und Moderne* (Munich: Klinkhardt & Biermann).

Zukowsky, John (ed.) (1986): *Mies Reconsidered: His Career, Legacy, and Disciples* (New York: Rizzoli).

Zukowsky, John (1994): *Karl Friedrich Schinkel 1781–1841: The Drama of Architecture* (Chicago: The Art Institute of Chicago; Tübingen/Berlin: Wasmuth).

Zukowsky, John (1994*a*): *The Many Faces of Modern Architecture: Building in Germany between the World Wars* (Munich & New York: Prestel).

Zurko, Edward Robert de (1957): *Origins of Functionalist Theory* (New York: Columbia University Press).

Publisher's Acknowledgements

We are grateful for permission to include the following copyright material in this book.

'Die Sechzehn Grundsätze des Städtebaus' from *Von deutschem Bauen*, by Lothar Bolz. Copyright © 1951. With permission from Verlag der Nation.

Extract from A. Bartlett Giamatti's Baccalaureate Address from 'Speeches and Articles by and about Presidents of Yale University' (RU 65). Manuscripts and Archives, Yale University.

Extract from *Buildings* by Robert A.M. Stern, copyright © 1996. With permission from The Monacelli Press.

The publisher and author have made every effort to trace and contact all copyright holders before publication. If notified, the publisher will be pleased to rectify any errors or omissions at the earliest opportunity.

Index

...the best book in the world would owe most to a good index,
and the worst..., if it had but a single good thought...,
might be kept alive by it...

HORACE BINNEY (1780–1875): *Letter to Samuel Austin Allibone* (8 April 1868).

Dates of persons are given where it has been possible to find these: where no dates are given, this is because, despite diligent research, no reliably verifiable dates have been established.

Note: Page numbers in **bold** refer to Plates; those in *italics* to Figures; those in ***bold italic*** to the epigraphs in the chapter headings; *n.* refers to Notes.